Critical Acclaim for John C. Dvorak's
PC Magazine 1992 Computer Buyer's Guide

"...highly recommended."

—**James A. Cox,** *The Bookwatch*

"...this book could spell trouble for consultants."

—**Larry Clark,** *Sacra Blue Users Group Newsletter*

"Even if you don't use the product lists to select your computer or peripherals, the text in between the lists could easily save you the $19.95 price of the book."

—**Hugh Bayless,** *Monterey Bay Users Group - Personal Computer Newsletter*

"Editor John C. Dvorak offers excellent hardware advice to help you choose the right system."

—**Brent Heslop and David Angell,** *PC Magazine*

"The book actually offers more than its title suggests. This book straightens out the array of choices in fresh, plain, non-buzzword English."

—**Peter McWilliams, Universal Press Syndicate**

PC Magazine 1994 Computer Buyer's Guide

PC Magazine 1994 Computer Buyer's Guide

Ziff-Davis Press
Emeryville, California

Edited by John C. Dvorak

Copy Editor	Jan Jue
Table Editor	K.D. Sullivan
Editorial Assistant	Kelly Green
Technical Reviewer	Dale Lewallen
Project Coordinator	Kim Haglund
Cover Photograph	Robert Sondgroth
Cover Design	Ken Roberts
Book Design	Laura Lamar/MAX, San Francisco
Technical Illustration	Cherie Plumlee Computer Graphics & Illustation and Steph Bradshaw
Word Processing	Howard Blechman, Cat Haglund, and Allison Levin
Page Layout	M.D. Barrera
Indexer	Valerie Haynes Perry

Ziff-Davis Press books are produced on a Macintosh computer system with the following applications: FrameMaker®, Microsoft® Word, QuarkXPress®, Adobe Illustrator®, Adobe Photoshop®, Adobe Streamline™, MacLink® *Plus*, Aldus® FreeHand™, Collage Plus™.

Ziff-Davis Press
5903 Christie Avenue
Emeryville, CA 94608

ISBN 1-56276-150-1

Manufactured in the United States of America
10 9 8 7 6 5 4 3 2 1

CONTENTS AT A GLANCE

TABLE OF CONTENTS

TABLE OF CONTENTS

TABLE OF CONTENTS

TABLE OF CONTENTS

TABLE OF CONTENTS

TABLE OF CONTENTS

TABLE OF CONTENTS

TABLE OF CONTENTS

TABLE OF CONTENTS

TABLE OF CONTENTS

TABLE OF CONTENTS

TABLE OF CONTENTS

ACKNOWLEDGMENTS

AS THIS BOOK EVOLVES into a definitive buyer's guide that can be used by experienced users and novices alike, I have to thank all those who made it possible. First of all, Mimi Dvorak gets the credit for fine-tuning the readability. When you write about computers all the time, it's very easy to forget that the average user (not to mention the newcomer) doesn't automatically know all the buzzwords and concepts that come packaged with today's computer system. Mimi has a knack for handling this oversight and making the writing approachable to all users. Credit also goes to the staff of *PC Magazine* along with the contributing editors, especially Winn Rosch, Alfred Poor, Matt Ross, Charles Petzold, Robin Raskin, Carol Levin, Don Wilmott, Jim Seymour, Bill Howard, Tom Stanton, Bruce Brown, Frank Bican, Ed Mendelson, Bill O'Brien and Mitt Jones. Special thanks go to Jim Galley and his staff at PC Labs for their never-ending testing of the equipment and their help in doing the tables found in this book.

Since this book is based on material that first appeared in *PC Magazine* I have to thank Michael Miller and the editors of the magazine for letting this project continue and evolve. Special thanks go to *PC Magazine* publisher Jim Stafford for producing one of the greatest magazines in history. Remember to read "Inside Track" when you pick up a copy!

Finally, I also want to thank the staff at ZD Press for getting this book out in time and making it look so good!

INTRODUCTION

WELCOME to *PC Magazine 1994 Computer Buyer's Guide*. This is a book designed to help you make smart buying decisions. You can use it as both an introduction to computer hardware and a reference tool. The first part of the book takes you through every hardware technology that you need to be familiar with. You will learn what the experts think and you will be carefully guided past the traps and pitfalls that newcomers and experts both encounter.

The idea for this book came along one day when a shelf of carefully organized *PC Magazine*s collapsed a solid oak bookshelf from their massive weight. I thought it might be a good idea to condense the material found in all those older issues and put the information in a concise book: a buyer's guide. This book is the result of that effort. While the book is no substitute for a subscription to *PC Magazine*, you'll find that it is a handy reference.

In this book you'll learn how a computer works. You'll learn what components are needed in a system that is just right for you. You'll become fluent in computerese—the awful language they speak on the computer store sales floor. You'll learn how modems work and how you can link your computer to other computers. You will understand how different printers work and which one is best for you. In short, you'll become an instant expert after reading this book. I hope you enjoy it.

A Quick Tour of the Chapters

The first two chapters of this book give you the building blocks for making an informed buying decision. Chapter 1, "Basics for Beginners," describes in simple terms what a PC is and what the different components are that make up a typical PC system. Chapter 2, "Smart PC Shopping," gives you the inside story on how and where to shop. Common sense rules, hints on mail-order purchasing, and tips on buying a used computer are just a few of the useful topics in this chapter.

The heart of the book is in Chapters 3-12. Here you'll find all the information you need on each of the components of a typical PC system. Chapter 3 covers computers—everything from the earliest, most primitive PCs to the current power-user 486s. Monitors of every type are discussed in Chapter 4, and information about video cards and graphic display standards is found in Chapter 5. Chapter 6 gives you the lowdown on printers—dot matrix, ink-jet, laser printers, and more—and teaches you how to decide which is the right one for you. Chapter 7 discusses backup and storage devices, including hard disks, tape drives, and CD-ROM drives. Chapter 8 covers input devices. You'll learn about keyboards and mice, as well as some interesting and unusual alternatives to the two. Modems are discussed in Chapter 9. You'll find a handy guide to the ever-changing terminology of modems and telecommunications, a dis-

INTRODUCTION

cussion of how modems work, and a survey of the different types of modems now available. Chapter 10 covers the basics of software buying, including tips on getting the best price and a guide to the many types of programs available. Chapter 11 will help you choose a portable or laptop computer, as well as guide you through the maze of features available on portables. Finally, Chapter 12 discusses computer accessories such as power strips, diagnostic software, and other recommended utilities that will help breathe life into your PC system.

The next part of the book is the product tables, Appendices A–L. These are elaborate condensed specifications for machines tested in the comparative reviews done in *PC Magazine*. Included are the famous *PC Magazine* Editor's Choices, which are determined at the time of testing by the project leaders and various editors. I have also included "Dvorak's picks," which are products that I personally have familiarity with and would recommend to others. You should note that these selections are subjective and open to debate. Many times the best product for you, the buyer, is something else.

Two more appendices and a glossary round out the book. Appendix M is an index of printer reviews that have appeared in *PC Magazine* over the past eight years. *PC Magazine* has earned a reputation for publishing the most extensive printer reviews in the industry, and over 300 are indexed in this appendix. Appendix N is a directory of computer equipment manufacturers. Over 600 names, addresses, phone numbers, and fax numbers are listed here so you can easily contact the manufacturers of the products mentioned in this book. The glossary is your guide to the always mercurial and sometimes confusing terms you'll encounter as you investigate computer equipment and make your buying decisions.

BASICS FOR BEGINNERS

BUYING YOUR FIRST COMPUTER can be a very frustrating experience. Often salespeople at computer stores don't know how to guide you to the right system, or they have a system they're "pushing." The lack of books and articles written for the computer novice compounds the frustration. And nothing's more aggravating than being told to "take a class" to learn the basics.

BASICS FOR BEGINNERS

CHAPTER 1 IS DESIGNED to help a beginning computer user learn some of the terms, concepts, and buzzwords of PC computing. Once you grasp the language and phrases, much of the gibberish will begin to make sense. You'll gain the ability to ask the right questions and make an intelligent purchase.

What Is a PC?

A PC (short for personal computer) is a machine. Like other machines, it has basic functions, and these functions can be applied to certain tasks.

A PC has four basic functions:

- To store and display information, or *data*

- To calculate information

- To talk to other computers and share information

- To control the operations of another machine, such as a printer

These functions can be directed toward many tasks. A PC may be used to control a robotic arm, calculate a spreadsheet, play a game, or compose music. But a computer cannot do any of these things without instructions, called *software programs* or *applications*. These sets of instructions tell the different elements of the computer to do something, such as perform a mathematical function, word-process, create a picture, connect to a telephone line, and more. There is good software and bad software, great software and dismal software. Badly written software will not perform well no matter how good the computer.

A minimum amount of programming (that is, software) is already in the computer when you buy it. This lets the computer know it's a computer and not a microwave oven, or simply a doorstop. The machine needs instructions for everything, no matter how simple.

What Are the Different Parts of a PC?

The computer system is made up of several different parts: a keyboard, a video screen, a box, and various cables. The box may also be called the system unit, central processing unit (CPU), or simply the computer. Additional parts may include a printer, a modem, and a mouse. All of these pieces are collectively referred to as the system *hardware* (see Figure 1.1).

It is a common misconception among beginners that all of these pieces of hardware must "go together"—in other words, that they must be made by one manufacturer and sold as a package.

BASICS FOR BEGINNERS

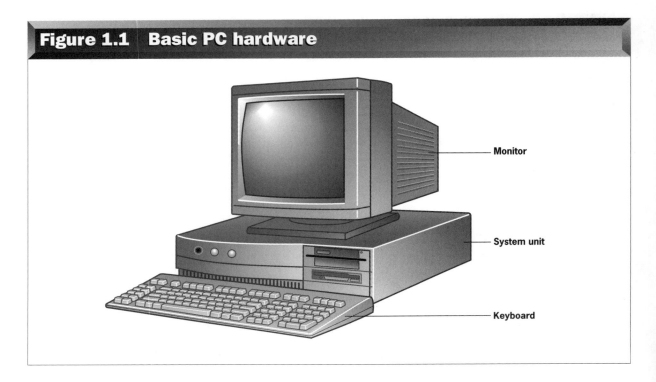

Figure 1.1 Basic PC hardware

Monitor

System unit

Keyboard

The different components must be *compatible* (designed to work together). The issue of compatibility has changed over the last few years. Historically, making computer components compatible was a big headache. It was a maze of "what-ifs" and exceptions to try to make different parts work correctly. With today's computers, this is almost a moot point. Manufacturers have worked very hard to correct the problems and the quirks of incompatibility. Now you can shop around for the different pieces of your computer system. Feel free to purchase your computer at one store, the printer at another, a keyboard through a mail-order company, and the monitor and video card at yet another outlet.

The computer is modular. Each and every piece may be swapped out when it ceases to work or when you want to *upgrade* it (change some parts to make a better computer).

The System Unit

The box part of the computer contains a whole world of hardware unto itself. The system unit is a case which holds a number of different components (see Figure 1.2). The box may be opened. There are usually four screws located on the back of the unit. Unscrew these and the entire case

BASICS FOR BEGINNERS

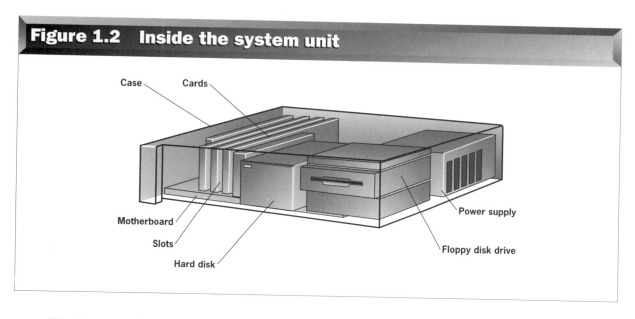

Figure 1.2 Inside the system unit

can lift off to reveal the innards of the computer. (Warning: The computer must be unplugged from the electrical outlet.)

A Dvorak tip: If you have young children, familiarize yourself with how to remove the cover of the machine and the disk drive because toddler-sized kids love to put pennies and other small objects into the open slot. Service time will add up if you rely on a serviceperson to pull out packages of Kool-Aid from the disk drive unit.

Inside the computer are the *cards* (also called boards). The cards are flat, rigid pieces of a hard, plastic-like green resin. They have different objects, square and rectangular raised pieces, brightly colored transistor diode-like things, and maybe even a set of little rocker switches soldered onto them. These cards plug into a panel. The panel is called a *bus* and the places where the card plugs in are called *slots*.

The bus is on the computer's *motherboard*, which is the biggest card in the computer. The processor chip, the bus, and the memory chips are all attached to the motherboard. The *processor chip* is the main chip—the brains of the computer. It oversees all the functions of the computer and processes all the data. (For a full discussion of the different processor chips, see Chapter 3.) In addition, the motherboard has open connectors for single in-line memory modules (SIMMs) so you can add more memory cheaply. You can buy SIMMs at any time to add more main memory, which is also known as random-access memory (RAM).

BASICS FOR BEGINNERS

THANKS FOR THE MEMORY

Memory is like money—what you have is never enough. The more memory your computer has, the better, but only to a point. Random-access memory (RAM) is short-term, temporary memory. If there is a power outage or if you turn off the machine, whatever is in the short-term memory will be lost. (For instance, if you're writing the great American novel and forget to save your work, it will become a bittersweet memory.)

Let's say you turn on your computer and see the C> prompt on the screen. When you type in the code or word that runs a program, that program is read from permanent memory on the hard disk to this RAM memory. That's why when you turn off the computer and turn it back on again, you'll see the C> prompt but not the word processing program. This short-term memory may be referred to as dynamic RAM (DRAM) or static RAM (SRAM). These terms are inconsequential to the user. They're just techie terms to describe the exact, precise, detailed way the chips work.

Flash memory, a brand-new kind of memory, is not widely available yet. This flash memory differs from RAM in that the data is not lost when the machine is powered down. Currently, it is used in palmtop computers and other tiny hand-held devices. Someday it may be found in the big, desktop computers.

Read-only memory (ROM) is the real brains behind the machine's operations. ROM, which cannot be overwritten, is permanently encoded programming that tells the computer how to operate. This includes the basic input/output system (BIOS). The input/output information governs how data is moved through the system—from the keyboard to the computer, from the computer to the monitor, and so on. It also governs how the machine boots (starts up) the system, and other operations as well. ■

Other cards which may be added to the box include a modem card, video card, small computer systems interface (SCSI) card, bus mouse card, joystick card, Sound Blaster card, and Windows accelerator card, among others. The box also houses a fan to cool the unit and a power supply which regulates electricity to the whole machine. The hard or floppy disk drives are inside the system unit, too. We'll discuss these in detail in a moment.

The Keyboard

A keyboard is usually included when you purchase the system. If you don't like a keyboard, if it stops working, or if you spill your cola on it, you can purchase a different one. We cover input devices in Chapter 8.

The keyboard looks a lot like a typewriter's, as shown in Figure 1.3. It's flatter, and there are extra keys on it, usually across the top and on the left, which are labeled F1 through F10 or F12. These *function keys* may be programmed for special functions. A number of different software programs will use these keys for specific commands. A keyboard may also have a numeric keypad, which is arranged much like a ten-key calculator.

BASICS FOR BEGINNERS

Figure 1.3 Typical keyboard layout

The Monitor

The monitor is a video screen. It looks like a television set in many ways. It may have vertical and horizontal control adjustment knobs and color adjustment knobs if it's a color monitor. The monitor "reports" the results of your commands and will display requested information. Monitors are either *monochrome* or *color*. Monochrome designates a two-color display: black and white, amber and white, or even green and black. Color screens typically display from 16 to 256 different colors, depending on the video card installed. There are also "full color" monitors which can display 16 million colors. Monitors are discussed fully in Chapter 4.

The Video Adapter Card

You can't just hook a monitor to a computer. It won't work. You need to purchase a video card. Many computers don't even have a place to plug the monitor in—it's on the video card. Video cards come in different varieties: EGA, VGA, CGA, SVGA, and XGA. Now there are cards designed for the VESA local bus, too. There are some compatibility problems between monitors and video adapter cards: A monochrome monitor won't work with a color video card, and a high-end advanced card will require an expensive, specialized monitor. The differences and conflicts between monitors and video cards are covered in Chapter 5.

The Disk Drive

The disk drive is also called the *floppy drive*. Floppy disks come in two sizes: $5^1/_4$- and $3^1/_2$-inch. The smaller disk is encased in rigid plastic, while the larger is in a flimsy, thin plastic case (see Figure 1.4). Disks must be used in the appropriately sized disk drives. Obviously, trying to use a

BASICS FOR BEGINNERS

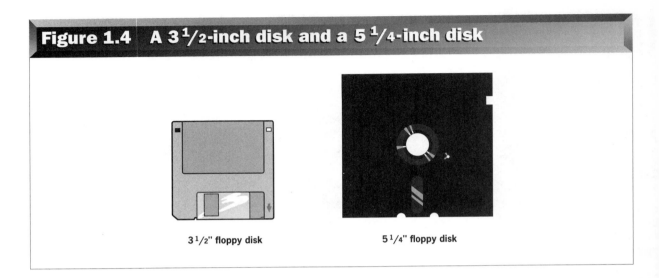

Figure 1.4   A 3 ¹/₂-inch disk and a 5 ¹/₄-inch disk

3 ¹/₂" floppy disk   5 ¹/₄" floppy disk

5¹/₄-inch disk in a 3¹/₂-inch disk drive is like shoving a quarter into the nickel slot of a parking meter. Computers come with one or two disk drives. If there are two drives, they may be both the same size or one of each size.

Inside the plastic cover of a floppy disk is a thin plastic wafer coated with a magnetic oxide. The coating can be magnetized in small sections. The magnetized patterns can be read as information by your computer's disk drive. The wafer is fragile, which is why a protective cover is placed over it. Inside, the disk is spun very quickly by the disk drive, like a record on a phonograph. The disk drive has *read heads* and *write heads*, which find data by reading the patterns or store data by magnetizing the disk's coating. The heads hover very close to the disk's spinning surface. Dirt, grit, and oily fingerprints can damage a disk and render it "unreadable" and "unwriteable."

Back in the "olden days" before hard disks, floppy disks held programs and stored data until you were ready to use them. A user would have a pile of disks on the desk and would have to sort through them to find the right program disk and then the right data disk. But since the emergence of hard disks, floppies have fallen into a lesser role. There are probably some computer users who have never even used a floppy, except to copy a program onto their hard disks. (Retail software programs come on floppies.) But floppy disks are very valuable in a few key ways. For instance, if your hard disk gets clogged up with too many files—some important and others simply copies—you can move the files to a floppy disk and remove them from your hard disk. This will give you extra hard disk

BASICS FOR BEGINNERS

COMPUTER CHEAT SHEET

If you're shopping for your first PC, it would be a good idea to know a few basic computer terms.

- **Application** A specific task a computer performs. Other words for this include software, program, or instructions.

- **Bit** The smallest piece of information a computer can process. Think of it as an electronic Morse code in which a bit is one dot or dash. Eight of these equal a *byte*. A *kilobyte* (K) is around a thousand bytes, a *megabyte* (Mb) is about a million bytes, and a *gigabyte* (G) is a billion bytes.

- **Chip** A very tiny square or rectangular sliver of material (usually silicon) with electrical components built into it. Some of the chips in a computer help to control the flow of information. Others help the computer to remember information. The most important chip is the microprocessor, which is the 8088, 286, 386, and so on, that every salesperson will speak of when talking about a specific machine's features.

- **CPU (central processing unit)** Also known as the system or the box, this is the functional "brain" of the computer.

- **Data** Another word for the information manipulated by a computer.

- **DOS (disk operating system)** A widely used operating system which gives the computer instructions. These instructions, along with the BIOS, enable the computer to work. Examples of DOS functions include displaying characters on the screen, reading and writing to a disk, printing, and accepting commands from the keyboard.

- **Function** An operation; a set of tasks for a computer to do.

- **Hardware** The various components of the computer you need to lug to your car after purchasing them. These include the CPU, keyboard, printer, and any other peripherals.

- **Software** The other stuff you need to buy to make a computer usable. Software instructs the computer to perform specific tasks. Word processing, games, spreadsheets, databases, and telecommunications programs are all software you may want to consider. Software can also be referred to as the application. ■

space or make room for a new program. Also, it's a good idea to back up important files by copying them to a floppy disk and keeping the disk in a safe place, just in case an accident or catastrophe occurs. For more on data storage and security, refer to Chapter 7, which covers backup and storage.

The Hard Disk

The hard disk functions like a floppy disk. The only difference is the hard disk can hold vast amounts of data. A hard disk allows you to store many different programs and data on your computer. This speeds things up considerably from back when a program had to be read off floppy disks in a disk drive for the program to work. Many software programs are so large that one floppy disk wouldn't hold enough instructions to allow the program to run. A hard disk is mandatory for today's personal computers.

BASICS FOR BEGINNERS

There are both internal and external hard disks. An internal disk is a necessary part of any computer system. External disks are for storing even more data or for specific needs like backing up data. Backing up data involves copying everything from the internal hard disk to a second location for security. This is common in the business world, but most home computer users just back up important data by making a copy to a floppy disk, called a *backup disk*. External hard disks are covered in Chapter 7.

Conclusion

These are the basics. There are many other details about computers which you can learn before you go out and buy one. Some of this information is important, but much of it isn't. What you have learned in this chapter and what you'll learn throughout the rest of this book will provide you with the knowledge base you'll need to be a wise consumer.

SMART PC SHOPPING

CHAPTER

2

WHEN YOU WALK into a computer store as a novice buyer, you can easily become overwhelmed by all the choices. The seemingly simple purchase of one peripheral—like a printer—becomes a massive undertaking. It's unnerving. The salesperson will speak in fancy high-techie terms like NLQ (near-letter-quality), ppm (pages per minute), ink-jet, laser, and dot matrix. Just reading the sales literature is like deciphering hieroglyphics or translating Finnish into English.

SMART PC SHOPPING

YOUR FIRST STEP in buying a new computer is to bone-up on this kooky "foreign" tongue: computerese. The best way to learn is to have a very patient friend (ideally, one who knows a lot about personal computers). Failing that, read, read, read. This book is a good start. Then go on to the magazines: *PC Magazine* and *PC/Computing*. Find out about user's groups in your area; usually a local computer store can point you in the right direction. And, of course, ask a lot of questions at the store.

Dvorak's Golden Rules

There are five things to keep in mind when shopping for a computer: Parts is parts; faster is better; little things add up; buy the newest technology you can afford; and shop, shop around. Don't let a salesperson sway you or persuade you to purchase a machine because "the parts are better," or "it will be fast enough for you," or even "you won't find a lower retail price anywhere."

Rule #1: Parts Is Parts

A PC clone is a PC clone is a PC clone. Most of the hundreds of different brands of PC clones use the same Taiwanese manufactured parts. Software programmers are very cautious, so most software works on a compatible clone just as well as on an IBM or Compaq machine. The most important thing to research when choosing a clone is whether the company has a reasonable maintenance program and good technical assistance. Your machine will be useless to you if getting it repaired is an impossible chore or getting the answer to a simple question involves calling Hong Kong.

In the past, IBM and Compaq had a head start in marketing the newest and fastest technology. It often took up to a year for clone makers to produce machines similar to the latest from the big computer companies. Nowadays, however, compatible computers appear at the same time that the major computer companies release their latest models. That means the prices on machines begin dropping as soon as the computers appear at the store. And this competition is a good thing for the computer buyer.

Today, the IBM standard for compatibles and the machines produced by IBM have diverged slightly. In 1987, IBM introduced the PS/2 (Personal System 2), which featured a new Micro Channel bus to help the computer's various expansion cards work together more efficiently. PS/2s can run IBM-compatible software, but the expansion cards a PS/2 uses differ from the ones used by other IBM-compatible computers.

The clone manufacturers continued to refine the IBM system, introducing faster and better machines without the Micro Channel technology. More manufacturers are making expansion cards for the compatibles than for the IBM PS/2, so the PS/2 has not become the new standard yet.

SMART PC SHOPPING

Instead, IBM compatibles with the old type of expansion cards have continued to be the IBM standard.

This means that there are certain advantages to owning a clone instead of the latest from IBM, including a wider (and cheaper) choice of expansion cards.

Rule #2: Faster Is Better

Purchase the fastest, most powerful unit you can afford. It should have a big, fast hard disk with at least 60Mb. The more memory, the better. It might sound like overkill, but memory is like money: You always wish you had more.

If you have a specific software program that you must use on your new machine, find out what chip it requires to run. If it requires a 386 chip, the software won't run on a 286. Most well-written software which was written for an earlier chip (such as a 286) will run on a new machine (such as a 386 or 486). This isn't a hard and fast rule, but is usually the case. Otherwise, as far as chips go, a good, fast 286 is functional but slow when compared to a 386 or 486. It all depends on the price you can afford and your individual requirements.

Rule #3: The Little Things Add Up

A competitive price is an important factor when buying, but your decisions also must be based on personal variables. What do you plan to do with the system? Do you need the vendor's warranty and support? In your haste to save money, don't forget these easily overlooked options.

The documentation that comes with a PC reveals something about the quality of a system. If the manual includes generic descriptions of components, this means the vendor uses whatever parts are available or cheapest at the moment. Because the system's components keep changing, there isn't any time to revise the documentation.

Specific documentation and a limited but adequate number of options (say, five or six hard-disk choices) usually guarantee a better overall quality. It also indicates higher compatibility, because the number of variables is controlled. A PC manufacturer that uses only one or two motherboard designs per processor type is in a better position to obtain Class B FCC ratings, and the machine will probably have greater compatibility with the computer peripherals.

Rule #4: Buy the Newest Technology You Can Afford

Computers become outdated in a very short time. What was top of the line six years ago is old and sluggish by today's standards. You might get a great deal on a "really cheap" 8088 PC, and it might serve you well, but it is already outdated. And if for some reason you use a friend's 386 or your

SMART PC SHOPPING

office gets a new 486, you will instantly become very unhappy with your painfully slow 8088.

Rule #5: Shop, Shop Around

First of all, know what you want. Do some comparative shopping. Visit dealers to ask about the services they provide. Pick up a copy of *PC Magazine* and start calling the direct marketers. What are their services and prices? Do you know the applications you'll want to run? What do they require? What video performance do you expect? What are your expectations for the speed and capacity of the disk? Put in the legwork up front, and you'll be happier with your system.

When considering price, remember that the list price and street price differ greatly. The *list price* is the manufacturer's suggested retail price, which has almost no basis in fact. (Well, perhaps a few government purchasing agents have paid the list price.) The *street price* is the discounted cost after the price wars between the discount computer chains, the direct-sales dealers, and special offers from the manufacturers themselves. The list and street prices can differ by as much as 40 percent.

Where Should You Purchase Your PC?

If you want a sandwich, you go to the deli. If you want a book, you go to the bookstore. But if you want to buy a new PC, things can get complicated. The options are endless. The large superstore with boxes piled high competes with the local computer store, which offers hands-on help and service. Then there's the mail-order house, where price is everything. If you want to get funky, go to the local computer swap meet. You can even buy a computer through the home shopping channel.

Those are just a few places to buy a computer or peripheral. You could also buy a used computer through a newspaper ad or a notice on a bulletin board. A relative or friend might give you an old, idle one. There is no one right place to buy your computer equipment. Let's examine some of the options and alternatives to see what's best for you.

Local Retail Stores

If you are a grass-green newcomer to computer ownership, you should purchase a new unit from a reliable source. This, for many users, means a local retail store. These stores can range from a nationwide chain to a mom-and-pop storefront clone builder. The key is they are local. This is convenient if something goes wrong, if you have a question, or if you need help hooking the computer up.

The prices may be 30 percent higher than a mail-order house's advertised price, but the local store will give you the support you're sure to need in the beginning. It's much easier to lug a computer back to the

SMART PC SHOPPING

store if something goes wrong than to pack it and ship it off to who-knows-where. In addition, if it's a minor connection problem or an intermittent one, the inconvenience and expense of shipping the computer back several times can eat up any savings you may have realized. Some direct-sales companies offer on-site service, it's true, but they don't offer the on-site handholding the first-time buyer sometimes needs. However, if you have friends who know the ropes, they can help you set up and run a mail-order machine. In fact, there is no one right way or one right place to buy your computer equipment.

The Clone Builders   These are guys with a screwdriver who know how to turn it to the right. They assemble computers from all the various parts to make a custom computer. A hot trend around the country is the "clone store." You walk in, figure out which components you want your machine made up of, and the clone builder slaps it together while you wait. One advantage to this—if you know what you're doing—is that you get some control over the components. If you aren't secure in your knowledge of computer parts and don't want to know (or care about) the details of every little thing, you might as well just purchase an already assembled clone from another type of vendor.

Computer Superstores   These giant stores focus on office supplies and computers. They have piles and piles of software, hardware, and peripherals, as well as office paper, pens, and other supplies. There are specials and "sale" tags on every item, and there's a quantity discount for everything. The problem with these stores is they've cropped up so quickly that few of the employees or the buyers have any experience with computers. While the store may have a variety of choices, these may not be well selected. The employees rarely know much about the products they're selling, which is an advantage of sorts; you can browse around without a pesky salesperson trying to help.

Mass-Market Superstores   These are the "membership" warehouse chains piled high with boxes and boxes of the same stuff. You can buy tires, beans, and toilet paper, as well as books, office supplies, and computers. You can't get in to shop—or get the best deal—unless you're a member. The places are crammed with everything, and fork lifts run up and down the aisles dodging people. They seem to offer a wide variety of computers, when in fact, there's only a lot of the same thing. The problem with these superstores is you're not able to do any comparison shopping. The price they quote as less than "retail" may not be such a significant savings. They rarely quote the street price—the price the item may actually

SMART PC SHOPPING

be selling for through most of the retail channels. (Computers, their peripherals, and software rarely sell for the retail price. The street price is often lower, occasionally lower by a significant amount.)

And Furthermore... Don't buy a computer from any retail store that has snooty help. If they try to make you feel like a complete dweeb and act like your questions are the stupidest ones they've ever heard, don't put up with it. There is no reason for a computer store to make you feel ill-at-ease. Look around for a computer store that has friendly, knowledgeable staff.

Mail-Order Houses

Mail-order houses can offer some great deals at low prices. If you know what you are purchasing, this can be a good way to go. Things to look for in a mail-order house include a toll-free order number, round-the-clock service, a money-back guarantee, an extended warranty, and speedy shipping.

Mail-Order Hints Here are some hints for purchasing mail-order equipment:

- Pay by credit card instead of by check. With a credit purchase you can stop payment, and the bank will act as your agent if there is a problem. Even if the amount has already been billed, you can dispute a charge, refuse to pay, and let the bank work out the dispute. Contact your credit card's issuing bank to clarify their policies before you start looking through the ads.

- When buying by mail order, insist on a firm shipping date and find out the method of delivery that the mail-order dealer uses. You need to know so that you'll have a good idea when your equipment will arrive.

- Confirm the exact configuration of the machine—right down to the make and model number of internal components such as hard disks. Shifting relationships between suppliers, fluctuations in the prices of components, and the constant revision and renaming of components mean vendors often make changes in their machines' internal configurations. Some vendors' ads will not reflect these changes, which affect both prices and shipping dates.

- Don't order anything from a mail-order company you or your friends have never heard of without checking the operation out. Check with your local users' group and find out what companies are on their hit and miss lists. Ask a friend if he or she is happy with the company that

SMART PC SHOPPING

shipped his or her system. You might want to call the Better Business Bureau and ask what they know about a specific company.

- Don't fall for a very low price that's accompanied by high-pressure phone tactics. If the price in the ad seems too incredible to be true, it probably is. When you see an amazingly low price on a machine, question the salesperson about that company's return policy (which should be a minimum of 30 days/money back). Check older issues of the magazine where you saw the ad and see if the company has been advertising for a fairly long time.

- If it's not right, send it back.

If you are a novice buyer trying out mail-order dealers, make sure you have friends who know the ropes. Your friends can help guide you through the difficulties during setup and can teach you how to use your mail-order machine. Check out a mail-order company's technical support before you purchase your PC. Many of these tech support groups are very good.

VARs (Value-Added Resellers)

VARs are dealers who specialize in selling a PC in a package complete with specialty software. If you are a real estate broker, for instance, you might want to look for a VAR selling a complete system that runs real estate software. The software packages are the "value added" to the computer system. Most computer buyers never deal with VARs, but they may prove useful to you in the future.

Television Shopping Shows

Recently, some television shopping shows have broken into the direct-sales computer market. The machines they sell are usually older design versions of either Apple IIs or PC clones. These machines are cheap, but unless you know exactly what you are buying, it's likely that the machine won't be what you hoped. Keep in mind that the telephone order takers know even less about their computer merchandise than the computer mail-order house order takers. These well-meaning people can lead you astray.

Another drawback is that they offer only a 30-day guarantee. If a problem develops after the warranty period, you must take the problem up with the manufacturer. The manufacturer might be an obscure clone maker on the other side of the country—or the world. A simple computer malfunction can become a complicated matter if you have to ship the entire unit to Taiwan.

SMART PC SHOPPING

Used Computers

For the budget minded, some great bargains can be found in the used-computer market. A used computer doesn't have a guarantee or warranty, however, which is a drawback. On the other hand, electronic equipment either works or it doesn't—if the computer works, it's likely to continue working for a long time. If the machine fails, don't fret. Few of the replacement parts are very expensive—power supplies and keyboards cost around a hundred dollars each.

Don't pay much for these older, used machines. Even if the computer cost thousands of dollars new, the retail value isn't more than 20 percent of the original cost, at most. If a friend or relative purchased an IBM XT in 1985 for $3,000, he can't expect to sell the machine for $1,500 or even $1,000.

Think about it: If you pay $1,000 for the machine, you'll still need to upgrade it. That IBM XT probably has a 10Mb hard disk (too little memory by today's standards). It may have a keyboard with a few sticking keys and may be missing its monitor. A new 60Mb hard disk will cost around $400, the keyboard $100, and a monitor another $200—which all adds up to a whopping $1,700 for a used piece of equipment.

Why buy the machine at all? You could purchase a new machine for that much money without all the time spent on the upgrades. If, however, you took that old unit off your friend's hands for $200 and then added on the $700 in upgrades, you'd have a great machine at a bargain price.

As for all that accumulated software that goes along with the used machine—don't pay for it. It should be thrown in for free. Software loses its value faster than hardware. Some of it might be useful, but the $150 spent in 1985 is worth about $1.50 today. It doesn't add to the machine's retail value any more than if you purchased a used car with an eight-track stereo system. An eight-track may have cost a mint way back when, but who cares?

Before you jump in and buy that used gem, shop around. Look at comparable new units, price replacement parts, call a few of the local computer repair and upgrade shops—find out everything you can. Read this book!

Whatever you do, don't fall for a pressure sale. Maybe there are a zillion people already interested in the deal, but so what? Remember, it's just like a used car purchase—buyer beware. Know what you want to buy and don't be in a rush.

Don't get talked into anything, either. An old CP/M computer might still work, but unless you have a museum or an old-computer collection, or need a good sturdy conversation piece doorstop, don't buy it. Software is almost impossible to find. Repairs are costly. Your friends will laugh at you.

SMART PC SHOPPING

THE BOSTON COMPUTER EXCHANGE

The Boston Computer Exchange (BoCoEx) produces weekly quotations of what popular used systems such as the IBM PC/AT or Compaq Deskpro 386/25 are worth, and they will assist you in purchasing one. Or you can use the prices as a starting point to purchase a used computer locally.

An old machine is one that was new just four or five years ago. Since any warranty or guarantee has long since expired, you must be willing to roll up your sleeves and do things yourself. If you're someone who thinks used cars are the only way to go, and thrift is your middle name, a used computer is for you.

A new service provided by the Boston Computer Exchange is "Fax Yourself Information." To get the information you want, call FYI at (617) 542-2345. Use your touch-tone phone to select the appropriate three digit-extension from this menu and give FYI your fax machine's phone number. Within a few minutes the service will fax the information requested.

FYI offers the following options:

300, Current BoCoEx Index

301, Information on BoCoEx Index

302, Listing Form (To offer equipment)

310, How We Do Business

312, Background Information on BoCoEx

314, Great Deals: Ready to Go

315, We Want to Buy

320, Research Analysis Forecasts Trends

321, Nine Year BoCoEx Price Comparison

322, How to Participate in TechTrade

333, Alex Randall's Used Computer Handbook: Contents and Order Form

BoCoEx Database of Products:

360, CPUs for Sale without Peripherals

361, CPUs with Monitor

362, CPUs with Monitor and Printer

363, Portables

364, Monitors

365, Printers

366, Miscellaneous

The Boston Computer Exchange can be contacted by phone at (617) 542-4414, (800) 262-6399 in the USA, or (800) 437-2470 in Canada; or write them at Box 1177, Boston, MA 02103. Their fax number is (617) 542-8849. ∎

What If It Breaks?

Service has always been an important feature—and selling point—for the pricey dealers and resellers. They can custom configure a system for large corporate accounts, and their service people usually show up quickly if anything goes wrong. Customers have grown tired of inadequately equipped dealers who charge high prices for service and repairs. It's enough to make customers look for other options.

For the individual, the mail-order manufacturers have outperformed the large dealer-distributed companies in service and price. This accounts for the overall success of mail-order business over the last few years.

SMART PC SHOPPING

SUPPORT COSTS MONEY

Is the era of free customer support drawing to a close? Software vendors are increasingly offering multiple levels of support, most at a price.

The most recent support scheme is a 900 number that charges the user on a per-call or per-minute basis. The worst aspect of this idea is that if you work in a large corporation, the 900 number may be blocked from your telephone system. Turning support into a revenue center encourages companies to produce inferior products that need support. This adds to the bottom line at the customer's expense. Not good.

With third-party, on-site service contracts, you get all the service you need for one flat fee. More and more, you will find on-site service contracts bundled with systems, included as part of the warranty (usually lasting a year), or available as an insurance policy to protect your system. An added option will extend the warranty of your system for an extra year or two, or as long as you choose to pay for the extra coverage.

With any service contract, find out up front what's covered: Who does the support? How far are you from the people responsible for the service? Are they familiar with this system? Undoubtedly, the areas of service and support are key to any would-be PC buyer. Check into the options; you'll be better off in the long run. ∎

Mail-order companies have discovered that buyers want faster and more convenient technical service. If the vendor can't resolve a problem over the phone, many will provide on-site service (provided the product is still under warranty). A number of direct marketers use the policy of mirror shipment. (The vendor returns your repaired PC by the same delivery method you used to send it.) If you need the computer back in a rush, ship it overnight. After a day or two of repairs, it's rushed back. If you're not so pressed, you can send it by ground delivery. (An important tip: Save your computer boxes, just in case you need to ship the system out for repairs.)

Some companies make provisions to ship parts to you by overnight express. They don't wait until the broken component is received. Once tech support determines that a faulty monitor needs replacing (from your frantic telephone call), the new part is on the way.

The amount of coverage and the degree of technical service varies from company to company (not to mention dealer to dealer). Some direct dealers offer free technical support over the phone, in the form of a toll-free number, for as long as you own the computer. Some provide 24-hour-a-day phone support and supplement support methods through a dedicated electronic bulletin board system (BBS) or a national service such as CompuServe. The service provided on these on-line forums usually includes answers to commonly asked questions and the posting of additional driver files.

SMART PC SHOPPING

Beware, there are still those fly-by-night companies that offer few or no fix-it services. Some of these companies may be on the up-and-up, but they might sacrifice technical support in order to offer the lowest price. To paraphrase the old saying: "Penny-wise, dollar-foolish." Saving a buck up front with these firms may end up costing more in the long run.

Now that you know a little about your options for purchasing a computer, you can begin checking out various dealers. If you have a question that hasn't been answered yet, read a little further in the book. Good luck!

COMPUTERS

CHAPTER

3

"COMPUTER" MEANS DIFFERENT THINGS to different people. Your local mechanic talks about the computer in your car, which controls the fuel injection. The airline can't tell you when Aunt Edna's flight will arrive because the computer is down. The stock clerk at the grocery store has some strange hand-held device; when you ask what it is, he says it's an inventory computer. These things are everywhere—from the VCR to the bread-making machine. Having said all that,

COMPUTERS

none of those kinds of computers are what we're talking about—or care about—in this guide. We're talking about the desktop computer found in businesses and in people's homes.

A Short History of the Microcomputer

The history of microcomputers doesn't compare with the history of ancient China. Microcomputers have been around for about a decade and a half, but in those few years there have been some milestones (and mill stones). It's good to have some knowledge of this short history to give you perspective on where we really are today.

Early Desktop Computers

The very first microcomputer machines were about as exciting as a do-it-yourself Heathkit Radio set—a thrill if you were an enthusiast, but just a pile of junk if you weren't. The early computers of the late '70s were functional, but crude by today's standards. The little machines couldn't out-perform the large mainframe and minicomputers that dominated the computing scene, but they were a lot more fun.

In the 1980s we witnessed an explosive growth of the personal computer scene. Early personal computers—or "micro" computers as they were originally dubbed—lacked a clear standard. The computer chip makers—Intel, Motorola, and Zilog—all competed in the microprocessor market in a rash of different computers from different manufacturers. None were compatible with any others. Perhaps the closest thing to a standard was the operating system, CP/M (control program for microprocessors). In its day it was a hot little operating system. As a matter of fact, much of DOS is based on the old CP/M program. Way back when DOS was first introduced, the die-hard CP/M aficionados swore that PC-DOS/MS-DOS was doomed to failure.

The real problem in the microcomputer scene was a lack of acceptance. "Big Business" was still reluctant to purchase any of these tabletop computers. Most corporations had been sold on the idea of giant mainframe CPUs, and smaller companies had a minicomputer stashed behind a Herman Miller partition. The basic business attitude was, "But we have a real computer. Why would we want a silly little micro?" So none of the manufacturers of the PCs were able to get their foot in the door.

Enter IBM

IBM's introduction of the IBM PC in August 1981 opened the eyes of many. Now a "real" computer manufacturer was in the PC market. IBM had scores of sales representatives well entrenched in corporations and businesses all across the country. The salesmen—used to selling big-ticket items and invoicing hundreds of thousands of dollars—were dressed in three-piece suits, and accustomed to a casual lunch with a corporate president. This was a big

COMPUTERS

advantage over the other microcomputer companies. Most of those guys had never been in a corporate president's waiting room or even owned a decent suit. Furthermore, they couldn't have cared less.

IBM, in their inimitable style, opened their own stores selling all IBM equipment, as well as their own brand of software. The software had been written by other companies but adapted for PC-DOS (IBM's proprietary operating system). IBM insisted the software all be packaged in the same standard plain white boxing and identical labeling. (It was very similar to the trend toward "generic" packaging of house-labeled items at grocery stores.) Distributors grumbled. Software manufacturers grumbled. The IBM PC was successfully followed by the PC/XT.

The CP/M machines just couldn't compete with IBM. Because IBM had chosen Intel and its 8088 processor, the Z-80 chip was essentially dead. The 8088 chip had a larger address space that would accommodate bigger, more involved software programs than the Z-80 could. (Intel subsequently developed the 80286, 80386, and 80486 chips now dominant in the PC marketplace.)

A number of companies began to produce machines that used the MS-DOS (Microsoft DOS) operating system. In the beginning, they were similar to PC-DOS machines but not true "compatibles." Software for PC-DOS would seldom run on an MS-DOS machine, and vice versa. It is not exactly clear when PC-DOS and MS-DOS merged and became one and the same. But today there is little distinction (if any) between the two. IBM-compatible clones and genuine IBM computers all run the same software.

IBM kept the pressure on with its next system release, its 6 MHz PC/AT, the first machine to use Intel's next-generation 80286 chip. The "power-user" computer was born, with improved EGA graphics (capable of 640 by 350 lines of resolution and 16 colors), an I/O and memory bus capable of moving data to and from the processor 16 bits at a time, and more internal hard-disk storage (at least 20Mb). Like every new generation of PCs, the AT quickly became a best-selling machine.

However, these first-generation ATs were plagued by frequent hard-disk failures. Without any warning, a user's disk would fail and data would be lost. The problem was widespread enough that IBM clone manufacturers started to erode IBM's dominance as early as the spring of 1986 with their own faster (8, 10, and 12 MHz), reliable systems.

Bring in the Clones

The IBM PC/AT's hard-disk failures allowed the PC-compatible makers to gain a foothold in the market. The AT clones were more reliable than IBMs—a fact which was quickly pointed out in numerous magazine articles.

COMPUTERS

IBM tried to knock the clone makers back with an improved offering later in 1986. IBM raised the 80286 clock speed to 8 MHz and began to use hardier, IBM-manufactured 30Mb hard disks. The AT 339 became the most popular IBM-made PC ever, and one of the most reliable.

But the clone competition continually improved PCs. PC clones were cheaper than IBM's machines, with larger hard disks (from 40Mb to 100Mb). Greater memory became standard, and options such as built-in serial and parallel ports were added to system boards. Clones often included displays, display adapters, and software in attractively priced bundles.

The PC/AT continued to sell well, but IBM's market share began to fall, even though it was selling more machines than ever. Other clone manufacturers (Compaq and Advanced Logic Research, for example) moved quickly on Intel's next big microprocessor evolution, the 32-bit 80386. In a daring move, IBM vied to win back dominance in the PC market by trying to change the standard.

PS/2

In 1987, IBM introduced its PS/2 line of PCs. Some say it was to avoid competition with the by now well-entrenched clone makers; other say it was to increase the performance of PCs. In any case, the PS/2 machines were characterized by an all-new proprietary input-output bus, which IBM termed Micro Channel architecture (MCA). The PS/2 lineup included the 80286-powered desktop Model 50 and the floor-standing Model 60. Both systems were slow performers, however. The Model 50 sold reasonably well because of its smaller "footprint" (the total space taken up on the desk by the CPU). The competition quickly caught on to that strategy and started to produce 286-powered PCs in smaller cases. These small-footprint machines occupied less desk space and were shorter in height than older machines like the AT. IBM later followed these machines with more powerful 386-based Model 70s.

OS/2

In 1987, IBM announced a new operating system, OS/2. Unlike the PS/2, there is no machine associated with this new standard. OS/2 will run on an IBM machine or any clone. OS/2 is like the Macintosh operating system in that it relies on a desktop as the base of operations. There are folders and icons, and other Mac-like features, but there are also command-line capabilities. It's really a hybrid of the DOS and Macintosh operating systems.

Since its introduction a few versions of OS/2 have been kicking about (most notable were versions 1.0 and 1.3), but none has garnered much attention. All that has changed with IBM's most recent version, 2.1. Version 2.1 allows you to run multiple DOS programs actively at the same time. It

COMPUTERS

lets you run Windows programs and use all of the available memory in your computer. It's high on the Dvorak recommended list—but only if you have a fast 386 machine with 8Mb of main memory. OS/2 is IBM's newest attempt to re-establish itself as the dominant force in personal computers. It may work.

Windows NT

The most recent operating system breakthrough has been the release in 1993 of the much-awaited Windows NT, which has all the characteristics of OS/2 but with the marketing clout of Microsoft. Windows NT won't be a factor in the business immediately, but when vendors begin to make machines with multiple processors in the years ahead, then NT, designed to run on multiple processors, will be necessary.

Pentium Processor

Finally, we cannot ignore the Pentium processor in our history. Although this chip is just now going into full production, it is the most talked-about chip in the industry. It will be discussed further in our overview of the chips that go into the PC.

In Conclusion

Now that you have a brief understanding of the history of microcomputers, it should be apparent that change is a part of the scene. This will continue until well into the next century—when some other device supplants the PC.

Desktop Computer Talk

Times have changed from way back about ten years ago when you could just say "I want an IBM," and the only computer available was an IBM PC. Now there is more to consider than just deciding you want a computer. Unfortunately it's tough to know what's what, especially if you're a beginner. Walk into a computer store, and the salesperson will overwhelm you with numbers and other computerese gibberish. It's like wandering into a foreign country. Let's try and make this easier for you by discussing some of the basic things you should know about a computer.

Chip Chat: Some Basic Information about Chips

The key component to any computer system is the microprocessor, or central processing unit (CPU). The actual "brains" of the machine is a little chip like that shown in Figure 3.1. The "legs" on the chip are the connectors, which allow the chip to be either snapped into place or soldered onto the card.

COMPUTERS

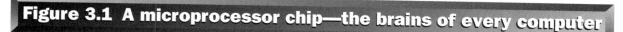

Figure 3.1 A microprocessor chip—the brains of every computer

There is a new chip socket which will become more common in the near future. This socket, called the Zero Insertion Force (ZIF) socket, is a way for a user to easily maneuver a chip out of the motherboard and insert a newer chip, instantly upgrading the computer. The ZIF socket has a lever which releases the chip's pins and then locks in a new chip's pins, a simple maneuver which makes the switch effortless.

Each CPU's designation (8088, 80286, 80386, and so on) is like a model number. Sometimes the number is expanded to denote speed and other attributes. For example, consider the 486SX-20 and the 486DX-25. SX designates the complexity of the chip (SX is simpler than DX), and 20 and 25 are the clock speeds in megahertz.

MHz (for megahertz) is the measurement of millions of cycles per second. It's used to gauge the speed at which a chip operates. We measure our own performance in seconds, minutes, and hours. A chip is measured in cycles per second. When we say a chip is operating at 20 MHz, it is running at 20 million cycles per second. The bigger the number, the faster the chip performs. Magazine articles often describe the difference between chip speeds as a percentage that measures how much faster one chip runs compared to another. For example, a 20 MHz chip is said to run about 20 percent faster than the 16 MHz version.

COMPUTERS

CHIP-NAMING CONFUSION

Intel is the main provider of CPUs for these computers, and they've managed to confuse the market by changing their naming scheme over the years. For example, what we like to call the 486 might also be referred to as the 80486 in one catalog or the iAPX486 in another. These are all the same chip. The American Micro Devices (AMD) version of the chip is usually called the AMD486, but it's also called the 80AMD486 or the 80AM486. Don't let all these names for the same thing confuse you. Most writers use 80486 interchangeably with 486 and 80386 with 386. Little attention is paid to the manufacturer of the chip unless the chip has some special attribute.   ∎

People often speak of the chip number when they talk about their PCs. They will say something like "my 386 is faster than my old 8088." This is similar to car buffs talking about the power of their vehicles' engines, but it's not quite the same. The speed of a very fast car usually depends on more variables than engine size. The model may have a high performance cam shaft, a specially geared transmission, special tires, and other racing features. If they're describing a stock car, they also discuss whether the vehicle has two or four doors, an automatic transmission or 5-speed, a convertible or hard top, a leather interior or the deluxe velour or special tuck-and-roll, and on and on.

When it comes to computers, the question of speed is simple: It's the chip. The chip *is* the computer. A fast chip makes a fast computer, while a slow chip makes a sluggish computer. (Other attributes are the hard-disk size, video/graphics speed, the I/O bus, and possibly a cache, but for now, we'll stick to chips.) When you go into a computer store, the first question you'll hear is always "What machine do you have?" The answer to this question isn't the manufacturer's name, but instead, the chip number. While there are a slew of computer makers, they all rely on only a few types of chips.

The big manufacturers such as IBM, Hewlett-Packard, and Zenith make computers with their name appearing boldly across the front. However, computers are often made by manufacturers who sell them to retailers who then put their own names on the machines and sell them. (These are referred to as original equipment manufacturer (OEM) machines.) Then, there are the various clone builders. This could be a guy assembling a computer in his garage for resale or a big factory in Taiwan spewing out thousands of machines a day.

The types of computers also vary. A manufacturer may make a variety of different machines to appeal to different segments of the market. So, purchasing a machine is not as simple as just saying "I want an IBM." The following sections briefly summarize the different chips which are the heart and guts of the computers on the market.

COMPUTERS

8088: The Dodo Bird of Microprocessors
The 8088 is slow by today's standards, but a decade ago it was a hot item. Compared to the newer chips, it's like racing a moped against a Kawasaki Ninja motorcycle.

8088-based systems are still available, but for a few extra dollars you can buy a 386. The 8088-based systems are almost always made from Taiwanese components in a mix-and-match fashion. An 8088 may be functional as a simple word processor or terminal, but there is no longer any reason to consider one in a personal computer.

80286: The Brain-Dead Microprocessor
A 286 is about three to four times faster than an 8088, but it's still slow. The biggest problems with a 286 chip are that it doesn't handle memory as well as a 386 and it has a different instruction set (the programming which tells a chip what to do) which is just slightly incompatible with the 386. In the future, these differences will make the 286 almost completely incompatible with new software.

The 286-based computers are cheap, but they handle only 16-bit chunks of data and have limited addressable memory compared to a 386. (*Addressable memory* is memory which can be talked to directly by the CPU. More addressable memory allows the computer to run larger, more complex programs efficiently.) Software development has moved beyond 16-bit performance, toward larger chunks (which speeds up performance) and toward larger programs which need greater space in addressable memory. The 286 is unable to keep up with these demands, which will ultimately spell its doom.

It's hard to justify such a system, however inexpensive it is. Some computer instructions are understood only by the 386 and newer processors. This is why almost every columnist writing about computers describes the 286 as "brain-dead." (Bill Machrone was the first to say it, by the way.) Software of the future is expected to use the 386 capabilities extensively.

80386SX and DX
The 386 has a huge amount of addressable memory compared to the 286. The 386 comes in two basic flavors—SX and DX—and in a whole range of speeds. The main difference between the two flavors is that the SX acts as a bridge between the 16-bit chunk grabbers and the 32-bit ones. The 386SX moves 16 bits of data, while the DX handles 32-bit chunks.

To run Windows 3.0 or 3.1 effectively, you'll need a 386SX or DX machine—the faster the better. The 386SX has become the corporate standard for entry-level spreadsheets, word processing, and network workstation computing.

The 386SX made its debut in mid-1988 with Compaq's introduction of the Deskpro 386SX. At that time, the 80386DX-based systems were prohibitively more expensive than 286s, so Intel created a hybrid chip, the

COMPUTERS

386SX. This chip gave manufacturers a less expensive way to produce a 386-based system at a cost not much higher than for a 286-based computer. The 386SX processes 32-bit instructions like a 386DX, but it transfers data to its system memory and the expansion bus in 16-bit chunks, like a 286. The 386SX typically runs at 20 or 25 MHz. (AMD is designing 33 and 40 MHz versions.)

The SX is the first item people look for if they want a computer. The success of the 16 MHz chip and now the faster 20 MHz chip has taken the market share away from 286-based systems. The 386SX has brought an end to the 16 and 20 MHz 286 and 386DX, leaving the 25, 33, and 40 MHz 386DX machines in the marketplace. If you are a graphics-oriented user in desktop publishing or computer-aided design (CAD) applications, you need the full 32-bit processing power of the 386 and the higher brute force clock speeds of the 33 MHz or 40 MHz 80386DX models.

The 33 and 40 MHz 386s stand in a good position to fill two roles: First, they are great for a corporate user's entry-level plunge into the world of both 32-bit memory and 32-bit data paths. Second, most 25 MHz 386s offer FCC Class B certification (for home use; see "Don't Forget the Government: What FCC Ratings Mean" later), but many faster 386s and 486s still lack it.

The 386 chip was a revolutionary change in personal computing. Higher clock speeds certainly boost performance, but the move from 16-bit to 32-bit computing is even more significant. Performance is doubled immediately, since twice as much data can be moved and used.

80486 When 25 MHz and 33 MHz 386-based machines were the fastest things with or without legs, they were touted as ideal network file servers, but 486s now fill that role better.

The 486 is a more efficient design than a 386. It incorporates a built-in 8K cache and cache controller, a math coprocessor (see the section "What about Coprocessors?" later), and better architecture and memory management for 32-bit operations. The cache gives a boost to overall performance while still using relatively inexpensive dynamic random-access memory (DRAM)—a volatile type of main memory. (A *cache*, in simple terms, is a way to help speed up the computer. The cache anticipates the next instruction based on what you're doing and stores it in a hiding place in memory. Then when the instruction or data is needed, it's retrieved from the hiding place more quickly than it could have been otherwise.) A 486 can process complex 32-bit instructions faster than any 386. DOS and most of today's software don't take advantage of this, because many applications and DOS itself were written with older 8- and 16-bit processing designs. OS/2, a multitasking operating system developed by IBM and Microsoft, and Windows NT are able to take full advantage of the 486's

COMPUTERS

features. The 50 MHz 486 has become the top-end desktop workhorse machine.

80486DX2　The 486DX2 is a peculiar chip that runs internally twice as fast as the external system. In other words, if a machine were designed to run a 25 MHz 486, you could put in the 50 MHz 486DX2 and it would work fine without any major changes to the rest of the computer. It would not run as fast as a 50 MHz 486DX, though. Only the innards of the CPU are running fast on a DX2 chip—the rest of the computer is running at the speed designed around the 25 MHz chip. This is a little confusing, but suffice it to say that a 50 MHz 486DX has more performance than a 50 MHz 486DX2.

80486SX　The 486SX is a slowed-down 486—it runs at 16, 20, and 25 MHz—with the math coprocessor circuitry disabled. Intel hopes that the 486SX is your ticket to low-cost 486 computing. It will excel at 32-bit computing because of its superior design over a 386. If you need a coprocessor, however, the 486SX doesn't make any sense. If your work will be under DOS and Windows or if the applications will not take advantage of 32-bit computing, a 33 or 40 MHz 386 will give you better performance through brute force. Unlike the 386SX (whose newer instruction set was a real advantage over the archaic 80286), the 486SX does not offer any clear advantages over the 386 machines. A true 486 or a 33–40 MHz 386 is a better choice.

　　In the last year or so the 66 MHz version of the 486DX2 has become the standard 486 to buy. Clone makers sell more of these than any other high-performance setup. And this is the chip we currently recommend.

80486DX3　IBM, meanwhile, has a license to build 486 chips, and it is now shipping the chips it calls Blue Thunder. These are clock-tripled 486 chips running at 75 MHz and 99 MHz (which everyone calls 100 MHz), and the company says it will produce a 120 MHz chip shortly. These chips can only be found on IBM motherboards, as their license with Intel does not allow IBM to ship raw chips to customers. Intel has the technology to do clock-tripled chips, and we can expect to see Intel, AMD, and Cyrix shipping 75 MHz 486 chips this year along with a few 100 MHz chips. The prices are not yet established.

Pentium　This chip should have been dubbed the 586, but instead was named the Pentium and was first shown publicly at COMDEX in late 1992. Only this year is the chip shipping in quantities. So far Intel has announced two clock speeds of 60 and 66 MHz with plans for faster speeds and clock doubling. It is now the standard for high-performance desktop computing.

COMPUTERS

DON'T FORGET THE GOVERNMENT: WHAT FCC RATINGS MEAN

The FCC (Federal Communications Commission) approves two classes of computers, Class A and Class B.

Class A approval signifies that a computer has sufficiently low radio frequency emissions for operation in a business locale. A Class A machine is more likely to act as a transmitter of interference, and therefore is unsuitable for the home or anywhere else that a TV, stereo, or AM/FM radio might be affected.

The more stringent Class B rating allows for home use as well, where computers are likely to be placed near radios and TVs. The Class B rating is much harder for a manufacturer to meet. The PC must be inspected first by an independent testing lab, and then it must be submitted to the FCC itself for direct approval. Class A machines merely conform to a published list of specifications, so Class A approval is a self-regulated process.

While a Class B rating is mandatory for any electronic devices operating in the home, it makes sense to get Class B-rated equipment for the office, too. This rating means that the system is less likely to send out emissions which might interfere with other electronic devices around the workplace. A machine with the Class B rating is also better protected from incoming electrical interference, which is a factor in offices where many computers and other electronic equipment are close to one another. Finally, Class B machines are generally better designed and engineered, and will likely prove to be more dependable over time. ∎

PowerPC   Right now this is a sleeper chip, designed by Motorola in concert with IBM and Apple. The first iteration of this chip is the 601 model and will be the basis for the new Macintosh. IBM has announced a division to make PCs with this chip, and since it is as powerful as the Pentium and costs half as much, we must watch the reaction of the market to the chip. As the chip is now designed it cannot directly run PC applications, but that may change.

Upgradable PCs

One of the newest PCs on the market is the so-called "upgradable" PC. This is a machine that can—conceivably—keep in step with the newest technology. Supposedly, an upgradable PC will stave off obsolescence, save money, and boost your productivity over the years. Much of that is true. However, upgradability by itself is not much of a reason to buy a particular PC. It's just another feature, like the size and layout of the case, the microprocessor locked inside, the disks, or the ports that come as standard equipment. A number of companies offer computers designed to be upgraded.

In reality, nearly any PC is upgradable if you're willing to replace the motherboard or pry out the microprocessor chip and plug an upgrade board in its place. The result is a workable, but confused, mess. One key

COMPUTERS

advantage that an "upgradable" PC has over a "regular" one is the ZIF (zero insertion force) socket on the motherboard. This allows you to easily pop off the current microprocessor and stick a more up-to-date one on the motherboard.

With the ZIF socket, you can upgrade as many times as you like. Because it's an easy socket to insert and extract a CPU from, you can perform as many upgrades as your pocketbook and the technology allows.

In the case of the non-ZIF upgrade socket, there are two sockets. This is the case where putting the new chip into the upgrade socket disables the other chip in the non-upgrade socket. Also, it's not true that you can only upgrade once. True, once you have put the chip into the non-ZIF socket, it's hard to remove it, but certainly not impossible if you have the right tools.

A number of machines called upgradable really aren't. Let's say a computer is said to be a 486, it runs at 50 MHz, and the salesperson says you can upgrade it. If you ask what chip is in the machine, the reply is, "A 486DX2." This means it's really a 25 MHz 486 with a clock doubler. This doubler makes the chip run twice as fast. But that's not the same as a true upgradable 50 MHz 486 machine.

This upgrading trend has a lot of "gotchas," since the specifications for the chips of the future keep changing, and although Intel says it keeps vendors apprised of the future architecture, it can't guarantee anything. It's possible that the "upgradable" PC you buy won't be upgradable after all.

Dvorak Recommends... When you're in the business of buying a machine that must stay current with the newest technological advancements, try to select one that can somehow be upgraded. It's a slightly new twist on the same old advice: Buy the newest technology you can afford, and make sure it's upgradable at least once.

In today's fast-paced world of technology, it's hard to get your money's worth out of a computer if you can't keep it current. A machine that will let you move from its current configuration to the next big step is a better choice in the long run. You need this flexibility. The actual cost for an upgradable machine versus a non-upgradable one is small. The two big questions to ask are: Does it have a ZIF socket on the motherboard, and does it have a 486DX2 chip? Obviously, go for the machine *with* the ZIF socket and with the fastest clock speed you can afford.

What about Coprocessors?

A *coprocessor* (also called a floating-point coprocessor) is a computer chip dedicated to high-speed math. The most efficient way to boost power for mathematics-intensive computing is by adding a math coprocessor.

COMPUTERS

Some software requires a math coprocessor chip to be installed in the computer. Most software does not, in which case the math coprocessor is simply ignored. Two major mathematical processors dominate the market: Intel's own 80387 FPU and Weitek Corporation's 3167 (for 386s) and 4167 (for 486s). Intel's chip is necessary to run AutoCAD, but only in the last several years have spreadsheet programs taken advantage of the added number-crunching power an FPU provides.

Weitek's math coprocessor is not widely supported, and tests performed in PC Labs indicate it does not provide better performance than other coprocessors in most commercial applications that support it. Weitek's Abacus series of coprocessors, which includes the 3167 and 4167, uses memory mapping and an architecture dissimilar to Intel's 80387 math coprocessor, so software supporting the 80387 does not necessarily support the 3167. According to Weitek, its coprocessors are supported by about 40 applications.

If you're really that concerned—and that willing to spend money on these high-performance/high-price items—then a 486-based system is probably what you really need. If you need even more processing power, Weitek chips can operate in addition to Intel 486s and 386/387 combinations. Just make sure your software can take advantage of them before you spend all that money.

The Computer Bus

Once you start looking around at computers, the issue of "which bus?" will arise (not which bus to take to the computer store, but which bus to put into your computer). The *expansion bus* is a data highway for information to travel on; the *bandwidth* is the number of lanes. The bigger the bandwidth the more data that can be sent. As examples, a 16-bit bandwidth means data can be sent in 16-bit chunks, and a 32-bit bandwidth sends data in 32-bit chunks.

An expansion bus is where cards connect to the computer. Cards have a connector edge, which fits snugly into the bus much like an electrical plug fits into a wall socket.

When cards are plugged into the bus, they communicate with the system, sometimes through the BIOS and other times not. (The *BIOS* is the basic input/output system that tells the computer how to move data from the different components.) The 16- or 32-bit bandwidth is an important consideration due to the communication time between the cards. Let's say you have a 32-bit 486 machine, and it's pumping out data at 32 bits; your video card (which connects to the monitor and is discussed in Chapter 5) is also 32 bits. If you have a 16-bit bus, it will become a bottleneck. It's like a four-lane highway connected to another four-lane highway by way of a two-lane connector. At rush hour, traffic movement will be sluggish.

COMPUTERS

You have the choice of four types of expansion bus: ISA, MCA, EISA, and Local Bus. There are some performance differences between the buses—and often a lot of discussion about them at gatherings of computer techno-nerds. Newer buses offer increased performance over the older technology buses. This performance is important in regard to networks and the newer multitasking operating systems (OS/2, Windows, Desqview X) which demand higher throughput. Generally speaking, the average user buying a first computer should buy the most common bus: ISA. But, there are exceptions to this rule, like almost every other rule in the computer world. (One such exception: If you buy an IBM PS/2 machine, you will get an MCA bus, since that's the only one they put in those machines.)

Industry Standard Architecture (ISA)   For most 386s, you can stick with the original AT bus, also called the ISA bus. This expansion bus originated in the IBM PC at an 8-bit bandwidth. IBM improved on the design with the PC/AT, raising its bandwidth to 16 bits. In a 16-bit computer, it's a fine match, but for the system of the future, it won't do.

Micro Channel Architecture (MCA)   386-based computers raised computing power on the desktop to the 32-bit level, leaving the expansion bus suddenly lagging behind the processor in performance. IBM introduced MCA in April 1987, forsaking its older architecture for a new 32-bit design. Not only did it offer a wider data path, but the process of bus-mastering was unveiled. *Bus-mastering* is a way to speed I/O transfers without losing processor performance. Intelligent peripherals on the expansion bus can take control of the bus to transfer information across it without the processor's having to arbitrate the process. An intelligent hard-disk controller can move data into memory without involving the CPU. It can continue to perform an instruction and have information it needs ready without controlling the movement of data. Performance is improved by task sharing.

Extended Industry Standard Architecture (EISA)   The MCA introduction was not well received by other manufacturers. A "Gang of Nine" consortium (including Compaq, Zenith, Hewlett-Packard, and several others) decided to create their own expansion bus architecture. It would be 32-bit, include bus-mastering, and remain compatible with older expansion cards.

The EISA connector was designed for full backward compatibility with ISA boards. All the connectors on the ISA bus are present in their ordinary positions, but a new, lower row of contacts is added to link up the advanced functions of the bus. The developers linked these new contacts to the expansion board circuitry by interleaving their connecting traces between the ISA contacts on the card, as shown in Figure 3.2.

COMPUTERS

Figure 3.2 Bus connectors

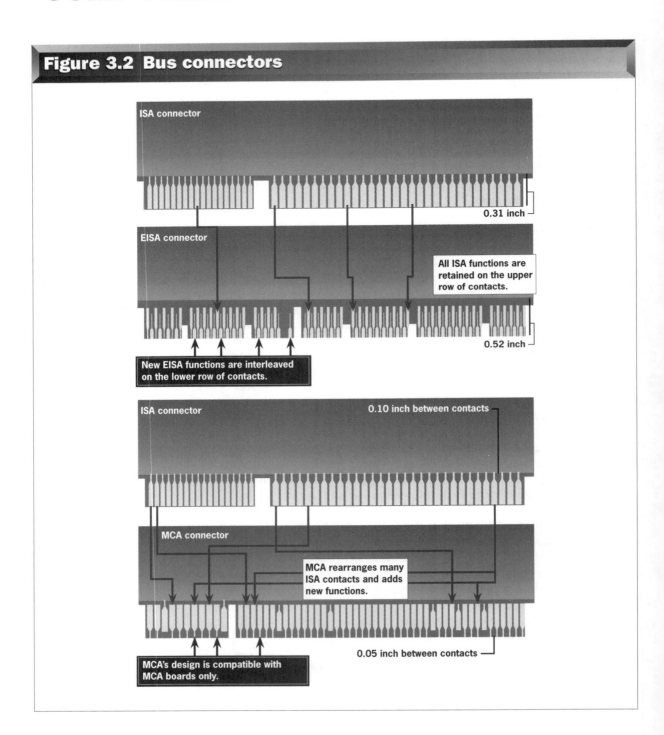

ISA connector

EISA connector

All ISA functions are retained on the upper row of contacts.

0.31 inch

0.52 inch

New EISA functions are interleaved on the lower row of contacts.

ISA connector

0.10 inch between contacts

MCA connector

MCA rearranges many ISA contacts and adds new functions.

MCA's design is compatible with MCA boards only.

0.05 inch between contacts

COMPUTERS

Micro Channel, on the other hand, forgoes hardware compatibility and guarantees only software compatibility with classic AT-bus computers. Thus, the MCA designers were free to alter the ISA layout completely, rearranging the functions of the contacts to minimize interference and to promote higher-speed operation. They added new functions as well. The result is that Micro Channel boards work only in Micro Channel slots. EISA slots will accommodate both ISA and EISA expansion boards, but this is a one-way compatibility: EISA boards cannot be used in ISA expansion slots.

When it was announced in August 1988, the extended industry standard architecture (EISA) promised too much. With its wealth of system-enhancing technologies, EISA promised to accelerate the performance of any peripheral through its bus-mastering, interrupt sharing, 32-bit bus width, high-speed transfer modes, and automated setup. But its success did not come easily.

Only recently have EISA systems come close to delivering on the promises the vendors made. Its original costs were disproportionately high: The first EISA machines demanded a $2,000 premium over their ISA kin. The premium still hovers around $800.

Despite the demonstrable improvements in performance made by this technology, the best advantages of the better bus design still lie ahead. EISA is a bundle of technologies, and most of today's quicker controllers cash in on only a single performance-improving aspect of the standard: EISA's 32-bit bandwidth. Future applications should implement EISA's higher-speed modes and allow data-transfer rates of up to 33Mb per second. (The AT bus is limited to about one-quarter of that speed.) The true power of bus-mastering, also, won't be realized until a new generation of software becomes available. This will include software drivers capable of bringing the advanced modes to life and versions of operating systems able to take advantage of this technology. The multitasking abilities of OS/2, Windows NT, and UNIX make EISA versions of these operating systems possible, but none of these are here yet.

Nevertheless, EISA outperforms the AT bus. Those performance-enhancing capabilities should soon migrate into peripherals other than disk controllers. Vendors including Cogent Data Technologies, Mylex, Novell, and Proteon already manufacture EISA network adapters, and 32-bit coprocessed graphics boards are on the way, promising even faster video performance.

Local Bus/VESA Bus The Intel processors that power the PC have the ability to be hooked directly to peripherals via something called a *local bus*. The Video Electronics Standards Association (VESA) saw that various manufacturers were toying with this bus in a nonstandard way to accelerate the graphics of the PC which was getting bogged down by Windows software.

COMPUTERS

WHAT'S AN MB?

Mb is short for megabyte. A megabyte is a million bytes, plus some change (1,048,576, or 1,024 times 1,024). Megabytes are used to measure the size of a hard or floppy disk and the total amount of RAM in the computer. Another term coming into common usage is a gigabyte (G), which is roughly a billion bytes. And looming on the horizon is the still larger terabyte (T), which is one trillion bytes.

When Mb describes a disk size, as in a 1.44Mb 3½-inch floppy drive, the 1.44 is just a more exact convention. In reality, 2Mb of RAM or 60Mb of hard disk should be more accurately written to two decimal places, but they just aren't. ∎

The VESA committee finally released a bus called the VESA bus, which is now the standard local bus for today's machines. Most PCs now come with one or more VESA slots in addition to the PC's other bus slots. These are used mostly for video, although hard-disk subsystems and even I/O such as parallel and serial ports may use these slots in the future. A competing bus from Intel called the PCI local bus is expected to emerge, too.

A Look at Some Typical Systems

The following sections briefly discuss some of the more common systems you can use as standards with which to compare your needs.

The Home Computer

This is a machine that will probably be used by everyone in the family. You will use it to play games, run educational programs, word-process, and handle family finances. The ideal system would be an inexpensive 33 MHz 486 machine with an 80Mb hard disk, a VGA color card, and a color monitor.

For a printer, the home computer user will find today's dot-matrix printer a perfect accompaniment. (See Chapter 6 for a full discussion of printer basics.)

Look for these specifications in a home computer:

- 33 MHz 486DX computer

- 4Mb of RAM

- 1.44Mb 3¹/₂-inch floppy drive

- 80Mb hard disk

- Standard VGA video card

- Standard VGA color monitor

COMPUTERS

A WORD ABOUT FLOPPY DRIVES

You may want your computer to have two floppy disk drives: one 5¼-inch 1.2Mb drive and one 3½-inch 1.44Mb drive. This is especially handy if you have a lot of old software or data stored on 5¼-inch disks. Most software now appears in the smaller disk drive size. If you have just one size floppy drive and the disks are not the size you need, you'll have to convert the disks to the proper size. While this inconvenience can be tolerated by some, it's a terrible inconvenience for the person who doesn't have the time to fuss with finding a friend or service to do this. When both drives are available, you'll never have a problem. It's also handy since you can put data or software on either size drive to exchange with a friend or colleague.

If you are going to purchase a system and want the two disk drive sizes, be sure to have the 3½-inch drive as drive A and the larger 5¼-inch disk as drive B. You'll need this arrangement because most of today's software comes with only 3½-inch disks. Newer software expects to be booted from drive A. If you have the smaller drive as drive B, the software won't be able to locate the disk and may not run. ∎

The Home Office Computer

This is similar to the home computer but it has more power. Although a 80386-based machine may have sufficed a year ago, it's now silly to buy anything less than a 486SX machine. An 80Mb hard disk is the minimum, although a larger hard disk would be more practical. A VGA card is recommended, along with a standard VGA monitor. The home office needs a near-letter-quality (NLQ) dot-matrix printer or a laser printer.

Look for these specifications in a home office computer:

- 66 MHz 486DX2 computer

- 8Mb of RAM

- 1.44Mb 3½-inch floppy drive

- 80Mb–400Mb hard disk

- Standard VGA video card

- VGA color monitor

- Mouse

- High-quality NLQ dot-matrix printer or laser printer

The Business Computer

The business computer should be able to run all available business software with speed. This means any 486 computer will do. When you're paid by the hour, time shouldn't be wasted waiting on the computer. Much of

COMPUTERS

today's business software is bloated and takes up a lot of disk space. Your best bet is to buy a minimum of 120Mb of hard-disk capacity or, ideally, as much as you can afford.

The business computer system should also include a high-quality laser printer.

A business computer system should meet these specifications:

- 66 MHz 486DX2 computer

- 16Mb of RAM

- 3½-inch 1.44Mb floppy drive

- 120Mb–500Mb hard disk

- Super VGA video card using VESA

- VGA color monitor

- Mouse

- Laser printer

The Engineering PC Workstation

This is the machine that is needed to do CAD/CAM work. It requires as much processing power as possible. This means a Pentium that incorporates a floating-point chip within the CPU. Since most CAD/CAM files use large amounts of disk space, at least a 500Mb hard disk is necessary. One major consideration is that CAD/CAM demands the best video you can afford. Super VGA and a multi-frequency monitor is the minimum for accommodating higher resolutions.

An engineering PC system should have the following:

- 66 MHz Pentium

- 16–32Mb of RAM

- 3½-inch 1.44Mb floppy drive

- 500Mb hard disk or larger

- Super VGA video card using VESA

- Multi-frequency VGA color monitor

- Mouse

- Laser printer

COMPUTERS

The Power-User Computer

An additional type of computer system is available for the class of user
called the power user. It's not much different than the engineering PC
workstation. Programmers will use such a system to do compilations. Show-
offs who want the fastest, best machine will also want this kind of system.
Intensive users of graphics software, desktop publishing software, and large
spreadsheets and databases will also benefit from a powerful, fast computer.

A power-user system should meet these specifications:

- 66 MHz Pentium

- 16–32Mb of RAM

- 3½-inch 1.44Mb floppy drive

- 1G hard disk or larger

- Super VGA video card using VESA

- Multi-frequency VGA color monitor

- Mouse

- Laser printer

MONITORS

CHAPTER
4

MONITORS ARE AN INTEGRAL PART of today's computer scene. They come in a variety of sizes, prices, and screen resolutions, some sharper than others. Back in 1977, it was as easy to purchase a monitor as it was a television set: "Yep, that one looks like it will work; won't clash with my wallpaper." Now specialized monitors are designed for explicit applications, and with them comes a multitude of compatibility issues, such as which specialty cards go with which

MONITORS

monitors. (A monitor won't work without a video card, which fits into the bus within your computer's case. The video card is the "middleman" which interprets the computer's data and sends it to the monitor. Chapter 5 covers these video cards in detail.)

The monitor is called by many names, including the video display terminal (VDT), the video display unit (VDU), the computer screen, or even outdated terms such as the cathode-ray tube (CRT) or the terminal.

How a Monitor Works

The main difference between the picture quality of a television and a monitor is the resolution. A monitor's screen display should be stable and of good quality, since you will sit very close to the monitor and will spend many hours reading the display. If the images are fuzzy (low resolution) or waver constantly, you'll have a raging headache and watering eyes in no time. (Although employing similar technology, a monitor is a better-built piece of equipment than a TV.)

Monitors have knobs to adjust for clarity. These include a brightness knob which adjusts the illumination of the entire screen, and a contrast knob which makes the letters lighter or darker in relation to the background screen. Particular monitors may have other adjustments, and color monitors may have a way to adjust the colors, but this is becoming unusual in the marketplace.

Color

A typical color screen works in much the same way as a color television. The inside of the picture tube is coated with three different phosphors: red, green, and blue. Phosphors are special chemical compounds that glow with characteristic colors when they are bombarded by a stream of electrons. The phosphor gets "excited." Thanks to the additive properties of colored light, you can use combinations of these three primary colors to produce every shade in the rainbow. When all three colors are mixed together in equal quantities, your eye perceives white light (see Figure 4.1).

This approach has its limitations. Since each type of phosphor must be excited by electrons fired from a different gun than the other two, the tubes must be constructed to fine tolerances. No matter how small the dots or how high the screen resolution, a little crispness and detail at the edge of a white line will be lost where a final row of one color pixel or another gives the edges of images a faint color tint. (Monochrome monitors have it much easier than their color cousins. They use one color phosphor which is uniformly coated across the inside of the screen. The precise placement of specific dots isn't an issue.)

MONITORS

VIDEO TALK: A GUIDE TO VIDEO TERMS

Discussions of monitors involve a particular kind of lingo. While most of these terms are computerese, many of them do describe the characteristics of a monitor. Here are some of the video terms you will come across in magazines, when you try to talk to a salesperson, and even as you read this book:

- **Aspect ratio** The aspect ratio is the ratio of a pixel's width to its height. In VGA and Super VGA mode, this ratio is 1:1, which means the pixels are as tall as they are wide.

- **Autosizing** True autosizing occurs when a monitor can maintain a constant image size when moving across low and high resolutions. Many monitors use preprogrammed factory settings to achieve a similar effect, but only for certain resolutions, usually VGA and Super VGA. Some manufacturers also provide user-determined settings. Autosizing is especially important for the newer multitasking operating systems, such as Windows, OS/2, and Desqview X.

- **Barrel distortion** Barrel distortion occurs at the edges of the screen and is the inverse of *pincushioning*. The sides of an image afflicted with this type of distortion seem to bow out, resembling a barrel.

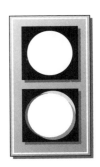

- **Convergence** Theoretically, each of the beams that generate the three color dots (red, green, and blue) should converge at appropriate distances from one another. When all three dots are being excited simultaneously and their relative distance is perfect, the result is pure white. Serious deviation from this harmony (mainly due to the relationship of the electron beams to each other) results in poor convergence. This can cause white pixels to show bits of color and can also decrease both picture sharpness and resolution.

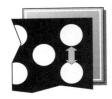

- **Dot pitch** Dot pitch describes the distance between the holes in the *shadow mask*; it therefore also indirectly describes how far apart the individual dots are on screen. The smaller the dot pitch, the finer the image's "grain." Some color monitors such as the Sony Trinitron, use a slot mask (also known as an aperture grille) which is perforated by strips, not holes, in the shadow mask. In this case, the dots are arranged linearly, and their density is called *striped dot pitch*. (Monochrome monitors do not use a shadow mask and therefore do not have a dot pitch.)

- **Drift** Drift, *jitter*, and *swim* are all terms that relate to an unwanted motion of a line. The only difference between the three terms is the amount of time used to measure on-screen wavers. A perfect image should be rock-steady on the screen.

- **Horizontal scan frequency** This is the frequency per second at which a monitor repaints the horizontal lines that make up an image. Horizontal scan frequency is measured in kHz (kilohertz). A standard VGA signal requires a 31.5 kHz horizontal scan frequency capability.

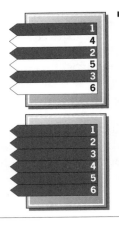

- **Interlaced and noninterlaced scanning** There are two basic schemes for painting an image on the screen: interlaced and noninterlaced. Interlaced scanning takes two passes, painting every other line on the first pass and filling in the rest of the lines on the second pass. Noninterlaced scanning paints all the lines in one pass and

Continued on next page

MONITORS

VIDEO TALK: A GUIDE TO VIDEO TERMS

Continued from previous page

then paints an entirely new frame. Noninterlaced scanning is preferable because it reduces screen flicker. However, it is more expensive.

- **Pincushioning**   Pincushioning describes an unwanted curve of an image which usually occurs at the edges of the screen. The sides of the image appear to curve inward.

- **Pixel**   A pixel is the smallest information building block of an on-screen image. On a color-monitor screen, each pixel is made of one or more triads. Resolution is usually expressed in terms of the number of pixels comprising the width and height of a complete on-screen image. In VGA, the resolution is 640×480 pixels; in Super VGA, it is 800×600 pixels or higher.

- **Roping**   Roping describes an image distortion that gives solid straight lines a helical or twisted appearance. This problem is caused by poor convergence.

- **Shadow mask**   A shadow mask is inside the monitor just behind the screen. It is drilled with small holes, each of which corresponds to a *triad*. The shadow mask helps guide the electron beam so that each beam hits only one phosphor dot in the triad.

- **Slot mask**   The slot mask, also known as the aperture grille, serves the same function as a shadow mask. The slot mask is made up of vertical wires stretched behind the screen. The spacing of these wires (or the slots between them) determines the finest detail that the monitor can display horizontally. The dot pitch for such a display measures the space between these slots.

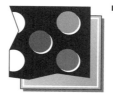

- **Triad**   A triad contains three phosphor-filled dots—one red, one green, and one blue—arranged in a triangle. Each of the three electron guns is dedicated to one of these colors (for example, the red gun excites only a triad's red phosphor dot). As the guns scan the screen, each active triad produces a single color. Which color it is depends on the combination of excited color dots and how active each dot is.

- **Vertical refresh rate**   The vertical refresh rate, also called the vertical scan frequency, is related to horizontal sweeps in that once an image has been entirely repainted (by horizontal sweeps), it has been vertically scanned or refreshed. Slow vertical refresh rates will increase screen flicker. Standard VGA has a vertical scan frequency of 60 Hz or 70 Hz, and Super VGA vertical refresh rates vary from industry guidelines of 56 Hz and 60 Hz to the official standard of 72 Hz.

- **Video bandwidth**   Video bandwidth represents the highest input frequency a monitor can handle. It determines the monitor's resolution capabilities. Video bandwidth is measured in MHz (megahertz).   ■

MONITORS

The sharpness of a color monitor's image is determined by three factors: the monitor's bandwidth, its dot pitch, and the accuracy of its convergence. Although the bandwidth and dot pitch are important to determine a good monitor, convergence is the real measurement.

Bandwidth   The *bandwidth* of a monitor is the range of signal frequencies that its circuits can handle. This frequency range determines what resolution the monitor can display. Most bandwidth figures do not represent absolute capabilities, but rather indicate the range at which the monitor achieves optimal operation. The visual effect of modestly exceeding the rated bandwidth is a slight softening of the sharp edges of each pixel (see Figure 4.2).

To estimate the minimum bandwidth that a monitor must display to attain a given graphics standard, you need to know the number of pixels and the frame rate associated with the standard. The bandwidth is equal to the total number of pixels (the number of horizontal pixels multiplied by the number of vertical pixels) multiplied by the frame rate. (This calculation assumes that each pixel represents a signal pulse.)

Figure 4.1   Making white with phosphors

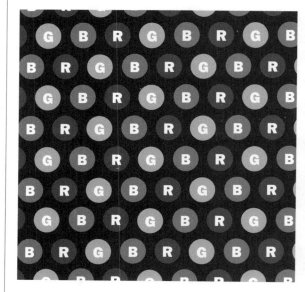 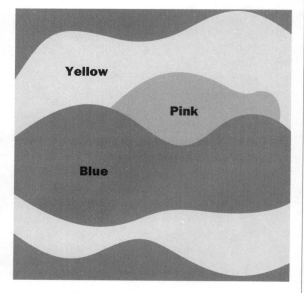

Close-up of the phosphors of an RGB color monitor   Close-up of the phosphors of a paper-white monitor

MONITORS

Figure 4.2 Bandwidth

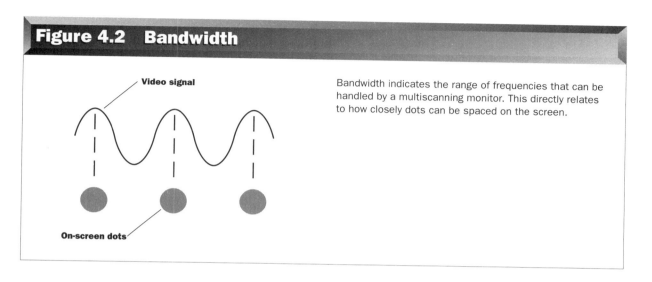

Video signal

On-screen dots

Bandwidth indicates the range of frequencies that can be handled by a multiscanning monitor. This directly relates to how closely dots can be spaced on the screen.

In the case of 800×600-pixel graphics and a frame rate of 60 Hz, this calculation (800×600×60) would give a bandwidth of 28.8 MHz. This is a low figure—in reality, such a resolution requires some overhead for *horizontal and vertical retrace*. This refers to the time it takes the monitor's circuitry to shift from the end of a line to the beginning of the next line, and from the bottom of one frame to the top of the next. A 30 MHz system would be barely adequate for 800×600-pixel graphics.

Dot Pitch   All monitors come with *dot pitch* specifications, a measure of pixel spacing given in millimeters (see Figure 4.3). Each pixel on a color screen consists of a trio of dots with each dot glowing in one of the primary colors of light: red, green, or blue. The pitch is determined by the spacing of the holes in what is called the *shadow (or slot) mask* of the monitor's CRT. The smaller a monitor's dot pitch rating, the sharper the on-screen image it can display.

Convergence   Convergence defines how accurately each of the three colored dots in a pixel is placed in relation to the other two (see Figure 4.4). In theory, the three electron beams should converge on a single point as they scan the inside of the CRT to create the monitor's image. In reality, they must be offset somewhat because the three phosphor colors of the tube are next to, rather than on top of, each other.

When convergence is perfect and all three guns are exciting the phosphor, the result is a pixel that appears perfectly white, but a number of factors conspire against this perfection: small irregularities in the electronics that control each color gun, tiny differences in the alignment of the

MONITORS

Figure 4.3 Dot pitch

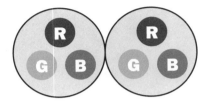

Every pixel on the screen is made from three dots of color, sorted out by the shadow mask of the picture tube. The dot pitch is determined by the spacing of holes in the shadow mask.

An effective dot pitch

guns, and variations in the magnetic fields that guide the electron beams. The result is that one or two colors may stray from ideal positioning, which gives the pixels a distinctly two- or three-color look. Because of the spread of the dot trios, the image also loses sharpness and resolution. The misconvergence results in a loss of true white (and black) on screen, causing text to appear fuzzy.

Convergence problems do not result from monitor design flaws, but rather from real-world imperfections. For this reason, the convergence of monitors of the same make and model varies. Convergence may even vary across the face of a screen. (Electron beams are more difficult to control near the corners of the image, so convergence problems usually arise there.)

Figure 4.4 Convergence

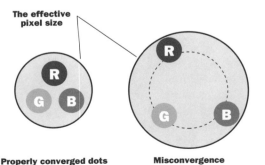

The effective pixel size

Convergence is a measure of how precisely the colored dots composing each pixel meet at the same point. When these dots don't converge properly, the pixels are enlarged (often doubled in size) and the image is blurred.

Properly converged dots   **Misconvergence**

MONITORS

MONITOR EMISSIONS: WHAT'S THE FUSS?

For years, a debate has been raging over how monitors affect our health. Studies have been conducted from all angles. In 1986, Sweden's National Board for Measurement and Testing (MPR) studied monitor emissions and published a set of standards. In 1988, Northern Kaiser Permanente Medical Care Program (in Oakland, California) observed 1,583 pregnant women in a study of environmental hazards. They found a correlation between an increased rate of miscarriages and the use of VDTs for more than 20 hours a week in the first trimester. (Some subsequent research has raised questions about these findings.)

In 1989, the University of Toronto's study showed no relation between miscarriages in mice and emissions of VDTs. In 1991, the *New England Journal of Medicine* was unable to reproduce results similar to the Kaiser study in a similar work situation. The conclusion, which the Kaiser study also notes, was that stress in the workplace may foster the miscarriages more than VDT signals.

It is agreed that higher-frequency radiation harms cells and is dangerous, but knowledge is lacking on the way low-frequency radiation may affect cells.

What Do Monitors Emit?

A VDT displays on-screen images. To do so, it generates electric and magnetic fields in extremely low frequency (ELF) and very low frequency (VLF). In recent studies, monitors have been measured in VLF radiation ranges from 3,000 to 30,000 Hz. These are primarily emitted by the deflection yokes of monitors and television sets.

The ELF range in monitors (nearly all electrical appliances emit ELF) is in the range of 30 to 300 Hz. ELF signals have been associated with a variety of negative health effects, both in laboratory experiments and epidemiological surveys. These effects include increased cancer rates, changes in biological clocks, and alteration of nerve-cell physiology. The studies have shown increased cancer rates for people living near power lines and using electrical blankets, both of which produce excessive electrical and magnetic ELF fields.

The ELF fields are strongest behind rather than in front of the monitor screens, but at this time, it is still debatable whether these fields are truly dangerous.

What to Do?

The University of California at Berkeley Wellness Letter (P.O. Box 420148, Palm Coast, FL 32142) recommends the following precautions:

- Sit at arm's length (a minimum of 28 inches) away from the computer screen.
- Sit at least four feet from a coworker's monitor.
- Turn off your monitor whenever you're not using it. (Just dimming the display doesn't diminish the emissions.)

In addition, monitor manufacturers are becoming increasingly sensitive to the issue of emissions. Many are producing low-emission models at a price competitive with their traditional counterparts. ∎

Convergence errors are often the chief limitation on a particular monitor's resolution. For example, a monitor may have a rated maximum convergence error of 0.6 mm—twice the dot pitch of the CRT tube. This would cause a very poor image quality, particularly at higher resolutions when more information is sent to the screen.

MONITORS

TERMINALS VS. MONITORS

A "terminal" usually means a keyboard/monitor combination (often as one "blended" unit). Many terminals are semi-smart machines and can perform functions on their own. Some of the old TeleVideo terminals could print directly from the screen to the printer—without going through the computer. (However, there are also dumb terminals which are little more than a keyboard and a monitor.) A terminal can also store information in a queue until it is *polled* (asked for information from a computer).

This is different from a monitor which can do nothing except display on the screen the information given to it by the computer. The monitor cannot store or queue information, nor can it request or answer a poll on its own. It is just a video display tube which is then hooked to a CPU. The keyboard is also hooked to the CPU. ∎

A Little Monitor History

Until the early 1980s, most monitors were terminals. These were boxy video display terminals (VDTs) combined with an attached keyboard. A terminal could be configured to work with just about any computer on the market (not that there was a wide selection of personal computers to choose from). Terminals attached to computers via a serial interface. In those days, the VDT was commonly referred to as a CRT (cathode-ray tube).

Before DOS, the dominant operating system for 8-bit computers was CP/M (control program for microprocessors). Early CP/M machines were originally designed to use separate memory-mapped video display devices and discrete keyboards that plugged into the machines—not unlike the video display cards used today. The most well-known was the VDM-1. Terminal manufacturers recognized this "lost market" and began to market mainframe and mini-style terminals to the CP/M community. The sales pitch of "just like a real computer" paid off: CP/M computers soon used terminals almost exclusively.

Apple II computers and the early game machines (such as those made by Atari) hooked to a monitor, not a terminal. (The Apple II was built with a keyboard as part of the system. All that was missing was a monitor.) These monitors—unlike terminals—looked like television sets without the tuner. In some cases they *were* television sets. (Many early computers could be used with any television set with a special RF adapter which hooked to the antenna.) Then IBM came out with PC-DOS computers, which were dubbed "three-piece" computers because they included three main components: the monitor, the keyboard, and the "box."

Ironically, when the IBM PC-DOS computers arrived on the scene—with separate monitor and keyboard—the monitor connected directly to the computer (just like the earliest personal computers) through a display device connection. These new monitors used video cards that were either

MONITORS

IBM monochrome (MDA), IBM color graphics adapter (CGA), or Hercules (the first third-party add-on card) cards.

Meanwhile, about the time these early personal computers were gaining some momentum, the big computers—mainframes—at large corporations were adding some pretty dazzling terminals. Compared to a terminal connected to a mainframe computer, the first monitors for personal computers were crude and unattractive. The early monitors had predominantly green or black and bluish-white displays. They were 40-column monitors, which meant that 40 characters could appear on the screen before the text wrapped to a new line. The Apple II had a 40-column, all uppercase display.

The next generation of personal computer monitors had 64 columns in stylish "eye-ease" amber. Add-in video cards would eventually change the display to a whopping 132 columns.

The Evolution of Resolution

The most dramatic technical advances in monitor development have been made in the area of resolution—the sharpness of the screen image. Early CGA monitors had a resolution of about 320×200 pixels; the noninterlaced monitors produced today have a resolution of 1,024×768 pixels. Current trends indicate that we can expect even greater improvements in resolution technology.

CGA (1981)   CGA (color graphics adapter) was one of the two display adapters IBM introduced for its original PC. CGA offered a palette of 16 colors in two modes: 320×200 resolution in four colors and 640×200 in two colors. The second adapter, MDA (monochrome display adapter), was less expensive. It offered higher resolution (720×350 pixels) but could display only text—no more than 25 lines of 80 characters each—in a single color. By 1982, power users were employing both adapters, MDA for text and CGA for then-new Lotus 1-2-3 graphics.

Hercules (1982)   The Hercules graphics adapter card was invented by Van Suwannukul (founder of Hercules Computer Technology) so he could use a standard PC and monitor to produce his doctoral thesis using his native Thai alphabet.

Before VGA (video graphics array), monochrome graphics meant one thing: the Hercules graphics adapter. Fully compatible with IBM's monochrome display adapter (MDA) for displaying text, the Hercules board added graphics capabilities to ordinary digital monochrome displays. Along the way, it brought the highest graphics resolution available to standard PC monitors before VGA—720×400 pixels.

For nearly five years, the Hercules card was the standard for monochrome graphics. Dozens of programs were rewritten to take advantage

MONITORS

of its capabilities, including the one that confirmed the success of the Hercules card—Lotus 1-2-3. But in 1987, the introduction of the VGA standard challenged Hercules's dominance.

EGA (1984)   Although today the standard EGA configuration is a card with 256K of DRAM which can provide 16 out of 64 colors at 640×350 resolution, the EGA card originally produced by IBM offered only 64K, enough to display only 16 colors at 320×200 resolution. Before long, the optional 192K memory addition was considered mandatory, even though it nearly doubled the cost of the card. Competitive EGA board makers offered 256K as a standard configuration.

At the same time it introduced EGA, IBM released PGC, the professional graphics controller. The PGC card was slow and expensive, so despite its 640×480 resolution, it failed to become a graphics standard.

Multiscanning Monitor (1985)   The first multiple-frequency (multiscanning) monitor, MultiSync from NEC Home Electronics (USA), could work with CGA, EGA, and PGC adapters.

VGA (1987)   The video graphics array adapter, introduced with IBM's PS/2 line, offered a palette of 262,144 colors. VGA provided 256 colors at 320×200 resolution or 16 at full 640×480 resolution. Though originally VGA was available only for Micro Channel machines, within a year, board manufacturers successfully created standard cards using the new VGA standard.

VGA improved the resolution above the Hercules standard only modestly. The text mode was slightly sharper at 720×400, due to two additional vertical dots in the matrix from which each character is made. In graphics mode, the VGA system can deliver 640×480 resolution, which is about 20 percent sharper than the 720×348 delivered by the Hercules board—not too dramatic an improvement. However, VGA held an important advantage over Hercules: It was compatible with color graphics software.

With VGA, monochrome and color were united under a single standard; the only operational difference between the two display modes (for which programmers need to allow) was the number of colors available on the screen. A color VGA system would show CGA and EGA graphics on its screen; a monochrome VGA system would do likewise, without the special drivers.

In addition, VGA monochrome displays used analog signals, so they had the potential to offer a near-infinite number of shades of gray. (MDA and Hercules display systems were limited to three levels—black, white, and highlighted—although with clever programming some video boards squeezed out up to 16 gray levels.)

MONITORS

Super VGA (1988) Promoted by a consortium of monitor and graphics-board manufacturers called the Video Electronics Standards Association (VESA), Super VGA (also called extended VGA or VGA Plus) offered 800×600 graphics resolution and 56 percent more on-screen pixels than VGA. It used 16 colors out of a palette of 256, which may not have satisfied serious graphics users, but should have sufficed for Microsoft Windows and text-mode users. Adapters capable of displaying 256 colors were readily available but were not addressed by VESA. Super VGA adapters cost little more than regular VGA adapters.

Today's Super VGA monitors provide all the resolution of the original release, a palette of colors (262,144 possibilities in all), and fast screen updates with high-speed 16-bit graphics adapters. They can adapt to any IBM video standard and graphics adapter, and some will even accommodate Apple II and Macintosh computers.

Noninterlaced 1,024×768 (1989) Beginning in 1989, Compaq promoted noninterlaced 1,024×768 resolution, targeting high-end graphics users such as CAD/CAM aficionados. Its boards offered 256 colors with a 512K memory addition.

Meanwhile, in the same market, IBM promoted interlaced 1,024×768 resolution with its 8514/A adapter, introduced in 1987 with the PS/2 line. The board came with 500K of memory, which allowed 16 colors to be displayed simultaneously. The interlaced display, however, was more likely to produce flicker. At present, not much software exists to support either adapter.

XGA (1991) XGA (extended graphics array) has recently become the new graphics standard, though it has yet to be widely accepted in the market. The current XGA design has a screen resolution of up to 1,024×768 with 256 colors. (At the lower resolution of 640×480 pixels, the color palette is 64,000 colors.) Future versions will include so-called "true color" (16 million simultaneous colors) and resolution of up to 4,000×4,000 pixels. It is downwardly compatible with the VGA standard.

Monitors in the Market

There are a number of different monitors on the market. The most common are VGA and Super VGA. If you go out shopping, these will be the ones you will most likely encounter.

All VGA and Super VGA monitors are divided into general classes, discussed below, according to the way they react to the synchronizing signals generated by your PC's VGA circuitry. These signals are used by the monitor to lock the screen image in place so that it doesn't roll like a 1950s television on the fritz.

MONITORS

Fixed-Frequency Monitors

Fixed-frequency monitors, such as the IBM and Compaq captive displays, are designed to lock onto a very narrow frequency range. These monitors demand that the signals from your VGA adapter be close to its nominal value—31.5 kHz for horizontal sync signals and both 60 and 70 Hz for vertical sync signals. Usually, you would choose a fixed-frequency monitor if you purchased your computer and monitor as a "package" deal. The monitors are designed to work only with the computer, and vice versa.

Multiple-Frequency Monitors

Multiple-frequency (or multiple-fixed-frequency) monitors are designed to operate at two or more frequency settings, each of which has a narrow band of acceptance like that of a fixed-frequency display. The best known of these monitors is IBM's 8514, a 16-inch monitor that accepts horizontal sync frequencies of either 31.5 kHz (for MCGA and VGA signals) or 35.5 kHz (for IBM's proprietary 1,024×768 interlaced graphics standard).

Multiscanning Monitors

Multiscanning monitors are specially designed for high-resolution graphics. To display graphic images, a monitor must be able to handle the two synchronizing frequencies used to form them: the horizontal scanning frequency (the rate at which one line is drawn across the width of the screen) and the vertical scanning frequency, also called the refresh or frame rate (the rate at which a complete screen is filled with an image). Each graphic standard requires a different combination of these scan rates; multiscanning monitors are so named because they can scan a range of horizontal and vertical frequencies.

It's important for the multiscanning monitor to operate within its limits, which means it requires a compatible video adapter card. (See Chapter 5 for a more complete discussion of video adapter cards.) If a video card puts out higher horizontal and vertical frequency rates than the monitor can handle, there may be problems. The frequency-handling limits determined by a monitor's manufacturer are noted to ensure safe operation (for example, to keep the operating temperatures of inductive components such as flyback transformers and semiconductors within acceptable limits) and long machine life; most monitors can exceed these limits within reason. But significantly higher scanning frequencies stress critical circuits more than lower frequencies do, which causes the circuits to produce more heat.

When you set a multiscanning monitor to display each different resolution graphics standard, the image is likely to appear in a different spot on the screen at first. Horizontal and vertical position controls allow you to move the image around. The controls help ensure that no part of the

MONITORS

image is cut off and that the black dead space around the image is equal on all four sides of the tube. Ideally, these controls should allow you to move the image beyond the edge of the screen on all four sides.

Specialty Monitors

There are some specialty monitors on the market which are designed for specific applications, such as desktop publishing, CAD/CAM, video editing, and illustration and graphic arts, among others. The monitors are expensive and often very large. They include 1,024 monitors, paper-white monitors, and big-screen (presentation) monitors.

1,024 Monitors   The 1,024 monitors, including big-screen and paper-white monitors, are specialty devices. Desktop publishing experts and those who use CAD/CAM programs like these monitors because their size and high resolution provide a crisp, legible display and because they can accommodate a two-page layout.

Paper-White Monitors   Paper-white monitors are designed for desktop publishing, CAD/CAM, and other specific uses. They have crisp white-and-black displays. This white light is displayed in a variety of ways, all of which involve color.

It may be surprising to discover that even these paper-white displays still rely on phosphors to produce different colors. Although we tend to refer to the display as white, close inspection reveals that the images are made up of a mixture of different colors. Most monitors use combinations of blue and yellow, and some use pink as well.

As you shop for a monitor, you may notice that some paper-white monitors have a blue tinge and some have a distinctly warmer tone. This is because some monitors are assembled by manufacturers and sold to OEMs (original equipment manufacturers). These middlemen purchase equipment components to sell under their own names and may shop through samples of varying phosphor mixtures to determine the exact shades they want for their products. Thus, the difference in shades is simply a matter of the buyer's personal taste and doesn't reflect the quality or cost of the monitor.

Big-Screen (Presentation) Monitors   Large-screen monitors measure at least 19 inches diagonally. The 19-inch measurement is significant; you need at least that size to display a legible two-page spread for a desktop publishing program. However, the 19-inch displays are still not able to display a full-scale image. You need at least 20 inches to produce a full 17-inch-wide image—enough to show two 8½-inch sheets side by side.

MONITORS

BIG-SCREEN ALTERNATIVES

There are alternatives to the big-screen monitors. One low-cost choice is an LCD projection panel on an overhead projector. Overhead projectors are fairly bright, in spite of all the light absorbed by the LCD, and the light weight of the panels makes them easy to set up and move. Unfortunately, LCD color panels remain extremely expensive and do not yet approach CRTs in terms of the range and quality of colors displayed.

Video projectors offer the same high quality as a CRT, at a slightly higher price. However, they are heavy and need tinkering to keep the image well-converged and sharp. Their displays are not very bright, so you must keep the room lights dim. You can improve the brightness by using special screens or rear projection, but these measures often limit the visibility range of the image. If you move off center (to the side), the picture will not be visible. ∎

These monitors are also referred to as *presentation* monitors if they reach the huge 25- to 35-inch picture tube sizes. These larger machines are stretching CRT technology to its limits. They are unable to keep up with Super VGA signals and usually drop back to a VGA resolution. The monitors work very well as conference-room monitors, since they are very readable by a group of people six feet away.

Keep in mind that despite the high resolutions offered by these larger tubes, you can still end up with a surprisingly low dots-per-inch (dpi) image. If you have 1,200 pixels spread across a 17-inch line, you get a display with only about 70 dpi—roughly the same resolution as a cheap dot-matrix printer. Still, it's actually not the dpi that counts as much as the large viewing area over which those 1 or 2 million pixels are spread.

One thing to keep in mind about the large-screen monitors is that monitor packages that offer total large-display solutions are preferable to the normal component approach, because many of the generic video cards don't have the right specs for the monitor and won't work properly, or at all. Video cards are finicky about which monitors they will cooperate with, and you must carefully match the monitor to the card. Chapter 5 covers video cards in detail.

Dvorak's Recommendations

When shopping for a monitor, you might be disappointed if you purchase the cheapest model. You should buy a monitor with the ability to adapt to different scanning frequencies. The buzzwords to look for are multiscanning and multiple frequency. These will give you the most flexibility in compatibility. This type of monitor will also allow you to upgrade your video card to keep up with the newer standards as they come along. Consider what you are going to use your computer for. Obviously, if you intend to

MONITORS

do CAD/CAM or demand high-end graphics, you won't be happy or able to function with a low-end monitor.

Keep in mind that—with the right choice—your monitor can have a longer usable life than your computer. It's not unusual to purchase a monitor for one machine—say a 386—and keep it through one or two upgrades—to a Pentium. A versatile monitor can keep up with technological improvements.

VIDEO CARDS

CHAPTER

5

IF YOU HAVE A COMPUTER AND A MONITOR, but no video display card, you're not going to have much luck using your machine. You must have a display adapter or video card to have any data appear on the screen. A computer seller will rarely bundle the monitor and the card as a package; they are usually purchased separately.

VIDEO CARDS

VIDEO CARDS, ADAPTER CARDS, OR ADD-IN BOARDS—whatever name you want to call them—run the gamut from an inexpensive monochrome display card (around $50) to a state-of-the-art graphics coprocessor that does everything but make coffee (with a price to make even the Department of Defense wince).

Card Basics

Add-in cards come in three basic flavors: 8-bit, 16-bit, and 32-bit. These terms refer to the number of data bits that the card sends out at one time. Ideally, a 16-bit video card sends an image to the monitor in half the time it would take for an 8-bit version to do so. It's important to know what kind of card your machine accepts. The older PCs and XTs usually have an 8-bit or PC bus, which accepts only the 8-bit cards. The newer machines use an ISA (Industry Standard Architecture) or AT 16-bit bus. Most cards are made for this bus.

Then there are the new IBM MCA (Micro Channel Architecture) and the EISA (Extended Industry Standard Architecture). ISA currently is the "bus of choice" for many applications. Right now, EISA and MCA offer some advantages for network servers, computer-aided design (CAD), and some future applications like multimedia, multitasking, and some high-end graphics. But in the near future—as prices drop and more applications appear which are better suited to an advanced bus—EISA and MCA will begin to appear on more machines.

An important point to remember here is that EISA is backward-compatible to ISA (an ISA card will fit into an EISA bus). ISA is backward-compatible with 8-bit cards (8-bit cards fit into ISA and EISA slots), but MCA will not work with either of the other two standards. (*Backward-compatible* means that the device works with all previous hardware technology, but it will not necessarily work with any new iterations.) In other words, if you move up to an EISA bus computer, the cards from your ISA bus computer will work in the new machine. If you move up to IBM's MCA machines, you're out of luck if you want to use your old cards. (See Chapter 3 for a more complete discussion of computer buses.)

Add-in cards are also described in terms of length—$^1/_2$-length, $^3/_4$-length, and full-size. This, along with the less common XT height, refers to the physical size of the card. These terms are loosely applied. There are no accepted standard sizes.

Graphic Display Standards and Compatibility

Not everyone needs the same resolution in a monitor. Some applications do require a high resolution for a really sharp color display and crisp letters. For this you will need to purchase an expensive monitor

VIDEO CARDS

VIDEO TERMS

As you shop for a video card, you'll come across an array of terms and jargon that can make a difficult task even harder. Here's a quick guide to some of the more commonly used video terms:

- **Alpha channel** The upper 8 bits of the 32-bit data path in some graphics adapters. The alpha channel is used by some software for controlling the color information in the lower 24 bits.

- **BitBLT (bit-block transfer)** An operation in which the pixel data residing in one area of the frame buffer is copied directly to another area of the frame buffer, and vice versa. By performing bit-block transfers, graphics coprocessors can dramatically improve video display speeds, since a displayed object is treated as one unit rather than as many individual pixels.

- **DAC (digital-to-analog converter)** A chip that converts the binary numbers representing particular colors to analog red, green, and blue signals that the monitor displays.

- **DRAM (dynamic RAM)** The most commonly used type of memory, found on video boards as well as on PC system boards. DRAM is usually slower than VRAM, since it has only a single data pathway.

- **Flicker** Describes two different effects. True flicker, where the screen seems to blink rapidly on and off, is caused by a slow refresh rate, or low vertical frequency. This means the screen isn't rewritten quickly enough to fool the eye into seeing a steady image. The second kind of flicker, which looks more like a jiggling of horizontal lines, is caused by interlacing. To avoid both kinds of flicker you need a high vertical frequency (at least 60 Hz, but often more) and a noninterlaced video scheme—currently an expensive combination.

- **Frame buffer** A large section of memory used to store an image to be displayed on screen, as well as parts of the image that lie outside the limits of the display.

- **Graphics coprocessor** Similar to a math coprocessor in concept, this is a programmable chip that speeds video performance by carrying out graphics processing independently of the CPU. It can speed up performance in two ways: by taking over tasks the main processor would lose time performing and by optimizing for graphics. Video adapters with graphics coprocessors are expensive compared with those without them, but they speed up graphics operations considerably.

- **Horizontal frequency** Measures how long it takes a monitor to draw one horizontal line across the screen. Monitors are designed and rated for one or more specific horizontal (and vertical) frequencies. Similarly, video modes are designed for specific frequencies. When you choose a graphics adapter and monitor, the frequencies of both must match. Horizontal frequencies are usually given in kHz.

- **Interlaced display** A display created by drawing images on screen in two passes. The first pass draws the odd-numbered lines, while the second pass draws the even-numbered lines. Interlaced displays usually tend to flicker noticeably.

- **JPEG (Joint Photographic Experts Group)** The image compression standard developed by an international committee of the same name. JPEG was developed to compress large, still images, such as photographs, single video frames, or scanned pictures, to reduce the amount of memory required to store them.

Continued on next page

VIDEO CARDS

VIDEO TERMS

Continued from previous page

- **Noninterlaced display** The opposite of an interlaced display. All the lines are drawn in one pass rather than two. This reduces the appearance of flicker.

- **Pass-through VGA** A method of handling VGA display that passes a VGA signal from another graphics board through a cable attached to the high-resolution adapter and out to the monitor. Other methods of handling VGA include on-board VGA (where a VGA controller is mounted on the high-resolution board) and daughter-card VGA (where the VGA controller and memory reside on a small daughterboard that plugs into the high-resolution board).

- **TMS 34010** A popular graphics coprocessor from Texas Instruments and one of the leading choices for coprocessed video boards. It is only the first generation in a promised series. In fact, the second generation—the 34020—is already available on some boards.

- **Vertical frequency** Also called the *refresh rate.* Indicates how long it takes to draw an entire screenful of lines from top to bottom. Monitors are designed for specific vertical (and horizontal) frequencies. Vertical frequency is a key factor in image flicker. Given a low enough vertical frequency (53 Hz, for example), virtually everyone will see a flicker because the screen isn't rewritten quickly enough. A high vertical frequency (70 Hz on a 14-inch monitor) will eliminate the flicker for most people.

- **VESA (Video Electronics Standards Association)** A consortium of manufacturers formed to establish and maintain industry-wide standards for video cards and monitors. VESA is responsible for establishing the Super VGA recommendations that many manufacturers follow today.

- **VGA pass-through** A feature present on the 8514/A and some other high-resolution boards. The VGA signal literally passes through the board. The VGA signal originates on a VGA board or system board-mounted VGA system and goes to a monitor connected to the high-resolution board. This feature lets you use a single monitor for both VGA and high-resolution levels.

- **VLSI (Very Large Scale Integration)** A bunch of different chips and their functions jammed onto a single silicon chip. Over 100,000 transistors can be integrated into one, and the amazing thing is that as one chip they consume little power and can perform extremely complex functions.

- **VRAM (video random access memory)** Special-purpose RAM with two data paths for access, rather than the one path in conventional RAM. The two paths let a VRAM board handle two functions at once: display refresh and processor access. VRAM doesn't force the system to wait for one function to finish before starting the other, so it permits faster operation for the video subsystem. ∎

VIDEO CARDS

and proprietary display adapter. Others, including most home users, can do just fine with a monochrome monitor and a plain-vanilla VGA card. The trick is to select the right video card for your monitor. There are a number of different video display schemes and standards on the market.

EGA Cards

The EGA (enhanced graphics adapter) was an IBM invention that started the migration toward higher-resolution color displays. Before the EGA, the display offerings were either monochrome or a four-color CGA (color graphics adapter) which was both crude and hard on the eyes. The EGA had a 640×350 resolution and 16 colors. The key difference, and main drawback, is that the EGA scheme was digital. (Most other displays were and still are analog.) The EGA, although it's still around, was never wholeheartedly accepted by the computer-buying masses. Compared to the widespread VGA, EGA cards are rare. Also, few monitors will work with an EGA video card since most monitors are analog. Although it's possible to locate a monitor which is switchable between digital and analog, the option can be pricey. For the most part, the EGA will continue to fade until it is simply a footnote in history.

VGA Cards

VGA, which stands for video graphics array, is simply a descriptive name for the circuitry used to bring the chip to life. IBM uses a large VLSI (very large-scale integration) chip containing a huge number of logic gates—a "gate array" chip—to implement the video circuitry. The result is an image, in graphics mode, that is 640×480×16. In other words, there are 640 picture elements (or pixels) in every row and 480 pixels in every column, and the screen can display 16 simultaneous colors from a palette of 262,144. The difference from the EGA standard (640×350×16) may seem slight, but VGA's wider palette and sharper image produces a much more realistic and pleasing display.

With the introduction of VGA, you could still run software written for the older standards, but you couldn't use the same monitor. The only exceptions to this were those multi-scanning monitors which were capable of handling the horizontal and vertical frequencies required by the new standard.

Super VGA

Super VGA often refers to any enhancements—such as more colors or greater resolution—that ensure VGA compatibility. The VESA recommendation calls for 800×600 resolution and 16 colors, but manufacturers often produce boards with 256 colors or may even refer to boards that offer 1,024×768 resolution as Super VGA.

VIDEO CARDS

The problem, however, is the astounding number of graphic display standards. The VGA standard itself incorporates 17 video modes—different methods to display an image on the monitor. Most of these provide backward compatibility to the most important of the earlier standards: the color graphics adapter (CGA), enhanced graphics adapter (EGA), and monochrome display adapter (MDA).

Even discounting the earlier standards, that leaves us with Super VGA (the nonstandard standard), IBM's 8514/A adapter for MCA machines, and IBM's new extended graphics array (XGA) standard. All of these standards deliver more colors or higher resolution than VGA. That doesn't include the adapters that make use of new continuous edge graphics (CEG) chips, which promise to put over 740,000 colors on your screen simultaneously.

Before you race out and buy any of these enhanced video adapters, keep one thought in mind: software. Most new software includes support for the standard VGA modes. With the other video cards, you can only hope the manufacturer includes drivers for the software. This is probably not a problem if you use Lotus 1-2-3, AutoCAD, Windows, or Ventura Publisher. Other than that, you'll want to make sure the manufacturer supplies the drivers you need before you buy a new card. This changes daily, so always ask if the driver is included.

Another important issue is whether the monitor you have can support the higher resolutions the card offers. If you have a CGA- or EGA-compatible monitor, chances are you'll need a new monitor to take advantage of a VGA or better video board. Older monitors used a digital interface, while the VGA specification requires an analog interface. Only the multi-scanning monitors allow you to use both a digital and an analog system. But not every multi-scanning monitor will work with a VGA card. The monitor must be able to work within the horizontal and vertical scanning frequencies required by the standard you intend to use. (For more information on monitors and their requirements, see Chapter 4.)

The 8514/A Card

The 8514/A card and 8514 monitor were introduced in 1987 by IBM as their high-end video hardware. The 8514/A offered 256 colors, a 640×480 resolution, and an interlaced 1,024×768 resolution with either 16 or 256 colors. Technically, 8514/A refers to the card and 8514 refers to the monitor, but the "/A" is often dropped when discussing the card. IBM is clearly aiming to replace the 8514/A standard with XGA in the Micro Channel world. Still, 8514-compatible boards may survive for some time on the ISA bus.

VIDEO CARDS

BUYING A PLAIN-VANILLA VGA CARD

Since 1990 the guts of the VGA circuitry have been incorporated into various VLSI chips, and the cards are now inexpensively made by most board makers. Dozens of them are cranked out in Taiwan. A plain VGA card costs $100–$150. Many of the newest computer systems actually incorporate the VGA circuitry on the machine's motherboard. This will become more and more common in future systems. Each time a new VLSI chip is released, these cards are redesigned. This makes testing the cards impractical.

Unfortunately, few low-end VGA cards or on-board systems are completely compatible with the original specification. This basic problem still exists with many of the newest, most inexpensive VGA cards. I recommend testing your favorite applications and demo programs on a card before buying it. Make sure you are offered a money-back guarantee when you do buy one. By the time all the cards discussed are perfectly compatible, XGA will be old-hat, and we'll have a new scheme. Meanwhile, we have to live with this situation. ∎

XGA Cards

XGA is IBM's latest high-resolution video scheme. It appears that this will be the next major video standard, so watch this trend carefully. XGA was introduced along with the PS/2 Models 90 and 95, and it puts 8514-level and VGA-level resolutions on the same board. The current IBM implementation is interlaced, but the specification does include support for noninterlaced modes. The XGA is expected to become the next standard and should be considered as boards are announced.

Super VGA (SVGA) for Windows

Until recently you probably have not given much thought to your graphics adapter. Whatever card came in your PC is probably the one you are using today. After all, it ran fine under DOS. But if you have moved into the Microsoft Windows arena, you need a faster board to get around the new graphics-intensive neighborhood.

But choosing the best video card for Windows is more complicated than simply shopping for the best price. Today's Super VGA marketplace is filled with tantalizing possibilities. It's all very exciting, but it is also confusing. Is the right video controller a frame buffer, a graphics accelerator board, or a coprocessor board? Is one chip set faster than the rest? Let's try to answer these questions.

The VL Bus

If you use any graphical application (including Windows and OS/2), you may want to buy a video card that runs on the local (VL or VESA [Video Electronics Standards Association]) bus. This card is fast and modern, but requires a VL-bus slot in your computer.

VIDEO CARDS

Look for a 72-Hz vertical refresh rate. The refresh rate refers to the number of times the screen is redrawn each second. The higher the rate, the less flicker you will see. For Super VGA modes, VESA has defined 72 Hz as its official standard vertical refresh rate. It has also defined 56 and 60 Hz as its manufacturer's guidelines (VGA has a vertical refresh rate of 60 or 70 Hz.)

The reason VESA chose 72 Hz—not 75 Hz or any other number—is because the same video bandwidth produces a 1,024×768-pixel mode at 60 Hz.

Get 1Mb of display memory. For a 1,024×768 resolution with 256 colors, you need 1Mb (actually, you need only 786,432 bytes, but since memory doesn't come in that configuration, look for 1Mb). With 512k you can go to only 16 colors in the high-resolution mode. Most 512k boards cannot handle the 72-Hz Super VGA refresh rate.

Weigh price against performance carefully. Super VGA boards are getting cheaper all the time. DRAM boards are less expensive than VRAM, but the latter is faster.

Faster, Faster   You can speed up Microsoft Windows either with software or hardware. The software approach means writing a driver that is optimized for the environment. Microsoft has recently begun to emphasize the role that hardware can play. To get the best video performance under Windows, buy a board with a fully programmable graphics coprocessor. A graphics coprocessor offers two advantages: It is specifically designed for video functions, and it lightens your CPU's workload. In most resolutions/color combinations, coprocessed boards outperform frame buffers (which have no built-in intelligence). The only downside to coprocessed boards is the price—they are expensive.

Graphics accelerator chips, which contain specific Windows functions as bitBLTs, area filling, and line drawing, also promise performance gains.

PRINTERS

PRINTERS ARE HIGH on new computer users' wish lists. Long before modems or speed-up cards or even a new desk, new computer owners want a printer. With a printer you can show people what you've done. You can print letters and memos, charts and spreadsheets, mailing labels for Christmas card lists, and much more.

PRINTERS

PRINTERS COME IN A WIDE VARIETY: dot-matrix, color dot-matrix, ink-jet, color ink-jet, color laser, plain laser, and PostScript laser printers—not to mention the tangle of fonts, drivers, and printer supplies. Beyond the standard array of printer choices, you'll also find some less desirable options, such as thermal-paper and daisy-wheel printers. The printer you choose will depend upon your needs and your pocketbook.

Print quality will ultimately affect your buying decision. Look for a consistent, deep black print with little or no white showing through. For simple home uses, a modest dot-matrix printer will suffice, but if you want to print graphics and other high-quality, "wow" output, then look to one of the laser printers.

Dot-Matrix Printers

A dot-matrix printer is one of the simplest, most rugged, and most serviceable machines in the computer industry. It consists of a plastic case containing only three or four moving parts and a small computer that communicates with your PC and controls the printing mechanism at the behest of the PC's commands. Dot-matrix printers are workhorses. They perform their job very well. (Almost too well, if you realize that many of your bills—water, electricity, telephone, store charges—are printed with commercial dot-matrix printers.) The small, lightweight, inexpensive personal-computer models are just as effective as the larger models.

How a Dot-Matrix Printer Works

A dot-matrix printer creates each character from an array of dots. The basic printing mechanism of a dot-matrix printer is simple: A print head houses one or more vertical rows of tiny metal rods called *pins*, and each pin is carefully positioned in a tube-like track (see Figure 6.1). The spring-loaded pins are held back from the ribbon and paper by electromagnets. When a pin's electromagnet is charged, the pin is released and the spring forces it into the ribbon, coloring a spot on the paper positioned between the printer's platen and the ribbon.

Pins are typically arranged in a single vertical row in 7- or 9-pin print heads; 18-pin models have two rows of nine pins, while 24-pin models have three vertical rows of eight pins each, usually arranged in a staggered pattern. The basic pin action is the same regardless of the number of pins in the print head.

The print head is mounted on a track so it can slide back and forth across the paper surface. The pins form characters on the paper by coloring an appropriate pattern of dots within a character box of horizontal and vertical dot positions in a rectangular—or matrix—pattern. The number of positions in the character box depends on the resolution of the printer. For better quality printing, the print head may pass over the character a

PRINTERS

Figure 6.1   Dot-matrix printer engine

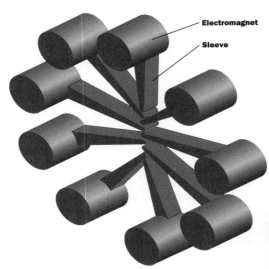

The 9-pin dot-matrix heads usually arrange all nine pins in a single vertical column, while 24-pin heads usually have three offset columns of eigth pins each. In order to fit all of these pins in close proximity, the magnets are often arranged in a radial pattern.

To put a dot on a page, a dot-matrix printer sends a pulse of current through the electromagnetic coils, making the pin shoot forward. The pin strikes the the paper through the inked ribbon and transfers the ink to the paper. A spring quickly retracts the pin so that it is ready to fire again.

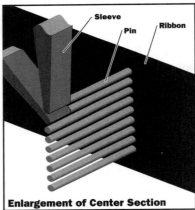

Enlargement of Center Section

number of times, each time filling in gaps between the dots. Lower-quality printing often has voids and scalloped edges, and occasionally the dots can be detected.

Tractor-feed Paper   When you print with a dot-matrix printer, most of the time you will use tractor-feed paper. Tractor-feed (or continuous-feed) paper has vertical holes on both sides of the page. These holes fit onto sprockets on the printer roller, which pull the paper through. The paper is perforated to make 8½-by-11-inch sheets. The part of the paper

PRINTERS

SOME DOT-MATRIX PRINTING TERMS

- **Burst** To separate track paper at the perforations to make standard-sized pieces of paper.

- **Paper-parking device** A mechanism that allows you to print on a single sheet while fanfold paper is still loaded in the printer. Instead of taking out the track paper, feeding in a single sheet, and then reloading the track paper, you use the paper-parking device. It moves the track paper out of the way (with the press of a button), and you can feed in a single sheet. Once you're done, the printer will move the track paper back into place.

- **Sheet feeder** An optional piece of hardware that enables a dot-matrix printer to use multiple single sheets of paper. Most printers will let you use a single sheet of paper, but you must feed each sheet in—one after another—much like a manual typewriter. The sheet feeder automates the process.

- **Tractor-feed paper** Also called computer paper, fanfold paper, tractor paper, or simply track paper. The paper is in one long sheet, and perforations divide it into standard-sized sheets. Tractor-feed paper has a gutter along the edges in which regularly spaced holes appear. This gutter may be easily detached. The holes fit onto a pair of sprockets in the printer. The sprockets pull the paper through the printing mechanism.

- **Zero tear-off** The printer advances the track paper so finished output can be removed, and then backs up the paper to begin printing the next job at the top of the page. ■

that has the holes is also perforated so it can be easily detached—the paper looks like "real" paper when it's "burst apart" (separated).

This paper tractor-feed device was invented for the mainframe environment. Mainframe computers crank out zillions upon zillions of bank statements, bills, and itemized reports and need a surefire way to feed paper through the printers with a minimum of paper jams.

Tractor-feed paper can be purchased by the box, which can be economical. A number of stationery stores have "home office" tractor-feed paper packages available. These aren't as economical as commercial packaging, but they are available in a greater variety than commercial paper. They include high-quality, specialty-colored papers and tractor-feed envelopes, as well as traditional white paper. Tractor-feed forms, labels, checks, and other specialty products are also available through stationery stores and mail-order houses.

Tractor-feed paper sometimes misfeeds when it is run through the printer. This is usually caused by the stack of unprinted-on paper behind the printer. If the printer cable is in the way or if the paper isn't in line with the printer, the paper will pull to one side and jam in the printer.

Tractor-feed paper is hardy. It isn't affected by the environment as much as laser printer paper is. It won't go bad over time, so you can buy it in bulk to save money. As long as it's kept dry and stored indoors, it

PRINTERS

shouldn't have any problems running through your printer. As a matter of fact, I've had a box of tractor-feed paper for about ten years. It sits in a storage room, and when I need a handful I get some. It's fine.

Improvements in Dot-Matrix Printers Paper handling, once the bane of every printer user, has been redesigned. It's much easier to load paper on the newer dot-matrix printers. Paper can be loaded from the front, back, or bottom, depending on the printer. There's even automatic paper loading; just stick the end of the tractor-feed paper into a slot and press a button—the printer takes care of the rest. Some have an output tray that holds the printed paper away from the paper being fed into the printer (to avoid those ferocious paper jams).

A sheet feeder can be attached to the newer dot-matrix printers to allow single-sheet printing. Some printers allow multiple bins for distinctive second sheets or even envelopes. This is a wonderful add-on if you've never liked the ragged-edge look of bursted, perforated, fanfold, tractor-feed computer paper. Even the high-cost paper still has the telltale fuzzy edges.

Dot-matrix printers are also quieter than they used to be. The head and traveler mechanisms that move them are now designed to run more smoothly, constructed of better materials, and assembled with greater emphasis on quality. Printers that aren't quieted by mechanical means are soundproofed. Other advances include covers that are easy to lift off and that stay put when you replace them, custom-built stands, and easier-to-use operating panels and switches.

Color printing, which used to require a special printer, is now just another feature requiring only a special ribbon. Mylar ribbon is commonplace; it enhances the output quality of matrix printers, especially the high-grade 24-pin models.

Many of these improvements are included with the printer, while others you must buy separately. The ones you choose will depend on your needs. A sheet feeder is worth paying for if your correspondence must be on the company letterhead. Add-on features must be weighed—cost versus benefit. With printers, as with all purchases, it's best to shop around and familiarize yourself with all the available options. One printer will stand out as the best choice for you.

Color Dot-Matrix Printers

Color printing with dot-matrix printers is in the early stages of software implementation and user acceptance. It's no coincidence that color dot-matrix technology is currently making a statement; as needs arise, the market responds. Major business uses of color printers have grown to include the production of business graphs and charts, as well as hard-copy presentation materials such as text charts with clip art.

PRINTERS

THE QUEST FOR LETTER QUALITY

Like display-screen engineers, printer engineers are constantly trying to squeeze more quality out of their display mechanism. Dot-matrix printers have inherently poorer quality than any continuous mechanism, such as a type ball or wheel with its fully formed characters. One approach to improving quality is to design printers with higher dot resolution (more dots per inch). That requires more pins in the print head; 24 pins seems to be the maximum allowed by the metals available for making pins.

Another approach is improving the character and graphics designs to use the available spots more effectively. Better use of the spots usually results in better printer resolution without increasing the number of pins in the print head. However, this high-resolution output comes at the cost of printer speed, which is impaired when the print head has to make extra trips across the same line.

At one time, 9-pin dot-matrix printers were not capable of letter-quality printing. Early attempts at improving print quality gave these printers the ability to emphasize characters by printing extra dots vertically, horizontally, or both at once. That technique gave some semblance of dark printing, but the results could hardly be called quality printing.

The first efforts to create serif fonts for 9-pin printers were unsuccessful. Better results were produced by very expensive, high-performance models such as Okidata's legendary Pacemark 2410, the Sherman tank of dot-matrix printers. But most company officers and managers didn't consider this letter-quality output.

That's all changed in a big way. Virtually all 9-pin dot-matrix printers, many of which cost well below $500, offer "near-letter-quality" fonts. Many of them are suitable for business correspondence, and home users should be happy with the results.■

Another valuable use for color dot-matrix printing is in the creation of drafts of output that will later be generated by a color page printer. Although color page printers are coming down in price, they are still significantly more expensive than a color dot-matrix printer.

Two factors should affect your buying decision: print quality and color-control command set compatibility. High-quality color printout should have clear color differentiation, deep, saturated colors with little or no white showing through, and true colors rather than off-shades.

The color-control command set is a group of instructions that allows for communication between the software and the printer. The software's print drivers and the printer's internal command set must be compatible. If they aren't, you'll end up with screwball colors in strange and inappropriate places. (One oddball color printer we saw had an incompatible command set. It printed all blue, except for an occasional unsolicited green, red, or black letter here and there.)

Your color printer may produce gorgeous images, but if the printer doesn't have a common color-printer compatibility, your application software is less likely to have printer drivers that can take advantage of the printer's capabilities. The major color-control command sets are for Epson and IBM color printers. (The standard is the Epson JX-80.)

PRINTERS

Don't expect color printing to be fast, especially if the print head has to make more than one pass to blend the colors.

Some mono-color dot-matrix printers can be modified to add color-print capability. This is surprisingly inexpensive. The necessary four-color ribbons of black, yellow, red, and blue bands allow the printer to blend dots to produce up to seven different colors. These ribbons cost two to three times as much as black fabric ribbons—more expensive, but not an intimidating premium.

If you use color only occasionally, it's a good idea to use a black ribbon and swap it for a four-color ribbon when you need the color. The color portions of ribbons dry out, which results in faded shades. To prevent this, store the color ribbons in a plastic bag when not in use.

Ink-jet Printers

An ink-jet printer forms letters and graphics by projecting squirts of ink onto the paper. The technology is very similar to the dot matrix, except there isn't any contact with the paper (no pins striking the paper), so the image looks much more smooth and even. The resolution is much finer than that of a dot-matrix printer, and the quality can approach that of a laser printer.

Ink-jets aren't a new technology; they have been in use for many years in the data-processing industry (since the 1960s) in a number of different devices. In 1976, IBM's 6640 ink-jet printer became a popular, reliable device which enjoyed widespread use.

One of two types of technological designs are employed in ink-jets: pulsing jet and continuous stream.

The first is when the ink is sprayed in a pulsing jet. There may be one or more of these jets mounted in the print head (usually more than one). Each jet ejects a single squirt at the page. Characters are printed as a matrix array, much like a dot-matrix printer. Print speeds may be as great as 400 characters per second. Printers with a greater number of jets offer a higher resolution and a crisper, more even print quality.

The second design is a print head with a single jet which shoots out in a constant-velocity, continuous stream. The characters are made as the ink shoots out of the jet and is passed through electrode plates. These plates alter the jet of ink, deflecting it in the necessary direction towards the paper (much like placing your thumb over the end of a hose to change the spray pattern of the water). This is a slower process, printing up to 100 characters per second.

The ink-jet is finding most of its popularity in portable printer applications, as well as in home "desktop" use. The printers are lightweight and small. They produce very good print quality for a relatively low price. Most of the ink-jet printers, however, are not suitable for high volume use,

PRINTERS

and a number of the lower-priced printers on the market require you to hand-feed sheets of paper into the printer—a drawback for multiple pages and/or high volume. In addition, ink cartridges are expensive (around $20) and tend to run out pretty quickly. But if you want quality approaching that of a laser printer for a low price, these ink-jets are an excellent choice.

Laser Printers

The laser printer (also called a page printer) is the printer everyone wants to own. It produces high-quality output quickly and uses regular, single sheet paper. It's quiet, too.

How a Laser Printer Works

The printer is more accurately called "electrophotographic." An image is made by a beam of light (hence the term *laser*) focused on a photoconductive drum which is uniformly electrically charged over its surface. The light beam causes a localized conductivity in the pattern of the light beam. The charged pattern attracts pigment: the toner particles. (The background repels the toner particles.) The image is then transferred to the paper by pressing the paper against the drum. The toner particles are fixed to the paper by intense heat and pressure. The technology is very similar to that used in office copiers. For a close-up of how a laser printer works, see Figure 6.2.

Laser Printer History

In 1984, PC Labs tested one laser printer for the annual *PC Magazine* printer issue. Not surprisingly, it was the Hewlett-Packard LaserJet. This was the printer that broke the dam and opened desktop computing to the superb quality and silent operation of laser printing. The only other page printer reviewed that year was the soon-to-be forgotten Diablo EPM-1 thermal transfer printer. Daisy-wheel printers, which ruled the letter-quality printing roost, were doomed once the laser printer appeared.

People didn't expect lasers to be hooked up to individual PCs when the LaserJet was introduced. At $3,495 plus font cartridges, it cost as much as or more than most PC configurations, and besides, not much software existed to support the then-new Printer Control Language (PCL) codes embodied in the Canon-made engine's driver. Local area networks seemed a more logical target for these expensive but speedy and quiet machines. Wrong: People prefer their own printer and will pay extra for the privilege if they have to.

The LaserJet took off like a shot. Office workers were tired of the hammering daisy-wheel printers and whining dot-matrix printers. The LaserJet's price didn't seem much to pay for a little peace and quiet and a lot of speed. The drawback? The inconveniences of the early LaserJet.

PRINTERS

Laser Technology

Scanning mirror

Laser beam

Collimator lens

Cylindrical lens

Mirror

Focusing lenses

Photosensitive drum

In a typical laser printer, a single laser beam is focused on a rotating polygon mirror. As the mirror spins, the beam is deflected through a focusing lens and scans across the rotating drum, which accepts the image line by line.

For example, the original Canon engine had space for only 100 sheets of paper in its input bin and output tray. In response, sheet feeders that could handle large capacities, multiple bins of paper, and even envelopes began showing up early in the laser game. Some units came with collators that could assemble multiple copies of reports into the correct page sequence (the original LaserJet couldn't assemble even one copy into its correct sequence); some even put letters together with their properly addressed envelopes.

Printer-sharing devices began to be touted as low-cost (non-LAN) answers to the high cost of laser printing. Many of them came with print-queuing and spooling capabilities that put mainframe operating systems to shame.

Software incompatibility provided a wide playing field for innovators. Third-party utilities that magically transformed output designed for other printers into LaserJet format started popping up everywhere. Third-party vendors also produced LaserJet printer drivers compatible with popular software products, especially word processors and spreadsheets.

PRINTERS

Similar fixes and patches became available both in user groups and on bulletin boards, where the price certainly was right. PC add-on cards appeared, and they too worked magic by transforming the LaserJet into something else. Boards that replaced the LaserJet's controller also came on the scene. Unfortunately, the LaserJet sometimes was transformed into something equally foreign to your software. A few products now can even turn a LaserJet into a PostScript printer.

Software vendors were likewise excited by the new laser technology, and sooner than many people expected, word processing and graphics vendors caught up with the LaserJet and began to ship compatible products, as well as fixes for existing products. That meant the LaserJet had come of age, and users could rely on supported compatibility from original software vendors rather than add-on products.

As software support spread, LaserJet clones came along, stiffening the competition for Hewlett-Packard. The challenge was quickly met by the LaserJet Plus, which accommodated more memory for graphics and downloadable fonts to replace or supplement the company's expensive font cartridges.

The clones kept coming anyway. Most met the capabilities of the LaserJet Plus, and many added more features. Some of them offered more memory and a better selection of fonts, while others increased paper capacity and even envelope handling. Still others had faster print engines and alternative printer emulations so the printer could be used with software that still didn't support the LaserJet. And many of those capabilities were offered at a lower price.

Getting the Most Out of Your Laser Printer

If your laser printer has ceased to amaze you, maybe it's time to push its limits. You can buy enhancement boards which plug into your computer to improve the quality of your laser's text and graphics. And while these boards add new features and capabilities to your printer, they take nothing away from the functions it already provides. Most of them will work on any printer built around a Canon laser engine. You can even add PostScript to your laser printer.

What Is PostScript?   PostScript is generally acknowledged to be the most versatile page description language (PDL) available, and it has set the standard for desktop publishing and many graphics applications.

Although the Hewlett-Packard LaserJet Series II and LaserJet III printers can handle the majority of desktop publishing tasks of a typical business, PCL (the LaserJet's native Printer Control Language) has its limitations. There are certainly occasions that call for PostScript.

PRINTERS

You need a PostScript printer if, for example, you send your final copy to a high-quality Linotronic typesetter and you want to create good-quality page proofs from the same code. And many desktop publishing programs have better drivers for PostScript than for the unenhanced LaserJet.

But don't chuck your LaserJet and start over with a new printer. There are a number of solutions—both hardware- and software-based—to bring PostScript to your LaserJet.

Adding PostScript to a Laser Printer   Most of the add-ins are composed of the same components: a board that you install in an unused expansion slot in your computer, another smaller board that fits into the expansion slot on your printer, a custom cable that connects these two cards, and special software drivers that allow them to work together. Some packages use genuine PostScript (licensed from Adobe Systems, the developer of the page description language). Other manufacturers use clone products. These clones do well overall with only minor incompatibilities.

PostScript capabilities can be added to your laser printer by using add-on boards, emulation software, or emulation cartridges. Add-in products may differ significantly in their operation, depending on how the PostScript code is treated. Most of the systems can be configured to take over one of your DOS printer ports (LPT1 through LPT3) to allow for direct use by any application that can send a stream of PostScript code to a printer. Another, less convenient approach is to print your PostScript code to a disk file. It's processed by a separate PostScript interpreter program to produce a printed page. For the most part, these boards are fast.

Printer Enhancement Boards   By far the best thing you can do to a page printer is to attach it to a printer enhancement board. With an enhancement board, text resolution can be improved almost to the quality of low-end typesetters. Unfortunately, most of the boards cannot increase the resolution of 300-dpi laser printers. Although most do not change the text print speed, graphics printing can be up to ten times faster. Enhancement boards come with their own printer drivers and scalable fonts that are usually compatible with PostScript printers. These enhancement boards can be costly, however, which might be their only drawback.

The add-in boards have a custom connection between the computer and the printer. The standard parallel or serial port connection is still in place. This means that the printer can still be used as a LaserJet without the PostScript.

These boards work by processing the regular LaserJet commands faster than the printer's controller. These products also give you features

PRINTERS

beyond the scope of PCL and support high-speed output from desktop publishing programs through proprietary drivers.

In either case, although you won't be able to print from the same Post-Script files your large typesetting machine uses, you should be able to print desktop publishing or presentation graphics pages much faster than with an unmodified LaserJet.

If you have an XT-compatible, your choices will be limited, because some cards require a 286- or 386-based machine. The cards fit well in 8-bit slots; even the cards with 16-bit edge connectors can be configured to work in 8-bit slots without a problem. IBM PS/2s with Micro Channel expansion slots, on the other hand, require Micro Channel connections.

Some of the boards do not work with network servers, and those that do can be limited in the types of networks they support. The nonstandard cables these products use may also create a problem. They may not be able to hook into a printer switchbox.

Emulation Software   But you don't have to buy an add-in board to print PostScript pages on a non-PostScript page printer. You can simply buy emulation software packages—if you have 1.5Mb of extended memory to spare. They work by printing PostScript files to a disk and then using the software to send the files to the printer.

Emulation Cartridges   Emulation cartridges are another way to add PostScript to your laser printer. An emulation cartridge plugs into an open, external slot (normally for fonts) on a laser printer. The cartridge makes the laser printer behave like a PostScript printer. Hewlett-Packard sells a cartridge such as this to answer the PostScript problem. It's not the best solution, but it is one solution.

Paper Is Paper, Right? Wrong

When you go into a stationery store, the paper selection can be confusing and baffling. You'll find laser paper in a wide variety of colors; with cotton and linen rag content; and in reams labeled "long grain," "hi-speed," and "xerographic." Some papers are called copier paper, while others are called laser paper. There's premium paper, coated and uncoated paper, exotic paper, opaque paper, presentation paper, onion skin, and vellum. There's paper weight (by the pound) and recycled paper. How do you choose? First you need to know a little about printer paper.

Factors to Consider When Choosing Paper   The first step is to understand the printing process. Laser printers rely on an electrical charge to hold the toner to the paper, and then heat and pressure to fuse the toner

PRINTERS

to the page. So it stands to reason that good laser paper will have special electrical- and heat-resistant properties, just as copier machine paper does.

Brightness is rated according to the amount of light reflected by the paper. A sheet with a brightness rating of 90 percent reflects 90 percent of the light striking it; a high brightness rating makes for a high contrast between the page and ink. Colored paper may be misleading as to brightness, because a dark purple sheet doesn't reflect light as well as a light tan of the same rating.

Electrical resistance results from a number of factors in the paper-making process. Paper manufacturers can either add resistant chemicals to the surface of the paper or mix them into the paper itself. The moisture content of the paper also has a significant impact on paper's resistance, which is why print quality can vary with humidity.

Moisture affects another aspect of the laser printing process: paper feeding. The greater the moisture content of paper, the more likely it is to curl. And if a page has too much curl, it can be more prone to jamming. As a result, it is important that you store paper carefully and take care to close the packaging on partial reams.

The paper-making process creates paper that has two distinctly different sides, though the difference is not always obvious to the eye or touch. The top is called the felt side, and the bottom is called the wire side—the rule is to print on the wire side first. Look at the label on the front of the ream wrapper for an arrow indicating the wire side, and keep this in mind when loading your printer's paper trays. And be aware of whether your printer's tray loads face-up or face-down.

Another factor that affects paper jamming is the weight of the paper. Basis weight is a standard measure based on 500 sheets of paper. Most paper is rated at 20 pounds, though some higher-quality paper is rated at 24 pounds or more. Paper that is too light or too heavy is more likely to jam.

Many people assume that "weight" means the same as "thickness" and "stiffness." In fact, the three measures tend to correlate, but they are not directly related. Stiffness is a measure of how much a page resists bending, while thickness describes the physical dimension. It is quite possible to have three sheets of different 20-pound paper, one significantly stiffer than the other two, and one noticeably thicker.

Cotton bond paper, as its name suggests, has cotton fibers mixed with the wood pulp that forms the paper. Paper with this mixture often has a high-quality feel and typically is stamped with a watermark as part of the manufacturing process.

There are other factors that affect print quality. *Wax pick* is the strength of the paper's surface; cheap papers can leave lots of lint inside your printer, compromising print quality and shortening engine life. *Opacity*

PRINTERS

describes how well a page prevents print on the back from showing through to the front. And *smoothness* measures the texture of the page; rough surfaces such as classic laid bonds often do not take toner evenly, but toner doesn't fuse well to very smooth surfaces either and is prone to flaking and falling off.

Types of Laser Printer Paper   Laser printers have special paper needs. It's no wonder that supply catalogs list dozens of types of laser printer paper; each manufacturer offers at least a half-dozen varieties of its own. How should you choose which paper to use?

Premium Papers   These are the highest quality papers available. They are made of the same fibers (wood, cotton and/or linen) as regular office paper, but the difference lies in the way the raw paper products are handled. In premium papers, the paper-making machines are slowed down to a crawl, which gives the paper pulp more time to "knit" the fibers and for water to drain off. The process is well inspected and controlled.

Premium papers may be either coated or uncoated. Coated paper is glossy, and is usually used in color brochures and slick magazine pages. Uncoated paper is used in all types of printing, from letterhead to books and posters.

Laser-Printer Papers   Laser-printer papers are very smooth and have a high brightness rating—about 85 percent or above. The moisture content for laser printer papers is lower than for many other grades of paper. Bond and xerographic papers will work in laser printers and look similar, but they are designed for copiers. They may not look as good or perform as well (expect jamming or smearing) because they were designed for a different purpose.

Xerographic Paper   The commonplace copy machines have a specific grade of papers designed just for them: xerographic grade. These, like laser papers, have less moisture to resist curling and are flexible enough to move through the copier innards. The main difference is they are not as smooth as laser-grade papers.

Bond   Bond, the standard business paper, was designed for use with pen and ink or in typewriters. It is heavy and durable, as well as thick and impressive. It feels good to hold. Bond can usually run through a laser printer pretty well without too much jamming. Most paper manufacturers are moving toward adding some of the xerographic and laser qualities to bond paper.

PRINTERS

Recycled Papers The trend towards recycled paper, as opposed to all-virgin stock, is becoming fairly commonplace, as well as ecologically correct. There are two advantages to recycled papers from a technical perspective: They lay flatter and are easier to fold. However, these same attributes are negative for high-speed copiers and laser printers. In these machines, the paper follows a curved path. Recycled paper is less stiff and has less curl than virgin paper, and when the static electricity and heat build up, the more malleable paper is prone to jamming inside the machine. (Paper manufacturers are attempting to solve this problem by making recycled stock designed specifically for laser printers.)

Specialty Papers When you leave the realm of blank paper and start looking at special supplies, the laser printer paper world gets even more complex.

A number of "handmade" papers will perform very well in a laser printer. The possibilities are endless. We've used some spectacular Japanese and Italian marbled handmade papers (cut to 8½-by-11 inches) with impressive results. A number of manufacturers are rising to the demand with some beautiful granite-look, marbled, or simulated handmade papers designed to be used in laser printers. It's fun to experiment with different papers for different effects.

If you wish to add color to your standard black-and-white output, you have a number of options. You can get pages that have been preprinted in another color. (Don't try to run raised-ink printing through your laser, however; the thermographic ink will melt in the fuser. Embossing also does not travel well through the heat and pressure of the fusing rollers.)

There are many colored papers and preprinted forms available for use with page printers. New products specifically designed for lasers are introduced all the time. These range from clear plastic "overhead" transparencies to prescored and preperforated mailers, and even die-cut Rolodex cards.

Laser-Printer Envelopes Envelopes tend to cause some of the biggest headaches for page printers. Hewlett-Packard has run extensive tests on envelopes and recommends those with diagonal seams and standard gummed flaps. This style results in the fewest layers of paper. Another tip from HP for reducing envelope printing problems is to make certain that the leading edge of the envelope has a sharp crease.

Labels Labels also have special requirements. Since the fusing rollers can be as hot as 200° or more, you must be sure that the label adhesive can withstand the heat. Labels for copiers are designed to handle these

PRINTERS

temperatures, but many labels designed for impact printers can't take the punishment.

Color Page Printers

Although these printers are commonly referred to as color laser printers, few of these devices actually use laser technology. Instead, they use various thermal-transfer technologies. The color transfer material is either wax or a plastic polymer. These devices all rely on heat to create a phase change at the time of impression. The wax or plastic is stored as a solid. Heat is applied to it so that it melts and sticks to the paper. The material then dries as a solid on the paper.

Some color print materials offer advantages over the others. For instance, the plastic material used is tough and durable. You could drive a truck across its printouts and not lift plastic from the paper. The cost of these prints—about 5¢ to 10¢ a copy—is a great advantage. The downside is that these prints show a texture—that is, the plastic shows on the paper.

Yet another technology uses a wax-transfer process that produces some of the brightest color prints you could ever hope for. However, the wax medium is delicate, and printouts can easily be marred under normal business abuse—paper clips, pencils, and so on.

Color page printers are not geared toward the home or small-business user yet. They are intended for the corporate art department or professional service bureau where users are willing to spend the "accountant-choking" initial price, as well as the $1.50 per print to get high-quality output.

Better quality and lower prices loom on the horizon for color page printers. It may be a while, though, before these printers are available at an affordable price for the home market.

Other Printers

When shopping for a printer, you will most likely buy a dot-matrix, ink-jet, or laser printer. However, there are a couple other types of printers you should be aware of.

Thermal Paper Printers

Thermal paper printers require a special kind of a paper that is sensitive to heat. The paper has a thermosensitive coating made up of two different colorless chemicals. When heated, one of the chemicals melts and combines with the second chemical to make a visible mark. (Many facsimile machines use thermal paper technology.)

Thermal paper printers are quiet and inexpensive, but are slow and have a very limited ability to print graphics. The print quality has a cheap, fuzzy look. Another significant drawback is that thermal paper tends to fade over time or if it's left in direct sunlight.

PRINTERS

Daisy-wheel Printers

Daisy-wheel printers were one of the early computer peripherals. Introduced by Diablo Systems in 1972, they had a whopping speed of 30 cps (characters per second). At their introduction, they were an impressive improvement over the low-speed typewriter-based printers in use. (Some of these were actually typewriters with special adapters and could be used either with a computer or manually.)

The main component of the daisy-wheel printer is the print device, a spoked wheel with each spoke ending in a character or number (a variation of and improvement over the old IBM Selectric "golf ball"). To change fonts, you remove the wheel and replace it with a different one.

The daisy-wheels went through a number of improvements. Speeds eventually rose to 65 cps. They produced a crisp, good-quality typewriter-style print, but were unable to print graphics or on envelopes or single sheets of paper.

Daisy-wheel printers once were one of the best choices for home printing needs, but they have limitations overcome by the newer printers. The dot-matrix printer is a better choice for basic printing needs.

Dvorak's Printer Buying Tips

Most people buy printers based on price. They find out if a particular printer is reliable, and then they search for the cheapest price.

Unfortunately, neither PC Labs nor anyone else has really given all printers a torture test. Most reliability questions are answered by word-of-mouth. This is yet another reason for joining a users' group.

I would suggest you go to a dealer or store that carries a lot of different printers from which you can get a printout. The quality of the print varies enormously, especially on dot-matrix printers. When you find a printer that you like, try to put price considerations aside and buy it.

Among laser printers, I prefer those that use the Canon engine, such as the HP and the Apple LaserWriter. A wide variety of toner cartridges is readily available for Canon-based laser printers. If you buy a Suzuki-nawa 45 laser printer with a Memphis Belle engine, you've bought something you'll never find supplies for. Ricoh, Panasonic, and others have good distribution, but Canon has great distribution.

BACKUP AND STORAGE

CHAPTER

7

ABOUT A DECADE AGO, before a hard disk was an option, everyone used the old way of loading programs: digging through piles of disks, finding the right ones, and shoving one after the other into the floppy drive to load the program. Today most software packages are very large—too large to run off floppy disks—so a hard disk is a necessity. It's much easier to have a regularly used program stored on the hard

BACKUP AND STORAGE

disk; at the DOS prompt you can just type in the program's start-up command to load in the file.

But what may seem like a huge amount of hard-disk storage when you first start out will become dinky and confining after just a few months. The space will soon become filled with programs, files, and utilities. But just because your computer has a small hard disk doesn't mean that you should toss out the machine and buy a new one. You can upgrade the hard disk. And, if the hard disk in your machine is beginning to fail, you can replace it. This chapter will give you enough information to guide you through the purchase of the next drive and to find the best buy. Along with hard disks, this chapter will also take a look at some alternative methods of backing up your data, including tape backups and optical drives.

Hard Disks: How They Work, How They Break

In simple terms, a hard disk is much like a record player (see Figure 7.1). There is a spinning disk (the record) and a read/write head (the old phonograph needle). The read/write head hovers over the disk and reads the data off the disk.

The disk, or platter, spins at very high speeds. The read/write head floats over the platter on a thin film of air without ever touching it. It's like a 747 airplane flying 700 miles an hour 1 inch over the ground. The data is magnetically encoded so the read/write head can detect these positive and negative magnetic patches and read data without ever coming in contact with the platter. When someone is said to have a *disk crash,* the read/write head has bumped into the hard disk and destroyed the disk's media, or surface. Although this is becoming a rare occurrence, it is not a repairable failure. Hard disks may have other problems, but most of these concern drive circuitry.

Disk Controllers

The disk controller is the brains of the hard disk. It's the part that tells the hard disk how to work, when to work, and what it should look for. It's the interface between the hard disk and the computer's brains—the microprocessor. Until recently the disk controller was a separate card that fit into the motherboard, but now, it's usually built into the hard disk, and a cable interface connects it to the motherboard.

The disk controller may develop some hardware problems that can be repaired. These problems usually occur suddenly, as do most hardware errors. If your hard disk just doesn't work and it's had no previous problems, you probably have a disk controller problem.

BACKUP AND STORAGE

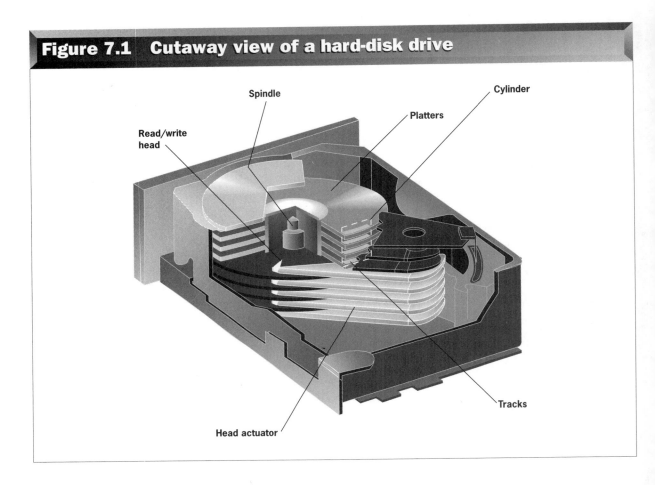

Figure 7.1   Cutaway view of a hard-disk drive

Do You Have a Bad Disk?

A hard disk may begin to fail because the material magnetically coded on the platter begins to lose its ability to hold a magnetic charge. These bad areas—called *sectors*—are unable to work properly, and you'll begin to see odd errors and discover that data is missing. Disk failure is most often caused by poor manufacturing. There is little you can do to prevent a bad hard disk from total failure. The best option is to replace the entire drive unit with a new one.

It is difficult to manufacture a 100 percent perfect hard disk. Most hard disks have a few bad sectors. These are detected when the hard disk is formatted (most come formatted from the manufacturer). The bad sectors are mapped and blocked off so data cannot be written to them. Programs that check a disk for accuracy may find a few bad sectors, and these

BACKUP AND STORAGE

will also be blocked off. If you begin to see new bad sectors showing up, this is not a good trend. It indicates a failing disk. Although it seems logical to reformat a hard disk to extend its life, it's not a good computing practice to entrust any data to a failing hard disk. Sooner or later it will fail completely (usually when you least expect it).

Disk errors, disk failure at start-up, and frequent system crashes all indicate a problem hard disk. At start-up (when you first turn your computer on) you may get an ominous error message, such as the often fatal numbers 1701. (In IBM code scheme, error messages prefaced with 17 indicate a problem in your hard-disk system.) Sometimes, hard-disk failure is a complete surprise, but other times it's a creeping problem. It's looming, and showing up just enough to remind you there's something wrong. It never quite goes away.

Good hard disks have few errors, and they aren't regular occurrences. Most hard disks are extremely reliable. Out of the dozens of computers I've used, only one hard disk died, and that was due to a bad bearing. The data was all recoverable. Hard-disk failure is something to be aware of and plan for even if it never happens. If you should have one of the rare lemons that is unstable, look into a replacement. Contrary to popular thought, disk drives don't wear out with overuse or "go bad" if you leave the machine on overnight. If a hard disk works, it works, and it will continue to do so for a very long time.

Unfortunately, you can no more predict the failure of your drive than you can predict ants showing up in your kitchen or a runaway truck hitting your house, so prepare for the worst and back up your data. While there is no foolproof way to gauge how long hard disks will last, manufacturers rate their products using a *mean time between failures* (MTBF) measurement. Statistically, the MTBF is the best estimation of how long your hard disk will run before it crashes. Your hard disk, however, will probably become obsolete long before it fails. Furthermore, warranties generally run out before the MTBF. For example, a drive with an advertised 50,000-hour MTBF typically carries a one-year warranty, which equals 8,760 hours.

Troubleshooting Problems   Your drive may give you a few hints of impending problems. For example, if you start to get an increased number of disk errors, you can be certain something is going wrong. Commercial disk-testing software can help locate and even minimize the effects of these errors on your files. Some of the best include:

Disk Technician Gold from PrimeSolutions, (800) 847-5000

SpinRite from Gibson Research Corp., (800) 736-0637

Mace Utilities from Fifth Generation Systems, (800) 777-5306

BACKUP AND STORAGE

GLOSSARY OF HARD-DISK TERMS

■ **Areal density**   The amount of data that can be stored in one area of a disk.

■ **ATA drive**   *See* IDE

■ **Average access time**   The time in milliseconds that the drive takes to find the right track in response to a request (the *seek time*) plus the time it takes to get to the right place on the track (the *latency*). IBM PC/XTs used 80- to 110-millisecond drives, while ATs used 28- to 40-ms drives, and today's 80386- and 80486-based systems use 15- to 20-ms drives.

■ **Back up**   To make a copy of a file, a group of files, or the entire contents of a hard disk. This ensures that you have a copy to "restore" lost files in the event of some terrible event—the hard disk crashing and dying, a fire, or the theft of a computer.

■ **Buffer**   An area of RAM (usually 512 bytes plus another 16 for overhead) in which DOS temporarily stores data.

■ **Cluster**   A group of sectors; the smallest storage unit recognized by DOS. On most modern hard disks, four 512-byte sectors make up a cluster, and one or more clusters make up a track.

■ **Cylinder**   A three-dimensional stack of vertical tracks from multiple platters. The number of cylinders in a drive corresponds to the name of different positions to which the read/write heads can be moved.

■ **Device**   Also known as a level interface, it uses an external controller to connect drives to the PC. Among its other functions, the controller converts the serial stream of data read from the drive into parallel data for the host computer's bus. ST-506 and ESDI are device-level interfaces.

■ **Drive array**   A storage system composed of several hard disks in which data is divided among the different drives for greater speed and higher reliability.

■ **ESDI (enhanced small device interface)**   A device-level interface designed as a successor to ST-506 but with a higher transfer rate (1.25Mb to 2.5Mb per second). Seldom used nowadays.

■ **GCR (group coded recording)**   A storage process in which bits are packaged as groups, each of which is assigned to and stored under a particular code; used by RLL drives.

■ **Head actuator**   The mechanism that moves the read/write head radially across the surface of the platters of a disk drive.

■ **IDE (integrated drive electronics)**   A system-level interface that conforms to ANSI's AT Attachment standard. This standard uses a variation on the AT expansion bus to connect a disk drive to the CPU, the maximum transfer rate being 4Mb per second. Originally, IDE was a generic term for any system-level interface (one that integrates controller electronics onto the drive).

■ **Interface**   The connection between the disk-drive mechanism and the system bus. The interface defines the way signals pass between the system bus and the hard disk, which in turn determines the speed at which information can be transferred between them. Examples are ESDI, IDE, SCSI, and ST-506.

■ **Interleaving**   A method of arranging disk sectors to compensate for relatively slow computers. Instead of sectors being arranged consecutively, they are spread apart. For example, 3:1 interleaving means your system reads one out of every three tracks on one rotation. The time required for the extra spins lets the read/write head catch up with the disk drive, which might otherwise outpace the head's ability to read the data. Thanks to track buffering and the speed of today's PCs, interleaving is obsolete. Look for "1:1 interleaving" (which actually indicates a noninterleaved drive).

Continued on next page

BACKUP AND STORAGE

GLOSSARY OF HARD-DISK TERMS

Continued from previous page

- **MFM (modified frequency modulation)** A method of magnetically encoding information that creates a one-to-one correspondence between data bits and flux transitions (magnetic changes) on a disk. It uses smaller storage densities and lower transfer speeds than RLL.

- **Platter** The actual disk inside a hard-disk drive; this is what carries the magnetic recording material. All but the thinnest disk drives have multiple platters, most of which have two sides that can be used for data storage. (On multiple-platter drives, one side of each platter is usually reserved for storing control information.)

- **Read/write head** The part of the hard-disk drive that writes data to or reads data from a platter. It functions like a coil of wire that reacts to a changing magnetic field by producing a minute current that can be detected and amplified by the electronics of the disk drive.

- **Restore** To replace files on a disk from a backup copy.

- **RLL (run length limited)** A method of encoding information magnetically that uses GCR to store blocks instead of single bits of data. It allows greater storage densities and higher transfer speeds than MFM.

- **SCSI (small computer system interface)** A system-level interface, designed for general-purpose applications, that allows up to seven devices to be connected to a single host adapter. It uses a parallel connection that produces a transfer rate faster than other currently available drive technologies. The term is pronounced "scuzzy."

- **Sector** The basic data storage unit on hard disks. On most modern hard disks, sectors are 512 bytes each, four sectors make up a cluster, and 17 to 34 sectors make up a track. Newer drives may have different numbers of sectors.

- **Spindle** The part of a hard-disk drive around which the platters rotate.

- **ST-506** A device-level interface; the first interface used with PCs. It provides a maximum data-transfer rate of less than 1Mb per second (625K per second with MFM encoding or 984K per second with RLL encoding).

- **System-level interface** A connection between the hard disk and its host system that puts control and data-separation functions on the drive itself (and not on the external controller). SCSI and IDE are system-level interfaces.

- **Track** The circular path traced across the spinning surface of a disk platter by the read/write head. The track consists of one or more clusters.

- **Track buffer** Memory sometimes built into disk drive electronics, sufficient to store the contents of one full track. This allows the drive to read the entire track quickly in one rotation and then slowly send the information to your CPU. It eliminates the need for interleaving and can speed up drive operation.

- **Transfer rate** The speed at which a disk drive can transfer information between its platters and your CPU. The transfer rate is typically measured in megabytes per second. The ST-506 interface has a transfer rate below 1Mb per second; today's SCSI drives can reach about 5Mb per second.

- **Winchester disk drive** A nickname for a hard disk with a spinning platter. IBM's original PC hard disk stored 30Mb on each side of a platter and was called a 3030, which reminded people of the Winchester 30-30 rifle.

- **Zone-bit recording** A storage process that arranges more sectors on the longer outer tracks of the disk but maintains a constant spin rate. It is designed to get more data on the disk but can be used only with intelligent interfaces. ■

BACKUP AND STORAGE

The Norton Utilities from Symantec Corp., (800) 441-7234

PC Tools from Central Point Software, (800) 445-4208

If sectors start going bad on your drive, you can no longer depend on it. It is time to consider a replacement.

Some hard-disk failures are easy to repair. When you start noticing problems, make sure a dead battery didn't cause your system to lose its setup memory and forget what kind of drive was installed. Then check your controller to ensure that it is properly seated in its socket and that all the cables between the controller and your drive are fully plugged in at both ends. Those quick experiments are all most people can do to repair an ailing drive. For anything more serious, you'll need a soldering iron, the knowledge to use it, and an environmentally controlled chamber, all of which is beyond the scope of this book.

You could send your old drive out for repair, but face it: You'll get back a piece of hardware that is not more reliable than it was before the failure. New drives are lower priced, higher capacity, and faster than the older ones.

These are the points to remember:

- Always back up

- Replace instead of repair

- Upgrade instead of tolerating a shrinking hard disk

The Only Reason to Repair   The only compelling reason to repair a failed hard disk is when you have important files on it and you failed to back them up. Then, your best bet is to contact a data recovery service. In the yellow pages these are listed under "Computer Service and Repair." You'll need to make a few calls to find out if they are able to do data recovery. Unfortunately, this service is expensive.

If there are no businesses in your area that are capable of data recovery, you can ship your drive to a service that specializes in it. One such service is Ontrack Data Recovery. You'll need to pull out the disk drive from your machine, pack it up, and ship it to them. They charge a flat fee of $200 to diagnose the disk's ailment (within 24 hours) and an additional $200 to $600 (not including shipping) to restore the data on a 40Mb drive. It can cost upwards of $1000 for a network server. (Note that the prices are accurate as of the time this is being written.) If your data is valuable, it's a necessary expense to get your files back. But for those prices, a good data backup system would be a better choice. (Keep in mind, they're making money on people's laziness—always a good business.)

BACKUP AND STORAGE

Contact Ontrack Data Recovery at (800) 872-2599, (612) 937-5161 in Minnesota, or on the West Coast in Irvine, California, at (714) 263-9245. Their address is 6321 Bury Drive, Ste. 15-19, Eden Prairie, MN 55346.

Choosing a New Hard Disk

When you select a new hard-disk drive, there are several factors to consider: Whether to get an internal or external disk, what kind of interface to get, how big a disk to get, and more.

Internal or External Disk?

You can purchase either an internal or an external hard disk. An external hard disk has a card that plugs into your motherboard, and a connector that pokes out the back of the machine, to which the external unit connects. External hard disks have many disadvantages: They're difficult to connect, they take up desk space, and they can be bumped or knocked to the floor with disastrous results. For these reasons external hard disks just aren't recommended. Stick with an internal hard disk.

Capacity

Another important feature to consider is capacity. No one makes 10Mb drives anymore, and 20Mb units have become specialized products, miniatures designed for the confines of a laptop and smaller computers. Full-size 5¼-inch drives storing 20Mb are as obsolete as your DOS 2.0 system disks.

The smallest drive you'll want will likely have a capacity of 40Mb and be available for under $200. These were once the most popular upgrades, but expectations have risen and costs have fallen so that today 60Mb to 80Mb drives are in the most demand. These drives can be found for under $300 through mail-order channels. For most desktop users, 100Mb is just the right size. That will give you enough storage for 30Mb of applications, 30Mb for the accompanying data files, and another 30Mb or more for expansion. You should have more megabytes if you have definite workstation or server plans for your PC. Server-size drives start where single-user products stop. (330Mb is a favored size.) For larger systems, the variety of 600Mb and larger drives is steadily increasing, and drives larger than 1 gigabyte are commonly available. (The thing to remember with hard disks is the bigger the better. It's like money: You never have enough.)

Speed

As for speed, get the fastest drive you can afford. A fast PC demands a fast hard disk; if you have a 486-based machine, you should get a 15- to 16-ms disk. Although a slow PC might not absolutely need such a fast drive, it can still benefit from one. Its response will improve on disk-intensive tasks.

BACKUP AND STORAGE

MFM VERSUS RLL

RLL (run length limited) is a way to store information magnetically that uses GCR (group coded recording) to pack up the bits into groups and to store these blocks as a unit instead of handling single bits of data. It allows for tighter packed storage and faster transfer speeds than MFM (modified frequency modulation), which stores the data bits individually on the disk.

The two storage schemes for hard disks—MFM versus RLL—used to be hotly debated. Since RLL is more efficient at packing data on disks, there could be little doubt about which technology would prove the eventual winner. RLL and its offspring are standard on most of today's advanced-technology hard disks. It's becoming so commonplace, in fact, that the term RLL itself is disappearing from the common computer lexicon.

In the past, you had to specify whether you wanted an MFM or RLL disk with a controller to match. The older interfaces, ST-506 and EDSI, delivered the raw data stream that was read from the disk to the disk controller. IDE and SCSI, as system-level interfaces, hide the data stream from you and your PC, so the form of disk modulation used is invisible to you.   ■

Mass storage speeds have only gotten faster over the years, but the average access times of PC-sized hard disks may be bottoming out. Check the specifications and you will see that most of today's better hard disks clock in close to an average access time of 15 ms. System overhead in disk transfers is such that faster disk drives will not appreciably improve system response.

Interfaces: ST-506, ESDI, IDE, or SCSI?

The interface for hard disks has changed over the years. In the early PCs, the interface was a full-size card, much like the old video adapter cards. But the trend has been toward moving most of the controller logic to the disk drive itself. The interface is now small, often no more than just a couple of chips and a connector (more accurately called a *host adapter*). The only possible exceptions to this little-card trend are a few of the specialized drives, SCSI, for example. The interface hooks into the motherboard. (You've probably gotten the drift by now—everything hooks into the motherboard at some point.) The interface determines the speed at which data can be transferred between the drive and the motherboard.

ST-506 and ESDI

The device-level ST-506 interface fell from fashion a year or two ago. No new drives use it. And it only hinders a drive with the speeds and capacities expected from a modern unit. The successor to ST-506 is ESDI (enhanced small device interface) but its popularity is on the decline as well. ESDI

BACKUP AND STORAGE

drives are available in quantity, but development work is concentrated on drives with other interfaces. In fact, this may be the last year that new ESDI drives are introduced. The data-transfer rates of ST-506 and ESDI interfaces are relatively slow; they actually impede the performance of 386- and 486-based machines.

IDE/ATA and SCSI

The two remaining interfaces—IDE (integrated drive electronics), sometimes called ATA for AT Attachment, and SCSI (small computer system interface)—are likely to be around for a while. Originally, IDE was a generic term for any system-level interface, but most people use it to mean a system-level interface that conforms to ANSI's AT Attachment standard (based on the PC/AT expansion bus) and that matches the bus in its potential throughput. IDE's and SCSI's higher-level connection allows them to use all the latest technologies to increase capacity and speed.

What Are Your Options?

If your PC is three or more years old, the hard disk probably uses an ST-506 interface, and its performance alone is good reason to upgrade. There are still some ST-506 drives on the market, but they are becoming increasingly rare as replacements. If you bought your PC more recently, it probably uses a more advanced interface—IDE or SCSI—which will allow you to upgrade your hard disk without making a costly change of interface. The IDE and SCSI interfaces put the controller electronics on the drive, so the "controller" you buy is really just a host adapter for connecting the drive to your PC. If you've got one of the advanced interfaces, stick with it: You will save yourself money (because you won't have to buy a new controller or host adapter) and some minor headaches (for example, switching from IDE often also requires tinkering with your PC to disable the IDE circuitry built into your system board).

Check your manual or invoice to determine what kind of drive is inside your PC. That is the easiest and most reliable indication of drive type. For example, you can't just tell by looking at a drive whether it uses an ST-506 or ESDI interface; all the cables and connections appear the same. To guard against future problems, you should label any new drive you get with its interface type, its capacity, and the drive type number your PC's setup program uses for it. See Table 7.1 for a comparison of the four interfaces.

Adding a Second Drive: Interface Considerations

When you want to add a second drive, your considerations vary depending on what interface you already have.

BACKUP AND STORAGE

Table 7.1 How the Interfaces Compare

Disk interface	ST-506	ESDI	IDE	SCSI
Integration	Device-level	Device-level	System-level	System-level
Transfer rate	Less than 1Mb per second	Up to 2.5Mb per second	Up to 4Mb per second	Up to 5Mb per second
PROS	Easiest upgrade path for systems with smaller ST-506 drives, if low capacity and slow performance are still acceptable.	Faster than ST-506; includes some advanced features. Available with large capacities and high speeds.	Faster than ST-506 and ESDI. Squeezes more capacity from small drives. Available with large capacities and high speeds. The best bet.	Faster than ST-506 and ESDI. Squeezes more capacity from small drives. Available with large capacities and high speeds. Can support up to seven devices, including printers, CD-ROM drives, and scanners.
CONS	Slow. Hard to find except in 20Mb to 40Mb capacities. Modulation methods (MFM or RLL) must match; controllers and drivers are not always compatible.	Slower than IDE and SCSI. Increasingly hard to find. Data-transfer rates must match.	Early specification ill-defined; compatibility with other drives not guaranteed. Switching to another interface requires disabling circuitry on the system board.	Different vendors implement different options, resulting in compatibility and installation headaches.

Adding a Second ST-506 Drive If you have ST-506, you can generally add a second ST-506 drive of any capacity supported by your PC (check the owner's manual or your PC's setup program to see what type drives are allowed). The only restriction is that both drives must use the same data coding scheme, MFM (modified frequency modulation) or RLL (run length limited). But you may have considerable trouble finding an ST-506 drive. For instance, a recent ad in *PC Magazine* for Hard Drive International, a major mail-order supplier, listed only two ST-506 drives out of the 27 advertised, and they were small: 20Mb and 30Mb.

Adding a Second ESDI or IDE Drive You can add a second ESDI drive with virtually any capacity, but you must match the transfer speed of the new drive to the controller. If you have a 10 MHz ESDI controller, you will want a 10 MHz drive. A controller can handle a slower drive but not a faster one. If you want a faster second drive, you will have to upgrade the controller to match, but it will generally be able to handle the old drive as well.

Adding a second IDE drive will force you to face compatibility issues. Because the original IDE specification was not well defined, some manufacturers' older drives would not work with those from other manufacturers.

BACKUP AND STORAGE

DON'T FORGET ABOUT FLOPPY DRIVES

When upgrading hard disks, don't forget about your floppy disk drives. Disk controllers for middle-aged computers, from the AT to the last generation of 386s, have combined the hard disk and floppy drive controllers. Earlier machines used separate boards for each; current machines are likely to use IDE interfaces on the system board. If you have one of these middle-aged machines and want to upgrade it, you will have to be sure to get floppy-disk control circuitry on your new host adapter controller or get a dedicated controller board for your floppy disk drives to accompany your new host adapter. ∎

While ANSI standardization of the IDE connection has solved the problem, odds are that the drive already in your PC was made before the standard was finalized. The best way to avoid compatibility problems is to make sure the new drive is manufactured by the same company that made your old drive or insist that the vendor let you return the new drive (without a restocking charge) if it proves incompatible. Your second IDE drive need not match the capacity of your first. It depends on your machine.

Adding a Second SCSI Drive   Adding a second (or third) SCSI drive might pose more problems than you would expect. Although, in theory, a single SCSI host adapter can handle seven peripherals, getting seven devices to work on a single SCSI connection is not easy. The original SCSI specification made many of its features optional, and various vendors have chosen to implement different options. Drives from two different vendors might not work together, and mixing peripheral types—CD-ROM drives, printers, and so forth—is even chancier. The advice is the same as for IDE: Either stick with the same manufacturer and make sure your vendor has a liberal return policy, or be prepared to stay up late for several frustrating nights. If you are replacing your hard disk with a new SCSI system, this won't be a problem, because you will buy a matched drive and host adapter.

In general, you can mix interfaces when you add a second drive. For instance, you might want to add a new SCSI drive to a system that already has an ST-506 unit, though you might occasionally encounter unpredictable hardware incompatibilities between some products.

Optimizing Your Hard Disk

Even when your hard disk is operating perfectly, there are still a few things you can do to optimize its performance, including defragmenting the data on the disk, adding a disk cache, and compressing the data.

BACKUP AND STORAGE

Defragment Your Disk

Every time you use your hard disk, it gets a little slower. This is because DOS was written when capacity was more important than speed. It tries to pack files on disk as conservatively as possible, dividing them into clusters and squeezing them as tightly as possible wherever there is a smidgen of room.

Whenever you erase (or delete) a file, a space is made on the disk. Then, when you save something new, this space can be filled with new data. If the space left is bigger than the new data, a little gap will remain. The next time you save something, some data will get squeezed into that opening, and the rest will be put in other little voids. Sometimes, when you've erased and saved data repeatedly, the data gets scattered over wide areas—a little here, a little there. But file clusters saved in this way cause DOS (and your hard disk's read mechanism) to search all over the disk for errant clusters. In addition, if something should happen to your hard disk, it makes complete file recovery difficult.

You can reorganize your disk by putting all of each file's clusters next to one another, so DOS and your disk drive do not have to search for them. You can do this easily with a special disk optimizer program (also referred to as a *disk defragmenter* or *disk compactor*). These programs are often included in hard-disk utility packages.

The cheap way to reorganize your hard disk is to back up (make a copy of everything on the disk), reformat, and restore all your files (copy them back onto the disk). It's a long, tedious job, but it's beneficial to the life of your hard disk and also reduces access time. A side benefit is a current backup of your hard disk.

Add a Disk Cache

The most effective software acceleration you can give your hard disk is a disk cache. This cache dynamically duplicates part of the contents of your hard disk in fast RAM so it can be read (and sometimes written to) at RAM speed. Unlike buffers, the disk cache has a memory management scheme that attempts to anticipate your program's requests for disk data, typically by retaining the data you've most recently accessed under the assumption that this is what you are most likely to need next. Disk caches are generally more versatile than RAM disks because they are larger. However, software disk caches may demonstrate incompatibilities with some applications. (One such program, considered one of the best, is PC-Kwik Power Pack from PC-Kwik Corp., (800) 395-5945.)

Another alternative is a caching disk controller. This hardware approach to disk caching is, however, expensive (between $700 and $1,800) and doesn't always offer a noticeable speed improvement over software disk caching in stand-alone user applications.

BACKUP AND STORAGE

Compress Your Data

Data compression is a way to take out extra spaces and repetitive characters in order to squeeze a file into the smallest possible amount of space on your hard disk. Data compression was originally used only in telecommunications, to shorten the transmission time (which lowered telephone bills), but soon moved into the realm of data storage for squeezing out every last bit of precious hard-disk space. It's a cheap way to double your disk capacity.

Today, you can buy software-based or combined hardware-and-software systems, such as Stacker or SpeedStor, to add data compression to existing PC systems. A hardware compression, or "internal compression," of a hard disk will render any add-on compression systems completely useless. Once a file is compressed, it cannot be compressed further. If you already have a hard disk that compresses data, don't waste your money on a software-based compression program in hopes of a further gain in storage capacity.

The major selling point of compression—both software- and hardware-based—is the promise of doubling the amount you can store on your hard disk. This is an impressive gain. On the other hand, one dark and dreary drawback to disk compression is that the data cannot be recovered if the disk fails. This is because the data is not recognizable as data—it's encrypted. It cannot be pulled out and pieced back together as regular uncompressed data. It is unrecoverable, a complete loss.

If you are religious about backup, and do it on a regular basis, a disk failure won't pose much of a problem. A compressed disk and the extra storage it offers may be the way to go. But if you're like most people, the threat of an unrecoverable failed disk makes you blanch. It's a decision only you can make.

File Backup

It can't be said often enough: Back up your important files. It may be both time-consuming and bothersome, but there are tools that make it less boring.

One good reason to back up important files is to avoid the heartache that will result if you inadvertently erase the file, or you have some major catastrophe—fire, theft, a virus, or a failed hard disk. It's not all that important to back up everything on your computer, but it is vital that you get into the habit of backing up important files. One bad loss usually remedies bad habits.

The most inexpensive, common, and readily available media to use for backup are floppy disks. Almost everyone begins by backing up data to floppies. However, this is tedious and time-consuming. If you must

BACKUP AND STORAGE

back up your entire hard disk on a regular basis, or if you have many files to keep secure, the only solution is a dedicated hardware backup device.

Ways to Back Up

Once you decide to back up, you must also decide on a method or strategy and how often to implement it: every day, once a week, or once a month. To back up whenever the "whim" strikes is a poor strategy. Another decision is what kind of backup you will do. A good backup system isn't just hardware, but a hardware and software combination that partially "automates" the system. Some software will work with a tape backup system to allow you to back up while you're absent. Software offers different choices for backup, including mirror, incremental, archival, and selective backups.

Mirror Backup   Mirror backup involves making a copy of everything on the hard disk. In high-volume situations (large inventory control systems, accounts payable/receivable), this often means there are two recording media—such as two hard disks or a hard disk and a tape backup system— and all the data is recorded on both at the same time. This provides an immediate "mirror" of the data.

A single mirror backup can also be done on floppy disks (you'll need a bunch of them). You can make a copy of everything on the hard disk— files, software, and so on. This is commonly done before reformatting a hard disk.

Incremental Backup   Incremental backup is useful only for updating the files that have changed since the last backup. Software backup programs do this automatically, by comparing the date and time of the last backup to the dates and times of files on the disk. The new version of the file will replace the previous version. The software also looks for files that have been deleted since the last backup.

Archival Backup   This will make a copy of an updated file, but it won't delete the previous version. In this way you'll have a trail of files, each one more current than the last. It's useful if you need to go back and check a previous version of a file for historical data (for instance, during an audit). A drawback to this system is that you'll need to have more and more backup media and storage for it. (Some companies have set-aside storage for three years, and then reuse the media.)

Selective Backup   A selective backup is when just a few files, usually the important ones, are backed up. This is usually how you'd do it if you

BACKUP AND STORAGE

were using a floppy disk to make a simple backup. Some software backup programs let you select the files to be backed up.

Backup Hardware

Adding a backup system to your machine is easy. The problem you may face is in the selection of the system. A number of different backup hardware options are available: tape, WORM, DAT, and disk. Some of these devices are technically excellent, while others are really "in" temporarily (with a great sales pitch).

Vendor stability is the key phrase. It's an important factor in choosing any system. There are so many choices and no effective standards. Because different systems use different media, and so much is "proprietary," few systems are compatible with any others. Look for a company that has been in business for a while and has a large installed base. If you have a popular, widely used system, you'll have a better chance of walking into a computer store after some catastrophic event and saying, "Here's my backup data tape. Now please build a computer system around it for me." Table 7.2 shows the date of introduction for the major categories of systems.

Dvorak's Rule: Consider the selection of a backup device by its popularity. Ask around. Price should not be the sole consideration.

Tape Backup Tape backup is fairly inexpensive, and it does the job. A tape backup unit may cost from $300 to $5,000 (for a DAT backup unit).

The data is stored on the magnetic tape in a sequential, linear way which makes finding a particular file difficult if only one file on your system is damaged. (Most other storage devices operate more like a disk drive, so a file can be located quickly.) But tape backup is a tried-and-true way to store data. It has been used on mainframes for years, and there are a number of different sizes of tapes to choose from. These tapes look much like standard cassette audio tapes. The popular tape formats include $1/2$-inch magnetic tape, $1/4$-inch magnetic tape and cartridge, and 4-mm digital audio tape.

One of the oldest tape drive storage devices is $1/2$-inch magnetic tape. The $1/2$-inch, open-reel tapes were developed for mainframes in the 1950s. For microcomputers, a smaller tape enclosed in a plastic cartridge is more common. The main difference between the regular magnetic audio tapes and data tapes is in the way the tape is pulled. The data cartridge is designed differently. The tape sits on a big flat spool, and the outer rim hub of the spool is rotated. This means the tape is pulled onto the spool at a constant speed no matter how much tape is on either side of the reel.

An audio tape is wound in like a fishing line onto a reel around and around a center hub. The more tape on the hub, the faster tape is wound on. Although the variance in speed is minimal, it's just enough to cause

BACKUP AND STORAGE

Table 7.2   From Floppy to Magneto-Optical: A Guide to Storage

Nobody has invented a storage solution that will satisfy all PC business users, so any choice you make will involve trade-offs among capacity, cost, and speed. To help you make the best choice for your applications, we have rated each medium, from the floppy disk to the magneto-optical disk, on its ability to perform the following functions: primary storage (for programs and data that must be available on-line, when maximum speed for reading and writing is essential), secondary storage (for programs and data that you want on hand, but when speed is not a critical factor), and backup (for backing up the contents of your primary storage area for safety and archival purposes).

The ratings (excellent, good, poor, or inappropriate) are based on the needs of the mainstream business user, but you may have a niche application that turns a normally poor choice into an excellent one. For example, an optical disk's removability may be more important to you (if you want your data securely locked overnight in a safe) than a hard disk's faster access times. And in a harsh environment, the rewritable optical disk's invulnerability to head crashes may be more important than a hard disk's faster speed for primary storage.

The table is organized in reverse chronological order.

	Date of introduction	Primary storage	Secondary storage	Backup
Magneto-optical and phase-change disks	1988	Poor	Excellent	Good
4-mm digital audio tape cartridge	1988	Inappropriate	Inappropriate	Excellent
8-mm helical scan tape cartridge	1987	Inappropriate	Inappropriate	Excellent
WORM disk	1985	Poor	Good	Poor
$1/4$-inch tape, DC-2000 minicartridge	1984	Inappropriate	Inappropriate	Excellent
Removable cartridge (Bernoulli Box)	1983	Good	Good	Good
Hard disk (Winchester)	1974	Excellent	Inappropriate	Good
$1/4$-inch tape, DC-6000 cartridge	1972	Inappropriate	Inappropriate	Excellent
Floppy disk	1971	Poor	Inappropriate	Poor

problems with data storage. For this reason, magnetic audio tapes are not recommended or used in tape backup.

Magnetic Cartridge Standards   Many different tape/cartridge combinations can be found on the market, the naming of which meets some conventional standards adopted by ANSI (American National Standards Institute). One such standard is DC, which stands for data cartridge. A number of ¼-inch magnetic tape cartridge sizes are on the market, including DC 600, DC 1000, DC 2000, DC 2000XL, and DC 6000. The numbers following the DC have little rhyme or reason. For instance, the DC 600 has 600 feet of tape, while the DC 1000 has 185 feet of tape.

Another designation, new to the market, is the QIC (¼-inch cartridge) standard for tape drives. This includes the QIC-40, the QIC-80, and the QIC-1350. The QICs use minicartridge ¼-inch tapes based on a dual-hub system developed by 3M Corporation two decades ago (usually used in the cartridges referred to as DC 2000). The QIC-80 minicartridge drives are expected to be an increasingly popular choice for data backup in the next few years.

BACKUP AND STORAGE

The QIC-80 improves on its QIC-40 predecessor by doubling its capacity. The QIC-80 standard also allows complete compatibility among drives following its format; this means you can format a tape on one maker's drive and use it in another's.

To become fully QIC-80 certified, a manufacturer must submit a system to the Pericomp Corporation of Natick, Maine, where it must pass a suite of tests defined by the QIC committee. The drives fall into three rough categories:

- **Non-QIC-80 compatible**   The drive doesn't work on the QIC-80 standard.

- **QIC-80 compatible**   The drive manufacturer claims to conform to the QIC-80 standard, but the drive has not yet been approved by the Pericomp testing facility.

- **QIC-80 approved**   The drive subsystem has been tested and certified compatible by Pericomp.

The Pericomp certification process involves evaluating a combination of hardware and software; that's why a company that uses its own proprietary software, for instance, won't necessarily pass the Pericomp tests. The same is true of a system that uses one of the QIC-certified drive mechanisms and even a modified version of the software that comes with that drive.

DAT   DAT (Digital Audio Tape), developed and patented by Sony, is an audio recording medium that can also be used for data. As an audio tape, it records the sound digitally, which eliminates any noise caused by the inherent problems of the tape and produces a superior, clean recording. As a data storage tape, it is excellent. DAT is said to be better suited to computer storage because it was originally created as a high-capacity digital medium. DAT has been capable of holding up to 1.3G of uncompressed data from its inception, and units with 5G (uncompressed) capacity are now available.

DAT technology has two important strengths: access speed and capacity. The 4-mm DAT medium was designed for rapid access to information; hence, a file can be located in about 15 seconds. This speed is generally more critical for restorations than for backups.

DAT tape is packed into 3-inch-by-2-inch cassettes that measure about 1/4-inch thick. You can buy these tapes in either 60- or 90-meter lengths, and they list for about $30 and $60, respectively.

DAT uses a type of recording method called *helical scan*. It is similar to the technology used by video recorders. The tape travels about 90 degrees around a drum spinning at 2000 rpm. The drum is at an angle of

BACKUP AND STORAGE

about 5 to 6 degrees to the tape. As the drum spins, the data is recorded in long diagonal strips across the tape, which create sections of a spiral helix of recorded data. The spinning drum has two read and two write heads, so data can be read and recorded at the same time. "Crossover" between the two recorded tracks is reduced, because each track is actually recorded at different *azimuth* angles. The two tracks make up a "frame" of 8K of data. The scheme efficiently uses the tape surface for about 60K per inch of storage capacity. Two principal data formats for 4-mm tape are DDS (digital data storage) and DAT.

Optical Drives   Optical drives come in three major categories: compact disc read-only memory (CD-ROM); write-once/read-many (WORM) drives; and magneto-optical drives. Optical drives use lasers instead of magnetic fields to read and write data. These drives can pack data tighter, squeezing as much as 650Mb on an optical disk smaller in size than a regular floppy disk. Optical drives can access data randomly rather than sequentially, just as a regular hard disk does, with access times below 30 milliseconds. With the use of a mechanical optical disk changer (like a jukebox), it is possible to have hundreds of gigabytes of data on line.

CD-ROM Drives   A data CD-ROM is similar in many ways to audio CD-ROM technology. Data is recorded with a laser beam which burns a bubble on the shiny surface. Data bits are represented by shiny spots alternating with flat spots. Unfortunately, CD-ROM is read-only, which makes it unusable for daily backup. Some service bureaus will convert data from regular floppies or backup tapes to CD-ROM for a permanent historical backup, but this is expensive. CD-ROM is used as a resource for bringing vast quantities of data—virtual libraries—to your fingertips. A number of publishers of CD-ROM information offer everything from encyclopedias, to nationwide telephone numbers, to copies of newspapers and old out-of-print books.

CD-ROMs can store an enormous amount of information, but accessing it rapidly is another story. Though their access times have improved over the last few years, even the best of today's CD-ROM drives are a great deal slower than hard disks. CD-ROM drives are slower than ordinary hard disks for a couple of reasons. First, a CD-ROM's sectors are arranged in a continuous spiral track, which is ideal for reading large blocks of sequential data, such as music. The spiral track also allows CD-ROM makers to take advantage of the equipment and infrastructure developed for mastering, pressing, and playing audio CDs. But it makes for slower random-access times than the concentric tracks used by hard disks (see Figure 7.2), whose sectors can be located faster because they are always found on a given track at a fixed distance from the center.

BACKUP AND STORAGE

Figure 7.2   Comparison of CD-ROM and hard disks

CD-ROM disk: Data stored in a continuous spiral track

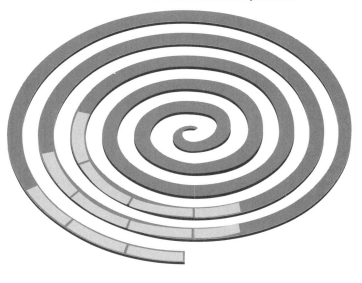

Hard disk: Data stored in concentric tracks

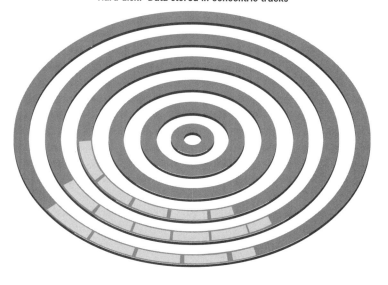

BACKUP AND STORAGE

The other reason for their slow access rates lies in the way sectors are arranged along the tracks. Hard disks use a constant angular velocity (CAV) encoding scheme, in which the disk spins at a constant rate of speed and each sector occupies the area subtended by a fixed angle. Sectors are placed at maximum density along the inside track of the disk; moving outward, however, the sectors must spread to cover the increasing track circumference, leading to "wasted" space between them and within them.

To make use of this space, CD-ROM disks use the constant linear velocity (CLV) encoding scheme, in which the length of a sector is constant regardless of whether it's located on the inside or the outside of the disk. This means the rotation speed of the disk must vary inversely with the radius; the motor must slow down the disk to read sectors located toward the outside of the disk and speed it up to read sectors located toward the inside. Doing this requires a more complicated drive mechanism that can overcome the inertia of the disk when accelerating and the momentum when decelerating, which slows the drive's random access times. But this encoding scheme also allows data to be packed at maximum density over the entire disk.

WORM (Write-Once/Read-Many) Drives WORM drives are much like CD-ROM drives, but they have a write laser. They can burn information onto the CD-ROM disk, but they can only do it once. The write lasers aren't as powerful as the ones which master CD-ROMs, but they do the job. A WORM drive is usable for backup, and the backed-up copy is permanent. WORM drives can store from 600Mb to nearly 1G of data, which makes them a good choice for high-end needs.

Magneto-Optical (MO) Disks This technology (also referred to as erasable optical drives) relies on both laser and magnetic technology. A laser beam heats a small area of the disk's surface. Then a magnetic write head magnetizes the area. When the area cools, the spot becomes stable. The entire idea is based on a screwy oddity of physics, namely, the *Kerr Effect*. When a laser is aimed at the spot, the reflection will show a detectable polar rotation based on the polarity of the magnetic media. When the spot is reheated, it can be rewritten to or erased. Vendors claim that this may be done up to a million times with no ill effects on the data. Unfortunately, the drive is slow to write data, which makes it a questionable choice for data backup.

INPUT DEVICES

CHAPTER

8

THERE ARE A LOT OF WAYS for the user to communicate directly with the computer. The most common is the keyboard, but there are also the joystick, the graphics tablet, and the mouse. Keyboards are provided with every new computer (with the exception of the newer pen-based computers), and the mouse is becoming a more common device as Windows continues to increase in popularity.

INPUT DEVICES

Keyboards

Most new computer users think of the keyboard as a fixed part of the computer. It's like owning an old Royal typewriter with a sticking L key; you get used to it. (It's cheaper than getting it fixed or buying a new typewriter.)

If your computer keyboard has keys that stick or don't feel right, there's an easy solution: Get a new keyboard. This may sound decadent (how many people have you known to buy a new typewriter because the "feel" was wrong?), but it's not. There is a keyboard out there for you, but they aren't all alike.

Keyboard History

Most keyboards conform—with minor variations—to the IBM Enhanced 101 Key Keyboard which IBM decreed as the standard in 1987. In fact, the Enhanced design was IBM's third keyboard standard for PCs.

The original IBM PC and XT keyboard had 83 keys (see Figure 8.1); ten function keys appeared on the left, and a combined number pad and cursor pad appeared on the right. The Ctrl, Left Shift, and Alt keys were arranged in a line next to the function keys; Esc was to the left of the numbers in the top row. To the right of the Right Shift key, an unshifted asterisk key let you type *.* without acrobatics. Between the tiny Left Shift and Z keys was a Backslash/Vertical key. The Enter key was narrow, vertically aligned, and easy to miss. The design was a mixture of sensible and absurd layout decisions combined with a splendidly positive touch that many users believe no other manufacturer has equaled.

IBM's next design was the original AT keyboard. This was incompatible with the PC/XT design, but could be programmed through the MODE command and other utilities to change both the rate at which a held-down key was repeated and the delay before the first repeat. The AT keyboard again had ten function keys on the left, but exiled Esc and the unshifted asterisk to the number pad. The Enter key was L-shaped, and the Backslash key (which occupied the spot that used to be the left half of the Backspace key) was reduced to the width of a single alpha key.

When IBM upgraded the AT, it introduced the Enhanced model, which was compatible with the original AT model, but had a drastically different layout. The Esc key and 12 function keys were now along the top, the number pad was moved to the right, and a new cursor pad was placed between the alpha keys and number pad. The cursor pad (which was actually split into two sets of keys) consisted of four arrow keys in an inverted T at the bottom and a separate bank of six keys at the top: Ins and Del, Home and End, and PgUp and PgDn. Computer users started pressing Del when they meant End, sometimes with disastrous results (for example, when a large block of text happened to be defined on

INPUT DEVICES

KEYBOARD KEY TALK

In any discussion of a keyboard, the description of the individual keys comes up. If you've never used a computer before, this may be confusing. We've compiled a list of the more common keys and their common abbreviations.

- **Alternate (Alt)** This is similar to the Control key. It is also like a Shift key in that when used in conjunction (simultaneously) with another key, it executes a command, or in certain applications, creates a graphics character. The Alt key is more common in telecommunications programs and TSR (terminate-and-stay-resident) programs than in regular application programs. It is used often in multitasking environments.

- **Arrow keys (Right, Left, Up, Down)** The arrow keys move the cursor up and down, left and right.

- **Control key (Ctrl)** This is like the Shift key or Alt key in that when used in conjunction (simultaneously) with another key, it makes a new graphics character or executes a command.

- **Delete (Del)** In most word processing programs, this will delete the characters to the right of the cursor. The longer you hold down the Delete key, the more characters are "sucked up." The cursor itself does not move. (It is different from the Backspace key, which does move the cursor.)

- **Enter (also called the Return key or Rtn key)** This key lets the computer know a command has been issued; in a word processing document, it adds a line feed similar to a typewriter.

- **Escape (Esc)** Usually it backs you out of a command, menu, dialog box, or program.

- **Function key (F-key)** Usually numbered from 1 to 12 (F1, F2, and so on), they perform special functions. They are also used to standardize software interfaces. For example, F1 in most software will produce a help screen. They also make word processing and other applications easier to use, because function keys are linked to common commands. So instead of typing in a command or using a number of control key/key combinations, you can just use a function key as a shortcut.

- **Home, End** Home is supposed to move the cursor to the upper-left corner of an application document. In reality, it does a number of variable things depending on the software program. In some programs, Home will move the cursor to the top of the current page, while in others it does nothing. The End key, in theory, should bring you to the bottom right of a document, but often it does nothing. Sometimes these keys must be used in conjunction with a Ctrl or Alt key to function properly.

- **Insert (Ins)** In many applications, this key is a "toggle" for Insert mode, meaning that if you depress the key, it will turn Insert mode on or off. If you turn off Insert mode, move your cursor into a line of text, and type, you will write over existing text instead of inserting text. With Insert mode on, you would thrust new text between the existing text.

- **Page Up, Page Down (PgUp, PgDn)** PgUp moves the cursor up 25 lines or a page (depending on the software). PgDn moves the cursor down 25 lines or a page. In a telecommunications program, these keys may be used to begin to send or receive files. ■

INPUT DEVICES

Figure 8.1   Original IBM XT and AT keyboards

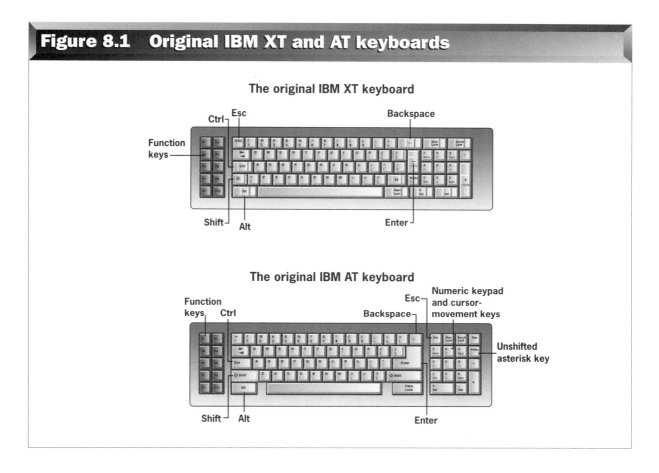

The original IBM XT keyboard

The original IBM AT keyboard

screen at the time). The Backspace returned to its original double width. The Backslash replaced the upper part of the two-row AT Enter key, and the Enter key now occupied a single row. Caps Lock migrated to the old site of the Ctrl Key, and twin Ctrl and Alt keys flanked the spacebar.

Variations on the Standard   Like it or not, the Enhanced layout has become the unshakable corporate standard, although many replacement keyboards alter this standard slightly by restoring the original AT's two-row L-shaped Enter key, single-width Backspace, and top-row Back-slash key. Your keyboard preference will depend on whether you press the wrong key more often when aiming for a single-width Backspace or when aiming for a single-row Enter key. Some keyboards also let you reverse Ctrl and Caps Lock, and some let you remove an IBM-standard

INPUT DEVICES

annoyance by locking the period and comma keys so that their shifted states generate a period and comma instead of angle brackets. All these keyboards are functionally equivalent to Enhanced keyboards despite differences in layout (see Figure 8.2).

How a Keyboard Works

The secret to the click of a keyboard is in the key-switch technology it uses. The four key-switch technologies commonly found inside PC keyboards are mechanical, capacitive, conductive rubber-dome, and membrane switches. All but the last one are hidden under key caps, but you can't tell much about a keyboard's switch technology just by popping off the cap. (Be careful if you do try—some keyboards can be broken if the key caps are removed.)

Although you might expect a keyboard's touch to be directly related to its switch technology, this is not always the case. Keyboards with mechanical switches tend to have the positive clicky touch you would expect, but keyboards that use capacitive, conductive rubber-dome, or membrane technology aren't always mushy.

Note that keyboards can differentiate up to about 300 characters per second—more than any human hands can produce. The computer can't always process the signals that quickly, however. In order to ensure that keystrokes can be saved for future execution, all of these keyboards send their signals into a special buffer on the motherboard that can hold up to 16 characters. The presence and activity of this buffer are unrelated to the key-switch technology a keyboard uses.

The switch technology a vendor uses is governed by how and where the keyboard will be used, how reliable it needs to be, and how much it will cost. Several vendors sell keyboards with a variety of switch technologies to cater to customer preference or application.

Mechanical Switches   Mechanical switches are one of the most popular technologies. Keyboards that use mechanical key switches tend to have a positive, tactile touch, which is produced by the spring tension used to return the key. These keyboards generate audible clicks when keys are depressed. The feel and sound result from the contact that occurs between conductive materials on the plunger; the conductors are often made of gold, gold alloy, or mylar with silver-carbon overlay.

One drawback to mechanical switches is the higher number of parts they require, which increases the cost. A mechanical-switch keyboard may use as many as three times the parts of a membrane-switch model (See Figure 8.3). Mechanical switches are reliable and have a relatively long life expectancy.

INPUT DEVICES

Figure 8.2   Variations on a theme

The **IBM Enhanced 101 Key Keyboard** is the keyboard that all the others imitate, with more or less minor modifications. The single-row Enter key and double-width Backspace are the features most likely to be modified in other layouts.

The **Northgate OmniKey/Ultra-T** improvises on the standard IBM design by including a double complement of function keys. It lets you modify IBM's layout by rearranging the Ctrl and Caps Lock keys so that the Ctrl, Shift, and Alt keys are in a vertical line, as in the original IBM-XT and -AT layouts.

DataDesk's elegantly finished **Switchboard** goes a step further—it can be split into three pieces and rearranged according to personal preferences. Note the Switchboard's extra Option keys, designed for the Macintosh, and key labels that display both Macintosh and PC functions.

INPUT DEVICES

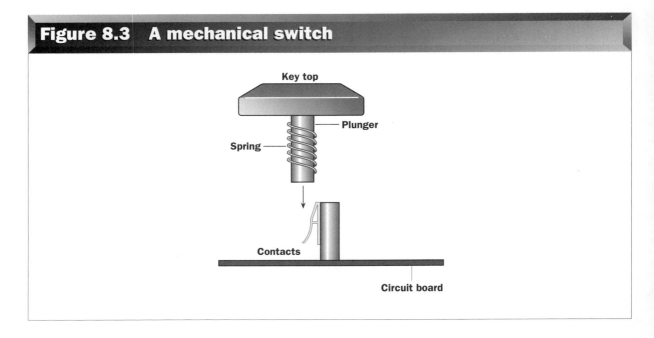

Figure 8.3   A mechanical switch

Capacitive Switches   Capacitive key switches don't make a mechanical contact between conductive elements (see Figure 8.4).

A mechanical contact between conductive elements is like a Rube Goldberg design: An act triggers another act. It functions like a typewriter key struck by the finger: As the key moves down, the arm moves up, strikes the ribbon, and leaves an inked impression on the paper. It relies on motion and force. A capacitive key switch uses another design.

Capacitive key switches are designed to detect a change in the electrical impulse of a circuit. The circuit—in true electric form—is either opened or closed (that is, on or off). When a keyboard key is pressed, it presses down a dielectric cushion (*dielectric* means the pad does not transfer electricity). This dielectric cushion forces the conductive elements farther apart or closer together—depending on the design—to create a change in the electric impulse of the circuit. This change in the circuit is what signals the computer to "recognize" the depressed key.

Keyboards with capacitive switches are expensive to design. The electronics are relatively complex, but they also offer high reliability and a long life. (These keyboards may have problems in harsh environments, especially in dusty or very humid workplaces.) Traditionally, capacitive switches use springs on the plunger to control stroke pressure and feel; the IBM Enhanced-style keyboards use this design. Other keyboards use

INPUT DEVICES

Figure 8.4   A capacitive switch

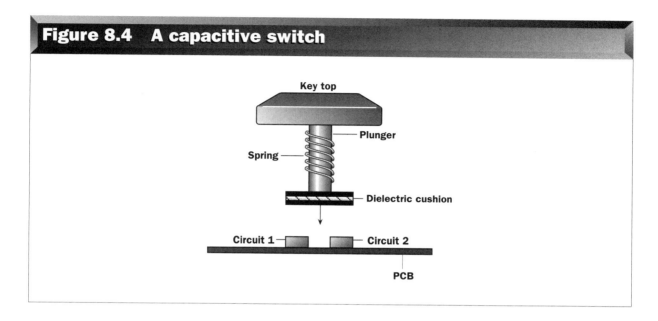

capacitive switches with a rubber-domed sheet to control pressure and feel. (This differs from a conductive rubber-dome key switch.)

Conductive Rubber-Dome Switches   In conductive rubber-dome technology, each switch has a carbon dot under the center of a raised rubber dome. When a key is pressed, the dome collapses, pushing the carbon dot down to complete a circuit between two contact pads (see Figure 8.5). This type of switch is very quiet and can have a good feel, depending upon the composition of the rubber that is used. The rubber domes themselves may be individual pads under separate keys or, more commonly, may be arranged on a single, thin sheet of rubber.

Conductive rubber-dome switches are relatively inexpensive and easy to assemble. Single-sheet rubber-dome keyboards give you some protection against spills, but if one part of the sheet goes bad, the whole thing must be replaced. Not surprisingly, conductive rubber-dome keyboards typically have a rubbery feel.

Membrane Switches   Membrane switches are now among the most popular technologies. Once the least reliable keyboard technology with the shortest life expectancy, current versions of membrane-switch keyboards are among the most reliable of all. Membrane switches use a very small number of parts, and current materials are durable and resistant to environmental changes.

INPUT DEVICES

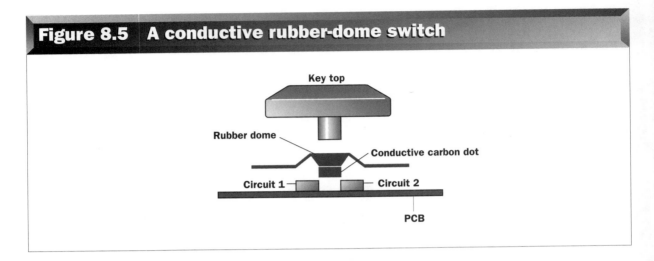

Figure 8.5   A conductive rubber-dome switch

Membrane switches consist of two layers of polyester film, each with a silk-screened pattern of conductive silver-carbon ink. A layer of insulation between the two membranes has small holes in strategic locations. When you press a key, a cushion—sometimes an inverted rubber dome—squeezes the conductive membranes, causing them to make contact and close the circuit (see Figure 8.6).

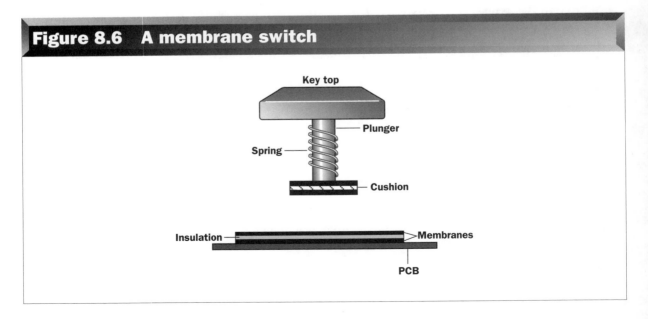

Figure 8.6   A membrane switch

INPUT DEVICES

There are other implementations. IBM uses a buckling spring and a pivot plate. When pushed, the spring causes the plate to rotate, which closes the circuit. The spring can be adjusted to return the key to its "up" position, similar to conductive rubber-dome technology.

Another point in favor of membrane switches is that they need not have a stiff mechanical touch. While some of the membrane entrants offer little better than slightly muted mechanical clicks, the current IBM and Tandy models provide the full clickiness of their capacitive-based predecessors. Like the IBM, the Tandy keyboard maintains its particular feel by employing the same kind of spring actuators used in its older models to trigger the membrane switches. IBM's keyboard technology is patented, so the Tandy can't exactly match its feel, but it comes close.

Buying a Keyboard

Replacement keyboards range in price from $50 to $150. All you have to do is plug them into the computer. Most computers use a 5-pin DIN connector for the keyboard cable, and almost all replacement keyboards have the 5-pin connector attached (see Figure 8.7).

IBM PS/2s and many other recent models use 6-pin mini-DIN connectors, and 5-pin to 6-pin adapters are readily available; however, 6-pin to 5-pin adapters are harder to find. IBM uses a detachable cable, and you can order a cable with either a 6-pin or 5-pin connector on the end.

Beyond this obvious issue, compatibility generally is not a problem unless you're choosing a keyboard to use with an older Novell network or you're replacing the keyboard on an XT-class machine or a not-quite-IBM-compatible machine such as the Tandy 1000 or AT&T 6300.

Figure 8.7   A 5-pin DIN and 6-pin mini-DIN connector

INPUT DEVICES

If you're upgrading the keyboard on an old XT, make sure the replacement is electrically compatible with the XT as well as later models. All PC-compatible machines communicate with the keyboard in the same way. The only exception is between the AT and XT. An AT keyboard is not compatible with an XT computer, and vice versa. Keyboards from most third-party vendors, however, have a switch at the back of the keyboard for either AT or XT.

Try It Out   To choose a keyboard, sit down and type. It needs to feel just right for you—a subjective thing. The top-of-the-line, gold-plated, pricey keyboard might not feel as good as a more modestly priced one. It might not perform any better, either.

Don't buy a used keyboard at a swap meet. It's possible to get a good one, but what's the point? Keyboards fail, they get gunk between the keys, a spring on a key gets broken, the connections get loose—all of which may not be apparent at first. There is nothing worse than trying to "make do" with a faulty keyboard.

Things to Consider   Keyboards vary. If you compare computer keyboards from different makers, you'll note that the Ctrl, Caps Lock, Num Lock, and Shift keys appear in different locations. The "throw" (the distance the finger travels to make a letter on the screen) and the key spacing would range from comfortable to alien, depending on personal tastes.

I'll give you an example. You have a keyboard at the office that's perfect—it fits like a glove. You've used the office computer for years and know the keyboard well. Then, you purchase a home computer. The computer doesn't "feel" right. You make mistakes. You fumble for the Ctrl key. You type half the page in caps. The home computer is frustrating; using it isn't a pleasurable experience.

Then you realize that it's not the computer at all—it's the keyboard. It's completely different from the one you use at work. The Caps Lock and Ctrl keys are switched. And that's not all: The keyboard feels mushy and your little finger can barely reach the Delete key. It's time to replace the keyboard.

The placement of the function keys might seem like a minor point, but it isn't. It's as important as the H key being next to the G key. Touch typing is a habit. Move one key and it's like going on a hike with a pebble in your boot.

When it comes to keyboards, there is no absolute best choice, just as there is no one perfect car for everyone. Individual taste, comfort, and habit are the guidelines for choosing a keyboard that suits you.

INPUT DEVICES

THE DVORAK KEYBOARD LAYOUT

There is a dedicated following for the famous Dvorak layout (no relation). The keys are laid out differently from the standard QWERTY configuration (named for the first six alphabetic keys at the upper-left corner). QWERTY was originally devised to slow down typists. Back in 1868, when the first workable typewriter was introduced, typewriters had a tendency to jam, especially with a speedy operator. So to keep the keys from piling up, the keys were arranged so the most common letters were spread apart and different fingers were called upon, with the most common letters on the left side of the keyboard. (Just think about touch typing: The little finger of the left hand hits the letter A, and the middle finger of the left hand must also travel up to hit E.) It was designed to be inefficient.

Modern technology has eliminated jams. The Dvorak keyboard was designed with a different key placement for more efficient typing, but the Dvorak is old hat now. You can get keyboards with this arrangement from a variety of sources, and there are even public-domain and shareware programs that will remap your keyboard to give you a Dvorak layout. ∎

Qwerty

Dvorak

INPUT DEVICES

Touch and Technology   The touch of a keyboard can be divided into two basic categories: those with a positive (or tactile), hard clicky touch versus keyboards with a relatively nontactile, silent (or soft clicky) touch. Mail-order dealers report that user preferences divide more or less evenly between the two categories.

IBM's keyboards are the leading examples of a clicky, tactile response. When you press an IBM key top, pressure builds until the contact is complete—or, as keyboard engineers say, the key is "made." At that point the user receives aural feedback through a loud mechanical click and positive tactile feedback by way of an abrupt drop in pressure. An audible click is far less important than precise tactile feedback, and you should probably avoid third-party keyboards that generate an annoying electronic click or add mechanisms solely to produce noise beyond that caused by the switch itself.

Compaq's desktop keyboards, with some recent exceptions, offer the most famous examples of silent, soft, and imprecise tactile feedback. Keyboards of this kind give less positive feedback and often have a soft, pliable feeling at the bottom. This feeling tells you when you've made the key, but it doesn't tell you precisely. Some users find these keyboards more restful, because there is none of the sharp, exact response you get from an IBM-style design.

Ergonomic Concerns (OUCH! My Aching Wrists!)

The hand-to-keyboard relationship is the most strained interface between you and your PC. Typing can be more than just a bothersome task; it can cause permanent damage to your hands and wrists. A study conducted by the South Australian Health Commission in 1984 found that 56 percent of keyboard operators had recurring symptoms of keyboard-caused injury, 8 percent of them so seriously that they had to contact a health-care provider.

The most serious health problem associated with keyboard use is the same ailment suffered by chicken pluckers and meat packers. The formal name for the ailment is *repetitive strain injury* (RSI). The name explains the cause: Straining to perform the same hand movements over and over again eventually leads to physical damage. The most common manifestation of RSI among typists is *Carpal Tunnel Syndrome (CTS)*. A similar ailment, wrist tendonitis, has also been associated with keyboard use.

The carpal tunnel is a narrow passageway in your wrist through which the median nerve passes; it carries sensations for your entire hand (see Figure 8.8). It also affects the finger flexor tendons, which link your fingers to the muscles in your lower arm. The tunnel is formed by walls of solid bone on three sides with the bottom enclosed by the transverse carpal ligament, a tough, inelastic cartilage.

INPUT DEVICES

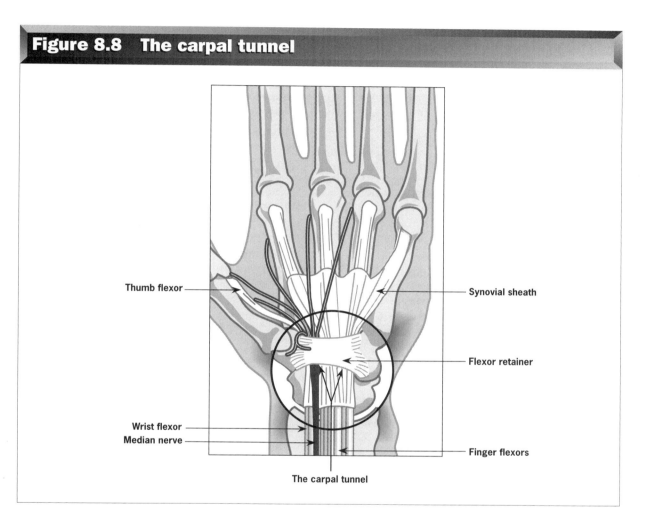

Figure 8.8   The carpal tunnel

Thumb flexor

Synovial sheath

Flexor retainer

Wrist flexor

Median nerve

Finger flexors

The carpal tunnel

 Carpal Tunnel Syndrome occurs when the tendons protect themselves from overuse. Each tendon is surrounded by a thick, fluid-filled sac called a synovial sheath, which swells with extra fluid to protect the tendon. Scientifically, this swelling is called tendonitis. When these sacs swell in the carpal tunnel, they can pinch the median nerve against the bones or the carpal ligament. The result can be loss of sensation in the hand and debilitating pain.

 Although the problem develops over a period of years, the onset of pain caused by Carpal Tunnel Syndrome is often sudden. Some sufferers have no symptoms at night and wake up the next morning in excruciating pain, unable to work, possibly for months. In most cases those afflicted

INPUT DEVICES

RSI (REPETITIVE STRAIN INJURY)

You can replace your keyboard, but not the hands you use for typing. It's important to take care of them. A growing number of office workers are being diagnosed with ailments that stem from long hours at the computer. RSI (Repetitive Strain Injury) results from executing the same motions over and over, and the much talked about CTS (Carpal Tunnel Syndrome) is caused primarily by bad keying habits. They progress from irritating (numbness and shooting pains in the arms) to debilitating (permanent inability to use the hand). Wrist surgery to repair the damage caused by CTS is the second most frequently performed surgical procedure in the United States.

RSI develops gradually and is often ignored until it becomes chronic. The symptoms of RSI include restricted joint movement and swelling of soft tissues. RSI can affect a keyboard user's nerves, tendons, and neurovascular structures. The most common disorders include Carpal Tunnel Syndrome, De Quervain's disease, tendonitis, and ganglionic cyst.

Frequent work breaks can help to prevent the onset of these injuries; however, use of a traditional keyboard requires inherently stressful postures. According to the Kinesis Corporation (whose alternative keyboard will be discussed in a moment), the postures to be avoided include:

- **Ulnar deviation** The wrist is bent outward in the direction of the little finger.

- **Abduction** The hands and arms are angled together in front of the body rather than at shoulder width.

- **Flexion** The wrist is bent down such that the fingers are lower than the wrist joint.

- **Extension** The wrist is bent up and back such that the fingers are higher than the wrist joint.

- **Pronation** A forearm and hand position in which the hand is open, palm down and parallel with the flat surface of the desk or floor.

If you must operate a keyboard for the entire workday, you can take some simple steps to lower your risk significantly:

- Try to keep your wrists straight while typing.

- Adjust your chair so that as you type, your elbows are at the same height as your wrists.

- Resting your wrists is important. If the center of your keyboard is less than two inches thick and you have enough room, rest your wrists on the desk as you type. Special contoured wrist-rest pads, which attach to the front of the keyboard, are also available.

- Every hour, rest your hands and wrists for five minutes. ∎

with Carpal Tunnel Syndrome have ignored all the pain warning signs: a minor pain in the wrist after a day of typing or some numbness in the thumb or fingers.

People have been typing for over 100 years, yet Carpal Tunnel Syndrome appears to be a recent phenomenon. The diagnosis is not new, and the condition is not caused by a recently evolved virus or bacterium. People's typing habits have actually changed.

Today, a typist's or word processor's fingers stay as close to the home row on the keyboard as possible. A simple press of the pinkie is all that's needed to issue a carriage return. Old typewriters required a definite

INPUT DEVICES

change of position and a resounding right hook to send the carriage back to the left after each page, and at the end of the page, the typist had to extract one sheet and roll a new one into the typewriter. All of these simple, necessary acts added variation to the typing process. Computers encourage extended use, resulting in hour upon hour of entering and editing text and data.

These differences between classic typing and modern keyboarding hint at one way of avoiding Carpal Tunnel Syndrome: Take frequent breaks.

Products claiming to increase keyboarding comfort and decrease the risk of Carpal Tunnel Syndrome have proliferated, but like the words "diet" and "lite," "ergonomic" is often only an advertiser's catchy marketing hype. Most experts agree that if a product aims to promote the ideal keyboard posture, that posture is the one that takes the least effort to hold.

Ergonomic (Specialty) Keyboards   A wild variety of new ergonomic keyboards has been designed, some of which are on the market and some of which aren't. (Thank goodness!) One model which came and went was a pole-shaped device that stood upright on your desk. You'd wrap your hands around it like a giant oboe.

Ergonomic keyboards have a dedicated following, but it's a matter of personal taste. Some people have had amazing relief of hand and wrist disorders and swear by their ergonomic keyboards. Others think they're awkward and silly looking.

The basic designs of these ergonomic keyboards focus on moving the hands further apart (straight with the shoulders) and keeping the wrists straight.

Ergonomic keyboards include the Comfort Keyboard, the Kinesis, and the PCD Maltron.

The Comfort Keyboard   The three sections of the Comfort Keyboard (left-hand, right-hand, and numeric keypad) can be independently separated, raised, lowered, rotated, and tilted into an infinite number of positions (see Figure 8.9). This can remove barriers to computer access and use for people with a variety of physical disabilities, including arthritis, spinal cord injuries, and orthopedic conditions such as Carpal Tunnel Syndrome. Specific adjustability applications are numerous. For example, the keyboard can accommodate orthopedic conditions, including those requiring the use of splints and braces; it can also adjust for use in a standing position to assist people with back problems. A person with cerebral palsy or arthritis might have hands that are angled, so the keyboard sections could be adjusted away from the body or arranged for one-handed use. In addition, quadriplegics can vary the angle of each section so a head-wand can be used comfortably and effectively.

INPUT DEVICES

Figure 8.9   The Comfort Keyboard

The keyboard uses a standard QWERTY key arrangement. (The purchase price is $590.) For more information, contact:

Health Care Keyboard Company, Inc.
N82 W15340 Appleton Ave., Suite L
Menomonee Falls, WI 53051
(414) 253-4131; Fax: (414) 253-4177

The Kinesis Keyboard   The Kinesis keyboard (see Figure 8.10) resembles a regular keyboard, except there are separated, concave, alphanumeric keypads for each hand. The separation is to minimize strain and stretching. The user's arms and hands are positioned at shoulder width, and the wrists remain straight.

The hands are raised at the thumb relative to the little finger, further reducing stress. Thumb keypads redistribute the workload from the relatively weak little fingers to the stronger and more flexible thumbs. The Kinesis keyboard uses thumb keys for such heavily used keys as Enter, Space, Backspace, and Delete. As a result, the workload is more evenly distributed and the lateral motions required to reach peripheral keys are reduced.

INPUT DEVICES

Figure 8.10 The Kinesis keyboard

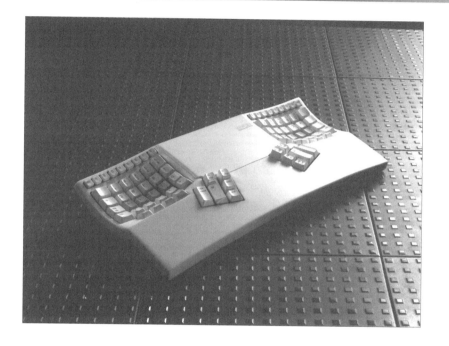

Keys are arranged in columns to reflect the natural motion of the fingers, and the keypads are sculpted and concave to fit the varying lengths of fingers. Palm supports with optional, self-adhesive pads increase comfort and reduce static postural effort. They also prohibit stressful wrist extension.

The key switches are engineered to provide mechanical and audible feedback with a minimal force and activation distance. The audible click is user-selected. The layout retains the standard QWERTY configuration (although a Dvorak configuration is planned for a future release). An optional numeric/cursor keypad can be positioned for right- or left-hand use. (The purchase price is around $700.) For more information, contact:

Kinesis Corporation
915 118th Ave. S.E.
Bellevue, WA 98005-3855
(206) 455-9220; Fax: (206) 455-9233

INPUT DEVICES

The PCD Maltron Ergonomic Keyboard   The PCD Maltron Ergonomic keyboard divides the alphabet keys into two groups and places them in hemispherical indentations on either side of the case. The function keys line the top, while numbers are arranged in the center of the keyboard. Shift, Enter, Ctrl, Alt, End, Home, and cursor keys are placed in mini-indentations near the lower corners of the alphabet keys—about where your thumbs would be if you were typing. (The price is around $600.) For more information, contact:

>   Applied Learning Corporation
>   1376 Glen Hardie Rd.
>   Wayne, PA 19087
>   (215) 688-6866

Special Keyboards and Aids for the Disabled

Some of the most innovative and unusual keyboards and input devices are special-purpose models for people with special needs. Nowhere is the PC's tremendous power more apparent than in the burgeoning field of assistive technologies.

The available types of assistive input devices are as various as the disabilities they overcome. There are customized keyboards for those who have difficulty with the size or tension of the standard keyboard. There are keyboards that range from regular keyboard layouts with enlarged keys, to braille keyboards, to programmable membrane surfaces, to single-switch entry systems that display a keyboard on screen, as well as other innovative solutions for almost every need. (For more information, contact Furalletech Systems of North Liberty, Iowa; EKEG Electronics of Vancouver, British Columbia; Polytel Computer Products of Tulsa, Oklahoma; and Koala Technologies of Santa Clara, California.)

The EyeTyper from Sentient Systems Technology of Pittsburgh, Pennsylvania, offers an alternative for the severely physically disabled user. The user briefly focuses on a tiny light on the desired key cap, and the letter is "typed" by a camera embedded in the keyboard.

Other companies specialize in custom systems that use infrared scanning technology and a sensitive visor to interpret input from a single brow or head movement, or eye blinks and eye movements. (For information, contact Words Plus of Sunnyvale, California, and Pointer Systems of Burlington, Vermont.)

Add-on speech synthesis units, such as Personal Reader (Kurzweil Computer Products of Cambridge, Massachusetts) and the Arkenstone Reader (Arkenstone of Santa Clara, California) actually speak the text.

Pioneer technologies, such as voice recognition, have a long way to go before they can be truly useful in the general market. Some voice-recognition devices are currently on the market, however. At best, they

INPUT DEVICES

KEYBOARD ALTERNATIVES

Far different from the standard keyboards are other devices based on other concepts. A court stenographer records every spoken word without a typewriter, and there have been attempts to duplicate this method with computer keyboard alternatives.

One product currently on the market is the BAT Chord Keypad. This is an interface made up of two identical keyboards, one for the left hand and one for the right. Each keypad is about seven by seven inches in size, and has seven keys: five white, one red, and one blue. (The thumb has the red, blue, and one of the white keys to move between.) Characters are entered by pressing combinations of keys, much like playing chords on a piano.

Computer commands are entered with a letter "chord" with the thumb on the red key. Punctuation is entered with a letter "chord" while the thumb is on the blue key.

The BAT Chord Keypads are separate and independent from each other. This means that with either the right or left keypad you can enter all the standard computer keyboard commands. (To increase efficiency, you can use both hands.) If you use only one hand, you are limited to a top speed of around 35 words per minute. With both pads, the top speed is around 80 words per minute.

For more information, contact:

Infogrip, Inc.
5800 Perkins Place 5-F
Baton Rouge, LA 70808
(504) 766-8082 or 766-4228   ■

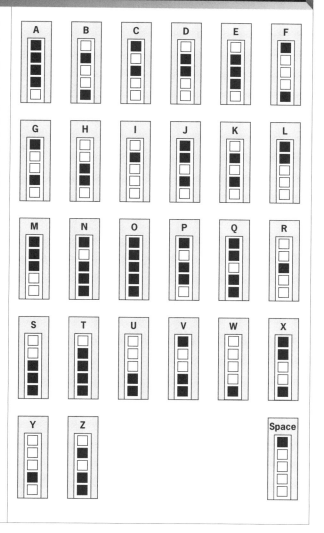

have an accuracy of 98 percent, with a vocabulary of up to 150 user-selected words.

For information about these products or for help in building a customized solution, contact the IBM National Support Center for People with Disabilities at (800) 426-2133 or Apple Computer's Office of Special Education and Rehabilitation at (408) 996-1010.

INPUT DEVICES

Keyboard Accessories

A variety of wrist supports are available for your keyboard. These help you maintain the best typing position. When typing at your workstation, your wrists should be naturally in line with your arms; flexing them forward or extending them backward for long periods of time will injure them. Forearms should be parallel to the floor (not half-raised as they are at most desks, which are generally three inches too high). And neither the wrists nor forearms are designed to support body weight, as they do when you rest them on your desk.

The simplest keyboard enhancements are wrist rests. The most readily available and cheapest rest can be fashioned out of a hand towel (rolled and rubber-banded). Commercial wrist rests are padded bars the same height as the keyboard; the wrists rest on them flatly, neither flexing nor extending. Most computer-supply sources offer wrist rests for desktop use or PC "pillows" for those who plop the keyboard in their laps. One such pillow is the CTS-Pillow from:

Ergo-Nomic Inc.
4102 E. 7th St., Suite 260
Long Beach, CA 90804-5310

Since the wrists should be kept straight, the angled keyboard supports offered by many vendors might not be useful for you; some authorities even recommend the keyboard lie flat on the typing surface. The Wrist Pro, from Ergonomic Solutions, is a wrist support system with an adjustable stairstep design. It supplies "neutral" wrist support (neither extended nor flexed) and lets you position the board comfortably beneath your fingers. MicroComputer Accessories's Keyboard Platform is another combination keyboard platform and wrist support.

If you've already done serious damage to your hands from keyboarding, you may need the full-body approach of the Compu-Rest Arm Support from Wholesale Ergonomic Products. This is an arm rest (which costs about $250 per arm) attached to a desktop on either side of the computer; it allows users to move their hands across the keyboard without moving their wrists or putting excessive strain on the arms and shoulders. It is designed for people with advanced CTS.

The Wrist Trolly from MicroComputer Accessories consists of two padded platforms on a rolling track attached to the edge of the desk. It also allows hand movements without wrist action, but it sells for under $100. Fox Bay Industries makes the CarpalRest, which supports the wrists, hands, and upper body on a padded contoured surface. It retails for about $60.

INPUT DEVICES

For more information, contact:

Fox Bay Industries
4150 B Place NW #101
Auburn, WA 98001
(800) 874-8527 or (206) 941-9155

MicroComputer Accessories
9920 Lacienega
Inglewood, CA 90302
(800) 521-8270 or (310) 301-9400

Wholesale Ergonomic Products
422 Larkfield Center Ste. 251
Santa Rosa, CA 95403
(707) 544-3020

Ergonomic Solutions
16100 N. Outer Forty, #250
St. Louis, MO 63017
(800) 348-8633 or (314) 532-2827

Mice

Mice are said to be intuitive devices. It ain't necessarily so. Take the case of the new clerk who I was showing how to use a Macintosh. I thought it would be an easy machine for her to learn, but I turned around to see her waving the mouse in the air in a vain attempt to get the cursor to move. I was stunned. It does show, however, that the mouse is anything but intuitive. Most of the things we call "intuitive" only seem natural after we've learned to use them.

A mouse is an add-on peripheral. Its function is to move the cursor around and execute commands—both of which can be done by the keyboard. The mouse is a "nice break" for some people, a way to get their hands off the keyboard. Others hate mice.

The device is a box with a ball on the bottom. As you roll the ball the cursor moves. Buttons on the mouse execute commands and "place" the cursor.

Some mice deliver on the promise of graphic computing environments better than others. To help you distinguish among the good, the bad, and the ugly, there are a few mouse basics you should be aware of. Most of this information applies to trackballs as well, since trackballs are essentially upside-down mice.

INPUT DEVICES

Serial Mouse versus Bus Mouse

There is no appreciable difference in performance between a serial and a bus mouse, so the choice depends on your system's port availability.

A *serial mouse* uses one of the two serial ports MS-DOS provides (four in MS-DOS 3.3 and up), which may cause problems if you have a mouse, a modem, and a serial printer. A *bus mouse* takes up one half-slot but may cost more.

Most serial mice include a short connector that lets you use either a 9- or 25-pin serial port. There also are two specialty connectors that let you use either Microsoft's InPort standard (which isn't really a standard, because hardly anybody uses it) or the similar connector for IBM's PS/2 models.

Two or Three Buttons?

Most mice have either two or three buttons. The number of buttons determines the number of possible choices that can be programmed for any given action. A two-button mouse offers three choices, which makes it easy to learn but may necessitate several steps to complete an action. Except for CAD programs, most software requires only two buttons.

The three-button mouse offers seven choices, which makes it more difficult to learn but may provide greater flexibility in applications. A three-button mouse can, however, be used as a two-button mouse, so there's no disadvantage there, except that the case is somewhat wider and less comfortable to handle.

Mouse Tracking Systems

The tracking system determines how accurately you can position the mouse cursor. There are three types of tracking systems; each has its pluses and minuses. The three are mechanical, optomechanical, and optical.

Mechanical Tracking   Mechanical tracking uses a hard rubber ball or wheels to turn rollers that send signals to move the cursor. Drawbacks to mechanical tracking are that the balls and rollers pick up hair and dirt. (Sugar-laden liquids can do terrible damage.) The moving parts wear out, and performance is affected. This system is usually used on a firm rubber pad to help cushion the mouse ball assembly, and therefore prolong life.

Optomechanical and Optical Tracking   The optomechanical mouse uses the same tracking mechanism, but the rollers use optical elements to send signals.

The high end of the mouse market is the optical mouse. An optical tracking system has no internal moving parts; instead, it bounces a light beam off a highly reflective pad with a grid pattern. Its strong point is

INPUT DEVICES

THE SHAPE OF MICE TO COME

Like so many developments now common on PCs, the mouse had its origins in the innovative work done two decades ago at the Xerox Palo Alto Research Center (PARC). The PARC mouse had two rollers for horizontal and vertical motion and a single button. The decidedly boxy shape was favored by many developers at PARC and has persisted throughout various mouse incarnations. New mice from other manufacturers have broken out of the box, led by the Microsoft mouse.

Microsoft Mice

Microsoft mice have always had an ergonomic design (even before ergonomics was fashionable). The broad teardrop shape with two buttons distinguished the Microsoft mice through various upgrades. The original green-buttoned model had a steel ball that spawned an industry in foam mouse pads. The next iteration had larger buttons, a larger body, and a rubber-coated ball, but only 100-dots-per-inch resolution. The next mouse, available through mid-1987, increased resolution to 200 dpi, but the shape remained essentially the same. Typical complaints included a soft feel to the buttons and a too-narrow front.

When Microsoft decided the mouse needed to be redesigned, it turned to Matrix Design of San Francisco, a company responsible for designing Wyse terminals and Tandon computers. Mike Nuttal, one of Matrix Design's founders, was intrigued by Microsoft's project: reshaping the exterior without altering the internal mechanism.

Matrix did change one internal element: the position of the mouse ball. "Almost the first thing we tried was to move the ball forward," Nuttal says. "In the older design, the ball sits under the palm, and there's a tendency to put your weight on your palm and the ball. By moving it forward, you can achieve greater accuracy, even though the mechanical resolution is the same." The trick is fairly simple: If you think of the mouse ball as moving in an arc with your wrist at the center, moving the ball farther from your wrist increases the radius of the arc, so the ball travels farther with less motion.

"We knew the buttons had to be bigger," Nuttal says. "We tried several button sizes, and in the process of designing, we ended up incorporating the buttons into the body of the mouse." Another change was in relative button size. "We felt the left button should be larger, and when we tested it, the results were better than we had expected, particularly with left-handed users. By making the left button larger, finger position is no longer a factor, so the index finger can curve from lower-left to upper-right (vice versa for lefties), as it does naturally." Rubber-dome switches were replaced with microswitches that had a short travel depression and better tactile feedback.

Matrix built more than 100 conceptual prototypes using surfboard foam. Fourteen working prototypes were tested over a nine-month period by ex-PARC staffer Bill VerPlank and Kate Oliver, associates of IDTwo, another San Francisco industrial design firm.

Nuttal says the design of the new mouse was shaped in part by products outside the computer industry. Nuttal eschewed textured surfaces for high-gloss white plastic on the body because it's easier to clean and doesn't show fingerprints. And the rounded heel that fits so well into the palm of your hand (it feels like an electric razor), the large buttons, and the smooth edges all have roots in that most universal of electrical/electronic products—the telephone. It turns out that Nuttal and Matrix Design worked on telephones before mice.

Logitech Responds

Logitech, which has been criticized for the boxy design of its mouse, hasn't ignored ergonomics—especially if you know how to hold the mouse correctly, Logitech says.

Logitech's first mouse was an international effort. Professor Niklaus Wirth of the University of Lausanne, Switzerland, spent a year on sabbatical at Xerox PARC in 1970 and returned to Europe to test mouse designs, working closely with Inria, a

Continued on next page

INPUT DEVICES

THE SHAPE OF MICE TO COME

Continued from previous page

French design center for office automation products. The final design was a round, 400-dpi mouse with front-mounted buttons. Much argument ensued over the position of the buttons, and the front position won out over the top.

However, Logitech soon found that the buttons on the front made the mouse jump backward slightly when clicked. The design was abandoned in favor of a wedge shape, followed by the rectangular shape used today, which features the buttons on top. Pierluigi Zappacosta, president of Logitech, believes mouse improvements spurred by technology and industry experience are more important than a new design. "We are in the mouse business, nothing else," says Zappacosta. "If we had received lots of requests for a new design, you would've seen it. But if consumers like the new (Microsoft) shape, we'll respond."

Zappacosta says the Logitech mouse has the ergonomic features users want: large switches, positive feedback, and (if you hold it correctly) a comfortable body. Instead of holding the mouse in your palm, place your wrist on the desk, rest the pad under the knuckles on the back edge, and let your fingers rest on the buttons. Zappacosta adds that if you place your wrist on a desk and relax your hands, your fingers will assume the correct position for his company's mouse. Because it has three buttons, the shell has to be a bit wider than that of a two-button mouse.

Traditionally, Logitech has contributed more to internal mouse technology than to ergonomic design. Its clients include Apple, Hewlett-Packard, and DEC, which blend Logitech's optomechanical mechanisms with their own exteriors. DEC's mouse recalls the round shape found in Logitech's first mouse, but the buttons wrap from top to bottom, so you can click either from the top or from the side. ∎

accuracy, which is critical in CAD and high-end desktop publishing applications, though not particularly noticeable in mainstream Windows applications. One drawback to the optical mouse is the space needed for the reflective pad.

Trackballs

Trackballs use the same technology as mice, but instead of rolling the mouse ball around on the desk, you move the ball with your fingers. They are stationary, which makes them easier to find on a cluttered desktop. Trackballs are not as popular as mice. They have their fans and their foes. Some people find the trackball easier to use because it doesn't involve as much arm movement.

A new category of trackballs and mice has emerged specifically for notebook and laptop computers. These include tiny trackballs (about the size of a matchbox), scaled down mice, and even a small joystick for games.

INPUT DEVICES

Other Pointing Devices

A light pen is an add-on device which you use with the screen, to point and to execute commands. It is connected in much the same way as a mouse, but a light pen is the size of a fat ballpoint pen—so it often gets lost in mounds of paper. Light pens, while they may not be as versatile as mice, come closest in function and design to the most intuitive of all pointing devices: the human finger. The light pen is a natural for specialized menu-oriented database software. Hospital record keeping, point-of-sale operations, and automotive maintenance are the biggest markets for these pens. The light pen's main drawback arises from constantly holding it up to a computer screen, which can be tiring to your arm. These pens prove cumbersome in data entry applications.

A digitizing tablet is a grid with sensors (about the size of an Etch-A-Sketch) which you write or draw on with a special stylus. Their application is mostly for graphics and CAD uses. As for recognizing human writing and storing it as digitized text—the digitizing tablets have a ways to go.

Using a touch screen is much like using a light pen, except that the screen itself is sensitized. When you touch a command it is executed. There is *no* practical application for home use of touch screens, but they are great for ATMs and marketing tools.

In the past few years, there have been a number of new twists: the IsoPoint, a below-the-spacebar rolling cylinder; GRiDPad's "electronic pen," which recognizes handwritten characters; CalComp's Wiz Mouse System, which bundles an electromagnetic mouse-like device with application-specific templates; foot pedals (as a stand-alone product in the case of PC Pedal, and as an adjunct to a trackball in the case of the Kraft Trackball); DataDesk's modular keyboard, which can be configured with different devices including a trackball; and Home Row, a technology being licensed to keyboard vendors that modifies the J key, turning it into a miniature trackball-like device. The only device to have had any measureable impact is the IBM TrakPoint—a small red nipple found in the middle of the IBM ThinkPad notebook computers. It's a reasonable substitute for a mouse.

Finally, we have to mention that there are a number of computer makers trying to make stylus- or pen-based computers work for the general user. So far these have been niche products and probably will remain so a little longer.

MODEMS

CHAPTER 9

TELECOMMUNICATE, TELECOMMUTE, AND TELE-
CONFERENCE are all things you can do with a modem. Modems are an add-on (a peripheral) to your computer system.
A modem lets you "talk" through the keyboard with remote
users, either directly or through an on-line service. You can
search through vast libraries or on-line databases. It's easy to
send and transmit files, memos, and letters either directly or
through an E-mail system (such as MCI or CompuServe).

MODEMS

THERE ARE NUMEROUS BULLETIN BOARDS for special interest groups where you can obtain *shareware* and *freeware* (software at nominal or no cost).

What Is a Modem?

Telephone lines are designed to carry sounds. Computers are digital. They emit silent electronic impulses. A *modem* translates these electronic impulses into sound, so that the transformed impulses can be sent over the telephone lines. At the other end, a modem decodes the sounds and reinterprets them as electronic impulses. In technical jargon, this is known as *mo*dulation and *dem*odulation, hence the name of the device: modem.

Modems are either internal or external. Internal modems reside on a card which fits snugly into your computer's bus. External ones come in their own containers and sit on the desk next to the computer; these connect to the serial port of your computer and come in all sizes—from the size of a bar of soap to large shoe-box size devices.

A variety of specialty modems are now on the market. These include cellular modems (which connect and transmit over the cellular telephone system) and wireless modems (which connect by means of special RF radio relay systems). Pocket modems for on-the-road telecommunications and fax/modem combination cards (which will allow you to send files either to another computer modem or to a fax machine) are other examples of specialty modems.

What Modems Do

A modem converts digital bits from your PC to analog tones which are more suitable for telephone lines (the ear-shattering "beep-beep-deet-beep-whistle-tweet" that you hear when you dial a line to which a modem or fax is connected). The receiving modem then converts the tones back to digital bits for subsequent processing by a PC.

When you make a voice call, the person at the receiving end usually answers "Hello." You respond with your name, and the conversation begins. Modems work in much the same way to establish communication. This initial exchange is called *handshaking*. When your modem calls another, the second modem responds with a set of answer tones. The two modems then "negotiate" to find out how to communicate with each other. The underlying procedure, called a *renegotiation protocol*, helps the modems determine which signaling, error-correction, and data compression protocols to follow.

The Protocol

Protocol is to modems what language is to humans. If someone answers the telephone, "Allô, allô. Parlez-vous français?" you respond (if you're

MODEMS

MODEM TALK—A FEW COMMON TERMS

- **AT Command Set**   An industry standard set of commands communications (also known as the Hayes Command Set). The computer uses these commands to control the modem. But, in reality, communications software is also required because the AT Command Set is limited. If a modem is called "Hayes-compatible," it uses the AT Command Set. Most modems use the AT Command Set and are Hayes-compatible.

- **ASCII**   American Standard Code for Information Interchange. This standard way of transmitting characters is used internationally by all computers, from big mainframes to small hand-held ones. It's the computers' universal character set.

- **Baud rate**   The rate symbols are transmitted per second. This is often used interchangeably with *bps* (bits per second), although technically, this is incorrect.

- **BBS (bulletin board system)**   A computer set up to receive calls and act as a host system. These computers often have messages, shareware software, games, and other special-interest information.

- **Bps (bits per second)**   The number of data bits sent per second between a pair of modems. Speeds of 2400 bps, 9600 bps, and 14.4 kbps (14,400 bits per second) are common. The higher the number, the faster the modem. The faster the modem, the shorter the telephone call.

- **COM (1, 2, 3, etc.)**   Short for communications port. Printers, mice, modems, scanners, and so on, all connect to a COM port. COM 1 (meaning the first communications port, also known as the first *serial port*) is usually "hard-wired" to the motherboard. Subsequent ports are numbered 2 through 4, currently. In the near future, COM ports 2 through 8 will be available.

- **Communications parameters**   These settings define how your communications software will handle incoming data and transmit outgoing

data. Parameters include bits per second, parity, data bits, and stop bits.

- **Data bits**   The bits sent by a modem. These bits make up the characters of the message being sent and don't include the bits which make up the communications parameters.

- **Download**   To receive a copy of a file from another modem/computer to your computer. Opposite of *upload*.

- **Electronic mail (E-mail)**   The exchange of messages via a bulletin board, on-line service, or local area network (LAN).

- **Handshaking**   The way one modem asks another "Are you there?" and the other one answers "I am here."

- **Host system**   Very generally, this refers to the system to which you are connected when you call a bulletin board system (BBS) or a large on-line service (such as CompuServe).

- **Local area network (LAN)**   A group of computers hooked together by cables in a confined area—an office, building, or group of adjacent buildings. Larger networks—encompassing a larger area—are called WANs (wide area networks).

- **Logoff/logon**   The first means to disconnect from another computer; the second, to connect to it. When you call an information service such as CompuServe or a BBS (bulletin board system), you will be asked to "logon." The host computer is asking you if you want to begin a session. To do this you must type in a user code (like a membership number) and possibly a personal password. Once this is done, you can then move through the host computer system and download files, receive and send E-mail, log on to conferences, and so on. Then, when you want to

Continued on next page

MODEMS

MODEM TALK—A FEW COMMON TERMS

Continued from previous page

end the session, you must "logoff." This tells the host computer that you are hanging up. Since many on-line services and BBSs charge a monthly fee for on-line time, the logon/logoff is needed to accurately calculate the charges.

- **Modem**   A combination of the words "*mo*dulate/*demo*dulate.*" A modem is a device that allows a computer to communicate with other computers over telephone lines.

- **On-line/off-line**   The modem state of being. When connected to another computer via modems and telephone lines, a modem is on-line. When disconnected, it's off-line.

- **Parity**   An unsophisticated means of error checking. After a set of bits is sent, an additional bit is sent to make the total number of bits sent either even or odd. Parity can be set to even, odd, or no parity. No parity is the most common setting for personal computer telecommunication.

- **Protocol**   A set of rules which governs a modem's transfer of information. It's much like playing poker—you must adhere to the set of rules of the particular game of poker you're playing. There are a number of different protocols (Kermit, Zmodem, Xmodem, Lynx, and so on), each of which has its own attributes. The most popular protocol right now is Zmodem.

- **Serial port** (also called a COM port)   This is a "male" connector (usually DB-9 or DB-25) located at the back of your computer. It sends out data one bit at a time. It is used by modems and, in years past, for daisy-wheel and other types of printers.

- **Stop bit**   Signals the end of a string of bits.

- **Telecommunications**   Another way to say modem communications.   ∎

bilingual) in French. If the caller doesn't speak English and you don't speak French, but you both speak Spanish, you will communicate that way. For modems, signaling is the "allô, allô," "hello, hello." The entire process is the "handshake." Error-correction is analogous to when a transatlantic telephone line gets static and suddenly you cannot hear what the other person said. You respond, "What? Repeat that? Pardon?"

The Handshake

When modems handshake, they go through a series of questions and answers to establish what kinds of modems they are and then what transfer rate (the speed at which modems can transmit) they are going to use. The transfer rate (also called the send rate, the signal rate, or the transmit rate) is measured in terms of bits per second (bps).

The handshake will find the fastest transfer rate between different speed modems. This rate is usually the fastest speed of the slowest modem—the highest common rate. Noise on the telephone line may

MODEMS

lower the transfer rate further. The transfer rate can be as slow as 110 bps, but this is uncommon.

Two modems of different speeds are able to communicate because this "handshake" establishes a common transfer rate. Next, the modems check to see if a hardware error-correction protocol is available. They use the highest common protocol level for error correction and data compression. Then the modems transfer control to the telecommunications software.

Telecommunications Software

Modems need instructions, and telecommunications programs provide them. The software tells the computer to send a set of characters (called a configuration string) to the modem. This tells the modem how to communicate with your computer, your phone line, and other modems. Usually the Hayes Standard AT Command Set or a derivative is used as the configuration string.

The program will then, at your command, direct the modem to open the telephone line and dial, connect, read or send mail, send files, receive files, and disconnect. If you are uploading or downloading a file, the program will give you options for the possible types of file transfers. This is called a transfer protocol.

Transfer Protocol

A protocol ensures that the information sent by the modem and the information received are the same. There are many different schemes for doing this, but most protocols use a form of *error correcting* in which extra data is attached to the beginning or end of a block of text being sent. This extra data must be verified as having been received intact at the other end for the block of text to be successfully transmitted. If the receiving computer detects changes in the verification data, it requests that the block of text be resent until the extra data is received intact. Errors may actually be transmitted in the block of text itself, but as long as the verification data is correctly transmitted, the block is accepted. This is how most telecommunications protocols work.

Protocol Types   A number of error-correcting file transfer protocols have been introduced over the years, but fewer than a dozen have met with any real acceptance. Each of the major telecommunications programs will offer a wide selection of these popular protocols, so the selection of one is up to you. There is no "one right" protocol. Some work better with some types of files, some better with some modems, some are slow, and some are *proprietary* (only supported by one telecommunications package, so they require that each end of the connection use the same program).

MODEMS

HAYES COMMANDS

You can send Hayes commands directly to your modem through your computer to place and answer phone calls. However, the commands are limited to basic modem functions, such as:

- Dial the line (pulse or tone)

- Redial a busy line

- Auto-redial

- Connect

- Force a connection if the modem hasn't answered a ringing (incoming) line

- Hang up

- Switch parity (on, off, or none)

- Turn Echo on and off (it's usually set to off)

- Turn the modem speaker on and off

With the AT Command Set, you can communicate with another party over your modem. If you want to do any "higher level" functions, such as transferring files over the modem line, you will need telecommunications software.

If you travel with a portable computer, it's handy to have available a list of the AT Command Set. In this way, you can enable and disable modem features in awkward situations, such as at a hotel with a strange "in house" dial tone which the modem cannot accept. ∎

Some of the more popular protocols include

- Kermit

- Xmodem

- Ymodem

- Zmodem

- Lynx

- Telelink

- CIS-B

Most telecommunications packages will offer a variety of different file transfer protocols. The important thing to remember is that the sender and receiver must use the same protocol, so you must find one which is common to both telecommunications packages. (There should be a number of choices.) Zmodem is a good one to start with when you are first learning to transfer files. It has a number of automatic options and is easy to use.

Data Compression

Data compression is a way to squeeze more data into a smaller unit. When you compress a file, the redundant or empty sections are removed.

MODEMS

The transmission time is decreased, and a shorter transmission time means less possibility of telephone line errors (and a lower telephone bill).

Most compression schemes use a combination of two approaches. One simple (and obvious) way to compress data is to remove all the spaces from a document. Another is to assign a character in place of common words, much like shorthand.

Several file compression utilities are available, the most popular of which are Lharc and PKZIP. They can be acquired through many users' groups and shareware services. You use them to compress files before you send them. The person who receives the files will need to decompress them in order to view them.

Most computer bulletin board systems store their files in compressed form. A word of warning: If you are using an MNP 5–compatible modem, turn off MNP 5 before downloading compressed files. (Precompression only confuses this protocol, which will then expand the file instead of compressing it.) There are no disadvantages to V.42bis.

The Need for Speed

PC users deserve credit for demanding technological improvements in modems. Way back before personal computers, there was only one modem company to speak of: Bell Telephone. Their two modems were the Bell 103 and Bell 212, at 300- and 1,200-baud, respectively. (Other manufacturers existed, but not in force.) These modems had no extra features, and were big, ugly, and expensive. But at the time, the only customers using modems were companies with large mini- and mainframe-computers. The telephone company had no motivation to make a faster modem. After all, the longer the line was being used to transmit data, the more money they raked in. They had the market coming and going.

Then with the break up of Big Bell into a number of Baby Bells and with the deluge of PC hardware, modem manufacturers figured out pretty quickly that the market demanded faster modem speeds. And PC hardware and software systems kept evolving. Files became bigger, and modems had to perform increasingly complex tasks.

Five years ago, Rockwell International Corporation and other manufacturers made chip sets available for modems following the international V.22bis standards. (See the next section for a description of V.x standards.) This increased the maximum transfer rate to 2,400 bps. The price of these modems is well under $100 today.

As PC users moved an ever-increasing volume of data through modems, they demanded even higher transfer rates. Hayes Microcomputer Products, Microcom, and U.S. Robotics rose to the challenge. They offered faster modems and proprietary transfer protocols. These early high-speed modems worked their magic when communicating with a twin

MODEMS

modem, but they regressed to the standard 2,400 and 1,200 bps when a modem from another manufacturer answered at the other end.

With the advent of the CCITT standards, the proprietary protocols fell by the wayside. Manufacturers changed to these international standards, and modems became "truly" high-speed. Today, a fast modem can communicate with other fast modems with no difficulty. This means you can send larger files faster, which saves on connect charges and your time.

Compatibility Issues

Even though the Hayes Command Set is a de facto standard, compatibility between modems is occasionally a problem. For example, very fast modems sometimes cannot communicate with very slow modems. (Think of it as a slow-talking Texan, with a drawl, trying to carry on a long, involved, technical conversation with a high-strung, nontechnical, hyper New Yorker.)

Modems made by different manufacturers may be incompatible for reasons that are not always apparent, but the finger often points to seemingly insignificant differences in timing or performance thresholds in the initial handshake. Each vendor uses its own method and sequence for conducting the protocol handshake, and some offer additional proprietary protocols. Since the handshake method and order of the protocols may influence the final protocol agreement, we strongly recommend that you purchase modems which adhere to the CCITT standards: V.32, V.32bis, V.42, and V.42bis.

What's All This CCITT Stuff?   CCITT stands for "Comité Consultatif Internationale Téléphonique et Télégraphique" (in the United States we call them the International Consultative Committee for Telephony and Telegraphy). This agency of the United Nations was established in the early 1970s to address the worldwide questions of modem compatibility and to create coordinated standards. This is a French group, so the naming standards are, well, very French. When a standard has been introduced and a second, improved version is released, the second is dubbed *bis*. If a third is released, it has the suffix *ter*, for third. You should be at least slightly familiar with the CCITT's "V-dot" standards when you are out shopping for a modem. There are five important standards applicable for today's modems. Let's look at each of them in turn.

V.32   The V.32 standard is the granddaddy. Introduced in 1985 to avert the creation of an electronic Tower of Babel by manufacturers with incompatible proprietary standards, the V.32 standard enables transmissions up to 14,400 bps, which was necessary for higher speed modems (faster than 300 bps) to communicate. The V.32 standard describes how

MODEMS

modems should talk to each other using two-way signaling at 4,800 and 9,600 bps over dial-up telephone lines.

Unfortunately, the V.32 standard did not provide a method for error control. V.32 signaling is more sensitive to noise on the telephone line than lower-speed protocols are.

MNP and MNP 5   MNP (Microcom Networking Protocol) is an independent standard created by Microcom, a modem manufacturer, to improve data transfer. Versions of MNP are now available in a variety of modems and communications software packages. MNP 4 (an error-correcting scheme) and MNP 5 (a compression method) are compatible with, but not supported by, the CCITT. However, many modem manufacturers use both MNP 4 and V.42 standards for the best possible combination of error detection and correction.

Microcom led the industry by introducing the MNP Class 5 data-compression protocol. It soon became a feature in many modems and some application programs. Software supporting the MNP 5 protocol can compress files to half their original size during transmission.

V.42 and V.42bis   In 1989, the CCITT issued a hardware-implemented error-correction standard called V.42, which describes two error-correction schemes. The primary protocol is named *link access procedure for modems* (LAPM). The secondary (or support) protocol is functionally the same as MNP Class 4. If you want to communicate between two modems which are V.42 compliant, you should connect them with the LAPM protocol. LAPM offers slightly better error recovery and reliability than MNP 4.

In late 1989, the CCITT issued the V.42bis standard, which describes how to implement data compression in hardware. Using the Lempel-Ziv compression algorithm, the new V.42bis protocol offers much greater data compression than MNP 5. For a 9,600-bps modem, there is a potential transfer of 38,400 bps for compressable files. For most file transfers, however, you can expect transfers of around 19,200 bps for files not previously compressed through other means.

V.32bis   In early 1991, the CCITT approved a revision of the V.32 standard. V.32bis adds 7,200-, 12,000-, and 14,400-bps transfer rates and a faster renegotiation protocol. V.32bis is able to renegotiate the protocol in less than 100 milliseconds.

On the 2,400-bps side, note the recent availability of V.22bis modems with 2,400-bps signaling and V.42bis data compression. Most new 2,400-bps modems should be V.42bis compatible.

MODEMS

IS YOUR UART CHIP A WEAK LINK?

Even with the fastest modem in town, you might not be ready to burn up the phone lines yet. There is another potential weak link in the communications chain.

Most serial cards have a chip that controls the serial port. These are called UART (universal asynchronous receiver/ transmitter) chips. They come in two flavors: 8250 (8-bit) or 16450 (16-bit). During modem communications, the PC's UART and the CPU transfer a great deal of information. Unfortunately, if the communications program asks the CPU to manage large changes on the screen or to move data to and from the hard disk, the UART on the receiving side may drop bits, particularly if it runs under a multitasking environment like DESQview X, Microsoft Windows, or OS/2.

The new 16550 UART solves the problem by creating a FIFO (first in, first out) buffer stack. (A buffer is like a queue. Data stacks up and waits its turn.) This buffer allows the UART to save any incoming data while it's waiting for the CPU. Although the 16550 can directly replace the 8250 and 16450, it needs communications software that initializes it to implement its FIFO stack. Luckily, most modern communications programs do this.

If your old 8250 or 16450 UART still occupies a socket, you can purchase a new 16550 and replace the chip for less than $15. Anyone interested in high-speed modem communications (including those running a 2,400-bps modem under a multitasking environment) will find this a worthwhile investment. ∎

Types of Modems

Common modem speeds on the market today include 2,400 bps, 2,400/9,600-bps modem/fax combos, 9,600 bps, and 14,400 bps. In the future you may see modems rated 19,200 bps or even higher. These modems may be internal cards, external, pocket modems, or one of the new wireless kind—cellular or radio.

Some modems are "feature heavy," while others are "bare bones." The feature-heavy modems may have extensions of the basic AT Command Set. To fully access all of these features, you might need to consult both the modem vendor and the vendor of your communications software to correctly initialize all of the modem's features.

External versus Internal Modems

Internal and external modems display few differences beyond their physical configuration. Your choice between an internal or external modem should be based solely on your needs and preferences. There are no differences in terms of efficiency or transfer rate.

Internal Modems   Internal modems have some advantages. You don't have to hassle with the proper configuration of an RS-232 connecting cable, the modem doesn't clutter desktop space, and you don't need a free AC wall plug. Internal modems don't have cabinets and power supplies. This means they are a little less expensive than their external kin.

MODEMS

Once they've saved money on these items, manufacturers can afford to throw in a perk or two. One common bundled-in extra is a communications software package.

External Modems   The external models are more entertaining because most of them have lights installed on the front panels that show when the modem is in operation. There are lights for carrier detect, read data, and terminal ready, among other functions. In addition, an external modem can be moved among PCs or used between a PC and an Apple Macintosh. (To move internal modems between PCs is a project, and an internal PC modem is unusable on an Apple Macintosh.)

Modem/Fax Combos

This is a modem (either external or internal) which has two different modem chips—a data modem and a fax modem. These two chips usually operate at different speeds; a 2,400-bps data modem might be paired with a 9,600-bps fax modem. Don't be fooled by some fast-talking salesperson who claims the 9,600-bps speed is applicable to both modems. It's not true. The data modem is limited by the data modem chip, and the fax modem is limited by the fax modem chip. The chips don't cross-communicate.

The fax uses a different CCITT set of standards than data modems. A fax modem cannot transmit to a data modem, and vice versa.

Pocket (Portable) Modems

You can take pocket modems on the road if your laptop or notebook computer lacks an internal modem. The power needs of these pocket modems vary. Some use a single 9-volt battery, while others are self-powered; they suck the juice out of the portable computer to establish the connection and then draw power from the telephone line to continue operations.

These may be used with a regular computer as well, but can easily get lost on the desk if your paperwork piles up. The speeds of these modems are limited to 2,400 bps. The circuits are low-powered, and high-speed modem circuitry has not been developed to take advantage of these advanced power tricks. Their prices are high compared to a regular 2,400-bps modem—in the $200 range.

Wireless Modems

Cellular and radio technologies create a wireless communications path. They use radio waves instead of phone lines to communicate. Modems are still needed, but the modems are specialized to either broadcast radio waves or use the existing cellular services.

MODEMS

Cellular Modems   Cellular phones use a series of transmitters/receivers (called *cells*) that work together to provide coverage over a large geographic area. The system can automatically pass calls from one cell to another as you travel from one destination to the next. This changing of cells is almost seamless, although occasionally you do hear noises. Many cellular companies have joined together to create "roam" service and to allow a client of one service to call a client of another service.

Cellular modems are now available to connect to cellular telephones (some handheld models optionally come with a female telephone connector (RJ11) to plug a modem into). The downside of telecommunications by cellular phones is that the technology was designed primarily for voice; cell changes may disrupt data transmissions.

Radio Modems   Radio modems use RF signals much like a ham radio does. The modem transmits these signals, which are then picked up by a base station. The station then either relays the signal to another base station or transmits the data to regular telephone lines. Finally, the information is carried by telephone lines to its destination. These radio networks were developed for and limited to data transmissions for a fairly reliable data exchange. Unlike cellular technology, which is available to anyone, these systems are proprietary. The two major systems are ARDIS and RAM Mobile Data Network.

In 1990, IBM and Motorola formed a joint venture to market ARDIS as a public data network. ARDIS holds FCC licenses for single-channel operation across more than 1,250 radio base stations placed in 400-plus areas, including Alaska and Hawaii. For more information, contact:

ARDIS
300 Knightsbridge Pkwy.
Lincolnshire, IL 60069
(800) 622-5328 or (708) 913-4700

RAM Mobil Data Network began commercial operation in February 1991, as a joint venture between RAM Broadcasting Corporation and Bell-South Enterprises, Inc. The network uses a public network technology known as Mobitex. It is a public, packet-switched, wireless data network designed to provide nationwide roaming. For more information, contact:

Motorola Wireless Enterprises
1201 Wiley Rd., Ste. 103
Schaumburg, IL 60173
(708) 576-1600

Proprietary modems are required to transmit to these systems (with few exceptions). To date, coverage for either of these RF systems is not as well developed as the cellular systems. And, contrary to popular belief,

MODEMS

satellite transmission of data is not currently a viable means of transmitting data.

Buying a Modem: Dvorak's Tips

Now that you have some background on modems and a slew of terms at your disposal, what should you buy? If you want to go out and buy a modem today that would serve you well for the next few years, I'd say that you should get a 14,400-bps one that uses V.32bis and V.42bis. Most modems with these two specifications will also feature various MNP protocols and a few other features. You might also consider buying a modem from U.S. Robotics which incorporates its proprietary HST protocol; this protocol is used by many of the computerized bulletin board systems (BBSs). Most V.32bis modems offer fax/modem capability. This can be very handy. Look for it.

The drawback to this recommendation is that such a modem will cost around $300. A slow 2,400-bps modem can be purchased for less than $100. The price difference is substantial, so you should carefully consider how you'll use the modem. If you plan to call a local BBS once a month to pick up electronic mail but little else, then it's hard to justify spending a fortune on a modem. But if you download many large files, the high-speed modem will save you lots of time. If these are long-distance calls, the modem will pay for itself.

Make sure the 2,400-bps modem is Hayes-compatible. However, as far as I'm concerned, avoid the overpriced 2,400-bps modems featuring V.42bis. They are supposed to be fast, but for the extra money you'd do better buying a "real" high-speed modem, such as a 14,400-bps modem.

BUYING SOFTWARE

CHAPTER

10

AFTER YOU PURCHASE YOUR FIRST COMPUTER
(or even your tenth!), you have to get software for it. Software, also called computer programs or applications, is what
makes computers compute. Without it they'd be large, cumbersome doorstops, or landfill. Software is a set of instructions that tell a computer how to carry out a specific job. The
trend nowadays is for the computer maker to "throw in"
some software—an operating system, for example. The

BUYING SOFTWARE

operating system is what controls the communications between the processor, all its peripherals (hard disk, keyboard, memory, printer, and so on), and the user. It also coordinates the activity of the installed application whether it be a word processor, a spreadsheet, or some other off-the-shelf software package. To fully understand this process, we recommend you purchase the books *How Computers Work* and *How Software Works* (Ziff-Davis Press).

This chapter discusses the different types of software available and explains how they can help you with your computing tasks. You'll also find some tips on how to shop for software.

Operating Systems

With today's PC you have few choices when it comes to operating systems. The most popular is called DOS or MS-DOS. Its clone, once called DR-DOS, is Novell DOS. The most popular add-on to DOS is Microsoft Windows. Most of the new software selling today is designed to run under the current version, Windows 3.1. There is much debate over whether Windows 3.1 is a true operating system or a DOS shell. A shell is a program that is used to simplify the functions of an operating system. Because it requires DOS to run, we prefer to call it a DOS shell. But unlike a typical DOS shell, it is very powerful and programs are written specifically to run on it. Another DOS shell is a product called Desqview, which allows the average PC to run more than one program at a time and was very popular until the release of Windows.

If you have a powerful enough system, you can go further and run OS/2, UNIX, NextStep, or Windows NT on your system. These require more hardware and have various levels of compatibility with existing DOS software. They are all true modern operating systems designed to be used on the powerful computers of tomorrow. Most of today's users will either buy the DOS/Windows combination or OS/2, which has the ability to run all the software that runs under DOS and Windows. The jury is still out on Windows NT and NextStep. UNIX has not found the PC platform to be too welcoming and is largely a niche product.

Development Software

These are primarily programming languages. You can compare programming your computer to "programming" your dishwasher. Dishwashers have a selection of buttons and/or dials to set your dishwashing preference. Let's say the dishwasher has five buttons on the left: rinse, light wash, regular wash, heavy wash, and pot scrubber. On the right are three buttons: dry off, dry, and sani-steam. If you choose regular wash and dry, you'd be programming the dishwasher. The washing and drying buttons are selected and the program instructions would read "off, off, on, off, off" and "off, on, off,"

BUYING SOFTWARE

respectively. The dishwasher is an electro-mechanical device, and it performs what it has been designed to do based on the on/off combinations of switch settings. The computer is similar but more sophisticated. Programs outline for the computer a series of steps for it to do. Programming languages make developing the program easy.

When people talk about coding, they are talking about using a programming language. The most popular languages used by professionals are Pascal, C, or C++. You may also have heard of assembly language programming, which is much more difficult. Some professionals and many amateurs use a language called BASIC or Visual Basic. BASIC is an easy-to-use, easy-to-learn language that is very powerful. Most languages can make the computer do just about anything. Choosing one language over another becomes a personal preference developed after working with the different languages.

Along with the languages there are various debugging aids and other helpful utilities that might be classified as development software.

Application Software

Most people use this type of software on their computer. These are the programs that do things such as word processing and bookkeeping. The major classes are word processing, spreadsheets, database management, and telecommunications. Application software also includes music software, educational software, and games.

Word Processing Programs

Word processing on a computer beats pounding on a typewriter. You can delete mistakes (save money on correction fluid), rearrange your sentences, and fix spelling errors, all without wasting time and paper. For simple letters or long, multipage documents, word processing is one good reason to own a computer. A host of additional software programs can help to make your pages perfect. These include spelling checkers, grammar checkers, thesauruses, and other writing aids.

Business Software

Spreadsheets, graph programs, and databases all have a multitude of business uses. Spreadsheets track every business cent earned and spent. The graph programs can make detailed visual representations. Databases can hold thousands of records which may be searched with ease. Databases are routinely used for mailing lists because names, addresses, and other vital information can quickly be searched for by zip code, type of business, or by other key information.

Personal information managers (PIMs) are a hot business item these days. With a PIM you can schedule your week, plan your time, and log your minutes.

BUYING SOFTWARE

CheckFree

CheckFree lets you make electronic payments with your computer, a telephone line, and a modem (see Chapter 9). Once you set up an account, you give CheckFree a list of your regular monthly payments to the payees who are set up to accept them. For those who aren't, CheckFree will have checks printed and sent. CheckFree updates your bank account balance whenever a bill is paid. You will need to enter any paper checks you've written.

For more information, contact CheckFree at:
CheckFree Corporation
720 Greenpress Dr.
Westerville, OH 43081
(614) 698-6000 ∎

Other useful software includes business-specific programs like CAD/CAM programs (computer-aided design/computer-aided manufacturing), multimedia programs, and accounts receivable/accounts payable billing programs.

Personal and Home Computing Programs

These programs include personal and household financial managers, income tax programs, educational software, and, of course, games.

Personal and financial managers help you to balance your checkbook, pay bills, and track your money. They make it easy to set up a household budget and figure out how to achieve your long-term financial goals.

One program, CheckFree, can be used to make electronic payments. With it your checking account is debited for such regular payments as gas and electric, telephone, and revolving charge accounts to department stores and bank cards.

Checkwriting programs are often integral to home money-management software. This software can balance your checkbook and track where your money goes (besides just "away"). If you keep the information current (by noting automated teller withdrawals, deposits, and recently written checks), this software can also generate reports, graphs, charts, and provide long-range planning.

Income tax programs are very popular in the home software market. All you do is plug in the right numbers, and the computer calculates the amount of tax you owe. These packages are good for calculating estimated taxes, which is especially helpful for self-employed people who must calculate a realistic quarterly payment.

Music Software

Music programs teach people to play music, help professionals synthesize music, create new sounds, and perform other specialized functions.

BUYING SOFTWARE

ONLY THE BEST: THE HIGHEST-RATED EDUCATIONAL SOFTWARE

This guide is the best reference for educational software. It has listings for PC-, Apple II-, and Macintosh-based programs. Programs are divided by type of program—art, computer science, early childhood education, and special-education programs. Each listing provides hardware requirements, cost, a brief description, tips, evaluation conclusions (from a variety of participating schools across the country), and in what magazine the product was reviewed. All of the software producers reviewed are listed by name, address, and telephone number.

For more information, contact
Educational News Service
P.O. Box 1789
Carmichael, CA 95609
(916) 483-6159

The leading magazine on the subject is *Electronic Musician*. If your bookstore doesn't carry it, contact
ACT III Publishing
6400 Hollis #12
Emeryville, CA 94608
(510) 653-3307

Educational Software and Games

Educational programs are wonderful if you have kids around the house. They have all the appeal of games but inspire none of the parental guilt associated with letting the kids waste time—because with educational programs the kids learn while they play.

Games have a certain charm and addictive quality. They require more mental power than watching television, and you are able to achieve a sense of accomplishment with a high score. These programs often are very popular with all members of a household. They are many people's first introduction to using a computer, since they can be less threatening than more "serious" programs. And they are more familiar, owing to the proliferation of video game machines.

Utility Programs

Often called simply "utilities," these programs support the operation of your computer. Though many of these support functions are supplied with the operating system, you may find you need additional utilities. For example, a utility program can enable you to recover a disk file if it is accidentally deleted, use enhanced file management functions, and check the health and performance of your computer with diagnostic and measurement programs.

BUYING SOFTWARE

Utilities can be purchased off the shelf or even downloaded via modem from electronic bulletin boards.

Shareware and Free Software

Not to be overlooked is the enormous amount of high-quality software that is sold as shareware. This is software you obtain for free; then if you like the software, you buy it. There are various kinds of shareware ranging from fully functional programs to programs that only have a few limited features. When you buy the whole package, you get all the features. Whatever the case, there is a lot of variety and it's usually inexpensive. In fact, some programs are free!

Exec-PC

The best way to collect and examine shareware is by using a modem to call a computerized bulletin board. Start with the biggest and best—Exec-PC—an enormous system in Elk Grove, Wisconsin. It has virtually every shareware program ever written.

Exec-PC has 280 phone lines going into the system, and it contains over 650,000 files. Here are three numbers you can call to get access to Exec-PC. Their nominal fee is money well-spent. For a 2400 baud modem, call (414) 789-4210 and for V.32bis (14.4 kbps) call (414) 789-4360. They even have an ISDN connection at (414) 341-2074.

Piracy

Finally, remember to carefully read your warranty card that comes with the software to see what the vendor is allowing in terms of copying and backing up your software. It's usually illegal to copy software and give it to a friend. It's also wrong to sell old software that has since been updated. Software is usually licensed, not sold outright, and different laws regarding ownership apply.

What to Look for When Buying Software

Each major category of program has a number of companies with products vying for your hard-earned dollar. Each one claims to be the best. Each one seems to have even more features than the one before. It can be confusing.

Software for tasks such as word processing may have a bunch of different products which all seem to do the same thing. What do you shop for? Price? Name recognition? Package design? It's not clear-cut. The best thing would be to sit down and try every one, but that's just too time-consuming.

Avoid the tendency to shop for features. Just because a program seems to be able to "do it all" doesn't mean it's the best choice. The larger

BUYING SOFTWARE

and more complex a program is, the harder it may be to learn and the more memory it will chew up on your computer. Don't buy a word processing program, for example, which will do graphing and has a mini-spreadsheet and a calculator, if you only need a word processing program.

On the side of each software box there should be a small listing telling you the system requirements. Always read this listing before buying anything. Make sure you have what is required on the box.

Buying through Mail Order versus Stores

A lot of users are confused by the variety of places where you can purchase software. In the trade these are called *channels*. The direct channel is where you call the vendor directly and buy from the source. When you do this, you are assured of getting the latest version. Software versions change so often that many people prefer this method.

The other major channel is the retail store. This can be a superstore, a small computer store, or a store specializing in software. The advantage of many retail outlets is that they sell software at a price lower than the vendor's price. This is a curiosity in the world of retail. Normally mail-order and direct sales are associated with discounts. With computer software the opposite is usually the case.

When people talk about computer software prices, they seldom talk about the retail price—they talk about the "street price" as if it were a drug deal. That's because it has become a tradition to lower the manufacturer's suggested retail price by about 25 percent and sell software at a competitive street price. This began when a chain of software-only stores sold all software at a discount. Nowadays software companies price their products with the eventual street price in mind.

Good hunting!

PORTABLE COMPUTERS

THE NAME OF THE GAME in portable computing, as in politics, is compromise. There are plenty of compromises to make when you decide on a portable computer. In theory, it ought to have all the zip and whiz of a desktop PC. In reality, expect the desktop machine to run as much as three times faster. You'll be disappointed with your laptop purchase if you think it's going to do everything your desktop computer can do. A portable isn't a substitute for a desktop machine.

PORTABLE COMPUTERS

WHAT THE PORTABLE DOES HAVE TO OFFER is light weight, portability, and compact computing. This chapter will run through the different types of portables and what they offer to meet your computing needs.

What Is a Portable?

Let's begin by deciding what is meant by the term "portable." "Portable" doesn't necessarily mean the same thing to you as to someone else, especially a salesperson. Portable computers can range from 1-pound "palm-tops" with limited DOS compatibility to 25-pound, 80486-based, AC-only "luggables." (The AC-only machines need a power outlet to work. This is hard to come by if you want to use your luggable on an airplane.)

Laptops and notebooks all rely on a battery power source. The batteries you use are not the AA kinds pushed by the Energizer Bunny. Instead you use rechargeable nickel cadmium power packs that you recharge by means of an adapter and an AC power source. The laptop or portable you purchase will come with its own battery pack—usually a proprietary design. (There isn't a standard size or style of these batteries, as yet.) Extra power packs for most laptops cost in the $200 range, and it's a good idea to purchase a second one.

Batteries—The Overlooked Component

Most rechargeable batteries currently installed in laptops are made from nickel and cadmium. How long your computer will run depends on the simple ratio of your nickel cadmium battery's work ability—measured in milliampere-hours—to the amount of current your portable uses.

A nickel cadmium battery can be effectively recharged as many as 1,000 times, giving it a life span of three years if you discharge it once a day. But a number of factors determine the amount of work your battery can do on a single charge, as well as the battery's actual life span.

The Memory Effect   Early rechargeable portable systems ran until the battery discharged completely. If you were working when your laptop's lights went out, you were out of luck.

To prevent this, systems were designed to warn you when the batteries were about to expire so you could safely save your data. These systems work by taking advantage of the voltage characteristics of nickel cadmium batteries. When fully charged, a nickel cadmium battery rated at 1.25 volts may have an actual measured level of 1.5 volts. As the battery discharges, its voltage level drops. Just before exhaustion, the level is about 1.1 volts. A voltage-sensing system detects this condition and sends a warning by means of a flashing LED, a beep, or both.

Unfortunately, this system's benefits can cause battery problems down the road. If your portable's voltage-sensing system varies in its accuracy

PORTABLE COMPUTERS

even by small amounts, you may be cued to recharge your batteries before they're fully discharged.

Over a consistent period of time (perhaps a month or two with daily use), your batteries will be "trained" to expect recharging at that level—say 1.2 volts instead of 1.1—and they will effectively lose some of their capacity. This is known in laptop circles as "the memory effect." It is as if your car's engine went dead because the gauge read "empty," even though you had a gallon of gas left in the tank.

Less Wait, More Heat   Another set of problems is caused by tradeoffs in charging techniques. In early laptops, recharging could take up to 18 hours. The laptop's AC transformer used a *trickle-charging* method that fed the battery pack at a very low amperage. Although trickle-charging drastically increased the recharge time, it was easiest on your nickel cadmium battery, promoting more work ability and longer life span. Nevertheless, the long recharge times made for awkwardness on the road, requiring users to carry extra batteries or face long periods of down-time.

Consequently, vendors have begun to supply portables with fast chargers that need as little as one hour per recharge. But this gain in usability is offset by damage to the battery. Newly fast-charged batteries are warm to the touch. The additional heat is a sign that the chemical reaction that creates electrical potential is occurring too quickly. Heat damages nickel cadmium batteries, and for the systems that charge the fastest, the life span of the battery pack is usually rated at about 500 recharges—half of the theoretical 1,000-charge life potential.

Worse still, although fortunately rare, are fast chargers that quickly overload a fully charged battery. All batteries begin to discharge immediately after they reach full charge, exactly as nonrechargeable batteries do. *Peak-detect* or *negative-voltage-change* chargers monitor the voltage and switch to trickle-charge when the battery is charged and the voltage begins to drop. At this point, true trickle-charging maintains the correct battery level no matter how long the charging continues. Chargers unable to trickle-charge will pour higher amperage into an already charged battery, damaging it further by creating more heat. Continued fast charging can burn out a battery pack overnight.

Charging Ahead   How do you keep your batteries in shape? The answer is to do manually what your laptop and charger won't do automatically.

To fight "the memory effect," once a month you should turn off the power-save features, turn up the display brightness, and let the machine run down until it stops on its own. This will help drop the battery's voltage to its original minimum and squeeze every drop of work ability out of it.

PORTABLE COMPUTERS

If your machine won't allow a complete power-down, let your portable system's AC power pack trickle-charge the machine overnight when the system is on. Again, turn up the screen brightness and shut off the power-save features. Do this once out of every three charges. In the morning you can zap the machine with a fast charge for the half an hour or so that it takes you to get ready.

To help mitigate the damage caused by fast-charge heating, try not to use your portable immediately after recharging the batteries. Instead, let the battery cool down for at least half an hour before you power up. Likewise, don't start a recharge cycle immediately after the battery is exhausted. This, too, generates damaging heat.

For a portable that sees daily use, an optimal situation would be to have three battery packs available. Use one while another is recharging and the third is resting. This will save you the price of a battery pack and a half over a three-year period.

Battery-Saving Features of Laptops   All portables use power-saving techniques to extend what is essentially a fixed ratio of battery strength to the power drained by all the components in your notebook—a strict one-to-one ratio based on electrical law. Thankfully, portable vendors have spent the last few years learning how to cheat that law.

Notebook power-saving techniques typically include screen blanking and hard-disk power-down, as well as a feature that downshifts the operating speed from, say, 16 to 8 (or even 2) MHz during periods of inactivity. Many notebook power-saving schemes also include a standby mode (sometimes called "suspend and resume"); standby can be implemented in several different ways, ranging from simply closing the lid to activate all the power-saving features at once, to pressing a key combination. Another way is for the standby mode to shut off every component of the system, including the processor, while keeping only the contents of memory active. Yet another way is for the laptop to have a separate nickel cadmium battery that preserves the contents of RAM for about 12 hours after the main battery has died.

Power-saving features are, of course, a shotgun approach to a problem. They minimize battery drain, but they cannot mitigate the other problems presented by the applications software, such as repeated disk accesses.

Of course, turning off the internal modem and speaker (when you can) is a good idea. That alone can save several hundred milliamps—even with the small piezoelectric speakers most notebooks use.

Your screen is the greatest battery killer of any notebook component. Running it in inverse mode (black type on a white background) can cost you as much as 25 percent of your battery time. Normal mode (white on

PORTABLE COMPUTERS

black) sends power only to those pixels that are displayed, not the entire screen. If you must run inverse, keep the brightness as low as possible.

Setting up the proper interval for hard-disk power-down will depend on what applications you're running. In general, it takes nearly three times as much power to restart your hard disk frequently as it does just to let it run. If you use programs like Windows, Microsoft Word, and others that frequently move data to and from the hard disk, you may find that you've reached the power-down interval just when the application wants to access the drive.

The best (though expensive) solution is to fill your portable with RAM and turn those extra megabytes into a RAM disk. Setting the RAM drive as the destination for any temporary disk files or making it the program's source drive (by transferring all the program and data files to the RAM disk and running it from there) takes much less power than using your hard disk would. You can also slow your system down, especially when you are running word processing and telecommunications applications.

This cannot be stressed enough—whenever possible, let both your main and standby batteries charge overnight. Fast charging may get you up and running quickly, but in most cases it brings your battery up to only 85 or 90 percent of its capacity. Finally, always carry a spare, fully charged battery. Your case may weigh a pound or two more, but you'll double your system's battery life.

The six tips for longer battery life are

1. Run white-on-black text.

2. Keep the brightness to its lowest acceptable level.

3. Turn off the modem and the communications port.

4. Run programs from a RAM disk.

5. Use the slowest processor speed, whenever possible.

6. Keep a fully charged spare battery handy.

Types of Portables

The basic categories of portable computers, starting with the smallest, are palmtops, notebooks, laptops, and transportables. Each is a different beast.

Palmtops

The palmtops (or sub-laptops, as they are also known) can fill the most basic needs you may have when you're away from your desktop computer. The most obvious advantage of any palmtop unit is its size. It is small enough to easily fit in a pocket or a purse, just like a calculator. This

PORTABLE COMPUTERS

allows you to jot down notes, check your schedule, or look up a telephone number quickly. The weight of a palmtop is normally in the neighborhood of 1 pound.

A palmtop computer should also provide software and cabling to transfer appointment, Rolodex, diary, and address databases to and from your desktop machine so that your files are identical in each. If an organizer doesn't make some provision for this kind of data transfer or if it doesn't store information in a format that your desktop computer can read, you shouldn't consider buying it.

Palmtops can be electronic organizers or more versatile DOS-compatible machines. Some are intended solely to perform simple word processing. One of the problems with using a palmtop for word processing, however, is that even if it has a standard QWERTY keyboard (the layout found on most typewriters and computer keyboards), the keyboard is so tiny that typing is a two-finger proposition. And the nonstandard key layouts can be even more maddening.

Other palmtops are actually hand-held, DOS-compatible computers that use plug-in ROM cards to load your DOS programs. They are the exception among these small, hand-held computers.

Palmtop computers are a handy package—relatively easy to use, compact, some with the power of an IBM XT. The general population can find these computers disguised as pocket reference guides, inventory-control machines, maps, and sales tools, among other novel types of packaging. People who consider PCs too complicated will use these incognito computers. It's a high-growth and innovative area, with potential unparalleled in other facets of the computer industry.

Organizers   Many palmtops are essentially electronic Filofaxes (the looseleaf memory-aid notebooks that hoards of business types cling to for dear life in the hope of becoming "organized"), and within that niche they are useful. This type of palmtop is called an *organizer.* Organizers can store phone numbers and names and record business expenses and short notes. Most of them provide some method for transferring files to your desktop machine.

Hand-held organizers and microcomputers can be a good choice if you mainly want to keep track of personal information and expenses while out of the office and if your computing needs are light. They are perfect for salespeople and executives who need quick, easy access to phone numbers, addresses, appointments, short notes, and the like.

However, you should be realistic about what palmtops can do for you. If you have already given up on a Filofax, or if you have personal information management (PIM) software on your desktop machine but don't keep it current, an organizer is a waste of money. If, on the other

PORTABLE COMPUTERS

hand, you use either of these methods regularly, then you are likely to find that an electronic organizer is just what you need.

If you find an organizer's inability to run DOS programs limiting but don't really need to work with large programs when you're out of the office, then you may find that a DOS-compatible palmtop will suit your portable computing needs.

DOS-Compatible Palmtops   Most palmtop computers are limited in their ability to mimic a full-sized DOS machine. Two manufacturers, Atari and Poqet, have attempted to address some of these limitations.

The Poqet PC is a fully DOS-compatible microcomputer that runs on AA batteries. It is a crossover that could just as easily be considered a notebook computer. The Atari Portfolio, on the other hand, is capable of running only a few small DOS programs. Both use versions of the 8088 microprocessor, and the Poqet's performance is actually better than the original 4.77-MHz IBM PC and the Toshiba T1000. Both also use static RAM for memory, but the Portfolio comes with just 128k standard memory, whereas the Poqet has 512k.

It is important to keep in mind that the range of DOS programs available for either of these machines is limited. Small programs can be loaded into RAM, but for the most part, the lack of commercial, readily available software for these minuscule machines is a drawback. Until they are better supported, these machines may not be the best choice for everyone.

As DOS-compatible palmtops become more popular, expect to see more power-saving technology. PCMCIA (ROM) program cards are one example. These cards, each about the size of a credit card, hold programs and are accessed like a hard disk. They can also have RAM memory to store files. They offer a compact, powerful, and lightweight vehicle to palmtop power.

ROM program cards in particular are likely to have an impact on the design of future computers. In fact, some experts believe that ROM cards will find their way to desktop computers as well, because some software developers see this technology as a way to protect their programs from being pirated.

Notebooks

Notebook portable computers are so named because their designers attempt to keep their dimensions close to those of a regular-size notebook, typically 10"×12"×2". Weight, or the lack of it, is also a distinguishing feature of the typical notebook computer. Seven pounds is too heavy for today's notebooks and marginally acceptable only in those with an 80486 chip and a color screen. The typical range is between 4 and 6 pounds.

PORTABLE COMPUTERS

Their light weight is not without a price, though. A notebook computer is intended for one function—to perform the limited computing chores that most users are likely to have on the road. For the most part, if your intention is to perform graphics-, disk-, or speed-intensive computing chores, or if you are looking for the "magical" computer that will travel from home to office to sales presentation, then a notebook computer is not for you—at least not quite yet.

The definition of a notebook computer is in transition. Although the majority of notebooks still fit the traditional definition of light weight and light computing, a new standard is being set. In a sense, these new notebooks are downsized versions of the latest laptop computers. Their low weight still carries a penalty of restricted storage capacity, but even that limitation is overcome by hard disks with a smaller form factor. In fact, you will now find 486 notebooks that come with between 60Mb and 180Mb hard drives.

Notebook computers have already begun to edge out laptops as the most popular type of portable computer. Mass-storage technology makes notebooks the choice of all but the most ravenous of power users.

Subnotebooks   The newest term in portable computing is "subnotebook." A result of the trend toward lighter weight monochrome computers, this usually refers to any machine that weighs less than 4 pounds. This category will soon replace the "notebook" category until the heavier color machines shrink to notebook size in the next few years. A subnotebook typically differs from a notebook in that it has no built-in floppy disk. It may or may not have a built-in hard disk; some just use pop-in PCMCIA cards that can hold about 20Mb—as much data as some hard disks (some PCMCIA cards actually contain a hard disk). Subnotebooks may also have a smaller than normal keyboard; users should see if the small keyboard is useable. Some people find it impossible to work with.

Laptops

Laptops are the most powerful of the battery-operated portable computers. Newer models run on the Intel 80486 and 80386 families of microprocessors and typically weigh between 5 and 9 pounds. Although they are usually not much bigger than their notebook cousins in length and width, they are usually twice as thick. What you find in these larger machines is higher-capacity hard-disk drives, more standard memory, crisp VGA displays, and all the speed and power you'll need to run even the most demanding applications.

Laptops trade their extra weight for as many of the amenities of desktop computing as the designers are able to squeeze into a small, battery-operated package. Although the weight is kept down to a practical minimum

PORTABLE COMPUTERS

and battery life is stretched to its limits, the laptop's real selling points are speed and power. Low weight and battery life are really secondary in this class of machine.

Many laptop users are satisfied if they can get more than an hour's worth of work done on an airplane. But when they get to their hotel room and plug their laptop into a wall socket, they expect to be able to do almost anything they can on a desktop machine. Some performance drop-off is acceptable and even expected, but only as long as it isn't too large a drop.

Some Minimum Laptop Requirements   If you could have everything you wanted in a laptop, you would probably want 8Mb of RAM; a 32-gray-scale monitor (or color!); a 14,400 bps, V.32bis data/fax modem; about 100 to 200Mb of hard-disk space; an 486SX or DX processor, and some expansion capabilities. Since no one machine offers all these features, you'll have to decide for yourself which ones you really need. Here are a few of my recommendations:

- 486DX CPU running at 33MHz

- At least 4Mb of RAM

- 2,400 bps modem with at least MNP 5 data compression and fax capability of 9,600 bps

- 3.5-inch high-density floppy-disk drive

- 120Mb hard disk

- At least a 16-gray-scale VGA monitor

- Screen size of 8 inches by 6 inches or 7 inches by 5 inches.

- At least one serial port, one parallel port, and an external 15-pin analog video port for connecting to a VGA monitor

These are minimums and, if you're considering a computer in this class, you will probably need to exceed these minimums in at least one area.

Expansion Options for Laptops   Other expansion options will depend on what you need access to, but an important one to keep in mind is an external expansion port. If you plan to use your laptop as a dual-purpose desktop/travel machine or if you need regular access to a network, you'll probably need a docking station, or expansion unit. These are pricey units, running from $1,000 to $1,500, but they can be invaluable to the businessperson who travels on a regular basis. The expansion unit has room for the add-on cards and storage units that just won't fit in a portable computer. It also allows you to quickly connect to and disconnect

PORTABLE COMPUTERS

LAPTOP OR NOTEBOOK?

Laptop computers are powerful tools for those who need them, but if you can get by with a notebook computer, that's probably the route you should take. Over the coming months notebook computers will begin to blur the line between simple "notetaking" machines and "serious" computers. The added weight of the laptop computer seems minimal when you buy it. It's only after you tote the machine from airport terminal to convention hall that you begin to appreciate the trade-off of weight vs. computing power.

If, after assessing your computing needs, you find that you cannot live on the road without 100Mb of disk space or huge amounts of RAM, or if you have decided to use one computer for all your computing needs (in the office, at home, and on the road), then you can justify the extra weight and expense of a laptop computer. No other class of computer can match the versatility and power of a 386-based laptop computer—not yet, at least. ∎

from those very same options by providing a single connection that tells your portable computer what it's attached to when you plug it in. If you do buy a docking station, make sure it is self-configuring.

Portables/Transportables

These big, heavy computers are more aptly called "luggables" than portables. They are largely specialty machines. If you work at multiple locations and need to carry the machine from one site to another, or require the machine for CAD (computer aided drafting) or other power-hungry applications and require the speed and power of these big guys, these AC-only portables are for you.

This category of computer is defined by its need for AC power. Some actually will run for a limited time on a battery pack, but they are so limited in this respect that they are not practical to use. What makes them desirable to the user is their power and expandability. The trade-offs for those features are bulk and power consumption.

The appeal of AC-powered portable computers is based on the premise that, if you own a portable computer, you probably do most of your computing at a few stationary locations (at home, in the office, at the plant or a branch office). If this is true for you, then it makes sense to use the same machine at all the locations at which you usually work. Why buy two or three computers when one will work just as well, if not better?

Even given these conditions, an AC-powered portable is not necessarily the best choice for the job. There are an increasing number of capable laptop computers that are more flexible, somewhat lighter, and not really that much slower. As is the case with other classes of portable computers, if you can get by with a lighter-weight package, then that's the type of

PORTABLE COMPUTERS

FCC CLASS B CERTIFICATION

A note of warning about portable computers: Pay attention to FCC Class B certification. Portable computers must have this certification, which ensures that the machine has adequate radio frequency emission shielding. This keeps the portable from interfering with television and radio reception and, most importantly, an airplane's navigational equipment.

Unlike desktop computers, no portable computer of any type can be legally sold without that FCC certification. Beware of oddball portable computers sold at swap-meets, through dubious mail-order firms, or by other shifty-eyed, fly-by-night merchandisers. FCC Class B certification stickers can be, and are, counterfeited. When in doubt, you can call the FCC to check. (FCC is listed in the federal government pages of the telephone book.) Just give the manufacturer's name and the model number of the machine to verify a Class B certification.∎

machine you should buy. On the other hand, if you use your computer for CAD applications or some similar performance-hungry task in multiple locations, then an AC-powered portable is probably just what you need.

As a minimum, an AC-powered portable should have at least these features:

- 66-MHz 486DX microprocessor
- A 16-gray-scale or active matrix color VGA display
- 3.5-inch 1.44Mb floppy-disk drive
- 200Mb hard-disk drive
- Room for 16Mb of RAM
- Two expansion slots
- Provisions for an optional docking bay

As with laptops, you'll want all the ports you can fit into your computer; whereas proprietary ports generally are acceptable in the smaller machines, however, with transportables you should expect standard connections. You'll also need the same kind of provisions for a docking station as those a laptop user might want.

What To Shop For: Features

There are a number of real and imagined features when it comes to portable—laptop, notebook, and palmtop—computers. Understand the trade-offs and your real requirements before you shop.

PORTABLE COMPUTERS

VGA Compatibility

Most laptops offer a high resolution, readable VGA display with a gray scale. Monochrome VGA graphics are available on most notebook and laptop computers. Color VGA graphics are now available on many laptop and notebook computers, and will be more standard in the years ahead. (Currently, they are priced at around $5,000.)

Screen Size

Look for a screen size of at least 6 inches by 8 inches. Anything smaller is impossible to read without a magnifying glass. Try to buy the largest screen size you can afford. There is nothing worse than straining to read a display—it's frustrating, causes headaches, and results in the computer's being left home and unused more often than not.

Screen Lighting

The screen lighting for monochrome portable computers is either back lighting or reflective lighting. The type that's best for you is a matter of personal choice. (A display that I don't like, my wife thinks is terrific.)

Back-lit displays use battery power to run, which limits the amount of computing time available. A back-lit screen is impossible to see in direct sunlight, so if you plan to do most of your computing on your yacht or at the beach, you'll probably be happier with a reflective display.

Reflective displays depend on the available light to reflect characters on the screen. Reflective screens are particularly hard to read in rooms lit with energy-saving fluorescent lights. If you'll be using your portable mainly in airport lobbies, on airplanes, in hotel rooms, and in other make-shift indoor offices, a back-lit screen may work best for you. However, reflective screens have the advantage of requiring less battery power, so your computing time is less limited in this regard.

The best way to find out which screen lighting works for you is to compare the displays of a number of portables. Try them out in sunlight and in the darkest part of the store until you find one that meets your needs.

Hard-Disk Drives

Hard-disk drives aren't a new feature in portable computers. The early Compaq had double floppy-disk drives for $5\frac{1}{4}$-inch floppies. The size of the drives contributed to the excessive weight of these early lap squishers (in the 20-pound range). Of course, these early attempts at "take-along" computing also had a video display tube, a case made of metal, and significantly larger components than their counterparts today. Later, the portables added the weighty and cumbersome $5\frac{1}{4}$-inch hard drives to their units.

When the $3\frac{1}{2}$-inch hard drives became commonplace in computer manufacturing, they were added to portables. The innovation made a

PORTABLE COMPUTERS

significant dent in the weight of the laptop computers—a reduction of more than a pound.

The newer, smaller, and lighter the technology, the higher the cost. The first drives held about 20Mb, but at the time of this writing, the newest evolution is in the 200Mb and higher range.

The new feature of the lightweight notebook computers is a small, 2½-inch fixed-disk drive. These petite drives (manufactured by Conner Peripherals, JVC, and Seagate) weigh no more than a pack of playing cards, and their capacity ranges from 20Mb for single-platter drives to 80Mb or more for those with two platters. These small drives have cropped up in some of the laptop-sized machines, which has resulted in a downturn of weight to about 5 pounds or even less. The latest iteration of this neverending shrinking disk trend is the 1.3-inch hard disk. (We'll be talking about that in next year's buyer's guide.)

If it's available, 40Mb is probably the smallest reasonable size for a hard disk, even for a relatively light computing load.

Processor Chips

The processor chip is the brain of the computer, the CPU. When considering the purchase of a laptop, notebook, or palmtop computer, ask about the processor chip the machine is built around. If your requirement is to run a particular piece of software, the chip will make all the difference in the world. Certain software can run only on the 386-and-above family of chips. It wouldn't make much sense to purchase a "bargain" laptop if it couldn't run the one piece of software you really needed to use.

These days the portable you choose should probably have at least an 80386SX chip.

Internal Modem

Your portable should have at least a 2,400-bps internal modem so that you can transfer files and connect with MCI Mail or another E-mail service. This, combined with a good file-transfer program (such as Lap Link, Brooklyn Bridge, or FastLynx), eliminates the need for a built-in floppy-disk drive. (A typical floppy-disk drive, at a little under a pound, would account for about 20 percent of the total weight of our optimum laptop.)

ROM Card Slot

One of the newer portable feature choices is PCMCIA (ROM) card slots. These are also called *JEIDA* cards. (See the sidebar on PCMCIA cards.) They are much like a hard-cased floppy disk (like a 3½-inch disk) except that the floppy has been replaced by a chip. The computer can read this chip, but unlike a floppy, cannot write to it. What the ROM card-slot assembly allows is a quick and efficient means to load a program into a

PORTABLE COMPUTERS

traveling computer. The ROM card is difficult to damage and perfect for on-the-road turmoil. The easiest way to use the ROM card is to load the program into RAM whenever you need to use it. This way, the program doesn't occupy precious memory space on the computer when you don't need to use it. A consortium of manufacturers has arrived at a standard for this type of data transfer, so we're likely to see a growing number of software companies adopt this technology as a way to protect their work from piracy and illegal copying.

Expansion Units

Expansion units, also called docking stations, are for using a portable in an office setting. These units provide enough storage and expansion options to allow a laptop computer to function as part of a network or to easily plug into a network while the user is on the road. The best docking stations provide configuration information to the portable computer so it is aware of any floppy-disk drives, hard disks, video cards, network adapters, or modems that it's currently attached to.

Battery Life

Battery life is still the major limitation with notebook and laptop computers. While you shouldn't accept a machine that provides less than two hours of intensive computing time, you won't find many that exceed that minimum by much more than half an hour. At least, you won't without paying a terrible weight penalty. The batteries are the heaviest component of these computers.

Keyboard

One item to consider when choosing a portable—and the most subjective—is the keyboard. With the exception of a couple of lunchbox-style portable computers, the keyboard does not have a standard 101-key arrangement. You can generally expect the standard key spacing of .75 inches and some variation on the QWERTY key layout, but the layout of the function, cursor, PgUp, PgDn, Home, and End keys will vary even within a manufacturer's product line. Separate numeric keypads are added as off-board options to a very few machines. With notebook and palmtop machines, the key spacing can be even tighter. Some of the notebook computers have a very good keyboard, surprisingly.

Palmtops have a very crowded keyboard. Some people find that they cannot touch-type on a palmtop, while others do fine. Try out the keyboard. Type for at least ten minutes before you decide on a machine. Some keyboards that have a good feel initially will begin to feel mushy, or have an uneven "bounce," after a few minutes of use. The best keyboard is a matter of taste.

PORTABLE COMPUTERS

PCMCIA CARDS

If you've ever looked at a Poqet computer, the HP palmtop, or any of a number of Japanese notebook computers, then you've seen what is loosely called a JEIDA (Japan Electronics Industry Development Association) card. The size of a credit card, a JEIDA card might hold a copy of Lotus 1-2-3 or substitute as a DRAM-based silicon hard disk in some systems. A small, round battery keeps the DRAM version alive for a year or more. This card is going to be one of the most important developments in personal computing.

In fact, the card should be referred to as the PC-MCIA PC-Card or the PC-Card, for short. PCMCIA is the Personal Computer Memory Card International Association, the governing body based in Sunnyvale, California, that has standardized the specifications for this card worldwide (phone 408-720-0107). While over the past few years users have perceived this card as a Japanese invention, it is, in fact, American. JEIDA works with the PCMCIA and the specifications are identical. Make no mistake: The PCMCIA is the lead organization when it comes to this card. It's amusing how we sometimes assume that any such new development, especially when it comes to anything regarding miniaturization, is from Japan. So let's start calling this card the PCMCIA PC-Card (or the PC-Card for short) and not the JEIDA card.

What do we know about the PCMCIA and what will be the benefit to users? The PCMCIA has over 150 member companies, including Fujitsu, Lotus, Maxell, Motorola, Intel, DuPont, Mitsubishi, Zenith, HP, and Epson. The first specification was released in May of 1990 and this became the standard PC-Card we've begun to see on certain laptops, palmtops, and notebook machines. The latest release of the PC-Card is version 2.0 (which is identical to JEIDA 4.1).

Release 2.0 is important to users because it will revolutionize portable computing. It may even become a standard on desktop machines worldwide because the PC-Card eliminates piracy and prevents certain types of virus infection. The original PC-Card was like a silicon hard disk. Programs were loaded from it into memory. Release 2.0 allows what is termed *XIP*—Execute in Place. The code is executed from the card itself. Designed primarily for ROM cards, it can work with any type of memory the card uses, including DRAM and flash.

More importantly, though, the new release of this card adds dual voltage operation to take advantage of the upcoming 3.3-volt standard and a second interface to take advantage of I/O operations. This means that the card can now be an I/O device such as a modem or LAN adapter. Imagine a 9,600-bps V.42bis modem on a credit card!

With memory prices forever declining there will be a point when the disk-drive makers finally give in. When they do, it will be to the PCMCIA PC-Card. You can be sure the semiconductor makers would love this to happen. Mitsubishi and others have already announced 12Mb DRAM PC-Cards that are being remarketed by OEMS. The current design of the card supports 64Mb of memory. Imagine the usefulness of a credit card holding 64Mb of fast silicon memory. For starters, you could make a PC-Card a mirror of a 64Mb partition of the hard disk on your desktop machine. It would be convenient backup and easily removable for use in your notebook machine while on the road. What could be easier?

I expect to see desktop computer makers installing a PC-Card slot in the front of their machines next year. It's already common to see this in systems sold in Asia. Acer, for example, makes a machine with this capability. A lot of Taiwanese board makers have add-in cards to drive the PC-Card slot, but we've seen only a few over here.

It's obvious that the PCMCIA PC-Card will be a tremendous success because it solves so many problems associated with portable computing. Since portables are considered to be the big growth market for the next few years it would be wise to familiarize yourself with this standard and the PCMCIA. I believe a lot of people are going to be caught off guard when this technology hits the home run. ∎

PORTABLE COMPUTERS

Weight

If you're considering a notebook computer, weight is probably a major concern for you. Most likely you plan to carry this computer with you extensively and don't feel like going into weight training to do so. While you probably won't notice the difference of a pound in weight, you should try to get the lightest machine that has the features you need. Remember, along with the computer itself, you're going to be carrying the battery in the machine, a spare battery, a recharger/wall adapter, a carrying case, and probably some manuals and floppy disks. Eventually it adds up to quite a bit more than the weight the manufacturer advertises.

Try Before You Buy

The only way to decide what's right for you is to try out any computer before you buy it. Any good retailer is willing to let you tap on the keys to your heart's content. Remember, you're going to have to live with the miserable keyboard that's permanently attached to that dreamy laptop, so pay attention not only to the layout and special key combinations needed to perform normal operations, but also to the feel of the keys themselves. If you hate it, then don't buy it. On the other hand, it's amazing what you can get used to.

The best way to try out any computer is to bring a sample file with you and perform the types of operations you'd expect to perform under normal circumstances. And don't assume that because a particular computer is running Windows that it will adequately run your full set of Windows programs.

One last thing to keep in mind when comparing machines, particularly concerning price and weight, is to make sure that you compare the same configuration. That means adding in the price and weight of an internal modem, if it does not come as standard equipment, and any extra memory you will need.

Convenience on the Go

Computing while on the road is not only becoming more commonplace, it's also becoming more complex. No longer are portable-computer users impressed—or even satisfied—with merely a movable processor. Portable power, speed, and data storage have all increased dramatically, and versatility has soared with them. An expanding number of on-the-go applications have created an almost overnight demand for new portable peripherals. But is a kit bag of assorted laptop add-ons really for you?

As you gain experience with portable computing, the missing pieces you take for granted at most desktop computing sites may become more important while you're on the road. You may find that you can't do without a portable printer, scanner, modem, fax machine, external hard disk,

PORTABLE COMPUTERS

tape drive, mouse, or even a convenient way to use the laptop and printer in your car.

Portable Printing

Printing while you are away from your office can be inconvenient at best when it requires a hookup to the printer in a client's office. For those who don't want to annoy their hosts, or who visit printerless offices or homes, portable printers that plug into your laptop are just the thing.

The minimum requirements for portable printers are small size and light weight. Battery operation is handy, but not crucial if you are going to use the printer in a hotel room or in someone's office.

External Hard Disks: Data Luggage for Laptops

External hard disks serve multiple purposes for portable computers. When paired with notebook and laptop computers that don't already have a hard disk, external units can serve as primary storage for programs and data that are either left at the office or carried along for access when AC power is available. If your portable already has an internal hard disk, you may want to consider buying an external one as a secondary large-capacity storage device or as a fast, software-accessible data backup unit.

Road Trackballs

The popularity of GUIs (graphical user interfaces), especially Microsoft Windows, has brought about the need for portable laptop pointing devices. The most common style of these pointing devices is a very small trackball that clips to the side of the laptop's keyboard. You use your thumb to move the cursor.

Other Products

A number of other products are available for portable computing. These include modems (covered in Chapter 9), some of which connect with cellular or other wireless systems, and extra add-ons like screen enhancers, lightweight plastic keyboard overlays and covers (to keep crumbs out of the keys), fancy carrying cases in nylon and leather, and joysticks, among other specialty products.

As with any buying decision, you'll have to prioritize your wants and needs in order to find the machine and the peripherals that are best for you.

ACCESSORIES

ONCE YOUR COMPUTER IS UP AND RUNNING, it's always fun to find new accessories to add. There is always some new thing on the market that is both useful and needed. Copy holders, mouse pads, computer dust covers, and the like are just the beginning. Here are just a few Dvorak recommendations.

ACCESSORIES

Preventing Crashes:
Power Supply Accessories and Diagnostics

Computers crash for a variety of reasons. If your computer is crashing frequently, chances are you may have a hardware problem. Power surges, overheating, bad wiring, and bad chips are all common problems that cause computers to crash. Here are some accessories to deal with these problems.

Power Strips

A power strip is that power shop standby. It's a simple way to turn your one wall outlet into enough plugs for the four, five, or six electrical plugs you need without rewiring the house. Power strips come in a number of different varieties.

Most of these outlets have a power switch to turn on the entire strip at once. One drawback to the toggle switch is most people put the power strip on the floor under their computer—and invariably, at one time or another, your foot will accidentally hit the switch and turn off the computer. (This, of course, only happens when you've been working on a long word-processed document and have neglected to save your work, thereby wiping out hours of work.)

The plain power strips sold in computer stores and hardware stores are essentially the same. And if you're shopping by price, the hardware store prices are usually better. But not all power strips are plain. There are higher priced models which have "surge protection." A *surge* refers to a fluctuation in the electrical current, which rarely flows steadily. When the refrigerator kicks on or someone turns on the vacuum cleaner, there will be a momentary drop in the power current. (You can often see this when the light dims for an instant as an appliance is turned on.) When the appliance motor is switched off, the current surges—a spike. Spikes and low power are more common than you might think. Computers are designed to handle these power fluctuations, but only to a point.

The ebb and flow of electricity can be greater, due to a problem at the power company, a bolt of lightening hitting a power line, or after a "brownout." Then a big gush of electricity rushes through the line. (It's like unkinking a hose!) The computer's circuitry could be damaged. The surge protector guards against such damage. Instead of the spike hitting the computer, it blows out the fuse in the power strip, so instead of buying a new computer, you just have to shell out the cash for a new power strip. The prices range from $10 to $30. Manufacturers include Curtis, Zero Surge, Telemax, PowerCenter, and Lunalite.

ACCESSORIES

Wire Testing

If you have a lot of unexplained crashes with your computer, the problem might be improper AC wiring and grounding. Many buildings, especially older ones, aren't wired correctly. There are little mistakes here and there which contribute to computer problems. A power strip with a surge protector won't help you with these wiring anomalies. You could hire an electrician to come and check each socket in your home or office for one of a multitude of possible errors: open neutrals, ground shorts, reversed polarity, ground and hot reversals, and all sorts of other problems, but that's expensive, given the number of sockets the average building has.

There is a device you can buy to check the sockets yourself: the Accu-Test II wiring integrity tester, from Ecos Electronics in Oak Park, Illinois (retail $198). This is a hand-held device which you plug into the socket. A panel of lights will diagnose any problems and isolate where the problem is. (Then you can call an electrician to fix it.) It's an excellent device and will pay for itself when it finds just one defective outlet.

Uninterruptible Power Supply (UPS)

A UPS (uninterruptible power supply) offers the ultimate in power peace-of-mind. These devices are battery backups which you plug your computer into. If the power suddenly fails, you'll hear a warning beep to alert you that the power isn't coming in. Then you'll have enough time to save your files and turn off your computer. The benefit of the UPS is you'll never be caught in the middle of a program at the mercy of a power outage. A UPS is also an excellent device to guard against electrical surges. It is expensive but well worth the investment if you're in an area with frequent outages.

Heat problems? Moi?

Put your finger on a powered-up 50-MHz 486. It's hot. Apparently, the DX2 version of the 486 is even hotter, so hot that the 66-MHz version of the chip might actually contribute to global warming. The market is just beginning to absorb 50-MHz 486s, and while the manufacturers are aware of the heat problem, the users aren't. Many report unusual crashes (especially when running processor-intensive Windows and OS/2 operating systems) and other screwy problems which will make you begin to think you're going crazy. You're not, it's just the processor overheating. (The Intel heat specification for the chip tops out at 185 degrees Fahrenheit.) When the heat of summertime comes, the problem may become more serious. You should expect to see manufacturers redesign the computer's box to better dissipate heat—someday.

In the meantime, there's a quick fix. From Norm Bailey comes the CPU Kooler. This is a $39.95 package consisting of a milspec (military

ACCESSORIES

MO' CRASHES, MO' CRASHES, MO' CRASHES

While on the subject of crashes, a fascinating new product has been announced by Computer Library, called Support On Site. Apparently they've accumulated almost every in-house tech note available from Microsoft, Borland, WordPerfect, and dozens of other companies. The idea is that your corporate in-house support people can use this database to look up wacky problems that occur on site. The disk is updated monthly, and it costs $1,295 a year. It should pay for itself at companies that have support staff and plenty of machines. One unadvertised feature I found when playing with this database is that you can discover known bugs and incompatibilities before you decide to buy that site license for some software product. You just punch in the system you have and then key in the software you want to buy, and you'll find out all the bad things you should know. Call Computer Library in New York at (212) 503-4400 for more information.■

specification) fan hooked to a heat sink. The fan is glued onto the top of the 486 chip with a special thermal compound which transfers most of the heat to the heat-sink fan. It's plugged into the power supply. According to the company, "A surface temperature of 170.2 degrees Fahrenheit was measured on a 80486-33 after one hour's operation. This reduces the life of the most costly component in the PC. With the CPU Kooler installed, the temperature increased only 7 degrees above ambient room temperature to 87.6 degrees."

For more information call PCubid Computer Technology in Sacramento, California, at (916) 338-1338 or fax them at (916) 725-0230.

Hardware Helper

There are diagnostic tools and there is PocketPOST, a $199 minicard that pops into any PC or ISA slot. Included with the card is a complete diagnostic system that can pinpoint any PC failure (including boot failure). It comes with a comprehensive book with hundreds of error codes that can crop up on the PocketPOST digital display and LED read outs. The product comes from Data Depot (1525 Sandy Lane, Clearwater, FL, 34615, (813) 446-3402). When combined with the company's Remote RX software ($100 when purchased with PocketPOST), there is no problem that can't be resolved. The software can even isolate a single bad memory chip and specifically show you what chip to pull. This is an amazing system that is equaled only by equipment selling for thousands of dollars. You'll be a hero in your company if you own PocketPOST and Remote RX from Data Depot. If you have anything to do with maintenance or repair, call these guys immediately. Also ask the company about their inexpensive (but outstanding) PC Certify—a program that certifies compatibility. I give the highest recommendation for the entire product line.

ACCESSORIES

Fun Stuff

There is a lot of fun stuff on the market for PCs that makes the computer seem like less of a tool and more of a toy. There are gadgets to stick onto the computer that look like a big wind-up key, a big tongue which will stick out of the small disk drive, and other silly items. Let's face it, computers don't have to be dull. Keep your eyes open for the occasional good, useful (but silly) gift items, interesting specialty catalogs, small utility software programs, and the occasional "conversation piece." They're fun.

The Corvette Mouse

How can anyone resist a product like the Corvette Mouse! Actually it's a little Corvette model that fits over a Macintosh or Microsoft mouse. The user presses on the hood of the 'Vette to activate the mouse button underneath. The company says, "instead of having a boring-looking mouse on your desk, you are driving a hot Corvette!" Cheap thrills at only $19.95. To order one of these nifty covers, contact:

Suntime
7817 N. Cameron Ave.
Tampa, FL 33614
(813) 886-1145

Genuinely Interesting Mail

Computer mail-order catalogs usually fall into two categories: the software catalog in which, in many cases, the vendors have to pay for inclusion, which creates a mish-mosh of ever-changing products; and the hardware catalog which sells the same old cables and connectors. But a new generation of specialty catalogs is emerging.

Specialty Paper   One excellent specialty catalog is from a company called Paper Direct. It specializes in something new: laser printer paper. Not just any laser printer paper, mind you, but exotic stuff like the Shimizu line that appears to be handmade Japanese one-of-a-kind paper. They also sell a strange foil that you can put through your laser printer to create a foil-stamped letterhead. The product line doesn't end there. There are recycled papers, tri-fold brochures, and greeting cards which will all run through your laser printer with ease. Get their catalog and you won't regret it. The company can be reached at (201) 507-5488, or fax them at (201) 507-0817 and ask for a catalog.

Price Trend Newsletter   If you like to watch computer price trends, there's a new and interesting newsletter available called *The PC Street Price Index*. It's 25 pages of price data reflecting street prices of everything from 386SX machines to AskSAM software. Not cheap at $195, the

ACCESSORIES

newsletter is a must-have for large corporations and vendors who want to know the real price of their competitor's products. The publisher is Metro Computing of Cherry Hill, New Jersey. Contact them at (609)784-8866 for more information or a subscription.

Utility Software

You can find lots of cute and valuable software on the market, not the big applications programs, but the small accessory programs which are helpful for more humble computing tasks. (They're like purchasing a vase for the living room; it's not a major purchase like a piece of furniture, but it's nice to have around.) Here is a small sampling of products that make your computer more "homey."

Tick-Tock   While many of you may discover various bugs in the clocks of your PC clone, there is one problem that seems to be common to all clocks. They lose a small amount of time every day—about 20 seconds. Worse, some applications throw the DOS clock out of sync with the system clock. Pacific Standard Time has a $19.95 utility called CLOCK that adjusts the clock appropriately and without hassle. It's worth a look. You can reach PST at (408) 246-0589.

Personal Fonts   Word process your handwriting? If you turn your handwriting into a font, then that's exactly what you'll end up doing. Lazy Dog Foundry (316 Bates Ave., St. Paul, MN, 55106, (612) 774-4717) can take your handwriting (printed or cursive) and make a font out of it that you can use for correspondence with a personal touch. The service is a steal at $179! For your money you get a complete Type 1 PostScript font with kerning hints and all. It's going to be the hot ticket in the next few years. Everyone will have a personal font. The direct-mail marketers will find them especially useful for envelope addressing and fake sincere letters to gullible rubes.

I've already received one such postcard with what appeared to be a handwritten address and personal note. Careful examination revealed a laser printer and a curious exactness to the handwriting—every capital F, for example, was identical. Still, only a few people would notice that this was actually a personal font based on the sloppy writing of an employee. Lazy Dog, in fact, has worked with a number of direct-mail firms to perfect this technology.

This will give many of the executives out there the opportunity to "hand write" those thank-you memos and terse notes that are actually written and signed by the secretary. The secretary will still do it, of course, but using the boss's unique penmanship. (A perfect gift for that egomaniacal art director!) Lazy Dog will also help you create custom fonts of any sort.

ACCESSORIES

Caller ID, Anyone?   One of the finest products I've seen in the last five years is Caller ID+Plus from Rochelle Communications (8920 Business Park Dr., #125, Austin, TX, 78759, (512) 794-0088, fax (512) 794-9997). This $295 gem of a product works with local phone systems that utilize the premium phone service called "Caller ID."

Caller ID lets phone users see the phone number from which they are receiving phone calls. This will virtually eliminate crank calls and stop anonymous harassment. But its real benefit will be when used in conjunction with a product such as Caller ID+Plus. The phone line is routed through the computer and when an incoming call is received, the Caller ID system alerts the computer which then looks up the person calling.

Once the database of associates is searched, you can expect to see the caller's name pop up on your screen as the phone rings. You'll also see whatever information you might have in the database. Unknowns are entered on the fly, too. The system also logs all calls in and out, and the user can make on-the-fly notes about each call, with the information going into a master log. This is a killer program for any salesperson.

KEY TO APPENDICES A–L

The tables in the following appendices were compiled from the last three years' worth of *PC Magazine*s. Because prices change quickly, we will specify the general price range to which each product belongs rather than specifying original list prices. Price ranges are denoted by dollar signs, as follows:

$	= $1400 or less
$$	= $1401–$2400
$$$	= $2401–$4000
$$$$	= $4001–$6000
$$$$$	= over $6000

The tables also use the following symbols and abbreviations:

N/A = Not applicable (the product does not have this feature)

INA = Information not available

● = Yes

○ = No

= *PC Magazine* Editor's Choice

= Dvorak's Pick

COMPUTERS

A.1 Computers

(Products listed in alphabetical order by company name)	AcerPower 486DX2/50 WU	AcerPower 486e DX2/66 Model 5657	ACMA 386/40	ACMA 486/33 EISA	ACMA 486/33 Engineering Workstation
Price	$$$$$	$$$	$$	$$$$	$$$$
Processor/speed	486DX2/50MHz	486DX2/66MHz	Am386/40MHz	486/33MHz	486/33MHz
Case type	Desktop	Desktop	Desktop	Tower	Tower
Dimensions (HWD, in inches)	INA	INA	INA	24.5 × 7.5 × 17.5	25.5 × 7.5 × 17.5
Installed RAM	INA	INA	INA	INA	8Mb
Bus architecture	ISA	EISA	INA	INA	INA
Warranty	1 year	1 year	1 year	INA	1 year on parts, 2 years on labor

MOTHERBOARD

Motherboard manufacturer	Acer	Acer	Helm Engineering	Free Technology	AMI
Chip set manufacturer	SIS	OPTi	SIS	Intel	C&T
System shadowing/video shadowing	●/●	INA	●/●	●/●	●/●
BIOS version	Acer 1.2R1	Acer 1.2R1.0	AMI 4.0	Award 4.0 (1990)	AMI (April 1990)
ZIF socket	○	○	INA	INA	INA
Coprocessor supported	INA	INA	80487/Weitek	INA	Weitek 4167

MEMORY AND PROCESSOR RAM CACHE

Installable RAM (minimum–maximum)	4Mb–64Mb	4Mb–256Mb	1Mb–64Mb	1Mb–64Mb	4Mb–24Mb
Cache controller	SIS	INA	Intel	Discrete logic	Discrete logic
Installed RAM cache	INA	INA	INA	64K	128K
Installable RAM cache	64K–256K	64K–256K	64K	256K	128K

DISK DRIVES

Drive bays	3 5.25-inch, 1 3.5-inch	3 5.25-inch, 2 3.5-inch	3 5.25-inch	6 half-height	6 half-height
Disk controller location	Card	ISA card	INA	Card	Card
Hard disk capacity	212Mb	213Mb	210Mb	360Mb	210Mb
Hard disk options	212Mb	120Mb–500Mb	105Mb–650Mb	150Mb–676Mb	80Mb–676Mb
Interface	INA	INA	INA	ESDI	IDE
Minimal floppy disk drive configuration	1.2Mb, 1.44Mb	1.2Mb, 1.44Mb	1.2Mb, 1.44Mb	1.2Mb, 1.44Mb	1.2Mb, 1.44Mb

EXPANSION BUS

8-bit slots	None	None	2 (1 open)	None	1
16-bit slots	8	2	5 (4 open)	2	6
32-bit:				6	1
EISA/MCA slots	None	5	None	INA	INA
Proprietary	None	1	1 (open)	INA	INA
Slots free in fully configured PC	INA	INA	INA	4	5
Parallel, serial, mouse ports on motherboard	0, 0, 1	1, 2, 1	INA	INA	INA
Integrated network adapter option	INA	None	INA	INA	INA

VIDEO

Display circuitry location	Card	Proprietary local bus	Card	Card	Card
Chip set manufacturer	ATI	ATI	Tseng	Tseng	Tseng

POWER SUPPLY

Power supply (watts)	200	200	250	INA	450
Number of device connectors	6	4	5	INA	5

●—Yes   ○—No   N/A—Not applicable   INA—Information not available

Table Continues →

Computers

	ACMA 486/50i	ACMA 486DX2/50	ACMA 486SX/25	ALR BusinessVEISA 486/33 Model 200	ALR Flyer 32DT 4DX2/66
Price	$$$	$$$	$$$	$$$	$$$
Processor/speed	486/50MHz	486DX2/50MHz	486SX/25MHz	486/33MHz	486DX2/66MHz
Case type	Tower	Desktop	Tower	Small-footprint	Slimline
Dimensions (HWD, in inches)	INA	INA	INA	INA	INA
Installed RAM	INA	INA	INA	INA	INA
Bus architecture	INA	EISA	EISA	INA	ISA
Warranty	1 year	1 year	1 year	1 year	1 year
MOTHERBOARD					
Motherboard manufacturer	Helm Engineering	Helm Engineering	Helm Engineering	ALR	ALR
Chip set manufacturer	SIS	Intel	SIS	Intel/ALR	UMC
System shadowing/video shadowing	●/●	●/●	INA	●/●	INA
BIOS version	AMI (May 1991)	Award 4.00	Award (July 1991)	Phoenix 4.03.03	Phoenix 1.01.10m
ZIF socket	INA	○	○	INA	○
Coprocessor supported	Weitek	INA	INA	80487/Weitek	INA
MEMORY AND PROCESSOR RAM CACHE					
Installable RAM (minimum–maximum)	1Mb–64Mb	1Mb–64Mb	2Mb–32Mb	1Mb–49Mb	4Mb–36Mb
Cache controller	SIS	Intel	INA	Proprietary	INA
Installed RAM cache	INA	INA	INA	INA	INA
Installable RAM cache	64K–256K	256K	64K–256K	64K–256K	0–256K
DISK DRIVES					
Drive bays	4 5.25-inch	3 5.25-inch	4 5.25-inch	2 5.25-inch, 1 3.5-inch	2 5.25-inch, 1 3.5-inch
Disk controller location	Card	Card	Card	Integrated	Motherboard
Hard disk capacity	425Mb	240Mb	245Mb	212Mb	200Mb
Hard disk options	52Mb–1.2G	240Mb	245Mb	80Mb–1.2G	80Mb–535Mb
Interface	INA	INA	INA	INA	INA
Minimal floppy disk drive configuration	1.2Mb, 1.44Mb	1.2Mb, 1.44Mb	1.2Mb, 1.44Mb	1.2Mb, 1.44Mb	1.2Mb, 1.44Mb
EXPANSION BUS					
8-bit slots	None	None	None	None	None
16-bit slots	7 (4 open)	None	None	2 (2 open)	3
32-bit:					
EISA/MCA slots	None	8	8	4 (3 open)	None
Proprietary	1 (none open)	None	None	3 (1 open)	3
Slots free in fully configured PC	INA	INA	INA	INA	INA
Parallel, serial, mouse ports on motherboard	INA	None	None	INA	2, 1, 0
Integrated network adapter option	INA	INA	INA	INA	None
VIDEO					
Display circuitry location	Card	Card	Card	Card	ISA card
Chip set manufacturer	ATI	ATI	ATI	Orchid	WD
POWER SUPPLY					
Power supply (watts)	250	250	250	145	145
Number of device connectors	5	5	6	4	4

●—Yes ○—No N/A—Not applicable INA—Information not available

Computers

	ALR Flyer 32DT 4SX/25	ALR PowerCache 33/4e	ALR PowerPro VM 486/33 Model 150	Altec 486DX2 Local Bus	Amax 486/33e
Price	$$$	$$$$	$$$$	$$$	$$$$
Processor/speed	486SX/25MHz	486/33MHz	486/33MHz	486DX2/50MHz	486/33MHz
Case type	Small-footprint	Tower	Tower	Tower	Tower
Dimensions (HWD, in inches)	INA	23.5 × 7.5 × 18.5	INA	INA	24.5 × 7.5 × 17.5
Installed RAM	INA	INA	INA	INA	INA
Bus architecture	ISA	INA	INA	ISA	INA
Warranty	1 year	INA	1 year	2 years	INA
MOTHERBOARD					
Motherboard manufacturer	ALR	ALR	ALR	Gigabyte	Free Technology
Chip set manufacturer	UMC, WD	Intel	ALR	UMC	Intel
System shadowing/video shadowing	INA	●/○	●/●	●/●	●/●
BIOS version	Phoenix 1.01	Phoenix 1.00.04 (January 1988)	Phoenix 4.03.03	AMI (May 1991)	Award 4.1 (1990)
ZIF socket	○	INA	INA	○	INA
Coprocessor supported	INA	INA	80487/Weitek	INA	INA
MEMORY AND PROCESSOR RAM CACHE					
Installable RAM (minimum–maximum)	4Mb–36Mb	8Mb–128Mb	5Mb–49Mb	1Mb–32Mb	1Mb–64Mb
Cache controller	INA	ALR	Proprietary	UMC	Discrete logic
Installed RAM cache	INA	128K	INA	INA	64K
Installable RAM cache	N/A	None	64K–256K	256K	256K
DISK DRIVES					
Drive bays	1 5.25-inch, 1 3.5-inch	1 full-height, 4 half-height	3 5.25-inch, 1 3.5-inch	6 5.25-inch	6 half-height
Disk controller location	Motherboard	Card	Card	Card	Card
Hard disk capacity	213Mb	330Mb	150Mb	212Mb	346Mb
Hard disk options	80Mb–535Mb	150Mb–1.2G	150Mb–1.2G	212Mb–678Mb	300Mb–1G
Interface	INA	ESDI	INA	INA	ESDI
Minimal floppy disk drive configuration	1.2Mb, 1.44Mb	1.2Mb	1.2Mb, 1.44Mb	1.2Mb, 1.44Mb	1.2Mb, 1.44Mb
EXPANSION BUS					
8-bit slots	None	1	None	1	None
16-bit slots	3	1	2 (2 open)	7	2
32-bit:		6			6
EISA/MCA slots	None	INA	8 (6 open)	None	INA
Proprietary	3	INA	2 (none open)	2	INA
Slots free in fully configured PC	INA	6	INA	INA	4
Parallel, serial, mouse ports on motherboard	1, 2, 0	INA	INA	None	INA
Integrated network adapter option	INA	INA	INA	INA	INA
VIDEO					
Display circuitry location	Motherboard	Card	Card	Card	Card
Chip set manufacturer	WD	Paradise	Orchid	S3	Tseng
POWER SUPPLY					
Power supply (watts)	145	INA	300	250	INA
Number of device connectors	3	INA	4	8	INA

●—Yes ○—No N/A—Not applicable INA—Information not available

Table Continues →

Computers

	Amax 486/50 ISAmax Power Station	Amax PC/486 Power Station	Amax 486DX2 Power Station	Amax 486SX/25 Power Station	American Mitac TL4466
Price	$$$	$$$	$$$	$$$	$$$
Processor/speed	486/50MHz	486/33MHz	486DX2/50MHz	486SX/25MHz	486DX2/66MHz
Case type	Desktop	Tower	Desktop	Desktop	Tower
Dimensions (HWD, in inches)	INA	25.5 × 7.5 × 17.5	INA	INA	INA
Installed RAM	INA	8Mb	INA	INA	INA
Bus architecture	INA	INA	EISA	EISA	EISA
Warranty	1 year	1 year	1 year	1 year	1 year
MOTHERBOARD					
Motherboard manufacturer	Helm Engineering	AMI	Amax	Amax	American Mitac
Chip set manufacturer	SIS	C&T	Intel	Intel	American Mitac/Intel
System shadowing/video shadowing	●/●	●/●	●/●	INA	INA
BIOS version	AMI (May 1991)	AMI (April 1990)	Award 4.00	Award 4.0	Phoenix VEA4033 R1.04
ZIF socket	INA	INA	○	○	○
Coprocessor supported	Weitek	Weitek 4167	INA	INA	INA
MEMORY AND PROCESSOR RAM CACHE					
Installable RAM (minimum–maximum)	1Mb–64Mb	1Mb–16Mb	1Mb–64Mb	4Mb–64Mb	1Mb–64Mb
Cache controller	SIS	Discrete logic	Intel	INA	INA
Installed RAM cache	INA	128K	INA	INA	INA
Installable RAM cache	64K–256K	128K	256K	64K–256K	1K–256K
DISK DRIVES					
Drive bays	3 5.25-inch	6 half-height	3 5.25-inch, 2 3.5-inch	3 5.25-inch	7 5.25-inch
Disk controller location	Card	Integrated	Card	Card	EISA card
Hard disk capacity	425Mb	355Mb	240Mb	240Mb	380Mb
Hard disk options	52Mb–1.2G	105Mb–600Mb	52Mb–1.4G	52Mb–1.4G	80Mb–380Mb
Interface	INA	SCSI	INA	INA	INA
Minimal floppy disk drive configuration	1.2Mb or 1.44Mb	1.2Mb, 1.44Mb	1.2Mb, 1.44Mb	1.2Mb, 1.44Mb	1.44Mb
EXPANSION BUS					
8-bit slots	None	1	None	None	None
16-bit slots	7 (4 open)	6	None	None	2
32-bit:		1			
EISA/MCA slots	None	INA	8	8	6
Proprietary	1(none open)	INA	None	None	None
Slots free in fully configured PC	INA	5	INA	INA	INA
Parallel, serial, mouse ports on motherboard	INA	INA	None	None	None
Integrated network adapter option	INA	INA	INA	INA	None
VIDEO					
Display circuitry location	Card	Card	Card	Card	EISA card
Chip set manufacturer	S3	Tseng	S3	Tseng	S3
POWER SUPPLY					
Power supply (watts)	250	250	250	250	302
Number of device connectors	5	4	6	6	5

●—Yes ○—No N/A—Not applicable INA—Information not available

Computers

	American Super Computer 486X2/e66	Amkly 486DX2/50E	Amkly 486SX/25E	Arche Legacy 386-40	Arche Legacy 486/50DX2
Price	$$$	$$$$	$$$	$$$	$$$$
Processor/speed	486DX2/66MHz	486DX2/50MHz	486SX/25MHz	Am386/40MHz	486DX2/50MHz
Case type	Tower	Small-footprint	Small-footprint	Desktop	Desktop
Dimensions (HWD, in inches)	INA	INA	INA	INA	INA
Installed RAM	INA	INA	INA	INA	INA
Bus architecture	EISA	EISA	EISA	INA	EISA
Warranty	2 years	1 year	1 year	2 years	2 years
MOTHERBOARD					
Motherboard manufacturer	BCM	Amkly	Amkly	Arche	Arche
Chip set manufacturer	Intel	Intel	Intel	Arche	OPTi
System shadowing/video shadowing	INA	●/●	INA	●/●	●/●
BIOS version	AMI (May 1991)	Phoenix 1.00	Phoenix 1.0	AMI/Arche 1.51	AMI (July 1991)
ZIF socket	○	●	○	INA	○
Coprocessor supported	INA	INA	INA	80487	INA
MEMORY AND PROCESSOR RAM CACHE					
Installable RAM (minimum–maximum)	4Mb–64Mb	1Mb–64Mb	4Mb–64Mb	1Mb–16Mb	4Mb–80Mb
Cache controller	INA	N/A	INA	Arche	OPTi
Installed RAM cache	INA	INA	INA	INA	INA
Installable RAM cache	64K–256K	N/A	N/A	64K–128K	256K
DISK DRIVES					
Drive bays	8 5.25-inch, 1 3.5-inch	2 5.25-inch, 1 3.5-inch	2 5.25-inch, 1 3.5-inch	2 5.25-inch	3 5.25-inch
Disk controller location	EISA card	N/A	Motherboard	INA	Card
Hard disk capacity	240Mb	397Mb	345Mb	202Mb	212Mb
Hard disk options	105Mb–544Mb	40Mb–2G	40Mb–2G	40Mb–650Mb	212Mb
Interface	INA	INA	INA	INA	INA
Minimal floppy disk drive configuration	1.2Mb, 1.44Mb	1.2Mb, 1.44Mb	1.2Mb, 1.44Mb	1.2Mb	1.2Mb
EXPANSION BUS					
8-bit slots	None	None	None	1 (open)	None
16-bit slots	1	None	None	6 (3 open)	None
32-bit:					
EISA/MCA slots	6	7	7	None	8
Proprietary	1	2	2	1 (open)	None
Slots free in fully configured PC	INA	INA	INA	INA	INA
Parallel, serial, mouse ports on motherboard	None	1,2,1	1, 2, 1	INA	None
Integrated network adapter option	None	INA	INA	INA	INA
VIDEO					
Display circuitry location	EISA card	Motherboard	Motherboard	Card	Card
Chip set manufacturer	ATI	Trident	Trident	Tseng	Tseng
POWER SUPPLY					
Power supply (watts)	230	200	200	200	200
Number of device connectors	6	4	4	4	6

●—Yes ○—No N/A—Not applicable INA—Information not available

Table Continues →

Computers

	Arche Legacy 486/66DX2	Arche Legacy 486SX/25	Arche Legacy ProFile 486-33	Ares 386/40 Sonic	Ares 486-50DX2 Sonic III
Price	$$$$	$$$$	$$$$	$$	$$$
Processor/speed	486DX2/66MHz	486SX/25MHz	486/33MHz	Am386/40MHz	486DX2/50MHz
Case type	Small-footprint	Desktop	Tower	Tower	Desktop
Dimensions (HWD, in inches)	INA	INA	23.5 × 6.5 × 18.8	INA	INA
Installed RAM	INA	INA	8Mb	INA	INA
Bus architecture	ISA	ISA	INA	INA	ISA
Warranty	2 years	2 years	2 years	2 years on parts, unlimited labor	2 years
MOTHERBOARD					
Motherboard manufacturer	Arche	Arche	Arche	Technology Power	Ares
Chip set manufacturer	Arche	Arche, Siemens	Arche	VLSI	VLSI
System shadowing/video shadowing	INA	INA	●/●	●/●	●/●
BIOS version	AMI 1.57	AMI (April 1992)	AMI/Arche (September 1990)	AMI 386 Hybrid F	AMI (May 1991)
ZIF socket	○	○	INA	INA	○
Coprocessor supported	INA	INA	Weitek 4167	Weitek	INA
MEMORY AND PROCESSOR RAM CACHE					
Installable RAM (minimum–maximum)	4Mb–32Mb	4Mb–32Mb	2Mb–64Mb	1Mb–64Mb	4Mb–64Mb
Cache controller	INA	INA	Discrete logic	Northport	Northport
Installed RAM cache	INA	INA	256K	INA	INA
Installable RAM cache	128K	128K	256K	64K–256K	128K–512K
DISK DRIVES					
Drive bays	3 5.25-inch	3 5.25-inch	2 full-height, 2 half-height, 2 3.5-inch	4 5.25-inch	2 5.25-inch, 2 3.5-inch
Disk controller location	ISA card	Card	Integrated	INA	Card
Hard disk capacity	212Mb	200Mb	338Mb	210Mb	240Mb
Hard disk options	80Mb–650Mb	80Mb–650Mb	44Mb–380Mb	52Mb–665Mb	120Mb–425Mb
Interface	INA	INA	ESDI	INA	INA
Minimal floppy disk drive configuration	1.2Mb, 1.44Mb	1.44Mb	1.2Mb	1.2Mb, 1.44Mb	1.2Mb, 1.44Mb
EXPANSION BUS					
8-bit slots	1	1	2	None	None
16-bit slots	7	7	6	7 (5 open)	6
32-bit:					
EISA/MCA slots	None	None	None	None	None
Proprietary	None	None	None	1 (open)	2
Slots free in fully configured PC	INA	INA	5	INA	INA
Parallel, serial, mouse ports on motherboard	None	1, 2, 0	INA	INA	None
Integrated network adapter option	None	INA	INA	INA	INA
VIDEO					
Display circuitry location	ISA card	Card	Card	Card	Card
Chip set manufacturer	Tseng	Tseng	Tseng	Tseng	S3
POWER SUPPLY					
Power supply (watts)	200	200	220	250	200
Number of device connectors	4	4	4	4	5

●—Yes ○—No N/A—Not applicable INA—Information not available

Computers

	Ares 486-66DX2 VL-Bus	Ariel 486DX2-50	Ariel 486DX2-66VLB	Ariel 486SX/25	AST Bravo 4/66d
Price	$$$	$$$	$$$$	$$	$$$$
Processor/speed	486DX2/66MHz	486DX2/50MHz	486DX2/66MHz	486SX/25MHz	486DX2/66MHz
Case type	Desktop	Tower	Tower	Tower	Slimline
Dimensions (HWD, in inches)	INA	INA	INA	INA	6.3 × 15.3 × 16.5
Installed RAM	INA	INA	INA	INA	2Mb
Bus architecture	ISA	ISA	ISA	ISA	ISA
Warranty	2 years on parts, lifetime on labor	1 year	1 year	1 year	1 year
MOTHERBOARD					
Motherboard manufacturer	Micronics	Micronics	Micronics	Micronics	AST
Chip set manufacturer	Micronics	Micronics	Micronics	C&T, Micronics	VLSI
System shadowing/video shadowing	INA	●/●	INA	INA	INA
BIOS version	Phoenix (August 1991)	Phoenix 2.0	Phoenix LB222	Phoenix (January 1988)	AST 1.03
ZIF socket	○	○	○	○	○
Coprocessor supported	INA	INA	INA	INA	Intel
MEMORY AND PROCESSOR RAM CACHE					
Installable RAM (minimum–maximum)	4Mb–64Mb	1Mb–64Mb	4Mb–64Mb	4Mb–64Mb	2Mb–64Mb
Cache controller	INA	Micronics	INA	INA	INA
Installed RAM cache	INA	INA	INA	INA	INA
Installable RAM cache	0–256K	256K	0–256K	64K–256K	256K
DISK DRIVES					
Drive bays	4 5.25-inch, 1 3.5-inch	4 5.25-inch	7 5.25-inch, 2 3.5-inch	4 5.25-inch	4 5.25-inch
Disk controller location	Motherboard	Card	ISA card	Card	Motherboard
Hard disk capacity	240Mb	240Mb	520Mb	234Mb	340Mb
Hard disk options	127Mb–1.2G	120Mb–520Mb	212Mb–2.1G	80Mb–535Mb	120Mb–520Mb
Interface	INA	INA	INA	INA	INA
Minimal floppy disk drive configuration	Dual	1.2Mb, 1.44Mb	1.2Mb, 1.44Mb	1.2Mb, 1.44Mb	1.2Mb, 1.44Mb
EXPANSION BUS					
8-bit slots	None	None	None	None	None
16-bit slots	8	8	8	8	4
32-bit:					
EISA/MCA slots	None	None	None	None	None
Proprietary	None	1	None	None	None
Slots free in fully configured PC	INA	INA	INA	INA	INA
Parallel, serial, mouse ports on motherboard	1, 2, 0	None	2, 1, 0	None	2, 1, 1
Integrated network adapter option	None	INA	None	INA	Ethernet
VIDEO					
Display circuitry location	ISA card	Card	VESA local bus	Card	Motherboard
Chip set manufacturer	WD	Tseng	ATI	S3	Cirrus
POWER SUPPLY					
Power supply (watts)	250	250	300	250	145
Number of device connectors	5	5	4	4	4

●—Yes   ○—No   N/A—Not applicable   INA—Information not available

Table Continues →

Computers

	AST Power Premium 4/50d	Atlas 486SX/25	ATronics ATI 486B/50	ATronics ATI-486/50DX2	ATronics ATI-486-66
Price	$$$$	$$	$$$	$$	$$$
Processor/speed	486DX2/50MHz	486SX/25MHz	486/50MHz	486DX2/50MHz	486DX2/66MHz
Case type	Small-footprint	Small-footprint	Mini-tower	Tower	Small-footprint
Dimensions (HWD, in inches)	6.3 × 15.3 × 16.5	INA	INA	INA	INA
Installed RAM	4Mb	INA	INA	INA	INA
Bus architecture	EISA	ISA	INA	ISA	ISA
Warranty	1 year	1 year	1 year	1 year	1 year
MOTHERBOARD					
Motherboard manufacturer	AST	Micronics	ATI	ATronics	ATronics
Chip set manufacturer	Intel	Micronics	UMC	UMC	UMC
System shadowing/video shadowing	●/●	INA	●/●	●/●	INA
BIOS version	AST 1.01	Phoenix (January 1988)	AMI (July 1991)	AMI (July 1991)	AMI (May 1991)
ZIF socket	○	○	INA	○	○
Coprocessor supported	Intel, Weitek	Weitek	Weitek	INA	INA
MEMORY AND PROCESSOR RAM CACHE					
Installable RAM (minimum–maximum)	4Mb–80Mb	4Mb–64Mb	1Mb–64Mb	1Mb–64Mb	1Mb–64Mb
Cache controller	N/A	INA	UMC	UMC	INA
Installed RAM cache	INA	INA	INA	INA	INA
Installable RAM cache	N/A	64K–256K	64K–256K	64K–256K	32K–256K
DISK DRIVES					
Drive bays	3 5.25-inch	3 5.25-inch, 2 3.5-inch	2 5.25-inch, 2 3.5-inch	3 5.25-inch, 2 3.5-inch	3 5.25-inch, 2 3.5-inch
Disk controller location	Motherboard	Card	Card	Card	ISA card
Hard disk capacity	210Mb	210Mb	340Mb	212Mb	340Mb
Hard disk options	1Mb–210Mb	40Mb–2G	40Mb–1.2G	115Mb–500Mb	80Mb–2.4G
Interface	INA	INA	INA	INA	INA
Minimal floppy disk drive configuration	1.2Mb	1.2Mb, 1.44Mb	1.2Mb or 1.44Mb	1.2Mb, 1.44Mb	1.2Mb, 1.44Mb
EXPANSION BUS					
8-bit slots	None	None	1	1	1
16-bit slots	None	8	6 (4 open)	7	7
32-bit:					
EISA/MCA slots	6	None	None	None	None
Proprietary	None	None	1	1	1
Slots free in fully configured PC	INA	INA	INA	INA	INA
Parallel, serial, mouse ports on motherboard	1, 2, 1	1, 2, 0	INA	None	None
Integrated network adapter option	INA	INA	INA	INA	None
VIDEO					
Display circuitry location	Motherboard	Card	Card	Card	ISA card
Chip set manufacturer	WD	S3	Trident	Tseng	S3
POWER SUPPLY					
Power supply (watts)	145	230	200	250	200
Number of device connectors	4	6	5	4	4

●—Yes ○—No N/A—Not applicable INA—Information not available

Computers

	ATronics ATI 486SX-25	Austin 466DX2 WinStation	Austin 486-33E Wintower	Austin 486-33i WinStation	Austin 486 WinStation DX2-50
Price	$$	$$$	$$$	$$	$$$
Processor/speed	486SX/25MHz	486DX2/66MHz	486/33MHz	486/33MHz	486DX2/50MHz
Case type	Small-footprint	Desktop	Tower	Small-footprint	Small-footprint
Dimensions (HWD, in inches)	INA	INA	INA	INA	INA
Installed RAM	INA	INA	INA	INA	INA
Bus architecture	ISA	ISA	INA	INA	EISA
Warranty	1 year	1 year	1 year	1 year	1 year
MOTHERBOARD					
Motherboard manufacturer	ATronics	Micronics	Intel	Austin	Austin
Chip set manufacturer	UMC	Micronics	Intel	OPTi	Intel
System shadowing/video shadowing	INA	INA	●/●	●/●	●/●
BIOS version	AMI (July 1991)	Phoenix 0.10-g2-2-LB	Phoenix 1.10.33	AMI (May 1991)	AMI (May 1991)
ZIF socket	○	○	INA	INA	○
Coprocessor supported	INA	INA	INA	80487/Weitek	INA
MEMORY AND PROCESSOR RAM CACHE					
Installable RAM (minimum–maximum)	1Mb–64Mb	4Mb–64Mb	8Mb–64Mb	4Mb–32Mb	4Mb–64Mb
Cache controller	INA	INA	Intel	OPTi	Discrete logic
Installed RAM cache	INA	INA	INA	INA	INA
Installable RAM cache	64K–256K	64K–256K	64K–128K	128K	64K–256K
DISK DRIVES					
Drive bays	3 5.25-inch, 2 3.5-inch	3 5.25-inch, 2 3.5-inch	6 5.25-inch	3 5.25-inch	3 5.25-inch
Disk controller location	Card	Motherboard	Card	Integrated	Card
Hard disk capacity	211Mb	220Mb	330Mb	210Mb	200Mb
Hard disk options	116Mb–500Mb	40Mb–1.2G	330Mb–1.6G	40Mb–426Mb	40Mb–1.2G
Interface	INA	INA	INA	INA	INA
Minimal floppy disk drive configuration	1.2Mb, 1.44Mb	1.2Mb, 1.44Mb	1.2Mb, 1.44Mb	1.2Mb, 1.44Mb	1.2Mb
EXPANSION BUS					
8-bit slots	1	None	None	1 (open)	None
16-bit slots	7	8	None	6 (5 open)	None
32-bit:					
EISA/MCA slots	None	None	8 (6 open)	None	6
Proprietary	1	None	None	None	1
Slots free in fully configured PC	INA	INA	INA	INA	INA
Parallel, serial, mouse ports on motherboard	None	2, 1, 0	INA	INA	1, 2, 0
Integrated network adapter option	INA	None	INA	INA	INA
VIDEO					
Display circuitry location	Card	VESA local bus	Card	Card	Card
Chip set manufacturer	S3	ATI	Silicon Subsystems	Diamond	WD
POWER SUPPLY					
Power supply (watts)	200	200	300	200	200
Number of device connectors	3	5	7	4	5

●—Yes ○—No N/A—Not applicable INA—Information not available

Table Continues →

ZIFF-DAVIS PRESS

Computers

	Axik Ace Cache 486DX2-50	Axik Ace Cache 486SX/25	Bi-Link Desktop i486DX2/66	Blackship 486/33I	BLK 486DX2/66
Price	$$$	$$$	$$$	$$$$	$$$
Processor/speed	486DX2/50MHz	486SX/25MHz	486DX2/66MHz	486/33MHz	486DX2/66MHz
Case type	Small-footprint	Tower	Tower	Desktop	Mini-tower
Dimensions (HWD, in inches)	14 × 7 × 16	INA	INA	6.5 × 21 × 16.8	INA
Installed RAM	4Mb	4Mb	INA	8Mb	INA
Bus architecture	ISA	ISA	ISA	INA	ISA
Warranty	13 months	13 months	1 year	1 year	1 year
MOTHERBOARD					
Motherboard manufacturer	Axik	Axik	AIR	ATronics	AMI
Chip set manufacturer	Contaq	Contaq	UMC	Discrete logic	AMI
System shadowing/video shadowing	●/●	INA	INA	●/●	INA
BIOS version	AMI (December 1991)	AMI (December 1991)	AMI 27C512	AMI (September 1990)	AMI (December 1991)
ZIF socket	●	●	○	INA	○
Coprocessor supported	INA	Weitek	INA	Weitek 4167	INA
MEMORY AND PROCESSOR RAM CACHE					
Installable RAM (minimum–maximum)	1Mb–32Mb	4Mb–32Mb	1Mb–32Mb	16Mb	1Mb–32Mb
Cache controller	Contaq	INA	INA	Discrete logic	INA
Installed RAM cache	INA	INA	INA	64K	INA
Installable RAM cache	64K–256K	64K–256K	64K–256K	32K, 64K	64K–256K
DISK DRIVES					
Drive bays	3 5.25-inch, 1 3.5-inch	3 5.25-inch, 2 3.5-inch	7 5.25-inch, 1 3.5-inch	5 half-height	2 5.25-inch, 3 3.5-inch
Disk controller location	Card	Card	ISA card	Integrated	Motherboard
Hard disk capacity	212Mb	245Mb	210Mb	202Mb	213Mb
Hard disk options	40Mb–1G	40Mb–3G	120Mb–530Mb	80Mb–676Mb	40Mb–22G
Interface	INA	INA	INA	ESDI	INA
Minimal floppy disk drive configuration	1.2Mb, 1.44Mb	1.2Mb, 1.44Mb	1.2Mb, 1.44Mb	1.2Mb	1.2Mb, 1.44Mb
EXPANSION BUS					
8-bit slots	None	None	1	2	None
16-bit slots	8	8	7	5	8
32-bit:				1	
EISA/MCA slots	None	None	None	INA	None
Proprietary	1	None	None	INA	None
Slots free in fully configured PC	INA	INA	INA	6	INA
Parallel, serial, mouse ports on motherboard	None	None	None	INA	1, 2, 0
Integrated network adapter option	INA	INA	None	INA	None
VIDEO					
Display circuitry location	Card	Card	Proprietary local bus	Card	ISA card
Chip set manufacturer	S3	S3	S3	Tseng	Tseng
POWER SUPPLY					
Power supply (watts)	230	250	300	220	250
Number of device connectors	5	8	6	4	5

●—Yes ○—No N/A—Not applicable INA—Information not available

Computers

	BLK 486SX/25	Blue Star 466D2U	Blue Star 486SX/25 Desktop	BOSS 466d	BOSS 486 Model 4633
Price	$$	$$$	$$	$$$$	$$$$
Processor/speed	486SX/25MHz	486DX2/66MHz	486SX/25MHz	486DX2/66MHz	486/33MHz
Case type	Desktop	Desktop	Desktop	Mini-tower	Tower
Dimensions (HWD, in inches)	INA	INA	INA	INA	24 × 7.2 × 17.2
Installed RAM	INA	INA	INA	INA	8Mb
Bus architecture	ISA	ISA	ISA	ISA	INA
Warranty	1 year	1 year	1 year	2 years	2 years
MOTHERBOARD					
Motherboard manufacturer	Free Technology	ZEN	Zenny	AMI	AMI
Chip set manufacturer	OPTi	UMC	UMC	AMI	Discrete logic
System shadowing/video shadowing	INA	INA	INA	INA	●/●
BIOS version	AMI (June 1991)	GA-30093 (April 1991)	AMI (July 1991)	AMI (December 1991)	AMI (April 1990)
ZIF socket	○	○	○	○	INA
Coprocessor supported	INA	INA	INA	INA	Weitek 4167
MEMORY AND PROCESSOR RAM CACHE					
Installable RAM (minimum–maximum)	4Mb–32Mb	1Mb–32Mb	1Mb–64Mb	1Mb–32Mb	1Mb–32Mb
Cache controller	INA	INA	INA	INA	Discrete logic
Installed RAM cache	INA	INA	INA	INA	128K
Installable RAM cache	64K–512K	128K–256K	64K–256K	64K–256K	128K
DISK DRIVES					
Drive bays	2 5.25-inch	4 5.25-inch, 1 3.5-inch	3 5.25-inch, 2 3.5-inch	4 5.25-inch, 2 3.5-inch	5 half-height, 2 3.5-inch
Disk controller location	Card	ISA card	Card	ISA card	Integrated
Hard disk capacity	203Mb	340Mb	213Mb	245Mb	200Mb
Hard disk options	40Mb–1.7G	106Mb–1.2G	40Mb–1.2G	106Mb–535Mb	80Mb–600Mb
Interface	INA	INA	INA	INA	SCSI
Minimal floppy disk drive configuration	1.2Mb	Dual	1.2Mb, 1.44Mb	1.2Mb, 1.44Mb	1.2Mb, 1.44Mb
EXPANSION BUS					
8-bit slots	None	None	2	1	2
16-bit slots	8	8	6	7	6
32-bit:					1
EISA/MCA slots	None	None	None	None	INA
Proprietary	None	1	None	None	INA
Slots free in fully configured PC	INA	INA	INA	INA	5
Parallel, serial, mouse ports on motherboard	1, 2, 0	None	None	1, 2, 0	INA
Integrated network adapter option	INA	None	INA	None	INA
VIDEO					
Display circuitry location	Card	ISA card	Card	ISA card	Card
Chip set manufacturer	Tseng	WD	Tseng	WD	C&T
POWER SUPPLY					
Power supply (watts)	250	250	250	300	300
Number of device connectors	4	4	4	6	4

●—Yes ○—No N/A—Not applicable INA—Information not available

Table Continues →

Computers

	Broadax 486DX2-66	c² Micro Systems 386/33	c² Micro Systems Saber/50	c² Micro Systems Saber 486 EISA	c² Micro Systems Saber DX/2
Price	$$	$$$	$$$	$$$$	$$$
Processor/speed	486DX2/66MHz	386/33MHz	486/50MHz	486/33MHz	486DX2/50MHz
Case type	Desktop	Tower	Tower	Tower	Tower
Dimensions (HWD, in inches)	INA	24.8 × 7 × 16.5	INA	25.5 × 7.5 × 17.5	INA
Installed RAM	INA	N/A	INA	INA	INA
Bus architecture	ISA	INA	INA	INA	ISA
Warranty	1 year	1 year	1 year	INA	1 year
MOTHERBOARD					
Motherboard manufacturer	TMC	AIR	ERI	Free Technology	ERI
Chip set manufacturer	OPTi	C&T	Symphony	Intel	Symphony
System shadowing/video shadowing	INA	●/●	●/●	●/●	●/●
BIOS version	AMI (June 1991)	AMI BIOS (March 1989)	AMI (May 1991)	Award 4.1 (April 1990)	AMI (July 1991)
ZIF socket	○	INA	INA	INA	○
Coprocessor supported	INA	80387 or Weitek 3167	Weitek/Cyrix	INA	INA
MEMORY AND PROCESSOR RAM CACHE					
Installable RAM (minimum–maximum)	1Mb–32Mb	INA	1Mb–64Mb	1Mb–64Mb	1Mb–64Mb
Cache controller	INA	Intel 82385	Symphony	Free Technology	Symphony
Installed RAM cache	INA	32K	INA	64K	INA
Installable RAM cache	64K–256K	32K	64K–1Mb	128K, 256K	64K
DISK DRIVES					
Drive bays	3 5.25-inch, 2 3.5-inch	7 half-height	4 5.25-inch	7 half-height	4 5.25-inch, 1 3.5-inch
Disk controller location	ISA card	INA	Card	Card	Card
Hard disk capacity	212Mb	INA	340Mb	339Mb	212Mb
Hard disk options	40Mb–1.5G	350Mb–675Mb	52Mb–1.2G	40Mb–675Mb	80Mb–212Mb
Interface	INA	INA	INA	ESDI	INA
Minimal floppy disk drive configuration	1.2Mb, 1.44Mb	INA	1.2Mb, 1.44Mb	1.2Mb, 1.44Mb	1.2Mb, 1.44Mb
EXPANSION BUS					
8-bit slots	2	2	1 (open)	None	1
16-bit slots	6	5	7 (3 open)	2	7
32-bit:				6	
EISA/MCA slots	None	1	None	INA	None
Proprietary	None	N/A	None	INA	None
Slots free in fully configured PC	INA	4	INA	4	INA
Parallel, serial, mouse ports on motherboard	None	INA	INA	INA	None
Integrated network adapter option	None	INA	INA	INA	INA
VIDEO					
Display circuitry location	ISA card	Card	Card	Card	Card
Chip set manufacturer	ATI	ATI	S3	Trident	S3
POWER SUPPLY					
Power supply (watts)	200	275	250	INA	250
Number of device connectors	5	7	4	INA	5

●—Yes ○—No N/A—Not applicable INA—Information not available

Computers

	C² Micro Systems Saber 486/e DX2-66	C² Micro Systems Saber 4X25	CAF Gold 6D2	Clover 486 EM II	Clover 486 Quick-I Series
Price	$$$$	$$$	$$$	$$$$	$$$
Processor/speed	486DX2/66MHz	486SX/25MHz	486DX2/66MHz	486DX2/50MHz	486DX2/66MHz
Case type	Tower	Small-footprint	Desktop	Desktop	Small-footprint
Dimensions (HWD, in inches)	INA	INA	INA	INA	INA
Installed RAM	INA	INA	INA	INA	INA
Bus architecture	EISA	ISA	ISA	EISA	ISA
Warranty	1 year	1 year	1 year	1 year	1 year
MOTHERBOARD					
Motherboard manufacturer	BCM	ERI	CAF	Mylex	Quickpath
Chip set manufacturer	Intel	Symphony	SIS	Proprietary	OPTi
System shadowing/video shadowing	INA	INA	INA	●/●	INA
BIOS version	AMI (April 1992)	AMI (July 1991)	AMI 1.02	Mylex (October 1991)	AMI (June 1991)
ZIF socket	○	○	○	○	●
Coprocessor supported	INA	INA	INA	INA	INA
MEMORY AND PROCESSOR RAM CACHE					
Installable RAM (minimum–maximum)	1Mb–64Mb	1Mb–64Mb	1Mb–32Mb	1Mb–32Mb	512K–32Mb
Cache controller	INA	INA	INA	Intel	INA
Installed RAM cache	INA	INA	INA	INA	INA
Installable RAM cache	64K–256K	64K–1Mb	64K–256K	128K	0–256K
DISK DRIVES					
Drive bays	8 5.25-inch, 1 3.5-inch	3 5.25-inch, 1 3.5-inch	3 5.25-inch, 4 3.5-inch	2 5.25-inch, 2 3.5-inch	3 5.25-inch, 4 3.5-inch
Disk controller location	EISA card	Card	ISA card	Card	ISA card
Hard disk capacity	358Mb	245Mb	213Mb	212Mb	245Mb
Hard disk options	42Mb–2G	105Mb–340Mb	40Mb–200Mb	212Mb–1.7G	120Mb–1.2G
Interface	INA	INA	INA	INA	INA
Minimal floppy disk drive configuration	1.2Mb, 1.44Mb	1.2Mb, 1.44Mb	1.2Mb, 1.44Mb	1.2Mb, 1.44Mb	1.2Mb, 1.44Mb
EXPANSION BUS					
8-bit slots	None	1	None	None	None
16-bit slots	1	7	8	None	8
32-bit:					
EISA/MCA slots	6	None	None	8	None
Proprietary	None	None	None	None	None
Slots free in fully configured PC	INA	INA	INA	INA	INA
Parallel, serial, mouse ports on motherboard	None	None	None	None	None
Integrated network adapter option	None	INA	None	INA	None
VIDEO					
Display circuitry location	ISA card	Card	Motherboard	Card	ISA card
Chip set manufacturer	WD	S3	WD	S3	S3
POWER SUPPLY					
Power supply (watts)	250	200	200	250	200
Number of device connectors	6	4	5	6	4

●—Yes ○—No N/A—Not applicable INA—Information not available

Table Continues →

Computers

	Club Falcon 386/40	Club Falcon 450 DX2	Club Falcon 450T	Club Hawk IIITi	Comex 486DX2/66
Price	$$	$$$	$$	$$$$	$$$
Processor/speed	Am386/40MHz	486DX2/50MHz	486/50MHz	486/33MHz	486DX2/66MHz
Case type	Desktop	Tower	Tower	Tower	Desktop
Dimensions (HWD, in inches)	INA	INA	INA	25.8 × 8.5 × 20.3	INA
Installed RAM	INA	INA	INA	8Mb	INA
Bus architecture	INA	ISA	INA	INA	ISA
Warranty	1 year	1 year	1 year	1 year	2 years
MOTHERBOARD					
Motherboard manufacturer	Club	Club	Club	Club	Micronics
Chip set manufacturer	VLSI	Club/VLSI	Club/VLSI	Discrete logic	C&T/Micronics
System shadowing/video shadowing	●/○	●/●	●/●	○/○	INA
BIOS version	AMI 386 Hybrid F	AMI (March 1991)	AMI (March 1991)	AMI (April 1990)	Phoenix 0.10 g20-2
ZIF socket	INA	○	INA	INA	○
Coprocessor supported	80487/Weitek	INA	Weitek/Cyrix	Weitek 4167	INA
MEMORY AND PROCESSOR RAM CACHE					
Installable RAM (minimum–maximum)	4Mb–64Mb	4Mb–64Mb	1Mb–64Mb	16Mb	1Mb–32Mb
Cache controller	Club	Club	Club	Discrete logic	INA
Installed RAM cache	INA	INA	INA	256K	INA
Installable RAM cache	64K–256K	256K	64K–256K	64K, 256K	64K–256K
DISK DRIVES					
Drive bays	3 5.25-inch	5 5.25-inch	5 5.25-inch	9 half-height	3 5.25-inch, 2 3.5-inch
Disk controller location	2	Card	Card	Integrated	ISA card
Hard disk capacity	213Mb	240Mb	425Mb	338Mb	202Mb
Hard disk options	52Mb–340Mb	120Mb–1.2G	52Mb–1.2G	44Mb–651Mb	30Mb–670Mb
Interface	INA	INA	INA	ESDI	INA
Minimal floppy disk drive configuration	1.2Mb	1.2Mb, 1.44Mb	1.2Mb or 1.44Mb	1.2Mb	1.2Mb, 1.44Mb
EXPANSION BUS					
8-bit slots	None	None	None	None	None
16-bit slots	7 (5 open)	7	7 (5 open)	7	8
32-bit:				1	
EISA/MCA slots	None	None	None	INA	1
Proprietary	1	1	1	INA	None
Slots free in fully configured PC	INA	None	INA	5	INA
Parallel, serial, mouse ports on motherboard	INA	INA	INA	INA	None
Integrated network adapter option	INA	INA	INA	INA	None
VIDEO					
Display circuitry location	Card	Card	Card	Card	ISA card
Chip set manufacturer	Tseng	Tseng	Tseng	Tseng	ATI
POWER SUPPLY					
Power supply (watts)	200	250	250	250	250
Number of device connectors	4	6	6	5	5

●—Yes ○—No N/A—Not applicable INA—Information not available

Computers

	Comex 486SX-25	Compaq 486/33L	Compaq Deskpro 50M	Compaq Deskpro 66	Compaq Deskpro 486/33M
Price	$$	$$$$	$$$$	$$$$	$$$$
Processor/speed	486SX/25MHz	486/33MHz	486DX2/50MHz	486DX2/66MHz	486/33MHz
Case type	Small-footprint	Desktop	Small-footprint	Desktop	Desktop
Dimensions (HWD, in inches)	INA	6.5 × 19.3 × 18	6 × 17 × 15	5.9 × 6.8 × 14.8	6 × 17 × 15
Installed RAM	INA	INA	8Mb	8Mb	4Mb
Bus architecture	ISA	INA	EISA	EISA	INA
Warranty	2 years	INA	1 year	1 year	1 year
MOTHERBOARD					
Motherboard manufacturer	Micronics	Compaq	Compaq	Compaq	Compaq
Chip set manufacturer	Micronics	Intel	Compaq	Intel	Compaq
System shadowing/video shadowing	INA	○/○	●/●	INA	●/●
BIOS version	Phoenix (January 1988)	Compaq 386E1 (August 1990)	Compaq (February 1992)	Compaq 66/M (June 1992)	Compaq 08.14.91
ZIF socket	○	INA	○	○	INA
Coprocessor supported	INA	INA	Weitek	Intel, Weitek	Intel
MEMORY AND PROCESSOR RAM CACHE					
Installable RAM (minimum–maximum)	4Mb–64Mb	4Mb–100Mb	8Mb–64Mb	8Mb–64Mb	4Mb–64Mb
Cache controller	INA	Discrete logic	Compaq	INA	None
Installed RAM cache	INA	128K	INA	INA	INA
Installable RAM cache	64K–256K	None	256K	256K	N/A
DISK DRIVES					
Drive bays	2 5.25-inch, 1 3.5-inch	5 half-height	1 5.25-inch, 1 3.5-inch	3 5.25-inch, 1 3.5-inch	3 5.25-inch
Disk controller location	Card	Card	Motherboard	Motherboard	Integrated
Hard disk capacity	212Mb	320Mb	212Mb	211Mb	200Mb
Hard disk options	212Mb–670Mb	150Mb–325Mb	60Mb–510Mb	84Mb–510Mb	120Mb–2.6G
Interface	INA	ESDI	INA	INA	INA
Minimal floppy disk drive configuration	1.2Mb, 1.44Mb	1.2Mb, 1.44Mb	1.2Mb, 1.44Mb	1.44Mb	1.44Mb
EXPANSION BUS					
8-bit slots	None	None	None	None	None
16-bit slots	8	None	None	None	None
32-bit:		9			
EISA/MCA slots	None	INA	5	5	5 (5 open)
Proprietary	1	INA	2	2	2 (2 open)
Slots free in fully configured PC	INA	3	INA	INA	INA
Parallel, serial, mouse ports on motherboard	None	INA	1, 2, 1	1, 2, 1	1, 2, 1
Integrated network adapter option	INA	INA	INA	None	INA
VIDEO					
Display circuitry location	Card	Card	Card	EISA card	Card
Chip set manufacturer	Tseng	Xilinx	Compaq	Compaq	Compaq
POWER SUPPLY					
Power supply (watts)	250	INA	240	240	240
Number of device connectors	5	INA	4	4	4

●—Yes   ○—No   N/A—Not applicable   INA—Information not available

Table Continues →

Computers

	Compaq Deskpro 486/50L	Compaq Deskpro 486S/25M	CompuAdd 433E Tower	CompuAdd 466E	CompuAdd Express 466DX2 Scalable
Price	$$$$	$$$	$$$	$$$$	$$$
Processor/speed	486/50MHz	486SX/25MHz	486/33MHz	486DX2/66MHz	486DX2/66MHz
Case type	Desktop	Small-footprint	Tower	Desktop	Slimline
Dimensions (HWD, in inches)	INA	INA	INA	INA	INA
Installed RAM	INA	INA	INA	INA	INA
Bus architecture	INA	EISA	INA	EISA	ISA
Warranty	1 year	1 year	1 year	1 year	1 year
MOTHERBOARD					
Motherboard manufacturer	Compaq	Compaq	CompuAdd	CompuAdd	CompuAdd
Chip set manufacturer	Compaq	Compaq	Intel	Intel	OPTi
System shadowing/video shadowing	●/●	INA	●/●	INA	INA
BIOS version	Compaq	Compaq (February 1992)	Phoenix 1.10	Phoenix 1.01	AMI/OPTi DXBB-F
ZIF socket	INA	○	INA	○	○
Coprocessor supported	None	INA	80487/Weitek	INA	INA
MEMORY AND PROCESSOR RAM CACHE					
Installable RAM (minimum–maximum)	8Mb–104Mb	4Mb–64Mb	4Mb–64Mb	4Mb–64Mb	1Mb–32Mb
Cache controller	Intel	INA	Proprietary	INA	INA
Installed RAM cache	INA	INA	INA	INA	INA
Installable RAM cache	256K	N/A	256K	256K	128K
DISK DRIVES					
Drive bays	3 5.25-inch	1 5.25-inch, 2 3.5-inch	4 5.25-inch	2 5.25-inch, 5 3.5-inch	1 5.25-inch, 2 3.5-inch
Disk controller location	Motherboard	Motherboard	Card	EISA card	Motherboard
Hard disk capacity	340Mb	212Mb	200Mb	212Mb	200Mb
Hard disk options	120Mb–510Mb	60Mb–510Mb	80Mb–1.2G	80Mb–500Mb	80Mb–340Mb
Interface	INA	INA	INA	INA	INA
Minimal floppy disk drive configuration	1.2Mb, 1.44Mb	1.44Mb	1.2Mb, 1.44Mb	1.2Mb, 1.44Mb	1.2Mb, 1.44Mb
EXPANSION BUS					
8-bit slots	None	None	None	None	2
16-bit slots	None	None	None	None	3
32-bit:					
EISA/MCA slots	8 (7 open)	5	8 (6 open)	8	None
Proprietary	2	2	None	None	None
Slots free in fully configured PC	INA	INA	INA	INA	INA
Parallel, serial, mouse ports on motherboard	INA	1, 2, 1	INA	None	1, 2, 0
Integrated network adapter option	INA	INA	INA	None	None
VIDEO					
Display circuitry location	Card	Card	Card	EISA card	Motherboard
Chip set manufacturer	Compaq	Compaq	Tseng	WD	Tseng
POWER SUPPLY					
Power supply (watts)	300	240	300	200	150
Number of device connectors	7	4	9	5	5

●—Yes   ○—No   N/A—Not applicable   INA—Information not available

Computers

	Compudyne 4DX/250	Compudyne 4SX/25	Computer Market Place Ultra 486-33	Computer Sales Professional Pro 486DX2/50	Computer Sales Professional Pro 486SX/25
Price	$$	$$	$$$	$$	$$
Processor/speed	486DX2/50MHz	486SX/25MHz	486/33MHz	486DX2/50MHz	486SX/25MHz
Case type	Small-footprint	Small-footprint	Tower	Tower	Small-footprint
Dimensions (HWD, in inches)	INA	INA	25.5 × 7.5 × 17.3	18.8 × 8.9 × 16.8	6 × 15.5 × 15.5
Installed RAM	INA	INA	8Mb	8Mb	4Mb
Bus architecture	ISA	ISA	INA	ISA	ISA
Warranty	1 year	1 year	1 year; 18 months on motherboard	1 year	1 year
MOTHERBOARD					
Motherboard manufacturer	Compudyne	Compudyne	Cache	Symphony	Computer Sales Professional
Chip set manufacturer	UMC	ACC Micro	OPTi	Symphony	VLSI
System shadowing/video shadowing	●/●	INA	●/●	●/●	INA
BIOS version	AMI 1.1	AMI486 1.0	BAT 486 1.07 (August 1990)	Diamond 4.23	AMI (July 1991)
ZIF socket	○	○	INA	○	○
Coprocessor supported	INA	INA	None	Intel	Intel
MEMORY AND PROCESSOR RAM CACHE					
Installable RAM (minimum–maximum)	1Mb–64Mb	1Mb–32Mb	16Mb	1Mb–32Mb	4Mb–32Mb
Cache controller	UMC	INA	OPTi	DFI	INA
Installed RAM cache	INA	INA	128K	INA	INA
Installable RAM cache	128K–256K	N/A	128K	256K–1Mb	256K
DISK DRIVES					
Drive bays	3 5.25-inch	3 5.25-inch	6 half-height	6 5.25-inch, 5 3.5-inch	3 5.25-inch, 1 3.5-inch
Disk controller location	Card	Card	Card	Card	Card
Hard disk capacity	212Mb	200Mb	211Mb	121Mb	212Mb
Hard disk options	120Mb–330Mb	80Mb–200Mb	106Mb–676Mb	80Mb–200Mb	120Mb–200Mb
Interface	INA	INA	IDE	INA	INA
Minimal floppy disk drive configuration	1.2Mb, 1.44Mb	1.2Mb, 1.44Mb	1.2Mb, 1.44Mb	1.2Mb, 1.44Mb	1.2Mb, 1.44Mb
EXPANSION BUS					
8-bit slots	2	None	1	None	None
16-bit slots	5	6	7	8	8
32-bit:					
EISA/MCA slots	None	None	None	None	None
Proprietary	1	None	None	None	1
Slots free in fully configured PC	INA	INA	5	INA	INA
Parallel, serial, mouse ports on motherboard	1, 2, 0	1, 2, 0	INA	1, 2, 0	1, 2, 0
Integrated network adapter option	INA	INA	INA	INA	INA
VIDEO					
Display circuitry location	Card	Card	Card	Card	Card
Chip set manufacturer	S3	WD	Xilinx	Tseng	WD
POWER SUPPLY					
Power supply (watts)	200	200	220	200	200
Number of device connectors	5	5	6	5	5

●—Yes   ○—No   N/A—Not applicable   INA—Information not available

Table Continues →

Computers

	Copam 486SXB/25	Comtrade 486 EISA Dream Machine	Comtrade 486 EISA WinStation	CORE Model 95	CSS MaxSys
Price	$$$	$$$	$$$	$$$$$	$$$$
Processor/speed	486SX/25MHz	486DX2/66MHz	486DX2/50MHz	486SX/25MHz	386/33MHz
Case type	Small-footprint	Tower	Tower	Tower	Tower
Dimensions (HWD, in inches)	INA	INA	INA	INA	25 × 7.5 × 16.5
Installed RAM	INA	INA	INA	INA	N/A
Bus architecture	ISA	EISA	EISA	MCA	INA
Warranty	1 year	2 years on parts, lifetime on labor	2 years	1 year	1 year
MOTHERBOARD					
Motherboard manufacturer	Copam	ECS	Elisa Technology	IBM	CSS Laboratories
Chip set manufacturer	UMC	SIS	OPTi	IBM	CSS Laboratories
System shadowing/video shadowing	INA	INA	●/●	INA	●/●
BIOS version	Phoenix 1.01	AMI (December 1991)	Award (September 1989)	IBM (March 1992)	AMI BIOS (3.04D) 3.0 (April 1989)
ZIF socket	○	○	○	○	INA
Coprocessor supported	INA	INA	INA	INA	80387
MEMORY AND PROCESSOR RAM CACHE					
Installable RAM (minimum–maximum)	1Mb–64Mb	1Mb–128Mb	4Mb–32Mb	8Mb–64Mb	INA
Cache controller	INA	INA	OPTi	INA	Intel 82385
Installed RAM cache	INA	INA	INA	INA	64K
Installable RAM cache	64K–256K	64K–256K	256K	N/A	64K
DISK DRIVES					
Drive bays	3 5.25-inch	3 5.25-inch, 5 3.5-inch	3 5.25-inch, 2 3.5-inch	3 5.25-inch, 2 3.5-inch	5 half-height
Disk controller location	Motherboard	EISA card	Card	Card	INA
Hard disk capacity	210Mb	212Mb	240Mb	520Mb	INA
Hard disk options	40Mb–310Mb	130Mb–510Mb	130Mb–1G	520Mb–4G	150Mb–600Mb
Interface	INA	INA	INA	INA	INA
Minimal floppy disk drive configuration	1.2Mb, 1.44Mb	1.2Mb, 1.44Mb	1.2Mb, 1.44Mb	1.44Mb	INA
EXPANSION BUS					
8-bit slots	None	None	None	None	3
16-bit slots	5	None	None	None	7
32-bit:					
EISA/MCA slots	None	7	7	8	2
Proprietary	None	None	3	1	N/A
Slots free in fully configured PC	INA	INA	INA	INA	7
Parallel, serial, mouse ports on motherboard	1, 2, 0	None	None	1, 1, 1	INA
Integrated network adapter option	INA	None	INA	INA	INA
VIDEO					
Display circuitry location	Motherboard	ISA card	Card	Card	Card
Chip set manufacturer	Trident	WD	S3	STB	Video Seven
POWER SUPPLY					
Power supply (watts)	160	230	230	335	270
Number of device connectors	4	5	4	3	6

●—Yes   ○—No   N/A—Not applicable   INA—Information not available

	CSS Preferred 425/50 GE	CUBE 425ATX Upgradable System	CUI Advantage 486–50CX	CyberMax 386/40	Dataworld Data 486-25
Price	$$$	$$$	$$$	$	$$$
Processor/speed	486DX2/50MHz	486SX/25MHz	486/50MHz	Am386/40MHz	486/25MHz
Case type	Desktop	Mini-tower	Tower	Small-footprint	Desktop
Dimensions (HWD, in inches)	INA	INA	INA	INA	6.5 × 21 × 16.5
Installed RAM	INA	INA	INA	INA	INA
Bus architecture	EISA	ISA	INA	INA	INA
Warranty	1 year	1 year	1 year	1 year	1 year
MOTHERBOARD					
Motherboard manufacturer	CSS	Deico	CUI	Fountain	Dataworld
Chip set manufacturer	Intel	Symphony	Symphony	Intel/VLSI	Intel
System shadowing/video shadowing	○/○	INA	●/●	●/●	●/●
BIOS version	AMI (May 1991)	AMI (December 1991)	AMI (May 1991)	Quadtel 3.05.07	AMI EPOB-1131-040990-K8
ZIF socket	○	○	INA	INA	INA
Coprocessor supported	INA	INA	Weitek	80487/Weitek	Weitek
MEMORY AND PROCESSOR RAM CACHE					
Installable RAM (minimum–maximum)	4Mb–64Mb	1Mb–64Mb	1Mb–64Mb	1Mb–31Mb	1Mb–16Mb
Cache controller	Intel	INA	Symphony	Intel	OPTi
Installed RAM cache	INA	INA	INA	INA	INA
Installable RAM cache	64K–128K	64K–256K	64K–256K	16K	128K
DISK DRIVES					
Drive bays	3 5.25-inch	2 5.25-inch, 2 3.5-inch	6 5.25-inch	3 5.25-inch, 1 3.5-inch	5 half-height
Disk controller location	Motherboard	Motherboard	Card	1	Card
Hard disk capacity	202Mb	212Mb	340Mb	210Mb	210Mb
Hard disk options	202Mb–1.2G	120Mb–540Mb	52Mb–1.2G	210Mb–380Mb	40Mb–676Mb
Interface	INA	INA	INA	INA	INA
Minimal floppy disk drive configuration	1.2Mb, 1.44Mb	1.2Mb, 1.44Mb	1.2Mb, 1.44Mb	1.2Mb, 1.44Mb	1.2Mb
EXPANSION BUS					
8-bit slots	None	1	None	None	None
16-bit slots	None	6	8 (5 open)	8 (6 open)	6 (4 open)
32-bit:					
EISA/MCA slots	7	None	None	None	None
Proprietary	1	None	None	None	2 (2 open)
Slots free in fully configured PC	INA	INA	INA	INA	INA
Parallel, serial, mouse ports on motherboard	1, 2, 1	1, 2, 1	INA	INA	INA
Integrated network adapter option	INA	INA	INA	INA	INA
VIDEO					
Display circuitry location	Card	Card	Card	Card	Card
Chip set manufacturer	S3	S3	Tseng	Tseng	Tseng
POWER SUPPLY					
Power supply (watts)	300	250	280	200	200
Number of device connectors	6	5	5	5	4

●—Yes ○—No N/A—Not applicable INA—Information not available   **Table Continues** →

Computers

	Dataworld Data 486/DX2-50	Dataworld Data 486i EISA	Deico Predator 486DX2/50	Deico Predator 486SX/25	Dell 466DE/2
Price	$$$	$$$$	$$$	$$	$$$$
Processor/speed	486DX2/50MHz	486/33MHz	486DX2/50MHz	486SX/25MHz	486DX2/66MHz
Case type	Tower	Tower	Small-footprint	Small-footprint	Small-footprint
Dimensions (HWD, in inches)	INA	24.4 × 6.8 × 27	INA	INA	INA
Installed RAM	INA	INA	INA	INA	INA
Bus architecture	ISA	INA	ISA	ISA	EISA
Warranty	1 year	INA	1 year	1 year, 2 years for motherboard	1 year
MOTHERBOARD					
Motherboard manufacturer	ELT	Intel	Deico	Deico	Dell
Chip set manufacturer	ETEQ, SIS	Intel	Symphony	C&T, Symphony	Dell
System shadowing/video shadowing	●/●	●/●	●/●	INA	INA
BIOS version	AMI (May 1991)	Phoenix (January 1991)	AMI 1.1	AMI 1.1	Phoenix/Dell (A06)
ZIF socket	○	INA	●	○	○
Coprocessor supported	INA	INA	INA	Intel	INA
MEMORY AND PROCESSOR RAM CACHE					
Installable RAM (minimum–maximum)	1Mb–64Mb	4Mb–64Mb	1Mb–64Mb	1Mb–64Mb	4Mb–96Mb
Cache controller	ETEQ	N/A	Symphony	INA	INA
Installed RAM cache	INA	N/A	INA	INA	INA
Installable RAM cache	64K–256K	N/A	128K	64K–256K	128K
DISK DRIVES					
Drive bays	3 5.25-inch, 2 3.5-inch	8 half-height	3 5.25-inch, 2 3.5-inch	3 5.25-inch, 2 3.5-inch	3 5.25-inch, 1 3.5-inch
Disk controller location	Card	Card	Motherboard	Motherboard	Motherboard
Hard disk capacity	212Mb	322Mb	200Mb	200Mb	230Mb
Hard disk options	212Mb–500Mb	120Mb–676Mb	80Mb–200Mb	40Mb–1G	80Mb–1.4G
Interface	INA	ESDI	INA	IDE	INA
Minimal floppy disk drive configuration	1.2Mb, 1.44Mb	1.2Mb, 1.44Mb	1.2Mb, 1.44Mb	1.2Mb, 1.44Mb	1.2Mb, 1.44Mb
EXPANSION BUS					
8-bit slots	None	None	1	1	None
16-bit slots	7	None	6	6	None
32-bit:		10			
EISA/MCA slots	None	INA	None	None	6
Proprietary	None	INA	None	None	None
Slots free in fully configured PC	INA	8	1, 2, 1	INA	INA
Parallel, serial, mouse ports on motherboard	None	INA	INA	1, 2, 1	2, 1, 1
Integrated network adapter option	INA	INA	INA	INA	None
VIDEO					
Display circuitry location	Card	Card	Card	Card	ISA card
Chip set manufacturer	S3	Tseng	NCR	NCR	ATI
POWER SUPPLY					
Power supply (watts)	230	INA	200	200	224
Number of device connectors	5	INA	6	6	4

●—Yes   ○—No   N/A—Not applicable   INA—Information not available

Computers

	Dell PowerLine 420DE	Dell PowerLine 433DE	Dell PowerLine 450DE	Dell System 425 TE	Dell System 486D/50
Price	$$$	$$$$	$$$$	$$$$	$$$
Processor/speed	486SX/20MHz	486/33MHz	486/50MHz	486/25MHz	486DX2/50MHz
Case type	Small-footprint	Small-footprint	Small-footprint	Tower	Small-footprint
Dimensions (HWD, in inches)	INA	6 × 16 × 16	6 × 16 × 16	24 × 7.6 × 22.3	INA
Installed RAM	INA	8Mb	8Mb	INA	INA
Bus architecture	INA	EISA	EISA	INA	ISA
Warranty	1 year	1 year	1 year	1 year	1 year
MOTHERBOARD					
Motherboard manufacturer	Dell	Dell	Dell	Dell	Dell
Chip set manufacturer	Dell/Intel	Dell/Intel	Dell/Intel	Intel	VLSI
System shadowing/video shadowing	○/●	●/●	●/●	●/●	●/●
BIOS version	Dell/Phoenix 1.00 A03	Phoenix/Dell 1.1	Phoenix 80486 Plus A06	Phoenix 1.00 A02	Phoenix 1.10A07
ZIF socket	INA	INA	INA	INA	○
Coprocessor supported	80487	80487/Weitek	Weitek	Weitek	INA
MEMORY AND PROCESSOR RAM CACHE					
Installable RAM (minimum–maximum)	4Mb–48Mb	4Mb–96Mb	4Mb–96Mb	4Mb–64Mb	4Mb–64Mb
Cache controller	None	Dell	Dell Asic	None	N/A
Installed RAM cache	INA	INA	INA	INA	INA
Installable RAM cache	N/A	128K	128K	N/A	None
DISK DRIVES					
Drive bays	3 5.25-inch	3 5.25-inch	3 5.25-inch	11 half-height	3 5.25-inch
Disk controller location	Integrated	Integrated	Motherboard	Card	Motherboard
Hard disk capacity	200Mb	202Mb	345Mb	190Mb	240Mb
Hard disk options	80Mb–650Mb	80Mb–650Mb	230Mb–500Mb	80Mb–650Mb	50Mb–1.4G
Interface	INA	INA	INA	INA	INA
Minimal floppy disk drive configuration	1.2Mb, 1.44Mb	1.2Mb, 1.44Mb	1.2Mb, 1.44Mb	1.2Mb, 1.44Mb	1.2Mb, 1.44Mb
EXPANSION BUS					
8-bit slots	None	None	None	None	None
16-bit slots	None	None	None	None	6
32-bit:					
EISA/MCA slots	6 (6 open)	6 (6 open)	6 (5 open)	8 (7 open)	None
Proprietary	1 (open)	1	1 (open)	None	None
Slots free in fully configured PC	INA	INA	INA	INA	INA
Parallel, serial, mouse ports on motherboard	INA	1, 2, 1	1, 2, 1	INA	1, 2, 1
Integrated network adapter option	INA	INA	INA	INA	INA
VIDEO					
Display circuitry location	Motherboard	Motherboard	Motherboard	Motherboard	Motherboard
Chip set manufacturer	Western Digital	Western Digital	Tseng	WD	Paradise/WD
POWER SUPPLY					
Power supply (watts)	220	224	224	300	224
Number of device connectors	5	4	4	6	5

●—Yes ○—No N/A—Not applicable INA—Information not available

Table Continues →

Computers

	Dell System 486D/25	DFI 486-66DX2	DFI Diamond Series Model 425SX	Diamond 486-33	Diamond DT 486DX2/50
Price	$$$	$$$	$$	$$$	$$
Processor/speed	486SX/25MHz	486DX2/66MHz	486SX/25MHz	486/33MHz	486DX2/50MHz
Case type	Small-footprint	Tower	Small-footprint	Tower	Mini-tower
Dimensions (HWD, in inches)	INA	INA	INA	25.5 × 7.5 × 17.5	INA
Installed RAM	INA	INA	INA	8Mb	INA
Bus architecture	ISA	ISA	ISA	INA	ISA
Warranty	1 year	1 year	1 year	15 months	15 months
MOTHERBOARD					
Motherboard manufacturer	Dell	DFI	DFI	AMI	Dash
Chip set manufacturer	VLSI	UMC	UMC	C&T	OPTi
System shadowing/video shadowing	INA	INA	INA	●/●	●/●
BIOS version	Phoenix (February 1992)	AMI (July 1991)	AMI (July 1991)	AMI (April 1990)	AMI (June 1991)
ZIF socket	○	○	○	INA	○
Coprocessor supported	INA	INA	INA	Weitek 4167	INA
MEMORY AND PROCESSOR RAM CACHE					
Installable RAM (minimum–maximum)	4Mb–64Mb	1Mb–32Mb	1Mb–64Mb	24Mb	1Mb–64Mb
Cache controller	INA	INA	INA	Discrete logic	OPTi
Installed RAM cache	INA	INA	INA	128K	INA
Installable RAM cache	N/A	32K–256K	64K–256K	128K	64K–256K
DISK DRIVES					
Drive bays	3 5.25-inch	6 5.25-inch	2 5.25-inch, 1 3.5-inch	6 half-height	3 5.25-inch, 1 3.5-inch
Disk controller location	Motherboard	ISA card	Card	Integrated	Card
Hard disk capacity	245Mb	202Mb	212Mb	360Mb	202Mb
Hard disk options	80Mb–1.4G	200Mb–675Mb	212Mb	100Mb–750Mb	202Mb–1.5G
Interface	INA	INA	INA	ESDI	INA
Minimal floppy disk drive configuration	1.2Mb, 1.44Mb	1.2Mb, 1.44Mb	1.2Mb, 1.44Mb	1.2Mb, 1.44Mb	1.2Mb, 1.44Mb
EXPANSION BUS					
8-bit slots	None	None	2	1	None
16-bit slots	6	7	5	6	8
32-bit:				1	
EISA/MCA slots	None	None	None	INA	None
Proprietary	None	1	1	INA	1
Slots free in fully configured PC	INA	INA	INA	5	None
Parallel, serial, mouse ports on motherboard	1, 2, 1	None	None	INA	INA
Integrated network adapter option	INA	None	INA	INA	INA
VIDEO					
Display circuitry location	Motherboard	UBSA local bus	Card	Card	Card
Chip set manufacturer	WD	Tseng	Tseng	Tseng	Tseng
POWER SUPPLY					
Power supply (watts)	224	250	200	220	200
Number of device connectors	4	5	6	6	5

●—Yes   ○—No   N/A—Not applicable   INA—Information not available

Computers

	Diamond DT 486SX-25	Diamond DX2-66	Digital DECpc 452ST	Digital DECpc 466d2 LP	DT 486-50
Price	$$	$$$	$$$$	$$$	$$
Processor/speed	486SX/25MHz	486DX2/66MHz	486DX2/50MHz	486DX2/66MHz	486/50MHz
Case type	Small-footprint	Tower	Mini-tower	Slimline	Tower
Dimensions (HWD, in inches)	INA	INA	18 × 7 × 19	3.5 × 16 × 15.6	INA
Installed RAM	INA	INA	4Mb	4Mb	INA
Bus architecture	ISA	EISA	EISA	ISA	INA
Warranty	15 months	15 months on parts, 2 years on labor	1 year	1 year	15–24 months

MOTHERBOARD

Motherboard manufacturer	S&A Laboratory	S&A Laboratory	Intel	Digital	AIR
Chip set manufacturer	OPTi	OPTi	Intel	C&T/OPTi	Intel, SIS
System shadowing/video shadowing	INA	INA	●/●	INA	○/●
BIOS version	Phoenix (April 1990)	AMI (July 1991)	Phoenix 1.00	Phoenix 1.01.02	Phoenix 1.01.04
ZIF socket	○	○	○	○	INA
Coprocessor supported	INA	INA	Weitek	Intel	Weitek

MEMORY AND PROCESSOR RAM CACHE

Installable RAM (minimum–maximum)	1Mb–32Mb	1Mb–128Mb	4Mb–192Mb	4Mb–64Mb	1Mb–64Mb
Cache controller	INA	INA	Intel	INA	Discrete logic
Installed RAM cache	INA	INA	INA	INA	INA
Installable RAM cache	N/A	64K–512K	64K–128K	128K–256K	64K–256K

DISK DRIVES

Drive bays	3 5.25-inch, 2 3.5-inch	3 5.25-inch, 4 3.5-inch	3 5.25-inch, 1 3.5-inch	4 3.5-inch	4 5.25-inch, 2 3.5-inch
Disk controller location	Card	EISA card	Motherboard	Motherboard	Card
Hard disk capacity	213Mb	245Mb	852Mb	240Mb	360Mb
Hard disk options	40Mb–1.7G	80Mb–1.2G	105Mb–852Mb	52Mb–426Mb	80Mb–3G
Interface	INA	INA	INA	INA	INA
Minimal floppy disk drive configuration	1.2Mb, 1.44Mb	1.2Mb, 1.44Mb	1.2Mb, 1.44Mb	1.44Mb	1.2Mb, 1.44Mb

EXPANSION BUS

8-bit slots	2	None	None	None	None
16-bit slots	6	None	None	3	None
32-bit:					
EISA/MCA slots	None	8	6	None	8 (6 open)
Proprietary	None	None	2	None	None
Slots free in fully configured PC	INA	INA	INA	INA	INA
Parallel, serial, mouse ports on motherboard	None	None	1, 2, 1	1, 2, 1	INA
Integrated network adapter option	INA	None	INA	None	INA

VIDEO

Display circuitry location	Card	ISA card	Card	Proprietary local bus	Card
Chip set manufacturer	S3	ATI	WD	S3	Tseng

POWER SUPPLY

Power supply (watts)	200	200	254	146	300
Number of device connectors	4	4	6	4	7

●—Yes   ○—No   N/A—Not applicable   INA—Information not available

Table Continues →

Computers

	DTK FEAT-3300	DTx Voyager Model 425S	Dynamic Decisions Dynex 486	Dyna Work Master 486 33 Cache	Dyna Work Master 486 33 EISA
Price	$$	$$$	$$$$	$$$$	$$$$
Processor/speed	486/33MHz	486SX/25MHz	486/33MHz	486/33MHz	486/33MHz
Case type	Tower	Small-footprint	Tower	Tower	Tower
Dimensions (HWD, in inches)	INA	INA	25.5 × 7.5 × 17.5	24.3 × 7.3 × 16.5	26 × 11 × 18
Installed RAM	INA	INA	8Mb	8Mb	INA
Bus architecture	INA	ISA	INA	INA	INA
Warranty	1 year	1 year	1 year; 9 months for hard disk	1 year	INA

MOTHERBOARD

Motherboard manufacturer	DTK	AMI	AMI	AIR	AIR
Chip set manufacturer	Discrete logic	AMI	C&T	C&T, discrete logic	Intel
System shadowing/video shadowing	○/○	INA	●/●	●/●	●/●
BIOS version	DTK 4.26	AMI (December 1991)	AMI (April 1990)	AMI (May 1990)	Phoenix 1.04 (October 1990)
ZIF socket	INA	○	INA	INA	INA
Coprocessor supported	80487/Weitek	INA	Weitek 4167	Weitek 4167	INA

MEMORY AND PROCESSOR RAM CACHE

Installable RAM (minimum–maximum)	1Mb–16Mb	1Mb–32Mb	32Mb	1Mb–16Mb	8Mb–64Mb
Cache controller	Discrete logic	INA	Discrete logic	Discrete logic	Discrete logic
Installed RAM cache	INA	INA	128K	256K	256K
Installable RAM cache	64K–256K	64K–256K	128K	256K	64K

DISK DRIVES

Drive bays	3 5.25-inch	3 5.25-inch, 2 3.5-inch	6 half-height	6 half-height	10 half-height
Disk controller location	Integrated	Card	Card	Integrated	Card
Hard disk capacity	240Mb	245Mb	213Mb	320Mb	320Mb
Hard disk options	40Mb–800Mb	120Mb–425Mb	300Mb	106Mb–383Mb	40Mb–600Mb
Interface	INA	INA	IDE	ESDI	ESDI
Minimal floppy disk drive configuration	1.2Mb, 1.44Mb	1.2Mb, 1.44Mb	1.2Mb, 1.44Mb	1.2Mb, 1.44Mb	1.2Mb, 1.44Mb

EXPANSION BUS

8-bit slots	1 (open)	1	1	None	None
16-bit slots	6 (4 open)	7	6	8	None
32-bit:			1		8
EISA/MCA slots	None	None	INA	None	INA
Proprietary	1 (open)	None	INA	None	INA
Slots free in fully configured PC	INA	INA	5	3	5
Parallel, serial, mouse ports on motherboard	INA	1, 2, 0	INA	INA	INA
Integrated network adapter option	INA	INA	INA	INA	INA

VIDEO

Display circuitry location	Card	Card	Card	Card	Card
Chip set manufacturer	Tseng	Tseng	Tseng	Tseng	Tseng

POWER SUPPLY

Power supply (watts)	250	200	230	250	INA
Number of device connectors	5	6	4	4	INA

●—Yes   ○—No   N/A—Not applicable   INA—Information not available

Computers

	Edge 486 DX2-50	Edge 466 Magnum	Eltech Model 486-33	Eltech Model 3400	Eltech Model 4200
Price	$$$	$$$	$$$	$$	$$
Processor/speed	486DX2/50MHz	486DX2/66MHz	486/33MHz	Am386/40MHz	486SX/25MHz
Case type	Small-footprint	Slimline	Desktop	Small-footprint	Small-footprint
Dimensions (HWD, in inches)	INA	INA	6.8 × 21 × 16.3	INA	INA
Installed RAM	INA	INA	8Mb	INA	INA
Bus architecture	ISA	EISA	INA	INA	ISA
Warranty	1 year	1 year	1 year	1 year	1 year
MOTHERBOARD					
Motherboard manufacturer	ECS	ECS	AMI	Eltech	Eltech
Chip set manufacturer	UMC	SIS	Discrete logic	OPTi	Symphony
System shadowing/video shadowing	●/●	INA	●/●	●/●	INA
BIOS version	AMI 1.1	AMI 1.0	AMI (April 1990)	Mr. BIOS 1.0E	AMI (January 1992)
ZIF socket	○	○	INA	INA	○
Coprocessor supported	INA	INA	Weitek 4167	80487/Weitek	INA
MEMORY AND PROCESSOR RAM CACHE					
Installable RAM (minimum–maximum)	1Mb–64Mb	1Mb–128Mb	2Mb–32Mb	1Mb–64Mb	1Mb–64Mb
Cache controller	UMC	INA	Discrete logic	OPTi	INA
Installed RAM cache	INA	INA	128K	INA	INA
Installable RAM cache	64K–256K	64K–256K	128K	64K–128K	N/A
DISK DRIVES					
Drive bays	3 5.25-inch	3 5.25-inch, 2 3.5-inch	5 half-height	3 5.25-inch, 2 3.5-inch	3 5.25-inch, 2 3.5-inch
Disk controller location	Card	EISA card	Integrated	None	Card
Hard disk capacity	240Mb	213Mb	314Mb	210Mb	202Mb
Hard disk options	80Mb–1.2G	213Mb–1.2G	600Mb	40Mb–1G	80Mb–1G
Interface	INA	INA	SCSI	INA	INA
Minimal floppy disk drive configuration	1.2Mb, 1.44Mb	Dual	1.2Mb, 1.44Mb	1.2Mb	1.2Mb, 1.44Mb
EXPANSION BUS					
8-bit slots	2	None	2	None	1
16-bit slots	6	7	6	7 (6 open)	7
32-bit:			1		
EISA/MCA slots	None	None	INA	None	None
Proprietary	1	None	INA	1 (open)	None
Slots free in fully configured PC	INA	INA	5	INA	INA
Parallel, serial, mouse ports on motherboard	None	None	INA	INA	None
Integrated network adapter option	INA	None	INA	INA	INA
VIDEO					
Display circuitry location	Card	Proprietary local bus	Card	Card	Card
Chip set manufacturer	S3	S3	Tseng	Trident	S3
POWER SUPPLY					
Power supply (watts)	200	200	200	200	200
Number of device connectors	7	5	4	5	4

●—Yes ○—No N/A—Not applicable INA—Information not available

Table Continues →

Computers

	Eltech Model 4500 DX2	EPS 486-50DX EISA	EPS 80486–50	EPS ISA 486 DX2/66	Epson Equity 486DX2/50 Plus
Price	$$	$$$	$$$	$$$	$$$
Processor/speed	486DX2/50MHz	486DX2/50MHz	486/50MHz	486DX2/66MHz	486DX2/50MHz
Case type	Small-footprint	Tower	Tower	Small-footprint	Desktop
Dimensions (HWD, in inches)	INA	INA	INA	INA	INA
Installed RAM	INA	INA	INA	4Mb	INA
Bus architecture	ISA	EISA	INA	ISA	ISA
Warranty	1 year	1 year	1 year	3 years	1 year
MOTHERBOARD					
Motherboard manufacturer	Eltech Research	Anigma	Contaq	Contaq	Epson
Chip set manufacturer	Symphony	Intel/Anigma	Contaq	Contaq	Epson
System shadowing/video shadowing	●/●	●/●	●/●	INA	●/●
BIOS version	AMI (July 1991)	Award 4.28	AMI (July 1991)	AMI (June 1992)	C&T 2.1.03B
ZIF socket	○	○	INA	○	○
Coprocessor supported	INA	INA	Weitek	INA	INA
MEMORY AND PROCESSOR RAM CACHE					
Installable RAM (minimum–maximum)	4Mb–64Mb	4Mb–64Mb	1Mb–32Mb	1Mb–32Mb	4Mb–16Mb
Cache controller	Symphony	Anigma	Contaq	INA	Intel
Installed RAM cache	INA	INA	INA	INA	INA
Installable RAM cache	128K–256K	128K–256K	128K–256K	64K–256K	32K
DISK DRIVES					
Drive bays	3 5.25-inch, 2 3.5-inch	4 5.25-inch, 2 3.5-inch	4 5.25-inch, 2 3.5-inch	4 5.25-inch, 1 3.5-inch	2 5.25-inch, 1 3.5-inch
Disk controller location	Card	Card	Card	ISA card	Motherboard
Hard disk capacity	202Mb	212Mb	340Mb	340Mb	240Mb
Hard disk options	202Mb–540Mb	130Mb–340Mb	80Mb–1.2G	80Mb–1.2G	40Mb–240Mb
Interface	INA	INA	INA	INA	INA
Minimal floppy disk drive configuration	1.2Mb, 1.44Mb	1.2Mb, 1.44Mb	1.2Mb, 1.44Mb	1.2Mb, 1.44Mb	1.2Mb, 1.44Mb
EXPANSION BUS					
8-bit slots	None	None	2 (1 open)	2	None
16-bit slots	7	None	6 (4 open)	6	6
32-bit:					
EISA/MCA slots	None	8	None	None	None
Proprietary	1	None	None	None	1
Slots free in fully configured PC	INA	INA	INA	INA	INA
Parallel, serial, mouse ports on motherboard	None	None	INA	1, 2, 0	1, 1, 1
Integrated network adapter option	INA	INA	INA	None	INA
VIDEO					
Display circuitry location	Card	Card	Card	ISA card	Motherboard
Chip set manufacturer	Tseng	Tseng	S3	ATI	C&T
POWER SUPPLY					
Power supply (watts)	200	300	300	200	200
Number of device connectors	4	5	6	5	5

●—Yes   ○—No   N/A—Not applicable   INA—Information not available

Computers

	Ergo Moby Brick 486DX	Ergo Moby Brick 486SX	Everex STEP 486DX2/50E	Everex Tempo C Series 486SX/25	Everex Tempo M Series 486 DX2/66
Price	$$$$	$$$	$$$$$	$$$	$$$$
Processor/speed	486/33MHz	486SX/25MHz	486DX2/50MHz	486SX/25MHz	486DX2/66MHz
Case type	Small-footprint	Small-footprint	Desktop	Slimline	Desktop
Dimensions (HWD, in inches)	INA	INA	INA	INA	INA
Installed RAM	INA	INA	INA	INA	INA
Bus architecture	INA	ISA	EISA	ISA	ISA
Warranty	1 year	1 year	1 year	1 year	1 year
MOTHERBOARD					
Motherboard manufacturer	Ergo	Ergo	Everex	Everex	Everex
Chip set manufacturer	VLSI	VLSI	Intel	Everex	Everex
System shadowing/video shadowing	●/●	INA	●/●	INA	INA
BIOS version	Ergo 2.09	Ergo 2.11	AMI (August 1991)	AMI (August 1991)	AMI 011589-K0
ZIF socket	INA	○	○	○	○
Coprocessor supported	INA	INA	INA	INA	INA
MEMORY AND PROCESSOR RAM CACHE					
Installable RAM (minimum–maximum)	4Mb–32Mb	4Mb–32Mb	4Mb–64Mb	4Mb–32Mb	1Mb–32Mb
Cache controller	None	INA	Everex	INA	INA
Installed RAM cache	INA	INA	INA	INA	INA
Installable RAM cache	N/A	N/A	256K	128K	128K–256K
DISK DRIVES					
Drive bays	1 3.5-inch	1 3.5-inch	5 5.25-inch	2 3.5-inch	5 5.25-inch
Disk controller location	Integrated	Motherboard	Card	Motherboard	Motherboard
Hard disk capacity	200Mb	212Mb	212Mb	211Mb	244Mb
Hard disk options	44Mb–510Mb	80Mb–1.2G	89Mb–16G	40Mb–1G	40Mb–1G
Interface	INA	INA	INA	INA	INA
Minimal floppy disk drive configuration	1.44Mb	1.44Mb	1.2Mb, 1.44Mb	1.44Mb	1.2Mb, 1.44Mb
EXPANSION BUS					
8-bit slots	1 (open)	1	None	None	1
16-bit slots	1 (open)	1	1	3	6
32-bit:					
EISA/MCA slots	None	None	6	None	None
Proprietary	None	2	1	None	1
Slots free in fully configured PC	INA	INA	INA	INA	INA
Parallel, serial, mouse ports on motherboard	INA	1, 2, 0	1, 2, 0	1, 2, 0	1, 2, 0
Integrated network adapter option	INA	INA	INA	INA	None
VIDEO					
Display circuitry location	Motherboard	Motherboard	Card	Motherboard	Motherboard
Chip set manufacturer	C&T	ATI	Tseng	Tseng	Tseng
POWER SUPPLY					
Power supply (watts)	42	42	200	145	200
Number of device connectors	1	N/A	4	6	4

●—Yes   ○—No   N/A—Not applicable   INA—Information not available

Table Continues →

Computers

	Expo 486 dX2/66	FCS 486-66	Fortron NetSet 433I	Fortron NetSet 486-33 EISA	FutureTech System 462E
Price	$$$	$$$	$$$	$$$$	$$$$
Processor/speed	486DX2/66MHz	486DX2/66MHz	486/33MHz	486/33MHz	486DX2/66MHz
Case type	Tower	Tower	Desktop	Tower	Tower
Dimensions (HWD, in inches)	INA	INA	6.5 × 21 × 16	24.5 × 9 × 25	INA
Installed RAM	INA	INA	8Mb	INA	INA
Bus architecture	ISA	ISA	INA	INA	EISA
Warranty	1 year	1 year on parts, 2 years on labor	1 year	INA	15 months
MOTHERBOARD					
Motherboard manufacturer	VTech	MCCI	AMI	AMI	Mylex
Chip set manufacturer	VTech	OPTi	C&T	Intel	Intel
System shadowing/video shadowing	INA	INA	●/●	●/●	INA
BIOS version	AMI (August 1992)	AMI (July 1991)	AMI (April 1990)	AMI 1.10 (October 1990)	Mylex 6.15
ZIF socket	○	○	INA	INA	○
Coprocessor supported	INA	INA	Weitek 4167	INA	INA
MEMORY AND PROCESSOR RAM CACHE					
Installable RAM (minimum–maximum)	4Mb–64Mb	1Mb–32Mb	4Mb–32Mb	1Mb–96Mb	4Mb–32Mb
Cache controller	INA	INA	Discrete logic	Intel	INA
Installed RAM cache	INA	INA	64K	64K	INA
Installable RAM cache	0–256K	256K	64K	128K, 256K, 512K	128K–256K
DISK DRIVES					
Drive bays	8 5.25-inch	5 5.25-inch	5 half-height	10 half-height	9 5.25-inch
Disk controller location	ISA card	ISA card	Integrated	Card	EISA card
Hard disk capacity	245Mb	330Mb	207Mb	330Mb	425Mb
Hard disk options	245Mb–426Mb	200Mb–2G	150Mb–300Mb	158Mb–1.02G	120Mb–2.4G
Interface	INA	INA	IDE	SCSI	INA
Minimal floppy disk drive configuration	1.2Mb, 1.44Mb	1.2Mb, 1.44Mb	1.2Mb	1.2Mb, 1.44Mb	1.2Mb, 1.44Mb
EXPANSION BUS					
8-bit slots	2	None	1	1	None
16-bit slots	8	7	6	None	None
32-bit:			1	7	
EISA/MCA slots	None	None	INA	INA	8
Proprietary	None	None	INA	INA	None
Slots free in fully configured PC	INA	INA	6	5	INA
Parallel, serial, mouse ports on motherboard	None	None	INA	INA	None
Integrated network adapter option	None	None	INA	INA	None
VIDEO					
Display circuitry location	ISA card	Motherboard	Card	Card	ISA card
Chip set manufacturer	ATI	S3	Western Digital	Paradise	ATI
POWER SUPPLY					
Power supply (watts)	300	300	200	INA	300
Number of device connectors	5	6	4	INA	6

●—Yes   ○—No   N/A—Not applicable   INA—Information not available

Computers

	FutureTech System 452E	Gateway 486/33C	Gateway 2000 25MHz/486SX	Gateway 2000 4DX2-66V	GCH EasyData 486DX-2/66
Price	$$$$	$$	$$	$$$	$$$
Processor/speed	486DX2/50MHz	486/33MHz	486SX/25MHz	486DX2/66MHz	486DX2/66MHz
Case type	Tower	Tower	Desktop	Desktop	Small-footprint
Dimensions (HWD, in inches)	INA	INA	INA	INA	INA
Installed RAM	INA	INA	INA	INA	INA
Bus architecture	EISA	INA	ISA	ISA	ISA
Warranty	15 months	1 year	1 year	1 year	1 year
MOTHERBOARD					
Motherboard manufacturer	Mylex	Micronics	Micronics	Micronics	GSS
Chip set manufacturer	Intel	Micronics	C&T, Micronics	Micronics	SIS
System shadowing/video shadowing	○/●	●/●	INA	INA	INA
BIOS version	Diamond 2.31	Phoenix 0.10.G17-2	Phoenix (January 1988)	Phoenix 1.10	AMI (December 1991)
ZIF socket	○	INA	○	○	○
Coprocessor supported	INA	80487/Weitek	INA	INA	INA
MEMORY AND PROCESSOR RAM CACHE					
Installable RAM (minimum–maximum)	1Mb–96Mb	4Mb–64Mb	4Mb–32Mb	4Mb–64Mb	1Mb–32Mb
Cache controller	Intel	Micronics	INA	INA	INA
Installed RAM cache	INA	INA	INA	INA	INA
Installable RAM cache	128K–512K	64K	N/A	64K–256K	64K–256K
DISK DRIVES					
Drive bays	5 5.25-inch	4 5.25-inch, 2 3.5-inch	3 5.25-inch	5 5.25-inch, 2 3.5-inch	3 5.25-inch, 2 3.5-inch
Disk controller location	Card	Integrated	Card	Motherboard	EISA card
Hard disk capacity	340Mb	200Mb	202Mb	340Mb	340Mb
Hard disk options	200Mb–1.2G	40Mb–1.2G	80Mb–1.2G	80Mb–1.2G	80Mb–1.2G
Interface	INA	INA	INA	INA	INA
Minimal floppy disk drive configuration	1.2Mb, 1.44Mb	1.2Mb, 1.44Mb	1.2Mb, 1.44Mb	1.2Mb, 1.44Mb	1.2Mb, 1.44Mb
EXPANSION BUS					
8-bit slots	None	None	2	None	1
16-bit slots	None	8 (6 open)	6	6	6
32-bit:					
EISA/MCA slots	8	None	None	None	None
Proprietary	None	None	1	None	None
Slots free in fully configured PC	INA	INA	INA	INA	INA
Parallel, serial, mouse ports on motherboard	None	INA	None	2, 1, 0	None
Integrated network adapter option	INA	INA	INA	None	None
VIDEO					
Display circuitry location	Card	Card	Card	Motherboard	EISA card
Chip set manufacturer	S3	Tseng	ATI	ATI	S3
POWER SUPPLY					
Power supply (watts)	300	200	200	200	220
Number of device connectors	6	6	5	5	4

Table Continues →

ZIFF-DAVIS PRESS

Computers

	Gecco 466E	GoldStar GS433	GRiD MFP/450	Hertz 486/33Ei	Hertz 486/D50X2e
Price	$$$	$$	$$$	$$$$	$$$
Processor/speed	486DX2/66MHz	486/33MHz	486DX2/50MHz	486/33MHz	486DX2/50MHz
Case type	Tower	Desktop	Slimline	Tower	Desktop
Dimensions (HWD, in inches)	INA	6 × 15 × 15	INA	INA	INA
Installed RAM	INA	4Mb	INA	INA	INA
Bus architecture	EISA	ISA	ISA	INA	ISA
Warranty	2 years	1 year	1 year	1 year	1 year
MOTHERBOARD					
Motherboard manufacturer	Kouwell	GoldStar	Tandy	Intel	Hertz
Chip set manufacturer	SIS	VLSI	VLSI	Intel	ETEQ
System shadowing/video shadowing	INA	●/●	○/○	●/●	●/●
BIOS version	AMI (April 1992)	Quadtel 3.0	Phoenix 1.10	Phoenix 1.10.33K1	AMI (July 1991)
ZIF socket	○	INA	○	INA	○
Coprocessor supported	INA	Intel, Weitek	INA	80487/Weitek	INA
MEMORY AND PROCESSOR RAM CACHE					
Installable RAM (minimum–maximum)	1Mb–128Mb	4Mb–32Mb	4Mb–32Mb	4Mb–64Mb	1Mb–32Mb
Cache controller	INA	None	N/A	Intel	ETEQ
Installed RAM cache	INA	INA	INA	INA	INA
Installable RAM cache	64K–128K	N/A	None	128K	64K–256K
DISK DRIVES					
Drive bays	4 5.25-inch, 3 3.5-inch	3 5.25-inch, 1 3.5-inch	1 5.25-inch, 1 3.5-inch	4 5.25-inch	3 5.25-inch, 2 3.5-inch
Disk controller location	EISA card	Integrated	Motherboard	Card	Card
Hard disk capacity	240Mb	200Mb	240Mb	200Mb	212Mb
Hard disk options	330Mb–1G	40Mb–200Mb	40Mb–440Mb	52Mb–2G	212Mb–2G
Interface	INA	INA	INA	INA	INA
Minimal floppy disk drive configuration	1.2Mb, 1.44Mb	1.2Mb, 1.44Mb	1.2Mb	1.2Mb or 1.44Mb	1.2Mb, 1.44Mb
EXPANSION BUS					
8-bit slots	None	None	None	None	2
16-bit slots	2	7 (5 open)	3	None	6
32-bit:					
EISA/MCA slots	6	None	None	10 (8 open)	None
Proprietary	None	1 (open)	None	None	None
Slots free in fully configured PC	INA	INA	INA	INA	INA
Parallel, serial, mouse ports on motherboard	None	1, 2, 0	1, 2, 1	INA	None
Integrated network adapter option	None	INA	INA	INA	INA
VIDEO					
Display circuitry location	EISA card	Card	Card	Card	Card
Chip set manufacturer	Tseng	Trident	WD/Paradise	Diamond	S3
POWER SUPPLY					
Power supply (watts)	250	200	100	396	230
Number of device connectors	5	3	3	6	5

●—Yes   ○—No   N/A—Not applicable   INA—Information not available

	HiQ 43FE	HiQ 425i	HiQ 486/33 EISA	HP Vectra 486/33T	HP Vectra 486/66U
Price	$$$	$$	$$$	$$$$	$$$$
Processor/speed	486DX2/50MHz	486/25MHz	486/33MHz	486/33MHz	486DX2/66MHz
Case type	Tower	Tower	Tower	Tower	Desktop
Dimensions (HWD, in inches)	INA	25.5 × 7.5 × 17.5	24.5 × 7.5 × 17.3	INA	INA
Installed RAM	INA	INA	INA	INA	INA
Bus architecture	EISA	INA	EISA	INA	EISA
Warranty	2 years	1 year on parts, 2 years on labor	INA	1 year	1 year
MOTHERBOARD					
Motherboard manufacturer	Free Technology	Free Technology	Free Technology	HP	HP
Chip set manufacturer	Intel	Intel	Intel	HP	HP/TI
System shadowing/video shadowing	●/●	●/●	●/●	●/●	INA
BIOS version	AMI (May 1991)	AMI (April 1990)	Award 4.1 (1990)	HP K.03.02	HP/Phoenix P.04.03
ZIF socket	○	INA	INA	INA	●
Coprocessor supported	INA	Weitek	INA	80487/Weitek	INA
MEMORY AND PROCESSOR RAM CACHE					
Installable RAM (minimum–maximum)	1Mb–64Mb	1Mb–16Mb	2Mb–64Mb	4Mb–64Mb	4Mb–64Mb
Cache controller	Free Technology	Discrete logic	TTL	HP	INA
Installed RAM cache	INA	INA	64K	INA	INA
Installable RAM cache	64K–256K	64K, 256K	256K	128K	128K
DISK DRIVES					
Drive bays	4 5.25-inch	6 half-height	3 full-height, 6 half-height	6 5.25-inch	2 5.25-inch, 1 3.5-inch
Disk controller location	Card	Card	Card	Integrated	Motherboard
Hard disk capacity	200Mb	200Mb	347Mb	168Mb	245Mb
Hard disk options	200Mb–535Mb	100Mb–350Mb	347Mb–680Mb	84Mb–1G	240Mb–430Mb
Interface	INA	INA	SCSI	INA	INA
Minimal floppy disk drive configuration	1.2Mb, 1.44Mb	1.2Mb, 1.44Mb	1.2Mb, 1.44Mb	1.44Mb	1.44Mb
EXPANSION BUS					
8-bit slots	None	None	1	None	None
16-bit slots	None	8 (5 open)	2	None	None
32-bit:			6		
EISA/MCA slots	8	None	INA	8 (8 open)	5
Proprietary	None	None	INA	4	None
Slots free in fully configured PC	INA	INA	5	INA	INA
Parallel, serial, mouse ports on motherboard	None	INA	INA	INA	1, 2, 1
Integrated network adapter option	INA	INA	INA	INA	None
VIDEO					
Display circuitry location	Card	Card	Card	Card	Motherboard
Chip set manufacturer	S3	Tseng	Tseng	HP	S3
POWER SUPPLY					
Power supply (watts)	250	230	INA	360	228
Number of device connectors	4	4	INA	6	5

●—Yes   ○— No   N/A—Not applicable   INA—Information not available

Table Continues →

Computers

	Hyundai 466D2	Hyundai Corporate Series 386/40	IBM PS/2 Model 77 486DX2	IBM PS/2 Model 90 XP 486	IBM PS/2 Model 95 XP 486SX/25
Price	$$$	$$$	$$$$	$$$$	$$$$$
Processor/speed	486DX2/66MHz	Am386/40MHz	486DX2/66MHz	486/33MHz	486SX/25MHz
Case type	Small-footprint	Small-footprint	Desktop	Desktop	Tower
Dimensions (HWD, in inches)	INA	INA	6.6 × 17.3 × 15.5	5.5 × 17.3 × 16.9	INA
Installed RAM	INA	INA	8Mb	8Mb	INA
Bus architecture	ISA	INA	MCA	MCA	MCA
Warranty	18 months	18 months	3 years	1 year	1 year
MOTHERBOARD					
Motherboard manufacturer	Hyundai	Motherboard Factory	IBM	IBM	IBM
Chip set manufacturer	OPTi	VLSI/Northport	IBM	IBM	IBM
System shadowing/video shadowing	INA	●/●	INA	●/●	INA
BIOS version	AMI (June 1992)	AMI 5.05	IBM 3G6921	IBM 1.02	IBM (March 1992)
ZIF socket	●	INA	○	INA	○
Coprocessor supported	INA	80487/Weitek	INA	80487/Weitek	INA
MEMORY AND PROCESSOR RAM CACHE					
Installable RAM (minimum–maximum)	1Mb–64Mb	1Mb–64Mb	2Mb–32Mb	8Mb–64Mb	8Mb–64Mb
Cache controller	INA	Proprietary	INA	IBM	INA
Installed RAM cache	INA	INA	INA	INA	INA
Installable RAM cache	128K–256K	64K–256K	None	256K	N/A
DISK DRIVES					
Drive bays	3 5.25-inch, 4 3.5-inch	3 5.25-inch	3 5.25-inch, 1 3.5-inch	1 5.25-inch, 1 3.5-inch	3 5.25-inch, 2 3.5-inch
Disk controller location	Motherboard	2	Motherboard	Card	Motherboard
Hard disk capacity	212Mb	200Mb	400Mb	160Mb	400Mb
Hard disk options	80Mb–540Mb	100Mb–300Mb	212Mb–400Mb	80Mb–400Mb	80Mb–1G
Interface	INA	INA	INA	INA	INA
Minimal floppy disk drive configuration	1.2Mb, 1.44Mb	1.2Mb	2.88Mb	1.44Mb	1.44Mb
EXPANSION BUS					
8-bit slots	None	None	None	None	None
16-bit slots	6	7 (6 open)	None	None	None
32-bit:					
EISA/MCA slots	None	None	5	4 (3 open)	8
Proprietary	None	1	None	3 (1 open)	1
Slots free in fully configured PC	INA	INA	INA	INA	INA
Parallel, serial, mouse ports on motherboard	1, 2, 1	INA	1, 2, 1	1, 2, 1	1, 1, 1
Integrated network adapter option	None	INA	None	INA	INA
VIDEO					
Display circuitry location	VESA local bus	Card	MCA card	Motherboard	Card
Chip set manufacturer	ATI	ATI	IBM	IBM	IBM
POWER SUPPLY					
Power supply (watts)	200	200	200	194	329
Number of device connectors	6	6	4	5	3

●—Yes ○—No N/A—Not applicable INA—Information not available

Computers

	IBM PS/2 Model 95 XP 486 25/50	i Corp Blazer IIs	IDS 466i2	Insight 486DX2-66I	Insight 486SX-25
Price	$$$$$	$$$$$	$$$	$$$	$$
Processor/speed	486DX2/50MHz	486SX/25MHz	486DX2/66MHz	486DX2/66MHz	486SX/25MHz
Case type	Tower	Tower	Small-footprint	Desktop	Small-footprint
Dimensions (HWD, in inches)	INA	INA	INA	INA	INA
Installed RAM	8Mb	8Mb	INA	INA	INA
Bus architecture	MCA	ISA	ISA	ISA	ISA
Warranty	1 year	2 years	1 year	1 year	1 year
MOTHERBOARD					
Motherboard manufacturer	IBM	Maha	AMI	Aten	Insight
Chip set manufacturer	IBM	Symphony	C&T	OPTi	OPTi
System shadowing/video shadowing	○/○	INA	INA	INA	INA
BIOS version	IBM (March 1992)	AMI (May 1991)	AMI 486 (December 1991)	AMI 4.01	AMI (June 1991)
ZIF socket	○	○	○	○	○
Coprocessor supported	INA	INA	INA	INA	INA
MEMORY AND PROCESSOR RAM CACHE					
Installable RAM (minimum–maximum)	8Mb–64Mb	8Mb–32Mb	1Mb–32Mb	1Mb–32Mb	4Mb–32Mb
Cache controller	IBM	INA	INA	INA	INA
Installed RAM cache	INA	INA	INA	INA	INA
Installable RAM cache	512K	64K–256K	64K–256K	64K–256K	64K–256K
DISK DRIVES					
Drive bays	2 5.25-inch, 3 3.5-inch	5 5.25-inch	3 5.25-inch, 2 3.5-inch	3 5.25-inch, 2 3.5-inch	3 5.25-inch, 1 3.5-inch
Disk controller location	Card	Card	Motherboard	ISA card	Card
Hard disk capacity	400Mb	1.4G	362Mb	490Mb	234Mb
Hard disk options	160Mb–1G	224Mb–2.2G	80Mb–2G	40Mb–2.1G	234Mb–1G
Interface	INA	INA	INA	INA	INA
Minimal floppy disk drive configuration	1.44Mb	1.2Mb, 1.44Mb	Dual	1.2Mb, 1.44Mb	1.2Mb, 1.44Mb
EXPANSION BUS					
8-bit slots	None	None	1	1	1
16-bit slots	None	8	7	7	7
32-bit:					
EISA/MCA slots	8	None	None	None	None
Proprietary	2	None	None	None	None
Slots free in fully configured PC	INA	INA	INA	INA	INA
Parallel, serial, mouse ports on motherboard	1, 1, 1	None	1, 2, 0	None	1, 2, 0
Integrated network adapter option	INA	INA	None	None	INA
VIDEO					
Display circuitry location	Card	Card	ISA card	ISA card	Card
Chip set manufacturer	IBM	TI	ATI	Cirrus	Tseng
POWER SUPPLY					
Power supply (watts)	195	230	200	200	200
Number of device connectors	3	8	5	4	5

●—Yes ○—No N/A—Not applicable INA—Information not available   **Table Continues** →

Computers

	Intelec INT 386-40	Intelec INT 486-50	International Instrumentation Blue Max Monolith 486D2/66UP	International Instrumentation Blue Max Monolith 486UP/25S	International Instrumentation Blue Max Monolith E486/500
Price	$	$$	$$$	$$	$$$
Processor/speed	Am386/40MHz	486/50MHz	486DX2/66MHz	486SX/25MHz	486DX2/50MHz
Case type	Desktop	Tower	Desktop	Small-footprint	Tower
Dimensions (HWD, in inches)	INA	INA	INA	INA	INA
Installed RAM	INA	INA	INA	INA	INA
Bus architecture	INA	INA	ISA	ISA	EISA
Warranty	1 year	1 year	1 year	1 year	1 year
MOTHERBOARD					
Motherboard manufacturer	Premio	Octek	International Instrumentation	Mylex	Mylex
Chip set manufacturer	ETEQ	OPTi	SIS/UNI Chip	OPTi	Mylex
System shadowing/video shadowing	●/●	●/●	INA	INA	●/○
BIOS version	AMI (February 1991)	AMI (July 1991)	AMI (December 1991)	Mylex 6.13	Mylex 6.14
ZIF socket	INA	INA	○	●	○
Coprocessor supported	80487/Weitek	Weitek/Cyrix	INA	INA	INA
MEMORY AND PROCESSOR RAM CACHE					
Installable RAM (minimum–maximum)	1Mb–64Mb	4Mb–64Mb	1Mb–128Mb	1Mb–32Mb	1Mb–96Mb
Cache controller	Discrete logic	OPTi	INA	INA	Discrete logic
Installed RAM cache	INA	INA	INA	INA	INA
Installable RAM cache	64K	64K–256K	64K–256K	64K–256K	128K–256K
DISK DRIVES					
Drive bays	3 5.25-inch, 1 3.5-inch	4 5.25-inch,	6 5.25-inch	2 5.25-inch, 1 3.5-inch	4 5.25-inch
Disk controller location	INA	Card	ISA card	Card	Card
Hard disk capacity	210Mb	340Mb	213Mb	340Mb	327Mb
Hard disk options	105Mb–330Mb	52Mb–1.2G	43Mb–2.2G	42Mb–2.2G	40Mb–2.2G
Interface	INA	INA	INA	INA	INA
Minimal floppy disk drive configuration	1.2Mb, 1.44Mb	1.2Mb, 1.44Mb	1.2Mb, 1.44Mb	1.2Mb, 1.44Mb	1.2Mb, 1.44Mb
EXPANSION BUS					
8-bit slots	1 (open)	1 (open)	2	1	None
16-bit slots	6 (5 open)	6 (3 open)	5	6	None
32-bit:					
EISA/MCA slots	None	None	None	None	8
Proprietary	1 (open)	1 (open)	1	None	2
Slots free in fully configured PC	INA	INA	INA	INA	INA
Parallel, serial, mouse ports on motherboard	INA	INA	1, 2, 0	1, 2, 0	None
Integrated network adapter option	INA	INA	None	INA	INA
VIDEO					
Display circuitry location	Card	Card	Local bus	Card	Card
Chip set manufacturer	Trident	Tseng	ATI/Tseng	S3	S3
POWER SUPPLY					
Power supply (watts)	200	250	250	250	250
Number of device connectors	4	4	7	5	6

●—Yes   ○—No   N/A—Not applicable   INA—Information not available

Computers

	International Instrumentation Blue Max Monolith 486/33	International Instrumentation Blue Max Monolith 486E/330CD	KEY486S-25 ISA	Keydata 486-50 DX2 EISA Station	Keydata 486DX2-66 KeyStation
Price	$$$$	$$$$	$$	$$$	$$$
Processor/speed	486/33MHz	486/33MHz	486SX/25MHz	486DX2/50MHz	486DX2/66MHz
Case type	Desktop	Desktop	Mini-tower	Small-footprint	Tower
Dimensions (HWD, in inches)	6.5 × 21 × 16	6.3 × 21.3 × 16.5	INA	INA	INA
Installed RAM	8Mb	INA	INA	INA	INA
Bus architecture	INA	INA	ISA	EISA	EISA
Warranty	1 year	INA	18 months	18 months	18 months
MOTHERBOARD					
Motherboard manufacturer	AMI	AMI	ASUS	ASUS	ASUS
Chip set manufacturer	Discrete logic	Intel	SIS	Intel	SIS
System shadowing/video shadowing	●/●	●/●	INA	●/●	INA
BIOS version	AMI (April 1990)	AMI EISA (August 1990)	AMI (May 1991)	Award 4.00	Award 1.0
ZIF socket	INA	INA	○	○	○
Coprocessor supported	Weitek 4167	INA	INA	INA	INA
MEMORY AND PROCESSOR RAM CACHE					
Installable RAM (minimum–maximum)	2Mb–16Mb	2Mb–96Mb	1Mb–64Mb	1Mb–64Mb	1Mb–128Mb
Cache controller	Discrete logic	Discrete logic	INA	Intel	INA
Installed RAM cache	128K	64K	INA	INA	INA
Installable RAM cache	128K	128K, 256K	256K	64K–256K	64K–256K
DISK DRIVES					
Drive bays	5 half-height	5 half-height, 4 full-height	3 5.25-inch, 1 3.5-inch	2 5.25-inch, 1 3.5-inch	5 5.25-inch, 3 3.5-inch
Disk controller location	Integrated	Card	Motherboard	Card	EISA card
Hard disk capacity	344Mb	300Mb	210Mb	212Mb	345Mb
Hard disk options	300Mb–600Mb	180Mb–1.02G	80Mb–340Mb	212Mb–340Mb	240Mb–600Mb
Interface	ESDI	ESDI	INA	INA	INA
Minimal floppy disk drive configuration	1.2Mb, 1.44Mb	1.2Mb, 1.44Mb	1.2Mb, 1.44Mb	1.2Mb, 1.44Mb	1.2Mb, 1.44Mb
EXPANSION BUS					
8-bit slots	2	1	1	None	None
16-bit slots	6	7	6	None	None
32-bit:	1	7			
EISA/MCA slots	INA	INA	None	8	8
Proprietary	INA	INA	1	None	None
Slots free in fully configured PC	5	5	INA	1, 2, 0	INA
Parallel, serial, mouse ports on motherboard	INA	INA	None	INA	None
Integrated network adapter option	INA	INA	INA	INA	None
VIDEO					
Display circuitry location	Card	Card	Card	Card	ISA card
Chip set manufacturer	G2	Tseng	S3	S3	NCR
POWER SUPPLY					
Power supply (watts)	230	INA	230	200	250
Number of device connectors	4	INA	5	4	4

●—Yes ○—No N/A—Not applicable INA—Information not available

Table Continues →

ZIFF-DAVIS PRESS

Computers

	Leading Edge D4/DX2-50	Lightning Omniflex 486SX25	Lightning ThunderBox	LodeStar 486-DX2/66 EISA WINstation	Matrix 486-33 EISA
Price	$$$	$$	$$$	$$$	$$$$
Processor/speed	486DX2/50MHz	486SX/25MHz	486DX2/66MHz	486DX2/66MHz	486/33MHz
Case type	Small-footprint	Desktop	Desktop	Tower	Tower
Dimensions (HWD, in inches)	INA	INA	INA	INA	23 × 6.5 × 19.1
Installed RAM	INA	4Mb	8Mb	INA	INA
Bus architecture	ISA	ISA	ISA	EISA	EISA
Warranty	1 year	2 years	2 years	2 years on parts, lifetime on labor	INA
MOTHERBOARD					
Motherboard manufacturer	Daewoo	AMI, HyQuest	Micronics	Giga	Micronics
Chip set manufacturer	OPTi	AMI, C&T, Siemens	C&T	OPTi	Intel
System shadowing/video shadowing	●/●	INA	INA	INA	○/●
BIOS version	Phoenix (April 1990)	AMI (December 1991)	Phoenix 1.01	AMI (September 1992)	Phoenix 1.00.11 (December 1988)
ZIF socket	○	○	○	○	INA
Coprocessor supported	INA	INA	INA	INA	INA
MEMORY AND PROCESSOR RAM CACHE					
Installable RAM (minimum–maximum)	4Mb–32Mb	1Mb–128Mb	4Mb–16Mb	1Mb–32Mb	1Mb–64Mb
Cache controller	OPTi	INA	INA	INA	Intel
Installed RAM cache	INA	INA	INA	INA	64K
Installable RAM cache	64K–256K	64K–256K	256K	64K–512K	128K, 256K
DISK DRIVES					
Drive bays	3 5.25-inch	2 5.25-inch, 2 3.5-inch	2 5.25-inch, 4 3.5-inch	6 5.25-inch, 5 3.5-inch	1 full-height, 2 half-height, 2 3.5-inch
Disk controller location	Card	Motherboard	ISA card	ISA card	Card
Hard disk capacity	240Mb	213Mb	363Mb	213Mb	330Mb
Hard disk options	130Mb–340Mb	213Mb–1G	100Mb–5.6G	40Mb–4G	106Mb–1G
Interface	INA	INA	INA	INA	ESDI
Minimal floppy disk drive configuration	1.2Mb, 1.44Mb	1.2Mb, 1.44Mb	1.2Mb, 1.44Mb	1.2Mb, 1.44Mb	1.2Mb
EXPANSION BUS					
8-bit slots	None	1	None	None	None
16-bit slots	8	7	6	2	1
32-bit:					7
EISA/MCA slots	None	None	None	6	INA
Proprietary	None	None	None	None	INA
Slots free in fully configured PC	INA	INA	INA	INA	4
Parallel, serial, mouse ports on motherboard	None	1, 2, 0	1, 2, 0	None	INA
Integrated network adapter option	INA	INA	None	None	INA
VIDEO					
Display circuitry location	Card	Card	VESA local bus	ISA card	Card
Chip set manufacturer	ATI	ATI	ATI	S3	Tseng
POWER SUPPLY					
Power supply (watts)	200	250	250	250	INA
Number of device connectors	4	6	6	6	INA

●—Yes ○—No N/A—Not applicable INA—Information not available

Computers

	Matrix 486-50 DX2	Media Micro Pro425SI	Mega Impact 486/50E	Mega Impact 486DX2/50E	Mega Impact 486DX2/66E+
Price	$$$	$$	$$$	$$$	$$$
Processor/speed	486DX2/50MHz	486SX/25MHz	486/50MHz	486DX2/50MHz	486DX2/66MHz
Case type	Small-footprint	Mini-tower	Tower	Tower	Tower
Dimensions (HWD, in inches)	INA	INA	INA	INA	INA
Installed RAM	INA	INA	INA	INA	INA
Bus architecture	ISA	ISA	INA	EISA	EISA
Warranty	1 year	1 year on parts, 5 years on labor	1 year	1 year	1 year

MOTHERBOARD

Motherboard manufacturer	Micronics	HyQuest	AIR	BCM	BCM
Chip set manufacturer	Micronics, C&T	UMC	Intel	Intel	Intel
System shadowing/video shadowing	●/●	INA	●/●	●/●	INA
BIOS version	Phoenix (January 1988)	AMI 1.0A	AMI (April 1991)	AMI (April 1991)	AMI 1.01
ZIF socket	○	○	INA	○	○
Coprocessor supported	INA	INA	Weitek/Cyrix	INA	INA

MEMORY AND PROCESSOR RAM CACHE

Installable RAM (minimum–maximum)	1Mb–64Mb	1Mb–64Mb	1Mb–64Mb	4Mb–64Mb	1Mb–64Mb
Cache controller	Micronics	INA	AIR	Intel	INA
Installed RAM cache	INA	INA	INA	INA	INA
Installable RAM cache	256K	0–256K	64K–256K	64K–256K	64K–256K

DISK DRIVES

Drive bays	3 5.25-inch, 2 3.5-inch	2 5.25-inch, 2 3.5-inch	4 5.25-inch	4 5.25-inch	5 5.25-inch, 3 3.5-inch
Disk controller location	Card	Card	Card	Card	EISA card
Hard disk capacity	212Mb	212Mb	340Mb	340Mb	340Mb
Hard disk options	40Mb–2G	40Mb–1G	120Mb–1G	210Mb–1.2G	210Mb–2G
Interface	INA	INA	INA	INA	INA
Minimal floppy disk drive configuration	1.2Mb, 1.44Mb	1.2Mb, 1.44Mb	1.2Mb, 1.44Mb	1.2Mb, 1.44Mb	1.2Mb, 1.44Mb

EXPANSION BUS

8-bit slots	None	None	None	None	None
16-bit slots	8	7	None	1	1
32-bit:					
EISA/MCA slots	None	None	8 (6 open)	6	6
Proprietary	None	None	None	1	1
Slots free in fully configured PC	INA	INA	INA	INA	INA
Parallel, serial, mouse ports on motherboard	None	None	INA	None	None
Integrated network adapter option	INA	INA	INA	INA	None

VIDEO

Display circuitry location	Card	Motherboard	Card	Card	ISA card
Chip set manufacturer	Tseng	Tseng	S3	S3	ATI

POWER SUPPLY

Power supply (watts)	200	200	250	250	250
Number of device connectors	5	5	6	4	5

●—Yes ○—No N/A—Not applicable INA—Information not available   **Table Continues →**

Computers

	Mega Impact 486SX/25E+	Memorex Telex 8080-25	Memorex Telex 8092-66	Micro Express ME 386-40	Micro Express ME 486-ISA/33
Price	$$	$$$	$$$$	$$	$$$$
Processor/speed	486SX/25MHz	486SX/25MHz	486DX2/66MHz	Am386/40MHz	486/33MHz
Case type	Tower	Small-footprint	Small-footprint	Small-footprint	Tower
Dimensions (HWD, in inches)	INA	INA	INA	6.5 × 14.8 × 16	24.5 × 9 × 23
Installed RAM	INA	INA	INA	4Mb	8Mb
Bus architecture	EISA	ISA	ISA	ISA	INA
Warranty	1 year	1 year	1 year	2 years	2 years
MOTHERBOARD					
Motherboard manufacturer	BCM	Cache Computers	Cache Computers	AMI	Micro Express
Chip set manufacturer	Intel	UMD	UMC	C&T/Discrete logic	Discrete logic
System shadowing/video shadowing	INA	INA	INA	●/●	●/●
BIOS version	AMI (May 1991)	AMI (July 1991)	AMI (December 1991)	AMI (August 1990)	AMI (May 1990)
ZIF socket	○	○	○	INA	INA
Coprocessor supported	INA	INA	INA	80487	Weitek 4167
MEMORY AND PROCESSOR RAM CACHE					
Installable RAM (minimum–maximum)	1Mb–64Mb	2Mb–64Mb	1Mb–32Mb	1Mb–64Mb	2Mb–16Mb
Cache controller	INA	INA	INA	Discrete logic	Discrete logic
Installed RAM cache	INA	INA	INA	INA	128K
Installable RAM cache	64K–256K	64K–256K	0–256K	64K–128K	128K
DISK DRIVES					
Drive bays	4 5.25-inch	3 5.25-inch	3 5.25-inch, 1 3.5-inch	2 5.25-inch, 1 3.5-inch	10 half-height
Disk controller location	Card	Motherboard	Motherboard	INA	Integrated
Hard disk capacity	340Mb	213Mb	213Mb	202Mb	330Mb
Hard disk options	200Mb–4.5G	213Mb–540Mb	80Mb–520Mb	80Mb–1.2G	200Mb–750Mb
Interface	INA	INA	INA	INA	ESDI
Minimal floppy disk drive configuration	1.2Mb, 1.44Mb	1.2Mb, 1.44Mb	1.2Mb, 1.44Mb	1.2Mb	1.2Mb, 1.44Mb
EXPANSION BUS					
8-bit slots	None	None	None	2 (2 open)	None
16-bit slots	1	7	7	6 (4 open)	8
32-bit:					
EISA/MCA slots	6	None	None	None	None
Proprietary	1	1	1	None	None
Slots free in fully configured PC	INA	INA	INA	INA	5
Parallel, serial, mouse ports on motherboard	None	1, 2, 1	1, 2, 0	1, 2, 0	INA
Integrated network adapter option	INA	INA	None	INA	INA
VIDEO					
Display circuitry location	Card	Card	ISA card	Card	Card
Chip set manufacturer	S3	ATI	ATI	Tseng	Tseng
POWER SUPPLY					
Power supply (watts)	250	200	230	200	250
Number of device connectors	4	5	5	5	5

●—Yes   ○—No   N/A—Not applicable   INA—Information not available

Computers

	Micro Express ME 486-50/DX2	Micro Express ME 486-Local Bus/DX2/66	Micro Express ME 486SX/Local Bus/25	Micro Generation LB-25SX	Micro Generation MG50DX2
Price	$$$	$$$	$$	$$	$$$
Processor/speed	486DX2/50MHz	486DX2/66MHz	486SX/25MHz	486SX/25MHz	486DX2/50MHz
Case type	Tower	Mini-tower	Mini-tower	Small-footprint	Tower
Dimensions (HWD, in inches)	24 × 10 × 17.5	INA	INA	INA	INA
Installed RAM	4Mb	INA	4Mb	INA	INA
Bus architecture	ISA	ISA	ISA	ISA	ISA
Warranty	2 years	2 years	2 years	1 year on parts, lifetime on labor	1 year
MOTHERBOARD					
Motherboard manufacturer	Micronics	Ergon	Ergon	High Candor	Continental
Chip set manufacturer	Micronics, C&T	OPTi	C&T, OPTi	OPTi	OPTi
System shadowing/video shadowing	●/●	INA	INA	INA	●/●
BIOS version	Phoenix 1.3	Phoenix/ATI BIOS (August 1992)	ETI/Phoenix 1.00	AMI (June 1991)	AMI (June 1991)
ZIF socket	○	●	●	○	○
Coprocessor supported	INA	INA	INA	INA	INA
MEMORY AND PROCESSOR RAM CACHE					
Installable RAM (minimum–maximum)	4Mb–64Mb	4Mb–32Mb	4Mb–32Mb	1Mb–32Mb	1Mb–32Mb
Cache controller	Micronics	INA	INA	INA	OPTi
Installed RAM cache	INA	INA	INA	INA	INA
Installable RAM cache	256K	256K	64K–256K	64K–256K	64K–256K
DISK DRIVES					
Drive bays	8 5.25-inch	4 5.25-inch, 2 3.5-inch	3 5.25-inch, 1 3.5-inch	3 5.25-inch, 1 3.5-inch	5 5.25-inch
Disk controller location	Card	ISA card	Motherboard	Card	Card
Hard disk capacity	240Mb	240Mb	240Mb	210Mb	212Mb
Hard disk options	240Mb–2G	80Mb–1.5G	80Mb–2G	80Mb–600Mb	80Mb–600Mb
Interface	INA	INA	INA	INA	INA
Minimal floppy disk drive configuration	1.2Mb, 1.44Mb	1.2Mb, 1.44Mb	1.2Mb, 1.44Mb	1.2Mb, 1.44Mb	1.2Mb, 1.44Mb
EXPANSION BUS					
8-bit slots	None	None	None	None	None
16-bit slots	8	7	7	8	8
32-bit:					
EISA/MCA slots	None	None	None	None	None
Proprietary	None	None	None	2	1
Slots free in fully configured PC	INA	INA	INA	INA	INA
Parallel, serial, mouse ports on motherboard	1, 2, 1	1, 1, 0	1, 2, 0	None	None
Integrated network adapter option	INA	None	INA	INA	INA
VIDEO					
Display circuitry location	Card	Local bus	Motherboard	Card	Motherboard
Chip set manufacturer	S3	Tseng	Tseng	S3	S3
POWER SUPPLY					
Power supply (watts)	375	200	200	230	230
Number of device connectors	10	5	5	5	8

●—Yes ○—No N/A—Not applicable INA—Information not available

Table Continues →

Computers

	Micro Telesis 486/33	Mitsuba Professional Upgradable	Myoda 486SX-25b	Naga Windows Workstation	National Micro Systems Flash 386-40C
Price	$$$$	$$$	$$	$$$	$
Processor/speed	486/33MHz	486SX/25MHz	486SX/25MHz	486DX2/66MHz	Am386/40MHz
Case type	Mini-tower	Small-footprint	Small-footprint	Desktop	Small-footprint
Dimensions (HWD, in inches)	16 × 8.5 × 19	INA	INA	INA	6 × 21 × 17
Installed RAM	8Mb	INA	INA	INA	4Mb
Bus architecture	INA	EISA	ISA	ISA	ISA
Warranty	13 months	1 year	1 year	2 years on parts, lifetime on labor	15 months on parts, 2 years on labor
MOTHERBOARD					
Motherboard manufacturer	SIC Research	Mitsuba	J-Bond Computer	ASUS	LAN Distributing
Chip set manufacturer	Discrete logic	Intel	ETEQ	SIS	Intel
System shadowing/video shadowing	○/○	INA	INA	INA	●/●
BIOS version	AMI (April 1990)	AMI (May 1991)	AMI (July 1991)	AMI (May 1991)	Quadtel 3.05.07
ZIF socket	INA	○	○	○	INA
Coprocessor supported	Weitek 4167	INA	INA	INA	80487/Weitek
MEMORY AND PROCESSOR RAM CACHE					
Installable RAM (minimum–maximum)	2Mb–16Mb	1Mb–64Mb	1Mb–32Mb	1Mb–64Mb	1Mb–32Mb
Cache controller	Discrete logic	INA	INA	INA	Intel
Installed RAM cache	64K, 128K	INA	INA	INA	INA
Installable RAM cache	128K	64K–256K	64K–256K	128K–256K	16K
DISK DRIVES					
Drive bays	5 half-height	3 5.25-inch	3 5.25-inch, 2 3.5-inch	3 5.25-inch, 2 3.5-inch	3 5.25-inch, 1 3.5-inch
Disk controller location	Card	Card	Card	ISA card	INA
Hard disk capacity	200Mb	213Mb	212Mb	340Mb	200Mb
Hard disk options	150Mb–1.2G	150Mb–300Mb	40Mb–675Mb	40Mb–1.7G	40Mb–1.2G
Interface	IDE	INA	INA	INA	INA
Minimal floppy disk drive configuration	1.2Mb, 1.44Mb	1.2Mb, 1.44Mb	1.2Mb, 1.44Mb	1.2Mb, 1.44Mb	1.44Mb
EXPANSION BUS					
8-bit slots	None	None	2	1	None
16-bit slots	7	None	6	8	8 (6 open)
32-bit:	1				
EISA/MCA slots	INA	6	None	None	None
Proprietary	INA	1	None	1	1 (open)
Slots free in fully configured PC	6	INA	INA	INA	INA
Parallel, serial, mouse ports on motherboard	INA	None	None	None	INA
Integrated network adapter option	INA	INA	INA	None	INA
VIDEO					
Display circuitry location	Card	Card	Card	ISA card	Card
Chip set manufacturer	Western Digital	Tseng	Tseng	Tseng	Tseng
POWER SUPPLY					
Power supply (watts)	200	200	200	200	200
Number of device connectors	4	5	6	4	5

●—Yes   ○—No   N/A—Not applicable   INA—Information not available

Computers

	National Micro Systems Flash 486-33	National Micro Systems Flash 486-33 EISA	National Micro Systems Flash 486–50C	National Micro Systems Flash 486DX2-50	National Micro Systems Flash 486DX2-66E
Price	$$$	$$$$	$$	$$	$$$
Processor/speed	486/33MHz	486/33MHz	486/50MHz	486DX2/50MHz	486DX2/66MHz
Case type	Tower	Tower	Tower	Small-footprint	Tower
Dimensions (HWD, in inches)	25.5 × 8 × 18	26 × 8 × 18	INA	INA	24 × 8 × 18
Installed RAM	8Mb	1Mb	INA	4Mb	8Mb
Bus architecture	ISA	EISA	INA	ISA	EISA
Warranty	15 months on parts, 2 years on labor	INA	15–24 months	15 months	15 months on parts, 2 years on labor

MOTHERBOARD

Motherboard manufacturer	AMI	AIR	AIR	AIR	AIR
Chip set manufacturer	Discrete logic	Intel	C&T, UMC	UMC, C&T	OPTi
System shadowing/video shadowing	●/●	●/●	●/●	●/●	INA
BIOS version	AMI (April 1990)	Phoenix 1.00.00 (January 1988)	AMI (May 1991)	AMI 1.1	AMI (December 1991)
ZIF socket	INA	INA	INA	●	○
Coprocessor supported	Weitek 4167	Weitek	Weitek/Cyrix	Weitek	Weitek, Cyrix

MEMORY AND PROCESSOR RAM CACHE

Installable RAM (minimum–maximum)	2Mb–24Mb	1Mb–64Mb	1Mb–64Mb	4Mb–64Mb	1Mb–128Mb
Cache controller	Discrete logic	Discrete logic	C&T	UMC	UMC
Installed RAM cache	128K	256K	INA	INA	256K
Installable RAM cache	128K	64K	64K–256K	64K–256K	64K–512K

DISK DRIVES

Drive bays	8 half-height	8 half-height	5 5.25-inch,	3 5.25-inch, 1 3.5-inch	7 5.25-inch, 3 3.5-inch
Disk controller location	Integrated	Card	Card	Card	EISA card
Hard disk capacity	344Mb	338Mb	340Mb	212Mb	312Mb
Hard disk options	150Mb–600Mb	150Mb–650Mb	40Mb–1.7G	40Mb–1.7G	40Mb–1.7G
Interface	ESDI	ESDI	INA	INA	INA
Minimal floppy disk drive configuration	1.2Mb, 1.44Mb	1.2Mb	1.2Mb, 1.44Mb	1.2Mb, 1.44Mb	1.2Mb, 1.44Mb

EXPANSION BUS

8-bit slots	2	None	None	None	None
16-bit slots	6	None	7 (4 open)	8	None
32-bit:	1	8			
EISA/MCA slots	INA	INA	None	None	7
Proprietary	INA	INA	1 (open)	1	None
Slots free in fully configured PC	5	5	INA	INA	INA
Parallel, serial, mouse ports on motherboard	1, 2, 0	1, 2, 0	INA	None	None
Integrated network adapter option	INA	INA	INA	INA	None

VIDEO

Display circuitry location	Card	Card	Card	Card	Local bus
Chip set manufacturer	Ahead	Tseng	Tseng	S3	S3

POWER SUPPLY

Power supply (watts)	230	INA	275	200	300
Number of device connectors	4	INA	5	5	5

●—Yes   ○—No   N/A—Not applicable   INA—Information not available *

Table Continues →

Computers

	Natinoal Micro Systems Flash 486SX-25C	NCR System 3335	NCR System 3350	NEC Express DX2/66e	NEC PowerMate 486/50i
Price	$$	$$$	$$$$	$$$$	$$$$
Processor/speed	486SX/25MHz	486DX2/50MHz	486DX2/66MHz	486DX2/66MHz	486DX2/50MHz
Case type	Small-footprint	Slimline	Small-footprint	Desktop	Small-footprint
Dimensions (HWD, in inches)	INA	INA	INA	INA	INA
Installed RAM	1Mb	INA	INA	INA	INA
Bus architecture	ISA	MCA	MCA	EISA	ISA
Warranty	15 months on parts, 2 years on labor	1 year	2 years	1 year	1 year
MOTHERBOARD					
Motherboard manufacturer	AIR	NCR	NCR	NEC	NEC
Chip set manufacturer	C&T, UMC	NCR	CSI Logic/ Intel/NCR/ VLSI	Intel	OPTi
System shadowing/video shadowing	INA	●/●	INA	INA	○/●
BIOS version	AMI (July 1991)	NCR 2.01	Phoenix 1.00.12	Phoenix 1.00.40	Phoenix 1.01
ZIF socket	○	○	○	○	○
Coprocessor supported	INA	INA	INA	INA	INA
MEMORY AND PROCESSOR RAM CACHE					
Installable RAM (minimum–maximum)	1Mb–64Mb	4Mb–192Mb	2Mb–192Mb	4Mb–256Mb	4Mb–36Mb
Cache controller	INA	N/A	INA	INA	OPTi
Installed RAM cache	INA	INA	INA	INA	INA
Installable RAM cache	0–256K	None	64K–128K	128K	64K–128K
DISK DRIVES					
Drive bays	3 5.25-inch, 2 3.5-inch	2 3.5-inch	1 5.25-inch, 3 3.5-inch	4 5.25-inch, 1 3.5-inch	2 5.25-inch
Disk controller location	Card	Card	Motherboard	Motherboard	Motherboard
Hard disk capacity	213Mb	212Mb	340Mb	535Mb	240Mb
Hard disk options	213Mb–535Mb	120Mb–535Mb	120Mb–1G	240Mb–1.5G	120Mb–240Mb
Interface	INA	INA	INA	INA	INA
Minimal floppy disk drive configuration	1.2Mb, 1.44Mb	1.44Mb	1.44Mb	1.44Mb	1.2Mb, 1.44Mb
EXPANSION BUS					
8-bit slots	None	None	None	None	None
16-bit slots	7	None	None	None	4
32-bit:					
EISA/MCA slots	1	8	4	5	None
Proprietary	None	4	2	1	None
Slots free in fully configured PC	INA	INA	INA	INA	INA
Parallel, serial, mouse ports on motherboard	None	1, 1, 1	1, 1, 1	1, 2, 0	1, 1, 1
Integrated network adapter option	INA	INA	None	None	INA
VIDEO					
Display circuitry location	Card	Motherboard	Motherboard	Motherboard	Motherboard
Chip set manufacturer	S3	NCR	NCR	Tseng	Tseng
POWER SUPPLY					
Power supply (watts)	200	218	182	285	110
Number of device connectors	5	4	4	6	4

●—Yes ○—No N/A—Not applicable INA—Information not available

Computers

	NEC PowerMate 486SX/25i	Netis 486/33 EISA	Netis EISA 450DX2	Netis ISA 425SX	Netis Ultra WinStation N466L
Price	$$$	$$$	$$$	$$	$$
Processor/speed	486SX/25MHz	486/33MHz	486DX2/50MHz	486SX/25MHz	486DX2/66MHz
Case type	Small-footprint	Tower	Small-footprint	Small-footprint	Desktop
Dimensions (HWD, in inches)	INA	24.5 × 7.5 × 17.5	INA	INA	INA
Installed RAM	INA	INA	INA	INA	INA
Bus architecture	ISA	INA	EISA	ISA	ISA
Warranty	1 year	INA	1 year	1 year	1 year

MOTHERBOARD

Motherboard manufacturer	NEC	Free Technology	Free Technology	Free Technology	Netis
Chip set manufacturer	OPTi	Intel	Intel	OPTi	Unichip
System shadowing/video shadowing	INA	●/●	●/●	INA	INA
BIOS version	Phoenix 1.01	Award 4.10 (December 1990)	AMI (May 1991)	AMI (June 1991)	AMI (December 1991)
ZIF socket	○	INA	○	○	○
Coprocessor supported	INA	INA	INA	INA	INA

MEMORY AND PROCESSOR RAM CACHE

Installable RAM (minimum–maximum)	4Mb–36Mb	1Mb–32Mb	4Mb–64Mb	4Mb–32Mb	1Mb–128Mb
Cache controller	INA	Discrete logic	Discrete Logic	INA	INA
Installed RAM cache	INA	64K	INA	INA	INA
Installable RAM cache	64K–128K	256K	1Mb–256Mb	64K–256K	64K–256K

DISK DRIVES

Drive bays	1 5.25-inch, 1 3.5-inch	6 half-height	3 5.25-inch, 1 3.5-inch	3 5.25-inch, 1 3.5-inch	1 5.25-inch, 2 3.5-inch
Disk controller location	Motherboard	Card	Card	Card	ISA card
Hard disk capacity	240Mb	200Mb	212Mb	212Mb	213Mb
Hard disk options	20Mb–245Mb	200Mb–1.2G	130Mb–1.2G	52Mb–1.2G	42Mb–520Mb
Interface	INA	SCSI	INA	INA	INA
Minimal floppy disk drive configuration	1.2Mb, 1.44Mb	1.2Mb, 1.44Mb	1.2Mb, 1.44Mb	1.2Mb, 1.44Mb	1.2Mb, 1.44Mb

EXPANSION BUS

8-bit slots	None	None	None	None	2
16-bit slots	4	2	2	8	5
32-bit:		6			
EISA/MCA slots	None	INA	6	None	None
Proprietary	None	INA	None	None	1
Slots free in fully configured PC	INA	5	INA	INA	INA
Parallel, serial, mouse ports on motherboard	1, 1, 1	INA	None	None	None
Integrated network adapter option	INA	INA	INA	INA	None

VIDEO

Display circuitry location	Motherboard	Card	Card	Card	Proprietary local bus
Chip set manufacturer	Tseng	WDC	S3	Tseng	Tseng

POWER SUPPLY

Power supply (watts)	110	INA	200	200	200
Number of device connectors	3	INA	5	4	5

●—Yes ○—No N/A—Not applicable INA—Information not available   **Table Continues** →

Computers

	Northgate 486e	Northgate Elegance 486/33	Northgate Elegance ZXP	Northgate Power Plus 486 ZXP	Northgate Slimline SP 386/40
Price	$$$	$$$$	$$$	$$	$$
Processor/speed	486DX2/50MHz	486/33MHz	486SX/25MHz	486/33MHz	Am386/40MHz
Case type	Small-footprint	Tower	Small-footprint	Tower	Small-footprint
Dimensions (HWD, in inches)	INA	26.3 × 7.3 × 16.5	INA	INA	INA
Installed RAM	INA	8Mb	4Mb	INA	INA
Bus architecture	EISA	INA	ISA	INA	INA
Warranty	1 year	1 year	1 year	1 year	1 year
MOTHERBOARD					
Motherboard manufacturer	TCM	Motherboard Factory	Northgate	Northgate	Motherboard Factory
Chip set manufacturer	OPTi	Discrete logic	OPTi	OPTi	VLSI/proprietary
System shadowing/video shadowing	●/●	○/○	INA	●/●	●/●
BIOS version	AMI 2.0	AMI (April 1990)	Mylex 6.10	Northgate 6.07	AMI B7VJN 1990
ZIF socket	○	INA	●	INA	INA
Coprocessor supported	INA	Weitek 4167	Weitek	80487/Weitek	80487/Weitek
MEMORY AND PROCESSOR RAM CACHE					
Installable RAM (minimum–maximum)	4Mb–128Mb	2Mb–16Mb	4Mb–32Mb	4Mb–32Mb	1Mb–32Mb
Cache controller	OPTi	Discrete logic	INA	OPTi	Northport
Installed RAM cache	INA	64K	INA	INA	INA
Installable RAM cache	256K	64K, 256K	64K–256K	64K	64K–256K
DISK DRIVES					
Drive bays	3 5.25-inch, 2 3.5-inch	7 half-height	3 5.25-inch, 2 3.5-inch	3 5.25-inch	1 5.25-inch, 2 3.5-inch
Disk controller location	Card	Card	Motherboard	Integrated	INA
Hard disk capacity	240Mb	200Mb	234Mb	212Mb	200Mb
Hard disk options	52Mb–2.4G	300Mb–600Mb	52Mb–1.2G	52Mb–1.2G	52Mb–535Mb
Interface	INA	IDE	INA	INA	INA
Minimal floppy disk drive configuration	1.2Mb, 1.44Mb	1.2Mb, 1.44Mb	1.2Mb, 1.44Mb	1.2Mb, 1.44Mb	1.2Mb
EXPANSION BUS					
8-bit slots	None	1	1	None	2 (2 open)
16-bit slots	None	6	6	8 (7 open)	3 (3 open)
32-bit:		1			
EISA/MCA slots	8	INA	None	None	None
Proprietary	None	INA	None	None	None
Slots free in fully configured PC	INA	5	INA	INA	INA
Parallel, serial, mouse ports on motherboard	1, 2, 0	INA	1, 2, 0	INA	INA
Integrated network adapter option	INA	INA	INA	INA	INA
VIDEO					
Display circuitry location	Card	Card	Card	Card	Motherboard
Chip set manufacturer	S3	Tseng	S3	S3	ATI
POWER SUPPLY					
Power supply (watts)	200	200	200	220	150
Number of device connectors	5	4	5	7	3

●—Yes ○—No N/A—Not applicable INA—Information not available

	Northgate SlimLine ZXP	Novas 486SX-20	Novas OPTimum 486 DX2-50	Novas OPTimum 486-25	Novas OPTimum 486-33
Price	$$$	$	$$$	$$$	$$$$
Processor/speed	486DX2/66MHz	486SX/20MHz	486DX2/50MHz	486/25MHz	486/33MHz
Case type	Slimline	Small-footprint	Desktop	Tower	Tower
Dimensions (HWD, in inches)	INA	INA	INA	24 × 7.5 × 17	24.5 × 8.8 × 20
Installed RAM	4Mb	INA	INA	INA	8Mb
Bus architecture	ISA	INA	EISA	INA	INA
Warranty	1 year	1 year	2 years	1 year on system, 2 years on parts	1 year
MOTHERBOARD					
Motherboard manufacturer	Northgate	Novacor	Novacor	Novacor	Novacor
Chip set manufacturer	Headland	OPTi	OPTi	OPTi	OPTi
System shadowing/video shadowing	INA	●/●	●/●	●/●	●/●
BIOS version	Northgate 9.01	Mr. BIOS 1.11	AMI (July 1991)	AMI (October 1990)	MR BIOS (1990)
ZIF socket	●	INA	○	INA	INA
Coprocessor supported	INA	80487/Weitek	INA	Weitek	Weitek 4167
MEMORY AND PROCESSOR RAM CACHE					
Installable RAM (minimum–maximum)	4Mb–128Mb	4Mb–32Mb	4Mb–256Mb	1Mb–16Mb	1Mb–32Mb
Cache controller	INA	OPTi	OPTi	OPTi	N/A
Installed RAM cache	INA	INA	INA	INA	N/A
Installable RAM cache	None	64K–256K	64K–512K	128K, 512K	N/A
DISK DRIVES					
Drive bays	2 5.25-inch, 1 3.5-inch	3 5.25-inch, 1 3.5-inch	3 5.25-inch	6 half-height	5 half-height, 2 full-height
Disk controller location	Motherboard	Integrated	Card	Card	Integrated
Hard disk capacity	245Mb	212Mb	240Mb	270Mb	212Mb
Hard disk options	100Mb–340Mb	40Mb–676Mb	240Mb–513Mb	40Mb–676Mb	40Mb–300Mb
Interface	INA	INA	INA	INA	IDE
Minimal floppy disk drive configuration	Dual	1.2Mb, 1.44Mb	1.2Mb, 1.44Mb	1.2Mb	1.2Mb, 1.44Mb
EXPANSION BUS					
8-bit slots	2	1 (open)	None	None	1
16-bit slots	3	7 (4 open)	None	6 (3 open)	5
32-bit:					2
EISA/MCA slots	None	None	8	None	INA
Proprietary	None	None	None	2 (2 open)	INA
Slots free in fully configured PC	INA	INA	INA	INA	4
Parallel, serial, mouse ports on motherboard	1, 2, 0	INA	None	INA	INA
Integrated network adapter option	None	INA	INA	INA	INA
VIDEO					
Display circuitry location	Motherboard	Card	Card	Card	Card
Chip set manufacturer	Headland	Tseng	S3	Tseng	C&T
POWER SUPPLY					
Power supply (watts)	150	200	230	275	275
Number of device connectors	3	6	5	6	6

●—Yes ○—No N/A—Not applicable INA—Information not available

Table Continues →

Computers

	Occidental 66MHz 486DX2	Osicom i450s	Osicom i466 MOD 420	Panther 486/33	Panther 486/33 EISA
Price	$$$	$$	$$$	$$$	$$$$
Processor/speed	486DX2/66MHz	486DX2/50MHz	486DX2/66MHz	486/33MHz	486/33MHz
Case type	Tower	Small-footprint	Small-footprint	Tower	Tower
Dimensions (HWD, in inches)	INA	INA	INA	25 × 7.5 × 16	25 × 7.5 × 16
Installed RAM	INA	INA	INA	8Mb	INA
Bus architecture	ISA	ISA	ISA	INA	INA
Warranty	1 year	1 year	1 year	1 year; 3 years for boards	INA
MOTHERBOARD					
Motherboard manufacturer	Occidental	Osicom	Osicom	Award	AMI
Chip set manufacturer	VLSI	UMC	OPTi	OPTi	Intel
System shadowing/video shadowing	INA	●/○	INA	●/○	●/●
BIOS version	AMI 1.04	AMI (July 1991)	AMI (June 1991)	Award 3.10 (1990)	AMI 4.1 (August 1990)
ZIF socket	●	○	○	INA	INA
Coprocessor supported	INA	INA	INA	None	INA
MEMORY AND PROCESSOR RAM CACHE					
Installable RAM (minimum–maximum)	1Mb–32Mb	4Mb–32Mb	1Mb–32Mb	2Mb–16Mb	1Mb–64Mb
Cache controller	INA	Microcom	INA	N/A	AMI
Installed RAM cache	INA	INA	INA	N/A	128K
Installable RAM cache	128K–256K	64K–256K	64K–256K	N/A	None
DISK DRIVES					
Drive bays	6 5.25-inch, 4 3.5-inch	3 5.25-inch, 1 3.5-inch	3 5.25-inch, 2 3.5-inch	6 half-height	3 full-height, 6 half-height
Disk controller location	Motherboard	Motherboard	ISA card	Integrated	Card
Hard disk capacity	245Mb	200Mb	420Mb	200Mb	329Mb
Hard disk options	170Mb–1.2G	200Mb–1G	100Mb–1.5G	300Mb–600Mb	325Mb–1G
Interface	INA	INA	INA	IDE	ESDI
Minimal floppy disk drive configuration	1.2Mb, 1.44Mb	1.2Mb, 1.44Mb	1.2Mb, 1.44Mb	1.2Mb, 1.44Mb	1.2Mb, 1.44Mb
EXPANSION BUS					
8-bit slots	1	1	2	None	1
16-bit slots	7	6	6	8	None
32-bit:					7
EISA/MCA slots	None	None	None	None	INA
Proprietary	None	1	None	None	INA
Slots free in fully configured PC	INA	INA	INA	5	5
Parallel, serial, mouse ports on motherboard	1, 2, 0	1, 2, 1	None	INA	INA
Integrated network adapter option	None	INA	None	INA	INA
VIDEO					
Display circuitry location	VESA local bus	Card	ISA card	Card	Card
Chip set manufacturer	NCR	Trident	S3	Paradise	ATI
POWER SUPPLY					
Power supply (watts)	200	200	200	200	INA
Number of device connectors	7	4	5	4	INA

●—Yes   ○—No   N/A—Not applicable   INA—Information not available

Computers

	PC Brand 386/40 Cache System	PC Brand 486/25 ISA	PC Brand 486/33	PC Brand 486/50 EISA Tower	PC Brand Leader Cache 486/DX2-66
Price	$$	$$$	$$$	$$$$	$$$
Processor/speed	Am386/40MHz	486/25MHz	486/33MHz	486DX2/50MHz	486DX2/66MHz
Case type	Desktop	Desktop	Desktop	Tower	Desktop
Dimensions (HWD, in inches)	INA	6.5 × 16 × 16.8	6.5 × 18.9 × 15.9	INA	INA
Installed RAM	INA	INA	8Mb	INA	INA
Bus architecture	INA	ISA	INA	EISA	ISA
Warranty	1 year	1 year	5 years on parts, 1 year on labor	1 year	1 year

MOTHERBOARD

Motherboard manufacturer	PC Brand	PC Brand	PC Brand	PC Brand	PC Brand
Chip set manufacturer	OPTi	OPTi	OPTi	Intel	Symphony
System shadowing/video shadowing	●/●	●/●	●/●	●/●	INA
BIOS version	AMI (February 1991)	MR V1.0C (1990)	Microid Research 1.08 (1990)	PC Brand (March 1992)	PC Brand 3.86
ZIF socket	INA	INA	INA	○	○
Coprocessor supported	80487/Weitek	Weitek	Weitek 4167	INA	INA

MEMORY AND PROCESSOR RAM CACHE

Installable RAM (minimum–maximum)	1Mb–64Mb	1Mb–16Mb	1Mb–32Mb	4Mb–64Mb	1Mb–32Mb
Cache controller	OPTi	OPTi	Intel	PC Brand	INA
Installed RAM cache	INA	INA	None	INA	INA
Installable RAM cache	128K–256K	128K	256K	64K	64K–256K

DISK DRIVES

Drive bays	3 5.25-inch, 1 3.5-inch	3 half-height, 2 3.5-inch	4 half-height, 2 3.5-inch	6 5.25-inch	2 5.25-inch, 2 3.5-inch
Disk controller location	INA	Card	Integrated	Motherboard	Motherboard
Hard disk capacity	211Mb	189Mb	200Mb	212Mb	170Mb
Hard disk options	40Mb–1.2G	44Mb–640Mb	40Mb–640Mb	212Mb–1.2G	105Mb–400Mb
Interface	INA	INA	IDE	INA	INA
Minimal floppy disk drive configuration	1.2Mb	1.2Mb or 1.44Mb	1.2Mb	1.2Mb, 1.44Mb	1.2Mb, 1.44Mb

EXPANSION BUS

8-bit slots	None	1 (open)	None	None	1
16-bit slots	6 (5 open)	6 (4 open)	7	1	4
32-bit:					
EISA/MCA slots	None	None	None	7	None
Proprietary	1 (open)	1 (open)	None	1	None
Slots free in fully configured PC	INA	INA	5	INA	INA
Parallel, serial, mouse ports on motherboard	INA	INA	INA	1, 2, 0	1, 2, 0
Integrated network adapter option	INA	INA	INA	INA	None

VIDEO

Display circuitry location	Card	Card	Card	Card	Motherboard
Chip set manufacturer	Tseng	Trident	Tseng	Tseng	WD

POWER SUPPLY

Power supply (watts)	200	200	200	300	200
Number of device connectors	4	4	4	5	5

●—Yes ○—No N/A—Not applicable INA—Information not available   **Table Continues** →

Computers

	PCI 486–50C128	PCI 486SX-25C256	PC Pros 486/66DX2 5550T	PC Pros/Touche 486-33 Model 5550	PC Pros/Touche 5550T/486 EISA-33
Price	$$$	$$$	$$$	$$$	$$$$
Processor/speed	486/50MHz	486SX/25MHz	486DX2/66MHz	486/33MHz	486/33MHz
Case type	Tower	Small-footprint	Tower	Tower	Tower
Dimensions (HWD, in inches)	INA	INA	INA	25 × 7.5 × 17.5	25.8 × 7.5 × 17.5
Installed RAM	INA	INA	INA	8Mb	INA
Bus architecture	INA	EISA	ISA	INA	EISA
Warranty	2 years	1 year	2 years	1 year	INA
MOTHERBOARD					
Motherboard manufacturer	Ideal	OPTi	AMI	AMI	AMI
Chip set manufacturer	Contaq	OPTi	C&T	C&T	Intel
System shadowing/video shadowing	●/●	INA	INA	○/●	●/●
BIOS version	AMI (May 1991)	AMI (July 1991)	AMI 1.2	AMI (April 1990)	AMI (August 1990)
ZIF socket	INA	○	○	INA	INA
Coprocessor supported	Weitek/Cyrix	INA	INA	Weitek 4167	INA
MEMORY AND PROCESSOR RAM CACHE					
Installable RAM (minimum–maximum)	1Mb–32Mb	1Mb–128Mb	1Mb–32Mb	4Mb–32Mb	1Mb–96Mb
Cache controller	Contaq	INA	INA	Proprietary	Discrete logic
Installed RAM cache	INA	INA	INA	128K	64K
Installable RAM cache	64K–256K	0–512K	64K–256K	256K	256K
DISK DRIVES					
Drive bays	4 5.25-inch	3 5.25-inch, 1 3.5-inch	6 5.25-inch, 3 3.5-inch	3 full-height, 6 half-height	6 half-height
Disk controller location	Card	Card	ISA card	Integrated	Card
Hard disk capacity	340Mb	245Mb	340Mb	338Mb	347Mb
Hard disk options	20Mb–1.2G	40Mb–1.2G	207Mb–1.35G	676Mb	203Mb–676Mb
Interface	INA	INA	INA	ESDI	ESDI
Minimal floppy disk drive configuration	1.2Mb, 1.44Mb	1.2Mb, 1.44Mb	1.2Mb, 1.44Mb	1.2Mb, 1.44Mb	1.2Mb, 1.44Mb
EXPANSION BUS					
8-bit slots	1 (open)	None	1	1	1
16-bit slots	6 (4 open)	None	7	6	None
32-bit:				1	7
EISA/MCA slots	None	8	None	INA	INA
Proprietary	None	None	None	INA	INA
Slots free in fully configured PC	INA	INA	INA	5	5
Parallel, serial, mouse ports on motherboard	INA	None	1, 2, 0	INA	INA
Integrated network adapter option	INA	INA	None	INA	INA
VIDEO					
Display circuitry location	Card	Card	ISA card	Card	Card
Chip set manufacturer	Contaq	ACU-MOS	S3	Tseng	Tseng
POWER SUPPLY					
Power supply (watts)	250	200	300	250	INA
Number of device connectors	4	4	4	4	INA

●—Yes ○—No N/A—Not applicable INA—Information not available

Computers

	PCS Double Pro-66	Peregrine 425T	Peregrine 486/33 Flyer	Poly 12/486-25A	Poly 486-25EISA
Price	$$$	$$$	$$$$	$$$	$$$
Processor/speed	486DX2/66MHz	486/25MHz	486/33MHz	486/25MHz	486/25MHz
Case type	Desktop	Tower	Tower	Tower	Desktop
Dimensions (HWD, in inches)	INA	24 × 7.5 × 16.5	24.5 × 7.5 × 18.5	24.5 × 7.5 × 17.5	6.5 × 21 × 16.5
Installed RAM	INA	INA	8Mb	INA	INA
Bus architecture	ISA	INA	INA	INA	EISA
Warranty	2 years	1 year	1 year	1 year on parts, 5 years on labor	1 year on parts, 5 years on labor

MOTHERBOARD

Motherboard manufacturer	AMI	Peregrine	AMI	Polywell	AIR
Chip set manufacturer	AMI Series 50	OPTi	Discrete logic	OPTi	Intel
System shadowing/video shadowing	INA	●/●	●/●	●/●	●/●
BIOS version	AMI (December 1991)	AMI (April 1990)	AMI (April 1990)	AMI EOBC-6188-101590-KF	Phoenix 1.00.04
ZIF socket	○	INA	INA	INA	INA
Coprocessor supported	INA	Weitek	Weitek 4167	Weitek	Weitek

MEMORY AND PROCESSOR RAM CACHE

Installable RAM (minimum–maximum)	1Mb–32Mb	1Mb–16Mb	1Mb–8Mb	1Mb–32Mb	1Mb–64Mb
Cache controller	INA	OPTi	Discrete logic	OPTi	Intel
Installed RAM cache	INA	INA	128K	INA	INA
Installable RAM cache	64K–256K	64K, 2Mb	128K	64K, 512K	64K

DISK DRIVES

Drive bays	3 5.25-inch, 1 3.5-inch	6 half-height, 2 3.5-inch	6 half-height	6 half-height, 1 3.5-inch	6 half-height
Disk controller location	Motherboard	Integrated	Integrated	Card	Card
Hard disk capacity	245Mb	200Mb	200Mb	200Mb	200Mb
Hard disk options	80Mb–425Mb	40Mb–650Mb	300Mb–600Mb	100Mb–2.5G	150Mb–2.5G
Interface	INA	INA	IDE	INA	INA
Minimal floppy disk drive configuration	1.2Mb, 1.44Mb	1.2Mb, 1.44Mb	1.2Mb, 1.44Mb	1.2Mb, 1.44Mb	1.2Mb, 1.44Mb

EXPANSION BUS

8-bit slots	1	2 (1 open)	1	2 (2 open)	None
16-bit slots	7	6 (4 open)	6	10 (7 open)	None
32-bit:			1		
EISA/MCA slots	None	None	INA	None	8 (6 open)
Proprietary	None	None	INA	None	None
Slots free in fully configured PC	INA	INA	6	INA	INA
Parallel, serial, mouse ports on motherboard	1, 1, 0	INA	INA	INA	INA
Integrated network adapter option	None	INA	INA	INA	INA

VIDEO

Display circuitry location	ISA card	Card	Card	Card	Card
Chip set manufacturer	Tseng	Tseng	Tseng	Tseng	Tseng

POWER SUPPLY

Power supply (watts)	200	300	300	250	220
Number of device connectors	4	5	10	4	4

●—Yes ○—No N/A—Not applicable INA—Information not available

Table Continues →

Computers

	Poly 486–50VF	Poly 486-50DX2	Poly 486-66LM	Poly 486SX-25Y	Proteus 486/33 EISA
Price	$$$	$$$	$$$	$$	$$$
Processor/speed	486/50MHz	486DX2/50MHz	486DX2/66MHz	486SX/25MHz	486/33MHz
Case type	Tower	Small-footprint	Tower	Tower	Mini-tower
Dimensions (HWD, in inches)	INA	INA	INA	INA	15.5 × 8.5 × 19.5
Installed RAM	INA	INA	INA	INA	INA
Bus architecture	INA	EISA	ISA	ISA	EISA
Warranty	2–5 years	2 years	2 years on parts, 5 years on labor	5 years on parts, 2 years on labor	INA
MOTHERBOARD					
Motherboard manufacturer	InterComp	InterComp	Orchid	Young Technology	AMI
Chip set manufacturer	OPTi	OPTi	OPTi	Symphony	Intel
System shadowing/video shadowing	●/●	●/●	INA	INA	●/●
BIOS version	AMI (September 1991)	AMI (July 1991)	AMI (July 1991)	AMI (July 1991)	AMI 1.10 (October 1990)
ZIF socket	INA	○	○	○	INA
Coprocessor supported	Weitek/Cyrix	INA	INA	INA	INA
MEMORY AND PROCESSOR RAM CACHE					
Installable RAM (minimum–maximum)	1Mb–32Mb	4Mb–128Mb	4Mb–32Mb	4Mb–32Mb	4Mb–96Mb
Cache controller	OPTi	OPTi	INA	INA	Discrete logic
Installed RAM cache	INA	INA	INA	INA	128K
Installable RAM cache	256K–512K	256K–512K	64K–256K	64K–256K	None
DISK DRIVES					
Drive bays	4 5.25-inch	3 5.25-inch, 2 3.5-inch	3 5.25-inch, 3 3.5-inch	3 5.25-inch, 2 3.5-inch	5 half-height
Disk controller location	Card	Card	ISA card	Card	Card
Hard disk capacity	340Mb	212Mb	320Mb	213Mb	200Mb
Hard disk options	200Mb–2.5G	340Mb–2.5G	120Mb–2G	213Mb–2G	200Mb–600Mb
Interface	INA	INA	INA	INA	ESDI
Minimal floppy disk drive configuration	1.2Mb, 1.44Mb	1.2Mb, 1.44Mb	1.2Mb, 1.44Mb	1.2Mb, 1.44Mb	1.2Mb, 1.44Mb
EXPANSION BUS					
8-bit slots	None	None	None	None	None
16-bit slots	8 (5 open)	None	7	8	None
32-bit:					8
EISA/MCA slots	None	8	None	None	INA
Proprietary	None	None	1	None	INA
Slots free in fully configured PC	INA	INA	INA	INA	5
Parallel, serial, mouse ports on motherboard	INA	None	None	None	INA
Integrated network adapter option	INA	INA	None	INA	INA
VIDEO					
Display circuitry location	Card	Card	Proprietary local bus	Card	Card
Chip set manufacturer	S3	S3	S3	S3	Tseng
POWER SUPPLY					
Power supply (watts)	250	230	250	230	INA
Number of device connectors	6	4	5	5	INA

●—Yes   ○—No   N/A—Not applicable   INA—Information not available

Computers

	QSI Klonimus 486DX2/66	Quill Qtech 486 4D2/66	Reason Square 4	SAI 486/25 ISA	SAI 486/33
Price	$$$	$$$	$$	$$	$$$
Processor/speed	486DX2/66MHz	486DX2/66MHz	486/25MHz	486/25MHz	486/33MHz
Case type	Small-footprint	Small-footprint	Small-footprint	Desktop	Desktop
Dimensions (HWD, in inches)	7 × 15 × 16.5	INA	6 × 16 × 15.3	6.3 × 17.5 × 18	6 × 21 × 16
Installed RAM	4Mb	INA	INA	INA	8Mb
Bus architecture	ISA	ISA	INA	ISA	INA
Warranty	2 years	1 year	2 years	1 year on parts, 3 years on labor	1 year on parts, 3 years on labor
MOTHERBOARD					
Motherboard manufacturer	Contaq	TMC	Reason	AIR	AIR
Chip set manufacturer	Contaq	OPTi	OPTi	Intel	Intel
System shadowing/video shadowing	INA	INA	●/●	●/●	●/●
BIOS version	AMI (December 1991)	AMI (June 1991)	AMI (1990)	AMI 0904 (1990)	AMI (May 1990)
ZIF socket	○	○	INA	INA	INA
Coprocessor supported	INA	INA	Weitek	Weitek	Weitek 4167
MEMORY AND PROCESSOR RAM CACHE					
Installable RAM (minimum–maximum)	1Mb–32Mb	1Mb–32Mb	4Mb–16Mb	2Mb–16Mb	2Mb–16Mb
Cache controller	INA	INA	OPTi	Discrete logic	Intel
Installed RAM cache	INA	INA	INA	INA	128K
Installable RAM cache	64K–256K	64K–256K	128K	128K, 256K	128K, 256K
DISK DRIVES					
Drive bays	4 5.25-inch, 1 3.5-inch	3 5.25-inch, 2 3.5-inch	3 half-height, 2 3.5-inch	5 half-height	5 half-height
Disk controller location	ISA card	ISA card	Card	Card	Integrated
Hard disk capacity	340Mb	334Mb	200Mb	200Mb	212Mb
Hard disk options	40Mb–1.2G	40Mb–1.2G	52Mb–676Mb	40Mb–1.2G	150Mb–300Mb
Interface	INA	INA	INA	INA	IDE
Minimal floppy disk drive configuration	1.2Mb, 1.44Mb	1.2Mb, 1.44Mb	1.2Mb, 1.44Mb	1.2Mb, 1.44Mb	1.2Mb, 1.44Mb
EXPANSION BUS					
8-bit slots	2	2	None	None	None
16-bit slots	6	5	7 (5 open)	8 (5 open)	8
32-bit:					
EISA/MCA slots	None	None	None	None	None
Proprietary	None	None	1 (open)	None	None
Slots free in fully configured PC	INA	INA	INA	INA	6
Parallel, serial, mouse ports on motherboard	None	None	INA	INA	INA
Integrated network adapter option	None	None	INA	INA	INA
VIDEO					
Display circuitry location	ISA card	ISA card	Card	Card	Card
Chip set manufacturer	ATI	S3	Tseng	Tseng	Western Digital
POWER SUPPLY					
Power supply (watts)	200	230	200	200	200
Number of device connectors	4	5	4	5	4

●—Yes   ○—No   N/A—Not applicable   INA—Information not available

Table Continues →

ZIFF-DAVIS PRESS

Computers

	SAI 486/33 EISA	Silicon SVC 450DXC I2–510	Silicon Pylon II 486DXi-212	Silicon SVC-I486SX25-212	SST 486DX2-50MWC
Price	$$$$	$$	$$$	$$	$$$
Processor/speed	486/33MHz	486/50MHz	486DX2/66MHz	486SX/25MHz	486DX2/50MHz
Case type	Desktop	Tower	Mini-tower	Small-footprint	Desktop
Dimensions (HWD, in inches)	5.9 × 21 × 15.9	INA	INA	INA	17 × 16 × 16
Installed RAM	INA	INA	INA	INA	4Mb
Bus architecture	EISA	INA	ISA	ISA	EISA
Warranty	INA	1 year	1 year	1 year	1 year
MOTHERBOARD					
Motherboard manufacturer	AIR	Silicon Valley	Silicon Valley	Silicon Valley	SST
Chip set manufacturer	Intel	OPTi	OPTi	OPTi	Intel
System shadowing/video shadowing	●/●	●/●	INA	INA	●/●
BIOS version	Phoenix 1.00.04 (March 1990)	SVC AT 4.01.dg	SVC 4020A	SVC 4.02	Award 486 V4.0
ZIF socket	INA	INA	○	○	○
Coprocessor supported	INA	Weitek/Cyrix	INA	INA	Intel, Weitek
MEMORY AND PROCESSOR RAM CACHE					
Installable RAM (minimum–maximum)	1Mb–64Mb	1Mb–64Mb	1Mb–64Mb	1Mb–64Mb	2Mb–32Mb
Cache controller	Discrete logic	OPTi	INA	INA	SIS
Installed RAM cache	256K	INA	INA	INA	INA
Installable RAM cache	None	64K–256K	64K–256K	N/A	64K
DISK DRIVES					
Drive bays	5 half-height	3 5.25-inch, 2 3.5-inch	3 5.25-inch, 4 3.5-inch	3 5.25-inch, 2 3.5-inch	5 5.25-inch
Disk controller location	Card	Card	ISA card	Card	Card
Hard disk capacity	200Mb	510Mb	212Mb	212Mb	212Mb
Hard disk options	150Mb–600Mb	40Mb–510Mb	42Mb–528Mb	42Mb–528Mb	120Mb–2G
Interface	ESDI	INA	INA	INA	INA
Minimal floppy disk drive configuration	1.2Mb, 1.44Mb	1.2Mb, 1.44Mb	1.2Mb, 1.44Mb	1.2Mb, 1.44Mb	1.2Mb, 1.44Mb
EXPANSION BUS					
8-bit slots	None	None	None	2	None
16-bit slots	None	8 (6 open)	8	6	None
32-bit:	8				8
EISA/MCA slots	INA	None	None	None	None
Proprietary	INA	1 (open)	None	None	None
Slots free in fully configured PC	6	INA	INA	INA	INA
Parallel, serial, mouse ports on motherboard	INA	INA	None	None	None
Integrated network adapter option	INA	INA	None	INA	INA
VIDEO					
Display circuitry location	Card	Card	ISA card	Card	Card
Chip set manufacturer	Tseng	Trident	S3	S3	S3
POWER SUPPLY					
Power supply (watts)	INA	230	220	220	200
Number of device connectors	INA	5	4	4	5

●—Yes ○—No N/A—Not applicable INA—Information not available

Computers

	Softworks Citus 486 TS 25i	Softworks Citus MDC	Softworks Citus MDC 486SX/25	Spear 486 Convertible	Spear Super 486SX/25
Price	$$$	$$$	$$$	$$	$$$
Processor/speed	486/25MHz	486DX2/50MHz	486SX/25MHz	486DX2/50MHz	486SX/25MHz
Case type	Tower	Small-footprint	Small-footprint	Tower	Tower
Dimensions (HWD, in inches)	25.3 × 7.5 × 16.9	INA	INA	INA	INA
Installed RAM	INA	INA	INA	INA	INA
Bus architecture	INA	ISA	ISA	ISA	EISA
Warranty	1 year	1 year	1 year	1 year	1 year
MOTHERBOARD					
Motherboard manufacturer	Softworks	SDC	Softworks	Quickpath	Elisa
Chip set manufacturer	OPTi	UMC	UMC	OPTi	OPTi
System shadowing/video shadowing	●/●	●/●	INA	●/●	INA
BIOS version	AMI (October 1990)	AMI (July 1991)	AMI (May 1991)	Pixel Engineering 1.3	Award V.4.20
ZIF socket	INA	○	○	●	●
Coprocessor supported	INA	INA	INA	INA	INA
MEMORY AND PROCESSOR RAM CACHE					
Installable RAM (minimum–maximum)	1Mb–64Mb	1Mb–32Mb	1Mb–32Mb	1Mb–32Mb	1Mb–128Mb
Cache controller	OPTi	UMC	INA	OPTi	INA
Installed RAM cache	INA	INA	INA	INA	INA
Installable RAM cache	64K, 128K	64K–256K	64K–256K	64K–256K	64K–512K
DISK DRIVES					
Drive bays	7 half-height	3 5.25-inch, 2 3.5-inch	3 5.25-inch, 2 3.5-inch	4 5.25-inch	2 5.25-inch, 2 3.5-inch
Disk controller location	Card	Card	Card	Card	Card
Hard disk capacity	213Mb	202Mb	130Mb	245Mb	213Mb
Hard disk options	40Mb–1.03G	40Mb–1.6G	40Mb–340Mb	120Mb–520Mb	40Mb–1.3G
Interface	INA	INA	INA	INA	INA
Minimal floppy disk drive configuration	1.2Mb or 1.44Mb	1.2Mb, 1.44Mb	1.2Mb, 1.44Mb	1.2Mb, 1.44Mb	1.2Mb, 1.44Mb
EXPANSION BUS					
8-bit slots	1 (open)	2	2	None	None
16-bit slots	7 (4 open)	5	5	8	None
32-bit:					
EISA/MCA slots	None	None	None	None	5
Proprietary	None	None	None	None	3
Slots free in fully configured PC	INA	INA	INA	INA	INA
Parallel, serial, mouse ports on motherboard	INA	None	None	None	1, 2, 0
Integrated network adapter option	INA	INA	INA	INA	INA
VIDEO					
Display circuitry location	Card	Card	Card	Card	Card
Chip set manufacturer	WD	WD	WD	S3	Tseng
POWER SUPPLY					
Power supply (watts)	220	300	300	250	230
Number of device connectors	6	6	4	5	8

●—Yes ○—No N/A—Not applicable INA—Information not available

Table Continues →

Computers

	SST 386-40MWC	SST 486-50MWC	SST 486DX2-66MWC	Standard 486/33	Standard Advantage 486 DX2/50
Price	$$	$$	$$$	$$$	$$$
Processor/speed	Am386/40MHz	486/50MHz	486DX2/66MHz	486/33MHz	486DX2/50MHz
Case type	Small-footprint	Small-footprint	Desktop	Mini-tower	Tower
Dimensions (HWD, in inches)	INA	INA	INA	14.5 × 8.5 × 16.5	INA
Installed RAM	INA	INA	INA	8Mb	INA
Bus architecture	INA	INA	ISA	INA	EISA
Warranty	1 year	1 year	1 year	1 year	2 years
MOTHERBOARD					
Motherboard manufacturer	TMC	TMC	SST	AMI	BCM
Chip set manufacturer	OPTi	C&T, OPTi	OPTi	C&T	Intel
System shadowing/video shadowing	●/●	●/●	INA	●/●	●/●
BIOS version	AMI 3.31	AMI (July 1991)	AMI (December 1991)	AMI (1990)	AMI 1.01
ZIF socket	INA	INA	○	INA	○
Coprocessor supported	80487/Weitek	Weitek	INA	Weitek 4167	INA
MEMORY AND PROCESSOR RAM CACHE					
Installable RAM (minimum–maximum)	1Mb–64Mb	1Mb–64Mb	4Mb–32Mb	1Mb–32Mb	8Mb–64Mb
Cache controller	OPTi	OPTi	INA	Discrete logic	Intel
Installed RAM cache	INA	INA	INA	128K	INA
Installable RAM cache	64K–256K	64K–256K	64K–256K	128K	256K
DISK DRIVES					
Drive bays	3 5.25-inch, 2 3.5-inch	3 5.25-inch, 2 3.5-inch	3 5.25-inch, 1 3.5-inch	3 half-height, 2 3.5-inch	6 5.25-inch
Disk controller location	INA	Card	ISA card	Integrated	Card
Hard disk capacity	200Mb	340Mb	212Mb	200Mb	240Mb
Hard disk options	44Mb–2.1G	40Mb–1.2G	80Mb–2G	100Mb–600Mb	240Mb–535Mb
Interface	INA	INA	INA	IDE	INA
Minimal floppy disk drive configuration	1.2Mb	1.2Mb, 1.44Mb	Dual	1.2Mb, 1.44Mb	1.2Mb, 1.44Mb
EXPANSION BUS					
8-bit slots	2 (2 open)	1 (open)	1	2	None
16-bit slots	6 (4 open)	6 (4 open)	7	6	1
32-bit:					
EISA/MCA slots	None	None	None	None	6
Proprietary	None	1 (open)	None	None	1
Slots free in fully configured PC	INA	INA	INA	5	INA
Parallel, serial, mouse ports on motherboard	INA	INA	None	INA	None
Integrated network adapter option	INA	INA	None	INA	INA
VIDEO					
Display circuitry location	Card	Card	ISA card	Card	Card
Chip set manufacturer	Tseng	S3	S3	Trident	ATI
POWER SUPPLY					
Power supply (watts)	200	200	200	200	250
Number of device connectors	5	5	2	5	6

●—Yes   ○—No   N/A—Not applicable   INA—Information not available

Computers

	Standard Windows Workstation Plus	Swan 486DX2-50DB	Swan 486DX2-66DB	Swan 486SX/25DB	Systems Integration Associates SIA 486/33
Price	$$$	$$$	$$$$	$$$	$$$$
Processor/speed	486DX2/66MHz	486DX2/50MHz	486DX2/66MHz	486SX/25MHz	486/33MHz
Case type	Desktop	Small-footprint	Desktop	Small-footprint	Tower
Dimensions (HWD, in inches)	INA	INA	INA	INA	29.5 × 9 × 23.5
Installed RAM	INA	INA	INA	INA	8Mb
Bus architecture	EISA	ISA	ISA	ISA	INA
Warranty	2 years	2 years	2 years	2 years	1 year
MOTHERBOARD					
Motherboard manufacturer	BCM	SCI	Swan	Swan	SIA
Chip set manufacturer	Intel	Syscon	Syscon	Syscon	Discrete logic
System shadowing/video shadowing	INA	●/●	INA	INA	●/●
BIOS version	AMI (May 1991)	AMI (September 1989)	AMI (May 1991)	AMI 1.0	AMI (April 1990)
ZIF socket	○	○	○	○	INA
Coprocessor supported	INA	INA	INA	INA	Weitek 4167
MEMORY AND PROCESSOR RAM CACHE					
Installable RAM (minimum–maximum)	4Mb–64Mb	4Mb–64Mb	4Mb–64Mb	4Mb–64Mb	1Mb–32Mb
Cache controller	INA	Syscon	INA	INA	Discrete logic
Installed RAM cache	INA	INA	INA	INA	128K
Installable RAM cache	64K–256K	128K	128K	128K	128K
DISK DRIVES					
Drive bays	3 5.25-inch, 2 3.5-inch	3 5.25-inch	5 5.25-inch, 1 3.5-inch	3 5.25-inch	10 half-height
Disk controller location	EISA card	Motherboard	Motherboard	Motherboard	Integrated
Hard disk capacity	240Mb	233Mb	318Mb	202Mb	322Mb
Hard disk options	130Mb–500Mb	50Mb–1.6G	120Mb–1.6G	60Mb–1.2G	90Mb–1.2G
Interface	INA	INA	INA	INA	ESDI
Minimal floppy disk drive configuration	1.2Mb, 1.44Mb	1.2Mb, 1.44Mb	1.2Mb, 1.44Mb	1.2Mb, 1.44Mb	1.2Mb
EXPANSION BUS					
8-bit slots	None	None	None	None	2
16-bit slots	1	6	6	5	6
32-bit:					
EISA/MCA slots	6	None	None	None	None
Proprietary	None	1	None	1	None
Slots free in fully configured PC	INA	INA	INA	INA	5
Parallel, serial, mouse ports on motherboard	None	1, 2, 0	1, 2, 0	1, 2, 0	INA
Integrated network adapter option	None	INA	None	INA	INA
VIDEO					
Display circuitry location	ISA card	Card	Proprietary local bus	Motherboard	Card
Chip set manufacturer	ATI	S3	S3	S3	SIA
POWER SUPPLY					
Power supply (watts)	200	200	200	200	450
Number of device connectors	4	5	5	5	8

●—Yes ○—No N/A—Not applicable INA—Information not available

Table Continues →

Computers

	Tandon 486/33 EISA	Tandy 4825 SX	Tangent Model 340	Tangent Model 425e	Tangent Model 425i
Price	$$$$	$$$	$$	$$$$	$$$
Processor/speed	486/33MHz	486SX/25MHz	Am386/40MHz	486/25MHz	486/25MHz
Case type	Tower	Slimline	Desktop	Tower	Mini-tower
Dimensions (HWD, in inches)	26.1 × 10.2 × 19.6	INA	INA	24.5 × 7.3 × 18	15.3 × 8.5 × 16
Installed RAM	INA	INA	INA	INA	INA
Bus architecture	EISA	ISA	INA	INA	INA
Warranty	INA	1 year	1 year	1 year for system, 2 years for motherboard	1 year

MOTHERBOARD
Motherboard manufacturer	Tandon	Tandy	Technology Power	Mylex	Dash
Chip set manufacturer	Intel	VLSI	VLSI	Intel	OPTi
System shadowing/video shadowing	●/●	INA	●/●	●/●	●/●
BIOS version	Tandon 3.62 (July 1990)	Phoenix 1.10	AMI 1.7	Phoenix 2.00, Mylex EISA 6.02	AMI EOBC 6150 (November 1990)
ZIF socket	INA	○	INA	INA	INA
Coprocessor supported	INA	INA	80487/Weitek	Weitek	Weitek

MEMORY AND PROCESSOR RAM CACHE
Installable RAM (minimum–maximum)	2Mb–64Mb	4Mb–32Mb	1Mb–64Mb	1Mb–32Mb	1Mb–32Mb
Cache controller	Discrete logic	INA	Northport	Mylex	Discrete logic
Installed RAM cache	64K	INA	INA	INA	INA
Installable RAM cache	None	N/A	64K–256K	128K	128K, 512K

DISK DRIVES
Drive bays	8 half-height	1 5.25-inch, 2 3.5-inch	3 5.25-inch	6 half-height	4 half-height, 1 3.5-inch
Disk controller location	Card	Motherboard	INA	Card	Card
Hard disk capacity	330Mb	240Mb	202Mb	207Mb	207Mb
Hard disk options	330Mb–1G	52Mb–440Mb	52Mb–2G	105Mb–7G	55Mb–1.2G
Interface	SCSI	INA	INA	INA	INA
Minimal floppy disk drive configuration	1.2Mb, 1.44Mb	1.2Mb, 1.44Mb	1.2Mb	1.2Mb	1.2Mb

EXPANSION BUS
8-bit slots	None	None	None	None	None
16-bit slots	2	3	7 (5 open)	None	8 (6 open)
32-bit:	6				
EISA/MCA slots	INA	None	None	8 (5 open)	None
Proprietary	INA	None	1	None	None
Slots free in fully configured PC	6	INA	INA	INA	INA
Parallel, serial, mouse ports on motherboard	INA	1, 2, 1	INA	INA	INA
Integrated network adapter option	INA	INA	INA	INA	INA

VIDEO
Display circuitry location	Card	Motherboard	Card	Card	Card
Chip set manufacturer	Tseng	WD	S3	Tseng/Edsun	Tseng/Sierra

POWER SUPPLY
Power supply (watts)	INA	100	200	270	275
Number of device connectors	INA	3	4	8	4

●—Yes ○—No N/A—Not applicable INA—Information not available

	Tangent Model 425se	Tangent 433e	Tangent 433i	Tangent Model 450ex	Tangent Model 466ex
Price	$$$	$$$	$$	$$$$	$$$
Processor/speed	486SX/25MHz	486/33MHz	486/33MHz	486DX2/50MHz	486DX2/66MHz
Case type	Small-footprint	Tower	Mini-tower	Mini-tower	Tower
Dimensions (HWD, in inches)	INA	INA	INA	INA	INA
Installed RAM	INA	INA	INA	INA	INA
Bus architecture	EISA	INA	INA	EISA	EISA
Warranty	1 year	1 year	1 year	1 year	1 year

MOTHERBOARD

Motherboard manufacturer	Nice USA	Mylex	Dash	Mylex	Micro Center
Chip set manufacturer	SIS	Intel	OPTi	Intel	SIS
System shadowing/video shadowing	INA	●/●	●/●	●/●	INA
BIOS version	AMI (December 1991)	Mylex 6.04	AMI (March 1991)	Mylex 6.0	SIS-EISA-F (December 1991)
ZIF socket	○	INA	INA	○	○
Coprocessor supported	INA	80487/Weitek	80487/Weitek	INA	INA

MEMORY AND PROCESSOR RAM CACHE

Installable RAM (minimum–maximum)	4Mb–128Mb	1Mb–32Mb	1Mb–64Mb	4Mb–32Mb	4Mb–128Mb
Cache controller	INA	Mylex	OPTi	Mylex	INA
Installed RAM cache	INA	INA	INA	INA	INA
Installable RAM cache	64K–256K	128K	64K–256K	128K	64K–256K

DISK DRIVES

Drive bays	3 5.25-inch, 1 3.5-inch	6 5.25-inch	3 5.25-inch	3 5.25-inch, 2 3.5-inch	3 5.25-inch, 3 3.5-inch
Disk controller location	Card	Card	Integrated	Card	EISA card
Hard disk capacity	212Mb	210Mb	210Mb	212Mb	340Mb
Hard disk options	212Mb–1G	52Mb–1.6G	52Mb–1.6G	210Mb–1G	200Mb–3G
Interface	INA	INA	INA	INA	INA
Minimal floppy disk drive configuration	1.2Mb, 1.44Mb	1.2Mb	1.2Mb	1.2Mb, 1.44Mb	Dual

EXPANSION BUS

8-bit slots	None	None	None	None	None
16-bit slots	2	None	8 (5 open)	None	2
32-bit:					
EISA/MCA slots	6	8 (5 open)	None	8	6
Proprietary	None	None	None	None	None
Slots free in fully configured PC	INA	INA	INA	INA	INA
Parallel, serial, mouse ports on motherboard	1, 2, 0	INA	INA	None	None
Integrated network adapter option	INA	INA	INA	INA	None

VIDEO

Display circuitry location	Card	Card	Card	Card	ISA card
Chip set manufacturer	S3	S3	S3	S3	WD

POWER SUPPLY

Power supply (watts)	300	300	300	300	200
Number of device connectors	4	4	6	4	4

●—Yes   ○—No   N/A—Not applicable   INA—Information not available

Table Continues →

Computers

	Tenex 486 Power Column	Touche 5550T/486-25	Touche 5550T/486-25E	Treasure Chest TC486-25	Tri-Star 66/DX2-VL
Price	$$	$$	$$$	$$	$$$
Processor/speed	486/25MHz	486/25MHz	486/25MHz	486/25MHz	486DX2/66MHz
Case type	Tower	Tower	Tower	Tower	Tower
Dimensions (HWD, in inches)	21 × 7.3 × 18.3	26 × 7.5 × 17.5	23.5 × 11 × 17.5	21 × 7.1 × 20	INA
Installed RAM	INA	INA	INA	INA	INA
Bus architecture	INA	INA	INA	INA	ISA
Warranty	1 year	1 year	1 year	1 year	2 years on parts, lifetime on labor
MOTHERBOARD					
Motherboard manufacturer	DTK	AMI	AMI	DTK	Micronics
Chip set manufacturer	VLSI	C&T	Intel	Intel	C&T/Micronics
System shadowing/video shadowing	○/○	●/●	●/●	●/●	INA
BIOS version	DTK 486 4.26	AMI (April 1990)	AMI 33235	AMI (April 1990)	Phoenix (January 1991)
ZIF socket	INA	INA	INA	INA	○
Coprocessor supported	Weitek	Weitek	Weitek	Weitek	INA
MEMORY AND PROCESSOR RAM CACHE					
Installable RAM (minimum–maximum)	1Mb–16Mb	1Mb–16Mb	1Mb–96Mb	1Mb–16Mb	4Mb–64Mb
Cache controller	Discrete logic	Proprietary	AMI	Austek	INA
Installed RAM cache	INA	INA	INA	INA	INA
Installable RAM cache	64K, 256K	128K	64K, 256K	64K, 256K	0–256K
DISK DRIVES					
Drive bays	5 half-height	3 full-height	10 half-height	6 half-height	8 5.25-inch
Disk controller location	Card	Card	Integrated	Card	Motherboard
Hard disk capacity	210Mb	200Mb	200Mb	211Mb	340Mb
Hard disk options	84Mb–676Mb	76Mb–1470Mb	76Mb–1470Mb	45Mb–1.05G	210Mb–1.7G
Interface	INA	INA	INA	INA	INA
Minimal floppy disk drive configuration	1.2Mb or 1.44Mb	1.2Mb, 1.44Mb	1.2Mb, 1.44Mb	1.2Mb, 1.44Mb	1.2Mb, 1.44Mb
EXPANSION BUS					
8-bit slots	1 (open)	1 (none open)	None	2 (2 open)	None
16-bit slots	6 (4 open)	6 (4 open)	None	6 (4 open)	6
32-bit:					
EISA/MCA slots	None	None	7 (5 open)	None	None
Proprietary	1 (open)	1 (open)	1 (open)	None	None
Slots free in fully configured PC	INA	INA	INA	INA	INA
Parallel, serial, mouse ports on motherboard	INA	INA	INA	INA	1, 2, 0
Integrated network adapter option	INA	INA	INA	INA	None
VIDEO					
Display circuitry location	Card	Card	Card	Card	VESA local bus
Chip set manufacturer	Tseng	Tseng	Tseng	Tseng	ATI
POWER SUPPLY					
Power supply (watts)	200	300	475	200	300
Number of device connectors	4	4	6	5	8

●—Yes ○—No N/A—Not applicable INA—Information not available

Computers

	Tri-Star Flash Cache 486	Tri-Star Flash Cache 486 EISA	Tri-Win 486SX/25	Tri-Win 486 DX2-50 EISA	Twinhead Superset 590/25C
Price	$$$$	$$	$$	$$$	$
Processor/speed	486/33MHz	486/33MHz	486SX/25MHz	486DX2/50MHz	386SX/25MHz
Case type	Tower	Tower	Slimline	Tower	Small-footprint
Dimensions (HWD, in inches)	24.3 × 8.8 × 19.3	INA	INA	INA	5 × 13.5 × 14.5
Installed RAM	8Mb	INA	INA	INA	1Mb
Bus architecture	INA	EISA	ISA	EISA	ISA
Warranty	2 years	2 years	2 years on parts, lifetime on labor	2 years	1 year

MOTHERBOARD

Motherboard manufacturer	TP Enterprise	Free Technology	Contaq	Free Technology	Twinhead
Chip set manufacturer	VLSI, discrete logic	Intel	Contaq	Intel	Intel/VLSI
System shadowing/video shadowing	○/○	●/●	INA	●/●	●/●
BIOS version	AMI (April 1990)	Award 15410005	AMI (July 1991)	AMI (May 1991)	Award 3.15C
ZIF socket	INA	INA	○	○	INA
Coprocessor supported	Weitek 4167	80487/Weitek	INA	INA	80387SX

MEMORY AND PROCESSOR RAM CACHE

Installable RAM (minimum–maximum)	1Mb–16Mb	4Mb–64Mb	4Mb–32Mb	4Mb–64Mb	1Mb–17Mb
Cache controller	Proprietary	Free Technology	INA	Discrete Logic	Intel
Installed RAM cache	64K	INA	INA	INA	INA
Installable RAM cache	64K, 256K	256K	INA	256K	16K

DISK DRIVES

Drive bays	3 full-height, 5 half-height	4 5.25-inch	3 5.25-inch, 2 3.5-inch	4 5.25-inch	3 5.25-inch
Disk controller location	Integrated	Card	Card	Card	Integrated
Hard disk capacity	200Mb	210Mb	210Mb	212Mb	INA
Hard disk options	65Mb–1.2G	40Mb–1.2G	105Mb–1.7G	80Mb–1.7G	40Mb–200Mb
Interface	IDE	INA	INA	INA	INA
Minimal floppy disk drive configuration	1.2Mb, 1.44Mb	1.2Mb, 1.44Mb	1.2Mb, 1.44Mb	1.2Mb, 1.44Mb	1.2Mb

EXPANSION BUS

8-bit slots	None	None	2	None	None
16-bit slots	6	2 (none open)	6	2	4 (4 open)
32-bit:	1				
EISA/MCA slots	INA	6 (5 open)	None	6	None
Proprietary	INA	None	None	None	None
Slots free in fully configured PC	6	INA	INA	INA	INA
Parallel, serial, mouse ports on motherboard	INA	INA	None	None	1, 2, 0
Integrated network adapter option	INA	INA	INA	INA	INA

VIDEO

Display circuitry location	Card	Card	Card	Card	Motherboard
Chip set manufacturer	Tseng	Tseng/Sierra	Tseng	S3	Trident

POWER SUPPLY

Power supply (watts)	250	230	200	230	150
Number of device connectors	6	4	5	8	4

●—Yes ○—No N/A—Not applicable INA—Information not available

Table Continues →

ZIFF-DAVIS PRESS

Computers

	Twinhead Superset 600/425C	Twinhead Superset 600/433	Twinhead Superset 600/433C	Twinhead Superset 600/462D	Ultra-Comp Ultra-Max 486-25
Price	$$	$$$$	$$$	$$$	$$$
Processor/speed	486SX/25MHz	486/33MHz	486/33MHz	486DX2/66MHz	486/25MHz
Case type	Slimline	Desktop	Small-footprint	Small-footprint	Desktop
Dimensions (HWD, in inches)	INA	5.8 × 15.8 × 15.8	5 × 16 × 16	INA	5.8 × 21 × 22.5
Installed RAM	4Mb	8Mb	4Mb	8Mb	INA
Bus architecture	ISA	INA	ISA	ISA	INA
Warranty	1 year	1 year	1 year	1 year	1 year
MOTHERBOARD					
Motherboard manufacturer	Twinhead	Twinhead	Twinhead	Twinhead	Micronics
Chip set manufacturer	Acer, Intel, Trident	C&T	Intel	ACC/Twinhead	Discrete logic
System shadowing/video shadowing	INA	●/●	●/●	INA	●/●
BIOS version	Award 3.15	Phoenix 1022 CA (1990)	Award 3.0	Phoenix 1.01	Phoenix 0.10F9
ZIF socket	○	INA	INA	○	INA
Coprocessor supported	INA	None	80487/Weitek	INA	Weitek
MEMORY AND PROCESSOR RAM CACHE					
Installable RAM (minimum–maximum)	1Mb–32Mb	1Mb–16Mb	4Mb–32Mb	1Mb–64Mb	4Mb–16Mb
Cache controller	INA	Proprietary	Twinhead	INA	C&T
Installed RAM cache	INA	64K	INA	INA	INA
Installable RAM cache	64K–256K	64K	64K	64K–256K	64K, 256K
DISK DRIVES					
Drive bays	3 5.25-inch	1 half-height, 2 one-third-height, 1 3.5-inch	1 5.25-inch, 2 3.5-inch	2 5.25-inch, 2 3.5-inch	5 half-height
Disk controller location	Motherboard	Integrated	Integrated	Motherboard	Card
Hard disk capacity	213Mb	204Mb	200Mb	212Mb	200Mb
Hard disk options	120Mb–213Mb	100Mb–500Mb	100Mb–500Mb	120Mb–500Mb	40Mb–541Mb
Interface	INA	IDE	INA	INA	INA
Minimal floppy disk drive configuration	1.2Mb, 1.44Mb	1.2Mb, 1.44Mb	1.2Mb	1.44Mb	1.2Mb, 1.44Mb
EXPANSION BUS					
8-bit slots	None	None	None	None	None
16-bit slots	4	4	4 (4 open)	4	8 (5 open)
32-bit:					
EISA/MCA slots	None	None	None	None	None
Proprietary	None	None	None	None	None
Slots free in fully configured PC	INA	4	INA	INA	INA
Parallel, serial, mouse ports on motherboard	1, 2, 0	INA	1, 2, 0	1, 2, 1	INA
Integrated network adapter option	INA	INA	INA	None	INA
VIDEO					
Display circuitry location	Motherboard	Motherboard	Motherboard	Motherboard	Card
Chip set manufacturer	Trident	Paradise	Trident	Cirrus	Tseng
POWER SUPPLY					
Power supply (watts)	150	145	165	150	220
Number of device connectors	5	4	4	5	4

●—Yes   ○—No   N/A—Not applicable   INA—Information not available

	Unisys PW² 800/486-25A	Unisys PW² 4506 Advantage	United Micro UM Galaxy 450-DX2	USA Flex 486DX2/50 System	USA Flex 486DX2/66
Price	$$$$	$$$$	$$	$$$	$$$
Processor/speed	486/25MHz	486DX2/50MHz	486DX2/50MHz	486DX2/50MHz	486DX2/66MHz
Case type	Tower	Desktop	Small-footprint	Small-footprint	Tower
Dimensions (HWD, in inches)	21 × 6 × 19	INA	INA	INA	INA
Installed RAM	INA	INA	INA	INA	INA
Bus architecture	INA	ISA	ISA	ISA	EISA
Warranty	1 year	1 year	2 years	1 year	1 year
MOTHERBOARD					
Motherboard manufacturer	Intel	Unisys	Pohai	Cache	Cache
Chip set manufacturer	Intel	C&T	OPTi	UMC	Cache
System shadowing/video shadowing	●/●	●/●	●/●	●/●	INA
BIOS version	Phoenix 1.10	Phoenix 1.01	AMI (June 1991)	AMI (July 1991)	Phoenix A45596
ZIF socket	INA	○	●	○	○
Coprocessor supported	Weitek	INA	INA	INA	INA
MEMORY AND PROCESSOR RAM CACHE					
Installable RAM (minimum–maximum)	8Mb–32Mb	4Mb–64Mb	1Mb–64Mb	4Mb–32Mb	1Mb–64Mb
Cache controller	None	N/A	OPTi	UMC	INA
Installed RAM cache	INA	INA	INA	INA	INA
Installable RAM cache	N/A	None	64K–256K	64K–256K	128K–256K
DISK DRIVES					
Drive bays	5 half-height	3 5.25-inch, 1 3.5-inch	3 5.25-inch, 1 3.5-inch	3 5.25-inch, 2 3.5-inch	6 5.25-inch
Disk controller location	Integrated	Card	Card	Motherboard	EISA card
Hard disk capacity	170Mb	244Mb	212Mb	200Mb	248Mb
Hard disk options	52Mb–340Mb	52Mb–338Mb	40Mb–1.7G	40Mb–425Mb	105Mb–1.2G
Interface	INA	INA	INA	INA	INA
Minimal floppy disk drive configuration	1.2Mb or 1.44Mb	1.2Mb, 1.44Mb	1.2Mb, 1.44Mb	1.2Mb, 1.44Mb	1.2Mb, 1.44Mb
EXPANSION BUS					
8-bit slots	1 (open)	None	1	None	None
16-bit slots	3 (2 open)	6	7	7	None
32-bit:					
EISA/MCA slots	None	None	1	None	7
Proprietary	4 (2 open)	None	None	1	None
Slots free in fully configured PC	INA	INA	INA	INA	INA
Parallel, serial, mouse ports on motherboard	INA	1, 2, 1	1, 2, 1	1, 2, 0	None
Integrated network adapter option	INA	INA	INA	INA	None
VIDEO					
Display circuitry location	Card	Motherboard	Card	Card	ISA card
Chip set manufacturer	Paradise	ATI	Tseng	S3	S3
POWER SUPPLY					
Power supply (watts)	302	200	200	200	250
Number of device connectors	5	5	4	5	6

●—Yes ○—No N/A—Not applicable INA—Information not available

Table Continues →

Computers

	USA Flex 486SX/25 System	U.S. Micro Jet 486DX2-66	U.S. Micro Jet 486SX-25	Wedge 486/33 EISA	Wyse Decision 486/50 DX2
Price	$$	$$$	$$	$$$$	$$$
Processor/speed	486SX/25MHz	486DX2/66MHz	486SX/25MHz	486/33MHz	486DX2/50MHz
Case type	Small-footprint	Desktop	Slimline	Desktop	Desktop
Dimensions (HWD, in inches)	INA	INA	INA	6.8 × 14.8 × 16.3	INA
Installed RAM	INA	8Mb	INA	INA	INA
Bus architecture	ISA	ISA	ISA	INA	ISA
Warranty	1 year	1 year on parts, 2 years on labor	1 year on parts, 2 years on labor	INA	1 year
MOTHERBOARD					
Motherboard manufacturer	Cache	ASUS	Soyo	Wedge	Wyse
Chip set manufacturer	UMC	SIS	ETEQ	Intel	OPTi
System shadowing/video shadowing	INA	INA	INA	●/●	●/●
BIOS version	AMI (July 1991)	AMI (May 1991)	AMI (July 1991)	Award 4.0 (1990)	Phoenix/Wyse (March 1991)
ZIF socket	○	○	○	INA	○
Coprocessor supported	INA	Weitek, Cyrix	INA	INA	INA
MEMORY AND PROCESSOR RAM CACHE					
Installable RAM (minimum–maximum)	4Mb–64Mb	1Mb–64Mb	1Mb–64Mb	2Mb–16Mb	2Mb–32Mb
Cache controller	INA	INA	INA	Intel	OPTi
Installed RAM cache	INA	INA	INA	128K	INA
Installable RAM cache	64K–256K	64K–256K	64K–256K	None	128K
DISK DRIVES					
Drive bays	3 5.25-inch, 2 3.5-inch	3 5.25-inch, 2 3.5-inch	3 5.25-inch, 2 3.5-inch	3 half-height, 2 3.5-inch	3 5.25-inch
Disk controller location	Motherboard	ISA card	Card	Card	Card
Hard disk capacity	203Mb	336Mb	203Mb	200Mb	200Mb
Hard disk options	105Mb–425Mb	40Mb–1.2G	47Mb–321Mb	200Mb–675Mb	110Mb–200Mb
Interface	INA	INA	INA	SCSI	INA
Minimal floppy disk drive configuration	1.2Mb, 1.44Mb	1.2Mb, 1.44Mb	1.2Mb, 1.44Mb	1.2Mb	1.2Mb, 1.44Mb
EXPANSION BUS					
8-bit slots	None	None	2	2	2
16-bit slots	7	7	6	None	6
32-bit:				6	
EISA/MCA slots	None	None	None	INA	None
Proprietary	1	1	1	INA	None
Slots free in fully configured PC	INA	INA	INA	5	INA
Parallel, serial, mouse ports on motherboard	1, 2, 0	None	None	INA	None
Integrated network adapter option	INA	None	INA	INA	INA
VIDEO					
Display circuitry location	Card	ISA card	Card	Card	Card
Chip set manufacturer	S3	Orchid	Tseng	Wedge	Tseng
POWER SUPPLY					
Power supply (watts)	200	230	230	INA	200
Number of device connectors	5	5	5	INA	4

●—Yes ○—No N/A—Not applicable INA—Information not available

Computers

	Wyse Decision 486si	ZDS Z-Station 466Xh Model 200	Zenith Z-486/33E	Zeos 486-25C	Zeos 486-33
Price	$$$	$$$$	$$$$	$$$	$$
Processor/speed	486DX2/66MHz	486DX2/66MHz	486/33MHz	486/25MHz	486/33MHz
Case type	Slimline	Slimline	Small-footprint	Tower	Tower
Dimensions (HWD, in inches)	4 × 17 × 17	INA	INA	24.5 × 7.5 × 17.5	INA
Installed RAM	4Mb	INA	INA	INA	INA
Bus architecture	ISA	ISA	INA	INA	INA
Warranty	1 year	1 year	1 year	1 year for system, 5 years for keyboard	1 year
MOTHERBOARD					
Motherboard manufacturer	Wyse	ZDS	Zenith	Mylex	Zeos
Chip set manufacturer	OPTi	ZDS	Intel	Discrete logic	VLSI
System shadowing/video shadowing	INA	INA	●/●	●/●	●/●
BIOS version	Wyse 251248-01 1.0	ZDS V4.1D	Zenith 3.7F	Mylex MAE-486 6.01 (November 1990)	Award 3.10
ZIF socket	●	○	INA	INA	INA
Coprocessor supported	Intel, Weitek	INA	80487/Weitek	Weitek	INA
MEMORY AND PROCESSOR RAM CACHE					
Installable RAM (minimum–maximum)	4Mb–64Mb	4Mb–64Mb	4Mb–64Mb	1Mb–32Mb	8Mb–32Mb
Cache controller	OPTi	INA	None	Discrete logic	Intel
Installed RAM cache	INA	INA	INA	INA	INA
Installable RAM cache	64K–256K	None	N/A	128K	128K
DISK DRIVES					
Drive bays	2 5.25-inch, 3 3.5-inch	3 5.25-inch, 2 3.5-inch	1 5.25-inch, 2 3.5-inch	6 half-height, 2 3.5-inch	4 5.25-inch
Disk controller location	Motherboard	Motherboard	Integrated	Card	Integrated
Hard disk capacity	213Mb	200Mb	200Mb	200Mb	210Mb
Hard disk options	120Mb–213Mb	120Mb–400Mb	200Mb–400Mb	42Mb–1.1G	42Mb–1.16G
Interface	INA	INA	INA	INA	INA
Minimal floppy disk drive configuration	1.2Mb, 1.44Mb	1.44Mb	1.44Mb	1.2Mb or 1.44Mb	1.2Mb, 1.44Mb
EXPANSION BUS					
8-bit slots	1	None	None	None	1 (open)
16-bit slots	5	4	None	None	7 (6 open)
32-bit:					
EISA/MCA slots	None	None	5 (3 open)	8 (5 open)	None
Proprietary	None	None	None	None	None
Slots free in fully configured PC	INA	INA	INA	INA	INA
Parallel, serial, mouse ports on motherboard	1, 2, 1	1, 1, 1	INA	INA	INA
Integrated network adapter option	None	Ethernet	INA	INA	INA
VIDEO					
Display circuitry location	Proprietary local bus	Motherboard	Card	Card	Card
Chip set manufacturer	Tseng	WD	TI	Tseng	Tseng
POWER SUPPLY					
Power supply (watts)	200	200	200	450	300
Number of device connectors	5	4	3	6	4

●—Yes ○—No N/A—Not applicable INA—Information not available   **Table Continues →**

Computers

	Zeos 486-33 EISA	Zeos 486DX2-50	Zeos 486DX2-66	Zeos 486SX-20C
Price	$$$$	$$$	$$$	$$
Processor/speed	486/33MHz	486DX2/50MHz	486DX2/66MHz	486SX/20MHz
Case type	Tower	Desktop	Desktop	Tower
Dimensions (HWD, in inches)	24.5 × 7.5 × 17.5	INA	INA	INA
Installed RAM	INA	INA	INA	INA
Bus architecture	INA	ISA	ISA	INA
Warranty	INA	1 year	1 year	1 year (5 years for keyboard)

MOTHERBOARD

Motherboard manufacturer	Mylex	Zeos	Zeos	Zeos
Chip set manufacturer	Intel	VLSI	VLSI	Intel/VLSI
System shadowing/video shadowing	●/●	●/●	INA	●/●
BIOS version	Mylex/Phoenix (November 1990)	Award 3.1	Phoenix 1.01	Award 3.10
ZIF socket	INA	○	●	INA
Coprocessor supported	INA	INA	INA	INA

MEMORY AND PROCESSOR RAM CACHE

Installable RAM (minimum–maximum)	1Mb–32Mb	1Mb–96Mb	2Mb–64Mb	1Mb–32Mb
Cache controller	Discrete logic	Intel	INA	Intel
Installed RAM cache	128K	INA	INA	INA
Installable RAM cache	64K	128K	0–256K	128K

DISK DRIVES

Drive bays	6 half-height, 2 3.5-inch	2 5.25-inch, 2 3.5-inch	4 5.25-inch, 3 3.5-inch	4 5.25-inch, 1 3.5-inch
Disk controller location	Card	Motherboard	Motherboard	Integrated
Hard disk capacity	200Mb	212Mb	245Mb	212Mb
Hard disk options	42Mb–1.05G	80Mb–1.1G	85Mb–1.1G	42Mb–1.1G
Interface	SCSI	INA	INA	INA
Minimal floppy disk drive configuration	1.2Mb, 1.44Mb	1.2Mb, 1.44Mb	1.2Mb, 1.44Mb	1.44Mb

EXPANSION BUS

8-bit slots	None	1	1	1 (open)
16-bit slots	1	7	7	7 (6 open)
32-bit:	8			
EISA/MCA slots	INA	None	None	None
Proprietary	INA	None	None	None
Slots free in fully configured PC	5	INA	INA	INA
Parallel, serial, mouse ports on motherboard	INA	1, 2, 0	1, 2, 0	INA
Integrated network adapter option	INA	INA	None	INA

VIDEO

Display circuitry location	Card	Card	VESA local bus	Card
Chip set manufacturer	Tseng	S3	Weitek	Tseng

POWER SUPPLY

Power supply (watts)	INA	200	300	300
Number of device connectors	INA	7	5	4

End ■

A.2 Upgradable PCs

(Products listed in alphabetical order by company name)	AcerPower 386/SX	AcerPower 486/SX	ALR Flyer 32DT	ALR Flyer 32LCT	ALR PowerFlex Flyer
Price	$	$$	$$$	$$$	$$$
Hard disk capacity	212Mb	212Mb	211Mb	325Mb	204Mb
Dealer/direct distribution channel	●/●	●/●	●/●	●/●	●/●
Case style	Small-footprint	Small-footprint	Slimline	Tower	Slimline
Bus architecture	ISA	ISA	ISA	ISA	ISA
Power supply (and number of connectors)	145.5 watts (5)	145 watts (4)	230 watts (8)	300 watts (8)	145 watts (5)
MOTHERBOARD AND CPU					
Motherboard manufacturer	Acer	Acer	ALR	ALR	ALR
Chip set manufacturer	Acer	Acer	UMC	UMC	OPTi
Processor upgrade path	Chip puller	Chip puller	Module	Module	Module
CPUs available	386SX/25, 486SX/25, 486DX2/50	486SX/20, 486SX/25, 486/33, 486DX2/50	486SX/25, 486/33, 486DX2/50, 486DX2/66	486SX/25, 486/33, 486DX2/50, 486DX2/66	486SX/20, 486SX/25
BIOS version (or date)	Acer 1.2 R3	Acer 1.2 R4	Phoenix 1.01.09	Phoenix 1.01.09M	Phoenix 1.01.05
Weitek/Cyrix coprocessor socket	○/○	●/○	○/○	○/○	○/○
MEMORY AND PROCESSOR RAM CACHE					
Installable RAM	2Mb–16Mb	2Mb–98Mb	4Mb–36Mb	4Mb–128Mb	1Mb–16Mb
External RAM cache	N/A	64K–256K	N/A	N/A	N/A
Cache architecture	N/A	Direct-mapped	N/A	N/A	N/A
Cache write design	N/A	Write-back	N/A	N/A	N/A
DISK DRIVES					
Drive bays (5.25", 3.5")	2, 2	1, 2	1, 2	6, 4	1, 2
Floppy disk drives (1.2Mb, 1.44Mb)	1, 1	1, 1	0, 1	1, 0	0, 1
Hard disk options	42Mb–245Mb	42Mb–245Mb	80Mb–535Mb	80Mb–535Mb	60Mb–535Mb
Disk controller location	Motherboard	Card	Card	Card	Motherboard
EXPANSION BUS					
8-bit/16-bit slots	0, 4	0, 4	0, 4	0, 10	0, 5
32-bit EISA/MCA/proprietary slots	None	None	0, 0, 2	0, 0, 2	None
Local-bus slots	None	None	None	None	None
Parallel, serial, mouse ports on motherboard	1, 2, 0	1, 2, 0	1, 2, 1	1, 2, 1	1, 2, 1
Integrated network adapter option	None	None	None	None	None
VIDEO					
Display circuitry location	Motherboard	Motherboard	Card	Motherboard	Motherboard
Video chip set manufacturer	ATI	ATI	WD	WD	WD
SOFTWARE					
DOS 5.0/Microsoft Windows 3.1	●/●	●/●	●/●	●/●	○/○
Other bundled software	○	○	○	○	○
MISCELLANEOUS					
Warranty	1 year	1 year	1 year	1 year	1 year

●—Yes ○—No N/A—Not applicable INA—Information not available

Table Continues →

Upgradable PCs

	Ariel 486SX/25	AST Power Premium	Atlas ProNet 486UX Series	ATronics ATI-B2 Series	Axik Ace Cache 486ALL! Series
Price	$$	$$$	$$$	$$	$$$
Hard disk capacity	213Mb	244Mb	212Mb	213Mb	210Mb
Dealer/direct distribution channel	○/●	○/●	●/○	●/●	●/●
Case style	Tower	Small-footprint	Tower	Tower	Tower
Bus architecture	ISA	EISA	ISA	ISA	ISA
Power supply (and number of connectors)	250 watts (5)	145 watts (4)	230 watts (3)	250 watts (6)	200 watts (3)
MOTHERBOARD AND CPU					
Motherboard manufacturer	Micronics	AST	Nice USA	ATI	Axik
Chip set manufacturer	Micronics	Intel	ETEQ	UMC	Contaq, Samsung
Processor upgrade path	Module	Module	Chip puller	Chip puller	ZIF socket
CPUs available	486SX/25, 486/33, 486DX2/50, 486DX2/66	386SX/25, 386/25, 386/33, 486SX/25, 486/33, 486DX2/50, 486DX2/66	486SX/20, 486SX/25, 486/33, 486DX2/50	486SX/20, 486SX/25, 486/33, 486/50, 486DX2/50, 486DX2/66	486SX/20, 486SX/25, 486/33, 486/50, 486DX2/50, 486DX2/66
BIOS version (or date)	Phoenix 0.10 G.20-2	AST 1.06	AMI (July 1991)	AMI (July 1991)	AMI 486 (December 1991)
Weitek/Cyrix coprocessor socket	○/○	●/○	●/○	●/○	●/○
MEMORY AND PROCESSOR RAM CACHE					
Installable RAM	4Mb–64Mb	1Mb–80Mb	1Mb–64Mb	1Mb–64Mb	1Mb–32Mb
External RAM cache	64K–256K	16K–20K	64K–256K	32K–256K	64K–256K
Cache architecture	Direct-mapped	Four-way set-associative	Direct-mapped	Direct-mapped	Direct-mapped
Cache write design	Write-through	Write-through	Posted write-through	Write-back	Write-back
DISK DRIVES					
Drive bays (5.25", 3.5")	4, 2	2, 3	3, 5	8, 0	3, 4
Floppy disk drives (1.2Mb, 1.44Mb)	1, 1	0, 1	1, 1	1, 1	1, 1
Hard disk options	80Mb–535Mb	80Mb–500Mb	40Mb–2G	120Mb–1G	40Mb–2G
Disk controller location	Card	Motherboard	Card	Card	Card
EXPANSION BUS					
8-bit/16-bit slots	0, 8	None	0, 7	1, 7	0, 7
32-bit EISA/MCA/proprietary slots	None	3, 0, 3	0, 0, 1	None	0, 0, 1
Local-bus slots	None	None	None	None	None
Parallel, serial, mouse ports on motherboard	None	1, 2, 1	None	None	2, 1, 0
Integrated network adapter option	None	None	None	None	None
VIDEO					
Display circuitry location	Card	Local bus	Card	Card	Card
Video chip set manufacturer	S3	WD	S3	S3	ATI
SOFTWARE					
DOS 5.0/Microsoft Windows 3.1	●/●	●/●	●/●	●/●	●/●
Other bundled software	○	○	○	○	○
MISCELLANEOUS					
Warranty	1 year	1 year	1 year	1 year	13 months

●—Yes   ○—No   N/A—Not applicable   INA—Information not available

Upgradable PCs

	Blue Star Upgradable	BOSS CEO	Clover 486-I Series	Club Falcon 325	Compaq Deskpro I
Price	$$	$$$$	$$$	$$	$$$
Hard disk capacity	211Mb	240Mb	200Mb	245Mb	210Mb
Dealer/direct distribution channel	●/●	●/○	●/●	●/●	●/○
Case style	Tower	Desktop	Tower	Desktop	Slimline
Bus architecture	ISA	EISA	ISA	ISA	ISA
Power supply (and number of connectors)	250 watts (4)	300 watts (4)	230 watts (5)	200 watts (4)	145 watts (4)
MOTHERBOARD AND CPU					
Motherboard manufacturer	ZEN	AMI	QuickPath	Club	Compaq
Chip set manufacturer	UMC	Intel	OPTi	Club, VLSI	Intel
Processor upgrade path	Chip puller	Module	ZIF socket	Module	Chip puller
CPUs available	386DX/25, 386DX/33, Am386/40, 486SX/20, 486SX/25, 486/25, 486/33, 486/50, 486DX2/50, 486DX2/66	Am386/40, 486SX/20, 486SX/25, 486/33, 486/50	486SX/20, 486SX/25, 486/33, 486/50, 486DX2/50, 486DX2/66	386/25, 386/33, 486SX/20, 486SX/25, 486/33, 486DX2/50, 486DX2/66	386/25, 386/33, 486SX/25, 486/33
BIOS version (or date)	AMI (July 1991)	AMI (July 1991)	Microid Research	AMI 1.27 (May 1991)	Compaq (May 1992)
Weitek/Cyrix coprocessor socket	●/●	○/○	●/○	●/●	○/○
MEMORY AND PROCESSOR RAM CACHE					
Installable RAM	1Mb–32Mb	1Mb–128Mb	1Mb–32Mb	2Mb–64Mb	4Mb–32Mb
External RAM cache	64K–256K	128K	64K–256K	64K–256K	16K–64K
Cache architecture	Direct-mapped	Direct-mapped	Direct-mapped	Direct-mapped	Two-way set-associative
Cache write design	Write-back	Write-back	Write-back	Write-back	Write-through
DISK DRIVES					
Drive bays (5.25", 3.5")	6, 2	6, 1	3, 5	3, 1	3, 0
Floppy disk drives (1.2Mb, 1.44Mb)	1, 1	1, 1	1, 1	1, 1	0, 1
Hard disk options	40Mb–525Mb	106Mb–1.7G	60Mb–1.2G	50Mb–1.2G	60Mb–510Mb
Disk controller location	Card	Card	Card	Card	Motherboard
EXPANSION BUS					
8-bit/16-bit slots	2, 6	None	0, 8	0, 7	0, 3
32-bit EISA/MCA/proprietary slots	0, 0, 1	7, 0, 0	None	0, 0, 1	None
Local-bus slots	None	None	None	None	None
Parallel, serial, mouse ports on motherboard	0, 1, 0	1, 2, 0	2, 2, 0	None	1, 1, 1
Integrated network adapter option	None	None	None	None	None
VIDEO					
Display circuitry location	Card	Card	Motherboard	Card	Motherboard
Video chip set manufacturer	S3	S3	S3	Tseng	Compaq
SOFTWARE					
DOS 5.0/Microsoft Windows 3.1	●/●	●/○	●/●	●/●	●/●
Other bundled software	●	○	●	○	○
MISCELLANEOUS					
Warranty	1 year	2 years	1 year (3 year on motherboard, I/O, video)	1 year	1 year

●—Yes ○—No N/A—Not applicable INA—Information not available

Table Continues →

Upgradable PCs

	Compaq Deskpro M	CompuAdd Scalable Systems	Comtrade 486 Local Bus Win-Station	CUBE ATX Upgradable System	Deico Predator
Price	$$$$	$$	$$	$$$	$$
Hard disk capacity	340Mb	212Mb	203Mb	212Mb	212Mb
Dealer/direct distribution channel	●/○	○/●	●/○	●/●	●/●
Case style	Small-footprint	Slimline	Mini-tower	Mini-tower	Desktop
Bus architecture	EISA	ISA	ISA	ISA	ISA
Power supply (and number of connectors)	240 watts (4)	145 watts (5)	250 watts (5)	250 watts (4)	230 watts (3)
MOTHERBOARD AND CPU					
Motherboard manufacturer	Compaq	BCM Advanced Research	Join Data	Deico	Deico
Chip set manufacturer	Compaq	OPTi	OPTi	Symphony	Symphony
Processor upgrade path	Module	Chip puller	Chip puller	Chip puller	Chip puller
CPUs available	386/25, 386/33, 486SX/16, 486SX/25, 486/33, 486DX2/50, 486DX2/66	386/25, 386/33, Am386/40, 486SX/25, 486/25, 486/33, 486DX2/50, 486DX2/66	486SX/25, 486/33, 486/50, 486DX2/50, 486DX2/66	Am386DXL/40, 486SX/25, 486/33, 486/50, 486DX2/50, 486DX2/66	386/25, 386/33, Am386/40, 486SX/20, 486SX/25, 486/25, 486/33, 486/50, 486DX2/50, 486DX2/66
BIOS version (or date)	Compaq (February 1992)	AMI 2.00	AMI (June 1991)	AMI 1.1	AMI (December 1991)
Weitek/Cyrix coprocessor socket	○/○	○/●	●/○	○/○	○/●
MEMORY AND PROCESSOR RAM CACHE					
Installable RAM	4Mb–32Mb	4Mb–32Mb	1Mb–128Mb	1Mb–64Mb	1Mb–64Mb
External RAM cache	64K–256K	128K	64K–256K	64K–256K	64K–256K
Cache architecture	Two-way set-associative	Direct-mapped	Direct-mapped	Direct-mapped	Direct-mapped
Cache write design	Write-back	Write-back	Write-back	Posted write-through	Posted write-through
DISK DRIVES					
Drive bays (5.25", 3.5")	4, 0	1, 2	3, 4	2, 4	3, 2
Floppy disk drives (1.2Mb, 1.44Mb)	1, 0	1, 1	1, 1	1, 1	1, 1
Hard disk options	60Mb–510Mb	80Mb–340Mb	125Mb–1G	120Mb–540Mb	80Mb–200Mb
Disk controller location	Motherboard	Motherboard	Card	Motherboard	Motherboard
EXPANSION BUS					
8-bit/16-bit slots	None	2, 3	0, 7	1,6	1, 6
32-bit EISA/MCA/proprietary slots	6, 0, 1	None	0, 0, 1	None	None
Local-bus slots	None	None	None	None	None
Parallel, serial, mouse ports on motherboard	1, 2, 1	1, 2, 1	None	1, 2, 1	1, 2, 1
Integrated network adapter option	None	None	None	None	None
VIDEO					
Display circuitry location	Card	Local bus	Card	Card	Card
Video chip set manufacturer	Compaq	Tseng	S3	S3	Tseng
SOFTWARE					
DOS 5.0/Microsoft Windows 3.1	●/●	●/●	●/●	●/●	●/●
Other bundled software	○	○	○	○	○
MISCELLANEOUS					
Warranty	1 year	1 year	2 years	1 year	1 year (2 year on motherboard)

●—Yes ○—No N/A—Not applicable INA—Information not available

Upgradable PCs

	Dell 486 D Family	Dell 486 DE Family	DFI Diamond Series Model 333D	Diamond DT486XI	Everex Tempo M Series
Price	$$$	$$$	$$	$$$	$$$
Hard disk capacity	244Mb	234Mb	118Mb	340Mb	211Mb
Dealer/direct distribution channel	●/●	●/●	●/●	○/●	●/○
Case style	Small-footprint	Small-footprint	Small-footprint	Tower	Small-footprint
Bus architecture	ISA	EISA	ISA	EISA	ISA
Power supply (and number of connectors)	224 watts (5)	224 watts (5)	200 watts (5)	230 watts (5)	200 watts (4)
MOTHERBOARD AND CPU					
Motherboard manufacturer	Dell	Dell	DFI	S&A Labs	Everex
Chip set manufacturer	VLSI	VLSI	UMC	OPTi	Everex
Processor upgrade path	Chip puller	Module	Module	ZIF socket	Module
CPUs available	486SX/25, 486/33, 486/50, 486DX2/50, 486DX2/66	486SX/25, 486/33, 486/50, 486DX2/50, 486DX2/66	386/25, 386/33, Am386/40, 486SX/20, 486SX/25, 486/33, 486/50	486SX/25, 486/25, 486/33, 486/50, 486DX2/50	386/33, 486SX/20, 486SX/25, 486/33, 486DX2/50, 486DX2/66
BIOS version (or date)	Dell A07	Dell A08	AMI (March 1991)	AMI (July 1991)	AMI 8035
Weitek/Cyrix coprocessor socket	○/○	●/○	●/●	●/○	●/○
MEMORY AND PROCESSOR RAM CACHE					
Installable RAM	4Mb–64Mb	4Mb–96Mb	1Mb–64Mb	4Mb–128Mb	1Mb–32Mb
External RAM cache	N/A	N/A	32K–256K	64K–512K	128K–256K
Cache architecture	N/A	N/A	Direct-mapped	Two-way set-associative	Direct-mapped
Cache write design	N/A	N/A	Write-back	Write-back	Write-back
DISK DRIVES					
Drive bays (5.25", 3.5")	3, 1	3, 2	3, 1	3, 4	6, 0
Floppy disk drives (1.2Mb, 1.44Mb)	1, 1	1, 1	1, 1	1, 1	1, 0
Hard disk options	80Mb–1.4G	80Mb–1.4G	120Mb–210Mb	40Mb–2G	43Mb–1G
Disk controller location	Motherboard	Motherboard	Card	Card	Motherboard
EXPANSION BUS					
8-bit/16-bit slots	0, 6	None	2, 4	None	1, 6
32-bit EISA/MCA/proprietary slots	None	6, 0, 1	0, 0, 1	8, 0, 0	0, 0, 1
Local-bus slots	None	None	None	None	None
Parallel, serial, mouse ports on motherboard	2, 2, 1	2, 2, 1	None	None	1, 2, 0
Integrated network adapter option	None	None	None	None	None
VIDEO					
Display circuitry location	Motherboard	Motherboard	Local bus	Card	Motherboard
Video chip set manufacturer	WD	Tseng	Tseng	WD	Tseng
SOFTWARE					
DOS 5.0/Microsoft Windows 3.1	●/●	●/●	●/●	●/●	●/●
Other bundled software	○	○	●	○	○
MISCELLANEOUS					
Warranty	1 year	1 year	1 year	15 months on parts, 2 years on labor	1 year

●—Yes   ○—No   N/A—Not applicable   INA—Information not available

Table Continues →

Upgradable PCs

	IBM PS/2 Model 90	IBM PS/2 Model 95	International Instrumentation Blue Max Monolith	KEY486SX-25	Lightning Omnicache 486E
Price	$$$$	$$$$	$$	$$	$$
Hard disk capacity	160Mb	400Mb	213Mb	212Mb	248Mb
Dealer/direct distribution channel	●/○	●/○	●/●	●/●	●/●
Case style	Desktop	Tower	Mini-tower	Mini-tower	Desktop
Bus architecture	MCA	MCA	ISA	ISA	EISA
Power supply (and number of connectors)	200 watts (3)	329 watts (4)	250 watts (5)	200 watts (5)	230 watts (5)
MOTHERBOARD AND CPU					
Motherboard manufacturer	IBM	IBM	Mylex	Chicony	Tyan
Chip set manufacturer	IBM	IBM	OPTi	SIS	OPTi
Processor upgrade path	Module	Module	ZIF socket	Chip puller	ZIF socket
CPUs available	486SX/25, 486/33, 486/50, 486DX2/50	486SX/25, 486/33, 486DX2/50	486SX/20, 486SX/25, 486/25, 486/33, 486DX2/50, 486DX2/66	486SX/20, 486SX/25, 486/25, 486/33, 486DX2/50	486SX/25, 486/25, 486/33, 486/50, 486DX2/50, 486DX2/66
BIOS version (or date)	IBM PN 41G9361	IBM 84F9154	Mylex 6.13	AMI (May 1991)	AMI OPEISA-F (July 1991)
Weitek/Cyrix coprocessor socket	○/○	○/○	○/○	●/○	●/○
MEMORY AND PROCESSOR RAM CACHE					
Installable RAM	4Mb–64Mb	4Mb–64Mb	1Mb–64Mb	1Mb–32Mb	1Mb–128Mb
External RAM cache	8K–256K	8K–512K	64K–256K	64K–256K	64K–512K
Cache architecture	Two-way set-associative	Two-way set-associative	Direct-mapped	Direct-mapped	Direct-mapped
Cache write design	Posted write-through	Posted write-through	Write-through	Write-back	Write-back
DISK DRIVES					
Drive bays (5.25", 3.5")	1, 3	7, 0	2, 4	4, 2	4, 2
Floppy disk drives (1.2Mb, 1.44Mb)	0, 1	1, 1	1, 1	1, 1	1, 1
Hard disk options	80Mb–1G	80Mb–1G	40Mb–2G	85Mb–660Mb	62Mb–2.1G
Disk controller location	Card	Card	Card	Card	Card
EXPANSION BUS					
8-bit/16-bit slots	None	None	1, 6	0, 7	None
32-bit EISA/MCA/proprietary slots	0, 4, 1	0, 8, 1	None	0, 0, 1	8, 0, 0
Local-bus slots	None	None	None	None	None
Parallel, serial, mouse ports on motherboard	1, 2, 1	1, 1, 1	1, 2, 0	None	None
Integrated network adapter option	None	None	None	None	None
VIDEO					
Display circuitry location	Card	Card	Card	Card	Card
Video chip set manufacturer	IBM	IBM	S3	S3	ATI
SOFTWARE					
DOS 5.0/Microsoft Windows 3.1	●/○	●/○	●/●	●/●	●/●
Other bundled software	●	●	○	●	○
MISCELLANEOUS					
Warranty	3 years	3 years	1 year	18 months	2 years

●—Yes   ○—No   N/A—Not applicable   INA—Information not available

Upgradable PCs

	Lightning Omniflex 486	Mega Impact	Micro Express ME 486-Local Bus	Micro Express MicroFLEX	Mitsuba Professional Upgradable
Price	$$	$$$	$$	$$	$$$
Hard disk capacity	245Mb	211Mb	244Mb	244Mb	213Mb
Dealer/direct distribution channel	●/●	●/●	●/●	●/●	●/○
Case style	Slimline	Tower	Small-footprint	Small-footprint	Desktop
Bus architecture	ISA	EISA	ISA	ISA	ISA
Power supply (and number of connectors)	175 watts (3)	250 watts(4)	200 watts (4)	200 watts (4)	200 watts (5)

MOTHERBOARD AND CPU

Motherboard manufacturer	AMI	BCM Advanced Research	Ergon	Forex	Mitsuba (PUMA)
Chip set manufacturer	AMI, C&T	Intel	C&T/OPTi	SIS/Forex	OPTi
Processor upgrade path	ZIF socket	Module	ZIF socket	ZIF socket	Module
CPUs available	486SX/25, 486/25, 486/33, 486/50, 486DX2/50, 486DX2/66	486SX/25, 486/33, 486/50, 486DX2/50, 486DX2/66	486SX/25, 486/25, 486/33, 486DX2/50, 486DX2/66	386/33, Am386/40, 486SX/25, 486/25, 486/33, 486DX2/50, 486DX2/66	486SX/25, 486/33, 486/50, 486DX2/50, 486DX2/66
BIOS version (or date)	AMI 1.2	AMI (May 1991)	Phoenix/Ergon 1.01	AMI (December 1991)	AMI (December 1991)
Weitek/Cyrix coprocessor socket	○/○	○/○	●/○	●/●	●/○

MEMORY AND PROCESSOR RAM CACHE

Installable RAM	1Mb–32Mb	1Mb–64Mb	1Mb–32Mb	1Mb–32Mb	1Mb–32Mb
External RAM cache	64K–256K	64K–256K	64K–256K	64K–256K	1K–256K
Cache architecture	Direct-mapped	Direct-mapped	Direct-mapped	Direct-mapped	Direct-mapped
Cache write design	Write-through	Write-through	Write-back	Write-back	Write-back

DISK DRIVES

Drive bays (5.25", 3.5")	4, 2	6, 2	3, 2	3, 2	2, 1
Floppy disk drives (1.2Mb, 1.44Mb)	1, 1	1, 1	1, 1	1, 1	1, 1
Hard disk options	120Mb–2G	210Mb–1.2G	170Mb–1.2G	300Mb–1.2G	40Mb–1.4G
Disk controller location	Card	Card	Motherboard	Motherboard	Card

EXPANSION BUS

8-bit/16-bit slots	1, 7	0, 1	0, 7	0, 8	1, 4
32-bit EISA/MCA/proprietary slots	None	6, 0, 1	None	None	0, 0, 3
Local-bus slots	None	None	None	None	3 proprietary
Parallel, serial, mouse ports on motherboard	None	None	None	None	None
Integrated network adapter option	None	None	None	None	I

VIDEO

Display circuitry location	Card	Card	Local bus	Card	Local bus
Video chip set manufacturer	ATI	S3	Tseng	S3	S3

SOFTWARE

DOS 5.0/Microsoft Windows 3.1	●/●	○/○	●/●	●/●	●/○
Other bundled software	○	○	○	○	○

MISCELLANEOUS

Warranty	2 years	1 year	2 years	2 years	1 year

●—Yes   ○—No   N/A—Not applicable   INA—Information not available   **Table Continues →**

Upgradable PCs

	National Micro Systems Flash 486 Series	NCC Impact V	NCR System 3330	NEC PowerMate Image Series	Northgate Elegance ZXP
Price	$$$	$$	$$$	$$$	$$$
Hard disk capacity	245Mb	203Mb	245Mb	245Mb	233Mb
Dealer/direct distribution channel	○/●	●/●	●/●	●/○	●/●
Case style	Mini-tower	Tower	Slimline	Desktop	Small-footprint
Bus architecture	ISA	ISA	ISA	ISA	ISA
Power supply (and number of connectors)	230 watts (6)	300 watts (3)	250 watts (5)	110 watts (4)	200 watts (5)
MOTHERBOARD AND CPU					
Motherboard manufacturer	Ergon	Vega	NCR	NEC	Mylex
Chip set manufacturer	C&T/OPTi	Symphony	C&T	OPTi	OPTi
Processor upgrade path	ZIF socket	Chip puller	Module	Chip puller	ZIF socket
CPUs available	486SX/20, 486SX/25, 486/25, 486/33, 486DX2/50	386/25, 386/33, Am386/40, 486SX/20, 486SX/25, 486/25, 486/33, 486/50, 486DX2/50	486SX/25, 486/25, 486/33, 486DX2/50, 486DX2/66	486SX/25, 486/33, 486/50, 486DX2/50	486SX/25, 486/33, 486/50, 486DX2/66
BIOS version (or date)	Phoenix 1.01	AMI 1.1	NCR E.02.01	Phoenix A486 1.01	Mylex 6.11
Weitek/Cyrix coprocessor socket	○/○	○/●	○/○	○/○	●/○
MEMORY AND PROCESSOR RAM CACHE					
Installable RAM	1Mb–32Mb	1Mb–32Mb	1Mb–32Mb	1Mb–36Mb	1Mb–32Mb
External RAM cache	64K–256K	64K–256K	64K–256K	64K–128K	64K–256K
Cache architecture	Direct-mapped	Direct-mapped	Direct-mapped	Four-way set-associative	Direct-mapped
Cache write design	Write-back	Write-through	Posted write-through	Write-through	Write-through
DISK DRIVES					
Drive bays (5.25", 3.5")	6, 0	6, 2	1, 2	0, 4	3, 2
Floppy disk drives (1.2Mb, 1.44Mb)	1, 1	1, 1	0, 1	0, 1	1,1
Hard disk options	80Mb–1.7G	40Mb–2.2G	80Mb–240Mb	60Mb–240Mb	100Mb–1.5G
Disk controller location	Card	Card	Motherboard	Motherboard	Motherboard
EXPANSION BUS					
8-bit/16-bit slots	0, 7	0, 8	0, 4	0, 4	1, 6
32-bit EISA/MCA/proprietary slots	None	None	None	None	None
Local-bus slots	None	None	None	None	None
Parallel, serial, mouse ports on motherboard	1, 2, 1	None	None	1, 1, 1	2, 2, 1
Integrated network adapter option	None	None	None	None	None
VIDEO					
Display circuitry location	Local bus	Card	Motherboard	Local bus	Card
Video chip set manufacturer	Tseng	Tseng	NCR	Tseng	S3
SOFTWARE					
DOS 5.0/Microsoft Windows 3.1	●/●	●/●	●/●	●/●	●/●
Other bundled software	○	○	○	○	●
MISCELLANEOUS					
Warranty	15 months on parts, 2 years on labor	1 year	1 year	1 year	1 year

●—Yes   ○— No   N/A—Not applicable   INA—Information not available

Upgradable PCs

	Sirius SST Local Bus Upgradable Series	Spear 486 ISA Convertible	Standard Advantage EISA	Swan Direct Bus Line	Tri-CAD 486 EISA
Price	$$	$$	$$$	$$$	$$$
Hard disk capacity	212Mb	245Mb	240Mb	213Mb	212Mb
Dealer/direct distribution channel	●/●	●/●	○/●	●/●	○/●
Case style	Small-footprint	Tower	Tower	Desktop	Tower
Bus architecture	ISA	ISA	EISA	ISA	EISA
Power supply (and number of connectors)	200 watts (5)	250 watts (4)	145 watts (4)	200 watts (4)	250 watts (6)
MOTHERBOARD AND CPU					
Motherboard manufacturer	TMC (PUMA)	QuickPath	BCM Advanced Research	Swan	Free Technology
Chip set manufacturer	OPTi	OPTi	Intel	Syscon	Intel
Processor upgrade path	Module	ZIF socket	ZIF Socket	Module	Chip puller
CPUs available	Am386DXL/25, 386/33, Am386/40, 486/33, 486SX/25, 486DX2/50, 486DX2/66	486SX/25, 486/25, 486/33, 486/50, 486DX2/50	486SX/25, 486/25, 486/33, 486/50, 486DX2/50, 486DX2/66	486SX/25, 486/33, 486/50, 486DX2/50, 486DX2/66	486SX/20, 486SX/25, 486/25, 486/33, 486/50, 486DX2/50, 486DX2/66,
BIOS version (or date)	AMI (December 1991)	Micoid Research Mr BIOS 486	AMI (May 1991)	AMI 1.0	AMI (May 1991)
Weitek/Cyrix coprocessor socket	●/●	●/○	●/○	○/○	●/○
MEMORY AND PROCESSOR RAM CACHE					
Installable RAM	1Mb–32Mb	1Mb–32Mb	1Mb–64Mb	4Mb–64Mb	4Mb–64Mb
External RAM cache	64K–256K	64K–256K	64K–256K	128K fixed	64K–256K
Cache architecture	Direct-mapped	Direct-mapped	Direct-mapped	Direct-mapped	Direct-mapped
Cache write design	Write-back	Write-back	Write-though	Write-back	Posted write-through
DISK DRIVES					
Drive bays (5.25", 3.5")	3, 2	6, 2	6, 0	3, 1	6, 2
Floppy disk drives (1.2Mb, 1.44Mb)	1, 1	1, 1	1, 1	1, 1	1, 1
Hard disk options	40Mb–2G	120Mb–2G	40Mb–65Mb	60Mb–400Mb	120Mb–1.7G
Disk controller location	Card	Card	Card	Motherboard	Motherboard
EXPANSION BUS					
8-bit/16-bit slots	1,4	0, 8	0, 1	0, 6	0, 2
32-bit EISA/MCA/proprietary slots	None	None	6, 0, 1	0, 0, 1	6, 0, 0
Local-bus slots	3 proprietary	None	None	None	None
Parallel, serial, mouse ports on motherboard	None	None	None	2, 2, 1	1, 2, 1
Integrated network adapter option	None	None	None	None	None
VIDEO					
Display circuitry location	Card	Card	Card	Local bus	Card
Video chip set manufacturer	S3	Tseng	ATI	S3	S3
SOFTWARE					
DOS 5.0/Microsoft Windows 3.1	●/●	●/●	●/●	●/●	●/●
Other bundled software	●	○	●	●	○
MISCELLANEOUS					
Warranty	1 year	1 year	2 years	2 years	2 years

●—Yes   ○—No   N/A—Not applicable   INA—Information not available

Table Continues →

Upgradable PCs

	Wyse Decision 486si	ZDS Z-Station 420SEh	ZDS Z-Station 420Sn
Price	$$$	$$$	$$$
Hard disk capacity	212Mb	212Mb	212Mb
Dealer/direct distribution channel	○/●	●/●	●/●
Case style	Slimline	Small-footprint	Slimline
Bus architecture	ISA	EISA	ISA
Power supply (and number of connectors)	200 watts (6)	300 watss (7)	250 watts (5)
MOTHERBOARD AND CPU			
Motherboard manufacturer	Wyse	ZDS	ZDS
Chip set manufacturer	OPTi	Intel	OPTi
Processor upgrade path	ZIF socket	Module	ZIF socket
CPUs available	486SX/25, 486/33, 486DX2/50, 486DX2/66	486SX/20, 486/33, 486DX2/50	486SX/20, 486/33
BIOS version (or date)	Phoenix (May 1992)	ZDS 1.0	ZDS 1.0
Weitek/Cyrix coprocessor socket	●/○	●/○	●/○
MEMORY AND PROCESSOR RAM CACHE			
Installable RAM	1Mb–64Mb	1Mb–128Mb	4Mb–64Mb
External RAM cache	N/A	N/A	N/A
Cache architecture	N/A	N/A	N/A
Cache write design	N/A	N/A	N/A
DISK DRIVES			
Drive bays (5.25", 3.5")	2, 3	1, 3	0, 2
Floppy disk drives (1.2Mb, 1.44Mb)	0, 1	0, 1	0, 1
Hard disk options	120Mb–210Mb	80Mb–400Mb	80Mb–400Mb
Disk controller location	Motherboard	Card	Motherboard
EXPANSION BUS			
8-bit/16-bit slots	1, 5	None	0, 2
32-bit EISA/MCA/proprietary slots	None	4, 0, 0	None
Local-bus slots	None	None	None
Parallel, serial, mouse ports on motherboard	1, 2, 1	1, 1, 1	1, 1, 1
Integrated network adapter option	None	Ethernet	Ethernet
VIDEO			
Display circuitry location	Local bus	Motherboard	Motherboard
Video chip set manufacturer	Tseng	WD	WD
SOFTWARE			
DOS 5.0/Microsoft Windows 3.1	●/●	●/●	●/●
Other bundled software	○	●	●
MISCELLANEOUS			
Warranty	1 year	1 year	1 year

●—Yes   ○—No   N/A—Not applicable   INA—Information not available

End ■

A.3 File Servers

(Products listed in alphabetical order by company name)	AcerFrame 1000/50	ALR ProVEISA VM 4/66d	AST Premium SE 4/66d	Compaq ProSignia 486DX2/66	Dell 466SE/DSA PowerLine Server
Price	$$$$$	$$$$$	$$$$$	$$$$$	$$$$$
Output (watts)	350	300	300	240	350
PROCESSOR AND MEMORY					
Processor	486DX/50	486DX2/66	486DX2/66	486DX2/66	486DX2/66
Maximum processors supported	2	2	1	1	1
Installable RAM on motherboard/card	64Mb/56Mb	256Mb/None	None/96Mb	128Mb/None	128Mb/None
Installable RAM cache	256K–512K	256K–1Mb	256K	256K	128K
EXPANSION BUS					
CPU bus structure	64-bit proprietary FrameBus	32-bit EISA	Cupid-32	32-bit Flexible Advanced System Architecture	32-bit EISA
32-bit bus-mastering slots	6	6	6	7	6
32-bit non-bus-mastering slots	2	2	4	None	2
Other slots	Two 64-bit proprietary for CPU/memory	Two 16-bit ISA	None	One 32-bit for NetFlex controller	None
Local-bus slots	None	None	None	None	None
DISK DRIVES					
Maximum installable drives	8	12	11	8	10
Drive manufacturer/Rated access time	Seagate/12 ms.	Maxtor/9 ms.	HP/10.5 ms.	Fujitsu, HP/11 ms.	Digital/15 ms.
Drive array:					
Capacity per drive	250Mb	1.2G	500Mb	550Mb	1G
Hard disk interface	SCSI-2	SCSI	Fast SCSI-2	Fast SCSI-2	SCSI
Hard disk type	EISA SCSI-2	EISA SCSI	EISA Fast SCSI	EISA SCSI-2	EISA SCSI-2
RAID level supported	0, 1, 4, 5	0, 1, 4, 5	0, 1, 5, AST 6 (RAID 0 and 1)	None	0, 1, 4, 5
RAID implementation	Hardware	Hardware	Hardware	N/A	Hardware
SOFTWARE					
Certified for DOS, NetWare, and Unix	●	●	●	●	●
Other compatible operating systems	OS/2, VINES	Microsoft Windows NT, OS/2, VINES	Microsoft LAN Manager, Microsoft Windows, OS/2, SCO Unix, VINES	Microsoft LAN Manager, OS/2, SCO Unix, VINES	Microsoft LAN Manager, OS/2, SCO Unix
FAULT TOLERANCE					
Fault-tolerant components:					
Processors	○	○	○	○	○
Drives	●	●	●	●	●
Controllers	●	○	●	○	●
Power supply	○	○	○	○	○
System management notification	None	None	None	Remote	On-screen, remote
SERVER MANAGEMENT					
Temperature sensor	○	●	○	●	○
Warranty	1 year	1 year	3 years	3 years	1 year

●—Yes ○—No N/A—Not applicable INA—Information not available   **Table Continues →**

File Servers

	Digital DECpc 450ST	HP Vectra 486/66ST PC Server	NEC PowerMate Express 486DX2/66	ZDS Z-Server 450DE
Price	$$$$$	$$$$$	$$$$$	$$$$$
Output (watts)	254	300	388	384
PROCESSOR AND MEMORY				
Processor	486DX/50	486DX2/66	486DX2/66	486DX/50
Maximum processors supported	1	1	1	1
Installable RAM on motherboard/card	64Mb/192Mb	64Mb/None	64Mb/192Mb	128Mb/256Mb
Installable RAM cache	256K	128K	128K	256K
EXPANSION BUS				
CPU bus structure	32-bit Intel Xpress	32-bit EISA	32-bit EISA	Strobed Asynchronous Modular Memory
32-bit bus-mastering slots	6	8	6	6
32-bit non-bus-mastering slots	None	None	4	2
Other slots	One 32-bit Xpress Bus for optional memory board	None	One 32-bit proprietary for CPU	One 32-bit for CPU, one 32-bit for memory
Local-bus slots	None	VL-Bus	None	None
DISK DRIVES				
Maximum installable drives	5	6	11	8
Drive manufacturer/Rated access time	HP/10.5 ms.	HP/9.8 ms.	Maxtor/12 ms.	Fujitsu/12 ms.
Drive array:				
Capacity per drive	245Mb, 1G	430Mb	525Mb	520Mb
Hard disk interface	SCSI-2	SCSI-2	IDE, SCSI	SCSI-2
Hard disk type	EISA SCSI-2	EISA SCSI-2	EISA IDE, SCSI	EISA SCSI-2
RAID level supported	None	1, 3	1	1,5
RAID implementation	N/A	Hardware	Hardware	Software
SOFTWARE				
Certified for DOS, NetWare, and Unix	●	●	●	●
Other compatible operating systems	DEC Pathworks, VINES	LAN Server, Microsoft LAN Manager, OS/2, VINES	DEC Pathworks, Microsoft LAN Manager, Microsoft Windows NT, OS/2, VINES	Microsoft LAN Manager, NetWare, SCO Unix, VINES
FAULT TOLERANCE				
Fault-tolerant components:				
Processors	○	○	○	○
Drives	○	○	○	●
Controllers	○	○	○	○
Power supply	○	○	○	○
System management notification	None	None	None	On-screen
SERVER MANAGEMENT				
Temperature sensor	○	○	○	●
Warranty	1 year	1 year	1 year	1 year

●—Yes ○—No N/A—Not applicable INA—Information not available

End ∎

MONITORS

APPENDIX

B

B.1 VGA Monitors

(Products listed in alphabetical order by company name)	Compaq Video Graphics Color Monitor	Electrohome 1310U	Electrohome 1312U	IBM 8512	IBM 8513
Price	$	$	$	$	$
PHYSICAL SPECIFICATIONS					
Measured screen size (diagonal in inches)	13	13.3	13.3	12.8	11
Maximum resolution	640 × 480	910 × 645	910 × 645	640 × 480	640 × 480
Case dimensions (HWD, in inches)	14 × 13.7 × 14.9	14.5 × 14.1 × 15.7	13.2 × 14.3 × 15.7	13.4 × 13.8 × 15.7	12.3 × 12.5 × 14.3
Tilt/swivel base	Included	Optional	Optional	Optional	Included
Bandwidth (MHz)	30	30	30	25.125–28.323	25.125–28.323
Vertical scanning frequency (Hz)	60–70	47–85	47–85	60–70	60–70
Horizontal scanning frequency (Hz)	31.5	15–34	15–34	31.5	31.5
Dot pitch (mm)	0.31	0.31	0.31	0.41	0.28
Glare protection	Etched screen	Etched screen	None	Etched screen	Etched screen
Text mode color	N/A	N/A	N/A	N/A	N/A
Cable detachable	○	●	●	○	○
INPUTS					
RGB	○	●	●	○	○
Analog	●	●	●	●	●
Connector types	15-pin VGA	DB-9, 5 BNC	DB-9, 5 BNC	15-pin VGA	15-pin VGA
CONTROLS					
Brightness	●	●	●	●	●
Contrast	●	●	●	●	●
Vertical position	○	●	●	○	○
Vertical size	○	●	●	○	○
Horizontal position	○	●	●	○	○
Horizontal size	○	●	●	○	○
Text mode	○	○	○	○	○
Text color	○	○	○	○	○
Control location	Front	Front, back	Front, back	Side	Side
OTHER COMPATIBLE ADAPTERS					
EGA	○	●	●	○	○
PGC	○	●	●	○	○
VGA	●	●	○	●	●

●—Yes ○—No N/A—Not applicable INA—Information not available

Table Continues →

VGA Monitors

	IBM 8514	Logitech AutoSync Monitor	Magnavox 8CM873	Nanao FlexScan 8060S	Princeton PSC-28
Price	$$	$	$	$	$
PHYSICAL SPECIFICATIONS					
Measured screen size (diagonal in inches)	14.3	13.3	13	13	11.6
Maximum resolution	1,024 × 768	800 × 560	926 × 580	820 × 620	770 × 570
Case dimensions (HWD, in inches)	14 × 15.7 × 16.4	13.7 × 14.8 × 15.3	13 × 14.1 × 15.5	14.6 × 14 × 15.6	12.4 × 12.3 × 14.2
Tilt/swivel base	Included	Included	None	Included	Included
Bandwidth (MHz)	44.9	40	25	30	30
Vertical scanning frequency (Hz)	43.48	45–80	50–70	50–80	50–70
Horizontal scanning frequency (Hz)	35.51–35.52	15.5–35	15–34	15.7–35	31.5
Dot pitch (mm)	0.31	0.31	0.31	0.28	0.28
Glare protection	Etched screen	Etched screen	Etched screen	Etched screen	Etched screen
Text mode color	N/A	White, amber, green	Green	White, amber	White, green, cyan
Cable detachable	○	○	●	●	●
INPUTS					
RGB	○	●	●	●	○
Analog	●	●	●	●	●
Connector types	15-pin VGA	DB-9	DB-9	DB-9	DB-25, 15-pin cable
CONTROLS					
Brightness	●	●	●	●	●
Contrast	●	●	●	●	●
Vertical position	○	●	●	●	○
Vertical size	○	●	●	●	○
Horizontal position	○	●	●	●	○
Horizontal size	○	●	○	●	○
Text mode	○	●	●	●	●
Text color	○	●	○	●	●
Control location	Side	Back, side	Front, back	Front, back	Side
OTHER COMPATIBLE ADAPTERS					
EGA	○	●	●	●	○
PGC	○	●	●	●	○
VGA	●	●	●	●	●

●—Yes   ○—No   N/A—Not applicable   INA—Information not available

VGA Monitors

	Princeton UltraSync	Relisys RE5155	Sony CPD-1303	Tatung CM-1495
Price	$	$	$	$
PHYSICAL SPECIFICATIONS				
Measured screen size (diagonal in inches)	11.6	13.3	13.3	13
Maximum resolution	770 × 570	800 × 560	800 × 600	800 × 560
Case dimensions (HWD, in inches)	12.4 × 12.3 × 14.2	13.7 × 14.8 × 15.2	13.5 × 14.1 × 16	13.2 × 14.5 × 15.4
Tilt/swivel base	Included	Included	Optional	Included
Bandwidth (MHz)	30	40	25	30
Vertical scanning frequency (Hz)	45–120	45–80	50–100	47–70
Horizontal scanning frequency (Hz)	15–35	15.5–35	15–35	15–35
Dot pitch (mm)	0.28	0.31	0.38	0.31
Glare protection	Etched screen	Etched screen	None	Etched screen
Text mode color	White, amber, green	White, amber, green	N/A	White, amber, green
Cable detachable	●	○	●	●
INPUTS				
RGB	●	●	●	●
Analog	●	●	●	●
Connector types	DB-25, 15-pin cable	DB-9	DB-9	DB-9
CONTROLS				
Brightness	●	●	●	●
Contrast	●	●	●	●
Vertical position	●	●	●	●
Vertical size	●	●	●	●
Horizontal position	●	●	●	●
Horizontal size	●	●	●	●
Text mode	●	●	○	●
Text color	●	●	○	●
Control location	Back, side	Back, side	Back, side	Front, back, top
OTHER COMPATIBLE ADAPTERS				
EGA	●	●	●	●
PGC	●	●	●	●
VGA	●	●	●	●

●—Yes   ○—No   N/A—Not applicable   INA—Information not available

End ■

B.2   VGA Monochrome Monitors

(Products listed in alphabetical order by company name)	Amdek AM432	AOC MN413	Compaq Monochrome Video Graphics Monitor	CTX-VGA Monochrome CM-24S2	Datafox DF-14S2
Price	$	$	$	$	$
PHYSICAL SPECIFICATIONS					
Diagonal screen size (inches)	13	12.5	10.75	12.25	12.5
Diagonal image size (inches)	11.75	11.75	9.875	11.25	11
Maximum resolution	640 × 480	640 × 480	640 × 480	640 × 480	640 × 480
Bandwidth (MHz)	25	30	30	30	35
Vertical scanning frequency (Hz)	50/60/70	50/60/70	60/70	60/70	50/60/70
Horizontal scanning frequency (Hz)	31.47	31.47	31.47	31.47	31.5
Text mode color	Amber or white	White	White	Amber, green, or white	White
Case dimensions (HWD, in inches)	12.5 × 12.5 × 13	12.25 × 12.75 × 12.5	12.25 × 11.7 × 12.6	11.75 × 12.75 × 12.5	13 × 12.75 × 13
Tilt/swivel base	●	●	●	●	●
Cable detachable	○	○	○	○	○
INPUTS					
RGB	○	○	○	○	○
Analog	●	●	●	●	●
Connector types	15-pin D-shell	15-pin D-shell	15-pin D-shell	15-pin D-shell	15-pin D-shell
CONTROLS					
Brightness	●	●	●	●	●
Contrast	●	●	●	●	●
Vertical position	○	○	○	●	○
Vertical size	○	○	○	●	○
Horizontal position	○	○	○	●	○
Horizontal size	○	○	○	○	○
COMPATIBLE ADAPTERS					
EGA	○	○	○	○	○
VGA	●	●	●	●	●

●—Yes   ○—No   N/A—Not applicable   INA—Information not available

VGA Monochrome Monitors

	Epson VGA Monochrome	GoldStar VGS Monochrome 1220 W	HP Vectra VGA Monochrome	Imtec 1261L	KDS KD-14S2
Price	$	$	$	$	$
PHYSICAL SPECIFICATIONS					
Diagonal screen size (inches)	11.75	11.5	12.25	11.25	12.5
Diagonal image size (inches)	11.25	11	11.25	11.25	11.75
Maximum resolution	640 × 480	640 × 480	640 × 480	640 × 480	640 × 480
Bandwidth (MHz)	30	30	30	30	35
Vertical scanning frequency (Hz)	60/70	60/70	60/70	60/70	50/60/70
Horizontal scanning frequency (Hz)	31.5	31.5	31.5	31.47	31.5
Text mode color	White	White	Amber, green, or white	White	White
Case dimensions (HWD, in inches)	13.2 × 12.9 × 12.2	11.2 × 12.9 × 12.2	12.75 × 13 × 12.75	12.25 × 12.25 × 11.75	13 × 12.8 × 13
Tilt/swivel base	●	●	●	●	●
Cable detachable	○	○	●	○	○
INPUTS					
RGB	○	○	○	○	○
Analog	●	●	●	●	●
Connector types	15-pin D-shell	15-pin D-shell	9-pin D-shell (includes 9/15-pin adapter)	15-pin D-shell	15-pin D-shell
CONTROLS					
Brightness	●	●	●	●	●
Contrast	●	●	●	●	●
Vertical position	○	○	○	○	○
Vertical size	○	○	○	○	○
Horizontal position	○	○	○	○	○
Horizontal size	○	○	○	○	○
COMPATIBLE ADAPTERS					
EGA	○	○	○	○	○
VGA	●	●	●	●	●

●—Yes   ○—No   N/A—Not applicable   INA—Information not available

Table Continues →

ZIFF-DAVIS PRESS

VGA Monochrome Monitors

	Magnavox Professional VGA Display 7BM749	NEC MultiSync GS	Packard Bell PB8503MG	Packard Bell PB8505MG	Princeton Graphics Systems Max-15
Price	$	$	$	$	$
PHYSICAL SPECIFICATIONS					
Diagonal screen size (inches)	12.5	12.5	11.25	11.5	12.5
Diagonal image size (inches)	12.5	12.25	10.75	10	11.75
Maximum resolution	640 × 480	640 × 480	640 × 480	640 × 480	1,024 × 768
Bandwidth (MHz)	22	30	30	30	45
Vertical scanning frequency (Hz)	60/70	50/60/70	59.95/70.08	50/60/70	45–120
Horizontal scanning frequency (Hz)	31.5	31.5	31.47	31.47	15–36
Text mode color	White	Amber, green, or white	White	White	White
Case dimensions (HWD, in inches)	14.25 × 13 × 11.5	13.25 × 13.25 × 13	11.5 × 12.5 × 11.5	12.25 × 12.5 × 12.25	12.25 × 12.5 × 13
Tilt/swivel base	●	●	●	●	●
Cable detachable	○	●	○	○	●
INPUTS					
RGB	○	●	○	○	●
Analog	●	●	●	●	●
Connector types	15-pin D-shell	9-pin D-shell (includes 9/15-pin adapter)	15-pin D-shell	15-pin D-shell	9-, 15-, and 25-pin D-shell, RCA composite jack
CONTROLS					
Brightness	●	●	●	●	●
Contrast	●	●	●	●	●
Vertical position	○	●	○	○	●
Vertical size	○	●	○	○	●
Horizontal position	○	●	○	○	●
Horizontal size	○	●	○	○	●
COMPATIBLE ADAPTERS					
EGA	○	●	○	○	●
VGA	●	●	●	●	●

●—Yes   ○—No   N/A—Not applicable   INA—Information not available

VGA Monochrome Monitors

	Quimax DM-3014	Relisys RE9503	Samsung ML2611	Samsung ML4571	Tandy VGM-100
Price	$	$	$	$	$
PHYSICAL SPECIFICATIONS					
Diagonal screen size (inches)	13.25	12.75	11.25	12.75	12.75
Diagonal image size (inches)	11.75	11.5	10.75	11.75	11.25
Maximum resolution	640 × 480	640 × 480	640 × 480	640 × 480	640 × 480
Bandwidth (MHz)	30	30	30	30	30
Vertical scanning frequency (Hz)	50/60/70	50/60/70	60/70	60/70	59.95/70.08
Horizontal scanning frequency (Hz)	31.47	31.47	31.47	31.47	31.47
Text mode color	White	White	White	White	White
Case dimensions (HWD, in inches)	13 × 12.75 × 13.25	13 × 12.5 × 12.75	12 × 12.25 × 11.75	13 × 13 × 12.5	13 × 13.25 × 12.75
Tilt/swivel base	●	●	●	●	○
Cable detachable	○	○	○	○	○
INPUTS					
RGB	○	○	○	○	○
Analog	●	●	●	●	●
Connector types	15-pin D-shell	15-pin D-shell	15-pin D-shell	15-pin D-shell	15-pin D-shell
CONTROLS					
Brightness	●	●	●	●	●
Contrast	●	●	●	●	●
Vertical position	○	○	○	○	○
Vertical size	○	●	○	○	○
Horizontal position	○	●	○	○	○
Horizontal size	○	○	○	○	○
COMPATIBLE ADAPTERS					
EGA	○	○	○	○	○
VGA	●	●	●	●	●

●—Yes ○—No N/A—Not applicable INA—Information not available

Table Continues →

VGA Monochrome Monitors

	Tatung MM1233	Tatung MM1295	Tatung MM1433	TVM MG-11	TVM MG-14
Price	$	$	$	$	$
PHYSICAL SPECIFICATIONS					
Diagonal screen size (inches)	11.25	11.5	12.75	12.75	12.75
Diagonal image size (inches)	10.5	11	11.75	11	11.5
Maximum resolution	640 × 480	800 × 600	640 × 480	1,024 × 768	640 × 480
Bandwidth (MHz)	30	30	30	30	30
Vertical scanning frequency (Hz)	50/60	50/60/70	50/60/70	45–75	45–75
Horizontal scanning frequency (Hz)	31.47	31.47	31.5	15–38	31.5
Text mode color	White	White	White	White	White
Case dimensions (HWD, in inches)	12.5 × 12.5 × 12.5	12.5 × 12.5 × 12.5	12.75 × 13 × 13.25	13 × 13 × 14.75	12.5 × 13 × 14.5
Tilt/swivel base	●	●	●	●	●
Cable detachable	○	●	○	●	○
INPUTS					
RGB	○	○	○	○	○
Analog	●	●	●	●	●
Connector types	15-pin D-shell	9- and 15-pin D-shell	15-pin D-shell	9- and 15-pin D-shell	15-pin D-shell
CONTROLS					
Brightness	●	●	●	●	●
Contrast	●	●	●	●	●
Vertical position	○	●	○	●	○
Vertical size	○	●	○	●	○
Horizontal position	○	●	●	○	●
Horizontal size	○	●	○	●	○
COMPATIBLE ADAPTERS					
EGA	○	○	○	●	○
VGA	●	●	●	●	●

●—Yes   ○—No   N/A—Not applicable   INA—Information not available

VGA Monochrome Monitors

	Wyse Technology WY550	Zenith MM149-P
Price	$	$
PHYSICAL SPECIFICATIONS		
Diagonal screen size (inches)	13	12.75
Diagonal image size (inches)	12.25	11.75
Maximum resolution	640 × 480	640 × 480
Bandwidth (MHz)	25	30
Vertical scanning frequency (Hz)	50/60/70	60/70
Horizontal scanning frequency (Hz)	31.47	31.49
Text mode color	Amber or white	Amber or white
Case dimensions (HWD, in inches)	15.6 × 15.2 × 13.1	10.25 × 13 × 12.75
Tilt/swivel base	●	○
Cable detachable	○	○
INPUTS		
RGB	○	○
Analog	●	●
Connector types	15-pin D-shell	15-pin D-shell
CONTROLS		
Brightness	●	●
Contrast	●	●
Vertical position	○	●
Vertical size	○	●
Horizontal position	○	●
Horizontal size	○	●
COMPATIBLE ADAPTERS		
EGA	○	○
VGA	●	●

●—Yes   ○—No   N/A—Not applicable   INA—Information not available   **End** ■

B.3 Super VGA Monitors

(Products listed in alphabetical order by company name)	AST Super VGA	CTX 5468 Super VGA Monitor	GoldStar 1460 Plus VGA	Hitachi/NSA 14MVX/LMF	Hyundai HCM-421E
Price	$	$	$	$	$
PHYSICAL SPECIFICATIONS					
Visible diagonal screen size (inches)	13	13	13	13	13
Monitor dimensions (HWD, in inches)	12 × 14 × 14	14 × 14 × 15	14 × 14 × 15	15 × 14 × 15	14 × 14 × 15
Weight (pounds)	31	26	29	33	30
SIGNAL COMPATABILITY					
1,024 × 768 (noninterlaced)	○	○	○	○	○
1,024 × 768 (interlaced)	●	●	●	●	●
Super VGA (800 × 600)	●	●	●	●	●
VGA (640 × 480)	●	●	●	●	●
MCGA	●	●	○	○	●
EGA	○	○	○	○	○
OPERATIONAL FEATURES					
Maximum noninterlaced resolution (pixels)	800 × 600	800 × 600	800 × 600	800 × 600	800 × 600
Maximum interlaced resolution (pixels)	1,024 × 768	1,024 × 768	1,024 × 768	1,024 × 768	1,024 × 768
Video bandwidth (MHz)	45	45	36	45	30
Vertical scanning frequency range (Hz)	56–87	50–90	50–87	50–120	56.2–87
Horizontal scanning frequency range (kHz)	31.5–35.5	30–38	31.5–35.5	30–40	31.5–35.5
Phosphor persistence	Medium-short	Medium-short	Medium-short	Short	Medium-short
Dot pitch (mm)	0.28	0.28	0.28	0.28	0.28
Input connectors:					
Analog D-sub	15-pin mini	15-pin mini	15-pin mini	15-pin mini	15-pin mini
Digital/TTL	○	○	○	○	○
CONTROLS					
Brightness	● (analog)	● (analog)	● (analog)	● (analog)	● (analog)
Contrast	● (analog)	● (analog)	● (analog)	● (analog)	● (analog)
Horizontal position	● (analog)	● (analog)	● (analog)	● (analog)	● (analog)
Vertical position	● (analog)	● (analog)	● (analog)	● (analog)	○
Horizontal size	○	○	● (analog)	● (analog)	○
Vertical size	● (analog)	● (analog)	● (analog)	● (analog)	● (analog)
Pincushioning	○	○	○	○	○
Convergence	○	○	○	○	○
Degaussing	○	○	○	○	○
120/240-volt switch	○	○	○	○	○

●—Yes ○—No N/A—Not applicable INA—Information not available

Super VGA Monitors

	Iiyama Idek MF-5015A	MAG Colorview/15	Mitsubishi Diamond Scan 14	NEC MultiSync 2A	NEC MultiSync 3DS
Price	$	$	$	$	$
PHYSICAL SPECIFICATIONS					
Visible diagonal screen size (inches)	14	14	13	13	13
Monitor dimensions (HWD, in inches)	14 × 14 × 15	12 × 14 × 16	13 × 14 × 15	14 × 14 × 16	14 × 14 × 16
Weight (pounds)	34	36	28	26	30
SIGNAL COMPATABILITY					
1,024 × 768 (noninterlaced)	○	●	○	○	○
1,024 × 768 (interlaced)	●	●	●	○	●
Super VGA (800 × 600)	●	●	●	●	●
VGA (640 × 480)	●	●	●	●	●
MCGA	●	●	●	●	●
EGA	●	○	●	○	●
OPERATIONAL FEATURES					
Maximum noninterlaced resolution (pixels)	800 × 600	1,280 × 1,024	800 × 600	800 × 600	800 × 600
Maximum interlaced resolution (pixels)	1,024 × 768	1,024 × 768	1,024 × 768	800 × 600	1,024 × 768
Video bandwidth (MHz)	30	100	30	38	45
Vertical scanning frequency range (Hz)	50–90	50–120	45–90	56–70	50–90
Horizontal scanning frequency range (kHz)	15.5–38.5	30–68	15.8–38	31.5–35	15.8–38
Phosphor persistence	Short	Medium-short	Medium-short	Medium-short	Medium-short
Dot pitch (mm)	0.31	0.28	0.31	0.31	0.28
Input connectors:					
Analog D-sub	15-pin standard	15-pin mini	25-pin mini	15-pin mini	15-pin mini
Digital/TTL	●	○	●	○	●
CONTROLS					
Brightness	● (analog)	● (analog)	● (analog)	● (analog)	● (analog)
Contrast	● (analog)	● (analog)	● (analog)	● (analog)	● (analog)
Horizontal position	● (analog)	● (digital)	● (analog)	● (analog)	● (digital)
Vertical position	● (analog)	● (digital)	● (analog)	● (analog)	● (digital)
Horizontal size	● (analog)	● (digital)	● (analog)	○	● (digital)
Vertical size	● (analog)	● (digital)	● (analog)	● (analog)	● (digital)
Pincushioning	○	○	○	○	○
Convergence	○	○	○	○	○
Degaussing	○	○	○	○	○
120/240-volt switch	○	○	○	○	●

●—Yes ○—No N/A—Not applicable INA—Information not available   **Table Continues →**

Super VGA Monitors

	Panasonic PanaSync C1381	Phillips Magnavox 6CM320	Relisys RE-9514	Samsung SyncMaster3	Seiko CM1450
Price	$	$	$	$	$
PHYSICAL SPECIFICATIONS					
Visible diagonal screen size (inches)	14	13	13	13	13
Monitor dimensions (HWD, in inches)	15 × 14 × 14	14 × 14 × 16	14 × 14 × 15	13 × 14 × 15	14 × 13 × 15
Weight (pounds)	25	31	25	26	33
SIGNAL COMPATABILITY					
1,024 × 768 (noninterlaced)	○	○	○	○	●
1,024 × 768 (interlaced)	●	○	●	●	●
Super VGA (800 × 600)	●	●	●	●	●
VGA (640 × 480)	●	●	●	●	●
MCGA	●	●	○	○	○
EGA	○	○	○	○	○
OPERATIONAL FEATURES					
Maximum noninterlaced resolution (pixels)	800 × 600	800 × 600	800 × 600	800 × 600	1,024 × 768
Maximum interlaced resolution (pixels)	1,024 × 768	800 × 600	1,024 × 768	1,024 × 768	1,024 × 768
Video bandwidth (MHz)	30	32	45	45	60
Vertical scanning frequency range (Hz)	50–90	60–70	50–90	56–86.8	50–90
Horizontal scanning frequency range (kHz)	30–37	31.5–37.8	31.5–35.5	31.5–35.5	31–50
Phosphor persistence	Short	Medium	Short	Medium-short	Medium-short
Dot pitch (mm)	0.28	0.28	0.28	0.28	0.25
Input connectors:					
Analog D-sub	15-pin mini	15-pin mini	15-pin mini	15-pin mini	15-pin mini
Digital/TTL	○	○	○	○	○
CONTROLS					
Brightness	● (analog)	● (analog)	● (analog)	● (analog)	● (analog)
Contrast	● (analog)	● (analog)	● (analog)	● (analog)	● (analog)
Horizontal position	● (analog)	● (analog)	● (analog)	● (analog)	● (analog)
Vertical position	● (analog)	● (analog)	● (analog)	● (analog)	● (analog)
Horizontal size	● (analog)	○	○	● (analog)	● (analog)
Vertical size	● (analog)	○	● (analog)	● (analog)	● (analog)
Pincushioning	○	○	○	●	○
Convergence	○	○	○	○	○
Degaussing	○	○	○	○	○
120/240-volt switch	○	○	○	○	○

●—Yes ○— No N/A—Not applicable INA—Information not available

Super VGA Monitors

	Sony CPD-1304 Multiscan HG	Tatung CM-1498T	Taxan MultiVision 795	TVM SuperSync 5A MD-15	TW Casper TM-5158
Price	$	$	$	$	$
PHYSICAL SPECIFICATIONS					
Visible diagonal screen size (inches)	13	13	14	14	14
Monitor dimensions (HWD, in inches)	14 × 14 × 16	14 × 14 × 16	14 × 14 × 15	15 × 15 × 16	14 × 14 × 14
Weight (pounds)	29	28	29	33	31
SIGNAL COMPATABILITY					
1,024 × 768 (noninterlaced)	●	○	●	●	○
1,024 × 768 (interlaced)	●	●	●	●	●
Super VGA (800 × 600)	●	●	●	●	●
VGA (640 × 480)	●	●	●	●	●
MCGA	●	●	○	●	●
EGA	○	○	○	○	○
OPERATIONAL FEATURES					
Maximum noninterlaced resolution (pixels)	1,024 × 768	800 × 600	1,024 × 768	1,024 × 768	800 × 600
Maximum interlaced resolution (pixels)	1,024 × 768	1,024 × 768	1,024 × 768	1,280 × 1,024	1,024 × 768
Video bandwidth (MHz)	50	45	50	65	30
Vertical scanning frequency range (Hz)	50–87	50–90	50–100	40–100	56–87
Horizontal scanning frequency range (kHz)	28–57	31.5, 35.5–38	30–57	31.5–48	31.5–35.5
Phosphor persistence	Medium-short	Medium-short	Medium-short	Medium-short	Long
Dot pitch (mm)	0.25	0.28	0.25	0.28	0.28
Input connectors:					
Analog D-sub	9-pin mini	15-pin mini	15-pin mini	15-pin mini	15-pin mini
Digital/TTL	○	○	○	○	○
CONTROLS					
Brightness	● (analog)	● (analog)	● (analog)	● (analog)	● (analog)
Contrast	● (analog)	● (analog)	● (analog)	● (analog)	● (analog)
Horizontal position	● (analog)	● (analog)	● (analog)	● (analog)	● (analog)
Vertical position	● (analog)	● (analog)	● (analog)	○	○
Horizontal size	● (analog)	● (analog)	● (analog)	○	○
Vertical size	● (analog)	● (analog)	● (analog)	● (analog)	● (analog)
Pincushioning	○	○	○	○	○
Convergence	○	○	○	○	○
Degaussing	○	○	○	○	○
120/240-volt switch	○	●	○	●	○

●—Yes ○—No N/A—Not applicable INA—Information not available

Table Continues →

Super VGA Monitors

	ViewSonic 5	Wyse WY-670
Price	$	$
PHYSICAL SPECIFICATIONS		
Visible diagonal screen size (inches)	13	13
Monitor dimensions (HWD, in inches)	13 × 14 × 16	13 × 14 × 15
Weight (pounds)	35	30
SIGNAL COMPATABILITY		
1,024 × 768 (noninterlaced)	●	○
1,024 × 768 (interlaced)	●	●
Super VGA (800 × 600)	●	●
VGA (640 × 480)	●	●
MCGA	○	●
EGA	○	○
OPERATIONAL FEATURES		
Maximum noninterlaced resolution (pixels)	1,024 × 768	800 × 600
Maximum interlaced resolution (pixels)	1,024 × 768	1,024 × 768
Video bandwidth (MHz)	65	45
Vertical scanning frequency range (Hz)	50–90	55–87
Horizontal scanning frequency range (kHz)	31–55	31.5, 34–38
Phosphor persistence	Medium-short	Medium-short
Dot pitch (mm)	0.25	0.28
Input connectors:		
Analog D-sub	15-pin mini	15-pin mini
Digital/TTL	○	○
CONTROLS		
Brightness	● (analog)	● (analog)
Contrast	● (analog)	● (analog)
Horizontal position	● (analog)	● (analog)
Vertical position	● (analog)	○
Horizontal size	● (analog)	● (analog)
Vertical size	● (analog)	● (analog)
Pincushioning	○	○
Convergence	○	○
Degaussing	○	○
120/240-volt switch	○	○

●—Yes ○—No N/A—Not applicable INA—Information not available

End ■

B.4   14-Inch Monitors

(Products listed in alphabetical order by company name)	Aamazing CM8428MX	ADI MicroScan 3E	ADI MicroScan 3E+	AOC CMLB-337	Arche 214MH VGA Monitor
Price	$	$	$	$	$
PHYSICAL SPECIFICATIONS					
Dimensions (HWD, in inches)	14 × 14.5 × 15.5	15 × 15 × 14	15 × 15 × 14	14.1 × 14 × 15	15 × 14 × 14
Weight (pounds)	27.6	28	28	27.2	25.4
Length of power cable (inches)	72	72	72	60	72
Adapter cable included	Captive to miniDB-15	Captive to miniDB-15	Captive to miniDB-15	Captive to DB-15	MiniDB-15 to miniDB-15
SIGNAL COMPATIBILITY					
1,280 × 1,024	○	●	●	○	○
1,024 × 768 (noninterlaced)	●	●	●	●	●
1,024 × 768 (interlaced)	●	●	●	●	●
Super VGA (800 × 600)	●	●	●	●	●
VGA (640 × 480)	●	●	●	●	●
MCGA/Hercules	●/○	●/○	●/○	○/○	○/○
Mac II/Apple II GS	○/○	○/○	○/○	●/●	○/○
OPERATIONAL FEATURES					
Fixed or variable frequency	Variable	Variable	Variable	Variable	Fixed
Maximum noninterlaced resolution (pixels)	1,024 × 768	1,024 × 768	1,024 × 768	1,024 × 768	1,024 × 768
Video bandwidth (MHz)	65	65	75	80	65
Vertical scanning frequency (Hz)	50–90	50–100	50–100	50–90	45–100
Horizontal scanning frequency (kHz)	32–48	30–50	30–58	30–60	32–49
Maximum vertical refresh rates (Hz)					
1,280 × 1,024	N/A	87	87	N/A	N/A
1,024 × 768 noninterlaced	60	60	72	72	60
Super VGA (800 × 600)	72	72	72	72	72
VGA (640 × 480)	72	72	72	72	72
Phosphor persistence	Medium-short	Medium-short	Medium-short	Medium-short	Medium-short
Dot pitch or aperture grill pitch (mm)	0.28	0.28	0.28	0.28	0.28
Analog or digital controls	Analog	Digital	Digital	Analog	Analog
Power consumption (watts)	90	85	85	80	90
Microprocessor included	○	●	●	○	○
Number of simultaneously stored settings	N/A	9	10	N/A	N/A
Number of user-definable settings	N/A	9	10	N/A	N/A
CONTROLS					
Brightness	●	●	●	●	●
Contrast	●	●	●	●	●
Color matching	○	○	○	○	○
Horizontal position	●	●	●	●	●
Vertical position	●	●	●	●	●
Horizontal size	●	●	●	●	○
Vertical size	●	●	●	●	●
Pincushioning	○	●	●	○	○
Barrel distortion	○	●	●	○	○
Degaussing	○	○	○	○	○
120-/240-volt switching	○	○	○	○	● (auto-sensing)
VLF/ELF radiation control	○/○	○/○	○/○	●/●	○/○

●—Yes   ○—No   N/A—Not applicable   INA—Information not available

Table Continues →

14-Inch Monitors

	Compaq 1024 Color Monitor	CTX CMS-1461	Darius HRN-1424	Dell UltraScan 14C	Dell UltraScan 14LR
Price	$	$	$	$	$
PHYSICAL SPECIFICATIONS					
Dimensions (HWD, in inches)	15 × 15 × 14	16 × 14.3 × 15	14 × 13.5 × 12.3	15 × 14 × 14.5	13.9 × 13.7 × 15.2
Weight (pounds)	28	22	24.8	27.3	26
Length of power cable (inches)	60	60	72	72	60
Adapter cable included	Captive to miniDB-15	Captive to DB-15	Captive to miniDB-15	Captive to miniDB-15	Captive to DB-15
SIGNAL COMPATIBILITY					
1,280 × 1,024	○	●	○	○	○
1,024 × 768 (noninterlaced)	●	●	●	●	●
1,024 × 768 (interlaced)	●	●	●	●	●
Super VGA (800 × 600)	●	●	●	●	●
VGA (640 × 480)	●	●	●	●	●
MCGA/Hercules	●/○	○/○	●/○	●/○	○/○
Mac II/Apple II GS	○/○	○/○	○/○	○/○	●/○
OPERATIONAL FEATURES					
Fixed or variable frequency	Variable	Variable	Variable	Variable	Variable
Maximum noninterlaced resolution (pixels)	1,024 × 768	1,024 × 768	1,024 × 768	1,024 × 768	1,024 × 768
Video bandwidth (MHz)	75	85	50	80	70
Vertical scanning frequency (Hz)	50–100	50–90	47–100	50–90	50–90
Horizontal scanning frequency (kHz)	30–58	30–60	31–60	30–60	30–58
Maximum vertical refresh rates (Hz)					
1,280 × 1,024	N/A	87	N/A	N/A	N/A
1,024 × 768 noninterlaced	72	70	70	72	72
Super VGA (800 × 600)	72	72	72	72	72
VGA (640 × 480)	75	72	72	72	73
Phosphor persistence	Medium-short	Medium-short	Medium-short	Medium-short	Medium-short
Dot pitch or aperture grill pitch (mm)	0.28	0.28	0.28	0.28	0.28
Analog or digital controls	Digital	Analog	Analog	Analog	Digital
Power consumption (watts)	85	80	75	110	90
Microprocessor included	●	○	○	○	●
Number of simultaneously stored settings	10	N/A	N/A	N/A	12
Number of user-definable settings	10	N/A	N/A	N/A	6
CONTROLS					
Brightness	●	●	●	●	●
Contrast	●	●	●	●	●
Color matching	○	○	○	○	○
Horizontal position	●	●	●	●	●
Vertical position	●	●	●	●	●
Horizontal size	●	●	●	●	●
Vertical size	●	●	●	●	●
Pincushioning	●	○	○	○	●
Barrel distortion	●	○	○	○	●
Degaussing	○	○	○	○	○
120-/240-volt switching	○	● (auto sensing)	○	○	○
VLF/ELF radiation control	○/○	Optional	○/○	○/○	●/●

●—Yes ○—No N/A—Not applicable INA—Information not available

14-Inch Monitors

	FORA Addonics C141	FORA Addonics C143	IBM PS/Value-Point 6312 Color Display	IBM PS/Value-Point 6314 Color Display	IOcomm ThinkSync 4E
Price	$	$	$	$	$
PHYSICAL SPECIFICATIONS					
Dimensions (HWD, in inches)	15 × 14 × 14.5	13.4 × 14 × 15	11 × 14 × 15	15 × 14 × 16	14.3 × 14.5 × 14.8
Weight (pounds)	27.3	24.2	24	33	26.2
Length of power cable (inches)	72	60	73	73	72
Adapter cable included	Captive to miniDB-15	Captive to miniDB-15	Captive to miniDB-15	MiniDB-15 to miniDB-15	Captive to miniDB-15
SIGNAL COMPATIBILITY					
1,280 × 1,024	○	○	○	○	●
1,024 × 768 (noninterlaced)	●	●	●	●	●
1,024 × 768 (interlaced)	●	●	●	●	●
Super VGA (800 × 600)	●	●	●	●	●
VGA (640 × 480)	●	●	●	●	●
MCGA/Hercules	●/○	○/○	●/○	●/○	●/○
Mac II/Apple II GS	○/○	○/○	○/○	○/○	○/○
OPERATIONAL FEATURES					
Fixed or variable frequency	Variable	Fixed	Variable	Variable	Variable
Maximum noninterlaced resolution (pixels)	1,024 × 768	1,024 × 768	1,024 × 768	1,024 × 768	1,024 × 768
Video bandwidth (MHz)	80	65	75	85	65
Vertical scanning frequency (Hz)	50–90	47–100	47–100	50–120	50–90
Horizontal scanning frequency (kHz)	30–60	32–48	31–50	30–60	32–48
Maximum vertical refresh rates (Hz)					
1,280 × 1,024	N/A	N/A	N/A	N/A	88
1,024 × 768 noninterlaced	72	60	60	72	60
Super VGA (800 × 600)	72	72	72	72	72
VGA (640 × 480)	72	72	75	75	72
Phosphor persistence	Medium-short	Medium-short	Short	Short	Medium-short
Dot pitch or aperture grill pitch (mm)	0.28	0.28	0.28	0.28	0.28
Analog or digital controls	Analog	Analog	Analog	Digital	Analog
Power consumption (watts)	110	100	85	80	89
Microprocessor included	○	○	○	●	○
Number of simultaneously stored settings	N/A	N/A	N/A	13	N/A
Number of user-definable settings	N/A	N/A	N/A	13	N/A
CONTROLS					
Brightness	●	●	●	●	●
Contrast	●	●	●	●	●
Color matching	○	○	○	●	○
Horizontal position	●	●	●	●	●
Vertical position	●	●	●	●	●
Horizontal size	●	●	●	●	○
Vertical size	●	●	●	●	○
Pincushioning	○	○	○	●	●
Barrel distortion	○	○	○	●	○
Degaussing	○	○	○	○	○
120-/240-volt switching	○	●	○	○	● (auto-sensing)
VLF/ELF radiation control	○/○	○/○	●/○	●/○	○/○

●—Yes ○—No N/A—Not applicable INA—Information not available

Table Continues →

14-Inch Monitors

	MAG LX1460	MAG MX14S	Mitsuba 710VX	Mitsubishi Diamond Pro 14	Neotec NT-1456
Price	$	$	$	$	$
PHYSICAL SPECIFICATIONS					
Dimensions (HWD, in inches)	14 × 14 × 15	14.3 × 14 × 16	14 × 14 × 14	13.9 × 13.7 × 15.2	14.3 × 14.3 × 16
Weight (pounds)	26.5	34.0	27.3	26.5	27.5
Length of power cable (inches)	60	60	70	60	72
Adapter cable included	Captive to miniDB-15	Captive to DB-15	Captive to miniDB-15	Captive to miniDB-15	Captive to DB-15
SIGNAL COMPATIBILITY					
1,280 × 1,024	●	●	○	○	○
1,024 × 768 (noninterlaced)	●	●	●	●	●
1,024 × 768 (interlaced)	●	●	●	●	●
Super VGA (800 × 600)	●	●	●	●	●
VGA (640 × 480)	●	●	●	●	●
MCGA/Hercules	●/○	○/○	○/○	○/○	●/○
Mac II/Apple II GS	●/○	●/○	○/○	●/○	○/○
OPERATIONAL FEATURES					
Fixed or variable frequency	Variable	Variable	Variable	Variable	Variable
Maximum noninterlaced resolution (pixels)	1,024 × 768	1,280 × 1,024	1,024 × 768	1,024 × 768	1,280 × 960
Video bandwidth (MHz)	80	100	65	70	75
Vertical scanning frequency (Hz)	50–100	50–120	56–87	50–90	50–120
Horizontal scanning frequency (kHz)	30–60	30–64	32–48	30–58	30–56
Maximum vertical refresh rates (Hz)					
1,280 × 1,024	87	60	N/A	N/A	N/A
1,024 × 768 noninterlaced	72	76	60	72	70
Super VGA (800 × 600)	85	76	72	72	72
VGA (640 × 480)	85	76	72	73	72
Phosphor persistence	Medium-short	Medium-short	Medium-short	Medium-short	Medium-short
Dot pitch or aperture grill pitch (mm)	0.28	0.25	0.28	0.28	0.28
Analog or digital controls	Analog	Digital	Analog	Digital	Analog
Power consumption (watts)	110	110	90	90	80
Microprocessor included	○	●	○	●	○
Number of simultaneously stored settings	N/A	17	N/A	12	N/A
Number of user-definable settings	N/A	8	N/A	6	N/A
CONTROLS					
Brightness	●	●	●	●	●
Contrast	●	●	●	●	●
Color matching	○	○	○	○	○
Horizontal position	●	●	●	●	●
Vertical position	●	●	●	●	●
Horizontal size	●	●	○	●	●
Vertical size	●	●	●	●	●
Pincushioning	●	○	○	●	○
Barrel distortion	○	○	○	●	○
Degaussing	●	○	○	○	○
120-/240-volt switching	●	○	○	○	○
VLF/ELF radiation control	○/○	●/●	○/○	●/●	○/○

●—Yes ○—No N/A—Not applicable INA—Information not available

14-Inch Monitors

	Optiquest 1000S	Optiquest 1500D	Packard Bell PB8548SVGL	Philips Magnavox MagnaScan/14 Model CM9214	Qume QM857
Price	$	$	$	$	$
PHYSICAL SPECIFICATIONS					
Dimensions (HWD, in inches)	14 × 14 × 14	15 × 15 × 14	12.5 × 14.5 × 15.75	13.8 × 14 × 15.5	13.5 × 14 × 15
Weight (pounds)	24.2	28	35	35	35
Length of power cable (inches)	72	72	72	78	60
Adapter cable included	Captive to miniDB-15	Captive to miniDB-15	Captive to miniDB-15	Captive to DB-15	Captive to DB-15
SIGNAL COMPATIBILITY					
1,280 × 1,024	○	●	○	○	○
1,024 × 768 (noninterlaced)	●	●	●	●	●
1,024 × 768 (interlaced)	●	●	●	●	●
Super VGA (800 × 600)	●	●	●	●	●
VGA (640 × 480)	●	●	●	●	●
MCGA/Hercules	○/○	●/○	○/○	○/○	○/○
Mac II/Apple II GS	○/○	○/○	○/○	●/○	●/○
OPERATIONAL FEATURES					
Fixed or variable frequency	Fixed	Variable	Fixed	Variable	Variable
Maximum noninterlaced resolution (pixels)	1,024 × 768	1,024 × 768	1,024 × 768	1,024 × 768	1,024 × 768
Video bandwidth (MHz)	65	75	65	75	65
Vertical scanning frequency (Hz)	47–100	50–100	50–90	50–100	50–90
Horizontal scanning frequency (kHz)	32–48	30–58	32–48	30–58	30–60
Maximum vertical refresh rates (Hz)					
1,280 × 1,024	N/A	87	N/A	N/A	N/A
1,024 × 768 noninterlaced	60	72	60	70	72
Super VGA (800 × 600)	72	72	72	72	72
VGA (640 × 480)	72	72	72	72	72
Phosphor persistence	Medium-short	Medium-short	Medium-short	Medium-short	Medium-short
Dot pitch or aperture grill pitch (mm)	0.28	0.28	0.28	0.28	0.28
Analog or digital controls	Analog	Digital	Analog	Analog	Analog
Power consumption (watts)	100	85	85	85	80
Microprocessor included	○	●	○	○	○
Number of simultaneously stored settings	N/A	10	N/A	N/A	N/A
Number of user-definable settings	N/A	10	N/A	N/A	N/A
CONTROLS					
Brightness	●	●	●	●	●
Contrast	●	●	●	●	●
Color matching	○	○	○	○	○
Horizontal position	●	●	●	●	●
Vertical position	●	●	●	●	●
Horizontal size	●	●	●	●	●
Vertical size	●	●	●	●	●
Pincushioning	○	●	○	○	○
Barrel distortion	○	●	○	○	○
Degaussing	○	○	○	○	○
120-/240-volt switching	●	○	●	○	○
VLF/ELF radiation control	○/○	○/○	●/○	○/○	Optional

●—Yes   ○—No   N/A—Not applicable   INA—Information not available

Table Continues →

14-Inch Monitors

	Relisys RE-1458	Sampo AlphaScan Plus	Samtron SC-428TX	Seiko CM1450	Sony CPD-1304S
Price	$	$	$	$	$
PHYSICAL SPECIFICATIONS					
Dimensions (HWD, in inches)	13.8 × 15 × 15.3	15 × 14 × 14.5	14 × 13.5 × 15	13.5 × 13.8 × 14	14 × 13.8 × 16.3
Weight (pounds)	35	27.3	35	35	35
Length of power cable (inches)	72	72	72	72	60
Adapter cable included	Captive to DB-15	Captive to miniDB-15	Captive to miniDB-15	Captive to miniDB-15	Captive to DB-15
SIGNAL COMPATIBILITY					
1,280 × 1,024	○	○	○	○	○
1,024 × 768 (noninterlaced)	●	●	●	●	●
1,024 × 768 (interlaced)	●	●	●	●	●
Super VGA (800 × 600)	●	●	●	●	●
VGA (640 × 480)	●	●	●	●	●
MCGA/Hercules	○/○	●/○	●/○	●/○	○/○
Mac II/Apple II GS	○/○	○/○	○/○	○/○	●/○
OPERATIONAL FEATURES					
Fixed or variable frequency	Variable	Variable	Fixed	Variable	Variable
Maximum noninterlaced resolution (pixels)	1,024 × 768	1,024 × 768	1,024 × 768	1,024 × 768	1,024 × 768
Video bandwidth (MHz)	75	80	65	60	60
Vertical scanning frequency (Hz)	50–120	50–90	50–90	50–90	55–110
Horizontal scanning frequency (kHz)	30–58	30–60	32–48	31–50	28–57
Maximum vertical refresh rates (Hz)					
1,280 × 1,024	N/A	N/A	N/A	N/A	N/A
1,024 × 768 noninterlaced	70	72	60	60	70
Super VGA (800 × 600)	72	72	72	72	72
VGA (640 × 480)	72	72	72	72	72
Phosphor persistence	Medium-short	Medium-short	Medium-short	Medium-short	Medium-short
Dot pitch or aperture grill pitch (mm)	0.28	0.28	0.28	0.25	0.25
Analog or digital controls	Analog	Analog	Analog	Analog	Analog
Power consumption (watts)	110	110	70	150	100
Microprocessor included	○	○	○	○	○
Number of simultaneously stored settings	N/A	N/A	N/A	N/A	N/A
Number of user-definable settings	N/A	N/A	N/A	N/A	N/A
CONTROLS					
Brightness	●	●	●	●	●
Contrast	●	●	●	●	●
Color matching	○	○	○	○	○
Horizontal position	●	●	●	●	●
Vertical position	●	●	●	●	●
Horizontal size	●	●	●	●	●
Vertical size	●	●	●	●	●
Pincushioning	○	○	○	○	○
Barrel distortion	○	○	○	○	○
Degaussing	○	○	○	○	○
120-/240-volt switching	● (auto-sensing)	○	○	○	● (auto-sensing)
VLF/ELF radiation control	○/●	○/○	●/●	○/○	●/●

●—Yes   ○—No   N/A—Not applicable   INA—Information not available

14-Inch Monitors

	Sunshine CM8+	TVM MediaScan 4A+	ViewSonic 5E	ViewSonic 6	WEN JK1466 Color Monitor
Price	$	$	$	$	$
PHYSICAL SPECIFICATIONS					
Dimensions (HWD, in inches)	13.8 × 14.3 × 15.5	15 × 15 × 15	14 × 14 × 15	15 × 14 × 15	14.5 × 14.5 × 14
Weight (pounds)	35	35	30.8	24.2	26.7
Length of power cable (inches)	72	60	54	60	72
Adapter cable included	Captive to miniDB-15	Captive to miniDB-15	Captive to miniDB-15	Captive to miniDB-15	Captive to miniDB-15
SIGNAL COMPATIBILITY					
1,280 × 1,024	○	○	○	○	○
1,024 × 768 (noninterlaced)	●	●	●	●	●
1,024 × 768 (interlaced)	●	●	●	●	●
Super VGA (800 × 600)	●	●	●	●	●
VGA (640 × 480)	●	●	●	●	●
MCGA/Hercules	○/○	●/○	●/○	●/○	●/●
Mac II/Apple II GS	○/○	○/○	○/○	○/○	●/●
OPERATIONAL FEATURES					
Fixed or variable frequency	Variable	Fixed	Variable	Variable	Variable
Maximum noninterlaced resolution (pixels)	1,024 × 768	1,024 × 768	1,024 × 768	1,024 × 768	1,024 × 768
Video bandwidth (MHz)	64	65	80	65	70
Vertical scanning frequency (Hz)	50–90	47–100	50–90	50–90	48–90
Horizontal scanning frequency (kHz)	30–48	32–48	31–60	30–50	30–59
Maximum vertical refresh rates (Hz)					
1,280 × 1,024	N/A	N/A	N/A	N/A	N/A
1,024 × 768 noninterlaced	60	60	72	60	72
Super VGA (800 × 600)	72	72	72	72	72
VGA (640 × 480)	70	72	72	72	72
Phosphor persistence	Medium-short	Medium-short	Medium-short	Medium-short	Medium-short
Dot pitch or aperture grill pitch (mm)	0.28	0.28	0.28	0.28	0.28
Analog or digital controls	Analog	Analog	Analog	Analog	Analog
Power consumption (watts)	75	100	100	85	80
Microprocessor included	○	○	○	○	○
Number of simultaneously stored settings	N/A	N/A	N/A	N/A	N/A
Number of user-definable settings	N/A	N/A	N/A	N/A	N/A
CONTROLS					
Brightness	●	●	●	●	●
Contrast	●	●	●	●	●
Color matching	○	○	○	○	○
Horizontal position	●	●	●	●	●
Vertical position	●	●	●	○	●
Horizontal size	○	●	●	●	○
Vertical size	●	●	●	●	●
Pincushioning	○	○	○	○	○
Barrel distortion	○	○	○	○	○
Degaussing	○	○	○	○	○
120-/240-volt switching	○	●	●	○	●
VLF/ELF radiation control	Optional	○/○	○/○	○/○	Optional

●—Yes ○—No N/A—Not applicable INA—Information not available

End ∎

B.5 15-Inch Monitors

(Products listed in alphabetical order by company name)	Aamazing CM1528FS	AcerView 56L	ADI MicroScan 4A	AOC CM-536	Compaq QVision 150
Price	$	$	$	$	$
PHYSICAL SPECIFICATIONS					
Dimensions (HWD, in inches)	14.3 × 14.3 × 15	14 × 14 × 15	15 × 15 × 15	14.5 × 14.5 × 15	16 × 16 × 17
Weight (pounds)	27.1	35	30	31.9	45
Length of power cable (inches)	72	72	72	60	80
Adapter cable included	MiniDB-15 to miniDB-15	Captive to miniDB-15	Captive to miniDB-15	Captive to DB-15	BNC-5 to miniDB-15
SIGNAL COMPATIBILITY					
1,280 × 1,024	●	○	●	●	○
1,024 × 768 (noninterlaced)	●	●	●	●	●
1,024 × 768 (interlaced)	●	●	●	●	○
Super VGA (800 × 600)	●	●	●	●	●
VGA (640 × 480)	●	●	●	●	●
MCGA/Hercules	●/○	●/○	●/○	○/○	●/●
Mac II/Apple II GS	○/○	●/○	○/○	●/●	●/●
OPERATIONAL FEATURES					
Fixed or variable frequency	Variable	Variable	Variable	Variable	Variable
Maximum noninterlaced resolution (pixels)	1,280 × 1,024	1,024 × 768	1,024 × 768	1,280 × 1,024	1,024 × 768
Video bandwidth (MHz)	85	80	75	100	75
Vertical scanning frequency (Hz)	47–104	50–90	50–100	50–90	50–100
Horizontal scanning frequency (kHz)	28–64	31–60	30–58	30–68	32–58
Maximum vertical refresh rates (Hz)					
1,280 × 1,024	72	N/A	87	60	N/A
1,024 × 768 noninterlaced	74	72	72	72	72
Super VGA (800 × 600)	74	72	72	72	72
VGA (640 × 480)	74	84	72	72	75
Phosphor persistence	Medium-short	Medium	Medium-short	Medium-short	Medium-short
Dot pitch or aperture grill pitch (mm)	0.28	0.28	0.28	0.28	0.26
Analog or digital controls	Analog	Digital	Digital	Digital	Digital
Power consumption (watts)	132	110	90	110	175
Microprocessor included	○	●	●	●	●
Number of simultaneously stored settings	N/A	32	10	36	14
Number of user-definable settings	N/A	32	10	36	6
CONTROLS					
Brightness	●	●	●	●	●
Contrast	●	●	●	●	●
Color matching	○	○	○	○	○
Horizontal position	●	●	●	●	●
Vertical position	●	●	●	●	●
Horizontal size	●	●	●	●	●
Vertical size	●	●	●	●	●
Pincushioning	○	●	●	○	○
Barrel distortion	○	●	●	○	○
Degaussing	○	○	○	○	○
120-/240-volt switching	○	○	○	● (auto-sensing)	○
VLF/ELF radiation control	○/○	●/●	○/○	Optional	●/●

●—Yes ○—No N/A—Not applicable INA—Information not available

15-Inch Monitors

	Dell UltraScan 15FS	Dell UltraScan 15LR	FORA Addonics C152/LR	Hitachi/Nissei SuperScan 15	IBM PS/Value-Point 6319 Color Display
Price	$	$	$	$	$
PHYSICAL SPECIFICATIONS					
Dimensions (HWD, in inches)	15 × 14 × 15	15.5 × 14.5 × 16.5	14 × 14 × 15	15 × 14 × 16	16 × 15 × 16
Weight (pounds)	35	40.2	35	37.8	34
Length of power cable (inches)	72	72	60	72	73
Adapter cable included	Captive to miniDB-15	Captive to miniDB-15	Captive to miniDB-15	Captive to DB-15	MiniDB-15 to miniDB-15
SIGNAL COMPATIBILITY					
1,280 × 1,024	○	○	○	○	○
1,024 × 768 (noninterlaced)	●	●	●	●	●
1,024 × 768 (interlaced)	●	●	●	●	●
Super VGA (800 × 600)	●	●	●	●	●
VGA (640 × 480)	●	●	●	●	●
MCGA/Hercules	●/○	●/○	●/○	○/○	●/○
Mac II/Apple II GS	○/○	○/○	●/○	●/○	○/○
OPERATIONAL FEATURES					
Fixed or variable frequency	Variable	Variable	Variable	Variable	Variable
Maximum noninterlaced resolution (pixels)	1,024 × 768	1,024 × 768	1,024 × 768	1,024 × 768	1,024 × 768
Video bandwidth (MHz)	80	75	80	75	85
Vertical scanning frequency (Hz)	50–90	55–90	50–90	50–100	50–120
Horizontal scanning frequency (kHz)	30–60	32–57	31–60	30–58	30–60
Maximum vertical refresh rates (Hz)					
1,280 × 1,024	N/A	N/A	N/A	N/A	N/A
1,024 × 768 noninterlaced	72	70	72	72	72
Super VGA (800 × 600)	72	72	72	72	72
VGA (640 × 480)	72	72	84	72	75
Phosphor persistence	Medium-short	Medium-short	Medium	Medium-short	Short
Dot pitch or aperture grill pitch (mm)	0.28	0.28	0.28	0.28	0.28
Analog or digital controls	Analog	Analog	Digital	Analog	Digital
Power consumption (watts)	120	120	110	110	80
Microprocessor included	○	○	●	○	●
Number of simultaneously stored settings	N/A	N/A	32	N/A	13
Number of user-definable settings	N/A	N/A	32	N/A	13
CONTROLS					
Brightness	●	●	●	●	●
Contrast	●	●	●	●	●
Color matching	○	○	○	○	●
Horizontal position	●	●	●	●	●
Vertical position	●	●	●	●	●
Horizontal size	●	●	●	●	●
Vertical size	●	●	●	●	●
Pincushioning	○	●	●	○	●
Barrel distortion	○	○	●	○	●
Degaussing	○	●	○	○	○
120-/240-volt switching	○	○	○	○	○
VLF/ELF radiation control	○/○	●/●	●/●	●/●	●/○

●—Yes   ○—No   N/A—Not applicable   INA—Information not available

Table Continues →

15-Inch Monitors

	IOcomm ThinkSync 5	MAG MX15F	Nanao Flexscan F340iW	NEC MultiSync 3FGX	NEC MultiSync 4FG
Price	$	$	$	$	$
PHYSICAL SPECIFICATIONS					
Dimensions (HWD, in inches)	14.3 × 14.5 × 15	14 × 14 × 16.5	14.9 × 14.4 × 16.2	15.6 × 14.6 × 16.3	15.6 × 14.6 × 16.3
Weight (pounds)	31	35.9	35.2	36.5	39.2
Length of power cable (inches)	72	60	80	72	72
Adapter cable included	MiniDB-15 to miniDB-15	Captive to DB-15	Captive to miniDB-15	Captive to DB-15	Captive to DB-15
SIGNAL COMPATIBILITY					
1,280 × 1,024	●	●	○	○	○
1,024 × 768 (noninterlaced)	●	●	●	●	●
1,024 × 768 (interlaced)	●	●	●	●	●
Super VGA (800 × 600)	●	●	●	●	●
VGA (640 × 480)	●	●	●	●	●
MCGA/Hercules	●/○	○/○	●/○	●/○	●/○
Mac II/Apple II GS	○/○	●/○	●/●	●/○	●/○
OPERATIONAL FEATURES					
Fixed or variable frequency	Variable	Variable	Variable	Variable	Variable
Maximum noninterlaced resolution (pixels)	1,280 × 1,024	1,280 × 1,024	1,024 × 768	1,024 × 768	1,024 × 768
Video bandwidth (MHz)	100	100	75	65	75
Vertical scanning frequency (Hz)	40–100	50–120	55–90	55–90	55–90
Horizontal scanning frequency (kHz)	30–65	30–68	27–61	32–49	27–57
Maximum vertical refresh rates (Hz)					
1,280 × 1,024	60	60	N/A	N/A	N/A
1,024 × 768 noninterlaced	76	76	76	60	70
Super VGA (800 × 600)	76	76	90	72	80
VGA (640 × 480)	72	76	90	72	90
Phosphor persistence	Medium-short	Medium-short	Medium-short	Medium-short	Medium-short
Dot pitch or aperture grill pitch (mm)	0.28	0.28	0.28	0.28	0.28
Analog or digital controls	Analog	Digital	Digital	Analog	Digital
Power consumption (watts)	110	110	100	100	105
Microprocessor included	○	●	●	○	●
Number of simultaneously stored settings	N/A	17	28	N/A	19
Number of user-definable settings	N/A	8	28	N/A	4
CONTROLS					
Brightness	●	●	●	●	●
Contrast	●	●	●	●	●
Color matching	○	○	●	○	●
Horizontal position	●	●	●	●	●
Vertical position	●	●	●	●	●
Horizontal size	●	●	●	●	●
Vertical size	●	●	●	●	●
Pincushioning	●	○	●	●	●
Barrel distortion	○	○	●	●	●
Degaussing	○	○	●	●	●
120-/240-volt switching	● (auto-sensing)	○	○	○	○
VLF/ELF radiation control	○/○	●/●	●/●	●/●	●/●

●—Yes ○—No N/A—Not applicable INA—Information not available

15-Inch Monitors

	Optiquest 2000D	Optiquest 2000DX	Relisys RE-1558	Sampo AlphaScan 15	Sunshine CM15C
Price	$	$	$	$	$
PHYSICAL SPECIFICATIONS					
Dimensions (HWD, in inches)	15 × 15 × 15	14 × 14 × 15	15.8 × 15 × 16.3	15 × 14 × 15	14.5 × 14.8 × 15.5
Weight (pounds)	30	35	35	35	35
Length of power cable (inches)	72	72	72	72	72
Adapter cable included	Captive to miniDB-15	Captive to miniDB-15	Captive to DB-15	Captive to miniDB-15	Captive to miniDB-15
SIGNAL COMPATIBILITY					
1,280 × 1,024	●	○	○	●	●
1,024 × 768 (noninterlaced)	●	●	●	●	●
1,024 × 768 (interlaced)	●	●	●	●	●
Super VGA (800 × 600)	●	●	●	●	●
VGA (640 × 480)	●	●	●	●	●
MCGA/Hercules	●/○	●/○	○/○	●/○	○/○
Mac II/Apple II GS	○/○	●/○	○/○	○/○	○/○
OPERATIONAL FEATURES					
Fixed or variable frequency	Variable	Variable	Variable	Variable	Variable
Maximum noninterlaced resolution (pixels)	1,024 × 768	1,024 × 768	1,024 × 768	1,280 × 1,024	1,280 × 1,024
Video bandwidth (MHz)	75	80	75	80	85
Vertical scanning frequency (Hz)	50–100	50–90	50–120	50–90	40–90
Horizontal scanning frequency (kHz)	30–58	31–60	30–58	30–64	30–64
Maximum vertical refresh rates (Hz)					
1,280 × 1,024	87	N/A	N/A	60	60
1,024 × 768 noninterlaced	72	72	70	72	76
Super VGA (800 × 600)	72	72	72	72	72
VGA (640 × 480)	72	84	72	72	70
Phosphor persistence	Medium-short	Medium	Medium-short	Medium-short	Medium-short
Dot pitch or aperture grill pitch (mm)	0.28	0.28	0.28	0.28	0.28
Analog or digital controls	Digital	Digital	Analog	Analog	Analog
Power consumption (watts)	90	110	110	120	100
Microprocessor included	●	●	○	○	○
Number of simultaneously stored settings	10	32	N/A	N/A	N/A
Number of user-definable settings	10	32	N/A	N/A	N/A
CONTROLS					
Brightness	●	●	●	●	●
Contrast	●	●	●	●	●
Color matching	○	○	○	○	○
Horizontal position	●	●	●	●	●
Vertical position	●	●	●	●	●
Horizontal size	●	●	●	●	●
Vertical size	●	●	●	●	●
Pincushioning	●	●	●	○	○
Barrel distortion	●	●	○	○	○
Degaussing	○	○	○	○	○
120-/240-volt switching	○	○	● (auto-sensing)	○	○
VLF/ELF radiation control	○/○	●/●	○/●	○/○	Optional

●—Yes ○—No N/A—Not applicable INA—Information not available   **Table Continues →**

15-Inch Monitors

	Taxan MultiVision 550	TVM LowRadiation 5A+	ViewSonic 6FS
Price	$	$	$
PHYSICAL SPECIFICATIONS			
Dimensions (HWD, in inches)	15 × 14 × 15	15.3 × 14.5 × 16	14 × 14 × 15
Weight (pounds)	35	35	35
Length of power cable (inches)	72	72	60
Adapter cable included	Captive to miniDB-15	Captive to miniDB-15	Captive to miniDB-15
SIGNAL COMPATIBILITY			
1,280 × 1,024	○	●	●
1,024 × 768 (noninterlaced)	●	●	●
1,024 × 768 (interlaced)	●	●	●
Super VGA (800 × 600)	●	●	●
VGA (640 × 480)	●	●	●
MCGA/Hercules	●/○	●/○	●/○
Mac II/Apple II GS	○/○	○/○	○/○
OPERATIONAL FEATURES			
Fixed or variable frequency	Variable	Variable	Variable
Maximum noninterlaced resolution (pixels)	1,024 × 768	1,024 × 768	1,024 × 768
Video bandwidth (MHz)	80	65	80
Vertical scanning frequency (Hz)	50–90	40–100	50–90
Horizontal scanning frequency (kHz)	30–60	30–57	31–60
Maximum vertical refresh rates (Hz)			
1,280 × 1,024	N/A	88	87
1,024 × 768 noninterlaced	70	72	72
Super VGA (800 × 600)	72	72	72
VGA (640 × 480)	72	72	84
Phosphor persistence	Medium-short	Medium-short	Medium
Dot pitch or aperture grill pitch (mm)	0.28	0.28	0.28
Analog or digital controls	Analog	Digital	Digital
Power consumption (watts)	110	90	110
Microprocessor included	○	●	●
Number of simultaneously stored settings	N/A	15	32
Number of user-definable settings	N/A	15	32
CONTROLS			
Brightness	●	●	●
Contrast	●	●	●
Color matching	○	○	○
Horizontal position	●	●	●
Vertical position	●	●	●
Horizontal size	●	●	●
Vertical size	●	●	●
Pincushioning	○	○	●
Barrel distortion	○	○	●
Degaussing	○	○	○
120-/240-volt switching	○	○	○
VLF/ELF radiation control	○/○	●/○	●/●

●—Yes   ○—No   N/A—Not applicable   INA—Information not available

End ■

B.6 16-Inch Monitors

(Products listed in alphabetical order by company name)	Dell Graphics Performance Display 16C	HP D1188A	Idek MF-5117	IOcomm ThinkSync 17 CM–7126	Mitsubishi Diamond Scan 16L
Price	$	$$$	$$	$$	$$
PHYSICAL SPECIFICATIONS					
Tilt/swivel base	●	○	●	●	●
Case dimensions (HWD, in inches)	16 × 15.8 × 17.8	14 × 15.8 × 17.9	16.3 × 15.8 × 16.3	15.3 × 16 × 16.5	14 × 15.8 × 17.9
Weight (pounds)	42	43	43	50	42
Type of connector(s) on monitor	DB-9, BNC-5	BNC-5	DB-15	BNC-5	BNC-5
COMPATABILITY					
1,280 × 1,024	○	●	○	●	●
1,024 × 768 (noninterlaced)	●	●	●	●	●
1,024 × 768 (interlaced)	●	●	●	●	●
Super VGA (800 × 600)	●	●	●	●	●
VGA (640 × 480)	●	●	●	●	●
MCGA	●	○	●	●	○
EGA	●	○	●	○	○
OPERATIONAL FEATURES					
Maximum resolution (pixels)	1,280 × 800	1,280 × 1,024	1,024 × 768	1,280 × 1,024	1,280 × 1,024
Video bandwidth (MHz)	50 (analog), 30 (digital/TLL)	100 (analog)	65 (analog)	136 (analog)	100 (analog)
Vertical scanning frequency range (Hz)	50–80	50–90	50–90	50–90	50–90
Horizontal scanning frequency range (kHz)	20–50	30–64	21.9–50	30–75	30–64
Can maintain image size across resolution modes	●	●	●	●	●
Phosphor persistence	Short	Medium	Short	Medium-short	Medium
Dot pitch (mm)	0.31	0.28	0.28	0.26	0.31
Inputs:					
Analog D-sub connector	9-pin mini	None	15-pin standard	None	None
Analog BNC coaxial connector (sync on green, composite sync, and separate sync)	●	●	●	●	●
Digital/TTL	●	○	●	○	○
CONTROLS					
Brightness	● (analog)	● (analog)	● (analog)	● (analog)	● (analog)
Contrast	● (analog)	● (analog)	● (analog)	● (analog)	● (analog)
Color	● (analog)	○	○	○	○
Horizontal position	● (analog)	● (analog)	● (analog)	● (digital)	● (analog)
Vertical position	● (analog)	● (analog)	● (analog)	● (digital)	● (analog)
Horizontal size	● (analog)	● (analog)	● (analog)	● (digital)	● (analog)
Vertical size	● (analog)	● (analog)	● (analog)	● (digital)	● (analog)
Pincushioning	● (analog)	○	● (digital)	● (digital)	● (digital)
Convergence	● (analog)	○	○	○	○
Degaussing	○	●	○	○	●
8/16/64-color switch	●	○	●	○	●
Text color switch	●	○	○	○	○
120/240-volt switch	○	●	●	○	●

●—Yes ○—No N/A—Not applicable INA—Information not available

Table Continues →

ZIFF-DAVIS PRESS

16-Inch Monitors

	Mitsubishi HL6615(TK)	Nanao FlexScan 9070U	Nanao FlexScan 9080i	NEC MultiSync 4D	Philips FC17AS
Price	$$	$$	$$	$$	$$$
PHYSICAL SPECIFICATIONS					
Tilt/swivel base	●	●	●	●	●
Case dimensions (HWD, in inches)	14 × 15.8 × 17.9	15.9 × 15.8 × 17.7	15.9 × 15.8 × 17.7	15.4 × 15.2 × 18.7	15.6 × 16.1 × 18.1
Weight (pounds)	44	42	42	50	51
Type of connector(s) on monitor	BNC-5	DB-9, BNC-5	DB-9	DB-15	BNC-5
COMPATABILITY					
1,280 × 1,024	●	○	●	○	●
1,024 × 768 (noninterlaced)	●	●	●	●	●
1,024 × 768 (interlaced)	●	●	●	●	●
Super VGA (800 × 600)	●	●	●	●	●
VGA (640 × 480)	●	●	●	●	○
MCGA	○	●	●	●	○
EGA	○	●	○	●	○
OPERATIONAL FEATURES					
Maximum resolution (pixels)	1,280 × 1,024	1,280 × 800	1,280 × 1,024	1,024 × 768	1,280 × 1,024
Video bandwidth (MHz)	110 (analog)	50 (analog), 30 (digital/TLL)	60 (analog)	75 (analog)	110 (analog)
Vertical scanning frequency range (Hz)	50–120	50–90	50–90	50–90	50–140
Horizontal scanning frequency range (kHz)	30–64	20–50	30–64	30–57	30–66
Can maintain image size across resolution modes	●	●	●	●	○
Phosphor persistence	Medium	Short	Short	Short	Medium-short
Dot pitch (mm)	0.31	0.28	0.28	0.28	0.26
Inputs:					
Analog D-sub connector	None	9-pin	9-pin	15-pin mini or 15-pin standard	None
Analog BNC coaxial connector (sync on green, composite sync, and separate sync)	●	●	●	●	●
Digital/TTL	○	●	○	○	○
CONTROLS					
Brightness	● (analog)	● (analog)	● (analog)	● (analog)	● (analog)
Contrast	● (analog)	● (analog)	● (analog)	● (analog)	● (analog)
Color	○	○	○	○	○
Horizontal position	● (analog)	● (analog)	● (digital)	● (digital)	● (analog)
Vertical position	● (analog)	● (analog)	● (digital)	● (digital)	● (analog)
Horizontal size	● (analog)	● (analog)	● (digital)	● (digital)	● (analog)
Vertical size	● (analog)	● (analog)	● (digital)	● (digital)	● (analog)
Pincushioning	● (digital)	● (analog)	● (digital)	○	○
Convergence	○	● (analog)	● (analog)	○	○
Degaussing	●	○	○	●	●
8/16/64-color switch	○	●	○	○	○
Text color switch	○	○	●	○	○
120/240-volt switch	●	○	○	○	●

●—Yes ○—No N/A—Not applicable INA—Information not available

End ∎

B.7 17-Inch Monitors

(Products listed in alphabetical order by company name)	AcerView 76	American Mitac M1758	CTX-1760	Epson Professional Series
Price	$	$	$	$$
Dimensions (HWD, in inches)	16 × 17 × 18	15.3 × 15.8 × 16	17 × 16.5 × 16.4	15.5 × 16.4 × 17.4
Weight (pounds)	42	44	52	55
SIGNAL COMPATABILITY				
1,280 × 1,024	○	○	●	○
1,024 × 768 (noninterlaced)	●	●	●	●
1,024 × 768 (interlaced)	●	●	●	●
Super VGA (800 × 600)	●	●	●	●
VGA (640 × 480)	●	●	●	●
MCGA	●	○	○	○
EGA	●	○	○	○
OPERATIONAL FEATURES				
Maximum noninterlaced resolution (pixels)	1,024 × 768	1,024 × 768	1,024 × 768	1,024 × 768
Video bandwidth (MHz)	80	85	100	70
Vertical scanning frequency range (Hz)	50–90	50–90	50–90	50–90
Horizontal scanning frequency range (kHz)	31–60	31.5–58	30–65	30–57
Maximum vertical refresh rates (Hz):				
1,280 × 1,024	N/A	N/A	60	N/A
1,024 × 768 (noninterlaced)	72	70	70	70
800 × 600	72	72	72	72
Phosphor persistence	Medium-short	Medium-short	Medium-short	Medium-short
Dot pitch or aperture grill pitch (mm)	0.31	0.31	0.31	0.26
INPUT CONNECTORS				
Analog D-sub connectors:				
9-pin mini	○	●	○	○
15-pin mini	●	○	●	○
15-pin standard	○	○	●	○
Analog BNC coaxial connectors:				
3-wire sync on green	○	○	○	●
4-wire external composite sync	○	○	○	○
5-wire external composite sync	○	○	○	○
CONTROLS				
Brightness	● (analog)	● (analog)	● (analog)	● (analog)
Contrast	● (analog)	● (analog)	● (analog)	● (analog)
Color matching	○	○	○	○
Horizontal position	● (analog)	● (analog)	● (digital)	● (analog)
Vertical position	● (analog)	● (analog)	● (digital)	● (analog)
Horizontal size	● (analog)	● (analog)	● (digital)	● (analog)
Vertical size	● (analog)	● (analog)	● (digital)	● (analog)
Pincushioning	● (analog)	○	○	● (analog)
120/240-volt switching	● (auto-sensing)	● (switch)	● (auto-sensing)	● (auto-sensing)
MISCELLANEOUS				
Fixed- or variable-frequency multiscan	Fixed	Variable	Variable	Variable
Low-emissions model	○	○	○	○
VLF radiation control	N/A	N/A	N/A	N/A
ELF radiation control	N/A	N/A	N/A	N/A

●—Yes ○— No N/A—Not applicable INA—Information not available

Table Continues →

17-Inch Monitors

	HP Ultra VGA 17-inch Display	Idek/Iiyama MF-5317	MAG MX17F	Mitsubishi Diamond Pro 17
Price	$$	$$	$$	$$
Dimensions (HWD, in inches)	16.8 × 16.3 × 17	16.4 × 15.8 × 16.3	16.5 × 16.5 × 19.9	15.8 × 15.8 × 17
Weight (pounds)	43	40	50.6	35
SIGNAL COMPATABILITY				
1,280 × 1,024	●	●	●	●
1,024 × 768 (noninterlaced)	●	●	●	●
1,024 × 768 (interlaced)	●	●	●	●
Super VGA (800 × 600)	●	●	●	●
VGA (640 × 480)	●	●	●	●
MCGA	○	○	●	○
EGA	○	○	○	○
OPERATIONAL FEATURES				
Maximum noninterlaced resolution (pixels)	1,280 × 1,024	1,280 × 1,024	1,280 × 1,024	1,280 × 1,024
Video bandwidth (MHz)	85	60	120	100
Vertical scanning frequency range (Hz)	50–90	50–90	50–120	50–130
Horizontal scanning frequency range (kHz)	30–64	30–65	30–68	30–64
Maximum vertical refresh rates (Hz):				
1,280 × 1,024	60	61	60	60
1,024 × 768 (noninterlaced)	70	72	76	80
800 × 600	72	72	85	72
Phosphor persistence	Medium-short	Short	Medium-short	Medium-short
Dot pitch or aperture grill pitch (mm)	0.28	0.28	0.26	0.26
INPUT CONNECTORS				
Analog D-sub connectors:				
9-pin mini	○	○	○	○
15-pin mini	●	○	●	●
15-pin standard	○	●	●	○
Analog BNC coaxial connectors:				
3-wire sync on green	○	○	○	○
4-wire external composite sync	○	○	●	○
5-wire external composite sync	○	●	●	○
CONTROLS				
Brightness	● (digital)	● (analog)	● (analog)	● (digital)
Contrast	● (digital)	● (analog)	● (analog)	● (digital)
Color matching	○	○	○	● (digital)
Horizontal position	● (digital)	● (analog)	● (digital)	● (digital)
Vertical position	● (digital)	● (analog)	● (digital)	● (digital)
Horizontal size	● (digital)	● (analog)	● (digital)	● (digital)
Vertical size	● (digital)	● (analog)	● (digital)	● (digital)
Pincushioning	○	○	○	● (digital)
120/240-volt switching	● (auto-sensing)	● (switch)	● (auto-sensing)	● (auto-sensing)
MISCELLANEOUS				
Fixed- or variable-frequency multiscan	Variable	Variable	Variable	Variable
Low-emissions model	●	●	○	●
VLF radiation control	●	●	N/A	●
ELF radiation control	●	●	N/A	●

●—Yes   ○—No   N/A—Not applicable   INA—Information not available

17-Inch Monitors

	Nanao Flexscan F550i	NEC MultiSync 5FG	Relisys RE1776 17-Inch High Resolution Multiscan Color Monitor	Seiko CM1760LR
Price	$$	$$	$$	$$
Dimensions (HWD, in inches)	16 × 15.8 × 17.8	18 × 16.5 × 20	17 × 16.5 × 16.3	17 × 16 × 17
Weight (pounds)	42	56.1	55	51
SIGNAL COMPATABILITY				
1,280 × 1,024	●	●	●	●
1,024 × 768 (noninterlaced)	●	●	●	●
1,024 × 768 (interlaced)	●	●	●	●
Super VGA (800 × 600)	●	●	●	●
VGA (640 × 480)	●	●	●	●
MCGA	●	●	○	○
EGA	○	●	○	○
OPERATIONAL FEATURES				
Maximum noninterlaced resolution (pixels)	1,280 × 1,024	1,280 × 1,024	1,280 × 1,024	1,280 × 1,024
Video bandwidth (MHz)	80	135	125	100
Vertical scanning frequency range (Hz)	55–90	55–90	40–120	50–90
Horizontal scanning frequency range (kHz)	30–65	27–79	30–76	31–64
Maximum vertical refresh rates (Hz):				
1,280 × 1,024	60	74	60	60
1,024 × 768 (noninterlaced)	78	88	70	78
800 × 600	72	90	72	72
Phosphor persistence	Medium-short	Medium-short	Medium-short	Medium-short
Dot pitch or aperture grill pitch (mm)	0.28	0.28	0.26	0.25
INPUT CONNECTORS				
Analog D-sub connectors:				
9-pin mini	●	○	○	○
15-pin mini	○	●	○	○
15-pin standard	○	●	○	●
Analog BNC coaxial connectors:				
3-wire sync on green	●	●	●	●
4-wire external composite sync	●	●	○	●
5-wire external composite sync	●	●	●	○
CONTROLS				
Brightness	● (digital)	● (digital)	● (analog)	● (analog)
Contrast	● (digital)	● (digital)	● (analog)	● (analog)
Color matching	○	● (digital)	○	○
Horizontal position	● (digital)	● (digital)	● (analog)	● (analog)
Vertical position	● (digital)	● (digital)	● (analog)	● (analog)
Horizontal size	● (digital)	● (digital)	● (analog)	● (analog)
Vertical size	● (digital)	● (digital)	● (analog)	● (analog)
Pincushioning	● (digital)	● (digital)	○	○
120/240-volt switching	● (auto-sensing)	○	● (auto-sensing)	○
MISCELLANEOUS				
Fixed- or variable-frequency multiscan	Variable	Variable	Variable	Variable
Low-emissions model	●	●	○	●
VLF radiation control	●	●	N/A	●
ELF radiation control	●	●	N/A	●

●—Yes ○—No N/A—Not applicable INA—Information not available

Table Continues →

17-Inch Monitors

	Sony CPD-1604S 17" Multiscan Trinitron Color Computer Monitor	Tatung CM-17MBD	Toshiba P17CM01	ViewSonic 76
Price	$$	$$	$$	$
Dimensions (HWD, in inches)	16.8 × 15.9 × 17.3	16.8 × 16.2 × 16.5	16.8 × 15.8 × 18.3	16.8 × 16 × 18.7
Weight (pounds)	48.4	44	57.2	60.5
SIGNAL COMPATABILITY				
1,280 × 1,024	○	●	●	●
1,024 × 768 (noninterlaced)	●	●	●	●
1,024 × 768 (interlaced)	●	●	●	●
Super VGA (800 × 600)	●	●	●	●
VGA (640 × 480)	●	●	●	●
MCGA	●	●	○	●
EGA	○	○	○	○
OPERATIONAL FEATURES				
Maximum noninterlaced resolution (pixels)	1,024 × 768	1,280 × 1,024	1,280 × 1,024	1,280 × 1,024
Video bandwidth (MHz)	60	100	100	110
Vertical scanning frequency range (Hz)	50–87	50–90	50–90	50–90
Horizontal scanning frequency range (kHz)	28–57	29–66	30–65	30–64
Maximum vertical refresh rates (Hz):				
1,280 × 1,024	N/A	60	60	60
1,024 × 768 (noninterlaced)	70	76	80	72
800 × 600	72	72	90	72
Phosphor persistence	Medium-short	Medium-short	Short	Short
Dot pitch or aperture grill pitch (mm)	0.25	0.26	0.31	0.28
INPUT CONNECTORS				
Analog D-sub connectors:				
9-pin mini	○	○	○	○
15-pin mini	○	●	●	●
15-pin standard	●	●	○	○
Analog BNC coaxial connectors:				
3-wire sync on green	○	●	●	●
4-wire external composite sync	○	●	●	●
5-wire external composite sync	○	●	●	●
CONTROLS				
Brightness	● (analog)	● (analog)	● (analog)	● (analog)
Contrast	● (analog)	● (analog)	● (analog)	● (analog)
Color matching	○	○	○	○
Horizontal position	● (analog)	● (digital)	● (digital)	● (digital)
Vertical position	● (analog)	● (digital)	● (digital)	● (digital)
Horizontal size	● (analog)	● (digital)	● (digital)	● (digital)
Vertical size	● (analog)	● (digital)	● (digital)	● (digital)
Pincushioning	○	● (digital)	● (digital)	○
120/240-volt switching	● (auto-sensing)	● (switch)	● (switch)	● (auto-sensing)
MISCELLANEOUS				
Fixed- or variable-frequency multiscan	Variable	Variable	Variable	Variable
Low-emissions model	●	○	●	●
VLF radiation control	●	N/A	●	●
ELF radiation control	●	N/A	○	●

●—Yes   ○—No   N/A—Not applicable   INA—Information not available

End ■

B.8 Presentation Monitors

(Products listed in alphabetical order by company name)	Barco Multidata OCM 2846	Barco Multidata OCM 3346	Barco Multidata SCM 2846	Mitsubishi AM-3501R	Mitsubishi AM-3151A
Price	$$$	$$$$	$$$	$$$$$	$$$$
PHYSICAL SPECIFICATIONS					
Measured diagonal screen size (inches)	26	31	26	35	31
Monitor case dimensions (HWD, in inches)	23 × 25 × 19	26 × 30 × 21	18 × 23 × 17	34 × 38 × 27	26 × 30 × 21
Weight (pounds)	95	148	93	266	143
SIGNAL COMPATABILITY					
1,280 × 1,024	○	○	○	○	○
1,024 × 768 (noninterlaced)	○	○	○	○	○
1,024 × 768 (interlaced)	●	●	●	●	●
Super VGA (800 × 600)	●	●	●	●	●
VGA (640 × 480)	●	●	●	●	●
MCGA	●	●	●	●	●
EGA	●	●	●	●	●
OPERATIONAL FEATURES					
Maximum resolution (pixels)	800 × 600	800 × 600	800 × 600	640 × 480	640 × 480
Video bandwidth (MHz)	30	30	30	15	15
Vertical scanning frequency range (Hz)	45–120	45–120	45–120	45–70	45–90
Horizontal scanning frequency range (kHz)	15–36	15–36	15–36	15–35.5	15.6–36
Phosphor persistence	Medium	Medium	Medium	Short	Medium-short
Dot pitch (mm)	0.80	0.80	0.80	1.0	0.83
Modes that maintain image size	None	None	None	None	MDA, CGA, EGA, VGA
Number of user-adjustable image settings	1	1	1	8	1
Input connectors:					
Analog D-sub	9-pin mini, 15-pin mini	9-pin, 15-pin	9-pin mini, 15-pin mini	25-pin	25-pin
Analog BNC coaxial:					
Sync on green	●	●	●	●	●
Composite sync	●	●	●	●	●
Separate sync	●	●	●	●	●
Digital/TTL	●	●	●	●	●
Composite video	●	●	●	●	●
NTSC	●	●	●	●	●
BNC	●	●	●	●	●
RCA jack	○	○	○	○	○
S-video	●	●	●	○	●
Output connectors:					
Analog D-sub	15-pin standard	15-pin standard	15-pin standard	None	None
Analog BNC coaxial:					
Sync on green	●	●	●	●	●
Composite sync	●	●	●	●	●
Separate sync	●	●	●	●	●
Digital/TTL	○	○	○	●	●
Composite video	●	●	●	●	●
NTSC	●	●	●	●	●
BNC	●	●	●	●	●
RCA jack	○	○	○	○	○
S-video	○	○	○	●	●

●—Yes   ○—No   N/A—Not applicable   INA—Information not available   **Table Continues →**

Presentation Monitors

	Mitsubishi HC3505SK	Mitsubishi XC-3310C	Mitsubishi XC-3715C	NEC DM-3000P
Price	$$$$$	$$$$	$$$$$	$$$$
PHYSICAL SPECIFICATIONS				
Measured diagonal screen size (inches)	26	33	37	30
Monitor case dimensions (HWD, in inches)	22 × 26 × 26	26 × 28 × 22	29 × 34 × 23	28 × 31 × 21
Weight (pounds)	122	172	216	137
SIGNAL COMPATABILITY				
1,280 × 1,024	○	○	○	○
1,024 × 768 (noninterlaced)	○	○	○	○
1,024 × 768 (interlaced)	●	●	●	●
Super VGA (800 × 600)	●	●	●	●
VGA (640 × 480)	●	●	●	●
MCGA	●	●	●	●
EGA	●	●	●	●
OPERATIONAL FEATURES				
Maximum resolution (pixels)	800 × 600	800 × 600	800 × 600	640 × 480
Video bandwidth (MHz)	50	30	35	20
Vertical scanning frequency range (Hz)	45–90	40–75	45–120	50–87
Horizontal scanning frequency range (kHz)	15.7–38	15.75–35	15.7–36	15–35.5
Phosphor persistence	Medium-short	Medium-short	Medium-short	Medium
Dot pitch (mm)	0.31	0.88–0.99	0.85–1.1	0.80
Modes that maintain image size	VGA, Super VGA, Mac II	CGA, EGA, VGA, MacII	CGA, EGA, VGA, Mac II	VGA, 8514/A
Number of user-adjustable image settings	6	4	6	1
Input connectors:				
Analog D-sub	15-pin mini	15-pin mini	15-pin standard	15-pin mini
Analog BNC coaxial:				
Sync on green	●	●	●	○
Composite sync	●	●	●	●
Separate sync	●	●	●	●
Digital/TTL	●	●	●	●
Composite video	○	●	●	●
NTSC	○	●	●	●
BNC	○	●	●	●
RCA jack	○	●	●	○
S-video	○	○	●	●
Output connectors:				
Analog D-sub	None	None	None	15-pin mini
Analog BNC coaxial:				
Sync on green	○	○	○	○
Composite sync	○	○	○	○
Separate sync	○	○	○	●
Digital/TTL	○	○	○	○
Composite video	○	○	○	●
NTSC	○	○	○	●
BNC	○	○	○	●
RCA jack	○	○	○	○
S-video	○	○	○	●

●—Yes ○—No N/A—Not applicable INA—Information not available

End ■

B.9 Multiscanning Monitors

(Products listed in alphabetical order by company name)	3Lynx IntelliSync SCC-1435	AOC Intl. CM-314	Casper TM-5155H	CTX 3435	Electrohome ECM 1310U, 1311U, and 1312U
Price	$	$	$	$	$
PHYSICAL SPECIFICATIONS					
Includes tilt/swivel	●	●	●	●	Optional
Includes cables	●	●	●	●	Optional
Visible screen size (diagonal, in inches)	12.875	13.25	13	13	13
Case dimensions (HWD, in inches)	13.375 × 13.5 × 15	14.5 × 14.25 × 14.5	14 × 14.25 × 15	14.5 × 14 × 15.75	13 × 14 × 15
Cable removable at monitor end	●	●	●	●	●
OPERATIONAL FEATURES					
Maximum resolution (pixels), width	940	800	800	800	910
Maximum resolution (pixels), height	600	600	560	560	675
Video bandwidth (MHz)	30	30	30	30	30
Vertical scanning frequency range (Hz)	45–120	50–80	47–70	50–70	47–85
Horizontal scanning frequency range (kHz)	15.7–35	15–35	15–35	15.5–35	15–34
Dot pitch (mm)	0.31	0.31	0.31	0.31	0.31
Autosizing	○	○	○	○	● (IBM only)
Inputs (separate socket or switch-selectable):					
Analog/TTL RGB	● (switch)	● (switch)	● (switch)	● (switch)	● (switch)
Composite	○	○	○	○	○
Separate sync	○	○	○	○	● (socket)
Outputs (separate socket or switch-selectable):					
Analog/TTL RGB	○	○	○	○	○
Composite	○	○	○	○	○
Separate sync	○	○	○	○	● (socket)
CONTROLS					
Brightness	●	●	●	●	●
Contrast	●	●	●	●	●
Horizontal position	●	●	●	●	●
Vertical position	●	●	●	●	●
Other	Manual/off, mono/ color/inverse	None	None	Auto/manual, monochrome/color	None
Horizontal size	●	●	●	●	●
Vertical size	●	●	●	●	●
Overscan (enlarges image)	○	○	○	○	○
Underscan (reduces image)	○	○	○	○	●
Vertical hold	○	●	○	●	○
Color selector for text	●	○	○	○	○
GRAPHICS STANDARDS COMPATIBILITY					
EGA	●	●	●	●	●
PGC	●	●	●	●	●
VGA	●	●	●	●	●
8514	○	○	○	○	●

●—Yes ○—No N/A—Not applicable INA—Information not available

Table Continues →

Multiscanning Monitors

	GoldStar 1440 Super	Leading Technology Imtec 1455N	Microvitec 1014/SP Auto-Sync	Mitsubishi Diamond Scan 14	Nanao 8060S
Price	$	$	$	$	$
PHYSICAL SPECIFICATIONS					
Includes tilt/swivel	●	●	●	Optional	● (tilt only)
Includes cables	●	●	Optional	●	●
Visible screen size (diagonal, in inches)	13.25	13.33	13.25	13	13
Case dimensions (HWD, in inches)	12 × 14 × 15	15 × 14.1875 × 14.75	13.125 × 16 × 15	12.75 × 14.25 × 14.75	15.75 × 14 × 15
Cable removable at monitor end	●	○	●	●	●
OPERATIONAL FEATURES					
Maximum resolution (pixels), width	800	800	930	800	820
Maximum resolution (pixels), height	560	560	604	600	620
Video bandwidth (MHz)	30	30	40	30	30
Vertical scanning frequency range (Hz)	45–85	58–72	45–100	45–90	50–80
Horizontal scanning frequency range (kHz)	15–35	15.5–35	15–37	15.6–36	15.75–35
Dot pitch (mm)	0.31	0.31	0.31	0.31	0.28
Autosizing	○	○	○	● (IBM only)	○
Inputs (separate socket or switch-selectable):					
Analog/TTL RGB	● (socket)	● (switch)	● (socket)	● (socket)	● (switch)
Composite	○	○	○	● (socket)	○
Separate sync	○	○	○	● (socket)	○
Outputs (separate socket or switch-selectable):					
Analog/TTL RGB	● (switch)	○	○	○	○
Composite	○	○	○	● (socket)	○
Separate sync	○	○	○	○	○
CONTROLS					
Brightness	●	●	●	●	●
Contrast	●	●	●	●	●
Horizontal position	●	●	●	●	●
Vertical position	●	●	●	●	●
Other	None	None	None	Analog/TTL/video	None
Horizontal size	●	○	●	●	●
Vertical size	●	●	●	●	●
Overscan (enlarges image)	○	○	○	●	○
Underscan (reduces image)	○	●	○	○	○
Vertical hold	○	●	○	○	○
Color selector for text	○	●	○	○	○
GRAPHICS STANDARDS COMPATIBILITY					
EGA	●	●	●	●	●
PGC	●	●	●	●	●
VGA	●	●	●	●	●
8514	○	○	●	●	○

●—Yes ○—No N/A—Not applicable INA—Information not available

Multiscanning Monitors

	NEC MultiSync Plus	Princeton Ultrasync	Relisys RE5155	Samsung Sync Master CN4551	Sony CPD-1302
Price	$	$	$	$	$
PHYSICAL SPECIFICATIONS					
Includes tilt/swivel	●	●	●	●	Optional
Includes cables	●	●	●	●	Optional
Visible screen size (diagonal, in inches)	13.5	11.5	13.375	13.375	13.125
Case dimensions (HWD, in inches)	15.33 × 14 × 16	12.5 × 12.33 × 14.1875	14 × 14.5 × 14.875	14.75 × 14.25 × 14.75	12 × 14 × 15
Cable removable at monitor end	●	●	●	●	●
OPERATIONAL FEATURES					
Maximum resolution (pixels), width	960	800	800	800	900
Maximum resolution (pixels), height	720	600	560	560	560
Video bandwidth (MHz)	55	30	40	30	30
Vertical scanning frequency range (Hz)	56–80	45–120	45–80	58–72	50–100
Horizontal scanning frequency range (kHz)	21.8–45	15–35	15.5–35	15.5–35	15–34
Dot pitch (mm)	0.33	0.28	0.31	0.31	0.26
Autosizing	●	● (IBM only)	● (IBM only)	● (IBM only)	● (IBM only)
Inputs (separate socket or switch-selectable):					
Analog/TTL RGB	● (switch)	● (switch)	● (switch)	● (switch)	● (switch)
Composite	● (socket)	○	○	○	○
Separate sync	● (socket)	○	○	○	○
Outputs (separate socket or switch-selectable):					
Analog/TTL RGB	○	○	○	○	○
Composite	○	○	○	○	○
Separate sync	○	○	○	○	○
CONTROLS					
Brightness	●	●	●	●	●
Contrast	●	●	●	●	●
Horizontal position	●	●	●	●	●
Vertical position	●	●	●	●	●
Other	BNC input voltage, manual scan mode	None	Auto/manual scan mode	Manual/preset	TTL mode
Horizontal size	●	●	○	●	●
Vertical size	●	●	●	●	●
Overscan (enlarges image)	○	○	○	○	○
Underscan (reduces image)	○	●	○	○	○
Vertical hold	○	○	○	○	○
Color selector for text	●	●	●	●	○
GRAPHICS STANDARDS COMPATIBILITY					
EGA	●	●	●	●	●
PGC	●	●	●	●	●
VGA	●	●	●	●	●
8514	●	○	●	○	●

●—Yes ○—No N/A—Not applicable INA—Information not available   **Table Continues →**

Multiscanning Monitors

	Tatung 159G	Taxan MultiVision 770 Plus
Price	$	$
PHYSICAL SPECIFICATIONS		
Includes tilt/swivel	●	Optional
Includes cables	●	●
Visible screen size (diagonal, in inches)	13.5	13
Case dimensions (HWD, in inches)	14.5 × 14.33 × 15.5	12 × 14 × 15
Cable removable at monitor end	●	●
OPERATIONAL FEATURES		
Maximum resolution (pixels), width	800	800
Maximum resolution (pixels), height	600	600
Video bandwidth (MHz)	30	30
Vertical scanning frequency range (Hz)	40–120	50–90
Horizontal scanning frequency range (kHz)	15–37	15–34
Dot pitch (mm)	0.31	0.31
Autosizing	○	●
Inputs (separate socket or switch-selectable):		
Analog/TTL RGB	● (switch)	● (switch)
Composite	○	○
Separate sync	○	○
Outputs (separate socket or switch-selectable):		
Analog/TTL RGB	○	● (switch)
Composite	○	○
Separate sync	○	○
CONTROLS		
Brightness	●	●
Contrast	●	●
Horizontal position	●	●
Vertical position	●	●
Other	PS/2/color/mono	None
Horizontal size	●	○
Vertical size	●	●
Overscan (enlarges image)	○	○
Underscan (reduces image)	○	○
Vertical hold	○	○
Color selector for text	○	○
GRAPHICS STANDARDS COMPATIBILITY		
EGA	●	●
PGC	●	●
VGA	●	●
8514	●	○

●—Yes ○—No N/A—Not applicable INA—Information not available

End ■

VIDEO CARDS

APPENDIX

C

C.1 VGA Boards

(Products listed in alphabetical order by company name)	Allstar Microsystems Peacock Plus EVGA	AST Research AST-VGA Plus	ATI Technologies VGA Wonder	Communication Inter-Globe Toucan VGA 1024	Genoa Systems SuperVGA Model 5400
Price (tested configuration)	$	$	$	$	$
Video memory	512K	512K	512K	512K	512K
Base price	$	$	$	$	$
Video memory	256K	256K	256K	256K	512K
Video BIOS	8-bit, 16-bit	8-bit, 16-bit	8-bit, 16-bit	8-bit, 16-bit	8-bit, 16-bit
Video RAM	8-bit, 16-bit	8-bit, 16-bit	8-bit, 16-bit	8-bit, 16-bit	8-bit
VIDEO STANDARDS					
CGA	●	●	●	●	●
EGA	●	●	●	●	●
VGA	●	●	●	●	●
Super VGA	●	●	●	●	●
1,024 × 768	●	○	●	●	●
CONNECTORS					
9-pin	●	○	●	●	●
15-pin	●	●	●	●	●
VGA	○	○	●	●	●
Mouse	○	○	●	○	○
OUTPUT					
TTL	●	○	●	●	●
Analog	●	●	●	●	●
MAXIMUM RESOLUTION					
Graphics (pixels)	1,024 × 768	800 × 600	1,024 × 768	1,024 × 768	1,024 × 768
Text (columns × rows)	132 × 44	132 × 43	132 × 60	132 × 44	132 × 60
Maximum number of colors in highest-resolution mode	256 (800 × 600)	256 (640 × 480)	256 (800 × 600)	256 (800 × 600)	256 (800 × 600)
Total number of colors	262,144	262,144	262,144	262,144	262,144
SOFTWARE DRIVERS					
Utilities	BIOS to RAM, font editor and shader, mode switching, monitor selection, nonstandard text modes, zoom	BIOS to RAM, diagnostics, mode switching	BIOS to RAM, diagnostics, mode switching, mouse driver, system information	BIOS to RAM, diagnostics, font loader, mode switching	ANSI.SYS emulator, BIOS to RAM, mode switching, smooth scroll

●—Yes ○—No N/A—Not applicable INA—Information not available

Table Continues →

ZIFF-DAVIS PRESS

VGA Boards

	HP Video Graphics Adapter	Intelligent VGA Model 650	Orchid Technology ProDesigner Plus VGA	Paradise Systems VGA Professional	Renaissance RVGA II
Price (tested configuration)	$	$	$	$	$
Video memory	512K	256K	512K	512K	256K
Base price	$	$	$	$	$
Video memory	256K	256K	512K	512K	256K
Video BIOS	8-bit, 16-bit	8-bit, 16-bit	8-bit, 16-bit	8-bit, 16-bit	8-bit, 16-bit
Video RAM	8-bit	8-bit, 16-bit	8-bit, 16-bit	8-bit, 16-bit	8-bit
VIDEO STANDARDS					
CGA	●	●	●	●	●
EGA	●	●	●	●	●
VGA	●	●	●	●	●
Super VGA	●	●	●	●	●
1,024 × 768	○	○	●	○	○
CONNECTORS					
9-pin	○	○	○	○	●
15-pin	●	●	●	●	●
VGA	●	●	●	●	●
Mouse	○	○	○	○	○
OUTPUT					
TTL	○	○	○	○	●
Analog	●	●	●	●	●
MAXIMUM RESOLUTION					
Graphics (pixels)	800 × 600	800 × 600	1,024 × 768	800 × 600	800 × 600
Text (columns × rows)	132 × 43	132 × 43	132 × 44	132 × 43	132 × 60
Maximum number of colors in highest-resolution mode	256 (640 × 480)	256 (640 × 400)	256 (800 × 600)	256 (640 × 480)	256 (320 × 200)
Total number of colors	262,144	262,144	262,144	262,144	262,144
SOFTWARE DRIVERS					
Utilities	Font loader, video mode set program	BIOS to RAM, 8/16-bit confirm operation test, mode switching, screen saver	ANSI.SYS emulator, BIOS to RAM, font editor, font loader, hotkey/hot zoom, mode switching	BIOS to RAM, 8/16-bit confirm operation test, mode switching, screen saver	BIOS to RAM, HGC emulator, mode switching

●—Yes   ○—No   N/A—Not applicable   INA—Information not available

VGA Boards

	SOTA VGA/16	STB Systems VGA EM-16	Tatung VGA	Tecmar VGA/AD	Video Seven V-RAM VGA
Price (tested configuration)	$	$	$	$	$
Video memory	512K	512K	256K	512K	512K
Base price	$	$	$	$	$
Video memory	256K	256K	256K	512K	256K
Video BIOS	8-bit, 16-bit	8-bit	8-bit, 16-bit	8-bit	8-bit, 16-bit
Video RAM	8-bit, 16-bit	8-bit, 16-bit	8-bit, 16-bit	8-bit, 16-bit	8-bit, 16-bit
VIDEO STANDARDS					
CGA	●	●	●	●	●
EGA	●	●	●	●	●
VGA	●	●	●	●	●
Super VGA	●	●	●	●	●
1,024 × 768	●	●	○	●	●
CONNECTORS					
9-pin	●	●	○	●	○
15-pin	●	●	●	●	●
VGA	●	●	○	●	●
Mouse	●	○	○	○	○
OUTPUT					
TTL	●	●	○	●	○
Analog	●	●	●	●	●
MAXIMUM RESOLUTION					
Graphics (pixels)	1,024 × 768	1,024 × 768	800 × 600	1,024 × 768	1,024 × 768
Text (columns × rows)	132 × 43	132 × 44	132 × 43	132 × 60	132 × 43
Maximum number of colors in highest-resolution mode	256 (800 × 600)	256 (800 × 600)	256 (640 × 400)	256 (800 × 600)	256 (800 × 600)
Total number of colors	262,144	262,144	262,144	262,144	262,144
SOFTWARE DRIVERS					
Utilities	ANSI.SYS emulator, diagnostics, memory upgrade, mode switching	BIOS to RAM, demo program, hotkey/hot zoom, mode switching	BIOS to RAM, CGA and HGC emulator, mode switching, screen saver	ANSI.SYS, BIOS to RAM, diagnostics, keyboard access, mode switching, screen saver	Directory utility, mode forcing, screen cleaning, text mode selection

●—Yes ○— No N/A—Not applicable INA—Information not available   **End** ■

C.2   1,024 × 786 Graphics Adapters

(Products listed in alphabetical order by company name)	Artist XJ10	Cardinal VGA600	Compaq Computer Advanced Graphics 1024	Dell GPX-1024/256	Enertronics Research Aurora 1024N
Price	$$$	$	$$	$	$
BUS TYPE					
ISA 8-bit	●	●	●	●	●
ISA 16-bit	●	●	●	●	●
MCA	○	○	○	○	○
EISA	○	○	○	○	○
PHYSICAL CHARACTERISTICS					
Board size (inches):					
Length	13.25	8	13.5	13.5	13.25
Height	4.5	4.25	4.5	4.5	4.5
Thickness	0.75	0.5	0.5	0.75	0.5
HIGH-RESOLUTION CHARACTERISTICS					
High-resolution graphics coprocessor	Hitachi	None	Texas Instruments	Texas Instruments	Texas Instruments
High-resolution memory	1Mb	N/A	1Mb	1Mb	1Mb
VGA CHARACTERISTICS					
VGA and high resolution on the same card	○	●	○	○	○
Accepts VGA daughtercard	●	N/A	○	●	○
Accepts VGA pass-through	●	N/A	●	●	●
Pass-through cable included	○	N/A	●	●	●
VGA BIOS ROM manufacturer	Cirrus Logic/Award	Cardinal	Compaq	Renaissance	Cirrus Logic/Award
VGA graphics processor	Cirrus Logic	C&T	Paradise	Renaissance	Cirrus Logic
VGA memory	256K	512K	256K	256K	256K
MAXIMUM RESOLUTION					
Graphics (pixels):					
Maximum addressable pixels	1,024 × 768	1,024 × 768	1,024 × 768	1,024 × 768	1,024 × 768
Maximum visible pixels	1,024 × 768	1,024 × 768	1,024 × 768	1,024 × 768	1,024 × 768
Text (columns × rows)	N/A	132 × 50	N/A	132 × 40	146 × 51
Colors in 1,024 × 768 mode:					
Palette	16,777,220	262,144	16,777,220	16,777,220	262,144
Maximum simultaneously displayable	256	16	16	16	256
VIDEO STANDARDS					
CGA	●	●	○	○	●
MDA	●	●	○	○	●
Hercules	●	●	○	○	●
EGA	●	●	○	○	●
VGA	●	●	●	●	●
Super VGA (800 × 600)	●	●	○	●	○
1,024 × 768	●	●	●	●	●
8514/A	○	○	○	●	●
OUTPUT					
TTL	○	●	○	○	●
Analog	●	●	●	●	●
CONNECTORS					
9-pin	○	●	○	○	○
9-pin to BNC	●	○	○	○	○
15-pin	○	●	●	●	●

●—Yes   ○—No   N/A—Not applicable   INA—Information not available

1,024 × 786 Graphics Adapters

	Genoa Systems Super VGA 6400	Headland Technology Video Seven VRAM VGA	Matrox PG-1024V	NEC MultiSync Graphics Engine	Number Nine Computer Corp. Pepper Pro 1024
Price	$	$	$$	$$	$$
BUS TYPE					
ISA 8-bit	●	●	○	○	●
ISA 16-bit	●	●	●	●	●
MCA	○	○	○	●	●
EISA	○	○	○	○	○
PHYSICAL CHARACTERISTICS					
Board size (inches):					
Length	8	13.5	13.25	13.25	13.25
Height	4.25	3	4.5	4.5	4
Thickness	0.5	0.5	0.75	0.5	0.5
HIGH-RESOLUTION CHARACTERISTICS					
High-resolution graphics coprocessor	None	None	Texas Instruments	Texas Instruments	Texas Instruments
High-resolution memory	N/A	N/A	512K	1Mb	1Mb
VGA CHARACTERISTICS					
VGA and high resolution on the same card	●	●	○	●	○
Accepts VGA daughtercard	N/A	N/A	○	N/A	○
Accepts VGA pass-through	N/A	N/A	●	N/A	●
Pass-through cable included	N/A	N/A	●	N/A	●
VGA BIOS ROM manufacturer	Genoa	Video Seven	N/A	C&T	N/A
VGA graphics processor	Genoa	Video Seven	N/A	C&T	N/A
VGA memory	512K	512K	N/A	256K	N/A
MAXIMUM RESOLUTION					
Graphics (pixels):					
Maximum addressable pixels	1,024 × 768	1,024 × 768	1,024 × 1,024	1,024 × 768	4,096 × 2,048
Maximum visible pixels	1,024 × 768	1,024 × 768	1,024 × 768	1,024 × 768	1,024 × 768
Text (columns × rows)	132 × 60	132 × 43	N/A	132 × 60	150 × 50
Colors in 1,024 × 768 mode:					
Palette	262,144	262,144	4,096	16,777,220	16,777,220
Maximum simultaneously displayable	16	16	16	256	256
VIDEO STANDARDS					
CGA	●	●	●	●	○
MDA	●	●	○	●	○
Hercules	●	●	○	●	○
EGA	●	●	○	●	○
VGA	●	●	○	●	●
Super VGA (800 × 600)	●	●	○	●	○
1,024 × 768	●	●	●	●	●
8514/A	●	○	○	●	○
OUTPUT					
TTL	○	○	○	○	○
Analog	●	●	●	●	●
CONNECTORS					
9-pin	○	○	○	○	○
9-pin to BNC	○	○	●	○	○
15-pin	●	●	○	●	●

●—Yes ○—No N/A—Not applicable INA—Information not available   **Table Continues →**

1,024 × 786 Graphics Adapters

	Orchid Technology ProDesigner Plus	PCG Photon Performa	Renaissance GRX Rendition II	Samsung SVGA16	STB VGA EM-16
Price	$	$	$$	$	$
BUS TYPE					
ISA 8-bit	●	●	●	●	●
ISA 16-bit	●	●	●	●	●
MCA	○	○	○	○	○
EISA	○	●	○	○	○
PHYSICAL CHARACTERISTICS					
Board size (inches):					
Length	13.25	8	13.25	9.75	8.5
Height	3	4.5	4.5	4	4
Thickness	0.5	0.5	0.75	0.5	0.5
HIGH-RESOLUTION CHARACTERISTICS					
High-resolution graphics coprocessor	None	PCG	Texas Instruments	None	None
High-resolution memory	N/A	512K	1Mb	N/A	N/A
VGA CHARACTERISTICS					
VGA and high resolution on the same card	●	●	○	●	●
Accepts VGA daughtercard	N/A	N/A	●	N/A	N/A
Accepts VGA pass-through	N/A	N/A	●	N/A	N/A
Pass-through cable included	N/A	N/A	●	N/A	N/A
VGA BIOS ROM manufacturer	Tseng	PCG	Renaissance	Tseng	STB/Award
VGA graphics processor	Tseng	PCG	Renaissance	Tseng	Tseng
VGA memory	512K	1Mb	256K	256K	512K
MAXIMUM RESOLUTION					
Graphics (pixels):					
Maximum addressable pixels	1,024 × 768	1,024 × 768	1,024 × 768	1,024 × 768	1,024 × 768
Maximum visible pixels	1,024 × 768	1,024 × 768	1,024 × 768	1,024 × 768	1,024 × 768
Text (columns × rows)	132 × 44	132 × 25	128 × 64	132 × 44	133 × 44
Colors in 1,024 × 768 mode:					
Palette	262,144	262,144	16,777,220	262,144	262,144
Maximum simultaneously displayable	16	16	256	16	16
VIDEO STANDARDS					
CGA	●	●	○	●	●
MDA	●	●	○	●	●
Hercules	●	●	○	●	●
EGA	●	●	○	●	●
VGA	●	●	●	●	●
Super VGA (800 × 600)	●	●	●	●	●
1,024 × 768	●	●	●	●	●
8514/A	○	○	●	○	○
OUTPUT					
TTL	○	●	○	●	●
Analog	●	●	●	●	●
CONNECTORS					
9-pin	○	●	○	●	●
9-pin to BNC	○	○	○	○	○
15-pin	●	●	●	●	●

●—Yes ○—No N/A—Not applicable INA—Information not available

1,024 × 786 Graphics Adapters

	Tecmar VGA/AD	Trident 8916	Vermont Microsystems Cobra Plus/HS
Price	$	$	$$$
BUS TYPE			
ISA 8-bit	●	●	●
ISA 16-bit	●	●	●
MCA	○	○	○
EISA	○	○	○
PHYSICAL CHARACTERISTICS			
Board size (inches):			
Length	11	8.5	13.5
Height	4	4.25	4.5
Thickness	0.5	0.75	0.5
HIGH-RESOLUTION CHARACTERISTICS			
High-resolution graphics coprocessor	None	None	Texas Instruments
High-resolution memory	N/A	N/A	1.5Mb
VGA CHARACTERISTICS			
VGA and high resolution on the same card	●	●	○
Accepts VGA daughtercard	N/A	N/A	○
Accepts VGA pass-through	N/A	N/A	●
Pass-through cable included	N/A	N/A	●
VGA BIOS ROM manufacturer	Tecmar	Trident	Video Seven
VGA graphics processor	Tseng	Trident	Video Seven
VGA memory	512K	1Mb	512K
MAXIMUM RESOLUTION			
Graphics (pixels):			
Maximum addressable pixels	1,440 × 720	1,024 × 768	1,024 × 768
Maximum visible pixels	1,440 × 720	1,024 × 768	1,024 × 768
Text (columns × rows)	132 × 60	132 × 60	N/A
Colors in 1,024 × 768 mode:			
Palette	262,144	16,777,220	16,777,220
Maximum simultaneously displayable	16	256	256
VIDEO STANDARDS			
CGA	●	●	○
MDA	●	●	○
Hercules	●	●	○
EGA	●	●	○
VGA	●	●	●
Super VGA (800 × 600)	●	●	○
1,024 × 768	●	●	●
8514/A	○	○	●
OUTPUT			
TTL	●	●	○
Analog	●	●	●
CONNECTORS			
9-pin	●	●	○
9-pin to BNC	○	○	●
15-pin	●	●	○

●—Yes ○—No N/A—Not applicable INA—Information not available   **End** ■

C.3 24-Bit Graphics Adapters

(Products listed in alphabetical order by company name)	BleuMont Truc	Everex Viewpoint TC	Matrox Impression/AT-S True-Color Graphics Controller	Opta Mona Lisa 24-Bit Color Display Board	RasterOps ColorBoard 1024MC Display Adapter	TrueVision 1024-32
Price	$$$	$	$$$	$$	$$$	$$$
Interfaces available:						
ISA (16-bit)	●	●	●	●	○	●
MCA	○	○	○	○	●	○
PERFORMANCE CHARACTERISTICS						
Graphics coprocessor	8514/A	None	TI 34020	TI 34020	None	TI 34020
Memory:						
DRAM (standard/maximum)	N/A	1Mb/1Mb	1Mb/1Mb	2Mb/4Mb	N/A	1Mb/16Mb
VRAM (standard/maximum)	3Mb/3Mb	N/A	3Mb/3Mb	2Mb/4Mb	3Mb/3Mb	3Mb/3Mb
VGA type	Pass-through	On-board	Pass-through	On-board	Pass-through	On-board
On-board VGA BIOS	N/A	Everex 1.01	N/A	Tseng ET 4000 AX	N/A	Tseng/TrueVision 1.4
On-board VGA chip set	N/A	Tseng	N/A	Tseng	N/A	Tseng
VGA memory	N/A	1Mb	N/A	512K	N/A	512K
VESA-compliant	N/A	●	N/A	○	N/A	●
Maximum resolution addressable (pixels)	1,024 × 1,024	1,664 × 1,280	1,152 × 882	1,152 × 900	1,024 × 1,024	1,024 × 768
Maximum resolution displayable (pixels)	1,024 × 768	1,280 × 1,024	1,152 × 882	1,152 × 900	1,024 × 768	1,024 × 768
Maximum columns and rows in text mode	132 × 44	132 × 44	N/A	132 × 44	N/A	132 × 50
COLORS						
Maximum colors at:						
640 × 480 resolution	16.8 million	16.8 million	N/A	16.8 million	N/A	16.8 million
800 × 600 resolution	16.8 million	256	N/A	16.8 million	N/A	16.8 million
1,024 × 768 resolution	16.8 million	256	16.8 million	16.8 million	16.8 million	16.8 million
RAM DAC manufacturer	Brooktree	Brooktree	Brooktree	Brooktree	Brooktree	Brooktree
OUTPUT CHARACTERISTICS						
Maximum vertical refresh rates (in hertz):						
1,024 × 768 (noninterlaced)	70	60	60	72	75	76
1,024 × 768 (interlaced)	N/A	79	N/A	72	N/A	87
Digital/TTL output	○	○	○	○	○	○
Analog output	●	●	●	●	●	●
Connectors	15-pin mini D-sub	15-pin mini D-sub	None	15-pin mini D-sub	None	15-pin mini D-sub
Adapter cable included	○	○	●	○	●	●
CUSTOMER SUPPORT						
Hardware warranty	1 year	2 years	1 year	1 year	3 years	1 year
Free technical support	●	●	●	●	●	●
Toll-free number	○	○	●	●	●	○
BBS	○	●	●	●	●	●
Fax	○	○	●	●	○	○

●—Yes ○—No N/A—Not applicable

C.4 Graphics Accelerators

(Products listed in alphabetical order by company name)	Actix GraphicsEngine Display Accelerator	Artist Graphics WinSprint 100	ATI Graphics Ultra	ATI Graphics Vantage	CSS Maxgraphics/16
Price	$	$	$	$	$
Graphics accelerator chip	S3 86C911	C&T 82C453	ATI Mach 8	ATI Mach 8	S3 86C911
ACCELERATOR CAPABILITIES					
BitBlts	●	○	●	●	●
Line draws	●	○	●	●	●
Area fills	●	○	●	●	●
Image transfers	●	○	○	○	●
Raster operations	●	○	●	●	●
Hardware cursor	●	○	○	○	●
Other	None	● (single-cycle read-modify-write operation)	● (zoom/clipping, pattern fill, font-scaling assist)	● (zoom/clipping, pattern fill, font-scaling assist)	None
VGA SUPPORT					
VGA BIOS manufacturer	AMI	C&T	ATI	ATI	AMI
Version number	1.04	453 VGA BIOS, Version 1.2.0	1130111513	1130111513	1.5
Revision date	October 31, 1991	November 22, 1991	N/A	N/A	September 20, 1991
VBE compatibility	Proprietary drivers	ROM BIOS	TSR	TSR	Proprietary drivers
VGA chip set manufacturer	S3	C&T	ATI	ATI	S3
Type of display memory	VRAM	VRAM	VRAM	DRAM	VRAM
Minimum display memory	512K	1Mb	512K	512K	1Mb
Maximum display memory	1Mb	1Mb	1Mb	1Mb	1Mb
Rated speed (nanoseconds)	100	100	100	80	80
DISPLAY CHARACTERISTICS					
Maximum addressable resolution (pixels)	2,048 × 1,024	1,024 × 768	2,048 × 2,048	2,048 × 2,048	1,280 × 1,024
Maximum displayable resolution (pixels)	1,280 × 1,024	1,024 × 768	1,024 × 768	1,024 × 768	1,280 × 1,024
Maximum displayable text (columns by rows)	132 × 44	132 × 44	132 × 44	132 × 44	132 × 44
High-color RAM DAC installed	None	None	None	None	Sierra
Other high-color RAM DAC available	Sierra	None	None	None	None
Number of colors simultaneously displayable at 800 × 600 pixels	256	256	256	256	256
8514/A register-level compatible	○	○	●	●	○
VIDEO STANDARDS					
1,280 × 1,024	●	○	●	●	○
1,280 × 960	●	○	○	○	●
1,024 × 768 (noninterlaced)	●	●	●	●	●
1,024 × 768 (interlaced)	●	●	●	●	○
800 × 600 (Super VGA)	●	●	●	●	●
640 × 480 (VGA)	●	●	●	●	●
CONNECTOR SUPPORT					
15-pin mini D-sub	●	●	●	●	●
Other	VESA feature connector	None	Mouse port	Mouse port	None

●—Yes ○—No N/A—Not applicable INA—Information not available

Table Continues →

Graphics Accelerators

	Diamond Stealth VRAM	Genoa Windows VGA	Glad UltraView	Hornet Rapix I	Orchid Fahrenheit 1280°
Price	$	$	$	$	$
Graphics accelerator chip	S3 86C911	S3 86C911	Glad Systems UV6000	Weitek W5086	S3 86C911
ACCELERATOR CAPABILITIES					
BitBlts	●	●	●	●	●
Line draws	●	●	●	●	●
Area fills	●	●	●	○	●
Image transfers	●	●	●	○	●
Raster operations	●	●	●	○	●
Hardware cursor	●	●	○	○	●
Other	None	None	None	None	None
VGA SUPPORT					
VGA BIOS manufacturer	Diamond	AMI	Glad Systems	Weitek	Orchid
Version number	1.0	1.5	16-0 0001	2.00	1.2
Revision date	November 22, 1991	September 1, 1991	May 8, 1991	November 12, 1991	September 18, 1991
VBE compatibility	ROM BIOS	Proprietary drivers	ROM BIOS	ROM BIOS	Proprietary drivers
VGA chip set manufacturer	S3	S3	Glad Systems	Hornet	S3
Type of display memory	VRAM	VRAM	DRAM	DRAM	VRAM
Minimum display memory	1Mb	1Mb	512K	512K	512K
Maximum display memory	1Mb	1Mb	2Mb	512K	1Mb
Rated speed (nanoseconds)	85	80	80	100	80
DISPLAY CHARACTERISTICS					
Maximum addressable resolution (pixels)	1,280 × 1,024	2,048 × 1,024	1,024 × 768	800 × 600	2,048 × 1,024
Maximum displayable resolution (pixels)	1,280 × 1,024	1,280 × 1,024	1,024 × 768	800 × 600	1,280 × 1,024
Maximum displayable text (columns by rows)	132 × 43	132 × 43	132 × 60	80 × 24	132 × 44
High-color RAM DAC installed	Sierra	Sierra	None	None	Sierra
Other high-color RAM DAC available	None	None	None	None	None
Number of colors simultaneously displayable at 800 × 600 pixels	256	256	256	256	256
8514/A register-level compatible	○	○	●	○	○
VIDEO STANDARDS					
1,280 × 1,024	●	●	●	○	●
1,280 × 960	●	●	○	○	●
1,024 × 768 (noninterlaced)	●	●	●	○	●
1,024 × 768 (interlaced)	●	●	●	○	●
800 × 600 (Super VGA)	●	●	●	●	●
640 × 480 (VGA)	●	●	●	●	●
CONNECTOR SUPPORT					
15-pin mini D-sub	●	●	●	●	●
Other	VESA feature connector	None	None	None	VESA feature connector

●—Yes   ○—No   N/A—Not applicable   INA—Information not available

Graphics Accelerators

	Pixel Turbo Windows Accelerator	Portacom Eclipse II	STB Wind/X
Price	$	$	$
Graphics accelerator chip	S3 86C911	S3 86C911	S3 86C911
ACCELERATOR CAPABILITIES			
BitBlts	●	●	●
Line draws	●	●	●
Area fills	●	●	●
Image transfers	●	●	●
Raster operations	●	●	●
Hardware cursor	●	●	●
Other	None	None	None
VGA SUPPORT			
VGA BIOS manufacturer	Pixel	AMI	STB
Version number	2.0	1.5	1.0
Revision date	October 10, 1991	September 1, 1991	October 16, 1991
VBE compatibility	Proprietary drivers	Proprietary drivers	Proprietary drivers
VGA chip set manufacturer	S3	S3	S3
Type of display memory	VRAM	VRAM	VRAM
Minimum display memory	512K	1Mb	1Mb
Maximum display memory	1Mb	1Mb	1Mb
Rated speed (nanoseconds)	80	80	80
DISPLAY CHARACTERISTICS			
Maximum addressable resolution (pixels)	2,048 × 1,024	2,048 × 1,024	1,280 × 1,024
Maximum displayable resolution (pixels)	1,280 × 1,024	1,280 × 1,024	1,024 × 768
Maximum displayable text (columns by rows)	132 × 43	132 × 60	132 × 44
High-color RAM DAC installed	None	None	None
Other high-color RAM DAC available	Sierra	Sierra	None
Number of colors simultaneously displayable at 800 × 600 pixels	256	256	262,144
8514/A register-level compatible	○	○	○
VIDEO STANDARDS			
1,280 × 1,024	●	●	●
1,280 × 960	●	●	●
1,024 × 768 (noninterlaced)	●	●	●
1,024 × 768 (interlaced)	●	●	●
800 × 600 (Super VGA)	●	●	●
640 × 480 (VGA)	●	●	●
CONNECTOR SUPPORT			
15-pin mini D-sub	●	●	●
Other	None	None	Mouse port

●—Yes ○—No N/A—Not applicable INA—Information not available

E n d ■

PRINTERS

D.1 Dot-Matrix Printers

(Products listed in alphabetical order by company name)	AMT Accel-212	AMT Accel-214	AMT Accel-242	AMT Accel-244	AMT Accel-292
Price (tested configuration)	$	$	$	$	$
PHYSICAL CHARACTERISTICS					
Dimensions (HWD, in inches)	INA	INA	INA	INA	INA
Weight (pounds)	INA	INA	INA	INA	INA
Carriage size	Narrow	Wide	Narrow	Wide	Narrow
Number of pins	9	9	24	24	Dual-head 9-pin
Maximum resolution (horizontal by vertical dots per inch)	240 × 216	240 × 216	360 × 360	360 × 360	240 × 216
Color capability	○	○	○	○	○
Memory	8K	8K	8K	8K	8K
Parallel interface	●	●	●	●	●
Serial interface	●	●	●	●	●
PAPER HANDLING					
Paper parking	●	●	●	●	●
Paper feeds:					
Pressure	●	●	●	●	●
Tractor	●	●	●	●	●
Internal	●	●	●	●	●
External	●	●	●	●	●
Push	●	●	●	●	●
Pull	●	●	●	●	●
Paper paths:					
Rear U path	●	●	●	●	●
Bottom vertical	●	●	●	●	●
Front L path	○	○	○	○	○
Rear L path	○	○	○	○	○
Rated maximum paper weight (pounds)	24	24	24	24	24
FONTS AND FEATURES					
Emulations	●	●	●	●	●
Typefaces:					
Courier	○	○	●	●	○
Gothic	○	○	○	○	○
Line printer	●	●	●	●	●
OCR-A	○	○	○	○	○
OCR-B	○	○	●	●	○
Orator	○	○	●	●	○
Prestige/Elite	○	○	●	●	○
Sans serif	●	●	●	●	●
Script	○	○	●	●	○
Times Roman	●	●	●	●	●
Supports scalable fonts	○	○	○	○	○
Postnet bar codes	Optional	Optional	Optional	Optional	Optional
Printer-specific Microsoft Windows 3.1 driver	○	○	○	○	○
Standard mode, quiet mode (dB)	55, N/A	55, N/A	55, 53	55, 53	57, N/A

●—Yes ○—No N/A—Not applicable INA—Information not available

Table Continues →

Dot-Matrix Printers

	AMT Accel-294	ALPS DMX800	Axonix MilWrite	Brother M-1309	Brother M-1324
Price (tested configuration)	$	$$	$	$	$
PHYSICAL CHARACTERISTICS					
Dimensions (HWD, in inches)	INA	7 × 24 × 17	INA	5 × 18 × 13	5 × 18 × 13
Weight (pounds)	INA	44	INA	11	11
Carriage size	Wide	Wide	Narrow	Narrow	Narrow
Number of pins	Dual-head 9-pin	18	9	18	24
Maximum resolution(horizontal by vertical dots per inch)	240 × 216	240 × 216	240 × 216	240 × 216	360 × 360
Color capability	○	●	○	○	○
Memory	8K	128K	8K	8K	8K
Parallel interface	●	●	●	●	●
Serial interface	●	●	Optional	○	●
PAPER HANDLING					
Paper parking	●	●	●	●	●
Paper feeds:					
Pressure	●	●	●	●	●
Tractor	●	●	●	●	●
Internal	●	●	●	●	●
External	●	Optional	○	●	●
Push	●	●	●	●	●
Pull	●	Optional	○	●	●
Paper paths:					
Rear U path	●	●	●	●	●
Bottom vertical	●	●	○	●	○
Front L path	○	○	○	○	○
Rear L path	○	●	●	●	●
Rated maximum paper weight (pounds)	24	22	21	24	24
FONTS AND FEATURES					
Emulations	●	●	○	●	●
Typefaces:					
Courier	○	●	●	●	●
Gothic	○	●	●	●	●
Line printer	●	○	○	INA	INA
OCR-A	○	●	○	○	○
OCR-B	○	●	○	○	●
Orator	○	○	○	○	○
Prestige/Elite	○	●	●	●	●
Sans serif	●	●	●	○	●
Script	○	○	●	○	●
Times Roman	●	●	○	○	●
Supports scalable fonts	○	○	○	INA	INA
Postnet bar codes	Optional	●	○	INA	INA
Printer-specific Microsoft Windows 3.1 driver	○	○	○	INA	INA
Standard mode, quiet mode (dB)	57, N/A	57, 55	55, 50	INA	INA

●—Yes   ○—No   N/A—Not applicable   INA—Information not available

Dot-Matrix Printers

	Brother M-4309A	CIE CI-250 LXP	CIE CI-500	C. Itoh ProWriter C-610II Document Printer	C. Itoh ProWriter C-615II Document Printer
Price (tested configuration)	$$	$$	$$$$	$	$
PHYSICAL CHARACTERISTICS					
Dimensions (HWD, in inches)	INA	7 × 24 × 23	13 × 28 × 20	INA	INA
Weight (pounds)	INA	33	110 (with stand)	INA	INA
Carriage size	Wide	Wide	Wide	Narrow	Wide
Number of pins	18	18	34	24	24
Maximum resolution(horizontal by vertical dots per inch)	240 × 216	240 × 216	205 × 288	360 × 360	360 × 360
Color capability	●	○	○	○	○
Memory	96K	8K	8K	26K	26K
Parallel interface	●	●	●	●	●
Serial interface	●	●	●	●	●
PAPER HANDLING					
Paper parking	●	●	●	●	●
Paper feeds:					
Pressure	●	●	○	●	●
Tractor	●	●	●	●	●
Internal	●	●	●	●	●
External	Optional	○	○	○	○
Push	●	●	●	●	●
Pull	Optional	●	●	○	○
Paper paths:					
Rear U path	●	●	○	INA	INA
Bottom vertical	●	●	●	INA	INA
Front L path	○	○	○	INA	INA
Rear L path	●	●	○	INA	INA
Rated maximum paper weight (pounds)	27	24	100	35	35
FONTS AND FEATURES					
Emulations	●	●	●	●	●
Typefaces:					
Courier	●	●	●	●	●
Gothic	●	○	○	○	○
Line printer	●	INA	INA	○	○
OCR-A	●	○	●	○	○
OCR-B	●	○	○	○	○
Orator	●	○	○	○	○
Prestige/Elite	●	○	○	○	○
Sans serif	●	●	●	●	●
Script	○	○	○	○	○
Times Roman	●	○	○	●	●
Supports scalable fonts	○	INA	INA	○	○
Postnet bar codes	●	INA	INA	○	○
Printer-specific Microsoft Windows 3.1 driver	○	INA	INA	○	○ (included)
Standard mode, quiet mode (dB)	57, 55	INA	INA	58, 55	58, 55

●—Yes   ○—No   N/A—Not applicable   INA—Information not available   **Table Continues →**

Dot-Matrix Printers

	Citizen GSX-130	Citizen GSX-140 Plus	Citizen GSX-145	Citizen GSX-240	Citizen PN48
Price (tested configuration)	$	$	$	$	$
PHYSICAL CHARACTERISTICS					
Dimensions (HWD, in inches)	5 × 16 × 13	5 × 16 × 13	6 × 23 × 13	5 × 17 × 13	2 × 12 × 4
Weight (pounds)	12	12	17	11	3 (with battery)
Carriage size	Narrow	Narrow	Wide	Narrow	Narrow
Number of pins	24	24	24	24	48
Maximum resolution (horizontal by vertical dots per inch)	360 × 360	360 × 360	360 × 360	360 × 360	360 × 360
Color capability	●	●	●	Optional	○
Memory	8K	8K	8K	8K	4K
Parallel interface	○	○	○	●	○
Serial interface	○	○	○	Optional	○
PAPER HANDLING					
Paper parking	●	●	●	●	○
Paper feeds:					
Pressure	●	●	●	●	●
Tractor	●	●	●	●	○
Internal	●	●	●	●	N/A
External	●	●	●	●	N/A
Push	●	●	●	●	N/A
Pull	●	●	●	●	N/A
Paper paths:					
Rear U path	●	●	●	○	○
Bottom vertical	●	●	●	●	●
Front L path	○	○	○	○	○
Rear L path	○	○	○	○	●
Rated maximum paper weight (pounds)	27	27	27	26	28
FONTS AND FEATURES					
Emulations	●	●	●	●	●
Typefaces:					
Courier	●	●	●	●	●
Gothic	○	○	○	○	○
Line printer	INA	INA	INA	●	INA
OCR-A	○	○	○	○	○
OCR-B	○	○	○	●	○
Orator	○	●	○	○	○
Prestige/Elite	●	●	●	●	○
Sans serif	●	●	●	●	○
Script	○	●	○	○	○
Times Roman	●	●	●	●	●
Supports scalable fonts	INA	INA	INA	●	INA
Postnet bar codes	INA	INA	INA	○	INA
Printer-specific Microsoft Windows 3.1 driver	INA	INA	INA	●	INA
Standard mode, quiet mode (dB)	INA	INA	INA	47, 43	INA

●—Yes ○—No N/A—Not applicable INA—Information not available

Dot-Matrix Printers

	Citizen 200GX Fifteen	Dataproducts LX 455	Datasouth Performax	Datasouth XL-300	DEC LA 75 Plus Companion Printer
Price (tested configuration)	$	$$$$	$$$	$$	$
PHYSICAL CHARACTERISTICS					
Dimensions (HWD, in inches)	5 × 23 × 13	INA	9 × 26 × 18	8 × 25 × 16	5 × 17 × 15
Weight (pounds)	17	INA	47	35	11
Carriage size	Wide	Wide	Wide	Wide	Narrow
Number of pins	9	33	18	9	24
Maximum resolution(horizontal by vertical dots per inch)	240 × 216	120 × 144	360 × 288	240 × 360	360 × 180
Color capability	●	○	○	○	●
Memory	8K	12K	128K	3K	8K
Parallel interface	○	●	●	●	●
Serial interface	○	●	●	●	●
PAPER HANDLING					
Paper parking	●	○	●	○	●
Paper feeds:					
Pressure	●	○	○	○	●
Tractor	●	●	●	●	●
Internal	●	●	●	●	●
External	●	○	○	○	○
Push	●	●	●	○	●
Pull	●	●	●	●	●
Paper paths:					
Rear U path	●	○	○	○	●
Bottom vertical	●	●	●	●	●
Front L path	○	○	●	●	○
Rear L path	○	○	○	○	○
Rated maximum paper weight (pounds)	27	120	24	35	24
FONTS AND FEATURES					
Emulations	●	●	●	●	○
Typefaces:					
Courier	●	●	●	●	●
Gothic	○	●	○	○	○
Line printer	INA	○	INA	INA	○
OCR-A	○	●	●	●	○
OCR-B	○	●	●	●	○
Orator	○	○	○	○	○
Prestige/Elite	○	○	●	●	○
Sans serif	●	●	○	○	○
Script	○	○	○	○	○
Times Roman	●	○	○	○	○
Supports scalable fonts	INA	○	INA	INA	○
Postnet bar codes	INA	●	INA	INA	○
Printer-specific Microsoft Windows 3.1 driver	INA	● (included)	INA	INA	● (included)
Standard mode, quiet mode (dB)	INA	55, N/A	INA	INA	53, 51

●—Yes   ○—No   N/A—Not applicable   INA—Information not available

Table Continues →

Dot-Matrix Printers

	DEC LA 424 MultiPrinter	Epson ActionPrinter 3250	Epson LQ-200	Epson LQ-570	Epson LQ-870
Price (tested configuration)	$	$	$	$	$
PHYSICAL CHARACTERISTICS					
Dimensions (HWD, in inches)	7 × 24 × 12	5 × 15 × 10	6 × 15 × 13	6 × 17 × 15	7 × 18 × 15
Weight (pounds)	32	12	15	15	20
Carriage size	Wide	Narrow	Narrow	Narrow	Narrow
Number of pins	24	24	24	24	24
Maximum resolution(horizontal by vertical dots per inch)	360 × 180	360 × 360	360 × 360	360 × 360	360 × 360
Color capability	●	○	○	○	○
Memory	8K	11K	8K	8K	8K
Parallel interface	●	●	●	●	●
Serial interface	●	○	○	●	○
PAPER HANDLING					
Paper parking	●	●	○	●	●
Paper feeds:					
Pressure	●	●	●	●	●
Tractor	●	●	●	●	●
Internal	●	Optional	○	●	●
External	○	○	●	○	○
Push	●	Optional	○	●	●
Pull	○	○	●	○	○
Paper paths:					
Rear U path	●	○	●	●	●
Bottom vertical	●	●	●	●	●
Front L path	○	●	○	●	●
Rear L path	○	●	○	●	●
Rated maximum paper weight (pounds)	24	24	22	22	22
FONTS AND FEATURES					
Emulations	○	○	●	●	●
Typefaces:					
Courier	●	●	●	●	●
Gothic	○	○	○	○	○
Line printer	○	●	INA	INA	INA
OCR-A	○	○	○	○	○
OCR-B	○	○	●	●	●
Orator	○	○	●	●	●
Prestige/Elite	○	●	●	●	●
Sans serif	○	●	●	●	●
Script	○	●	●	●	●
Times Roman	○	●	●	●	●
Supports scalable fonts	○	●	INA	INA	INA
Postnet bar codes	○	○	INA	INA	INA
Printer-specific Microsoft Windows 3.1 driver	●	● (in Windows)	INA	INA	INA
Standard mode, quiet mode (dB)	56, 53	50, N/A	INA	INA	INA

●—Yes   ○—No   N/A—Not applicable   INA—Information not available

Dot-Matrix Printers

	Epson LQ-1170	Fujitsu DL1200 PC PrintPartner	Fujitsu DL3600	Fujitsu DL5800 Power PrintPartner	Genicom 3840E
Price (tested configuration)	$	$	$	$$	$$$
PHYSICAL CHARACTERISTICS					
Dimensions (HWD, in inches)	7 × 25 × 15	INA	9 × 23 × 14	INA	12 × 27 × 14
Weight (pounds)	27	INA	27	INA	52
Carriage size	Wide	Wide	Wide	Wide	Wide
Number of pins	24	24	24	24	18
Maximum resolution(horizontal by vertical dots per inch)	360 × 360	360 × 360	360 × 360	360 × 360	400 × 144
Color capability	○	Optional	●	○	○
Memory	8K	32K	24K	32K	64K
Parallel interface	●	●	●	●	●
Serial interface	○	Optional	○	●	●
PAPER HANDLING					
Paper parking	●	●	●	●	●
Paper feeds:					
Pressure	●	●	●	●	○
Tractor	●	●	●	●	●
Internal	●	●	●	●	●
External	○	○	○	Optional	○
Push	●	●	●	●	●
Pull	○	●	○	Optional	●
Paper paths:					
Rear U path	●	○	●	●	○
Bottom vertical	●	○	○	●	●
Front L path	●	○	○	●	●
Rear L path	●	●	●	○	●
Rated maximum paper weight (pounds)	22	22	22	22	110
FONTS AND FEATURES					
Emulations	●	●	●	○	●
Typefaces:					
Courier	●	●	●	●	●
Gothic	○	○	○	○	●
Line printer	INA	○	INA	○	INA
OCR-A	○	○	○	○	○
OCR-B	●	○	○	○	○
Orator	●	○	○	○	●
Prestige/Elite	●	●	●	●	○
Sans serif	●	○	○	○	○
Script	●	○	○	○	○
Times Roman	●	○	○	○	○
Supports scalable fonts	INA	○	INA	○	INA
Postnet bar codes	INA	○	INA	○	INA
Printer-specific Microsoft Windows 3.1 driver	INA	● (included)	INA	● (via BBS)	INA
Standard mode, quiet mode (dB)	INA	52, N/A	INA	55, N/A	INA

●—Yes ○—No N/A—Not applicable INA—Information not available

Table Continues →

Dot-Matrix Printers

	Genicom 4440 XT	IBM Personal Printer Series II 2380	IBM Personal Printer Series II 2381	IBM Personal Printer Series II 2390	IBM Personal Printer Series II 2391
Price (tested configuration)	$$$$$	$	$	$	$
PHYSICAL CHARACTERISTICS					
Dimensions (HWD, in inches)	INA	10 × 19 × 15	10 × 25 × 15	10 × 19 × 15	10 × 25 × 15
Weight (pounds)	INA	15	19	15	19
Carriage size	Wide	Narrow	Wide	Narrow	Wide
Number of pins	66	9	9	24	24
Maximum resolution(horizontal by vertical dots per inch)	140 × 144	240 × 144	240 × 144	360 × 360	360 × 360
Color capability	○	○	○	○	○
Memory	2K	11K	11K	32K	32K
Parallel interface	●	●	●	●	●
Serial interface	●	○	○	○	○
PAPER HANDLING					
Paper parking	○	●	●	●	●
Paper feeds:					
Pressure	○	●	●	●	●
Tractor	●	●	●	●	●
Internal	●	●	●	●	●
External	○	○	○	○	○
Push	●	●	●	●	●
Pull	●	●	●	●	●
Paper paths:					
Rear U path	○	○	○	○	○
Bottom vertical	●	●	●	●	●
Front L path	○	●	●	●	●
Rear L path	○	○	○	○	○
Rated maximum paper weight (pounds)	100	24	24	24	24
FONTS AND FEATURES					
Emulations	●	●	●	●	●
Typefaces:					
Courier	●	●	●	●	●
Gothic	●	●	●	●	●
Line printer	○	INA	INA	INA	INA
OCR-A	●	○	○	○	○
OCR-B	●	○	○	○	○
Orator	○	○	○	●	●
Prestige/Elite	○	○	○	●	●
Sans serif	○	○	○	○	○
Script	○	○	○	●	●
Times Roman	○	○	○	○	○
Supports scalable fonts	○	INA	INA	INA	INA
Postnet bar codes	●	INA	INA	INA	INA
Printer-specific Microsoft Windows 3.1 driver	○	INA	INA	INA	INA
Standard mode, quiet mode (dB)	55, N/A	INA	INA	INA	INA

●—Yes ○—No N/A—Not applicable INA—Information not available

Dot-Matrix Printers

	IBM Proprinter 24P	IBM 4226 Printer	Mannesmann Tally MT82	Mannesmann Tally MT150/9	Mannesmann Tally MT150/24
Price (tested configuration)	$	$$	$	$	$
PHYSICAL CHARACTERISTICS					
Dimensions (HWD, in inches)	5 × 16 × 14	12 × 25 × 11	10 × 16 × 12	6 × 18 × 13	6 × 18 × 13
Weight (pounds)	18	46	13	21	21
Carriage size	Narrow	Wide	Narrow	Narrow	Narrow
Number of pins	24	9	24	9	24
Maximum resolution(horizontal by vertical dots per inch)	360 × 360	240 × 144	360 × 180	240 × 216	360 × 360
Color capability	○	○	○	○	○
Memory	32K	22K	11K	10K	24K
Parallel interface	●	●	●	●	●
Serial interface	○	●	○	Optional	Optional
PAPER HANDLING					
Paper parking	●	○	●	●	●
Paper feeds:					
Pressure	●	○	●	●	●
Tractor	●	●	●	●	●
Internal	●	●	●	●	●
External	○	○	○	○	○
Push	●	●	●	●	●
Pull	○	○	○	Optional	Optional
Paper paths:					
Rear U path	●	○	○	●	●
Bottom vertical	○	○	○	●	●
Front L path	○	○	○	●	○
Rear L path	○	○	●	○	○
Rated maximum paper weight (pounds)	24	24	24	24	24
FONTS AND FEATURES					
Emulations	●	●	●	●	●
Typefaces:					
Courier	●	●	○	●	●
Gothic	●	●	○	○	○
Line printer	INA	INA	INA	●	●
OCR-A	○	○	○	○	●
OCR-B	○	○	○	○	●
Orator	●	○	○	○	○
Prestige/Elite	●	○	○	○	●
Sans serif	○	○	●	●	●
Script	●	○	○	○	●
Times Roman	○	○	●	○	●
Supports scalable fonts	INA	INA	INA	○	○
Postnet bar codes	INA	INA	INA	○	○
Printer-specific Microsoft Windows 3.1 driver	INA	INA	INA	○	○
Standard mode, quiet mode (dB)	INA	INA	INA	53, N/A	53, N/A

●—Yes   ○—No   N/A—Not applicable   INA—Information not available

Table Continues →

Dot-Matrix Printers

	Mannesmann Tally MT151/9	Mannesmann Tally MT151/24	Mannesmann Tally MT661	NEC Pinwriter P3200	NEC Pinwriter P3300
Price (tested configuration)	$	$	$$$$$	$	$
PHYSICAL CHARACTERISTICS					
Dimensions (HWD, in inches)	INA	INA	45 × 32 × 22	6 × 17 × 14	6 × 23 × 14
Weight (pounds)	INA	INA	77	19	25
Carriage size	Wide	Wide	Wide	Narrow	Wide
Number of pins	9	24	66	24	24
Maximum resolution(horizontal by vertical dots per inch)	240 × 216	360 × 360	240 × 240	360 × 360	360 × 360
Color capability	○	○	○	○	○
Memory	10K	24K	8K	8K	8K
Parallel interface	●	●	●	●	●
Serial interface	Optional	Optional	●	○	○
PAPER HANDLING					
Paper parking	●	●	○	●	●
Paper feeds:					
Pressure	●	●	○	●	●
Tractor	●	●	●	●	●
Internal	●	●	●	●	○
External	○	○	○	●	●
Push	●	●	●	●	●
Pull	Optional	Optional	●	○	○
Paper paths:					
Rear U path	●	●	○	●	●
Bottom vertical	●	●	●	○	○
Front L path	○	○	○	○	○
Rear L path	○	○	○	○	○
Rated maximum paper weight (pounds)	24	24	100	24	24
FONTS AND FEATURES					
Emulations	●	●	●	●	●
Typefaces:					
Courier	●	●	●	●	●
Gothic	○	○	●	●	●
Line printer	●	●	INA	INA	INA
OCR-A	○	●	●	●	●
OCR-B	○	●	●	●	●
Orator	○	○	○	○	○
Prestige/Elite	○	●	○	●	●
Sans serif	●	●	○	●	●
Script	○	●	○	○	○
Times Roman	○	●	○	●	●
Supports scalable fonts	○	○	INA	INA	INA
Postnet bar codes	○	○	INA	INA	INA
Printer-specific Microsoft Windows 3.1 driver	○	○	INA	INA	INA
Standard mode, quiet mode (dB)	53, N/A	53, N/A	INA	INA	INA

●—Yes ○—No N/A—Not applicable INA—Information not available

Dot-Matrix Printers

	NEC Pinwriter P9300	Okidata Microline 184 Turbo	Okidata Pacemark 3410	OTC Euroline 400	OTC Euroline 600
Price (tested configuration)	$	$	$$	$$$$	$$$$$
PHYSICAL CHARACTERISTICS					
Dimensions (HWD, in inches)	8 × 24 × 15	3 × 14 × 11	15 × 25 × 19	INA	INA
Weight (pounds)	33	10	63	INA	INA
Carriage size	Wide	Narrow	Wide	Wide	Wide
Number of pins	24	9	9	Dual-head 21-pin	Triple-head 21-pin
Maximum resolution(horizontal by vertical dots per inch)	360 × 360	240 × 216	240 × 216	240 × 216	240 × 216
Color capability	○	○	○	○	○
Memory	80K	2K	64K	7.8K	7.8K
Parallel interface	●	●	●	●	●
Serial interface	○	Optional	●	●	●
PAPER HANDLING					
Paper parking	●	○	●	○	○
Paper feeds:					
Pressure	●	●	●	○	○
Tractor	●	●	●	●	●
Internal	●	●	●	●	●
External	○	Optional	Optional	○	○
Push	●	●	●	○	○
Pull	○	Optional	Optional	●	●
Paper paths:					
Rear U path	●	●	○	○	●
Bottom vertical	●	●	●	●	●
Front L path	○	○	○	○	○
Rear L path	○	○	○	○	○
Rated maximum paper weight (pounds)	24	24	24	120	120
FONTS AND FEATURES					
Emulations	●	○	○	●	●
Typefaces:					
Courier	●	○	●	○	○
Gothic	●	○	●	○	○
Line printer	INA	●	●	●	●
OCR-A	●	○	○	○	○
OCR-B	●	○	○	○	○
Orator	○	○	○	○	○
Prestige/Elite	●	○	○	○	○
Sans serif	●	○	○	○	○
Script	○	○	○	○	○
Times Roman	●	○	○	○	○
Supports scalable fonts	INA	○	○	○	○
Postnet bar codes	INA	○	●	●	●
Printer-specific Microsoft Windows 3.1 driver	INA	● (included)	● (included)	○	○
Standard mode, quiet mode (dB)	INA	55, N/A	58, N/A	53, 48	53, 48

●—Yes   ○—No   N/A—Not applicable   INA—Information not available

Table Continues →

Dot-Matrix Printers

	OTC DuraLine	Panasonic KX-P1123	Panasonic KX-P1124i	Panasonic KX-P2123	Panasonic KX-P2124
Price (tested configuration)	$$$	$	$	$	$
PHYSICAL CHARACTERISTICS					
Dimensions (HWD, in inches)	6 × 27 × 17	5 × 16 × 13	6 × 17 × 14	6 × 18 × 14	6 × 19 × 15
Weight (pounds)	110	16	19	19	19
Carriage size	Wide	Narrow	Narrow	Narrow	Narrow
Number of pins	27	24	24	24	24
Maximum resolution(horizontal by vertical dots per inch)	240 × 216	360 × 360	360 × 360	360 × 360	360 × 360
Color capability	○	○	○	Optional	Optional
Memory	2K	10K	12K	14K	20K
Parallel interface	●	●	●	●	●
Serial interface	●	○	○	Optional	Optional
PAPER HANDLING					
Paper parking	○	●	●	●	●
Paper feeds:					
Pressure	○	●	●	●	●
Tractor	●	●	●	●	●
Internal	●	●	●	●	●
External	○	○	○	○	○
Push	○	●	●	●	●
Pull	○	●	●	●	●
Paper paths:					
Rear U path	○	●	●	●	●
Bottom vertical	●	●	●	●	●
Front L path	●	●	●	○	○
Rear L path	○	○	○	○	○
Rated maximum paper weight (pounds)	104	24	24	24	24
FONTS AND FEATURES					
Emulations	●	●	●	●	●
Typefaces:					
Courier	○	●	●	●	●
Gothic	○	○	○	○	○
Line printer	INA	INA	INA	○	○
OCR-A	○	○	○	○	○
OCR-B	○	○	○	○	●
Orator	○	●	●	○	●
Prestige/Elite	○	●	●	●	●
Sans serif	○	●	●	●	●
Script	○	●	●	●	●
Times Roman	○	○	●	●	●
Supports scalable fonts	INA	INA	INA	○	○
Postnet bar codes	INA	INA	INA	○	○
Printer-specific Microsoft Windows 3.1 driver	INA	INA	INA	● (via BBS)	● (via BBS)
Standard mode, quiet mode (dB)	INA	INA	INA	47, 44	47, 44

●—Yes   ○—No   N/A—Not applicable   INA—Information not available

Dot-Matrix Printers

	Panasonic KX-P2180	Panasonic KX-P2624	Printronix P3240	Seikosha BP 5780	Seikosha LT 20
Price (tested configuration)	$	$	$$$$$	$$	$
PHYSICAL CHARACTERISTICS					
Dimensions (HWD, in inches)	6 × 18 × 14	7 × 23 × 16	42 × 27 × 29	10 × 24 × 12	2 × 15 × 11
Weight (pounds)	19	34	210	44	8
Carriage size	Narrow	Wide	Wide	Wide	Narrow
Number of pins	9	24	34	18	24
Maximum resolution(horizontal by vertical dots per inch)	240 × 216	360 × 360	180 × 96	240 × 216	360 × 180
Color capability	Optional	○	○	○	○
Memory	4K	26K	2K	20K	1K
Parallel interface	●	●	●	●	●
Serial interface	Optional	○	●	●	○
PAPER HANDLING					
Paper parking	●	●	○	●	○
Paper feeds:					
Pressure	●	●	○	●	●
Tractor	●	●	●	●	○
Internal	●	●	●	●	N/A
External	○	○	○	○	N/A
Push	●	●	○	●	N/A
Pull	●	●	●	○	N/A
Paper paths:					
Rear U path	●	●	○	○	○
Bottom vertical	●	●	●	○	○
Front L path	○	●	○	○	○
Rear L path	○	○	○	●	○
Rated maximum paper weight (pounds)	24	24	100	24	21
FONTS AND FEATURES					
Emulations	●	●	●	●	●
Typefaces:					
Courier	●	●	○	○	○
Gothic	○	○	○	○	○
Line printer	○	INA	INA	INA	INA
OCR-A	○	○	○	○	○
OCR-B	○	○	○	○	○
Orator	○	●	○	○	○
Prestige/Elite	●	●	○	○	○
Sans serif	●	●	●	●	●
Script	●	●	○	○	○
Times Roman	●	●	○	●	●
Supports scalable fonts	○	INA	INA	INA	INA
Postnet bar codes	○	INA	INA	INA	INA
Printer-specific Microsoft Windows 3.1 driver	● (via BBS)	INA	INA	INA	INA
Standard mode, quiet mode (dB)	48, 45	INA	INA	INA	INA

●—Yes   ○—No   N/A—Not applicable   INA—Information not available

Table Continues →

Dot-Matrix Printers

	Seikosha SP-2400	Seikosha SP-2415	Star Micronics NX-1001 Multi-Font	Star Micronics NX-1020 Rainbow	Star Micronics NX-2420 Multi-Font
Price (tested configuration)	$	$	$	$	$
PHYSICAL CHARACTERISTICS					
Dimensions (HWD, in inches)	4 × 15 × 11	5 × 21 × 11	5 × 17 × 16	6 × 19 × 17	7 × 19 × 14
Weight (pounds)	7	9	11	14	15
Carriage size	Narrow	Wide	Narrow	Narrow	Narrow
Number of pins	9	9	9	9	24
Maximum resolution(horizontal by vertical dots per inch)	240 × 216	240 × 216	216 × 240	216 × 240	360 × 360
Color capability	○	○	○	●	○
Memory	1K	17K	4K	16K	7K
Parallel interface	●	●	●	●	●
Serial interface	○	●	○	○	○
PAPER HANDLING					
Paper parking	●	●	●	●	●
Paper feeds:					
Pressure	●	●	●	●	●
Tractor	●	●	●	●	●
Internal	●	●	●	●	●
External	○	○	○	○	○
Push	●	●	●	●	●
Pull	○	○	○	●	●
Paper paths:					
Rear U path	●	●	○	○	○
Bottom vertical	○	○	○	●	●
Front L path	○	○	○	○	○
Rear L path	○	○	●	●	●
Rated maximum paper weight (pounds)	21	21	24	24	24
FONTS AND FEATURES					
Emulations	○	○	●	●	●
Typefaces:					
Courier	●	●	●	●	●
Gothic	●	●	○	○	○
Line printer	○	○	INA	INA	INA
OCR-A	○	○	○	○	○
OCR-B	○	○	○	○	○
Orator	○	○	●	●	○
Prestige/Elite	●	●	○	○	●
Sans serif	●	●	●	●	●
Script	●	●	○	●	●
Times Roman	○	○	○	○	●
Supports scalable fonts	○	○	INA	INA	INA
Postnet bar codes	○	○	INA	INA	INA
Printer-specific Microsoft Windows 3.1 driver	○	○	INA	INA	INA
Standard mode, quiet mode (dB)	56, 55	57, 55	INA	INA	INA

●—Yes ○—No N/A—Not applicable INA—Information not available

Dot-Matrix Printers

	Star Micronics NX-2420 Rainbow	Star Micronics NX-2430 Multi-Font	Star Micronics XB-2420 Multi-Font	Star Micronics XB-2425 Multi-Font	Star Micronics XR-1020 Multi-Font
Price (tested configuration)	$	$	$	$	$
PHYSICAL CHARACTERISTICS					
Dimensions (HWD, in inches)	7 × 19 × 14	6 × 17 × 13	7 × 19 × 20	7 × 25 × 20	7 × 19 × 20
Weight (pounds)	15	14	22	27	21
Carriage size	Narrow	Narrow	Narrow	Wide	Narrow
Number of pins	24	24	24	24	9
Maximum resolution(horizontal by vertical dots per inch)	360 × 360	360 × 360	360 × 360	360 × 360	216 × 240
Color capability	●	○	●	●	●
Memory	30K	16K	29K	76K	32K
Parallel interface	●	●	●	●	●
Serial interface	○	Optional	○	○	○
PAPER HANDLING					
Paper parking	●	●	●	●	●
Paper feeds:					
Pressure	●	●	●	●	●
Tractor	●	●	●	●	●
Internal	●	●	●	●	●
External	○	Optional	○	○	○
Push	●	●	●	●	●
Pull	●	Optional	○	○	○
Paper paths:					
Rear U path	○	●	○	○	○
Bottom vertical	●	●	●	●	●
Front L path	○	○	○	○	○
Rear L path	●	○	●	●	●
Rated maximum paper weight (pounds)	24	24	24	24	24
FONTS AND FEATURES					
Emulations	●	●	●	●	●
Typefaces:					
Courier	●	●	●	●	●
Gothic	○	○	○	○	○
Line printer	INA	○	INA	INA	INA
OCR-A	○	○	○	○	●
OCR-B	○	○	○	○	●
Orator	○	○	●	●	●
Prestige/Elite	●	●	●	●	●
Sans serif	●	●	●	●	●
Script	●	●	●	●	●
Times Roman	●	●	●	●	●
Supports scalable fonts	INA	○	INA	INA	INA
Postnet bar codes	INA	○	INA	INA	INA
Printer-specific Microsoft Windows 3.1 driver	INA	○	INA	INA	INA
Standard mode, quiet mode (dB)	INA	54, 51	INA	INA	INA

●—Yes ○—No N/A—Not applicable INA—Information not available

Table Continues →

ZIFF-DAVIS PRESS

Dot-Matrix Printers

	Star Micronics XR-1520 Multi-Font	Tandy DMP 135	Tandy DMP 136	Tandy DMP 202	Tandy DMP 310 Slimline Printer	Unisys AP 1371
Price (tested configuration)	$	$	$	$	$	$$$
PHYSICAL CHARACTERISTICS						
Dimensions (HWD, in inches)	7 × 25 × 20	5 × 15 × 14	6 × 17 × 14	5 × 16 × 14	2 × 11 × 15	INA
Weight (pounds)	26	8	11	9	6	INA
Carriage size	Wide	Narrow	Narrow	Narrow	Narrow	Wide
Number of pins	9	9	9	24	24	18
Maximum resolution(horizontal by vertical dots per inch)	216 × 240	240 × 215	240 × 215	360 × 180	360 × 180	240 × 144
Color capability	●	○	●	○	○	●
Memory	32K	1K	24K	12K	11K	32K
Parallel interface	●	●	●	●	●	●
Serial interface	○	○	○	○	○	●
PAPER HANDLING						
Paper parking	●	●	●	●	○	●
Paper feeds:						
Pressure	●	●	●	●	●	●
Tractor	●	●	●	●	○	Optional
Internal	●	●	●	●	○	Optional
External	○	○	○	○	○	Optional
Push	●	●	●	●	○	○
Pull	○	○	●	○	○	○
Paper paths:						
Rear U path	○	●	●	●	INA	●
Bottom vertical	●	○	●	○	INA	●
Front L path	○	○	○	○	INA	●
Rear L path	●	○	○	○	INA	●
Rated maximum paper weight (pounds)	24	20	27	20	21	32
FONTS AND FEATURES						
Emulations	●	●	●	●	○	●
Typefaces:						
Courier	●	●	●	●	●	●
Gothic	○	●	●	○	○	○
Line printer	INA	INA	INA	INA	●	○
OCR-A	●	○	○	○	○	○
OCR-B	●	○	○	○	○	●
Orator	●	○	○	○	○	○
Prestige/Elite	●	●	○	○	○	●
Sans serif	●	●	●	○	○	●
Script	●	○	○	○	○	○
Times Roman	●	○	●	○	○	○
Supports scalable fonts	INA	INA	INA	INA	○	○
Postnet bar codes	INA	INA	INA	INA	○	●
Printer-specific Microsoft Windows 3.1 driver	INA	INA	INA	INA	○	● (in Windows)
Standard mode, quiet mode (dB)	INA	INA	INA	INA	57, 55	Less than 55, 51

●—Yes   ○—No   N/A—Not applicable   INA—Information not available

End ■

D.2 Ink-Jet Printers

(Products listed in alphabetical order by company name)	Canon BJ-20 Bubble Jet Printer	Canon BJ-300 Bubble Jet Printer	Canon BJ-330 Bubble Jet Printer	Canon BJC-800 Bubble Jet Printer	DECmultiJET 2000	Eastman Kodak Diconix Color 4 Printer
Price (tested configuration)	$	$	$	$$$	$	$$
PHYSICAL CHARACTERISTICS						
Dimensions (HWD, in inches)	INA	13 × 19 × 13	14 × 24 × 13	INA	INA	4 × 20 × 18
Weight (pounds)	INA	15	19	INA	INA	13
Carriage size	Narrow	Narrow	Wide	Wide	Narrow	Narrow
Number of jets	64	64	64	64	50	12
Maximum resolution(horizontal by vertical dots per inch)	360 × 360	360 × 360	360 × 360	360 × 360	300 × 300	192 × 192
Color capability	○	○	○	●	○	●
Memory	37K	30K	30K	7K	8K	64K
Parallel interface	●	●	●	●	●	●
Serial interface	○	○	○	○	○	○
PAPER HANDLING						
Rated maximum paper weight (pounds)	28	34	34	24	36	24
Paper parking	N/A	●	●	N/A	●	○
Paper feeds:						
Pressure	●	●	●	●	●	●
Tractor	○	●	●	○	Optional	●
Internal	INA	●	●	INA	INA	●
External	INA	○	○	INA	INA	○
Push	INA	●	●	INA	INA	●
Pull	INA	○	○	INA	INA	○
Paper paths:						
Rear U path	○	○	○	○	○	●
Bottom vertical	●	○	○	○	○	○
Front L path	○	●	●	●	○	○
Rear L path	○	●	●	○	●	●
Media supported:						
Card stock	●	INA	INA	○	●	INA
Transparencies	●	INA	INA	●	●	INA
Envelopes	●	INA	INA	●	●	INA
Landscape printing	○	INA	INA	○	●	INA
FONTS AND FEATURES						
Emulations	●	●	●	N/A	○	●
Typefaces:						
Courier	●	●	●	●	●	○
Gothic	○	○	○	○	●	●
OCR-A	INA	○	○	INA	INA	○
OCR-B	INA	○	○	INA	INA	○
Orator	●	○	○	○	○	○
Prestige/Elite	●	●	●	○	○	●
Sans serif	●	●	●	●	○	○
Script	●	○	○	○	○	○
Times Roman	●	○	○	●	●	○
Includes scalable fonts	○	INA	INA	○	○	INA
Printer-specific Microsoft Windows 3.1 driver	○	INA	INA	●	●	INA

●—Yes ○—No N/A—Not applicable INA—Information not available   **Table Continues →**

Ink-Jet Printers

	HP DeskJet 500C	HP DeskJet 550C	HP PaintJet XL300	IBM ExecJet Printer	Royal CJP 450	Star Micronics StarJet SJ-48
Price (tested configuration)	$	$	$$$	$	$	$
PHYSICAL CHARACTERISTICS						
Dimensions (HWD, in inches)	8 × 17 × 15	8 × 18 × 15	10 × 30 × 20	14 × 24 × 13	INA	7 × 12 × 8
Weight (pounds)	14	15	45	19	INA	4
Carriage size	Narrow	Narrow	Wide	Wide	Narrow	Narrow
Number of jets	50 (black) 48 (color)	50 (black) 48 (color)	50	64	50	64
Maximum resolution(horizontal by vertical dots per inch)	300 × 300	300 × 300	300 × 300	360 × 360	300 × 300	360 × 360
Color capability	●	●	●	○	○	○
Memory	48K	80K	2Mb	30K	10.5K	28K
Parallel interface	●	●	●	●	●	●
Serial interface	○	○	○	○	○	○
PAPER HANDLING						
Rated maximum paper weight (pounds)	24	36	24	34	24	28
Paper parking	N/A	N/A	N/A	●	N/A	○
Paper feeds:						
Pressure	●	●	●	●	●	●
Tractor	○	○	○	●	○	○
Internal	INA	INA	INA	●	INA	N/A
External	INA	INA	INA	○	INA	N/A
Push	INA	INA	INA	●	INA	N/A
Pull	INA	INA	INA	○	INA	N/A
Paper paths:						
Rear U path	INA	INA	INA	○	INA	○
Bottom vertical	INA	INA	INA	○	INA	●
Front L path	INA	INA	INA	●	INA	○
Rear L path	INA	INA	INA	●	INA	○
Media supported:						
Card stock	○	○	●	INA	●	INA
Transparencies	●	●	●	INA	●	INA
Envelopes	●	●	○	INA	●	INA
Landscape printing	●	●	●	INA	●	INA
FONTS AND FEATURES						
Emulations	N/A	N/A	N/A	●	○	●
Typefaces:						
Courier	●	●	●	●	●	○
Gothic	●	●	○	○	●	○
OCR-A	INA	INA	INA	○	INA	○
OCR-B	INA	INA	INA	○	INA	○
Orator	○	○	○	○	○	○
Prestige/Elite	○	○	○	●	○	○
Sans serif	○	○	○	○	○	●
Script	○	○	○	○	○	○
Times Roman	●	●	○	○	○	●
Includes scalable fonts	○	○	●	INA	○	INA
Printer-specific Microsoft Windows 3.1 driver	●	●	●	INA	●	INA

●—Yes ○—No N/A—Not applicable INA—Information not available

End ∎

D.3 Desktop Laser Printers

(Products listed in alphabetical order by company name)	Apple LaserWriter IIf	Apple LaserWriter IIg	Apple Personal LaserWriter NTR	Bézier BP4040	Brother HL-4PS
Price (tested configuration)	$$$	$$$$	$$	$$	$$$
PHYSICAL CHARACTERISTICS					
Dimensions (HWD, in inches)	INA	INA	8 × 15 × 18	8 × 28 × 14	8 × 16 × 14
Weight (pounds)	INA	INA	30	26	27
ENGINE					
Engine type	Laser	Laser	Laser	Laser	Laser
Model	Canon SX	Canon SX	Canon LX	Canon LX	Canon LX
Rated speed (pages per minute)	8	8	4	4	4
Single-cartridge toner/developer/drum	●	●	●	●	●
Toner capacity (copies)	5,000	5,000	3,500	3,500	3,500
Memory	32Mb	32Mb	4Mb	2Mb	2Mb
Maximum resolution (horizontal by vertical dots per inch)	300 × 300	300 × 300	300 × 300	300 × 300	300 × 300
Controller with RISC processor	○	○	●	●	○
INTERFACES					
Parallel	○	○	●	●	●
Serial	●	●	●	●	●
SCSI	● (hard disk only)	● (hard disk only)	○	INA	INA
AppleTalk	●	●	●	●	●
Ethernet	○	●	○	INA	INA
Automatic interface switching	●	●	●	●	○
Simultaneously active ports	○	○	○	●	○
PAPER HANDLING					
Number of paper cassettes	INA	INA	INA	1	1
Cassette capacity (sheets)	200	200	70	70	50
Duplexing	○	○	○	○	○
Rated maximum paper weight (pounds)	28	28	28	28	28
FONTS AND FEATURES					
HP PCL support	PCL 4	PCL 4	PCL 4	PCL 4	PCL 4
Supports scalable fonts	INA	INA	INA	○	●
Accepts HP-compatible font cartridges	○	○	○	○	○
PostScript language support	Adobe PostScript Level 2	Adobe PostScript Level 2	Adobe PostScript Level 2	Microsoft TrueImage	Brother BR-Script
Supports Type 1 fonts	●	●	●	●	●
Supports resolution enhancement	●	●	○	INA	INA
Supports automatic emulation switching	○	○	○	○	○
Accepts proprietary font cards	INA	INA	INA	○	●
Printer-specific Microsoft Windows 3.1 driver available	○	○	○	INA	INA

●—Yes ○—No N/A—Not applicable INA—Information not available

Table Continues →

Desktop Laser Printers

	Brother HL-4Ve	Brother HL-8V	Brother HL-10V	C. Itoh ProWriter CI-4	C. Itoh ProWriter Desktop Laser Printer CI-8
Price (tested configuration)	$$	$$$	$$	$	$$
PHYSICAL CHARACTERISTICS					
Dimensions (HWD, in inches)	INA	9 × 18 × 25	11 × 16 × 15	8 × 14 × 23	INA
Weight (pounds)	INA	44	37	29	INA
ENGINE					
Engine type	Laser	Laser	Laser	Laser	Laser
Model	Canon LX	Canon SX	Brother HL-10V	TEC 1321C	TEC 1323D
Rated speed (pages per minute)	4	8	10	4	8
Single-cartridge toner/developer/drum	●	●	●	○	○
Toner capacity (copies)	3,500	4,000	4,000	2,500	2,000
Memory	5Mb	1Mb	5Mb	512K	5Mb
Maximum resolution (horizontal by vertical dots per inch)	300 × 300	300 × 300	300 × 300	300 × 300	300 × 300
Controller with RISC processor	○	○	○	○	●
INTERFACES					
Parallel	●	●	●	●	●
Serial	●	●	●	●	●
SCSI	○	INA	○	INA	○
AppleTalk	○	○	Optional	○	Optional
Ethernet	○	INA	○	INA	○
Automatic interface switching	○	●	○	○	○
Simultaneously active ports	○	○	○	○	○
PAPER HANDLING					
Number of paper cassettes	INA	1	INA	1	INA
Cassette capacity (sheets)	70	200	250	100	250
Duplexing	○	○	○	○	○
Rated maximum paper weight (pounds)	21	36	36	32	34
FONTS AND FEATURES					
HP PCL support	PCL 5	PCL 5	PCL 5	PCL 4	PCL 5
Supports scalable fonts	INA	●	INA	○	INA
Accepts HP-compatible font cartridges	○	●	●	●	●
PostScript language support	BR-Script (optional)	None	BR-Script (optional)	None	Destiny PDL (optional)
Supports Type 1 fonts	●	○	●	○	●
Supports resolution enhancement	●	INA	●	INA	●
Supports automatic emulation switching	●	○	●	○	○
Accepts proprietary font cards	INA	●	INA	○	INA
Printer-specific Microsoft Windows 3.1 driver available	○	INA	○	INA	○

●—Yes ○—No N/A—Not applicable INA—Information not available

Desktop Laser Printers

	C. Itoh ProWriter Desktop Laser Printer CI-8E	Dataproducts LZR 960	Eastman Kodak Ektaplus 7008	Epson ActionLaser II	Epson EPL-7000
Price (tested configuration)	$$	$$$	$	$	$
PHYSICAL CHARACTERISTICS					
Dimensions (HWD, in inches)	INA	11 × 13 × 14	9 × 15 × 16	INA	8 × 20 × 25
Weight (pounds)	INA	34	38	INA	40
ENGINE					
Engine type	Laser	Laser	Laser	Laser	Laser
Model	TEC 1323CE	Sharp JX-95	TEC 1306C	Ricoh LP-1200	Minolta SP101
Rated speed (pages per minute)	8	9	8	6	6
Single-cartridge toner/developer/drum	○	○	○	○	●
Toner capacity (copies)	2,000	3,000	1,500	5,000	6,000
Memory	5Mb	2Mb	1.5Mb	5.5Mb	512K
Maximum resolution (horizontal by vertical dots per inch)	300 × 300	300 × 300	300 × 300	300 × 300	300 × 300
Controller with RISC processor	○	●	○	○	○
INTERFACES					
Parallel	●	●	●	●	●
Serial	●	●	●	●	●
SCSI	○	INA	○	○	INA
AppleTalk	○	●	○	○	○
Ethernet	○	INA	○	○	INA
Automatic interface switching	○	●	○	●	●
Simultaneously active ports	○	●	○	●	●
PAPER HANDLING					
Number of paper cassettes	INA	1	1	INA	1
Cassette capacity (sheets)	250	250	200	100	250
Duplexing	○	○	○	○	○
Rated maximum paper weight (pounds)	34	31	34	42	42
FONTS AND FEATURES					
HP PCL support	PCL 5	PCL 4	PCL 4	PCL4	PCL 4
Supports scalable fonts	INA	○	○	INA	○
Accepts HP-compatible font cartridges	●	○	○	●	●
PostScript language support	Destiny PDL (optional)	Adobe Level 2	None	Adobe PostScript (optional)	None
Supports Type 1 fonts	●	●	○	●	○
Supports resolution enhancement	●	INA	INA	○	INA
Supports automatic emulation switching	○	○	○	○	○
Accepts proprietary font cards	INA	●	●	INA	○
Printer-specific Microsoft Windows 3.1 driver available	○	INA	INA	○	INA

●—Yes ○—No N/A—Not applicable INA—Information not available

Table Continues →

Desktop Laser Printers

	Epson EPL-7500	Epson EPL-8000	Fujitsu Print Partner 10	GCC BLP II	GCC BLP IIS
Price (tested configuration)	$$$	$$	$$	$$	$$$
PHYSICAL CHARACTERISTICS					
Dimensions (HWD, in inches)	8 × 20 × 25	11 × 19 × 15	INA	5 × 17 × 23	5 × 17 × 23
Weight (pounds)	40	40	INA	23	23
ENGINE					
Engine type	Laser	Laser	Laser	LED array	LED array
Model	Minolta SP101	Minolta NC-10	Minolta SP10	Oki Electric OL-400	Oki Electric OL-800
Rated speed (pages per minute)	6	10	10	4	8
Single-cartridge toner/developer/drum	●	●	●	○	○
Toner capacity (copies)	6,000	8,000	8,000	2,500	2,500
Memory	2Mb	7.5Mb	9Mb	2Mb	2Mb
Maximum resolution (horizontal by vertical dots per inch)	300 × 300	300 × 300	300 × 300	300 × 300	300 × 300
Controller with RISC processor	●	○	●	○	○
INTERFACES					
Parallel	●	●	●	○	○
Serial	●	●	●	○	○
SCSI	INA	○	○	●	●
AppleTalk	●	○	Optional	●	●
Ethernet	INA	○	○	○	○
Automatic interface switching	○	●	●	N/A	N/A
Simultaneously active ports	○	●	●	N/A	N/A
PAPER HANDLING					
Number of paper cassettes	1	INA	INA	1	1
Cassette capacity (sheets)	250	250	250	200	200
Duplexing	○	○	○	○	○
Rated maximum paper weight (pounds)	42	42	41	34	34
FONTS AND FEATURES					
HP PCL support	PCL 4	PCL 5	PCL 5	None	None
Supports scalable fonts	○	INA	INA	N/A	N/A
Accepts HP-compatible font cartridges	○	●	●	N/A	N/A
PostScript language support	Adobe Level 1	Adobe Postscript (optional)	Microsoft TrueImage (optional)	Adobe Level 1	Adobe Level 1
Supports Type 1 fonts	●	●	●	●	●
Supports resolution enhancement	INA	●	●	INA	INA
Supports automatic emulation switching	○	●	● (via software)	○	○
Accepts proprietary font cards	○	INA	INA	●	●
Printer-specific Microsoft Windows 3.1 driver available	INA	○	○	INA	INA

●—Yes ○—No N/A—Not applicable INA—Information not available

Desktop Laser Printers

	HP LaserJet 4	HP LaserJet 4M	HP LaserJet IIP Plus	HP LaserJet IIIP	IBM Laser Printer 5e
Price (tested configuration)	$$	$$$	$	$$	$$
PHYSICAL CHARACTERISTICS					
Dimensions (HWD, in inches)	INA	INA	INA	8 × 14 × 25	12 × 14 × 21
Weight (pounds)	INA	INA	INA	22	33
ENGINE					
Engine type	Laser	Laser	Laser	Laser	Laser
Model	Canon P-270	Canon P-270	Canon LX	Canon LX	IBM/Lexmark 4029 Model 10
Rated speed (pages per minute)	8	8	4	4	5
Single-cartridge toner/developer/drum	●	●	●	●	●
Toner capacity (copies)	6,000	6,000	3,500	3,500	4,000
Memory	34Mb	26Mb	4.5Mb	1Mb	1Mb
Maximum resolution (horizontal by vertical dots per inch)	600 × 600	600 × 600	300 × 300	300 × 300	300 × 300
Controller with RISC processor	●	●	○	○	○
INTERFACES					
Parallel	●	●	●	●	●
Serial	●	●	○	●	●
SCSI	○	○	○	INA	INA
AppleTalk	Optional	●	○	○	○
Ethernet	Optional	Optional	○	INA	INA
Automatic interface switching	●	●	N/A	○	○
Simultaneously active ports	●	●	N/A	○	○
PAPER HANDLING					
Number of paper cassettes	INA	INA	INA	1	1
Cassette capacity (sheets)	250, 100	250, 100	70	70	200
Duplexing	○	○	○	○	○
Rated maximum paper weight (pounds)	28	28	28	28	24
FONTS AND FEATURES					
HP PCL support	Enhanced PCL 5	Enhanced PCL 5	PCL 4	PCL 5	PCL 4
Supports scalable fonts	INA	INA	INA	●	○
Accepts HP-compatible font cartridges	●	●	●	●	○
PostScript language support	Adobe PostScript Level 2 (optional)	Adobe PostScript Level 2	Adobe PostScript (optional)	None	None
Supports Type 1 fonts	●	●	●	○	●
Supports resolution enhancement	●	●	○	INA	INA
Supports automatic emulation switching	●	●	○	○	○
Accepts proprietary font cards	INA	INA	INA	●	●
Printer-specific Microsoft Windows 3.1 driver available	● (included)	● (included)	● (in Windows 3.1 and via BBS)	INA	INA

●—Yes ○—No N/A—Not applicable INA—Information not available   **Table Continues** →

Desktop Laser Printers

	IBM LaserPrinter 6	IBM LaserPrinter 6P	IBM LaserPrinter 10	IBM LaserPrinter 10P	Kyocera Ecosys a-Si Printer FS-1500A
Price (tested configuration)	$$	$$	$$	$$$	$$
PHYSICAL CHARACTERISTICS					
Dimensions (HWD, in inches)	12 × 14 × 21	INA	12 × 14 × 21	INA	9 × 14 × 14
Weight (pounds)	33	INA	33	INA	30
ENGINE					
Engine type	Laser	Laser	Laser	Laser	LED array
Model	IBM/Lexmark 4029 Model 20	IBM/Lexmark 4029	IBM/Lexmark 4029 Model 30	IBM/Lexmark 4029	Ecosys
Rated speed (pages per minute)	6	6	10	10	10
Single-cartridge toner/developer/drum	●	●	●	●	○*
Toner capacity (copies)	4,000	7,000 (9,500 with high-yield toner)	4,000	7,000 (9,500 with high-yield toner)	5,000
Memory	1Mb	9Mb	1Mb	9Mb	5Mb
Maximum resolution (horizontal by vertical dots per inch)	300 × 300	300 × 300	300 × 300	600 × 600	300 × 300
Controller with RISC processor	○	○	○	○	○
INTERFACES					
Parallel	INA	●	INA	●	●
Serial	●	●	●	●	●
SCSI	INA	○	INA	○	○
AppleTalk	●	Optional	●	Optional	Optional
Ethernet	INA	Optional	INA	Optional	Optional
Automatic interface switching	○	○	●	○	●
Simultaneously active ports	○	○	○	○	●
PAPER HANDLING					
Number of paper cassettes	1	INA	1	INA	INA
Cassette capacity (sheets)	200	200	200	200	250
Duplexing	○	○	○	○	Optional
Rated maximum paper weight (pounds)	24	35	24	35	24
FONTS AND FEATURES					
HP PCL support	PCL 4	PCL 4	PCL 4	PCL 4	PCL 5
Supports scalable fonts	○	INA	○	INA	INA
Accepts HP-compatible font cartridges	○	○	○	○	●
PostScript language support	None	Adobe PostScript	None	Adobe PostScript	Kyocera PDL (optional)
Supports Type 1 fonts	●	●	●	●	●
Supports resolution enhancement	INA	●	INA	●	●
Supports automatic emulation switching	○	● (via software)	○	● (via software)	○
Accepts proprietary font cards	●	INA	●	INA	INA
Printer-specific Microsoft Windows 3.1 driver available	INA	● (included)	INA	● (included)	●

*This printer uses refillable toner and a permanently installed photoconductor and drum
●—Yes   ○—No   N/A—Not applicable   INA—Information not available

Desktop Laser Printers

	LaserMaster TrueTech 800/4	LaserMaster TrueTech 1000	LaserMaster Unity 1000	LaserMaster Unity 1200xl	LaserMaster WinPrinter 800
Price (tested configuration)	$$$	$$$$$	$$$$$	$$$$$	$$
PHYSICAL CHARACTERISTICS					
Dimensions (HWD, in inches)	$9 \times 28 \times 14$	$9 \times 18 \times 26$	INA	$8 \times 19 \times 18$	$8 \times 14 \times 16$
Weight (pounds)	24	38	INA	51	24
ENGINE					
Engine type	Laser	Laser	Laser	Laser	Laser
Model	Canon LX	Canon SX	Canon SX	Toshiba TN-7270	Canon LX
Rated speed (pages per minute)	4	8	8	8	4
Single-cartridge toner/developer/drum	●	●	●	○	●
Toner capacity (copies)	3,500	3,500	3,000	5,000	3,500
Memory	6Mb	9Mb	48Mb	48Mb	None
Maximum resolution (horizontal by vertical dots per inch)	800×800	$1,000 \times 1,000$	$1,000 \times 1,000$	$1,200 \times 1,200$	800×800 (600 × 600 with 5Mb RAM)
Controller with RISC processor	●	●	○	○	○
INTERFACES					
Parallel	INA	○*	●	●	○
Serial	○*	○	●	●	○
SCSI	INA	INA	○	○	○
AppleTalk	○	○	●	●	○
Ethernet	INA	INA	Optional	Optional	○
Automatic interface switching	●	N/A	●	●	N/A
Simultaneously active ports	N/A	N/A	●	●	N/A
PAPER HANDLING					
Number of paper cassettes	2	1	INA	INA	INA
Cassette capacity (sheets)	50, 250	250	200	150	50
Duplexing	○	○	○	○	○
Rated maximum paper weight (pounds)	28	35	35	34	32
FONTS AND FEATURES					
HP PCL support	None	None	PCL 4	PCL 4	PCL 4
Supports scalable fonts	N/A	N/A	INA	INA	INA
Accepts HP-compatible font cartridges	N/A	N/A	○	●	●
PostScript language support	Microsoft TrueImage	Microsoft TrueImage	LaserMaster Enhanced TrueImage	LaserMaster Enhanced TrueImage	LaserMaster Enhanced TrueImage
Supports Type 1 fonts	●	●	●	●	●
Supports resolution enhancement	INA	INA	●	●	●
Supports automatic emulation switching	●	○	●	●	●
Accepts proprietary font cards	○	○	INA	INA	INA
Printer-specific Microsoft Windows 3.1 driver available	INA	INA	● (included)	● (included)	● (included)

*This product uses a video I/O interface

●—Yes ○— No N/A—Not applicable INA—Information not available

Table Continues →

Desktop Laser Printers

	Mannesmann Tally MT735	Mannesmann Tally MT908	Mannesmann Tally MT911 PS	Microtek TrueLaser	NEC Silentwriter Model 95
Price (tested configuration)	$	$$	$$$	$$$	$$
PHYSICAL CHARACTERISTICS					
Dimensions (HWD, in inches)	2 × 11 × 9	9 × 16 × 16	9 × 18 × 24	9 × 25 × 16	INA
Weight (pounds)	8	31	42	35	INA
ENGINE					
Engine type	Thermal	Laser	Laser	Laser	Laser
Model	Mannesmann Tally 735	TEC 1323D	Konica LP3110	TEC INF 1305-Z	Minolta
Rated speed (pages per minute)	6	8	10	6	6
Single-cartridge toner/developer/drum	○	○	○	○	●
Toner capacity (copies)	150	1,500	2,000	1,500	8,000
Memory	1Mb	5Mb	2.5Mb	2Mb	5Mb
Maximum resolution (horizontal by vertical dots per inch)	300 × 300	300 × 300	300 × 300	300 × 300	300 × 300
Controller with RISC processor	○	●	○	●	○
INTERFACES					
Parallel	●	●	●	●	●
Serial	○	●	●	●	●
SCSI	INA	○	INA	○	○
AppleTalk	○	Optional	○	●	●
Ethernet	INA	○	INA	○	Optional
Automatic interface switching	N/A	○	○	●	●
Simultaneously active ports	N/A	○	○	●	●
PAPER HANDLING					
Number of paper cassettes	1	INA	2	1	INA
Cassette capacity (sheets)	80	250	200, 200	150	250
Duplexing	○	○	○	○	○
Rated maximum paper weight (pounds)	24	34	32	34	41
FONTS AND FEATURES					
HP PCL support	PCL 4	PCL 5	PCL 4	PCL 4	PCL 5
Supports scalable fonts	○	INA	○	○	INA
Accepts HP-compatible font cartridges	○	●	○	○	●
PostScript language support	None	Destiny PDL (optional)	Microsoft Interpreter	Microsoft TrueImage	Adobe PostScript Level 2
Supports Type 1 fonts	○	●	●	●	●
Supports resolution enhancement	INA	●	INA	INA	●
Supports automatic emulation switching	○	○	○	○	● (via software)
Accepts proprietary font cards	○	INA	●	●	INA
Printer-specific Microsoft Windows 3.1 driver available	INA	○	INA	INA	● (included)

●—Yes ○—No N/A—Not applicable INA—Information not available

Desktop Laser Printers

	NEC Silentwriter2 990	NewGen TurboPS/300p	NewGen TurboPS/400p	NewGen TurboPS/630En	NewGen TurboPS/660
Price (tested configuration)	$$$$	$$	$$$	$$$	$$$
PHYSICAL CHARACTERISTICS					
Dimensions (HWD, in inches)	11 × 25 × 17	8 × 16 × 14	8 × 16 × 14	9 × 18 × 26	9 × 18 × 26
Weight (pounds)	49	24	24	44	44
ENGINE					
Engine type	Laser	Laser	Laser	Laser	Laser
Model	Canon LBBP-UX	Canon LX	Canon LX	Canon SX	Canon SX
Rated speed (pages per minute)	8	4	4	8	8
Single-cartridge toner/developer/drum	●	●	●	●	●
Toner capacity (copies)	4,000	3,500	3,500	4,000	4,000
Memory	2Mb	16Mb	16Mb	32Mb	32Mb
Maximum resolution (horizontal by vertical dots per inch)	300 × 300	300 × 300	400 × 400	600 × 300	600 × 600
Controller with RISC processor	●	●	●	●	●
INTERFACES					
Parallel	●	●	●	●	●
Serial	●	●	●	●	●
SCSI	INA	Optional (hard disk only)	Optional (hard disk only)	● (hard disk only)	● (hard disk only)
AppleTalk	●	●	●	●	●
Ethernet	INA	○	○	●	Optional
Automatic interface switching	○	●	●	●	●
Simultaneously active ports	○	●	●	●	●
PAPER HANDLING					
Number of paper cassettes	1	INA	INA	INA	INA
Cassette capacity (sheets)	200	70	70	200	200
Duplexing	○	○	○	○	○
Rated maximum paper weight (pounds)	34	28	28	35	35
FONTS AND FEATURES					
HP PCL support	PCL 4	PCL 4	PCL 4	PCL 4	PCL 4
Supports scalable fonts	●	INA	INA	INA	INA
Accepts HP-compatible font cartridges	○	○	○	○	○
PostScript language support	Adobe Level 1	NewGen PDL	NewGen PDL	NewGen PDL	NewGen PDL
Supports Type 1 fonts	●	●	●	●	●
Supports resolution enhancement	INA	○	●	○	●
Supports automatic emulation switching	●	●	●	●	●
Accepts proprietary font cards	○	INA	INA	INA	INA
Printer-specific Microsoft Windows 3.1 driver available	INA	● (included)	● (included)	● (included)	● (included)

●—Yes   ○—No   N/A—Not applicable   INA—Information not available

Table Continues →

Desktop Laser Printers

	NewGen TurboPS/840e	NewGen TurboPS/880	Okidata OL810 LED Page Printer	Okidata OL830	Panasonic KX-P4410
Price (tested configuration)	$$$	$$$$	$$	$$	$
PHYSICAL CHARACTERISTICS					
Dimensions (HWD, in inches)	13 × 23 × 22	9 × 18 × 26	8 × 18 × 18	6 × 18 × 18	9 × 15 × 16
Weight (pounds)	56	44	24	37	31
ENGINE					
Engine type	Laser	Laser	LED array	LED	Laser
Model	Canon SX	Canon SX	Oki Electric OL-800	Oki Electric OL-800	Panasonic 4400
Rated speed (pages per minute)	8	8	8	8	5
Single-cartridge toner/developer/drum	●	●	○	○	○
Toner capacity (copies)	4,000	4,000	2,500	2,500	3,000
Memory	32Mb	32Mb	5Mb	2Mb	4.5Mb
Maximum resolution (horizontal by vertical dots per inch)	800 × 400	800 × 800	300 × 300	300 × 300	300 × 300
Controller with RISC processor	●	●	○	○	○
INTERFACES					
Parallel	●	●	●	●	●
Serial	●	●	Optional	○	○
SCSI	● (hard disk only)	● (hard disk only)	○	INA	○
AppleTalk	●	●	Optional	○	○
Ethernet	Optional	●	○	INA	○
Automatic interface switching	●	●	●	N/A	N/A
Simultaneously active ports	●	●	●	N/A	N/A
PAPER HANDLING					
Number of paper cassettes	INA	INA	INA	1	INA
Cassette capacity (sheets)	200	200	200	200	200
Duplexing	○	○	○	○	○
Rated maximum paper weight (pounds)	35	35	24	24	35
FONTS AND FEATURES					
HP PCL support	PCL 4	PCL 4	PCL 5	PCL 4	PCL 4
Supports scalable fonts	INA	INA	INA	N/A	INA
Accepts HP-compatible font cartridges	○	○	○	○	●
PostScript language support	NewGen PDL	NewGen PDL	Adobe PostScript (optional)	Adobe Level 1	None
Supports Type 1 fonts	●	●	INA	●	○
Supports resolution enhancement	●	●	●	INA	○
Supports automatic emulation switching	●	●	○	●	○
Accepts proprietary font cards	INA	INA	INA	●	INA
Printer-specific Microsoft Windows 3.1 driver available	● (included)	● (included)	● (included)	INA	●

●—Yes   ○—No   N/A—Not applicable   INA—Information not available

Desktop Laser Printers

	Panasonic KX-P4430	Panasonic KX-P4455 Laser Partner	QMS PS-815	QMS PS-815 MR	QMS PS-825
Price (tested configuration)	$$	$$$	$$$$	$$$$	$$$$
PHYSICAL CHARACTERISTICS					
Dimensions (HWD, in inches)	9 × 15 × 16	15 × 28 × 17	9 × 18 × 25	9 × 18 × 25	12 × 18 × 25
Weight (pounds)	31	60	44	44	55
ENGINE					
Engine type	Laser	Laser	Laser	Laser	Laser
Model	Panasonic 4400	Matsushita KX-P4455	Canon SX	Canon SX	Canon SX
Rated speed (pages per minute)	5	11	8	8	8
Single-cartridge toner/developer/drum	○	○	●	●	●
Toner capacity (copies)	3,000	5,000	4,000	4,000	4,000
Memory	5Mb	2Mb	2Mb	6Mb	2Mb
Maximum resolution (horizontal by vertical dots per inch)	300 × 300	300 × 300	300 × 300	600 × 600	300 × 300
Controller with RISC processor	○	○	○	○	○
INTERFACES					
Parallel	●	●	●	●	●
Serial	●	●	●	●	●
SCSI	○	○	INA	INA	INA
AppleTalk	○	●	●	●	●
Ethernet	○	○	INA	INA	INA
Automatic interface switching	●	○	●	●	●
Simultaneously active ports	○	○	●	●	●
PAPER HANDLING					
Number of paper cassettes	INA	2	1	1	2
Cassette capacity (sheets)	200	250, 250	200	200	200, 200
Duplexing	○	○	○	○	○
Rated maximum paper weight (pounds)	35	24	36	36	36
FONTS AND FEATURES					
HP PCL support	PCL 5	PCL 4	PCL 4	PCL 4	PCL 4
Supports scalable fonts	INA	N/A	○	○	○
Accepts HP-compatible font cartridges	●	○	●	●	●
PostScript language support	None	Adobe Level 1	Adobe Level 1	Adobe Level 1	Adobe Level 1
Supports Type 1 fonts	○	●	●	●	●
Supports resolution enhancement	●	INA	INA	INA	INA
Supports automatic emulation switching	○	○	●	●	●
Accepts proprietary font cards	INA	●	●	●	●
Printer-specific Microsoft Windows 3.1 driver available	●	INA	INA	INA	INA

●—Yes ○—No N/A—Not applicable INA—Information not available

Table Continues →

Desktop Laser Printers

	Samsung Finalé 8000	Sharp JX-9500H	Sharp JX-9500PS	Star Micronics LaserPrinter 4	Star Micronics LaserPrinter 4 StarScript
Price (tested configuration)	$$	$$	$$$	$	$$
PHYSICAL CHARACTERISTICS					
Dimensions (HWD, in inches)	INA	11 × 13 × 14	11 × 13 × 14	9 × 25 × 14	9 × 25 × 14
Weight (pounds)	INA	33	33	25	25
ENGINE					
Engine type	Laser	Laser	Laser	Laser	Laser
Model	Samsung F8000	Sharp JX-95	Sharp JX-95	Canon LX	Canon LX
Rated speed (pages per minute)	8	9	6	4	4
Single-cartridge toner/developer/drum	○	○	○	●	●
Toner capacity (copies)	5,000	3,000	3,000	3,500	3,500
Memory	18Mb	512K	2.5Mb	1Mb	2Mb
Maximum resolution (horizontal by vertical dots per inch)	300 × 300 (600 × 600 with optional Image-Resolution Kit)	300 × 300	300 × 300	300 × 300	300 × 300
Controller with RISC processor	●	○	○	●	●
INTERFACES					
Parallel	●	●	●	●	●
Serial	●	●	○	●	●
SCSI	○	INA	INA	INA	●
AppleTalk	Optional	○	○	○	INA
Ethernet	Optional	INA	INA	INA	INA
Automatic interface switching	●	○	N/A	○	○
Simultaneously active ports	●	○	N/A	○	○
PAPER HANDLING					
Number of paper cassettes	INA	1	1	1	1
Cassette capacity (sheets)	250, 250	250	250	50	50
Duplexing	○	○	○	○	○
Rated maximum paper weight (pounds)	35	34	34	28	28
FONTS AND FEATURES					
HP PCL support	PCL 5	PCL 4	PCL 4	PCL 4	PCL 4
Supports scalable fonts	INA	○	○	○	○
Accepts HP-compatible font cartridges	●	○	○	●	●
PostScript language support	Samsung PDL	None	Adobe Level 1	None	Star Micronics StarScript
Supports Type 1 fonts	●	○	●	○	●
Supports resolution enhancement	Optional	INA	INA	INA	INA
Supports automatic emulation switching	● (via software)	○	○	○	○
Accepts proprietary font cards	INA	●	●	○	●
Printer-specific Microsoft Windows 3.1 driver available	●	INA	INA	INA	INA

●—Yes ○—No N/A—Not applicable INA—Information not available

Desktop Laser Printers

	Tandy LP 950	TI microLaser Turbo	Toshiba PageLaser GX200	Xante Accel-a-Writer 8000
Price (tested configuration)	$$	$$	$$	$$$
PHYSICAL CHARACTERISTICS				
Dimensions (HWD, in inches)	11 × 13 × 15	11 × 13 × 14	INA	9 × 18 × 19
Weight (pounds)	33	33	INA	42
ENGINE				
Engine type	Laser	Laser	Laser	Laser
Model	Sharp JX-95	Sharp JX-9500	TEC LB-1323	Canon SX
Rated speed (pages per minute)	6	9	8	8
Single-cartridge toner/developer/drum	○	○	○	●
Toner capacity (copies)	3,000	3,000	3,000	4,000
Memory	512K	10.5Mb	5Mb	16Mb
Maximum resolution (horizontal by vertical dots per inch)	300 × 300	300 × 300	300 × 300	600 × 600
Controller with RISC processor	○	●	○	●
INTERFACES				
Parallel	●	●	●	●
Serial	●	Optional	●	●
SCSI	INA	Optional (hard disk only)	○	● (hard disk only)
AppleTalk	○	Optional	○	●
Ethernet		Optional	Optional	○
Automatic interface switching	●	●	○	○
Simultaneously active ports	○	●	○	●
PAPER HANDLING				
Number of paper cassettes	1	INA	INA	INA
Cassette capacity (sheets)	250	250	250	200
Duplexing	○	○	○	○
Rated maximum paper weight (pounds)	35	34	32	36
FONTS AND FEATURES				
HP PCL support	PCL 4	PCL 4	PCL 5	PCL 4
Supports scalable fonts	○	INA	INA	INA
Accepts HP-compatible font cartridges	●	●	●	○
PostScript language support	None	Adobe PostScript Level 2	Toshiba PDL (optional)	Phoenix
Supports Type 1 fonts	○	●	●	●
Supports resolution enhancement	INA	○	●	●
Supports automatic emulation switching	○	●	○	○
Accepts proprietary font cards	●	INA	INA	INA
Printer-specific Microsoft Windows 3.1 driver available	INA	○	○	○

●—Yes ○—No N/A—Not applicable INA—Information not available

E n d ■

D.4 Shared Laser Printers

(Products listed in alphabetical order by company name)	AMT TracJet Laser Printer	ALPS LSX1600	Compaq PageMarq 15	Compaq PageMarq 20	Dataproducts LZR 1555
Price (tested configuration)	$$$$	$$$	$$$	$$$$	$$$
PHYSICAL CHARACTERISTICS					
Dimensions (HWD, in inches)	INA	11 × 18 × 20	17 × 20 × 17	19 × 20 × 17	13 × 22 × 22
Weight (pounds)	INA	80	65	83	69
ENGINE					
Engine type	Laser	Laser	Laser	Laser	Laser
Model	Pentax PL-F0301	MKE Matsushita V50	Fuji Xerox	Fuji Xerox	Fuji Xerox XP-15
Rated speed (pages per minute)	16	16	15	20	15
Single-cartridge toner/developer/drum	○	○	●	●	●
Toner capacity (copies)	4,000	10,000	12,000	12,000	12,000
Memory (as tested)	8Mb	7Mb	18Mb	20Mb	16Mb
Maximum resolution (horizontal by vertical dots per inch)	300 × 300	300 × 300	800 × 400	800 × 400	400 × 400
Controller with RISC processor	○	○	●	●	○
INTERFACES					
Parallel	●	●	●	●	●
Serial	●	●	●	●	●
AppleTalk	○	○	Optional	Optional	○
SCSI port	○	○	○	○	○
Ethernet	○	○	Optional	Optional	○
Token-Ring	○	○	Optional	Optional	○
Automatic interface switching	○	○	●	●	○
Simultaneously active ports	○	○	●	●	●
Paper support	Continuous-form	Cut-sheet	Cut-sheet	Cut-sheet	Cut-sheet
PAPER HANDLING					
Input-cassette capacity (sheets)	N/A	500, 250	500, 250	500, 500, 500	250, 250
Letter-size paper (8.5 × 11 inches)	INA	●	●	●	●
Legal-size paper (8.5 × 14 inches)	INA	●	●	●	●
B-size paper (11 × 17 inches)	○	○	●	●	●
Output-cassette capacity (sheets)	N/A	500	500	500	250 (facedown), 250 (faceup)
Duplexing	○	●	○	○	○
Rated maximum paper weight (pounds)	20	35	32	32	32
FONTS AND FEATURES					
HP PCL support	PCL 4	PCL 4	PCL 5	PCL 5	PCL 5
Supports scalable fonts	INA	INA	INA	INA	INA
Accepts HP-compatible font cartridges	●	●	○	○	●
PostScript language support	None	ALPScript PDL (optional)	Adobe PostScript Level 2	Adobe PostScript Level 2	None
Supports Type 1 fonts	N/A	●	●	●	N/A
Supports resolution enhancement	○	○	●	●	○
Supports automatic emulation switching	○	○	●	●	○
Accepts proprietary font cards	INA	INA	INA	INA	INA
Printer-specific Microsoft Windows 3.1 driver	○	● (in Windows 3.1)	● (included)	● (included)	● (included)

●—Yes   ○—No   N/A—Not applicable   INA—Information not available

Shared Laser Printers

	Dataproducts LZR 1560	DEClaser 3250	Eastman Kodak Ektaplus 7016 PS	Genicom Model 7170	HP LaserJet IIISi
Price (tested configuration)	$$$	$$$$	$$$$	$$$$	$$$$
PHYSICAL CHARACTERISTICS					
Dimensions (HWD, in inches)	13 × 20 × 22	INA	16 × 28 × 21	13 × 19 × 18	17 × 22 × 24
Weight (pounds)	75	INA	85	58	106
ENGINE					
Engine type	Laser	Laser	LED array	Laser	Laser
Model	Fuji Xerox XP-15	Fuji Xerox 4213	Kodak LED QEXP-QT99	Toshiba G750	Canon
Rated speed (pages per minute)	15	13	16	17	17
Single-cartridge toner/developer/drum	●	○	○	●	●
Toner capacity (copies)	12,000	6,000	4,000	13,000	8,000
Memory (as tested)	16Mb	10.5Mb	2Mb	9Mb	1Mb
Maximum resolution (horizontal by vertical dots per inch)	400 × 400	300 × 300	300 × 300	300 × 300	300 × 300
Controller with RISC processor	●	○	○	○	●
INTERFACES					
Parallel	●	●	●	●	●
Serial	●	●	●	●	●
AppleTalk	●	○	○	Optional	●
SCSI port	● (for hard disk storage only)	○	○	○	○
Ethernet	○	Optional	○	Optional	○
Token-Ring	○	○	○	Optional	○
Automatic interface switching	○	○	○	○	●
Simultaneously active ports	●	○	●	○	○
Paper support	Cut-sheet	Cut-sheet	INA	Cut-sheet	INA
PAPER HANDLING					
Input-cassette capacity (sheets)	250, 250	250, 250	500	250, 250	1,000
Letter-size paper (8.5 × 11 inches)	●	INA	●	●	●
Legal-size paper (8.5 × 14 inches)	●	INA	○	●	●
B-size paper (11 × 17 inches)	●	○	○	○	○
Output-cassette capacity (sheets)	250 (facedown), 250 (faceup)	500	200	350 (facedown), 500 (faceup)	500
Duplexing	○	●	○	Optional	○
Rated maximum paper weight (pounds)	32	32	24	36	28
FONTS AND FEATURES					
HP PCL support	PCL 4	PCL 4	PCL 4	PCL 5	PCL 4, PCL 5
Supports scalable fonts	INA	INA	○	INA	●
Accepts HP-compatible font cartridges	○	○	○	●	●
PostScript language support	Adobe PostScript Level 2	Xerox PDL	Adobe Level 1	GeniScript PDL (optional)	None
Supports Type 1 fonts	●	●	●	●	○
Supports resolution enhancement	○	○	INA	●	INA
Supports automatic emulation switching	○	● (via software)	○	●	○
Accepts proprietary font cards	INA	INA	●	INA	●
Printer-specific Microsoft Windows 3.1 driver	● (included)	● (available on request)	INA	● (included)	INA

●—Yes ○—No N/A—Not applicable INA—Information not available

Table Continues →

Shared Laser Printers

	IBM LaserPrinter 10L	Kentek K30D	Kyocera F-5000A	LaserMaster TrueTech 1200	NewGen TurboPS/1200T
Price (tested configuration)	$$$	$$$$$	$$$$$	$$$$$	$$$$$
PHYSICAL CHARACTERISTICS					
Dimensions (HWD, in inches)	17 × 14 × 21	INA	13 × 42 × 19	14 × 37 × 21	19 × 23 × 26
Weight (pounds)	43	INA	95	121	INA
ENGINE					
Engine type	Laser	LED array	Laser	Laser	Laser
Model	IBM proprietary	Kentek K30D	Kyocera LBP27	Hitachi Laserbeam 2000	Copal SLB-6000
Rated speed (pages per minute)	10	30	12	20	12
Single-cartridge toner/developer/drum	●	○	○	○	○
Toner capacity (copies)	15,000	13,000	5,000	3,000	5,000
Memory (as tested)	1Mb	22Mb	3Mb	17Mb	48Mb
Maximum resolution (horizontal by vertical dots per inch)	300 × 300	300 × 300	300 × 300	1,200 × 800	1,200 × 600
Controller with RISC processor	○	●	○	●	●
INTERFACES					
Parallel	●	●	●	○	●
Serial	●	●	●	○	●
AppleTalk	○	○	○	○	●
SCSI port	○	○	○	○	● (for hard disk storage only)
Ethernet	○	Optional	○	○	●
Token-Ring	○	○	○	○	○
Automatic interface switching	○	○	●	N/A	●
Simultaneously active ports	○	○	○	N/A	●
Paper support	INA	Cut-sheet	INA	INA	Cut-sheet
PAPER HANDLING					
Input-cassette capacity (sheets)	700	550, 250	250	250	250, 250
Letter-size paper (8.5 × 11 inches)	●	INA	●	●	●
Legal-size paper (8.5 × 14 inches)	●	INA	●	●	●
B-size paper (11 × 17 inches)	○	○	●	●	●
Output-cassette capacity (sheets)	250	550	150	250	250
Duplexing	○	●	○	○	○
Rated maximum paper weight (pounds)	175	24	24	24	34
FONTS AND FEATURES					
HP PCL support	PCL 4	PCL 5	PCL 4	PCL 4	PCL 4
Supports scalable fonts	○	INA	○	○	INA
Accepts HP-compatible font cartridges	○	○	○	○	○
PostScript language support	None	PhoenixPage PDL (optional)	None	Microsoft TrueImage	NewGen PostScript PDL
Supports Type 1 fonts	○	●	○	●	●
Supports resolution enhancement	INA	○	INA	INA	●
Supports automatic emulation switching	○	○	○	●	●
Accepts proprietary font cards	●	INA	○	○	INA
Printer-specific Microsoft Windows 3.1 driver	INA	○	INA	INA	● (included)

●—Yes ○—No N/A—Not applicable INA—Information not available

Shared Laser Printers

	OTC LaserMatrix 1000 Model 5	Printronix L1016 Continuous Form Laser Printer	QMS-PS 1700	Sharp JX-9700	Synergystex CF1000 Continuous Form Laser Printer
Price (tested configuration)	$$$$	$$$$$	$$$$$	$$$	$$$$
PHYSICAL CHARACTERISTICS					
Dimensions (HWD, in inches)	INA	INA	INA	$11 \times 16 \times 17$	INA
Weight (pounds)	INA	INA	INA	52	INA
ENGINE					
Engine type	Laser	Laser	Laser	Laser	Laser
Model	Asahi Optical FL1	Pentax PL-F0301	Canon NX	Sharp JX-97	Pentax PL-F0301
Rated speed (pages per minute)	16	16	17	16	16
Single-cartridge toner/developer/drum	○	○	●	○	○
Toner capacity (copies)	4,000	8,000	8,000	5,000	4,000
Memory (as tested)	9Mb	24Mb	32Mb	1Mb	8Mb
Maximum resolution (horizontal by vertical dots per inch)	300×300	300×300	600×600	300×300	300×300
Controller with RISC processor	●	○	●	○	○
INTERFACES					
Parallel	●	●	●	●	●
Serial	●	●	●	●	●
AppleTalk	○	○	●	○	○
SCSI port	○	○	● (for hard disk storage only)	○	○
Ethernet	○	○	Optional	○	○
Token-Ring	○	○	Optional	○	○
Automatic interface switching	●	○	●	○	○
Simultaneously active ports	●	○	●	○	○
Paper support	Continuous-form	Continuous-form	Cut-sheet	INA	Continuous-form
PAPER HANDLING					
Input-cassette capacity (sheets)	N/A	N/A	500, 500	250	N/A
Letter-size paper (8.5 × 11 inches)	INA	INA	INA	●	INA
Legal-size paper (8.5 × 14 inches)	INA	INA	INA	●	INA
B-size paper (11 × 17 inches)	○	○	○	○	○
Output-cassette capacity (sheets)	N/A	N/A	500 (facedown), 100 (faceup)	250	N/A
Duplexing	○	○	Optional	○	○
Rated maximum paper weight (pounds)	40	24	36	34	24
FONTS AND FEATURES					
HP PCL support	PCL 5	None	PCL 4	PCL 4	PCL 4
Supports scalable fonts	INA	INA	INA	○	INA
Accepts HP-compatible font cartridges	●	N/A	○	○	●
PostScript language support	None	PhoenixPage PDL (optional)	Adobe PostScript Level 1	None	None
Supports Type 1 fonts	N/A	●	●	○	N/A
Supports resolution enhancement	○	○	○	INA	○
Supports automatic emulation switching	○	○	●	○	○
Accepts proprietary font cards	INA	INA	INA	●	INA
Printer-specific Microsoft Windows 3.1 driver	○	○	● (included)	INA	○

●—Yes ○—No N/A—Not applicable INA—Information not available

Table Continues →

Shared Laser Printers

	TI microLaser XL PS35	TI microLaser XL Turbo	Toshiba PageLaser GX400
Price (tested configuration)	$$$	$$$	$$$$
PHYSICAL CHARACTERISTICS			
Dimensions (HWD, in inches)	11 × 16 × 17	11 × 17 × 16	INA
Weight (pounds)	55	45	INA
ENGINE			
Engine type	Laser	Laser	Laser
Model	Sharp JX-97	Sharp JX-9700	Toshiba G750
Rated speed (pages per minute)	16	16	17
Single-cartridge toner/developer/drum	○	○	●
Toner capacity (copies)	6,000	6,000	13,000
Memory (as tested)	1.5Mb	10.5Mb	9Mb
Maximum resolution (horizontal by vertical dots per inch)	300 × 300	300 × 300	300 × 300
Controller with RISC processor	○	●	○
INTERFACES			
Parallel	●	●	●
Serial	○	Optional	●
AppleTalk	○	Optional	Optional
SCSI port	○	Optional (for hard disk storage only)	○
Ethernet	○	Optional	Optional
Token-Ring	○	○	Optional
Automatic interface switching	○	●	○
Simultaneously active ports	○	●	○
Paper support	INA	Cut-sheet	Cut-sheet
PAPER HANDLING			
Input-cassette capacity (sheets)	250	250	250, 250
Letter-size paper (8.5 × 11 inches)	●	●	INA
Legal-size paper (8.5 × 14 inches)	●	●	INA
B-size paper (11 × 17 inches)	○	○	○
Output-cassette capacity (sheets)	250	250	350 (facedown), 100 (faceup)
Duplexing	○	○	Optional
Rated maximum paper weight (pounds)	24	34	36
FONTS AND FEATURES			
HP PCL support	PCL 4	PCL 4	PCL 5
Supports scalable fonts	○	INA	INA
Accepts HP-compatible font cartridges	○	○	●
PostScript language support	Adobe Level 1	Adobe PostScript Level 2	Toshiba PDL (optional)
Supports Type 1 fonts	●	●	●
Supports resolution enhancement	INA	○	●
Supports automatic emulation switching	○	●	●
Accepts proprietary font cards	●	INA	INA
Printer-specific Microsoft Windows 3.1 driver	INA	● (included)	● (included)

●—Yes ○—No N/A—Not applicable INA—Information not available

(Products listed in alphabetical order by company name)	Brother HT-500PS	CalComp ColorMaster Plus 6613PS	Mitsubishi DiamondColor Print 300PS	Mitsubishi CHC-S446i ColorStream/DS	NEC Colormate PS Model 40
Price (tested configuration)	$$$$	$$$$$	$$$$$	$$$$$	$$$$$
PHYSICAL CHARACTERISTICS					
Dimensions (HWD, in inches)	11 × 17 × 17	INA	INA	INA	17 × 16 × 18
Weight (pounds)	65	INA	INA	INA	55
ENGINE					
Engine type	Thermal wax transfer	Thermal wax transfer	Dye sublimation	Dye sublimation	Thermal wax transfer
Model	Mitsubishi G370	CalComp 6613	Mitsubishi S3600-30U	Shinko CHC-S446i	NEC Colormate
Memory (tested configuration)	21Mb	34Mb	32Mb (printer), 38Mb (controller)	38Mb	4Mb
Maximum resolution (horizontal by vertical dots per inch)	300 × 300	300 × 300	300 × 300	300 × 300	300 × 300
Controller	Brother HT-500PS	CalComp 6613	Quintar Q-Script 2000	Mitsubishi i-PCB	INA
Controller with RISC processor	None	16-MHz i960KB	20-MHz AMD 29000	25-MHz AMD 29050	None
INTERFACES					
Parallel	●	●	●	●	●
Serial	●	●	●	●	●
AppleTalk	●	●	●	●	●
SCSI port	● (for hard disk)	● (for hard disk)	○	●	●
Automatic interface switching	●	●	●	●	○
Simultaneously active ports	○	●	○	●	○
PAPER HANDLING					
Accepts plain paper	○	○	○	○	○
Paper capacity (sheets)	INA	INA	INA	INA	100
Letter-size paper (8.5 × 11 inches)	●	●	●	●	●
Size of printable area (inches)	8.1 × 9	8.1 × 10.6	8.1 × 9	8.2 × 9.3	8.1 × 9
Legal-size paper (8.5 × 14 inches)	●	●	●	●	○
Size of printable area (inches)	8.1 × 12	8.1 × 10.6	8.1 × 11	8.5 × 12.3 (on super A–size paper)	N/A
B-size paper (11 × 17 inches)	○	●	○	○	○
Size of printable area (inches)	N/A	10.6 × 16.6	N/A	N/A	N/A
Duplexing	○	●	○	○	○
Rated maximum paper weight (pounds)	INA	INA	INA	INA	24
FONTS AND FEATURES					
PostScript language support	INA	INA	INA	INA	Adobe
Supports Type 1 fonts	●	●	●	●	●
Printer-specific Microsoft Windows 3.1 driver	● (on request)	● (included)	● (included)	● (included)	INA
Automatic emulation switching	●	●	○	●	INA
Pantone certified	○	●	○	○	INA
Color separations	●	●	○	●	INA
CONTROLS					
Control panels	●	●	● (on printer and controller)	●	INA
LCD	●	●	● (on printer and controller)	●	INA
Number of characters	32	32	64 (on printer), 16 (on controller)	16	INA
Control panel buttons:					
Color separation	●	●	○	○	INA
Paper size	●	○	○	○	INA
Image size	○	●	○	○	INA
Ribbon type	○	●	○	○	INA

●—Yes ○—No N/A—Not applicable INA—Information not available

Table Continues →

Color PostScript Printers

	Océ Graphics G5241-PS	QMS ColorScript 100 Model 10p	QMS ColorScript 100 Model 30si	Seiko ColorPoint PSX Model 4	Seiko ColorPoint PSX Model 14
Price (tested configuration)	$$$$$	$$$$$	$$$$$	$$$$$	$$$$$
PHYSICAL CHARACTERISTICS					
Dimensions (HWD, in inches)	10 × 16 × 24	12 × 17 × 22	INA	8 × 14 × 25	8 × 18 × 31
Weight (pounds)	42	65	INA	41	47
ENGINE					
Engine type	Thermal wax transfer	Thermal wax transfer	Thermal wax transfer	Thermal wax transfer	Thermal wax transfer
Model	Shinko 445	Mitsubishi G370	Mitsubishi G650	Seiko CH5504-DX10	Seiko CH5514-RX18
Memory (tested configuration)	8Mb	4Mb	12Mb (included)	10Mb	18Mb
Maximum resolution (horizontal by vertical dots per inch)	300 × 300	300 × 300	300 × 300	300 × 300	300 × 300
Controller	INA	INA	QMS 30si	INA	INA
Controller with RISC processor	None	None	None	Intel 80960	intel 80960
INTERFACES					
Parallel	●	●	●	●	●
Serial	●	●	●	●	●
AppleTalk	●	●	●	●	●
SCSI port	●	●	● (for hard disk)	○	○
Automatic interface switching	○	○	○	●	●
Simultaneously active ports	○	○	○	●	●
PAPER HANDLING					
Accepts plain paper	○	○	○	○	○
Paper capacity (sheets)	100	100	INA	145	80
Letter-size paper (8.5 × 11 inches)	●	●	●	●	●
Size of printable area (inches)	8.2 × 9.3	8.1 × 9	8.1 × 8.9	8.2 × 10.7	8.2 × 10.7
Legal-size paper (8.5 × 14 inches)	○	○	○	○	○
Size of printable area (inches)	N/A	N/A	N/A	N/A	N/A
B-size paper (11 × 17 inches)	○	○	●	○	●
Size of printable area (inches)	N/A	N/A	10.6 × 14.9	N/A	10.8 × 16
Duplexing	○	○	○	○	○
Rated maximum paper weight (pounds)	24	INA	INA	22	22
FONTS AND FEATURES					
PostScript language support	Adobe	Adobe	INA	PhoenixPage	PhoenixPage
Supports Type 1 fonts	●	●	●	●	●
Printer-specific Microsoft Windows 3.1 driver	INA	INA	● (via BBS and in Windows 3.1)	INA	INA
Automatic emulation switching	INA	INA	● (via software)	INA	INA
Pantone certified	INA	INA	●	INA	INA
Color separations	INA	INA	●	INA	INA
CONTROLS					
Control panels	INA	INA	●	INA	INA
LCD	INA	INA	○	INA	INA
Number of characters	INA	INA	N/A	INA	INA
Control panel buttons:					
Color separation	INA	INA	○	INA	INA
Paper size	INA	INA	○	INA	INA
Image size	INA	INA	●	INA	INA
Ribbon type	INA	INA	○	INA	INA

●—Yes　○—No　N/A—Not applicable　INA—Information not available

Color PostScript Printers

	Tektronix Phaser II PXe	Tektronix Phaser II PXi	Tektronix Phaser IIsd	Tektronix Phaser III PXi
Price (tested configuration)	$$$$	$$$$$	$$$$$	$$$$$
PHYSICAL CHARACTERISTICS				
Dimensions (HWD, in inches)	INA	15 × 17 × 27	INA	14 × 25 × 27
Weight (pounds)	INA	73	INA	90
ENGINE				
Engine type	Thermal wax transfer	Thermal wax transfer	Dye sublimation	Solid ink
Model	Sharp/Tek 4694	Sharp 4694	Sharp/Tek 4684	Tektronix 4698
Memory (tested configuration)	8Mb	6Mb	64Mb	18Mb
Maximum resolution (horizontal by vertical dots per inch)	300 × 300	300 × 300	300 × 300	300 × 300
Controller	Tektronix 4694PXe	INA	Tektronix 4684SD	Tektronix 4698 PXi
Controller with RISC processor	16-MHz AMD 29000	AMD 29000	24-MHz AMD 29000	24-MHz AMD 29000
INTERFACES				
Parallel	●	●	●	●
Serial	●	●	●	●
AppleTalk	●	●	●	●
SCSI port	○	●	● (for hard disk)	● (for hard disk)
Automatic interface switching	●	●	●	●
Simultaneously active ports	●	●	●	●
PAPER HANDLING				
Accepts plain paper	○	○	○	●
Paper capacity (sheets)	INA	100	INA	200
Letter-size paper (8.5 × 11 inches)	●	●	●	●
Size of printable area (inches)	8.1 × 8.8	8.1 × 8.8	8.1 × 8.8	8.1 × 10.5
Legal-size paper (8.5 × 14 inches)	●	●	●	●
Size of printable area (inches)	8.1 × 10.8	8.1 × 11.6	8.1 × 10.8	8.1 × 13.5
B-size paper (11 × 17 inches)	○	○	○	●
Size of printable area (inches)	N/A	N/A	N/A	10.6 × 16.5
Duplexing	○	○	○	○
Rated maximum paper weight (pounds)	INA	20	INA	INA
FONTS AND FEATURES				
PostScript language support	INA	Adobe Level 2	INA	INA
Supports Type 1 fonts	●	●	●	●
Printer-specific Microsoft Windows 3.1 driver	● (included and in Windows 3.1)	INA	● (included and in Windows 3.1)	● (in Windows 3.1)
Automatic emulation switching	● (via software)	INA	○	● (via software)
Pantone certified	●	INA	●	●
Color separations	○	INA	○	○
CONTROLS				
Control panels	○	INA	○	●
LCD	N/A	INA	N/A	●
Number of characters	N/A	INA	N/A	48
Control panel buttons:				
Color separation	N/A	INA	N/A	○
Paper size	N/A	INA	N/A	○
Image size	N/A	INA	N/A	○
Ribbon type	N/A	INA	N/A	○

●—Yes   ○—No   N/A—Not applicable   INA—Information not available

End ■

D.6 Portable Printers

(Products listed in alphabetical order by company name)	Brother HJ-100i Ink Jet Printer	Canon BJ-10ex Bubble Jet Printer	Citizen PN48 Notebook Printer	DECjet 1000	Eastman Kodak Diconix 180si Printer
List price	$	$	$	$	$
Battery option	$50	$50	$95	None	Third-party batteries
Cut-sheet feeder	$90	$90	None	$80	None
PHYSICAL CHARACTERISTICS					
Technology	Ink jet	Ink jet	Thermal fusion	Ink jet	Ink jet
Number of pins or jets	64	64	48	50	12
Carriage size	Narrow	Narrow	Narrow	Narrow	Narrow
Maximum resolution (dpi)	360 × 360	360 × 360	360 × 360	300 × 300	192 × 192
Installed memory	37K	37K	4K	8K	2K
Parallel/serial interface	●/○	●/○	●/○	●/○	●/$20
Microsoft Windows driver	○	○	● (via BBS)	● (in Windows 3.1)	● (included)
PAPER HANDLING					
Auto-load feature	○	○	●	○	○
Paper feeds:					
Pressure	●	●	●	●	●
Tractor	○	○	○	○	●
Internal	N/A	N/A	N/A	N/A	●
External	N/A	N/A	N/A	N/A	○
Push	N/A	N/A	N/A	N/A	○
Pull	N/A	N/A	N/A	N/A	●
Paper paths	Rear U path	Rear U path	Bottom vertical, rear L path	Front L path	Rear L path
Rated maximum paper weight (pounds)	28	28	28	24	24
Rated maximum paper width (inches)	8	8	10	9	9
Media supported:					
Card stock	●	●	●	●	○
Transparencies	○	○	●	●	●
Envelopes	●	●	●	●	○
Landscape printing	○	○	○	●	○
TYPEFACES					
Courier	●	●	●	●	○
Gothic	○	○	○	●	●
Prestige Elite	●	●	○	●	●
Sans serif	●	●	●	○	●
Times Roman	●	●	●	○	○
Other	None	None	None	Times Nordic	None
CONTROL-PANEL BUTTONS					
Typeface	●	●	●	●	●
Emulations	○	○	○	○	●
Print mode	●	●	N/A	●	●

●—Yes   ○—No   N/A—Not applicable   INA—Information not available

Portable Printers

	Eastman Kodak Diconix 701 Printer	Toshiba ExpressWriter 201
List price	$	$
Battery option	Third-party battery pack	$125
Cut-sheet feeder	Built-in	None
PHYSICAL CHARACTERISTICS		
Technology	Ink jet	Thermal fusion
Number of pins or jets	50	24
Carriage size	Narrow	Narrow
Maximum resolution (dpi)	300 × 300	180 × 180
Installed memory	23K	500 bytes
Parallel/serial interface	●/○	●/○
Microsoft Windows driver	● (included)	○
PAPER HANDLING		
Auto-load feature	●	○
Paper feeds:		
Pressure	●	●
Tractor	○	○
Internal	N/A	N/A
External	N/A	N/A
Push	N/A	N/A
Pull	N/A	N/A
Paper paths	Top U path	Bottom vertical, rear L path
Rated maximum paper weight (pounds)	24	25
Rated maximum paper width (inches)	8.5	10
Media supported:		
Card stock	○	○
Transparencies	●	○
Envelopes	○	○
Landscape printing	●	○
TYPEFACES		
Courier	●	●
Gothic	●	○
Prestige Elite	○	●
Sans serif	●	○
Times Roman	○	○
Other	None	None
CONTROL-PANEL BUTTONS		
Typeface	●	○
Emulations	●	○
Print mode	●	N/A

●—Yes ○—No N/A—Not applicable INA—Information not available

End ■

TAPE BACKUP

APPENDIX

Tape Backup

(Products listed in alphabetical order by company name)	Alloy Retriever/250ce	Colorado Memory Systems Jumbo 250 External	COREtape Light	Everex Excel 120F	Irwin AccuTrak Plus A250E
Price	$	$	$	$	$
Device type	External	External	External	External	External
Dimensions (HWD, in inches)	2 × 6 × 9.5	2.5 × 4.5 × 9	3 × 4.5 × 7	2.5 × 6 × 10.5	2.5 × 5 × 7.5
STANDARD COMPONENTS					
Number of DC-2000 tape cartridges included	1	None	1	1	1
Manufacturer	3M	N/A	3M	3M	3M
Standard-configuration controller	●	○	○	○	●
Accelerated	○	N/A	N/A	N/A	●
ISA 8-bit	●	N/A	N/A	N/A	●
OPTIONS					
Accelerated controller	○	●	○	○	●
Interface type	N/A	ISA 16-bit	N/A	N/A	ISA 8-bit
Other available controllers or interfaces	EISA, MCA	None	MCA	EISA, MCA	MCA
PHYSICAL CHARACTERISTICS					
Media speed (inches per second):					
Standard configuration	34	34	73	50	86
With optional accelerated controller	N/A	68	N/A	N/A	86
Power source	Host	Host	Host	Direct AC plug	Host
SOFTWARE CHARACTERISTICS					
Software (tested configuration)	ResQ120, Version 2.0	Jumbo Tape, Version 2.50	COREfast, Version 2.0	FTape, Version 3.0	EzTape, Version 2.22
Background operation	○	○	●	○	● (Microsoft Windows version)
Compatible third-party software	Central Point Backup	Central Point Backup, Norton Backup	Central Point Backup, PC Tools, Sytos	None	Central Point Backup, PC Tools
BACKUP AND RESTORE CHARACTERISTICS					
Backup and restore types permitted:					
Image	○	○	●	●	○
Modified image	○	●	○	○	○
File-by-file	●	●	●	●	●
Backup and restore range types:					
Entire disk	●	●	○	●	●
Multiple disks or partitions	●	●	○	●	●
Copies hidden and system files during backups:					
Image	N/A	N/A	●	●	N/A
File-by-file	User option	●	User option	User option	User option
NETWORK CHARACTERISTICS					
Networks supported	NetWare, PC LAN, 3+Open	NetWare, 3+Open	NetWare, 3+Open	NetWare	Microsoft LAN Manager, NetWare, PC LAN, 3+Open
Backup system resides on workstation/server	●/●	●/○	●/○	●/○	●/○
Workstation automatically logs off network after unattended backup	○	○	●	●	○
Tape system supports multiple volumes on single tape	●	●	●	●	●
INTERNAL TAPE DRIVES					
Optional internal tape drive	●	●	●	●	●
Form factor (in inches)	3.5	5.25	3.5	5.25, 3.5	5.25

●—Yes ○— No N/A—Not applicable INA—Information not available

Table Continues →

Tape Backup

	Maynard ArchiveXL 5580e Tape Backup	Micro Solutions Backpack Tape Drive	Mountain FileSafe External 8000Plus	Summit Express SE250 Tape Backup	Tallgrass FS250e
Price	$	$	$	$	$
Device type	External	External	External	Internal	External
Dimensions (HWD, in inches)	2.5 × 5 × 9	2.5 × 4 × 8	2.3 × 5 × 11	2 × 4 × 6.5	4.5 × 4 × 8.5
STANDARD COMPONENTS					
Number of DC-2000 tape cartridges included	1	None	None	None	1
Manufacturer	3M	N/A	N/A	N/A	3M
Standard-configuration controller	○	○	○	○	○
Accelerated	N/A	N/A	N/A	N/A	N/A
ISA 8-bit	N/A	N/A	N/A	N/A	N/A
OPTIONS					
Accelerated controller	○	○	●	●	○
Interface type	N/A	N/A	ISA 8-bit	ISA 8-bit	N/A
Other available controllers or interfaces	MCA	EISA, MCA	ISA 16-bit, MCA	ISA 16-bit, MCA	EISA, MCA
PHYSICAL CHARACTERISTICS					
Media speed (inches per second):					
Standard configuration	50	25	68	34	34
With optional accelerated controller	N/A	N/A	68	68	N/A
Power source	Host	External transformer	Direct AC plug	Host	Direct AC plug
SOFTWARE CHARACTERISTICS					
Software (tested configuration)	*QICstream*, Version 2.0XL	*BPBackup*, Version 1.30.03	*FileSafe*, Version 2.35	*Central Point Backup*, Version 7.1	*FileSECURE*, Version 1.52
Background operation	○	○	○	●	○
Compatible third-party software	*Central Point Backup, PC Tools*	None	*Central Point Backup, PC Tools*	None	*Central Point Backup*
BACKUP AND RESTORE CHARACTERISTICS					
Backup and restore types permitted:					
Image	○	○	●	○	○
Modified image	○	○	○	○	●
File-by-file	●	●	●	●	●
Backup and restore range types:					
Entire disk	●	○	●	●	●
Multiple disks or partitions	○	○	●	●	●
Copies hidden and system files during backups:					
Image	N/A	N/A	●	N/A	N/A
File-by-file	User option	User option	●	User option	●
NETWORK CHARACTERISTICS					
Networks supported	*NetWare, 3+Open*	*NetWare, 3+Open*	*LANtastic, NetWare*	*NetWare*	Any NetBIOS network, *NetWare*
Backup system resides on workstation/server	●/○	●/○	●/○	●/○	●/○
Workstation automatically logs off network after unattended backup	○	○	○	○	●
Tape system supports multiple volumes on single tape	●	●	●	●	●
INTERNAL TAPE DRIVES					
Optional internal tape drive	●	○	●	*	●
Form factor (in inches)	5.25, 3.5	N/A	5.25	3.5	3.5

*This product is an internal tape drive.
●—Yes ○—No N/A—Not applicable INA—Information not available

Tape Backup

	Tallgrass FS300e	Tecmar MiniVault 250	Wangtek E3080PK
Price	$	$	$
Device type	External	External	External
Dimensions (HWD, in inches)	4.5 × 4 × 8.5	3.5 × 5.5 × 8	3.5 × 5.5 × 8
STANDARD COMPONENTS			
Number of DC-2000 tape cartridges included	1	1	1
Manufacturer	3M	3M	3M
Standard-configuration controller	●	○	○
Accelerated	●	N/A	N/A
ISA 8-bit	●	N/A	N/A
OPTIONS			
Accelerated controller	●	●	●
Interface type	ISA 8-bit	ISA 8-bit	ISA 8-bit
Other available controllers or interfaces	EISA, MCA	MCA	EISA
PHYSICAL CHARACTERISTICS			
Media speed (inches per second):			
Standard configuration	68	34	34
With optional accelerated controller	N/A	68	68
Power source	Direct AC plug	Host	Host
SOFTWARE CHARACTERISTICS			
Software (tested configuration)	*FileSECURE*, Version 1.52	*MiniVault*, Version 1.3	*Central Point Backup*, Version 7.1
Background operation	○	○	●
Compatible third-party software	*Central Point Backup*	*Central Point Backup*	*Sytos*
BACKUP AND RESTORE CHARACTERISTICS			
Backup and restore types permitted:			
Image	○	●	○
Modified image	○	●	○
File-by-file	●	●	●
Backup and restore range types:			
Entire disk	●	○	●
Multiple disks or partitions	●	○	●
Copies hidden and system files during backups:			
Image	N/A	●	N/A
File-by-file	●	User option	User option
NETWORK CHARACTERISTICS			
Networks supported	Any NetBIOS network, *NetWare*	*LANtastic, NetWare, PC-Net, 3+Open*	*NetWare*
Backup system resides on workstation/server	●/○	●/○	●/○
Workstation automatically logs off network after unattended backup	●	●	○
Tape system supports multiple volumes on single tape	●	●	●
INTERNAL TAPE DRIVES			
Optional internal tape drive	●	●	●
Form factor (in inches)	3.5	5.25	5.25

●—Yes ○—No N/A—Not applicable INA—Information not available   **End ■**

CD-ROM DRIVES

APPENDIX

F

CD-ROM Drives

(Products listed in alphabetical order by company name)	CD Porta-Drive Model T3201	CD Porta-Drive Model T3301	Chinon CDC-435	Chinon CDX-431	Genesis GenSTAR 2000
Price	$	$	$	$	$
PHYSICAL CHARACTERISTICS					
Mechanism manufacturer	Toshiba	Toshiba	Chinon	Chinon	GoldStar
External/internal	●/●	●/●	●/●	●/○	●/○
External case characteristics:					
Dimensions (HWD, in inches)	1.7 × 5.9 × 8.2	2 × 6 × 9.6	2.4 × 6.1 × 10	2.2 × 6 × 10	3 × 13.5 × 11
Weight (pounds)	4.2	3	5.5	5.5	38.2
Length of supplied cables	6 ft.	2 ft.	5 ft.	4 ft. 10 in.	3 ft. 2 in.
Switchable voltage (110/220)	●	●	○	○	○
Power/busy indicators	○/●	●/●	●/●	●/●	●/●
Caddy manufacturer	Sony	CD Technology	Sony	Sony	Sony
Operates vertically	●	●	●	●	○
Audio support:					
Headphone jack	●	●	●	●	●
RCA jacks	●	●	●	●	●
Volume knob	●	●	●	●	●
PERFORMANCE RATINGS					
Buffer size	64K	64K	64K	32K	32K
Average access time	325 ms.	325 ms.	350 ms.	350 ms.	450 ms.
Data transfer rate:					
Average or sustained	150 KBps	150 KBps	150 KBps	150 KBps	150 KBps
Burst	1,500 KBps	1,500 KBps	2,200 KBps	2,200 KBps	600 KBps
Average latency:					
Inner	60 ms.	60 ms.	70 ms.	70 ms.	66 ms.
Outer	120 ms.	150 ms.	150 ms.	150 ms.	150 ms.
Mean time between failures (hours)	50,000	50,000	25,000	25,000	20,000
CONTROLLER CHARACTERISTICS					
Controller manufacturer	Trantor	Future Domain	Chinon	Chinon	GoldStar
Interface type	SCSI	SCSI II	SCSI	SCSI	Proprietary
Interface board (ISA):					
IRQs supported	3, 5, 7	3, 5	None	None	3, 5, 7
Number of selectable addresses	4	6	16	16	256
Maximum units in daisy chain	7	7	7	7	8
Alternate interfaces:					
Micro Channel	●	●	●	○	○
Macintosh	●	●	●	●	○
SOFTWARE SUPPORT					
Device driver supplier	Trantor	Future Domain	Chinon	Chinon	GoldStar
Version tested	1.2	2.20	3.0	2.2	2.20
RAM used	16K	INA	INA	31K	33K
OS/2 support	●	●	○	○	○
Includes MS/DOS CD-ROM extensions	●	2.2	2.21	●	●
Includes *Multimedia Extensions for Windows*	○	○	○	○	○
Installation software supplied	●	INA	INA	●	●
CD-ROM disks bundled with drive	1	INA	INA	1	None

●—Yes ○—No N/A—Not applicable INA—Information not available

Table Continues →

CD-ROM Drives

	Hitachi CDR-1750S	Hitachi CDR-3700	Hitachi CDR-3750	IBM PS/2 External CD-ROM Drive	Liberty 115 Series CD-ROM
Price	$	$	$	$	$
PHYSICAL CHARACTERISTICS					
Mechanism manufacturer	Hitachi	Hitachi	Hitachi	IBM	Sony
External/internal	●/●	○/●	○/●	●/●	●/○
External case characteristics:					
Dimensions (HWD, in inches)	2.9 × 9 × 12.8	N/A	N/A	1.6 × 5.8 × 8	1.9 × 6.8 × 9.6
Weight (pounds)	9.3	N/A	N/A	3.5	4.5
Length of supplied cables	4 ft. 2 in.	N/A	N/A	N/A	2 ft.
Switchable voltage (110/220)	○	N/A	N/A	●	●
Power/busy indicators	●/●	●/●	●/●	●/●	●/●
Caddy manufacturer	Sony	INA	INA	IBM	Sony
Operates vertically	○	●	●	●	●
Audio support:					
Headphone jack	●	●	●	●	●
RCA jacks	●	○	○	●	●
Volume knob	●	●	●	●	●
PERFORMANCE RATINGS					
Buffer size	64K	64K	64K	64K	64K
Average access time	320 ms.	300 ms.	300 ms.	380 ms.	380 ms.
Data transfer rate:					
Average or sustained	153.6 KBps	150 KBps	150 KBps	150 KBps	150 KBps
Burst	1,300 KBps	1,270 KBps	1,270 KBps	1,500 KBps	1,500 KBps
Average latency:					
Inner	55 ms.	56 ms.	56 ms.	56.6 ms.	60 ms.
Outer	150 ms.	150 ms.	150 ms.	150 ms.	155 ms.
Mean time between failures (hours)	20,000	50,000	50,000	55,000	25,000
CONTROLLER CHARACTERISTICS					
Controller manufacturer	Future Domain	Hitachi	Future Domain	IBM	Trantor
Interface type	SCSI	Proprietary	SCSI II	SCSI	SCSI, parallel-to-SCSI
Interface board (ISA):					
IRQs supported	3, 5	None	3, 5	None	3, 5, 7
Number of selectable addresses	4	8	6	None	4
Maximum units in daisy chain	8	8	8	7	7
Alternate interfaces:					
Micro Channel	●	○	○	●	●
Macintosh	●	○	○	○	●
SOFTWARE SUPPORT					
Device driver supplier	Future Domain	Hitachi	Future Domain	IBM	Trantor
Version tested	2.13	2.2	2.21	1.01	1.46F
RAM used	21K	INA	INA	10K	INA
OS/2 support	○	○	○	●	●
Includes MS/DOS CD-ROM extensions	●	2.21	2.21	○	2.21
Includes *Multimedia Extensions for Windows*	○	○	○	○	●
Installation software supplied	●	INA	INA	●	INA
CD-ROM disks bundled with drive	None	INA	INA	None	INA

●—Yes ○—No N/A—Not applicable INA—Information not available

CD-ROM Drives

	LMS CM225	LMSI CM 231	MacProducts Magic CDR74	MacProducts Magic 3301 Toshiba	NEC InterSect CDR-37
Price	$	$	$	$	$
PHYSICAL CHARACTERISTICS					
Mechanism manufacturer	LMS CM	Philips/LMSI	NEC	Toshiba	NEC
External/internal	●/●	●/●	●/●	●/●	●/○
External case characteristics:					
Dimensions (HWD, in inches)	2.5 × 9.8 × 10.5	3.4 × 12.5 × 11.3	3 × 9 × 10	2.8 × 8.8 × 9.4	1.7 × 5.6 × 8.7
Weight (pounds)	6.5	9	7.7	8	2.2
Length of supplied cables	3 ft.	3 ft. 2 in.	3 ft.	3 ft.	3 ft.
Switchable voltage (110/220)	●	●	●	●	○
Power/busy indicators	●/●	●/●	●/●	●/●	●/●
Caddy manufacturer	N/A	Philips	NEC	Toshiba	N/A
Operates vertically	○	○	●	●	○
Audio support:					
Headphone jack	●	●	●	●	●
RCA jacks	●	●	●	●	○
Volume knob	●	●	●	●	●
PERFORMANCE RATINGS					
Buffer size	32K	64K	64K	64K	64K
Average access time	375 ms.	400 ms.	280 ms.	325 ms.	450 ms.
Data transfer rate:					
Average or sustained	150 KBps	153.6 KBps	300 KBps	150 KBps	150 KBps
Burst	2,000 KBps	1,000 KBps	1,500 KBps	1,500 KBps	1,500 KBps
Average latency:					
Inner	60 ms.	60 ms.	Less than 100 ms.	60 ms.	Less than 100 ms.
Outer	155 ms.	155 ms.	Less than 100 ms.	150 ms.	Less than 100 ms.
Mean time between failures (hours)	15,000	35,000	25,000	30,000	10,000
CONTROLLER CHARACTERISTICS					
Controller manufacturer	LMS	Future Domain	Trantor	Trantor	Trantor
Interface type	Proprietary	SCSI	SCSI II	SCSI II	SCSI
Interface board (ISA):					
IRQs supported	3–6	3, 5	3	3	0–2
Number of selectable addresses	4	3	4	4	4
Maximum units in daisy chain	N/A	7	7	7	7
Alternate interfaces:					
Micro Channel	●	●	●	●	●
Macintosh	○	●	●	●	●
SOFTWARE SUPPORT					
Device driver supplier	LMS	LMSI	Trantor	Trantor	Trantor
Version tested	1.2	2.2	4.51B	4.51B	T128
RAM used	INA	2K	INA	INA	INA
OS/2 support	○	○	●	●	○
Includes MS/DOS CD-ROM extensions	2.21	●	2.21	2.21	2.21
Includes *Multimedia Extensions for Windows*	○	○	○	○	○
Installation software supplied	INA	●	INA	INA	INA
CD-ROM disks bundled with drive	INA	None	INA	INA	INA

●—Yes ○—No N/A—Not applicable INA—Information not available

Table Continues →

CD-ROM Drives

	NEC InterSect CDR-73	NEC InterSect CDR-74	Philips CM-205XRS	PLI CD-ROM Drive	Procom Allegro Series Model PXCD650S
Price	$	$	$	$	$
PHYSICAL CHARACTERISTICS					
Mechanism manufacturer	NEC	NEC	LMS	Sony	Sony
External/internal	●/●	●/●	○/●	●/●	●/●
External case characteristics:					
Dimensions (HWD, in inches)	3 × 9 × 9.5	3 × 9 × 10	N/A	2.4 × 9.8 × 9.8	2 × 6 × 12
Weight (pounds)	7.5	7.7	N/A	6.2	5.8
Length of supplied cables	3 ft. 3 in.	3 ft.	N/A	1 ft. 9 in.	3 ft.
Switchable voltage (110/220)	●	●	N/A	●	●
Power/busy indicators	●/●	●/●	●/●	○/●	○/●
Caddy manufacturer	Sony	Sony	N/A	Sony	Sony
Operates vertically	●	●	○	●	●
Audio support:					
Headphone jack	●	●	●	●	●
RCA jacks	●	●	●	●	●
Volume knob	●	●	●	●	●
PERFORMANCE RATINGS					
Buffer size	64K	64K	32K	64K	8K
Average access time	300 ms.	280 ms.	375 ms.	380 ms.	340 ms.
Data transfer rate:					
Average or sustained	150 KBps	300 KBps	150 KBps	150 KBps	150 KBps
Burst	1,500 KBps	1,500 KBps	2,000 KBps	1,500 KBps	600 KBps
Average latency:					
Inner	35 ms.	Less than 100 ms.	60 ms.	60 ms.	55 ms.
Outer	75 ms.	Less than 100 ms.	155 ms.	155 ms.	130 ms.
Mean time between failures (hours)	20,000	30,000	15,000	10,000	25,000
CONTROLLER CHARACTERISTICS					
Controller manufacturer	Trantor/NEC	Trantor	LMS	Future Domain/PLI	Procom
Interface type	SCSI	SCSI	Proprietary	SCSI II	Proprietary
Interface board (ISA):					
IRQs supported	3, 5, 7	0–2	3–6	3, 5, 10–12, 14, 15	None
Number of selectable addresses	4	4	4	4	64
Maximum units in daisy chain	7	7	N/A	6	2
Alternate interfaces:					
Micro Channel	●	●	○	●	●
Macintosh	●	●	○	●	●
SOFTWARE SUPPORT					
Device driver supplier	Trantor	Trantor	LMS	Future Domain	Procom
Version tested	2.20a	T128	1.2	2.20	1.0
RAM used	8K	INA	INA	INA	6K
OS/2 support	○	○	○	○	○
Includes MS/DOS CD-ROM extensions	●	2.21	2.21	2.2	●
Includes *Multimedia Extensions for Windows*	○	○	○	●	○
Installation software supplied	●	INA	INA	INA	●
CD-ROM disks bundled with drive	None	INA	INA	INA	6

●—Yes ○—No N/A—Not applicable INA—Information not available

CD-ROM Drives

	Procom PXCDL	Procom SXCDS-C8	Sony CDU-31A-02	Sony CDU-7205	Sony CDU-7211
Price	$	$	$	$	$
PHYSICAL CHARACTERISTICS					
Mechanism manufacturer	LMS	Sony	Sony	Sony	Sony
External/internal	●/●	●/●	○/●	●/○	●/●
External case characteristics:					
Dimensions (HWD, in inches)	2.1 × 6.2 × 12.5	2.1 × 6.2 × 12.5	N/A	2 × 7 × 13	2 × 7.1 × 13.3
Weight (pounds)	3.4	3.9	N/A	6.4	6.4
Length of supplied cables	3 ft. 1.5 in.	6 ft.	N/A	3 ft. 6 in.	3 ft.
Switchable voltage (110/220)	○	○	N/A	○	●
Power/busy indicators	○/●	○/●	○/●	●/●	○/●
Caddy manufacturer	N/A	Sony	N/A	Sony	Sony
Operates vertically	●	●	○	●	●
Audio support:					
Headphone jack	●	●	●	●	●
RCA jacks	●	●	○	●	●
Volume knob	●	●	●	●	●
PERFORMANCE RATINGS					
Buffer size	32K	64K	64K	8K	64K
Average access time	375 ms.	380 ms.	550 ms.	340 ms.	380 ms.
Data transfer rate:					
Average or sustained	150 KBps	150 KBps	150 KBps	150 KBps	150 KBps
Burst	2,000 KBps	1,500 KBps	2,100 KBps	600 KBps	1,500 KBps
Average latency:					
Inner	60 ms.	60 ms.	55 ms.	55 ms.	55 ms.
Outer	155 ms.	155 ms.	130 ms.	130 ms.	130 ms.
Mean time between failures (hours)	15,000	10,000	25,000	25,000	25,000
CONTROLLER CHARACTERISTICS					
Controller manufacturer	Procom	Procom	Sony	Sony	Future Domain
Interface type	Proprietary	SCSI II	Proprietary	IDE	SCSI II
Interface board (ISA):					
IRQs supported	2–7	2–7	3–6	2–5	2
Number of selectable addresses	4	4	4	19	4
Maximum units in daisy chain	N/A	7	4	4	7
Alternate interfaces:					
Micro Channel	○	●	○	○	●
Macintosh	○	●	○	○	○
SOFTWARE SUPPORT					
Device driver supplier	Procom	Procom	Sony	Sony	Future Domain
Version tested	DK0086 v. 1.01	DK0081 v. 1.00	1.21	2.20	2.13
RAM used	INA	INA	INA	9K	INA
OS/2 support	○	○	○	○	●
Includes MS/DOS CD-ROM extensions	2.21	2.21	2.21	●	2.21
Includes *Multimedia Extensions for Windows*	○	○	○	○	○
Installation software supplied	INA	INA	INA	●	INA
CD-ROM disks bundled with drive	INA	INA	INA	6	INA

●—Yes   ○—No   N/A—Not applicable   INA—Information not available   **Table Continues** →

CD-ROM Drives

	Storage Devices SCD-683	Tandy CDR-1000 CD-ROM Drive	Tandy CDR-1100	Texel DM-5021	Texel DM-5024
Price	$	$	$	$	$
PHYSICAL CHARACTERISTICS					
Mechanism manufacturer	Toshiba	Tandy	LMS	Texel	Texel
External/internal	●/○	○/●	○/●	●/●	●/●
External case characteristics:					
Dimensions (HWD, in inches)	2 × 9 × 11	N/A	N/A	1.7 × 5.8 × 14.8	2.4 × 9.7 × 11.2
Weight (pounds)	6	N/A	N/A	6	6.6
Length of supplied cables	3 ft.	N/A	N/A	3 ft.	3 ft.
Switchable voltage (110/220)	●	N/A	N/A	●	●
Power/busy indicators	●/●	○/●	●/●	○/●	●/●
Caddy manufacturer	Toshiba	N/A	N/A	Sony	INA
Operates vertically	●	○	●	○	●
Audio support:					
Headphone jack	●	●	●	●	●
RCA jacks	○	●	●	○	●
Volume knob	●	●	●	●	●
PERFORMANCE RATINGS					
Buffer size	64K	N/A	32K	64K	64K
Average access time	300 ms.	1,000 ms.	375 ms.	340 ms.	265 ms.
Data transfer rate:					
Average or sustained	150 KBps	150 KBps	150 KBps	150 KBps	300 KBps
Burst	1,500 KBps	1,400 KBps	1,367 KBps	153.6 KBps	1,500 KBps
Average latency:					
Inner	120 ms.	INA	60 ms.	56 ms.	57 ms.
Outer	320 ms.	INA	155 ms.	119 ms.	150 ms.
Mean time between failures (hours)	25,000	10,000	50,000	30,000	30,000
CONTROLLER CHARACTERISTICS					
Controller manufacturer	Storage Devices	Tandy	LMS	Trantor	Trantor
Interface type	Parallel-to-SCSI	Proprietary	Proprietary	SCSI	SCSI II
Interface board (ISA):					
IRQs supported	None	2, 3, 5	3–6	3, 5–7	3, 5, 7
Number of selectable addresses	3	5	4	4	4
Maximum units in daisy chain	7	N/A	N/A	7	7
Alternate interfaces:					
Micro Channel	○	○	○	●	●
Macintosh	○	○	○	●	●
SOFTWARE SUPPORT					
Device driver supplier	Freeport Data	Tandy	LMS	Trantor	Trantor
Version tested	2.5	1.00	1.2	1.30	1.46D
RAM used	INA	64K	INA	10K	INA
OS/2 support	●	○	○	○	●
Includes MS/DOS CD-ROM extensions	2.0	●	2.21	●	2.21
Includes *Multimedia Extensions for Windows*	●	○	●	○	○
Installation software supplied	INA	●	INA	●	INA
CD-ROM disks bundled with drive	INA	None	INA	None	INA

●—Yes ○—No N/A—Not applicable INA—Information not available

CD-ROM Drives

	Todd TCDR-6000	Todd TCDR 7000	Todd TCDR 7050	Toshiba TXM-3301-E1
Price	$	$	$	$
PHYSICAL CHARACTERISTICS				
Mechanism manufacturer	Hitachi	Hitachi	Hitachi	Toshiba
External/internal	●/●	●/●	●/●	●/●
External case characteristics:				
Dimensions (HWD, in inches)	2.2 × 6 × 13.5	2.2 × 6 × 13.5	2.2 × 6 × 13.5	2.7 × 8.7 × 9
Weight (pounds)	7.9	7.9	7.9	4.3
Length of supplied cables	4 ft.	3 ft. 5.7 in.	3 ft.	4 ft.
Switchable voltage (110/220)	○	○	○	●
Power/busy indicators	●/●	●/●	●/●	●/●
Caddy manufacturer	Sony	Ikka	Ikka	Sony
Operates vertically	○	●	●	●
Audio support:				
Headphone jack	●	●	●	●
RCA jacks	○	○	○	●
Volume knob	●	●	●	●
PERFORMANCE RATINGS				
Buffer size	32K	64K	64K	64K
Average access time	340 ms.	300 ms.	300 ms.	325 ms.
Data transfer rate:				
Average or sustained	175.2 KBps	150 KBps	150 KBps	153.7 KBps
Burst	INA	1,270 KBps	1,270 KBps	1,500 KBps
Average latency:				
Inner	50 ms.	56 ms.	56 ms.	60 ms.
Outer	150 ms.	150 ms.	150 ms.	150 ms.
Mean time between failures (hours)	25,000	50,000	50,000	30,000
CONTROLLER CHARACTERISTICS				
Controller manufacturer	Todd	Todd	Trantor	Future Domain
Interface type	Proprietary	Proprietary	SCSI II	SCSI
Interface board (ISA):				
IRQs supported	3 or 5	5, 7	None	3, 5
Number of selectable addresses	64	8	4	4
Maximum units in daisy chain	8	8	7	7
Alternate interfaces:				
Micro Channel	●	●	●	●
Macintosh	●	○	●	●
SOFTWARE SUPPORT				
Device driver supplier	Hitachi	Hitachi	Trantor	Future Domain
Version tested	2.2	4D	1.30B	2.14
RAM used	25.4K	INA	INA	23.8K
OS/2 support	○	●	●	○
Includes MS/DOS CD-ROM extensions	●	2.21	2.21	●
Includes *Multimedia Extensions for Windows*	●	○	○	●
Installation software supplied	●	INA	INA	●
CD-ROM disks bundled with drive	None	INA	INA	1

●—Yes   ○—No   N/A—Not applicable   INA—Information not available   **E n d** ■

INPUT DEVICES

A P P E N D I X

G

G.1 Replacement Keyboards

(Products listed in alphabetical order by company name)	ALPS MDS101	Cherry G80-1000	Cherry G80-3000	Chicony KB-5181	DataDesk Switchboard
Price	$	$	$	$	$
PHYSICAL FEATURES					
Case material	Plastic	Plastic	Plastic	Plastic	Plastic
Cord length (inches)	72	72	72	72	96
Number of angle settings	1	1	1	2	2
Pencil-tray depth (inches)	2	2	N/A	2	N/A
KEY DESIGN					
Key-switch type	Conductive rubber-dome	Mechanical	Mechanical	Mechanical	Mechanical
Operating force required (ounces)	2	2.1	2.1	2	2.5
Key travel distance (mm)	3.5	4	4	4.5	3.5
KEYBOARD DESIGN					
Special keys (beyond the usual 101)	○	○	○	○	●
Exchangeable Ctrl and CapsLock (with extra key caps provided)	○	○	○	○	●
SYSTEM COMPATIBILITIES					
IBM-XT	●	●	●	●	●
IBM AT/Enhanced AT	●	●	●	●	●
IBM PS/2 (Model 50 or later)	●	●	●	●	●
Stated incompatibilities	None	None	None	None	None
PROGRAMMABILITY					
Software-programmable	○	○	○	○	○
Hardware-programmable	○	○	○	○	●
MISCELLANEOUS					
Stated current drain	300 mA	200 mA	200 mA	100 mA	150 mA
Optional Dvorak keyboard models	○	○	○	○	○
Optional keyboard connectors	Mini-DIN adapter	Mini-DIN adapter	Mini-DIN adapter	Mini-DIN adapter	None
PC manufacturers that bundle this keyboard	INA	INA	INA	Amkly, AST, Insight	INA

●—Yes   ○—No   N/A—Not applicable   INA—Information not available   **Table Continues** →

Replacement Keyboards

	DataDesk Turbo-101	Honeywell 101 WN	IBM Enhanced 101 Key Keyboard	Key Tronic MB101 PLUS	Maxi Switch MaxiPRO
Price	$	$	$	$	$
PHYSICAL FEATURES					
Case material	Plastic	Plastic	Plastic	Plastic	Plastic
Cord length (inches)	96	84	72	72	72
Number of angle settings	1	2	1	1	1
Pencil-tray depth (inches)	N/A	N/A	1.7	1.6	1
KEY DESIGN					
Key-switch type	Mechanical	Membrane	Membrane	Membrane	Conductive rubber-dome
Operating force required (ounces)	2.5	1.9	2.5	1.8	1.9
Key travel distance (mm)	3.5	3.8	4	3.8	3.8
KEYBOARD DESIGN					
Special keys (beyond the usual 101)	○	○	○	○	●
Exchangeable Ctrl and CapsLock (with extra key caps provided)	○	○	○	○	○
SYSTEM COMPATIBILITIES					
IBM-XT	●	●	○	●	●
IBM AT/Enhanced AT	●	●	●	●	●
IBM PS/2 (Model 50 or later)	●	●	●	●	●
Stated incompatibilities	None	None	None	AT&T 6300, IBM AT 286/6, Tandy 1000	None
PROGRAMMABILITY					
Software-programmable	○	○	●	○	●
Hardware-programmable	○	○	○	○	●
MISCELLANEOUS					
Stated current drain	150 mA	125 mA	275 mA	350 mA	200 mA
Optional Dvorak keyboard models	○	○	○	●	○
Optional keyboard connectors	None	Mini-DIN adapter	None	Mini-DIN adapter	None
PC manufacturers that bundle this keyboard	INA	Philips, Unisys, Wang, Zenith	IBM	None	INA

●—Yes   ○—No   N/A—Not applicable   INA—Information not available

Replacement Keyboards

	Maxi Switch Tuscon-101	NMB RT-101+ Mechanical	NMB RT-101+ Membrane	Northgate OmniKey/101	Northgate OmniKey/Ultra-T
Price	$	$	$	$	$
PHYSICAL FEATURES					
Case material	Plastic	Plastic	Plastic	Plastic with metal base	Plastic with metal base
Cord length (inches)	96	72	72	84	84
Number of angle settings	1	1	1	1	1
Pencil-tray depth (inches)	2	2	2	1	1
KEY DESIGN					
Key-switch type	Conductive rubber-dome	Mechanical	Membrane	Mechanical	Mechanical
Operating force required (ounces)	1.9	2	2	2.5	2.5
Key travel distance (mm)	3.8	3.6	3.6	3.5	3.5
KEYBOARD DESIGN					
Special keys (beyond the usual 101)	○	○	○	●	●
Exchangeable Ctrl and CapsLock (with extra key caps provided)	○	○	○	●	●
SYSTEM COMPATIBILITIES					
IBM-XT	●	●	●	●	●
IBM AT/Enhanced AT	●	●	●	●	●
IBM PS/2 (Model 50 or later)	●	●	●	●	●
Stated incompatibilities	None	None	None	IBM PS/2 Model 25	IBM PS/2 Model 25
PROGRAMMABILITY					
Software-programmable	○	○	○	●	●
Hardware-programmable	○	○	○	●	●
MISCELLANEOUS					
Stated current drain	200 mA	300 mA	300 mA	200 mA	200 mA
Optional Dvorak keyboard models	○	○	○	●	●
Optional keyboard connectors	Mini-DIN adapter	None	None	Mini-DIN adapter	Mini-DIN adapter
PC manufacturers that bundle this keyboard	ACMA, California Microsystems, Digicom, DynaSystems, Gateway 2000, IDS, Informix, Micro Express, Mini Micro, National Microsystems, PC Craft, Tandon	INA	INA	Northgate	Northgate

●—Yes ○—No N/A—Not applicable INA—Information not available   **Table Continues →**

Replacement Keyboards

	Tandy 101-Key Enhanced Keyboard
Price	$
PHYSICAL FEATURES	
Case material	Plastic with metal base
Cord length (inches)	72
Number of angle settings	1
Pencil-tray depth (inches)	1.3
KEY DESIGN	
Key-switch type	Membrane
Operating force required (ounces)	2
Key travel distance (mm)	3.8
KEYBOARD DESIGN	
Special keys (beyond the usual 101)	○
Exchangeable Ctrl and CapsLock (with extra key caps provided)	○
SYSTEM COMPATIBILITIES	
IBM-XT	●
IBM AT/Enhanced AT	●
IBM PS/2 (Model 50 or later)	●
Stated incompatibilities	None
PROGRAMMABILITY	
Software-programmable	●
Hardware-programmable	●
MISCELLANEOUS	
Stated current drain	500 mA
Optional Dvorak keyboard models	○
Optional keyboard connectors	Mini-DIN adapter
PC manufacturers that bundle this keyboard	Tandy

●—Yes   ○—No   N/A—Not applicable   INA—Information not available

End ■

G.2 Mice and Trackballs

(Products listed in alphabetical order by company name)	Antec Mouse AM-21 Plus	CalComp Wiz Mouse System	Chicony Keyboard KB-5581	CH Products RollerMouse	CMS Mini Mouse (Hi-res)
Price	$	$	$	$	$
HARDWARE FEATURES					
Type of device	Mouse	Mouse	Keyboard with built-in trackball	Trackball	Mouse
Manufacturer	Artec	CalComp	Chicony America	CH Products	INA
Interfaces supported	Serial	Serial, PDP	Serial	Serial, bus, PS/2	Serial, bus
IRQs supported	3, 4	2, 3, 4, 5	4	3, 4	2, 3, 4, 5
Base (hardware) resolution (ppi)	356	1,000	200	100, 200, 400	340
Number of buttons	3	6	3	4	3
Position sensor used	Optomechanical	Electromagnetic	Mechanical	Optomechanical	Mechanical
Mouse pad included	●	●	N/A	N/A	N/A
Ball removable for cleaning	●	N/A	○	●	●
Warranty	Five years parts and labor	Five years parts and labor	One year parts and labor	One year parts and labor	Lifetime parts and labor
Cord length (inches)	81	32	81	60	71
Weight of device only (pounds)	0.25	0.17	3.41	0.8	0.25
SOFTWARE FEATURES					
Number of bytes in CONFIG.SYS device driver	4,927	N/A	12,242	10,976	10,768
Number of bytes in command line driver	N/A	30,720	12,366	10,496	10,288
Disk format of supplied driver	5.25	5.25, 3.5	5.25	5.25	5.25
Version of tested driver	1.01	1.0.1.1	1.0	6.24A	6.11
Driver can be uninstalled from DOS	N/A	●	●	●	●
Ballistic tracking supported	○	○	○	●	○
Minimum resolution supported	N/A	N/A	N/A	1	N/A
Maximum resolution supported	N/A	N/A	N/A	2,880	N/A
Driver upgrades available	○	●	●	●	●
Other mouse emulations included	Microsoft, Mouse Systems	○	Microsoft, Mouse Systems	Microsoft	Mouse Systems
Supports Microsoft Mouse driver in Microsoft Windows	●	●	●	●	●
Mouse driver supports interrupt 33	●	●	●	●	●
Driver for Microsoft Windows included	○	●	○	●	○
Driver for AutoCAD included	○	●	○	●	○

●—Yes ○—No N/A—Not applicable INA—Information not available   **Table Continues →**

Mice and Trackballs

	CMS Mini Mouse (Standard)	Commax Fancy Mouse	Commax Witty Ball	Commax Witty Mouse	Dell Serial Mouse
Price	$	$	$	$	$
HARDWARE FEATURES					
Type of device	Mouse	Mouse	Trackball	Mouse	Mouse
Manufacturer	INA	Commax	Commax	Commax	Logitech
Interfaces supported	Serial, bus	Serial	Serial	Serial	Serial
IRQs supported	2, 3, 4, 5	0, 3, 7, 8	0, 3, 7, 8	0, 3, 7, 8	4
Base (hardware) resolution (ppi)	250	360	300	360	200
Number of buttons	3	3	3	3	2
Position sensor used	Mechanical	Optomechanical	Optomechanical	Optomechanical	Optomechanical
Mouse pad included	N/A	●	N/A	○	N/A
Ball removable for cleaning	●	●	○	●	●
Warranty	Lifetime parts and labor	One year parts and labor	One year parts and labor	One year parts and labor	One year parts and labor
Cord length (inches)	71	62.25	62	62.25	72
Weight of device only (pounds)	0.25	0.22	0.52	0.22	0.19
SOFTWARE FEATURES					
Number of bytes in CONFIG.SYS device driver	10,768	N/A	N/A	N/A	14,336
Number of bytes in command line driver	10,288	19,526	19,526	19,526	14,336
Disk format of supplied driver	5.25	5.25	5.25	5.25	5.25, 3.5
Version of tested driver	6.11	4.1	4.1	4.1	3.43
Driver can be uninstalled from DOS	●	●	●	●	●
Ballistic tracking supported	○	●	○	●	○
Minimum resolution supported	N/A	360	N/A	360	N/A
Maximum resolution supported	N/A	1,050	N/A	1,050	N/A
Driver upgrades available	●	●	●	●	●
Other mouse emulations included	Mouse Systems	Microsoft, Mouse Systems	Microsoft, Mouse Systems	Microsoft, Mouse Systems	Microsoft
Supports Microsoft Mouse driver in Microsoft Windows	●	●	●	●	●
Mouse driver supports interrupt 33	●	●	●	●	○
Driver for Microsoft Windows included	○	●	●	●	●
Driver for AutoCAD included	○	●	●	●	●

●—Yes ○—No N/A—Not applicable INA—Information not available

Mice and Trackballs

	DFI Inc. DMS-200 Mouse	DFI Inc. DMS-200H Mouse	Focus FT-100 Tracker	Fulcrum Computer Products Trackball Plus	IBM PS/2 Mouse
Price	$	$	$	$	$
HARDWARE FEATURES					
Type of device	Mouse	Mouse	Trackball	Trackball	Mouse
Manufacturer	DFI	DFI	Focus	Fulcrum	Alps
Interfaces supported	Serial	Serial	Serial	Serial	PS/2
IRQs supported	3, 4	3, 4	1, 2	1, 2	12
Base (hardware) resolution (ppi)	200	200	160	100	200
Number of buttons	3	3	3	6	2
Position sensor used	Optomechanical	Optomechanical	Optomechanical	Optomechanical	Mechanical
Mouse pad included	●	●	N/A	N/A	N/A
Ball removable for cleaning	●	●	●	○	●
Warranty	One year parts and labor	One year parts and labor	One year parts and labor	Six months parts and labor	One year parts and labor
Cord length (inches)	71	71	59.5	48	108
Weight of device only (pounds)	0.24	0.24	0.75	0.86	0.11
SOFTWARE FEATURES					
Number of bytes in CONFIG.SYS device driver	15,657	15,657	817,152	11,120	N/A
Number of bytes in command line driver	15,569	15,569	272,384	16,888	10,384
Disk format of supplied driver	5.25	5.25	5.25	5.25, 3.5	3.5
Version of tested driver	3.0	3.0	1.02	6.24B	1.1
Driver can be uninstalled from DOS	○	○	●	●	○
Ballistic tracking supported	○	●	●	●	○
Minimum resolution supported	N/A	5	160	100	N/A
Maximum resolution supported	N/A	700	500	25,000	N/A
Driver upgrades available	●	●	○	●	○
Other mouse emulations included	Microsoft, Mouse Systems	Microsoft, Mouse Systems	Microsoft, Mouse Systems	Microsoft, Mouse Systems	○
Supports Microsoft Mouse driver in Microsoft Windows	●	●	●	●	●
Mouse driver supports interrupt 33	●	●	●	●	●
Driver for Microsoft Windows included	○	○	○	○	○
Driver for AutoCAD included	○	○	○	○	○

●—Yes   ○—No   N/A—Not applicable   INA—Information not available   **Table Continues →**

Mice and Trackballs

	IMSI Mouse	International Machine Control Systems The MousePen	International Machine Control Systems The MousePen	ITAC Systems Mouse-Trak (2 button)	ITAC Systems Mouse-Trak (3 button)
Price	$	$	$	$	$
HARDWARE FEATURES					
Type of device	Mouse	Mouse	Mouse	Trackball	Trackball
Manufacturer	Z-Nix	IMCS	IMCS	ITAC Systems	ITAC Systems
Interfaces supported	Serial, bus	Serial	PS/2	Serial, bus PS/2, InPort	Serial, bus PS/2, InPort
IRQs supported	4	0, 3, 4	0, 3, 4	3, 4, 5, 7, 10, 11, 12, 15	3, 4
Base (hardware) resolution (ppi)	250	100	100	200	200
Number of buttons	2	2	2	2	3
Position sensor used	Mechanical	Optomechanical	Optomechanical	Optomechanical	Optomechanical
Mouse pad included	N/A	N/A	N/A	N/A	N/A
Ball removable for cleaning	●	●	●	●	●
Warranty	Lifetime parts and labor	Unconditional one year parts and labor, lifetime afterward	Unconditional one year parts and labor, lifetime afterward	One year parts and labor	One year parts and labor
Cord length (inches)	69	118	118	60	60
Weight of device only (pounds)	0.25	0.06	0.06	0.94	0.94
SOFTWARE FEATURES					
Number of bytes in CONFIG.SYS device driver	10,544	10,960	10,496	11,000	11,000
Number of bytes in command line driver	9,952	10,480	10,000	10,000	10,000
Disk format of supplied driver	5.25	5.25, 3.5	5.25, 3.5	5.25	5.25
Version of tested driver	6.11	6.24A	6.24A	6.11	6.11
Driver can be uninstalled from DOS	○	●	●	●	●
Ballistic tracking supported	○	●	●	● (bus only)	● (bus only)
Minimum resolution supported	N/A	50	50	20	20
Maximum resolution supported	N/A	1,000	1,000	800	800
Driver upgrades available	●	●	●	●	●
Other mouse emulations included	Microsoft	Microsoft	Microsoft	Microsoft, Mouse Systems	Microsoft, Mouse Systems
Supports Microsoft Mouse driver in Microsoft Windows	●	●	●	●	●
Mouse driver supports interrupt 33	●	●	●	●	●
Driver for Microsoft Windows included	○	○	○	○	○
Driver for AutoCAD included	○	○	○	○	○

●—Yes   ○—No   N/A—Not applicable   INA—Information not available

Mice and Trackballs

	Kensington Expert Mouse	Key Tronic Professional Series Mouse	Kraft Trackball	KYE International Genius Mouse GM-6X	KYE International Genius Mouse GM-6000
Price	$	$	$	$	$
HARDWARE FEATURES					
Type of device	Trackball	Mouse	Trackball	Mouse	Mouse
Manufacturer	Kensington Microware	Key Tronic	Kraft Systems	KYE International	KYE International
Interfaces supported PS/2	Serial, bus	Serial, bus	Serial	Serial	Serial
IRQs supported	2, 3, 4, 5, 7, 10, 11, 12, 15	2, 3, 4, 5	3, 4	1, 2, 3, 4, 5	1, 2, 3, 4, 5
Base (hardware) resolution (ppi)	200	200	200	200	350
Number of buttons	2	2	3	3	3
Position sensor used	Optomechanical	Mechanical	Optomechanical	Optomechanical	Optomechanical
Mouse pad included	N/A	○	N/A	○	●
Ball removable for cleaning	●	●	●	●	●
Warranty	One year parts and labor	One year limited	Five years parts and labor	Lifetime parts and labor	Lifetime parts and labor
Cord length (inches)	72	58	96	70	71
Weight of device only (pounds)	0.89	0.32	0.75	0.26	0.26
SOFTWARE FEATURES					
Number of bytes in CONFIG.SYS device driver	15,392	10,688	11,887	N/A	13,083
Number of bytes in command line driver	20,894	10,224	13,525	12,649	13,664
Disk format of supplied driver	5.25, 3.5	5.25	5.25	5.25	5.25
Version of tested driver	2.03	1.1	1.06	8.20	9.03
Driver can be uninstalled from DOS	●	○	●	●	●
Ballistic tracking supported	●	○	○	●	●
Minimum resolution supported	20	N/A	10*	50	87.5
Maximum resolution supported	10,000	N/A	1,150*	800	1,400
Driver upgrades available	●	●	●	●	●
Other mouse emulations included	Microsoft, IBM PS/2	Microsoft	○	Microsoft, Mouse Systems	Microsoft, Mouse Systems
Supports Microsoft Mouse driver in Microsoft Windows	●	●	●	●	●
Mouse driver supports interrupt 33	●	●	●	●	●
Driver for Microsoft Windows included	●	○	○	○	○
Driver for AutoCAD included	○	○	●	○	○

* The product features adjustable resolution, but not ballistic tracking.

●—Yes   ○—No   N/A—Not applicable   INA—Information not available

Table Continues →

Mice and Trackballs

	KYE International Genius Mouse GM-F302/F303	Liuski International ProCorp Mouse (serial)	Liuski International ProCorp Mouse (bus)	Logitech Dexxa Mouse	Logitech TrackMan Stationary Mouse
Price	$	$	$	$	$
HARDWARE FEATURES					
Type of device	Mouse	Mouse	Mouse	Mouse	Trackball
Manufacturer	KYE International	P.R.O. Corp.	P.R.O. Corp.	Logitech	Logitech
Interfaces supported	Serial, PS/2	Serial	Bus	Serial, bus	Serial, bus
IRQs supported	1, 2, 3, 4, 5	3, 4	2, 3, 4, 5	2, 3, 4, 5	2, 3, 4, 5
Base (hardware) resolution (ppi)	350	250	340	200	320
Number of buttons	3	3	3	2	3
Position sensor used	Optomechanical	Mechanical	Mechanical	Optomechanical	Optomechanical
Mouse pad included	●	●	●	●	N/A
Ball removable for cleaning	●	●	●	●	●
Warranty	Lifetime parts and labor	One year parts and labor	One year parts and labor	Limited lifetime	Limited lifetime
Cord length (inches)	70	70	69.75	72	108
Weight of device only (pounds)	0.87	0.27	0.27	0.16	0.5
SOFTWARE FEATURES					
Number of bytes in CONFIG.SYS device driver	13,659	10,768	10,768	13,312	14,336
Number of bytes in command line driver	13,664	10,288	10,288	13,312	14,336
Disk format of supplied driver	5.25	5.25	5.25	5.25	5.25, 3.5
Version of tested driver	9.03	6.11	6.11	3.43	4.10
Driver can be uninstalled from DOS	●	●	●	○	●
Ballistic tracking supported	●	○	○	●	●
Minimum resolution supported	87.5	N/A	N/A	50	50
Maximum resolution supported	1,400	N/A	N/A	750	15,000
Driver upgrades available	●	●	●	●	●
Other mouse emulations included	Microsoft, Mouse Systems	○	○	○	Microsoft, Mouse Systems
Supports Microsoft Mouse driver in Microsoft Windows	●	●	●	○	●
Mouse driver supports interrupt 33	●	●	●	●	●
Driver for Microsoft Windows included	○	●	●	○	○
Driver for AutoCAD included	○	●	●	○	○

●—Yes ○—No N/A—Not applicable INA—Information not available

Mice and Trackballs

	Lynx Turbo Trackball	Marconi Marcus RB2-305/306	Microsoft Mouse	MicroSpeed FastTRAP	MicroSpeed PC-Trac
Price	$	$	$	$	$
HARDWARE FEATURES					
Type of device	Trackball	Trackball	Mouse	Trackball	Trackball
Manufacturer	Lynx	Marconi	Alps	MicroSpeed	MicroSpeed
Interfaces supported	Serial, bus, PS/2	Serial, bus	Serial, bus, PS/2, InPort	Serial, bus	Serial, bus, PS/2, InPort
IRQs supported	2, 3, 4, 5	2, 3, 4, 5	2, 3, 4, 5	2, 3, 4, 5, 7	2, 3, 4, 5, 7
Base (hardware) resolution (ppi)	250	76	400	200	200
Number of buttons	2	3	2	3	3
Position sensor used	Mechanical	Optomechanical	Mechanical	Optomechanical	Optomechanical
Mouse pad included	N/A	N/A	○	N/A	N/A
Ball removable for cleaning	●	○	●	●	●
Warranty	Lifetime replacement	One year parts and labor	One year parts and labor	One year parts and labor	One year parts and labor
Cord length (inches)	72	45.75	104	69	67
Weight of device only (pounds)	0.5	1.3	0.28	0.82	0.75
SOFTWARE FEATURES					
Number of bytes in CONFIG.SYS device driver	10,544	3,163	14,336	17,378	18,055
Number of bytes in command line driver	9,952	13,119	14,336	17,234	17,911
Disk format of supplied driver	5.25	5.25, 3.5	5.25, 3.5	5.25	5.25 or 3.5
Version of tested driver	6.11	6.21	7.04	2.06A	2.1
Driver can be uninstalled from DOS	●	●	●	○	○
Ballistic tracking supported	●	●	●	●	●
Minimum resolution supported	50	10	0	50	50
Maximum resolution supported	960	76	Infinite	1,000	1,000
Driver upgrades available	●	●	●	●	●
Other mouse emulations included	○	Microsoft	○	Microsoft, Mouse Systems	Microsoft, Mouse Systems
Supports Microsoft Mouse driver in Microsoft Windows	●	●	●	●	●
Mouse driver supports interrupt 33	●	●	●	●	●
Driver for Microsoft Windows included	○	●	●	●	●
Driver for AutoCAD included	○	●	○	●	●

Mice and Trackballs

	Mouse Systems OmniMouse II	Mouse Systems PC Mouse	Mouse Systems PC Mouse III	Mouse Systems PC Trackball	Mouse Systems The White Mouse
Price	$	$	$	$	$
HARDWARE FEATURES					
Type of device	Mouse	Mouse	Mouse	Trackball	Mouse
Manufacturer	Mouse Systems	Mouse Systems	Mouse Systems	Mouse Systems	Mouse Systems
Interfaces supported	Serial, bus	Serial, bus, PS/2	Serial, bus, PS/2	Serial, PS/2	Serial, bus, PS/2
IRQs supported	2, 3, 4, 5, 7	2, 3, 4, 5, 7	2, 3, 4, 5, 7	2, 3, 4, 5, 7	2, 3, 4, 5, 7
Base (hardware) resolution (ppi)	200	100	300	200	350
Number of buttons	2	3	3	3	3
Position sensor used	Optomechanical	Optical	Optical	Optomechanical	Optomechanical
Mouse pad included	○	●	●	N/A	●
Ball removable for cleaning	●	N/A	N/A	●	●
Warranty	Lifetime parts and labor	Lifetime parts and labor	Lifetime parts and labor	Lifetime parts and labor	Lifetime parts and labor
Cord length (inches)	69	58.5	96	75	69
Weight of device only (pounds)	0.18	0.18	0.17	0.52	0.24
SOFTWARE FEATURES					
Number of bytes in CONFIG.SYS device driver	12,288	12,288	12,288	12,288	12,288
Number of bytes in command line driver	17,408	17,408	18,432	17,408	17,408
Disk format of supplied driver	5.25	5.25	5.25, 3.5	5.25	5.25, 3.5
Version of tested driver	6.23	6.23	7.0	6.23	6.23
Driver can be uninstalled from DOS	●	●	●	●	●
Ballistic tracking supported	●	●	●	●	●
Minimum resolution supported	20	20	30	20	20
Maximum resolution supported	11,200	11,200	30,000	11,200	11,200
Driver upgrades available	●	●	●	●	●
Other mouse emulations included	Microsoft	Mouse Systems, IBM PS/2	Microsoft, Mouse Systems, IBM PS/2	Microsoft	Microsoft, Mouse Systems, IBM PS/2
Supports Microsoft Mouse driver in Microsoft Windows	●	○	●	●	●
Mouse driver supports interrupt 33	●	●	●	●	●
Driver for Microsoft Windows included	○	●	●	○	○
Driver for AutoCAD included	○	○	○	○	○

●—Yes ○—No N/A—Not applicable INA—Information not available

Mice and Trackballs

	Numonics Manager Mouse Cordless	Penny + Giles Controls TrackerMouse/TM1	Penny + Giles Controls TrackerMouse/TM1 Plus 16	Penny + Giles Controls TrackerMouse/TM1 Plus 32	Practical Solutions The Cordless Mouse
Price	$	$	$	$	$
HARDWARE FEATURES					
Type of device	Mouse	Trackball	Trackball	Trackball	Mouse
Manufacturer	Numonics	Penny + Giles Computer Products	Penny + Giles Computer Products	Penny + Giles Computer Products	INA
Interfaces supported	Serial	Serial, PS/2	Serial	Serial, PS/2	Serial, PS/2
IRQs supported	1, 2, 3, 4	3, 4	3, 4	3, 4	3, 4
Base (hardware) resolution (ppi)	200	40	40	40	200
Number of buttons	3	2	16	32	3
Position sensor used	Optomechanical	Optomechanical	Optomechanical	Optomechanical	Optomechanical
Mouse pad included	○	N/A	N/A	N/A	○
Ball removable for cleaning	○	●	●	●	●
Warranty	One year parts and labor	One year parts and labor	One year parts and labor	One year parts and labor	One year parts and labor
Cord length (inches)	80.5	53	53	53	N/A
Weight of device only (pounds)	0.24	0.53	0.6	0.6	0.27
SOFTWARE FEATURES					
Number of bytes in CONFIG.SYS device driver	12,288	12,801	12,801	12,801	N/A
Number of bytes in command line driver	12,288	14,240	14,240	14,240	11,289
Disk format of supplied driver	5.25	5.25, 3.5	5.25, 3.5	5.25, 3.5	5.25, 3.5
Version of tested driver	2.06	3.1	3.1	3.1	4.2
Driver can be uninstalled from DOS	●	○	○	○	○
Ballistic tracking supported	●	●	●	●	●
Minimum resolution supported	50	40	40	40	10
Maximum resolution supported	1,000	400	400	400	1,200
Driver upgrades available	●	●	●	●	●
Other mouse emulations included	Microsoft, Mouse Systems	○	○	○	Mouse Systems
Supports Microsoft Mouse driver in Microsoft Windows	○	●	●	●	●
Mouse driver supports interrupt 33	●	●	●	●	●
Driver for Microsoft Windows included	○	●	●	●	●
Driver for AutoCAD included	○	●	●	●	●

●—Yes   ○—No   N/A—Not applicable   INA—Information not available

Table Continues →

Mice and Trackballs

	ProHance PowerMouse 100	Qualitas Trading Co. Samurai Mouse	SmarTEAM Mouse	Suncom Technologies MouseTrac	Suncom Technologies SunMouse
Price	$	$	$	$	$
HARDWARE FEATURES					
Type of device	Programmable mouse	Mouse	Mouse	Trackball	Mouse
Manufacturer	ProHance Technologies	NEOS Electronics	TEAM Technology	INA	INA
Interfaces supported	Serial	Serial	Serial, bus	Serial	Serial
IRQs supported	All	3, 4	None	3, 4	3, 4
Base (hardware) resolution (ppi)	200	200	250	200	200
Number of buttons	40	2	3	3	3
Position sensor used	Optomechanical	Optomechanical	Mechanical	Optomechanical	Optomechanical
Mouse pad included	○	○	○	N/A	○
Ball removable for cleaning	●	●	●	●	●
Warranty	One year parts and labor	One year parts and labor	Limited lifetime	One year parts and labor	One year parts and labor
Cord length (inches)	70	58	70	104	56
Weight of device only (pounds)	0.44	0.27	0.26	0.70	0.28
SOFTWARE FEATURES					
Number of bytes in CONFIG.SYS device driver	N/A	16,976	10,704	N/A	N/A
Number of bytes in command line driver	15,913	16,784	10,224	N/A	N/A
Disk format of supplied driver	5.25, 3.5	5.25	5.25	N/A	N/A
Version of tested driver	5.23	4.0	6.11	N/A	N/A
Driver can be uninstalled from DOS	●	●	●	○	N/A
Ballistic tracking supported	●	●	○	○	○
Minimum resolution supported	200	100	N/A	N/A	N/A
Maximum resolution supported	400	1,000	N/A	N/A	N/A
Driver upgrades available	●	○	●	N/A	N/A
Other mouse emulations included	●	Microsoft	Microsoft	N/A	N/A
Supports Microsoft Mouse driver in Microsoft Windows	○	●	●	●	●
Mouse driver supports interrupt 33	●	●	●	N/A	N/A
Driver for Microsoft Windows included	●	○	○	○	○
Driver for AutoCAD included	○	○	○	○	○

●—Yes ○—No N/A—Not applicable INA—Information not available

Mice and Trackballs

	Tandy Serial Mouse	Tandy 2-Button Mouse
Price	$	$
HARDWARE FEATURES		
Type of device	Mouse	Mouse
Manufacturer	Tandy	Tandy
Interfaces supported	Serial	PS/2
IRQs supported	3, 4	0
Base (hardware) resolution (ppi)	200	200
Number of buttons	2	2
Position sensor used	Mechanical	Optomechanical
Mouse pad included	○	○
Ball removable for cleaning	●	●
Warranty	90-day replacement	90-day replacement
Cord length (inches)	60	62
Weight of device only (pounds)	0.22	0.20
SOFTWARE FEATURES		
Number of bytes in CONFIG.SYS device driver	13,793	13,793
Number of bytes in command line driver	13,950	13,950
Disk format of supplied driver	5.25, 3.5	5.25, 3.5
Version of tested driver	6.10	6.10
Driver can be uninstalled from DOS	○	
Ballistic tracking supported	●	●
Minimum resolution supported	200	200
Maximum resolution supported	19,000	19,000
Driver upgrades available	○	○
Other mouse emulations included	Microsoft	Microsoft
Supports Microsoft Mouse driver in Microsoft Windows	●	●
Mouse driver supports interrupt 33	●	●
Driver for Microsoft Windows included	○	○
Driver for AutoCAD included	○	○

●—Yes ○—No N/A—Not applicable INA—Information not available

End ■

G.3   Portable Pointing Devices

(Products listed in alphabetical order by company name)	Appoint MousePen Professional	Appoint Thumbelina	GRiD Systems Corp. GRiD IsoPoint	IBM Corp. IBM PS/2 Trackpoint	Kraft Systems Inc. TopTrak
Price	$	$	$$$$$ (as part of GRiDCase)	$	$
HARDWARE FEATURES					
Type of device	Optomechanical mouse	Optomechanical mouse	Mechanical mouse	Optomechanical trackball/mouse	Optomechanical trackball
Connector	PS/2	PS/2	None	PS/2	DB-9 serial
Additional connector (adapter)	DB-9 serial	DB-9 serial	N/A	None	DB-25 serial
IRQs supported	3, 4	3, 4	3–5	None	3, 4
Base hardware resolution (points per inch)	150	150	450	200	200
Composition of ball	Delrin	Delrin	N/A	Phenolic	Phenolic
Ball removable for cleaning	●	○	N/A	○	●
Method of attaching device to laptop	N/A	Z-bracket	Built-in	N/A	N/A
BUTTONS					
Unduplicated	2	2	2	2	2
Total	2	2	4	4	2
Drag-lock	None	1	None	2	1
Other switches	Fixed/ballistic	None	None	None	Simultaneous left/right
PHYSICAL SPECIFICATIONS					
Length of interface cable (inches)	56	45	N/A	44	95
Weight (ounces)	2	2	N/A	5	11
Ball diameter (inches)	0.4	0.3	N/A	1.3	1.5
OTHER FEATURES					
Size of CONFIG.SYS device driver	15K	15K	14K	N/A	10K
Size of command line driver	15K	15K	14K	14K	10K
Disk format of supplied drivers	5.25, 3.5	5.25, 3.5	3.5	3.5	5.25, 3.5
Version number of tested driver	2.00	7.04	7.4	7.04	6.24
Driver can be disabled from DOS	●	●	●	●	●
Driver supports ballistic tracking	●	●	●	●	●
AutoCAD driver	○	○	○	○	●
Resolutions supported (points per inch)	150–1,000	150–1,000	100–1,000	N/A	10–1,150
Other mouse emulations included	None	None	None	Microsoft	Microsoft
Software bundled	None	None	None	None	LCS's Telepaint

●—Yes   ○—No   N/A—Not applicable   INA—Information not available

Portable Pointing Devices

	Logitech Inc. TrackMan Portable	Microsoft Corp. BallPoint Mouse	Mouse Systems The Little Mouse/PC	Suncom Technologies ICONtroller
Price	$	$	$	$
HARDWARE FEATURES				
Type of device	Optomechanical trackball	Mechanical trackball	Optical mouse	Mini-joystick
Connector	DB-9 serial	DB-9 serial	DB-9 serial	DB-9 serial
Additional connector (adapter)	DB-25 serial	PS/2	DB-25 serial, PS/2	DB-25 serial
IRQs supported	3, 4	All (0–15)	2–15	3, 4
Base hardware resolution (points per inch)	200	400	300	(approximately) 200
Composition of ball	Polycarbonate	Compression-molded plastic	N/A	N/A
Ball removable for cleaning	●	●	N/A	N/A
Method of attaching device to laptop	Detachable clip	Detachable clip	N/A	Duo-Lock
BUTTONS				
Unduplicated	3	2	2	3
Total	3	4	2	4
Drag-lock	2	None	None	1
Other switches	None	○	○	Resolution, compatibility, joystick button
PHYSICAL SPECIFICATIONS				
Length of interface cable (inches)	26	52 (coiled)	70	36 (coiled)
Weight (ounces)	4	6	5	3
Ball diameter (inches)	1	1.1	N/A	N/A
OTHER FEATURES				
Size of CONFIG.SYS device driver	16K	N/A	13K	13.5K
Size of command line driver	34K	16K	12K	13K
Disk format of supplied drivers	3.5	3.5	5.25, 3.5	5.25, 3.5
Version number of tested driver	6.0	1.00	7.01	1.00
Driver can be disabled from DOS	●	●	●	●
Driver supports ballistic tracking	●	●	●	○
AutoCAD driver	○	○	○	○
Resolutions supported (points per inch)	50–10,000	0.75–22,400	300–30,000	N/A
Other mouse emulations included	Microsoft	None	Microsoft, PS/2	Microsoft
Software bundled	Windows hotkeys	Mouse menus	Pop-up menus, utilities	Testing and tutor programs

●—Yes ○—No N/A—Not applicable INA—Information not available   **E n d** ■

PORTABLE/LAPTOP COMPUTERS

H.1 Color Portable/Laptop Computers

(Products listed in alphabetical order by company name)	AST Premium Exec 386SX/25C	Compaq Portable 486C	Dell System 325NC	Dolch P.A.C. 386–33C	Dolch P.A.C. 486-33E
List price (tested configuration)	$$$	$$$$$	$$$$	$$$$$	$$$$$
Processor type and speed	AMD Am386SXL/25	Intel 486DX/33	Intel 386SL/25	Intel 386DX/33	Intel 486DX/33
Hard disk capacity	80Mb	120Mb	84Mb	420Mb	420Mb
Microsoft Windows 3.1	●	○	●	○	○
Distribution channel	Dealers	Dealers	Direct	Dealers	Dealers
Dimensions (HWD, in inches)	2.5 × 11.5 × 9	5.5 × 15.6 × 11	2.5 × 11 × 8.5	9.5 × 15.5 × 8.5	9.5 × 15.5 × 8.5
Weight/travel weight (pounds)	7.5, 8.7	17	7.3, 8.6	19.5	20.5
Display area (H × W, in inches)	5.3 × 7.3	6.5 × 8.5	5.6 × 7.4	6.5 × 8.5	6.5 × 8.5
Keys: total, function, cursor	82, 10, 8	101, 12, 4	85, 12, 4	86, 12, 4	86, 12, 4
MOTHERBOARD					
Motherboard manufacturer	AST	Compaq	Dell	Dolch	AIR
Chip set manufacturer	WD	Compaq	Intel	UMC	Intel
BIOS version (or date)	AST 2.00	Compaq 386E3	Phoenix 1.01A	AMI (July 1991)	Phoenix 1.01
Setup in ROM/Password in ROM	●/●	●/●	●/●	○/●	●/○
System shadowing/Video shadowing	●/●	●/●	●/●	●/●	●/●
MEMORY AND DISK DRIVES					
Installable RAM	4Mb–8Mb	2Mb–32Mb	4Mb–12Mb	4Mb–32Mb	4Mb–32Mb
User-installable	●	●	●	○	○
External processor RAM cache	None	None	64K	64K	128K
Available hard disk sizes	60Mb, 80Mb, 120Mb	120Mb, 210Mb	60Mb, 84Mb	120Mb, 240Mb, 420Mb	120Mb, 240Mb, 420Mb
I/O AND EXPANSION					
Parallel, serial, mouse ports	1, 1, 0	1, 1, 1	1, 1, 1	1, 1, 0	1, 1, 0
Proprietary expansion port	○	●	○	○	○
Expansion slots	None	2 32-bit EISA	None	6 16-bit ISA	6 32-bit EISA
Expansion unit	○	○	○	○	○
VIDEO					
Screen manufacturer	Sanyo	Sharp	Sharp	Hitachi	Hitachi
Type of display	Passive	Active	Passive	Active	Active
Maximum simultaneous colors	16	256	16	256	256
Video chip set manufacturer	Cirrus	Compaq	WD	C&T	C&T
MODEM					
Internal modem options	2,400-bps, 9,600-bps fax, 9,600-bps send-fax	2,400-bps	9,600-bps: fax, fax with MNP 5, data/fax	2,400-bps	2,400-bps
AC ADAPTER AND BATTERY					
AC adapter size (inches)	5.5 × 2.3 × 1.5	N/A	2 × 5.5 × 3.1	N/A	N/A
Rated battery life (hours)	2	N/A	3	N/A	N/A
ZDigit, Battery Rundown test scores (hours:minutes)	2:31, 2:12	N/A	4:59, 2:53	N/A	N/A
Charge time while on, off(hours)	3, 3	N/A	8, 3.5	N/A	N/A
Battery weight, amp/hour rating	0.9 lbs, 5.7 Ah	N/A	1.6 lbs, 2.2 Ah	N/A	N/A
Display/hard disk power-down	●/●	N/A	●/●	N/A	N/A
CUP/peripherals power-down	●/●	N/A	●/●	N/A	N/A
Standby/Hibernation	●/○	N/A	●/●	N/A	N/A

●—Yes   ○—No   N/A—Not applicable   INA—Information not available

Table Continues →

Color Portable/Laptop Computers

	Dolch P.A.C. 486-50E	IBM PS/2 Model CL57SX	Micronics Mport 450	NEC ProSpeed 486SX/C	NEC UltraLite SL/25C
List price (tested configuration)	$$$$$	$$$$$	$$$$$	$$$$$	$$$$
Processor type and speed	Intel 486DX/50	Intel 386SX/20	Intel 486DX2/50	Intel 486SX/20	Intel 386SL/25
Hard disk capacity	420Mb	80Mb	230Mb	120Mb	80Mb
Microsoft Windows 3.1	○	○	●	●	●
Distribution channel	Dealers	Dealers	Dealers	Dealers	Dealers
Dimensions (HWD, in inches)	9.5 × 15.5 × 8.5	3 × 13 × 11	4 × 16 × 12.3	4.3 × 15.5 × 14.8	2.5 × 11.5 × 9.5
Weight/travel weight (pounds)	21.1	11.4, 13.7	14.6, 18.4	17.8	7.2, 8.8
Display area (H × W, in inches)	6.5 × 8.5	6.5 × 8.5	6 × 8	6.5 × 8.5	6 × 7.5
Keys: total, function, cursor	86, 12, 4	84, 12, 4	82, 10, 0	91, 12, 4	78, 12, 4
MOTHERBOARD					
Motherboard manufacturer	AIR	IBM	Micronics	NEC	NEC
Chip set manufacturer	Intel	IBM	C&T	Intel	Intel
BIOS version (or date)	Phoenix 1.01	IBM (February 1992)	Phoenix 0.10 P18	Phoenix E486SX 1.0	Phoenix 386SL 1.0
Setup in ROM/Password in ROM	●/○	●/●	●/○	○/●	●/●
System shadowing/Video shadowing	○/●	○/●	●/●	●/●	●/●
MEMORY AND DISK DRIVES					
Installable RAM	4Mb–32Mb	2Mb–16Mb	0–32Mb	2Mb–20Mb	2Mb–10Mb
User-installable	○	●	●	●	○
External processor RAM cache	128K	None	None	None	64K
Available hard disk sizes	120Mb, 240Mb, 420Mb	80Mb	120Mb, 230Mb	120Mb, 240Mb	80Mb, 120Mb
I/O AND EXPANSION					
Parallel, serial, mouse ports	1, 1, 0	1, 1, 0	1, 2, 0	1, 1, 2	1, 1, 1
Proprietary expansion port	○	●	○	●	●
Expansion slots	6 32-bit EISA	None	1 16-bit ISA	1 32-bit EISA	None
Expansion unit	○	○	○	○	●
VIDEO					
Screen manufacturer	Hitachi	DTI	Sharp	Hitachi	NEC
Type of display	Active	Active	Active	Active	Active
Maximum simultaneous colors	256	256	256	256	16
Video chip set manufacturer	C&T	IBM	Cirrus	WD	Cirrus
MODEM					
Internal modem options	2,400-bps	9,600-bps fax	None	2,400-bps, 9,600-bps fax	2,400-bps, 9,600-bps fax
AC ADAPTER AND BATTERY					
AC adapter size (inches)	N/A	3.5 × 8 × 2	N/A	N/A	2 × 2.5 × 8
Rated battery life (hours)	N/A	1	N/A	N/A	1
ZDigit, Battery Rundown test scores (hours:minutes)	N/A	1:09, 0:50	N/A	N/A	2:17, 1:11
Charge time while on, off(hours)	N/A	2, 1	N/A	N/A	15, 3
Battery weight, amp/hour rating	N/A	0.8 lbs, 1.4Ah	N/A	N/A	1 lb, 1.7Ah
Display/hard disk power-down	N/A	●/●	N/A	N/A	●/●
CUP/peripherals power-down	N/A	●/●	N/A	N/A	●/●
Standby/Hibernation	N/A	●/●	N/A	N/A	●/●

●—Yes   ○—No   N/A—Not applicable   INA—Information not available

Color Portable/Laptop Computers

	Toshiba T4400SXC	Toshiba T5200C	Toshiba T6400DXC	Toshiba T6400SXC
List price (tested configuration)	$$$$$	$$$$$	$$$$$	$$$$$
Processor type and speed	Intel 486SX/25	INA 386/20	Intel 486DX/33	Intel 486SX/25
Hard disk capacity	85Mb	200Mb	200Mb	120Mb
Microsoft Windows 3.1	○	INA	○	○
Distribution channel	Dealers	INA	Dealers	Dealers
Dimensions (HWD, in inches)	2 × 8 × 11.5	4.3 × 14.6 × 15.6	4.5 × 15.5 × 10.5	4.5 × 15.5 × 10.5
Weight/travel weight (pounds)	7.8, 9.5	18.9	13.3	13.3
Display area (H × W, in inches)	6 × 7.5	6.3 × 8.4	6.5 × 8.5	6.5 × 8.5
Keys: total, function, cursor	82, 12, 8	91, 12, 4	101, 12, 8	101, 12, 8
MOTHERBOARD				
Motherboard Manufacturer	Toshiba	Toshiba	Toshiba	Toshiba
Chip set manufacturer	Toshiba	Toshiba	Toshiba	Toshiba
BIOS version (or date)	Toshiba 3/06E92	Toshiba	Toshiba 1.30	Toshiba 1.30
Setup in ROM/Password in ROM	●/●	INA	○/●	○/●
System shadowing/Video shadowing	●/○	○/○	●/○	●/○
MEMORY AND DISK DRIVES				
Installable RAM	4Mb–20Mb	2Mb–14Mb	4Mb–20Mb	4Mb–20Mb
User-installable	●	INA	●	●
External processor RAM cache	None	32K	None	None
Available hard disk sizes	85Mb, 120Mb	INA	120Mb, 200Mb	120Mb, 200Mb
I/O AND EXPANSION				
Parallel, serial, mouse ports	1, 1, 1	INA	1, 1, 1	1, 1, 1
Proprietary expansion port	●	INA	●	●
Expansion slots	None	1 16-bit, 1 full-length, 1 half-length	1 16-bit, 1 8-bit ISA	1 16-bit, 1 8-bit ISA
Expansion unit	●	INA	○	○
VIDEO				
Screen manufacturer	Sharp	INA	Sharp/DTI	Sharp/DTI
Type of display	Active	INA	Active	Active
Maximum simultaneous colors	256	INA	256	256
Video chip set manufacturer	WD	Paradise	WD	WD
MODEM				
Internal modem options	2,400-bps, 2,400-bps V.42bis, 9,600-bps data/fax	INA	2,400-bps, 2,400-bps V.42bis, 9,600-bps data/fax	2,400-bps, 2,400-bps V.42bis, 9,600-bps data/fax
AC ADAPTER AND BATTERY				
AC adapter size (inches)	6 × 3 × 2	INA	N/A	N/A
Rated battery life (hours)	3	N/A	N/A	N/A
ZDigit, Battery Rundown test scores (hours:minutes)	4:05, 2:26	INA	N/A	N/A
Charge time while on, off(hours)	4, 1.5	N/A	N/A	N/A
Battery weight, amp/hour rating	2.3 lbs, 2.4Ah	INA	N/A	N/A
Display/hard disk power-down	●/●	INA	N/A	N/A
CUP/peripherals power-down	●/●	INA	N/A	N/A
Standby/Hibernation	●/○	INA	N/A	N/A

●—Yes ○—No N/A—Not applicable INA—Information not available

End ■

H.2 Monochrome Portable/Laptop Computers

(Products listed in alphabetical order by company name)	Acer AnyWare V386SL	ALR Ranger M425-120	ALR Ranger M425s-120	ALR Ranger MC425-120	ALR Ranger MC425s-120
Price	$$	$$$	$$$	$$$$	$$$
Processor type and speed	Intel 386SL/25	Intel 486DX/25	Intel 486SX/25	Intel 486DX/25	Intel 486SX/25
Hard disk capacity	81Mb	120Mb	120Mb	120Mb	120Mb
Microsoft Windows 3.1	●	●	●	●	●
Distribution channel	Dealers	Dealers, direct	Dealers, direct	Dealers, direct	Dealers, direct
Dimensions (HWD, in inches)	2 × 11.4 × 8.5	2.3 × 11.8 × 8.5	2.3 × 11.8 × 8.5	2.3 × 11.8 × 8.5	2.3 × 11.8 × 8.5
Weight/travel weight (pounds)	5.9, 7.2	7.4, 8.6	7.7, 9	7.5, 9	7.8, 9
Display area (H × W, in inches)	6 × 7.8	5.3 × 6.8	5.3 × 6.8	5.3 × 6.8	5.3 × 6.8
Keys: total, function, cursor	82, 12, 8	82, 10, 8	82, 10, 8	82, 10, 8	82, 10, 8
MOTHERBOARD					
Motherboard manufacturer	Acer	ALR	ALR	ALR	ALR
Chip set manufacturer	Intel	WD	WD	WD	WD
BIOS version (or date)	Acer (July 1992)	Phoenix (July 1992)	Phoenix (April 1990)	Phoenix (July 1992)	Phoenix (July 1992)
Setup in ROM/Password in ROM	●/●	●/●	●/●	●/●	●/●
System shadowing/Video shadowing	●/●	○/●	○/●	○/●	●/●
MEMORY AND DISK DRIVES					
Installable RAM	4Mb–12Mb	4Mb–16Mb	4Mb–16Mb	4Mb–16Mb	4Mb–16Mb
User-installable	●	●	●	●	●
External processor RAM cache	64K	None	None	None	None
Available hard disk sizes	80Mb, 120Mb	60Mb, 80Mb, 120Mb	60Mb, 80Mb, 120Mb	80Mb, 120Mb	60Mb, 80Mb, 120Mb
I/O AND EXPANSION					
Parallel, serial, mouse ports	1, 2, 1	1, 1, 1	1, 1, 1	1, 1, 1	1, 1, 1
Proprietary expansion port	●	○	○	○	○
PCMCIA slot	●	○	○	○	○
Expansion unit	●	○	○	○	○
Internal modem options	2,400-bps/9,600-bps MNP 5 send/receive fax	2,400-bps/9,600-bps send-only fax, 2,400-bps/9,600-bps MNP 5 send/receive fax	2,400-bps/9,600-bps send-only fax, 2,400-bps/9,600-bps MNP 5 send/receive fax	2,400-bps/9,600-bps send-only fax, 2,400-bps/9,600-bps MNP 5 send/receive fax	2,400-bps/9,600-bps send-only fax
VIDEO					
Screen manufacturer	Sharp	Sharp	Sharp	Sharp	Sharp
Maximum shades of gray	32	32	32	16	16
Video chip set manufacturer	Cirrus	WD	WD	N/A	N/A
AC ADAPTER AND BATTERY					
AC adapter size (inches)	1.5 × 6 × 1.9	2 × 3.5 × 5.7	2 × 3.5 × 5.8	2 × 3.5 × 5.8	2 × 3.5 × 5.8
Rated battery life (hours)	4.5	3.5	3.5	3.5	3.5
ZDigit, battery rundowns (hr:min)	3:02, 1:56	7:41, 2:26	6:18, 2:32	4:27, 2:06	3:44, 1:46
Charge time while on, off (hours)	N/A, 2	2.5, 2	2.5, 2	2.5, 2	2.5, 2
Battery weight, amp/hour rating	0.9 lbs, 3.9Ah	1.8 lbs, 1.6Ah	1.8 lbs, 1.6Ah	1.8 lbs, 1.6Ah	1.8 lbs, 1.6Ah
Display/hard disk power-down	●/●	●/●	●/●	●/●	●/●
CPU/peripherals power-down	●/○	●/●	●/●	●/●	●/●
Standby/Hibernation	●/●	○/○	○/○	○/○	○/○

●—Yes ○—No N/A—Not applicable INA—Information not available

Monochrome Portable/Laptop Computers

	Altec 386SX/25 Notebook	Altima 325 80386SL	Altima 433 80486DX	American Mitac 3025F	American Mitac 3027F
Price	$$$	$$$	$$$	$$	$$
Processor type and speed	AMD Am386SXL/25	Intel 386SL/25	Intel 486DX/33	Intel 386SX/25	Intel 386SL/25
Hard disk capacity	80Mb	80Mb	120Mb	80Mb	81Mb
Microsoft Windows 3.1	●	●	●	●	●
Distribution channel	Direct	Dealers	Dealers	Dealers, direct	Dealers, direct
Dimensions (HWD, in inches)	2 × 11 × 8.5	1.6 × 11 × 8.5	1.6 × 11 × 8.5	2.5 × 11.5 × 8.5	2 × 11 × 9.2
Weight/travel weight (pounds)	6.3, 7.9	5.9, 7.6	6.1, 7.7	6.9, 8.8	6.3, 7.7
Display area (H × W, in inches)	6 × 7.5	5.8 × 7.7	5.8 × 7.7	5.8 × 7.5	5.2 × 7
Keys: total, function, cursor	81, 10, 4	84, 10, 8	84, 10, 8	82, 12, 4	84, 12, 8
MOTHERBOARD					
Motherboard manufacturer	Sampo	Twinhead	Twinhead	American Mitac	American Mitac
Chip set manufacturer	VLSI	Intel	ACC	Headland	Intel
BIOS version (or date)	Phoenix 1.1	Quadtel (April 1992)	Phoenix (May 1992)	Phoenix (April 1990)	Phoenix (November 1991)
Setup in ROM/Password in ROM	●/●	●/●	●/○	●/○	●/●
System shadowing/Video shadowing	●/●	●/●	●/●	●/●	●/●
MEMORY AND DISK DRIVES					
Installable RAM	3Mb–8Mb	2Mb–6Mb	4Mb–20Mb	1Mb–6Mb	2Mb–10Mb
User-installable	●	●	●	○	○
External processor RAM cache	None	64K	None	None	16K
Available hard disk sizes	60Mb, 80Mb	80Mb, 120Mb	120Mb	60Mb, 80Mb	60Mb, 80Mb, 120Mb
I/O AND EXPANSION					
Parallel, serial, mouse ports	1, 1, 0	1, 1, 1	1, 1, 1	1, 1, 0	1, 1, 1
Proprietary expansion port	●	●	●	●	●
PCMCIA slot	○	○	○	○	○
Expansion unit	○	●	●	○	○
Internal modem options	4,800-bps send-fax	2,400-bps/9,600-bps MNP 5 send/receive fax	2,400-bps/9,600-bps MNP 5 fax, 2,400-bps/4,800-bps send-only fax	2,400-bps/9,600-bps send/receive fax	2,400-bps/9,600-bps send-only fax
VIDEO					
Screen manufacturer	Sharp	Sharp	Sharp	Sharp	Sharp
Maximum shades of gray	32	64	64	32	32
Video chip set manufacturer	Cirrus	Cirrus	Cirrus	Cirrus	Cirrus
AC ADAPTER AND BATTERY					
AC adapter size (inches)	2 × 3.5 × 6	2 × 6.5 × 3.1	1.9 × 6.5 × 4.3	2.3 × 9.3 × 1.3	2.2 × 5.5 × 3.2
Rated battery life (hours)	3	6	2.5	3	3
ZDigit, battery rundowns (hr:min)	4:47, 2:53	3:01, 2:44	2:47, 2:12	3:01, 2:31	3:01, 2:20
Charge time while on, off (hours)	5, 3	2, 2	2, 2	10, 2	14, 2
Battery weight, amp/hour rating	1.1 lbs, 2.8Ah	1.3 lbs, 1Ah	1.3 lbs, 1Ah	1.2 lbs, 1.4Ah	1.1 lbs, 2.8Ah
Display/hard disk power-down	●/●	●/●	●/●	●/○	●/●
CPU/peripherals power-down	●/●	●/●	●/●	●/○	●/●
Standby/Hibernation	○/○	●/●	●/●	●/○	●/○

●—Yes ○—No N/A—Not applicable INA—Information not available

Table Continues →

Monochrome Portable/Laptop Computers

	Amrel MLT486DXU33	Aquiline NT33	Aquiline Aspen 433	AST Premium Exec 386SX/20	AST Premium Exec 386SX/25
Price	$$$	$$$	$$$	$$$	$$$
Processor type and speed	Intel 486DX/33	Intel 386DX/33	Intel 486DX/33	Intel 386SX/20	AMD Am386SXL/25
Hard disk capacity	130Mb	170Mb	245Mb	80Mb	80Mb
Microsoft Windows 3.1	●	○	●	●	●
Distribution channel	Dealers, direct	Direct, VARs	Dealers, direct	Dealers	Dealers
Dimensions (HWD, in inches)	2.5 × 11.5 × 8.5	2.3 × 11 × 10	2.5 × 11 × 8.8	2.5 × 11 × 8.5	2 × 11 × 8.5
Weight/travel weight (pounds)	7.3, 9	8.5, 10.2	8.5, 10.2	6.7, 8.4	6.6, 7.9
Display area (H × W, in inches)	6 × 7.1	5.2 × 7	5 × 6.8	5.2 × 7	5.2 × 7
Keys: total, function, cursor	85, 12, 4	83, 10, 8	82, 10, 8	82, 10, 8	82, 10, 8
MOTHERBOARD					
Motherboard manufacturer	Amrel	Aquiline	NTC	AST	AST
Chip set manufacturer	ACC	C&T	NTC	WD	WD
BIOS version (or date)	AMI (January 1992)	Award 3.20	Award 3.03	AST 1.06	AST 1.15
Setup in ROM/Password in ROM	●/●	○/○	●/○	●/●	●/●
System shadowing/Video shadowing	○/●	●/●	●/●	●/●	●/●
MEMORY AND DISK DRIVES					
Installable RAM	4Mb–32Mb	2Mb–16Mb	2Mb–16Mb	4Mb–8Mb	4Mb–8Mb
User-installable	●	●	●	●	●
External processor RAM cache	128K	32K	None	None	None
Available hard disk sizes	80Mb, 130Mb, 200Mb	120Mb, 170Mb, 213Mb	120Mb, 170Mb, 240Mb	40Mb, 60Mb, 80Mb, 120Mb	60Mb, 80Mb, 120Mb
I/O AND EXPANSION					
Parallel, serial, mouse ports	1, 1, 0	1, 1, 0	1, 2, 0	1, 1, 0	1, 1, 0
Proprietary expansion port	●	○	●	○	○
PCMCIA slot	○	○	○	○	○
Expansion unit	●	●	●	○	○
Internal modem options	2,400-bps/9,600-bps MNP 5 send/receive fax	9,600-bps MNP 5 fax	None	2,400-bps, 9,600-bps send-fax, 9,600-bps data/fax	2,400-bps, 9,600-bps send-fax, 9,600-bps data/fax
VIDEO					
Screen manufacturer	Sharp	Sharp	Sanyo	Epson	Epson
Maximum shades of gray	64	32	32	32	32
Video chip set manufacturer	Cirrus	Cirrus	Cirrus	Cirrus	Cirrus
AC ADAPTER AND BATTERY					
AC adapter size (inches)	2.3 × 3 × 6.5	2.3 × 3 × 6.5	2.3 × 6.8 × 3	2 × 3 × 6.5	1.5 × 2.3 × 6.5
Rated battery life (hours)	2	3	2	3	2
ZDigit, battery rundowns (hr:min)	2:47, 2:08	1:51, 1:37	2:05, 1:45	2:18, 1:47	6:12, 3:55
Charge time while on, off (hours)	3, 2	3, 3	8, 2	N/A, 3	N/A, 3
Battery weight, amp/hour rating	1.3 lbs, 1Ah	2.2 lbs, 2.8Ah	2.2 lbs, 2.6Ah	1.2 lbs, 5Ah	1.2 lbs, 5Ah
Display/hard disk power-down	●/●	●/●	●/●	●/●	●/●
CPU/peripherals power-down	●/○	●/○	○/○	●/●	●/●
Standby/Hibernation	●/○	○/○	○/○	●/○	●/○

●—Yes ○—No N/A—Not applicable INA—Information not available

Monochrome Portable/Laptop Computers

	Austin 386SX-25 Notebook	Austin 386SXL-25 Notebook	AVI ANB3-386SXL-25	BCC Avanti 025	BCC SL007
Price	$$	$$	$$$	$$$$	$$$$
Processor type and speed	AMD Am386SXL/25	AMD Am386SXL/25	AMD Am386SXL/25	AMD Am386SXL/25	AMD Am386SXL/20
Hard disk capacity	60Mb	60Mb	180Mb	130Mb	80Mb
Microsoft Windows 3.1	○	●	○	●	●
Distribution channel	Company-owned stores, dealers	Dealers, direct	Dealers	Dealers	Dealers
Dimensions (HWD, in inches)	2 × 11 × 8.5	2 × 10.9 × 8.4	1.8 × 11 × 9	3 × 11.5 × 9	2.5 × 11 × 8.5
Weight/travel weight (pounds)	6.8, 8.7	6.2, 8	5.4, 7.1	6.5, 7.8	6.6, 7.6
Display area (H × W, in inches)	6 × 7.5	5.6 × 7.6	5.8 × 7.8	6 × 7.5	5.7 × 7.7
Keys: total, function, cursor	80, 12, 4	79, 10, 4	84, 10, 8	80, 10, 4	80, 12, 4
MOTHERBOARD					
Motherboard manufacturer	Sampo	Austin	AVI	BCC	BCC
Chip set manufacturer	VLSI, Intel	VLSI	Acer	WD	Intel
BIOS version (or date)	Phoenix 1.1	Phoenix (April 1990)	AMI (May 1991)	Award (February 1992)	Award (February 1992)
Setup in ROM/Password in ROM	●/●	●/○	●/●	●/●	●/●
System shadowing/Video shadowing	●/●	○/●	○/●	●/●	●/●
MEMORY AND DISK DRIVES					
Installable RAM	1Mb–8Mb	2Mb–8Mb	2Mb–8Mb	2Mb–8Mb	4Mb–8Mb
User-installable	●	●	●	●	●
External processor RAM cache	None	None	None	None	64K
Available hard disk sizes	60Mb	60Mb, 120Mb	60Mb, 80Mb, 130Mb, 180Mb	60Mb, 80Mb, 130Mb	80Mb, 130Mb
I/O AND EXPANSION					
Parallel, serial, mouse ports	1, 1, 0	1, 1, 0	1, 2, 0	1, 1, 0	1, 1, 1
Proprietary expansion port	○	○	○	○	○
PCMCIA slot	○	○	○	○	○
Expansion unit	○	○	○	○	○
Internal modem options	4,800-bps fax	2,400-bps/9,600-bps send-only fax, 4,800-bps/9,600-bps send/receive fax	2,400-bps/9,600-bps send/receive fax	9,600-bps fax	9,600-bps fax
VIDEO					
Screen manufacturer	Sharp	Seiko	Sharp	Sharp	Sharp
Maximum shades of gray	32	32	32	32	32
Video chip set manufacturer	Cirrus	Cirrus	Cirrus	WD	WD
AC ADAPTER AND BATTERY					
AC adapter size (inches)	2.3 × 3.5 × 6	1.6 × 3.1 × 5.7	2 × 6.5 × 3	2 × 2.5 × 6	1.5 × 2.5 × 5.8
Rated battery life (hours)	2	4	2.5	2–8	2–8
ZDigit, battery rundowns (hr:min)	4:48, 2:56	4:42, 3:23	3:02, 1:58	2:45, 1:59	N/A, 1:49
Charge time while on, off (hours)	2.5, 2	6, 2	3, 3	10, 1	10, 4
Battery weight, amp/hour rating	1.1 lbs, 2.8Ah	1.3 lbs, 1.3Ah	0.8 lbs, 2.4Ah	1.8 lbs, 1.7Ah	1.2 lbs, 1.7Ah
Display/hard disk power-down	●/●	●/●	●/●	●/●	●/●
CPU/peripherals power-down	●/○	●/●	●/○	●/●	●/●
Standby/Hibernation	●/●	○/○	●/○	●/●	●/●

●—Yes ○—No N/A—Not applicable INA—Information not available

Table Continues →

Monochrome Portable/Laptop Computers

	Blackship NB320S	BLK 386SL/25NBF	Blue Star 386DX/25 Notebook	Blue Star 386SX/25 Notebook	Bondwell 386SL/F Notebook
Price	$$	$$	$$$	$$	$$$
Processor type and speed	Intel 386SX/20	Intel 386SL/25	Intel 386DX/25	Intel 386SX/25	Intel 386SL/25
Hard disk capacity	85Mb	80Mb	120Mb	80Mb	80 Mb
Microsoft Windows 3.1	○	●	●	●	○
Distribution channel	Direct	Dealers, direct	Dealers, direct	Dealers, direct	Dealers, direct
Dimensions (HWD, in inches)	2.1 × 11 × 8.5	1.5 × 11.3 × 8.5	2.5 × 11 × 8.3	1.7 × 12 × 9.5	1.5 × 11.5 × 8.5
Weight/travel weight (pounds)	6.7, 8.6	5.5, 6.7	7.5, 9.1	7.9, 9.4	5.5, 6.8
Display area (H × W, in inches)	5.5 × 7	5.8 × 7.8	7 × 8.5	5.5 × 7.5	5 × 7
Keys: total, function, cursor	80, 10, 4	86, 10, 8	84, 12, 4	83, 10, 8	81, 10, 4
MOTHERBOARD					
Motherboard manufacturer	Intra	Chaplet	Amrel	MCC	Bondwell
Chip set manufacturer	VLSI	ACC	SIS	Headland	Intel
BIOS version (or date)	AMI 1.3	Quadtel (June 1992)	AMI (June 1990)	AMI (June 1990)	Quadtel 3.06
Setup in ROM/Password in ROM	●/●	●/●	●/○	○/○	●/●
System shadowing/Video shadowing	●/●	●/●	●/●	●/●	●/●
MEMORY AND DISK DRIVES					
Installable RAM	1Mb–5Mb	4Mb–8Mb	2Mb–8Mb	4Mb–8Mb	2Mb–8Mb
User-installable	●	●	●	○	●
External processor RAM cache	None	32K	128K	None	16K
Available hard disk sizes	60Mb, 85Mb	60Mb, 80Mb, 120Mb	60Mb, 80Mb, 120Mb	60Mb, 80Mb, 130Mb	60Mb, 80Mb
I/O AND EXPANSION					
Parallel, serial, mouse ports	1, 1, 0	1, 2, 0	1, 1, 0	1, 1, 0	1, 1, 0
Proprietary expansion port	●	○	●	○	●
PCMCIA slot	○	○	○	○	○
Expansion unit	○	○	●	○	○
Internal modem options	9,600-bps fax	None	9,600-bps fax	None	2,400-bps V.42bis
VIDEO					
Screen manufacturer	Sanyo	Sharp	Sanyo	Sanyo	Hitachi
Maximum shades of gray	16	64	64	64	64
Video chip set manufacturer	Cirrus	Cirrus	Cirrus	C&T	Cirrus
AC ADAPTER AND BATTERY					
AC adapter size (inches)	2 × 3.1 × 6.5	1.8 × 2.5 × 6	2 × 3 × 6.5	1.5 × 3 × 7	1.5 × 5 × 5.5
Rated battery life (hours)	1.5	5.5	3	4–6	3.5
ZDigit, battery rundowns (hr:min)	2:59, 1:45	2:32, 1:15	2:59, 2:12	4:21, 3:03	2:03, 1:37
Charge time while on, off (hours)	12, 6	2, 2	2.5, 2	2.5, 2	12, 1
Battery weight, amp/hour rating	1.1 lbs, 2.5Ah	0.7 lbs, 1.5Ah	1.3 lbs, 2Ah	1 lb, 4Ah	0.8 lbs, 2.2Ah
Display/hard disk power-down	●/●	●/○	●/●	●/●	●/●
CPU/peripherals power-down	●/○	●/●	○/○	○/○	●/●
Standby/Hibernation	●/●	●/●	○/○	○/○	●/●

●—Yes ○—No N/A—Not applicable INA—Information not available

Monochrome Portable/Laptop Computers

	Chaplet 386 SL25 Notebook	Compaq Contura 3/20	Compaq Contura 3/25	Compaq LTE 386s/20	Compaq LTE Lite/20
Price	$$	$$	$$	$$$$	$$$
Processor type and speed	Intel 386SL/25	Intel 386SL/20	Intel 386SX/25	Intel 386SX/20	Intel 386SL/20
Hard disk capacity	120Mb	84Mb	60Mb	60Mb	80Mb
Microsoft Windows 3.1	○	○	○	○	○
Distribution channel	Dealers	Dealers	Dealers	Dealers, superstores	Dealers, superstores
Dimensions (HWD, in inches)	1.8 × 11.3 × 8.5	2 × 11.5 × 9	2 × 11 × 9	2.3 × 11 × 8.5	1.7 × 11 × 8.5
Weight/travel weight (pounds)	5.2, 6.9	6.2, 7.6	6.2, 7.6	7.6, 9.3	6.1, 7.3
Display area (H × W, in inches)	6 × 8	5.8 × 7.5	5.8 × 7.5	5.5 × 7.5	5.5 × 7.5
Keys: total, function, cursor	86, 10, 8	79, 10, 8	79, 10, 8	80, 10, 4	80, 12, 4
MOTHERBOARD					
Motherboard manufacturer	Chaplet	Compaq	Compaq	Compaq	Compaq
Chip set manufacturer	Intel	Intel	Intel	Compaq	Compaq
BIOS version (or date)	System Soft (July 1992)	Compaq (June 1992)	Compaq (June 1992)	Compaq (February 1992)	Compaq (January 1992)
Setup in ROM/Password in ROM	●/○	●/●	●/●	●/○	●/●
System shadowing/Video shadowing	●/●	●/○	●/○	○/●	●/●
MEMORY AND DISK DRIVES					
Installable RAM	2Mb–8Mb	2Mb–10Mb	4Mb–12Mb	2Mb–10Mb	2Mb–10Mb
User-installable	●	●	●	○	●
External processor RAM cache	16K	None	None	4K	None
Available hard disk sizes	60Mb, 80Mb, 120Mb	40Mb, 84Mb	60Mb, 120Mb	30Mb, 60Mb	40Mb, 60Mb, 80Mb
I/O AND EXPANSION					
Parallel, serial, mouse ports	1, 2, 0	1, 1, 1	1, 1, 1	2, 1, 1	1, 1, 1
Proprietary expansion port	○	○	○	●	○
PCMCIA slot	○	○	○	○	○
Expansion unit	○	○	○	●	●
Internal modem options	2,400-bps/9,600-bps MNP 5 send/receive fax	2,400-bps/9,600-bps MNP 5 send/receive fax	2,400-bps/9,600-bps MNP 5 send/receive fax	2,400-bps, 9,600-bps data/fax	2,400-bps, 9,600-bps data/fax
VIDEO					
Screen manufacturer	Citizen	Compaq	Compaq	Compaq	Compaq
Maximum shades of gray	64	64	64	16	16
Video chip set manufacturer	Cirrus	Compaq	Compaq	Compaq	Compaq
AC ADAPTER AND BATTERY					
AC adapter size (inches)	1.5 × 6 × 4.5	1.5 × 5.4 × 3.4	1.5 × 5.3 × 3.3	2.5 × 3 × 5.1	1.4 × 3.3 × 5.3
Rated battery life (hours)	2	3.5	3.5	3	4.5
ZDigit, battery rundowns (hr:min)	1:51, 1:23	4:53, 2:28	4:11, 2:15	4:07, 2:59	3:26, 2:16
Charge time while on, off (hours)	2, 2	1.5, 1	1.5, 1	3, 1.5	1.5, 1
Battery weight, amp/hour rating	0.7 lbs, 1.5Ah	1.1 lbs, 3Ah	1.1 lbs, 3Ah	1.8 lbs, 1.7Ah	1.3 lbs, 2.2Ah
Display/hard disk power-down	●/●	●/●	●/●	●/●	●/●
CPU/peripherals power-down	●/●	●/●	●/●	●/●	●/●
Standby/Hibernation	●/●	●/●	●/●	●/●	●/●

●—Yes   ○—No   N/A—Not applicable   INA—Information not available

Table Continues →

Monochrome Portable/Laptop Computers

	Compaq LTE Lite/25	Compaq LTE Lite/25E	CompuAdd Express 325NXL	CompuAdd Express 425CXL-80	Compudyne 386SXL/25
Price	$$$$	INA	$$	$$	$$
Processor type and speed	Intel 386SL/25	Intel 386SL/25	AMD Am386SXL/25	Cyrix CX486SLC/25	AMD Am386SXL/25
Hard disk capacity	80Mb	80Mb	60Mb	80Mb	60Mb
Microsoft Windows 3.1	○	●	○	●	●
Distribution channel	Dealers, superstores	Dealers	Direct	Direct	Direct
Dimensions (HWD, in inches)	1.7 × 11 × 8.5	2 × 11 × 8.5	2 × 11 × 8.5	2 × 11 × 8.5	1.5 × 11 × 8.5
Weight/travel weight (pounds)	6.1, 7.3	6.4, 8.4	5, 6.6	5.2, 6.9	5.9, 7.6
Display area (H × W, in inches)	5.5 × 7.5	5.3 × 6.8	6 × 8	5.8 × 7.8	6 × 7.5
Keys: total, function, cursor	80, 12, 4	80, 10, 4	84, 12, 4	86, 12, 8	84, 10, 4
MOTHERBOARD					
Motherboard manufacturer	Compaq	Compaq	ASIC	TI	Twinhead
Chip set manufacturer	Compaq	Intel	WD	WD	VLSI
BIOS version (or date)	Compaq (January 1992)	Compaq (September 1992)	Phoenix 1.03	Phoenix (April 1990)	Phoenix 1.01
Setup in ROM/Password in ROM	●/●	●/●	●/●	●/○	○/○
System shadowing/Video shadowing	●/●	●/●	●/●	○/●	●/●
MEMORY AND DISK DRIVES					
Installable RAM	4Mb–10Mb	4Mb–20Mb	4Mb–16Mb	1Mb–16Mb	2Mb–6Mb
User-installable	●	●	●	●	●
External processor RAM cache	16K	64K	None	None	None
Available hard disk sizes	40Mb, 60Mb, 80Mb	84Mb, 120Mb	60Mb	80Mb, 120Mb	60Mb, 80Mb
I/O AND EXPANSION					
Parallel, serial, mouse ports	1, 1, 1	1, 1, 1	1, 1, 1	1, 1, 1	1, 1, 1
Proprietary expansion port	○	●	○	○	●
PCMCIA slot	○	○	○	○	○
Expansion unit	●	●	○	○	○
Internal modem options	2,400-bps, 9,600-bps data/fax	2,400-bps/9,600-bps send/receive fax	9,600-bps fax	2,400-bps/9,600-bps send/receive fax	4,800-bps fax, 9,600-bps fax
VIDEO					
Screen manufacturer	Compaq	Compaq	Sharp	Sharp	Sharp
Maximum shades of gray	16	16	64	64	64
Video chip set manufacturer	Compaq	Compaq	WD	WD	Cirrus
AC ADAPTER AND BATTERY					
AC adapter size (inches)	1.4 × 3.3 × 5.3	1.4 × 5.3 × 3.3	2 × 2.5 × 3.5	3.3 × 2.6 × 2.2	1.8 × 3 × 6.5
Rated battery life (hours)	4.5	3	4	2	3
ZDigit, battery rundowns (hr:min)	3:26, 2:17	4:11, 2:38	5:28, 1:31	2:48, 2:09	3:26, 2:44
Charge time while on, off (hours)	1.5, 1	1.5, 1	N/A, 1.5	7, 1.5	6, 3
Battery weight, amp/hour rating	1.3 lbs, 2.2Ah	1.2 lbs, 2.2Ah	0.5 lbs, 1.4Ah	0.7 lbs, 1.4Ah	1.3 lbs, 1.7Ah
Display/hard disk power-down	●/●	●/●	●/●	●/●	○/●
CPU/peripherals power-down	●/●	●/●	●/●	●/●	○/○
Standby/Hibernation	●/●	●/●	●/○	●/●	●/●

●—Yes   ○—No   N/A—Not applicable   INA—Information not available

Monochrome Portable/Laptop Computers

	Compudyne 486DX/33	Compudyne Slimnote 386SL/25-80	Compudyne Slimnote 486SX/25-80	Cumulus Express 386SX/20 Notebook	Dauphin 1050 Lapbook
Price	$$$	$$	$$	$$	$$$$
Processor type and speed	Intel 486DX/33	Intel 386SL/25	Intel 486SX/25	Intel 386SX/20	Intel 386SX/20
Hard disk capacity	130Mb	80Mb	80Mb	60Mb	124Mb
Microsoft Windows 3.1	●	●	●	●	○
Distribution channel	Direct	Dealers, direct	Direct	Dealers, superstores	Direct
Dimensions (HWD, in inches)	1.6 × 11 × 8.5	11.6 × 11 × 8.5	11.6 × 11 × 8.5	2 × 11 × 8.5	2.2 × 12.5 × 11.2
Weight/travel weight (pounds)	5.9, 7.6	5.9, 7.6	6, 6.6	6.5, 8	7.6, 9.3
Display area (H × W, in inches)	5.5 × 7.5	5.8 × 7.7	5.8 × 7.7	5.5 × 7	6 × 8
Keys: total, function, cursor	84, 10, 4	84, 10, 8	84, 10, 8	85, 12, 10	79, 12, 4
MOTHERBOARD					
Motherboard manufacturer	Twinhead	Twinhead	Twinhead	Jetta Computer	ASIC
Chip set manufacturer	Intel	Intel	ACC	VLSI	WD
BIOS version (or date)	Phoenix 1.6	System Soft (April 1992)	Phoenix (May 1992)	Award 3.1	Phoenix 1.01
Setup in ROM/Password in ROM	○/○	●/●	●/○	○/○	●/○
System shadowing/Video shadowing	●/●	●/●	●/●	●/●	●/○
MEMORY AND DISK DRIVES					
Installable RAM	4Mb–20Mb	2Mb–6Mb	4Mb–20Mb	2Mb–16Mb	4Mb–8Mb
User-installable	●	●	○	●	○
External processor RAM cache	None	64K	None	None	None
Available hard disk sizes	130Mb	80Mb	80Mb, 120Mb	60Mb	60Mb, 80Mb, 124Mb
I/O AND EXPANSION					
Parallel, serial, mouse ports	1, 1, 1	1, 1, 1	1, 1, 1	1, 1, 1	1, 1, 1
Proprietary expansion port	●	●	●	●	●
PCMCIA slot	○	○	○	○	○
Expansion unit	○	○	○	○	●
Internal modem options	4,800-bps fax, 9,600-bps fax	2,400-bps/9,600-bps MNP 5 send/receive fax	2,400-bps/9,600-bps MNP 5 send/receive fax	9,600-bps send-fax	9,600-bps fax
VIDEO					
Screen manufacturer	Sharp	Sharp	Sharp	Hitachi	Seiko/Epson
Maximum shades of gray	64	64	64	16	32
Video chip set manufacturer	Cirrus	Cirrus	Cirrus	Cirrus	WD
AC ADAPTER AND BATTERY					
AC adapter size (inches)	1.8 × 3 × 6.5	2 × 6.5 × 3.1	1.9 × 6.5 × 3.1	2 × 3 × 7.5	2 × 3 × 6.5
Rated battery life (hours)	2.5	3.5	2.5	2	3
ZDigit, battery rundowns (hr:min)	N/A, 2:12	3:44, 2:20	3:30, 2:27	2:18, 1:36	2:16, 1:42
Charge time while on, off (hours)	2, 1.5	4, 2	4, 2	N/A, 8	8, 3
Battery weight, amp/hour rating	1.3 lbs, 1.7Ah	1.3 lbs, 1Ah	1.3 lbs, 1Ah	1.4 lbs, 5Ah	1.2 lbs, 1.7Ah
Display/hard disk power-down	●/●	●/●	●/●	●/●	●/●
CPU/peripherals power-down	●/●	●/●	●/●	●/●	●/●
Standby/Hibernation	●/○	●/○	●/○	○/○	●/●

●—Yes ○—No N/A—Not applicable INA—Information not available

Table Continues →

Monochrome Portable/Laptop Computers

	Dell Dimension NL20	Dell System NL25	Dell System 320SLi	Dell System 325N	Dell 320LT
Price	$$	$$$	$$$	$$	$$
Processor type and speed	Intel 386SL/20	Intel 386SL/25	Intel 386SL/20	Intel 386SL/25	386SX/20MHz
Hard disk capacity	60Mb	80Mb	60Mb	60Mb	40Mb
Microsoft Windows 3.1	●	●	●	●	INA
Distribution channel	Dealers, direct	Direct, superstores, VARs	Dealers, direct	Dealers, direct	
Dimensions (HWD, in inches)	1.8 × 11 × 8.3	1.5 × 11 × 8.3	1.3 × 11 × 7.8	2.3 × 11 × 8.5	3.5 × 12.8 × 14.3
Weight/travel weight (pounds)	6.1, 7.6	6.3, 7.7	3.8, 4.8	6.4, 7.4	15
Display area (H × W, in inches)	5.1 × 6.8	6 × 7.5	5.5 × 7.7	5.8 × 7.5	6 × 7.9
Keys: total, function, cursor	85, 12, 8	85, 12, 4	85, 12, 8	85, 12, 8	83, 12, 8
MOTHERBOARD					
Motherboard manufacturer	Dell	Dell	Dell	Dell	Dell
Chip set manufacturer	Intel	Intel	Intel	Intel	Kyocera
BIOS version (or date)	Quadtel/Phoenix A03	Quadtel 3.06	Phoenix (September 1992)	Phoenix (July 1992)	Phoenix 1.10 A00 (July 1990)
Setup in ROM/Password in ROM	●/●	●/●	●/●	●/●	INA
System shadowing/Video shadowing	●/●	●/●	●/●	●/●	●/●
MEMORY AND DISK DRIVES					
Installable RAM	2Mb–8Mb	2Mb–8Mb	2Mb–10Mb	4Mb–12Mb	1Mb–8Mb
User-installable	●	●	●	●	INA
External processor RAM cache	None	16K	None	64K	None
Available hard disk sizes	40Mb, 60Mb	60Mb, 80Mb	60Mb, 80Mb, 120Mb	60Mb, 80Mb, 120Mb	INA
I/O AND EXPANSION					
Parallel, serial, mouse ports	1, 1, 1	1, 1, 1	1, 1, 1	1, 1, 1	INA
Proprietary expansion port	○	○	○	○	INA
PCMCIA slot	○	○	●	○	INA
Expansion unit	○	○	○	○	INA
Internal modem options	2,400-bps/9,600-bps MNP 5 send-only fax	9,600-bps send-fax	2,400-bps	2,400-bps/9,600-bps send/receive fax	INA
VIDEO					
Screen manufacturer	Sharp	Sharp	Sharp	Sharp	INA
Maximum shades of gray	32	32	64	32	INA
Video chip set manufacturer	Cirrus	Intel	Cirrus	WD	C&T
AC ADAPTER AND BATTERY					
AC adapter size (inches)	1.8 × 3 × 6.1	3 × 4 × 5	1.8 × 2.5 × 4.6	1.5 × 3.2 × 5.5	INA
Rated battery life (hours)	2.5	2.5	2.5	3	2.3
ZDigit, battery rundowns (hr:min)	3:30, 3:12	3:26, 2:26	N/A, 3:08	5:07, 3:41	INA
Charge time while on, off (hours)	10, 2.5	N/A, 2.5	6, 2	N/A, 3.5	24, 1.5
Battery weight, amp/hour rating	1.5 lbs, 1.3Ah	1.3 lbs, 1.7Ah	0.7 lbs, 2Ah	1.6 lbs, 2Ah	INA
Display/hard disk power-down	●/●	●/●	●/●	●/●	INA
CPU/peripherals power-down	○/●	●/●	●/●	●/●	INA
Standby/Hibernation	●/●	●/●	●/●	●/●	INA

●—Yes ○—No N/A—Not applicable INA—Information not available

Monochrome Portable/Laptop Computers

	Digital DECpc 32 Notebook	Digital DECpc 325p	DTK Grafika 3N	Epson NB-SL/20	Epson NB-SL/25
Price	$$	$$$	$$	$$$	$$$
Processor type and speed	Intel 386SX/20	Intel 386SL/25	AMD Am386SXL/25	Intel 386SL/20	Intel 386SL/25
Hard disk capacity	40Mb	125Mb	120Mb	80Mb	80Mb
Microsoft Windows 3.1	●	●	●	○	○
Distribution channel	Dealers, direct	Dealers, direct	Dealers	Dealers, superstores	Dealers, superstores
Dimensions (HWD, in inches)	1.7 × 12 × 10	1.8 × 11.7 × 8.5	2 × 11.5 × 8.2	2 × 11.5 × 9	2 × 11.5 × 9
Weight/travel weight (pounds)	6.4, 7.7	5.9, 7.2	6.4, 7.6	7, 8.2	7.2, 9
Display area (H × W, in inches)	5.5 × 7	6 × 8	5.5 × 7	6 × 7.7	6 × 7.7
Keys: total, function, cursor	84, 12, 8	84, 12, 8	85, 12, 8	84, 12, 4	84, 12, 4
MOTHERBOARD					
Motherboard manufacturer	Matsushita	Matsushita	SOTEC	Seiko/Epson	Seiko/Epson
Chip set manufacturer	Headland	C&T	VLSI	Intel	Intel
BIOS version (or date)	Phoenix 3.1D	Phoenix (May 1992)	AMI (March 1992)	Epson/Seiko/ Quadtel 1.51	Quadtel 3.06
Setup in ROM/Password in ROM	○/○	○/○	●/○	●/●	●/●
System shadowing/Video shadowing	○/○	○/○	○/○	●/○	●/○
MEMORY AND DISK DRIVES					
Installable RAM	2Mb–8Mb	2Mb–8Mb	1Mb–5Mb	2Mb–14Mb	4Mb–20Mb
User-installable	●	●	●	●	●
External processor RAM cache	None	16K	None	64K	64K
Available hard disk sizes	40Mb, 80Mb	80Mb, 120Mb	60Mb, 80Mb, 120Mb	40Mb, 60Mb, 80Mb	40Mb, 60Mb, 80Mb
I/O AND EXPANSION					
Parallel, serial, mouse ports	1, 1, 1	1, 1, 0	1, 1, 1	1, 1, 1	1, 1, 1
Proprietary expansion port	○	●	○	●	●
PCMCIA slot	○	○	○	○	○
Expansion unit	○	●	○	●	●
Internal modem options	2,400-bps, 9,600-bps data/fax	2,400-bps/9,600-bps MNP 5 send/receive fax	2,400-bps/9,600-bps send/receive fax	9,600-bps fax, 9,600-bps data/fax	9,600-bps fax, 9,600-bps data/fax
VIDEO					
Screen manufacturer	Sharp	Sharp	Epson	Hitachi	Epson
Maximum shades of gray	16	32	16	16	16
Video chip set manufacturer	Cirrus	Cirrus	WD	Cirrus	Cirrus
AC ADAPTER AND BATTERY					
AC adapter size (inches)	1.8 × 2.8 × 5.5	1.6 × 2.5 × 5.5	2.5 × 5 × 1.5	1.5 × 3 × 6.5	1.5 × 3 × 6.5
Rated battery life (hours)	2.5	4	1	3	2
ZDigit, battery rundowns (hr:min)	3:26, 2:09	3:30, 2:31	3:29, 2:03	3:29, 2:33	3:39, 2:17
Charge time while on, off (hours)	1, 0.5	5, 2	8.5, 2	N/A, 1.5	N/A, 3.5
Battery weight, amp/hour rating	0.8 lbs, 1.4Ah	1 lb, 0.9Ah	0.9 lbs, 1.5Ah	0.7 lbs, 1.7Ah	0.7 lbs, 1.7Ah
Display/hard disk power-down	●/●	○/●	●/●	●/●	●/●
CPU/peripherals power-down	●/●	●/●	●/○	●/●	●/●
Standby/Hibernation	●/●	●/○	●/○	●/○	●/○

●—Yes   ○— No   N/A—Not applicable   INA—Information not available   **Table Continues →**

Monochrome Portable/Laptop Computers

	Ergo 486DX-33 NoteBrick II	Everex Carrier SL/25	Everex Tempo Carrier 386SX/20	Gateway Nomad 325SXL	Gateway Nomad 420SXL
Price	$$$	$$$	$$$	$$	$$$
Processor type and speed	Intel 486DX/33	Intel 386SL/25	Intel 386SX/20	AMD Am386SXL/25	Intel 486SX/20
Hard disk capacity	210Mb	81Mb	80Mb	80Mb	80Mb
Microsoft Windows 3.1	●	●	●	●	●
Distribution channel	Dealers, direct	Dealers	Dealers, superstores	Direct	Direct
Dimensions (HWD, in inches)	2.5 × 11 × 8.8	2 × 11 × 8.5	1.8 × 11 × 8.5	2 × 11 × 8.5	2 × 11 × 8.5
Weight/travel weight (pounds)	8.5, 10.2	6, 7.5	5.3, 7	5.7, 7.1	5.8, 7.2
Display area (H × W, in inches)	5 × 6.8	5.2 × 7	6.2 × 10	6 × 8	6 × 8
Keys: total, function, cursor	82, 10, 8	81, 12, 0	80, 12, 4	79, 10, 4	79, 10, 4
MOTHERBOARD					
Motherboard manufacturer	NTC	Everex	Everex	TI	TI
Chip set manufacturer	ETEQ	Intel	C&T	TI	TI
BIOS version (or date)	Award 3.03	AMI/Everex (June 1992)	AMI (February 1988)	Phoenix 1.01	Phoenix 0.98
Setup in ROM/Password in ROM	●/○	●/●	●/●	●/●	●/○
System shadowing/Video shadowing	●/●	●/●	●/●	●/●	●/●
MEMORY AND DISK DRIVES					
Installable RAM	1Mb–16Mb	2Mb–20Mb	2Mb–8Mb	2Mb–6Mb	4Mb–20Mb
User-installable	●	●	○	●	●
External processor RAM cache	None	64K	None	None	None
Available hard disk sizes	120Mb, 210Mb, 340Mb	85Mb, 120Mb, 180Mb	40Mb, 80Mb	80Mb	80Mb
I/O AND EXPANSION					
Parallel, serial, mouse ports	1, 2, 0	1, 1, 0	1, 2, 0	1, 1, 1	1, 1, 1
Proprietary expansion port	●	○	○	●	●
PCMCIA slot	○	○	○	○	○
Expansion unit	●	○	○	●	●
Internal modem options	2,400-bps	2,400-bps/9,600-bps send-only fax	9,600-bps send-fax	4,800-bps send-fax, 9,600-bps data/fax	4,800-bps send-fax, 9,600-bps data/fax
VIDEO					
Screen manufacturer	Sanyo	Sharp	Sharp	Sharp	Sharp
Maximum shades of gray	32	16	32	64	64
Video chip set manufacturer	Cirrus	Cirrus	C&T	Cirrus	Cirrus
AC ADAPTER AND BATTERY					
AC adapter size (inches)	1.6 × 3.1 × 5.7	1.7 × 5.7 × 2.5	1.8 × 2.6 × 5.9	1.5 × 2 × 6	1.5 × 2 × 6
Rated battery life (hours)	2	1.5	2	2.5–6	2.5–6
ZDigit, battery rundowns (hr:min)	2:05, 1:40	2:21, 1:56	2:31, 1:46	5:41, 3:34	4:34, 3:41
Charge time while on, off (hours)	2, 2	1, 1	1.5, 1.5	4, 3	4, 3
Battery weight, amp/hour rating	2.2 lbs, 2.5Ah	0.8 lbs, 2.2Ah	0.7 lbs, 2.4Ah	1.3 lbs, 5.7Ah	1.3 lbs, 5.7Ah
Display/hard disk power-down	●/●	●/●	●/●	●/●	●/●
CPU/peripherals power-down	○/○	●/○	●/●	●/●	●/●
Standby/Hibernation	○/○	●/●	●/●	●/○	●/○

●—Yes   ○—No   N/A—Not applicable   INA—Information not available

Monochrome Portable/Laptop Computers

	Gateway Nomad 425DXL	GRiD 1660	GRiD 1755 486SLC	GRiD Convertible	IBM PS/2 Model P75 486
Price	$$$	$$$	$$$	$$$	$$$$
Processor type and speed	Intel 486DX/25	Intel 386SL/25	Cyrix CX486SLC/25	Intel 386SL/25	486/33MHz
Hard disk capacity	120Mb	120Mb	80Mb	120Mb	160Mb
Microsoft Windows 3.1	●	●	●	●	INA
Distribution channel	Direct	Dealers	Dealers	Dealers	
Dimensions (HWD, in inches)	2 × 11 × 8.5	1.8 × 11.6 × 8.5	1.5 × 12.3 × 10	1.6 × 11.5 × 9.4	12.1 × 18.3 × 6.1
Weight/travel weight (pounds)	5.8, 7.2	5.9, 7.1	6.4, 7.7	5.5, 7.2	22.1
Display area (H × W, in inches)	6 × 8	6 × 8	5.1 × 7	6 × 7.6	6.4 × 8.3
Keys: total, function, cursor	79, 10, 4	84, 12, 8	84, 12, 8	79, 10, 8	101, 12, 4

MOTHERBOARD

Motherboard manufacturer	TI	Matsushita	Matsushita	Tandy	IBM
Chip set manufacturer	TI	C&T	Headland	Intel	IBM
BIOS version (or date)	Phoenix 0.98	Phoenix (April 1992)	Phoenix (May 1992)	Phoenix (June 1992)	IBM (November 1990)
Setup in ROM/Password in ROM	●/○	●/●	●/●	●/●	INA
System shadowing/Video shadowing	●/●	●/●	●/●	○/○	●/●

MEMORY AND DISK DRIVES

Installable RAM	4Mb–20Mb	2Mb–20Mb	2Mb–8Mb	2Mb–8Mb	8Mb–16Mb
User-installable	●	●	●	●	INA
External processor RAM cache	None	64K	1Mb	None	None
Available hard disk sizes	120Mb	125Mb	80Mb	120Mb	INA

I/O AND EXPANSION

Parallel, serial, mouse ports	1, 1, 1	1, 1, 1	1, 1, 1	1, 1, 0	INA
Proprietary expansion port	●	○	○	○	INA
PCMCIA slot	○	○	○	○	INA
Expansion unit	●	○	○	○	INA
Internal modem options	4,800-bps send-fax, 9,600-bps data/fax	2,400-bps/9,600-bps MNP 5 send/receive fax	2,400-bps/9,600-bps MNP 5 send/receive fax	2,400-bps/9,600-bps send/receive fax, 14,400-bps send/receive fax	INA

VIDEO

Screen manufacturer	Sharp	Sharp	Sharp	Sharp	INA
Maximum shades of gray	64	64	64	64	INA
Video chip set manufacturer	Cirrus	Cirrus	Cirrus	Cirrus	IBM

AC ADAPTER AND BATTERY

AC adapter size (inches)	1.5 × 2 × 6	1.6 × 2.5 × 5.5	1.8 × 2.8 × 5.3	1.5 × 3 × 7.8	INA
Rated battery life (hours)	2.5–6	3	2.5	3	N/A
ZDigit, battery rundowns (hr:min)	4:34, 3:41	4:11, 2:09	2:47, 1:53	1:39, 1:21	INA
Charge time while on, off (hours)	4, 3	5, 2	5, 2	1.5, 1.5	N/A
Battery weight, amp/hour rating	1.3 lbs, 5.7Ah	0.9 lbs, 0.9Ah	0.7 lbs, 1.4Ah	0.8 lbs, 1.3Ah	INA
Display/hard disk power-down	●/●	○/●	●/●	●/●	INA
CPU/peripherals power-down	●/●	○/●	○/●	○/●	INA
Standby/Hibernation	●/○	●/○	●/○	○/○	INA

●—Yes   ○—No   N/A—Not applicable   INA—Information not available

Table Continues →

Monochrome Portable/Laptop Computers

	IBM PS/note N45sl	Identity 386SX/20 Notebook	Identity 386SXL-25 Notebook Computer	Insight 386-25SXL Notebook	Intelec Halikan 386SX/20
Price	$$	$$$	$$$	$$	$$
Processor type and speed	Intel 386SL/25	Intel 386SX/20	AMD Am386SXL/25	AMD Am386SXL/25	Intel 386SX/20
Hard disk capacity	80Mb	124Mb	210Mb	80Mb	80Mb
Microsoft Windows 3.1	○	●	●	○	●
Distribution channel	Dealers, direct	Dealers, superstores	Dealers	Direct	Direct
Dimensions (HWD, in inches)	2 × 12.3 × 8.3	2.2 × 11 × 8.5	2.3 × 11 × 8.6	2 × 11 × 8.5	2 × 11.7 × 8.5
Weight/travel weight (pounds)	7, 8.9	6.4, 7.7	5.7, 8	5.7, 7.1	6.5, 8.3
Display area (H × W, in inches)	5.8 × 7.6	5 × 7	5 × 6.9	6 × 8	5 × 7
Keys: total, function, cursor	82, 12, 8	80, 12, 4	84, 12, 8	79, 10, 4	80, 12, 4
MOTHERBOARD					
Motherboard manufacturer	IBM	Cirrus	ARC	Insight	Chaplet
Chip set manufacturer	Intel	Phoenix	AMD	VLSI	Intel
BIOS version (or date)	ZDS (February 1992)	Phoenix 1.01	Phoenix (April 1990)	Phoenix 1.01	AMI 1.30
Setup in ROM/Password in ROM	●/●	○/○	●/●	●/●	●/●
System shadowing/Video shadowing	○/●	●/●	●/●	●/●	●/●
MEMORY AND DISK DRIVES					
Installable RAM	2Mb–8Mb	1Mb–5Mb	1Mb–8Mb	2Mb–8Mb	1Mb–4Mb
User-installable	●	●	●	○	●
External processor RAM cache	64K	None	None	None	None
Available hard disk sizes	80Mb, 120Mb	60Mb, 80Mb, 124Mb	500Mb	40Mb, 80Mb, 130Mb	40Mb, 60Mb, 80Mb, 120Mb
I/O AND EXPANSION					
Parallel, serial, mouse ports	1, 1, 1	1, 1, 0	1, 2, 0	1, 1, 1	1, 1, 0
Proprietary expansion port	○	○	○	○	●
PCMCIA slot	○	○	○	○	○
Expansion unit	○	○	○	○	●
Internal modem options	2,400-bps/9,600-bps send/receive fax	None	None	2,400-bps, 9,600-bps fax	None
VIDEO					
Screen manufacturer	Epson	Sanyo	Sanyo	Sharp	Epson
Maximum shades of gray	32	16	32	64	16
Video chip set manufacturer	WD	Cirrus	Cirrus	Cirrus	Cirrus
AC ADAPTER AND BATTERY					
AC adapter size (inches)	2 × 3.4 × 6.6	1.8 × 3 × 5	1.3 × 3.5 × 5	1.8 × 3 × 4.5	2 × 3.5 × 7
Rated battery life (hours)	3	2	2.5	2–3	2
ZDigit, battery rundowns (hr:min)	3:44, 2:57	2:18, 1:45	2:34,1:45	2:18, 1:45	2:30, 1:53
Charge time while on, off (hours)	3, 1.5	8, 4	8, 4	12, 3–4	6, 3
Battery weight, amp/hour rating	1.4 lbs, 1.3Ah	1.1 lbs, 2.8Ah	1 lb, 2.8Ah	0.7 lbs, 1.7Ah	1.3 lbs, 2.5Ah
Display/hard disk power-down	●/●	●/●	●/●	●/●	●/●
CPU/peripherals power-down	○/●	●/●	●/●	●/○	○/○
Standby/Hibernation	●/●	●/●	●/○	●/●	○/○

●—Yes ○—No N/A—Not applicable INA—Information not available

Monochrome Portable/Laptop Computers

	Jetta Jetbook 486DX/33	Keynote 386SX-25	Keynote 486SLC	KRIS Master 386SX/25	Leading Edge N3/SL25 Plus
Price	$$$	$$	$$	$$	$$$
Processor type and speed	Intel 486DX/33	AMD Am386SXL/25	Cyrix CX486SLC/25	AMD Am386SXL/25	Intel 386SL/25
Hard disk capacity	85Mb	85Mb	85Mb	80Mb	85Mb
Microsoft Windows 3.1	○	●	●	●	●
Distribution channel	Dealers	Dealers, direct	Dealers, direct	Dealers, OEMs, VARs	Dealers
Dimensions (HWD, in inches)	2.3 × 11.5 × 9	2 × 11.8 × 8.3	1.9 × 11.8 × 8.3	2 × 11 × 8.5	2 × 13.5 × 8.6
Weight/travel weight (pounds)	6.6, 8.1	7.1, 8.4	6.6, 8.3	6.7, 8.5	6.8, 8.1
Display area (H × W, in inches)	5.8 × 7.8	5.8 × 7.5	5.8 × 7.5	5.5 × 7	5.8 × 7.6
Keys: total, function, cursor	84, 12, 8	83, 10, 8	83, 10, 8	80, 12, 4	100, 12, 8
MOTHERBOARD					
Motherboard manufacturer	Jetta	Chicony	Chicony	Compal	Leading Edge
Chip set manufacturer	C&T	VLSI	WD	VLSI	Intel
BIOS version (or date)	AMI (July 1992)	AMI (May 1992)	AMI (May 1991)	Phoenix 1.01	Phoenix (April 1990)
Setup in ROM/Password in ROM	●/●	●/●	●/●	●/●	●/●
System shadowing/Video shadowing	●/●	●/●	●/●	●/●	○/●
MEMORY AND DISK DRIVES					
Installable RAM	4Mb–32Mb	1Mb–5Mb	2Mb–10Mb	2Mb–16Mb	2Mb–8Mb
User-installable	○	●	●	●	●
External processor RAM cache	32K	None	None	None	32K
Available hard disk sizes	80Mb, 125Mb	60Mb	85Mb, 125Mb	40Mb, 60Mb, 80Mb, 130Mb	80Mb, 120Mb
I/O AND EXPANSION					
Parallel, serial, mouse ports	1, 2, 1	1, 2, 0	1, 2, 0	1, 1, 0	1, 1, 1
Proprietary expansion port	●	○	●	●	○
PCMCIA slot	○	○	○	○	○
Expansion unit	●	○	●	●	○
Internal modem options	2,400-bps/9,600-bps send/receive fax	2,400-bps/9,600-bps MNP 5 send/receive fax	2,400-bps/9,600-bps MNP 5 send/receive fax	2,400-bps, 9,600-bps V.42bis fax	2,400-bps/4,800-bps MNP 5 send-only fax
VIDEO					
Screen manufacturer	Hitachi	Sanyo	Sanyo	Sharp	Hitachi
Maximum shades of gray	64	16	16	16	64
Video chip set manufacturer	Cirrus	Cirrus	Cirrus	Cirrus	Cirrus
AC ADAPTER AND BATTERY					
AC adapter size (inches)	1.8 × 6 × 2.5	1.4 × 6 × 1.3	1.5 × 6.5 × 3.3	2.3 × 3 × 6.5	1.8 × 5.7 × 2.8
Rated battery life (hours)	3.5	2	3	3	2.5
ZDigit, battery rundowns (hr:min)	3:15, 2:54	3:02, 1:58	N/A, 2:07	3:12, 2:41	1:51, 1:22
Charge time while on, off (hours)	2, 2	4, 2	2, 2	N/A, 3	3, 1.5
Battery weight, amp/hour rating	1.8 lbs, 2Ah	1 lb, 2.4Ah	1.3 lbs, 1.8Ah	1.4 lbs, 5Ah	0.7 lbs, 1.5Ah
Display/hard disk power-down	●/●	○/○	●/●	●/●	●/●
CPU/peripherals power-down	●/○	○/○	●/●	●/●	○/●
Standby/Hibernation	●/○	●/○	●/○	●/●	●/●

●—Yes   ○—No   N/A—Not applicable   INA—Information not available

Table Continues →

Monochrome Portable/Laptop Computers

	Librex R386SL	Librex T386SX	Lightning Thundernote 486DX/33	Matrix 386SX/20 Notebook	Matrix 486SX-25Mhz Notebook
Price	$$$	$$$	$$	$$	$$
Processor type and speed	Intel 386SL/25	Intel 386SX/20	Intel 486DX/33	Intel 386SX/20	Intel 486SX/25
Hard disk capacity	80Mb	40Mb	130Mb	60Mb	80Mb
Microsoft Windows 3.1	●	○	●	○	○
Distribution channel	Dealers	Dealers	Dealers, direct	Dealers	Dealers
Dimensions (HWD, in inches)	2 × 11.7 × 8.5	1.5 × 11.7 × 8.5	1.8 × 11 × 8.8	2 × 11 × 8.5	2 × 11 × 8.8
Weight/travel weight (pounds)	6.7, 7.9	5.3, 7.6	4.9, 8	7.3, 8.9	6.8, 8
Display area (H × W, in inches)	5.8 × 7.6	5.8 × 7.6	5.8 × 7.5	5.5 × 7	5.7 × 7.6
Keys: total, function, cursor	85, 12, 8	82, 12, 4	84, 10, 8	79, 12, 4	82, 12, 8
MOTHERBOARD					
Motherboard manufacturer	VLSI	Nippon Steel	Twinhead	Matrix	Quanta
Chip set manufacturer	VLSI	VLSI	ACC	Intel	NTC/ACC
BIOS version (or date)	AMI (July 1992)	Award (June 1992)	Phoenix (August 1992)	Award 3.04D	Award (July 1992)
Setup in ROM/Password in ROM	●/●	●/●	●/●	●/●	●/●
System shadowing/Video shadowing	●/●	●/●	●/●	●/●	●/●
MEMORY AND DISK DRIVES					
Installable RAM	2Mb–20Mb	4Mb–12Mb	4Mb–20Mb	2Mb–8Mb	4Mb–20Mb
User-installable	●	●	●	●	●
External processor RAM cache	None	None	None	None	None
Available hard disk sizes	80Mb, 120Mb	40Mb, 80Mb	80Mb, 124Mb, 180Mb	60Mb, 120Mb	80Mb, 120Mb
I/O AND EXPANSION					
Parallel, serial, mouse ports	1, 1, 0	1, 1, 1	1, 1, 0	1, 1, 1	1, 1, 1
Proprietary expansion port	○	○	●	○	●
PCMCIA slot	○	●	○	○	○
Expansion unit	○	○	○	●	○
Internal modem options	2,400-bps/9,600-bps MNP 5 send/receive fax	None	2,400-bps/9,600-bps send/receive fax	9,600-bps send-fax	2,400-bps/9,600-bps send/receive fax
VIDEO					
Screen manufacturer	Seiko	Sanyo	Sharp	Sharp	Sharp
Maximum shades of gray	64	64	64	32	64
Video chip set manufacturer	WD	Cirrus	Cirrus	Cirrus	Cirrus
AC ADAPTER AND BATTERY					
AC adapter size (inches)	1.7 × 2.3 × 5	1.5 × 2.5 × 5.5	1.8 × 6.8 × 3.3	2 × 3 × 7.5	1.8 × 4.5 × 2.9
Rated battery life (hours)	3	2.5	3	2.5	2
ZDigit, battery rundowns (hr:min)	2:48, 1:35	3:30, 2:23	2:05, 1:46	4:20, 3:06	4:12, 2:01
Charge time while on, off (hours)	5, 1.8	8, 2	2, N/A	N/A, 3	16, 2.5
Battery weight, amp/hour rating	0.9 lbs, 2.5Ah	1 lb, 1.3Ah	1.3 lbs, 0.8Ah	1.4 lbs, 5Ah	1.5 lbs, 2.2Ah
Display/hard disk power-down	●/●	●/●	●/●	●/●	●/●
CPU/peripherals power-down	●/○	○/○	○/○	●/○	○/●
Standby/Hibernation	○/○	○/○	○/○	●/○	●/○

●—Yes   ○—No   N/A—Not applicable   INA—Information not available

Monochrome Portable/Laptop Computers

	Micro Express NB486DX	Micro Express NB913 Notebook PC	Micro Express NB925	Micro Express NB2500 Notebook	Micro Express NP933
Price	$$$	$$	$$	$$$	$$
Processor type and speed	Intel 486DX/33	AMD Am386SXL/20	Intel 386SX/25	AMD Am386DXL/25	AMD Am386DX/33
Hard disk capacity	120Mb	120Mb	120Mb	120Mb	120Mb
Microsoft Windows 3.1	●	●	●	●	●
Distribution channel	Direct	Direct	Direct	Direct	Direct
Dimensions (HWD, in inches)	1.5 × 11.5 × 8.5	2 × 11.5 × 9.5	2 × 12.5 × 9.5	2.5 × 11 × 8.2	1.8 × 12 × 9.5
Weight/travel weight (pounds)	7.3, 9	7.9, 9.5	8, 9.5	7.4, 9.1	7.6, 8.9
Display area (H × W, in inches)	6 × 7.8	6 × 8	5.5 × 7.5	7 × 8.5	6.5 × 7.8
Keys: total, function, cursor	85, 12, 4	83, 12, 4	83, 10, 4	84, 12, 4	83, 10, 8
MOTHERBOARD					
Motherboard manufacturer	Micro Express	Micro Express	Micro Express	Micro Express	Micro Express
Chip set manufacturer	ACC	C&T, Headland	C&T	SIS, Acer	ACC
BIOS version (or date)	AMI (January 1992)	AMI 1.13	AMI 1.13	AMI (June 1990)	AMI (July 1991)
Setup in ROM/Password in ROM	●/●	●/○	○/○	●/○	●/●
System shadowing/Video shadowing	●/●	●/●	●/●	●/●	○/●
MEMORY AND DISK DRIVES					
Installable RAM	4Mb–32Mb	2Mb–8Mb	2Mb–8Mb	2Mb–8Mb	4Mb–8Mb
User-installable	○	○	○	○	○
External processor RAM cache	128K	None	None	128K	None
Available hard disk sizes	120Mb	60Mb, 80Mb, 120Mb	60Mb, 80Mb, 120Mb	60Mb, 80Mb, 120Mb	80Mb, 120Mb
I/O AND EXPANSION					
Parallel, serial, mouse ports	1, 1, 0	1, 1, 0	1, 1, 0	1, 1, 0	1, 1, 0
Proprietary expansion port	●	●	●	●	●
PCMCIA slot	○	○	○	○	○
Expansion unit	○	○	●	●	○
Internal modem options	Included	2,400-bps, 9,600-bps fax	2,400-bps, 9,600-bps fax	9,600-bps fax	2,400-bps/9,600-bps MNP 5 send/receive fax
VIDEO					
Screen manufacturer	Panasonic	Sanyo	Sanyo	Sanyo	Sanyo
Maximum shades of gray	64	64	64	64	64
Video chip set manufacturer	Cirrus	C&T	C&T	Cirrus	Cirrus
AC ADAPTER AND BATTERY					
AC adapter size (inches)	2.8 × 6.5 × 3	1.5 × 3 × 6.5	1.5 × 3 × 6.5	1.5 × 3 × 6.5	1.5 × 6 × 2.5
Rated battery life (hours)	3	2.5	2.5	3	5
ZDigit, battery rundowns (hr:min)	3:01, 2:33	4:20, 3:20	4:06, 2:56	2:31, 2:28	3:57, 2:42
Charge time while on, off (hours)	8, 3	8, 6	8, 6	7.5, 2.5	8, 3
Battery weight, amp/hour rating	1.3 lbs, 2Ah	1 lb, 2.8Ah	1 lb, 5Ah	1.3 lbs, 2Ah	1.9 lbs, 1Ah
Display/hard disk power-down	●/●	●/●	●/●	●/●	●/●
CPU/peripherals power-down	○/○	●/○	●/○	○/○	●/●
Standby/Hibernation	●/○	○/○	○/○	○/○	●/●

●—Yes ○—No N/A—Not applicable INA—Information not available

Table Continues →

Monochrome Portable/Laptop Computers

	MicroStar NoteStar NP-913 386SX/20	MicroStar NoteStar NP-925 386SX/25	Mitsuba Ninja 386SX/20	Mitsuba Ninja 486SX	NBCC 386SL/20
Price	$$	$$	$$	$$	$$
Processor type and speed	Intel 386SX/20	Intel 386SX/25	Intel 386SX/20	Intel 486SX/25	Intel 386SL/20
Hard disk capacity	120Mb	120Mb	60Mb	86Mb	40Mb
Microsoft Windows 3.1	●	●	○	●	○
Distribution channel	Dealers	Dealers	Dealers	Dealers	Dealers
Dimensions (HWD, in inches)	2.1 × 12.2 × 9.5	2.1 × 12.2 × 9.5	2 × 11 × 8.7	2 × 11 × 8.8	2.5 × 12 × 8.5
Weight/travel weight (pounds)	7.9, 10.2	7.9, 10.2	7.3, 9	6.8, 7.8	7.1, 8.8
Display area (H × W, in inches)	6 × 8	5.5 × 7.5	5.2 × 7	5.8 × 7.5	6 × 7.5
Keys: total, function, cursor	83, 12, 4	83, 10, 4	78, 12, 4	80, 12, 4	82, 10, 4
MOTHERBOARD					
Motherboard manufacturer	Citizen	Citizen	Quantum	Quanta	NBCC
Chip set manufacturer	Headland	Headland	Intel	ACC	AT&T, C&T
BIOS version (or date)	AMI 1.13	AMI 1.13	AMI 3.04D	Award (July 1992)	Quadtel 3.00
Setup in ROM/Password in ROM	●/○	○/○	●/●	●/●	●/●
System shadowing/Video shadowing	●/●	●/●	●/●	●/●	●/●
MEMORY AND DISK DRIVES					
Installable RAM	1Mb–8Mb	1Mb–8Mb	2Mb–8Mb	4Mb–20Mb	2Mb–8Mb
User-installable	●	●	●	○	●
External processor RAM cache	None	None	None	None	16K
Available hard disk sizes	20Mb, 40Mb, 60Mb, 80Mb, 130Mb	20Mb, 40Mb, 60Mb, 80Mb, 130Mb	60Mb, 80Mb, 120Mb	80Mb, 120Mb	40Mb, 60Mb, 80Mb, 120Mb
I/O AND EXPANSION					
Parallel, serial, mouse ports	1, 1, 0	1, 1, 0	1, 1, 1	1, 1, 1	1, 1, 0
Proprietary expansion port	●	●	●	○	●
PCMCIA slot	○	○	○	○	○
Expansion unit	○	○	●	○	●
Internal modem options	9,600-bps fax	9,600-bps fax	9,600-bps fax	2,400-bps/9,600-bps MNP 5 send-only fax	9,600-bps fax
VIDEO					
Screen manufacturer	Sanyo	Sanyo	Sharp	Sharp	Sharp
Maximum shades of gray	64	64	16	32	32
Video chip set manufacturer	Headland	Headland	Cirrus	Cirrus	Cirrus
AC ADAPTER AND BATTERY					
AC adapter size (inches)	1.8 × 3 × 6.8	1.8 × 3 × 6.8	2 × 3 × 7.5	1.5 × 4.5 × 3	1.5 × 2 × 4.5
Rated battery life (hours)	2.5	2.5	3.5	2	3
ZDigit, battery rundowns (hr:min)	4:34, 3:34	4:48, 3:09	4:07, 2:02	3:44, 1:47	2:44, 2:02
Charge time while on, off (hours)	8, 6	8, 6	N/A, 2.5	16, 2.5	5–7, 1
Battery weight, amp/hour rating	1 lb, 2.8Ah	1 lb, 2.8Ah	1.4 lbs, 5Ah	1.1 lbs, 1.2Ah	.08 lbs, 1.2Ah
Display/hard disk power-down	●/●	●/●	●/●	●/●	●/●
CPU/peripherals power-down	●/○	●/○	●/○	●/●	●/●
Standby/Hibernation	○/○	○/○	●/○	●/●	●/●

●—Yes   ○—No   N/A—Not applicable   INA—Information not available

Monochrome Portable/Laptop Computers

	NCR Safari NSX/20	NCR System 3170	NEC UltraLite SL/20	NEC UltraLite III	Olivetti Notebook S20
Price	$$$	$$$$	$$$	$$$	$$$
Processor type and speed	Intel 386SX/20	Intel 386SL/25	Intel 386SL/20	Intel 386SX/20	AMD Am386SXL/25
Hard disk capacity	80Mb	80Mb	80Mb	60Mb	64Mb
Microsoft Windows 3.1	●	●	●	●	●
Distribution channel	Dealers	Dealers	Dealers	Dealers	Direct
Dimensions (HWD, in inches)	2 × 12 × 9.5	2 × 11 × 8	2.5 × 11.5 × 9.5	1.5 × 11.5 × 9	2 × 11.5 × 8.2
Weight/travel weight (pounds)	7.2, 8.3	5.2, 6.6	6.4, 7.9	4.7, 5.8	7, 8.6
Display area (H × W, in inches)	6 × 8	6 × 7.5	6 × 7.5	6 × 7.8	5 × 7
Keys: total, function, cursor	82, 12, 4	78, 10, 3	78, 12, 4	78, 12, 4	83, 10, 8
MOTHERBOARD					
Motherboard manufacturer	Matsushita	Matsushita	NEC	NEC	Olivetti
Chip set manufacturer	Headland	Intel	Intel	Intel	VLSI
BIOS version (or date)	Phoenix 1.01	Phoenix 1.01	Phoenix 1.01 (April 1990)	Phoenix 1.01	Olivetti
Setup in ROM/Password in ROM	●/●	●/●	○/●	●/●	●/●
System shadowing/Video shadowing	●/●	●/●	●/●	●/●	●/●
MEMORY AND DISK DRIVES					
Installable RAM	4Mb–8Mb	2Mb–20Mb	2Mb–8Mb	2Mb–10Mb	2Mb–6Mb
User-installable	○	●	○	○	●
External processor RAM cache	None	64K	16K	None	None
Available hard disk sizes	40Mb, 80Mb	80Mb, 120Mb	80Mb, 125Mb	60Mb	64Mb
I/O AND EXPANSION					
Parallel, serial, mouse ports	1, 1, 1	1, 1, 1	1, 1, 1	1, 1, 1	1, 1, 1
Proprietary expansion port	●	●	●	●	●
PCMCIA slot	○	●	○	○	○
Expansion unit	●	●	●	●	●
Internal modem options	9,600-bps fax, 14,400-bps data/fax	14,400-bps data/9,600-bps fax	2,400-bps, 9,600-bps fax	9,600-bps MNP 5 fax	2,400-bps, 9,600-bps fax
VIDEO					
Screen manufacturer	Sharp	Matsushita	NEC	NEC	Seiko/Epson
Maximum shades of gray	32	32	16	16	32
Video chip set manufacturer	Cirrus	Cirrus	WD	WD	Cirrus
AC ADAPTER AND BATTERY					
AC adapter size (inches)	1.8 × 2.8 × 5.1	2 × 3 × 6	1.5 × 3.5 × 6.5	1.5 × 3.5 × 6.5	2 × 3.3 × 6.5
Rated battery life (hours)	4–6	3	3	2	4
ZDigit, battery rundowns (hr:min)	5:15, 4:06	1:50, 1:38	3:45, 2:05	1:50, 1:45	2:45, 2:34
Charge time while on, off (hours)	6, 6	N/A, 1.5	15, 3	8, 1	N/A, 3
Battery weight, amp/hour rating	0.8 lbs, 1.4Ah	0.8 lbs, 1.4Ah	1 lb, 1.7Ah	0.7 lbs, 1.7Ah	1.7 lbs, 1.8Ah
Display/hard disk power-down	●/●	●/●	●/●	●/●	●/●
CPU/peripherals power-down	●/●	●/●	●/●	●/●	●/●
Standby/Hibernation	●/●	●/●	●/●	●/●	●/●

●—Yes   ○—No   N/A—Not applicable   INA—Information not available

Table Continues →

Monochrome Portable/Laptop Computers

	Packard Bell 386SX/20 Notebook	PC Brand 386SX-25 Notebook	PC&C Dynova SLic 3000	Poly NB320T	Poly NB325T
Price	$$	$$	$$	$$	$$
Processor type and speed	Intel 386SX/20	Intel 386SX/25	Intel 386SL/25	Intel 386SX/20	Intel 386SXLV/25
Hard disk capacity	80Mb	60Mb	130Mb	130Mb	86Mb
Microsoft Windows 3.1	●	●	○	●	○
Distribution channel	Dealers	Direct	Dealers, direct	Direct	Dealers, direct
Dimensions (HWD, in inches)	2 × 11 × 8.5	1.5 × 11 × 8.5	2.2 × 11.4 × 8.5	2 × 11 × 8.5	2 × 11 × 8.5
Weight/travel weight (pounds)	7, 8.6	7, 8.8	7, 8.4	6.9, 8.7	6.8, 8.6
Display area (H × W, in inches)	5.5 × 7	5.5 × 7.3	5.3 × 7.2	5.3 × 7	5.5 × 7.3
Keys: total, function, cursor	80, 12, 4	81, 12, 4	82, 12, 4	80, 12, 4	80, 12, 8
MOTHERBOARD					
Motherboard manufacturer	Packard Bell	PC Brand	PC&C Research	LES	Compal
Chip set manufacturer	C&T	Intel	Intel	VLSI	Topcat
BIOS version (or date)	Award 3.04D	PC Brand (January 1992)	Quadtel/System Soft (July 1992)	Phoenix 1.00	Phoenix (April 1990)
Setup in ROM/Password in ROM	●/●	●/●	●/●	●/●	●/●
System shadowing/Video shadowing	●/●	●/●	○/●	●/●	●/○
MEMORY AND DISK DRIVES					
Installable RAM	4Mb–8Mb	2Mb–16Mb	2Mb–32Mb	4Mb–16Mb	2Mb–16Mb
User-installable	●	●	○	●	●
External processor RAM cache	None	None	64K	None	None
Available hard disk sizes	80Mb	60Mb, 80Mb, 120Mb	85Mb, 130Mb, 220Mb, 230Mb	40Mb, 130Mb	40Mb, 130Mb, 200Mb
I/O AND EXPANSION					
Parallel, serial, mouse ports	1, 1, 1	1, 2, 0	1, 1, 1	1, 2, 0	1, 2, 0
Proprietary expansion port	●	●	○	●	●
PCMCIA slot	○	○	○	○	○
Expansion unit	○	●	○	●	●
Internal modem options	9,600-bps send-fax	2,400-bps, 9,600-bps MNP 5 fax	2,400-bps/9,600-bps MNP 5 send/receive fax	2,400-bps, 9,600-bps fax	2,400-bps/9,600-bps MNP 5 send/receive fax, 2,400-bps data
VIDEO					
Screen manufacturer	Packard Bell	Sharp	Hitachi	Toshiba	Sharp
Maximum shades of gray	32	32	64	32	16
Video chip set manufacturer	Cirrus	C&T	Cirrus	Cirrus	Cirrus
AC ADAPTER AND BATTERY					
AC adapter size (inches)	1.5 × 3 × 7.5	2 × 3 × 6.3	1.8 × 2.6 × 6	2 × 3 × 6.5	2 × 3 × 6.5
Rated battery life (hours)	3	3	3.5	3	5
ZDigit, battery rundowns (hr:min)	3:40, 2:34	2:45, 2:28	3:45, 2:25	3:52, 3:07	3:29, 2:42
Charge time while on, off (hours)	N/A, 3	N/A, 2	2.1, 2.1	N/A, 2.5	N/A, 3
Battery weight, amp/hour rating	1.4 lbs, 5Ah	1.4 lbs, 5Ah	1.4 lbs, 1Ah	1.4 lbs, 4.5Ah	0.7 lbs, 0.5Ah
Display/hard disk power-down	●/●	●/●	●/●	●/●	●/●
CPU/peripherals power-down	●/○	●/○	●/●	○/●	○/●
Standby/Hibernation	●/○	●/○	●/●	●/○	○/○

●—Yes   ○—No   N/A—Not applicable   INA—Information not available

Monochrome Portable/Laptop Computers

	Poly NBC25	Positive PC320ND	Primax Eagle 425SX	Primax NightHawk 325SXL	Proteus 386-20NB
Price	$$	$$	$$	$$	$$
Processor type and speed	Intel 386SL/25	Intel 386SX/20	Intel 486SX/25	AMD Am386SXL/25	Intel 386SX/20
Hard disk capacity	80Mb	60Mb	80Mb	60Mb	60Mb
Microsoft Windows 3.1	●	●	○	○	●
Distribution channel	Dealers, direct	Dealers	Dealers, direct	Dealers, direct	Dealers, direct
Dimensions (HWD, in inches)	1.5 × 11.3 × 8.5	2 × 11 × 8.5	1.8 × 11 × 8.6	2.5 × 11.5 × 8.5	2 × 11.5 × 8
Weight/travel weight (pounds)	5.1, 6.9	6.9, 8.7	6.4, 8.1	6.5, 7.8	6, 7.1
Display area (H × W, in inches)	5.8 × 7.8	5.5 × 7	5.8 × 7.6	5.8 × 7.5	5.5 × 7
Keys: total, function, cursor	86, 10, 8	80, 12, 4	82, 12, 4	85, 12, 8	85, 12, 4
MOTHERBOARD					
Motherboard manufacturer	Chaplet	Compal	Quanta	Acer	Vysotec
Chip set manufacturer	Intel	Intel, VLSI	ACC	Acer	WD
BIOS version (or date)	Quadtel (June 1992)	IBM (December 1991)	Award (August 1992)	Acer (October 1992)	AMI 1.0
Setup in ROM/Password in ROM	●/○	●/●	●/●	●/●	●/●
System shadowing/Video shadowing	●/●	●/●	●/●	●/●	●/●
MEMORY AND DISK DRIVES					
Installable RAM	2Mb–8Mb	2Mb–16Mb	4Mb–20Mb	2Mb–8Mb	2Mb–5Mb
User-installable	●	●	●	●	●
External processor RAM cache	16K	None	None	None	None
Available hard disk sizes	40Mb, 130Mb, 200Mb	40Mb, 60Mb, 80Mb, 120Mb	120Mb	80Mb, 120Mb	60Mb, 80Mb, 120Mb, 230Mb
I/O AND EXPANSION					
Parallel, serial, mouse ports	1, 1, 0	1, 1, 0	1, 1, 1	1, 1, 1	1, 1, 1
Proprietary expansion port	○	●	●	○	●
PCMCIA slot	○	○	○	○	○
Expansion unit	○	○	○	○	●
Internal modem options	2,400-bps/9,600-bps MNP 5 send/receive fax	9,600-bps fax	2,400-bps/9,600-bps MNP 5 send/receive fax	2,400-bps/9,600-bps send/receive fax	9,600-bps fax
VIDEO					
Screen manufacturer	Sharp	Sharp	Sharp	Sharp	Hitachi
Maximum shades of gray	64	16	64	32	16
Video chip set manufacturer	Cirrus	Cirrus	Cirrus	Cirrus	WD
AC ADAPTER AND BATTERY					
AC adapter size (inches)	1.8 × 2.5 × 6	2 × 3 × 6.3	1.7 × 7 × 3.2	1.5 × 6 × 2.5	1.5 × 2.1 × 5
Rated battery life (hours)	3	2	3.5	2.5	1
ZDigit, battery rundowns (hr:min)	3:10, 2:35	2:32, 2:02	3:29, 2:44	2:20, 1:33	1:24, 1:14
Charge time while on, off (hours)	4, 2	N/A, 3	3.5, 2	3, 1.8	8, 1
Battery weight, amp/hour rating	0.7 lbs, 0.5Ah	1.4 lbs, 4.5Ah	1.4 lbs, 0.8Ah	1.1 lbs, 3.9Ah	0.7 lbs, 1.7Ah
Display/hard disk power-down	○/●	●/●	●/●	●/●	●/●
CPU/peripherals power-down	○/○	●/●	○/●	●/●	●/○
Standby/Hibernation	○/○	●/○	●/○	●/○	●/○

●—Yes ○—No N/A—Not applicable INA—Information not available

Table Continues →

Monochrome Portable/Laptop Computers

	QSI Klonimus Lite 386SL/25	Samsung NoteMaster 386L/25	Sanyo MBC-18NB6H	Sharp PC-6781 Notebook	Swan 386SX/20 Notebook
Price	$$	$$	$$$	$$$	$$
Processor type and speed	AMD Am386SXL/25	Intel 386SL/25	Intel 386SX/20	Intel 386SL/20	AMD Am386SXL/20
Hard disk capacity	123Mb	64Mb	60Mb	80Mb	60Mb
Microsoft Windows 3.1	●	○	○	○	●
Distribution channel	Dealers, direct	Dealers	Dealers	Dealers	Dealers
Dimensions (HWD, in inches)	1.7 × 12 × 9.5	1.8 × 11 × 8.5	2 × 12 × 10	1.6 × 11 × 8.5	2.1 × 11 × 8.5
Weight/travel weight (pounds)	7.5, 9.1	5.8, 7.1	7, 8.8	4.9, 6.2	7, 8.8
Display area (H × W, in inches)	5.8 × 7.5	5.8 × 7.5	6 × 8	6 × 8	6 × 8
Keys: total, function, cursor	84, 12, 8	80, 10, 4	82, 12, 4	79, 12, 4	80, 10, 4
MOTHERBOARD					
Motherboard manufacturer	Modern Computer	Samsung	Sanyo	Sharp	Samsung
Chip set manufacturer	C&T	Intel	Oak Technology	Intel	C&T
BIOS version (or date)	AMI (June 1990)	Phoenix (January 1991)	Phoenix 1.10	Phoenix (April 1990)	C&T 2.1
Setup in ROM/Password in ROM	●/○	●/○	●/●	●/●	●/○
System shadowing/Video shadowing	○/●	●/●	●/●	●/●	●/●
MEMORY AND DISK DRIVES					
Installable RAM	1Mb–8Mb	2Mb–8Mb	1Mb–5Mb	2Mb–8Mb	1Mb–8Mb
User-installable	●	●	○	●	●
External processor RAM cache	None	64K	None	16K	None
Available hard disk sizes	40Mb, 60Mb, 80Mb, 120Mb	40Mb, 60Mb, 80Mb	60Mb	80Mb	40Mb, 60Mb, 120Mb
I/O AND EXPANSION					
Parallel, serial, mouse ports	1, 1, 0	1, 1, 0	1, 1, 0	1, 1, 0	1, 1, 1
Proprietary expansion port	●	○	○	●	●
PCMCIA slot	○	○	○	●	○
Expansion unit	○	○	○	●	○
Internal modem options	2,400-bps/9,600-bps MNP 5 send/receive fax	2,400-bps/9,600-bps MNP 5 send/receive fax	2,400-bps	2,400-bps MNP 5 data/fax	2,400-bps, 9,600-bps fax
VIDEO					
Screen manufacturer	Sanyo	Sharp	Sanyo	Sharp	Samsung
Maximum shades of gray	64	256	8	32	64
Video chip set manufacturer	Headland	WD	WD	WD	C&T
AC ADAPTER AND BATTERY					
AC adapter size (inches)	1.7 × 3.2 × 7	2 × 4.8 × 3.3	2 × 3 × 8	1.4 × 3.5 × 6.4	2 × 3.5 × 5.7
Rated battery life (hours)	6	2	2	1.5	2.5
ZDigit, battery rundowns (hr:min)	4:25, 3:45	N/A, 1:29	3:39, 2:15	2:04, 1:47	3:52, 2:39
Charge time while on, off (hours)	8, 8	4, 4	8, 1	8, 2	4, 3
Battery weight, amp/hour rating	0.9 lbs, 2.5Ah	0.7 lbs, 1.6Ah	1.1 lbs, 1.7Ah	0.8 lbs, 1.8Ah	1.4 lbs, 5Ah
Display/hard disk power-down	●/●	●/●	●/●	●/●	●/●
CPU/peripherals power-down	●/○	●/○	●/●	●/●	●/○
Standby/Hibernation	○/○	●/○	●/○	●/●	●/●

●—Yes ○—No N/A—Not applicable INA—Information not available

Monochrome Portable/Laptop Computers

	Swan 386SX/25 Notebook	Tandy 3800 HD	Tandy 3830 SL	Tandy 4860 HD	Tartan NP-925
Price	$$$	$$$	$$$	$$$	$$
Processor type and speed	AMD Am386SXL/25	Cyrix CX486SLC/20	Intel 386SL/25	Intel 486DX/33	AMD Am386SXL/25
Hard disk capacity	80Mb	60Mb	80Mb	60Mb	124Mb
Microsoft Windows 3.1	●	●	●	●	●
Distribution channel	Dealers	Dealers	Company-owned stores, dealers	Company-owned stores, dealers	Dealers, OEMs, VARs
Dimensions (HWD, in inches)	1.8 × 11 × 8.5	1.6 × 12 × 10	2 × 11 × 8.5	2 × 11 × 8.5	1.7 × 12 × 9.5
Weight/travel weight (pounds)	5.8, 6.9	6.2, 6.8	5.9, 7.1	5.8, 7.5	7.9, 9.4
Display area (H × W, in inches)	6 × 8	4.8 × 7.5	6 × 8	6 × 7.5	6 × 7.5
Keys: total, function, cursor	80, 10, 4	84, 12, 8	84 10, 4	84, 10, 4	84, 10, 4
MOTHERBOARD					
Motherboard manufacturer	Samsung	Tandy	Matsushita	Twinhead	Modern Computer
Chip set manufacturer	C&T	TI	Intel	Intel	Acer, Headland
BIOS version (or date)	C&T 2.1	Phoenix (July 1992)	Phoenix 1.1	Phoenix 1.1	AMI (June 1990)
Setup in ROM/Password in ROM	●/○	○/○	●/○	●/○	○/○
System shadowing/Video shadowing	●/●	●/○	●/●	●/●	●/●
MEMORY AND DISK DRIVES					
Installable RAM	1Mb–8Mb	2Mb–4Mb	2Mb–8Mb	4Mb–20Mb	2Mb–8Mb
User-installable	●	●	●	●	●
External processor RAM cache	None	64K	16K	8K	None
Available hard disk sizes	40Mb, 80Mb, 120Mb	60Mb	80Mb	60Mb	80Mb, 124Mb
I/O AND EXPANSION					
Parallel, serial, mouse ports	1, 1, 1	1, 1, 0	1, 1, 1	1, 1, 0	1, 1, 0
Proprietary expansion port	●	○	●	○	●
PCMCIA slot	○	○	○	○	○
Expansion unit	○	○	●	○	○
Internal modem options	2,400-bps, 9,600-bps fax	2,400-bps/9,600-bps send/receive fax, 2,400-bps/9,600-bps send-only fax	9,600-bps fax	9,600-bps fax	2,400-bps, 2,400-bps MNP 5, 9,600-bps fax
VIDEO					
Screen manufacturer	Samsung	Sharp	Sharp	Sharp	Sanyo
Maximum shades of gray	64	32	64	64	64
Video chip set manufacturer	C&T	Cirrus	Cirrus	Cirrus	C&T
AC ADAPTER AND BATTERY					
AC adapter size (inches)	1.8 × 3.2 × 4.7	3.8 × 2.3 × 1.4	1.5 × 2.5 × 5.5	1.3 × 3 × 6.5	1.5 × 3 × 7
Rated battery life (hours)	2.5	2	3	2.5–3	3–5
ZDigit, battery rundowns (hr:min)	2:04, 1:36	2:48, 2:26	N/A, 2:39	2:23, 2:15	4:20, 3:48
Charge time while on, off (hours)	4, 3	8, 4	5, 2	5, 2	3–5, 3
Battery weight, amp/hour rating	0.8 lbs, 1.7Ah	0.5 lbs, 1.3Ah	0.9 lbs, 1.4Ah	1.3 lbs, 1.7Ah	1 lb, 2.8Ah
Display/hard disk power-down	●/●	●/●	●/●	●/●	●/●
CPU/peripherals power-down	●/○	●/●	●/●	●/●	●/○
Standby/Hibernation	●/●	●/○	●/○	●/○	●/○

●—Yes   ○—No   N/A—Not applicable   INA—Information not available

Table Continues →

Monochrome Portable/Laptop Computers

	Tenex NB25SX	TI TravelMate 3000 WinSX	TI TravelMate 4000 WinDX/25	TI TravelMate 4000 WinSX/25	Toshiba Satellite TI800
Price	$$	$$$	$$$	$$$	$$
Processor type and speed	AMD Am386SXL/25	Intel 386SX/20	Intel 486DX/25	Intel 486SX/25	Intel 386SX/20
Hard disk capacity	80Mb	120Mb	121Mb	121Mb	60Mb
Microsoft Windows 3.1	●	●	●	●	○
Distribution channel	Direct, VARs	Dealers, superstores	Dealers	Dealers	Dealers
Dimensions (HWD, in inches)	2 × 11 × 8.5	2 × 11 × 8.5	2.2 × 11 × 8.5	1.8 × 11 × 8.5	2 × 11.5 × 8
Weight/travel weight (pounds)	6.3, 8	6, 7.8	5.5, 6.7	5.5, 6.8	7, 8
Display area (H × W, in inches)	6 × 7.5	6 × 8	6 × 8	6 × 8	5.8 × 7.5
Keys: total, function, cursor	82, 10, 4	79, 12, 4	79, 10, 4	79, 10, 4	82, 12, 8
MOTHERBOARD					
Motherboard manufacturer	Sampo	TI	TI	TI	Toshiba
Chip set manufacturer	VLSI	TI	Intel/TI	Intel/TI	Toshiba
BIOS version (or date)	Phoenix (January 1988)	Phoenix 1.01	Phoenix (August 1992)	Phoenix (May 1992)	Toshiba (July 1992)
Setup in ROM/Password in ROM	●/●	●/●	●/○	●/○	●/●
System shadowing/Video shadowing	●/●	●/●	●/○	●/○	●/○
MEMORY AND DISK DRIVES					
Installable RAM	4Mb–8Mb	4Mb–6Mb	4Mb–20Mb	4Mb–20Mb	2Mb–10Mb
User-installable	●	○	●	●	●
External processor RAM cache	None	None	8K	8K	None
Available hard disk sizes	60Mb, 80Mb	60Mb, 80Mb	120Mb, 200Mb	120Mb	60Mb
I/O AND EXPANSION					
Parallel, serial, mouse ports	0, 1, 0	1, 1, 1	1, 1, 1	1, 1, 1	1, 1, 1
Proprietary expansion port	●	●	●	●	●
PCMCIA slot	○	●	○	○	○
Expansion unit	○	●	○	○	○
Internal modem options	4,800-bps fax	9,600-bps send-fax, 9,600-bps V.42bis data/fax	2,400-bps/9,600-bps MNP 5 send-only fax	2,400-bps/9,600-bps MNP 5 send-only fax, 2,400-bps/9,600-bps send/receive fax	2,400-bps/9,600-bps MNP 5 send-only fax
VIDEO					
Screen manufacturer	Sharp	Sharp	Sharp	Sharp	Toshiba
Maximum shades of gray	32	32	64	64	64
Video chip set manufacturer	Cirrus	WD	Cirrus	Cirrus	Toshiba
AC ADAPTER AND BATTERY					
AC adapter size (inches)	2 × 3.3 × 5.8	2 × 3.5 × 5.8	1.5 × 6 × 2.2	1.5 × 6 × 2.2	1 × 5.5 × 3
Rated battery life (hours)	3	3–4	4	4	3.5
ZDigit, battery rundowns (hr:min)	5:15, 3:25	3:12, 2:29	4:25, 3:28	3:59, 3:46	4:13, 3:18
Charge time while on, off (hours)	10, 2	18, 4–5	12, 4	12, 3.5	2, 2
Battery weight, amp/hour rating	1.1 lbs, 2.8Ah	1.2 lbs, 1.2Ah	1.3 lbs, 4.5Ah	1.3 lbs, 4.5Ah	1.6 lbs, 1.4Ah
Display/hard disk power-down	●/●	●/●	●/●	●/●	●/●
CPU/peripherals power-down	○/○	●/●	○/●	●/○	○/●
Standby/Hibernation	●/○	●/○	○/○	○/●	●/○

●—Yes   ○—No   N/A—Not applicable   INA—Information not available

Monochrome Portable/Laptop Computers

	Toshiba T2200SX	Toshiba T3300SL	Toshiba T4400SX (plasma)	Toshiba T4400SX (LCD)	Transource Verxion 386SX/20
Price	$$$	$$$	$$$$	$$$$	$$
Processor type and speed	Intel 386SX/20	Intel 386SL/25	Intel 486SX/25	Intel 486SX/25	Intel 386SX/20
Hard disk capacity	80Mb	120Mb	80Mb	80Mb	64Mb
Microsoft Windows 3.1	○	○	○	○	●
Distribution channel	Dealers	Dealers	Dealers	Dealers	Dealers, direct
Dimensions (HWD, in inches)	1.5 × 11 × 8.5	1.8 × 11.5 × 8.5	2 × 11.5 × 8.2	2 × 11.5 × 8.2	2 × 12 × 8
Weight/travel weight (pounds)	5.6, 6.9	5.9, 7.2	7.5, 9.4	7.5, 9.4	6.8, 7.1
Display area (H × W, in inches)	5 × 7	5.8 × 7.8	6 × 7.5	6 × 7.5	6 × 8
Keys: total, function, cursor	82, 12, 8	82, 12, 8	82, 12, 4	82, 12, 4	83, 12, 4
MOTHERBOARD					
Motherboard manufacturer	Toshiba	Toshiba	Toshiba	Toshiba	Top PC
Chip set manufacturer	Toshiba	Toshiba	Toshiba	Toshiba	Headland
BIOS version (or date)	Toshiba 1.2	Toshiba (February 1992)	Toshiba 1.2	Toshiba 1.2	AMI (April 1991)
Setup in ROM/Password in ROM	●/○	●/●	●/●	●/●	●/●
System shadowing/Video shadowing	●/●	○/●	●/●	●/●	●/●
MEMORY AND DISK DRIVES					
Installable RAM	2Mb–8Mb	2Mb–6Mb	2Mb–16Mb	2Mb–16Mb	1Mb–4Mb
User-installable	●	●	●	●	○
External processor RAM cache	None	64K	None	None	None
Available hard disk sizes	40Mb, 60Mb, 80Mb	80Mb, 120Mb	80Mb, 120Mb	80Mb, 120Mb	80Mb, 100Mb
I/O AND EXPANSION					
Parallel, serial, mouse ports	1, 1, 1	1, 1, 1	1, 1, 1	1, 1, 1	1, 1, 1
Proprietary expansion port	●	●	●	●	○
PCMCIA slot	○	●	○	○	○
Expansion unit	●	●	●	●	○
Internal modem options	2,400-bps MNP 5	2,400-bps/9,600-bps MNP 5 send/receive fax	2,400-bps, 2,400-bps V.42bis	2,400-bps, 2,400-bps V.42bis	None
VIDEO					
Screen manufacturer	Toshiba	Toshiba	Matsushita	Toshiba	Hitachi
Maximum shades of gray32	32	32	16	64	16
Video chip set manufacturer	WD	WD	WD	WD	Cirrus
AC ADAPTER AND BATTERY					
AC adapter size (inches)	1 × 3 × 5.5	1 × 5.5 × 3	1 × 3 × 5.5	1 × 3 × 5.5	2 × 3 × 5.5
Rated battery life (hours)	3.5	3	3	3	3
ZDigit, battery rundowns (hr:min)	4:06, 3:22	5:08, 3:19	3:55, 3:12	4:19, 3:40	3:12, 2:34
Charge time while on, off (hours)	N/A, 2	2, 2	4, 1.5	4, 1.5	4, 2
Battery weight, amp/hour rating	1.5 lbs, 2.2Ah	1.5 lbs, 1.1Ah	2.3 lbs, 2.4Ah	2.3 lbs, 2.4Ah	0.7 lbs, 5.6Ah
Display/hard disk power-down	●/●	●/●	●/●	●/●	●/●
CPU/peripherals power-down	●/●	●/●	●/●	●/●	○/○
Standby/Hibernation	●/●	●/●	●/○	●/○	●/○

●—Yes ○—No N/A—Not applicable INA—Information not available

Table Continues →

Monochrome Portable/Laptop Computers

	Twinhead Slimnote 486DX/33	WYSE DecisionMate 486SLC	Z-Note 320L	Z-Note 320Lb
Price	$$$	$$$	$$$	$$
Processor type and speed	Intel 486DX/33	Cyrix CX486SLC/25	Intel 386SL/20	Intel 386SL/20
Hard disk capacity	130Mb	127Mb	64Mb	64Mb
Microsoft Windows 3.1	●	●	●	●
Distribution channel	Dealers, direct	Dealers	Dealers, direct	Dealers, direct
Dimensions (HWD, in inches)	1.6 × 11 × 8.5	1.8 × 11 × 8.9	2.2 × 11.8 × 8.5	2.2 × 11.8 × 8.5
Weight/travel weight (pounds)	6.1, 7.8	4.9, 7.5	5.9, 7.7	5.7, 7.7
Display area (H × W, in inches)	5.8 × 7.7	5.2 × 6.8	5.6 × 7.6	5.8 × 7.6
Keys: total, function, cursor	84, 10, 8	79, 10, 4	82, 12, 8	82, 12, 8

MOTHERBOARD

Motherboard manufacturer	Twinhead	WYSE	ZDS	ZDS
Chip set manufacturer	ACC	Headland	Intel	Intel
BIOS version (or date)	Phoenix (June 1992)	Award (October 1991)	ZDS (April 1992)	ZDS (April 1992)
Setup in ROM/Password in ROM	●/●	●/●	●/●	●/●
System shadowing/Video shadowing	●/●	●/●	●/●	○/●

MEMORY AND DISK DRIVES

Installable RAM	4Mb–16Mb	1Mb–8Mb	2Mb–12Mb	2Mb–12Mb
User-installable	●	●	●	●
External processor RAM cache	None	None	None	None
Available hard disk sizes	80Mb, 130Mb	84Mb, 120Mb, 200Mb	60Mb, 85Mb, 120Mb	60Mb, 85Mb, 120Mb

I/O AND EXPANSION

Parallel, serial, mouse ports	1, 1, 1	1, 1, 1	1, 1, 1	1, 1, 1
Proprietary expansion port	●	○	●	●
PCMCIA slot	○	○	○	○
Expansion unit	●	○	●	●
Internal modem options	2,400-bps/9,600-bps send/receive fax	2,400-bps/9,600-bps MNP 5 send/receive fax	2,400-bps/9,600-bps MNP 5 send/receive fax	2,400-bps/9,600-bps MNP 5 send/receive fax

VIDEO

Screen manufacturer	Sharp	Sharp	Sanyo	Sanyo
Maximum shades of gray	64	32	64	64
Video chip set manufacturer	Cirrus	Cirrus	Cirrus	Cirrus

AC ADAPTER AND BATTERY

AC adapter size (inches)	1.9 × 6.5 × 3.1	1.8 × 5.9 × 3	2 × 6.8 × 3.4	0.7 × 5.5 × 3.6
Rated battery life (hours)	2.5	3	4	2.5
ZDigit, battery rundowns (hr:min)	2:33, 2:04	2:20, 1:29	6:03, 4:27	3:57, 1:58
Charge time while on, off (hours)	4, 2	4, 3	3, 3	N/A, 3
Battery weight, amp/hour rating	1.3 lbs, 1Ah	0.9 lbs, 18.2Ah	1.2 lbs, 1.3Ah	1.2 lbs, 1.3Ah
Display/hard disk power-down	●/●	●/●	●/●	●/●
CPU/peripherals power-down	●/●	○/○	●/●	●/●
Standby/Hibernation	●/○	○/○	●/●	●/●

●—Yes ○—No N/A—Not applicable INA—Information not available

Monochrome Portable/Laptop Computers

	Z-Note 325L	Z-Sport 325S
Price	$$$	$$$
Processor type and speed	Intel 386SL/25	Intel 386SX/25
Hard disk capacity	121Mb	85Mb
Microsoft Windows 3.1	●	○
Distribution channel	Dealers, direct	Dealers, direct
Dimensions (HWD, in inches)	2.2 × 11.8 × 8.5	2 × 11 × 8.5
Weight/travel weight (pounds)	5.9, 7.5	6.1, 7.5
Display area (H × W, in inches)	5.8 × 7.7	5.8 × 7.7
Keys: total, function, cursor	82, 12, 8	86, 12, 8
MOTHERBOARD		
Motherboard manufacturer	ZDS	ZDS
Chip set manufacturer	Intel	WD
BIOS version (or date)	ZDS (April 1992)	Phoenix (August 1992)
Setup in ROM/Password in ROM	●/●	●/●
System shadowing/Video shadowing	●/●	●/●
MEMORY AND DISK DRIVES		
Installable RAM	2Mb–12Mb	2Mb–8Mb
User-installable	●	●
External processor RAM cache	64K	None
Available hard disk sizes	60Mb, 85Mb, 120Mb	60Mb, 80Mb
I/O AND EXPANSION		
Parallel, serial, mouse ports	1, 1, 1	1, 1, 1
Proprietary expansion port	●	●
PCMCIA slot	○	○
Expansion unit	●	●
Internal modem options	2,400-bps/9,600-bps MNP 5 send/receive fax	2,400-bps/9,600-bps MNP 5 send/receive fax
VIDEO		
Screen manufacturer	Sanyo	Matsushita
Maximum shades of gray	64	64
Video chip set manufacturer	Cirrus	Cirrus
AC ADAPTER AND BATTERY		
AC adapter size (inches)	1.9 × 6.8 × 3.4	2.1 × 7.1 × 3
Rated battery life (hours)	4	2.5
ZDigit, battery rundowns (hr:min)	5:36, 4:21	2:47, 2:03
Charge time while on, off (hours)	N/A, 3	3.5, 1.5
Battery weight, amp/hour rating	1.2 lbs, 1.3Ah	1 lb, 2.2Ah
Display/hard disk power-down	●/●	●/●
CPU/peripherals power-down	●/●	●/●
Standby/Hibernation	●/●	●/●

●—Yes ○—No N/A—Not applicable INA—Information not available   **End** ■

FAX MODEMS

A P P E N D I X

I.1   Fax Modems

(Products listed in alphabetical order by company name)	Computer Peripherals ViVa 14.4/FAX Modem	Hayes Optima 96+ FAX96	Hayes Optima 144+ FAX144	Intel SatisFAXtion Modem 400/e
List price	$	$	$	$
STANDARD CONFIGURATION				
Dimensions (HWD, in inches)	5.4 × 2.1 × 5.7	1.5 × 5.5 × 9.5	1.5 × 5.5 × 9.5	1.3 × 5.5 × 9.6
Chip set	Rockwell 144DP	Proprietary	Proprietary	Rockwell RC144AC
RS-232 included	○	○	○	○
Phone cable included	●	●	●	●
Software included	QuickLink II, WinFax Lite	Smartcom EZ, Smartcom FAX	Smartcom EZ, Smartcom FAX	SatisFAXtion
CAS supported	○	●	●	●*
Fax BIOS supported	○	○	○	○
Configurable through software	●	●	●	●
Configurable through DIP switches	○	○	○	○
STATUS LIGHTS				
Transmit data	●	●	●	●
Carrier detect	●	●	●	●
Auto-answer	●	●	●	●
Modem ready	●	●	●	●
2,400 bps	●	●	○	●
Request to send	○	○	○	○
Test	○	○	○	○
Receive data	●	●	●	●
Off-hook	●	●	●	●
Error control	○	●	●	●
Terminal ready	●	●	●	●
High-speed indicator	●	●	●	●
Clear to send	●	○	○	○
DATA/FAX MODULATION AND ERROR CONTROL				
V.32/V.32bis	●/●	○/●	●/●	●/●
V.29/V.22bis	●/●	●/○	●/○	●/○
V.42/V.42bis	●/●	○/○	●/●	●/○
Group 2/Group 3/V.17 fax	○/●/●	●/●/○	●/●/○	●/●/○
MNP levels supported	1–5	2–5	2–5	2–5

*via device driver

●—Yes   ○—No   N/A—Not applicable   INA—Information not available

Table Continues →

Fax Modems

	Practical Peripherals Practical Modem 14400FXSA	Supra SupraFAX Modem V.32bis	U.S. Robotics Courier HST Dual Standard Fax	U.S. Robotics Courier V.32bis Fax
List price	$	$	$	$
STANDARD CONFIGURATION				
Dimensions (HWD, in inches)	3 × 5 × 10	4.6 × 6.5 × 1	6.3 × 10.3 × 1.5	6.3 × 10.3 × 1.5
Chip set	AT&T 14.4 MA	Rockwell RC144AC	Proprietary	Proprietary
RS-232 included	○	●	○	○
Phone cable included	●	●		●
Software included	QuickLink II	FaxTalk Plus, WinFax Lite	BlastFax PC 1.01	BlastFax PC 1.01
CAS supported	○	○	○	○
Fax BIOS supported	○	○	○	○
Configurable through software	●	●	●	●
Configurable through DIP switches	○	○	●	●
STATUS LIGHTS				
Transmit data	●	●	●	●
Carrier detect	●	●	●	●
Auto-answer	●	●	●	●
Modem ready	●	●	●	●
2,400 bps	●	●	●	●
Request to send	●	●	●	●
Test	●	●	●	●
Receive data	●	●	●	●
Off-hook	●	●	●	●
Error control	●	●	●	●
Terminal ready	●	●	●	●
High-speed indicator	●	●	●	●
Clear to send	●	●	●	●
DATA/FAX MODULATION AND ERROR CONTROL				
V.32/V.32bis	●/●	●/●	●/●	●/●
V.29/V.22bis	●/○	●/●	●/●	●/●
V.42/V.42bis	●/●	●/●	●/●	●/●
Group 2/Group 3/V.17 fax	○/●/○	○/●/●	○/●/○	○/●/○
MNP levels supported	1–5	2–5, 10	2–5	2–5

●—Yes ○—No N/A—Not applicable INA—Information not available

Fax Modems

	U.S. Robotics Sportster 9600 Fax	U.S. Robotics Sportster 14400 Fax	Zoom VFX V.32	Zoom VFX V.32bis
List price	$	$	$	$
STANDARD CONFIGURATION				
Dimensions (HWD, in inches)	6.6 × 5 × 1.8	6.6 × 5 × 1.8	6.1 × 8.5 × 1.6	6.1 × 8.5 × 1.6
Chip set	Proprietary	Proprietary	Rockwell RC96AC	Rockwell RC144AC
RS-232 included	○	○	○	○
Phone cable included	●	●	●	●
Software included	BlastFax PC 1.01	BlastFax PC 1.01	MTEZ with ExpressFax 1.17	MTEZ with ExpressFax 1.17
CAS supported	○	○	○	○
Fax BIOS supported	○	○	○	○
Configurable through software	●	●	●	●
Configurable through DIP switches	●	●	●	○
STATUS LIGHTS				
Transmit data	●	●	●	●
Carrier detect	●	●	●	●
Auto-answer	●	●	●	●
Modem ready	●	●	●	●
2,400 bps	●	●	●	●
Request to send	●	●	●	●
Test	●	●	●	●
Receive data	●	●	●	●
Off-hook	●	●	●	●
Error control	●	●	●	●
Terminal ready	●	●	●	●
High-speed indicator	●	●	●	●
Clear to send	●	●	●	●
DATA/FAX MODULATION AND ERROR CONTROL				
V.32/V.32bis	○/●	●/●	○/●	●/●
V.29/V.22bis	●/●	●/●	●/●	●/●
V.42/V.42bis	●/●	●/●	●/●	●/●
Group 2/Group 3/V.17 fax	○/●/○	○/●/○	○/●/○	○/●/●
MNP levels supported	2–5	2–5	1–5	1–5

●—Yes ○—No N/A—Not applicable INA—Information not available

End ■

I.2 Portable High-Speed Modems

(Products listed in alphabetical order by company name)	Compaq Enhanced 9600-bps Internal Modem	Dallas Fax 9696P	Megahertz C596FM Laptop FAX/Modem	Megahertz P296FMV Pocket Laptop FAX/Modem
List price	$	$	$	$
GENERAL INFORMATION				
Fax capability	○	●	●	●
Cellular capability	○	○	○	○
Warranty period	1 year	Lifetime	5 years	5 years
Communications software bundled with modem	None	MTEZ, QuickLink II, or WinFax	MTEZ	MTEZ
PHYSICAL FEATURES				
Modem type	Internal	External	Internal	External
Dimensions (HWD, in inches)	N/A	0.9 × 2.4 × 4.3	N/A	1.2 × 2.4 × 3.3
Weight including batteries (in ounces)	N/A	5.5	N/A	6.5
Number of LEDs	N/A	1	N/A	None
Location of power switch	N/A	Right side	N/A	None
Number of predefined setup strings	1	2	2	2
Number of user-definable setup strings	2	2	2	2
CUSTOMIZATION AND USAGE				
Amount of buffer memory for transmitting and receiving	380 bytes	32K	4K	4K
Two-wire leased-line capabilities	○	●	●	●
Synchronous mode	●	○	○	○
Hayes auto-sync mode	●	●	○	○
CCITT MODULATION PROTOCOLS SUPPORTED				
V.21	●	●	●	●
V.23	●	●	●	●
V.32bis	○	○	○	○
MISCELLANEOUS				
Most similar modem	Hayes Ultra 96	Microcom AX	Microcom AX	Microcom AX
Supports V.25bis command set	●	○	○	○
Carrying case provided	○	○	○	●
2,400-bps data-only modem available	●	○	●	●
2,400-bps-data and 9,600-bps-fax modem available	○	●	●	●

●—Yes   ○—No   N/A—Not applicable   INA—Information not available

Portable High-Speed Modems

	Megahertz T396FM Laptop FAX/Modem	Piiceon Dispatcher V.32bis Cellular Ready Data/Fax Modem	Telebit QBlazer
List price	$	$	$
GENERAL INFORMATION			
Fax capability	●	●	○
Cellular capability	○	●	○
Warranty period	5 years	Lifetime	2 years
Communications software bundled with modem	MTEZ	MTEZ	MTEZ
PHYSICAL FEATURES			
Modem type	Internal	Internal	External
Dimensions (HWD, in inches)	N/A	N/A	2.3 × 2.5 × 2.5
Weight including batteries (in ounces)	N/A	N/A	8
Number of LEDs	N/A	N/A	8
Location of power switch	N/A	N/A	Right side
Number of predefined setup strings	2	2	1
Number of user-definable setup strings	2	2	2
CUSTOMIZATION AND USAGE			
Amount of buffer memory for transmitting and receiving	4K	2K	512 bytes
Two-wire leased-line capabilities	●	●	○
Synchronous mode	○	○	○
Hayes auto-sync mode	○	●	○
CCITT MODULATION PROTOCOLS SUPPORTED			
V.21	●	●	○
V.23	●	●	○
V.32bis	○	●	○
MISCELLANEOUS			
Most similar modem	Microcom AX	Microcom AX	WorldPort 2400
Supports V.25bis command set	○	●	○
Carrying case provided	○	○	●
2,400-bps data-only modem available	●	●	○
2,400-bps-data and 9,600-bps-fax modem available	●	●	○

●—Yes   ○—No   N/A—Not applicable   INA—Information not available

End ■

ZIFF-DAVIS PRESS

VGA-TO-NTSC BOARDS

APPENDIX

J

VGA-to-NTSC Boards

Products listed in alphabetical order by company name	ADDA VGA-AVer	Aitech ProVGA/TV Plus	Cardinal SNAPplus	Everex Vision VGA with Overlay
List price (tested configuration)	$	$	$	$
VGA-to-NTSC Characteristics				
Encoder-chip manufacturer	Motorola	Sony	Sony	Motorola
Connectors:				
RCA	●	●	○	●
BCN	○	●	○	○
S-Video	Optional	●	●	●
Input/output formats supported:				
Composite NTSC	●	●	●	●
PAL	●	○	●	○
SECAM	○	○	○	○
S-Video	●	●	●	●
RBG analog	●	○	●	●
Still-Video System (SVS)	○	○	●	●
RF modulator	○	●	●	●
NTSC Output				
Maximum resolution (pixels)	720 × 400	640 × 480	640 × 480	512 × 480
Maximum number of colors	256	256	16.7 million	256
Supports separate sync	○	○	○	●
Allows screen blanking	○	●	●	●
Overscan/underscan controls	●/●	●/●	●/●	●/●
Vertical/horizontal controls	●/●	●/●	●/●	●/●
Video Effects and Editing				
Software-controlled keying	●	○	●	●
Grabs video in single frame	○	●	●	○
Freezes video in a frame	○	○	●	○
Converts video-in to gray 1–1 scale	○	○	●	○
Converts video-in to negative	○	○	●	○
Provides image fade-in or fade-out	○	●	●	○
Changes RGB values	○	○	●	○
Hue/Saturation	○/○	○/○	●/●	●/●
Brightness/Contrast	○/○	○/○	●/●	●/●
Anti-jitter/anti-flicker filter	○/●	○/●	○/○	●/●
VGA Characteristics				
VGA	Pass-through	Pass-through	On-board	On-board
VGA controller	N/A	N/A	Tseng ET4000	Tseng ET4000
BIOS version	N/A	N/A	Cardinal 2.01	Everex 1.01
On-board display memory	N/A	N/A	1Mb	1Mb
Video standards:				
1,280 × 1,024	N/A	N/A	●	●
1,024 × 768 noninterlaced	N/A	N/A	●	●
1,024 × 768 interlaced	N/A	N/A	●	●
Super VGA (800 × 600)	N/A	N/A	●	●
VGA (640 × 480)	N/A	N/A	●	●
Maximum addressable resolution	N/A	N/A	1,024 × 768	1,280 × 1,024
Maximum displayable resolution	N/A	N/A	1,024 × 768	1,280 × 1,024
Maximum number of colors simultaneously displayable (resolution)	N/A	N/A	65,000 (1,024 × 768)	256 (1,224 × 768)
Drivers	N/A	N/A	AutoCad, Gem, Lotus 1-2-3, Microsoft Windows, OS/2, Ventura Publisher, WordPerfect	AutoCad, Gem, Lotus 1-2-3, Microsoft Windows, OS/2, Symphony, WordPerfect
Technical Support and Warranty				
Technical support hours (Eastern time)	12:00–8:00 M–F	12:00–8:30 M–F	9:00–5:00 M–F	11:00–8:00 M–F
Toll-free number	○	●	○	●
BBS	○	●	●	●
Warranty	1 year	1 year	1 year	2 years

●—Yes ○—No N/A—Not applicable INA—Information not available

Table Continues →

VGA-to-NTSC Boards

	Genoa VGA2TV	Magni VGA Producer Pro	TrueVision VideoVGA	Willow GVA-TV GE/O
List price (tested configuration)	$	$	$	$
VGA-to-NTSC Characteristics				
Encoder-chip manufacturer	Genoa	Magni	Truevision	Motorola
Connectors:				
RCA	●	●	●	●
BCN	○	●	○	○
S-Video	●	●	●	●
Input/output formats supported:				
Composite NTSC	●	●	●	●
PAL	○	○	○	○
SECAM	○	○	○	○
S-Video	●	●	●	● (output only)
RBG analog	●	● (output only)	○	● (output only)
Still-Video System (SVS)	○	○	○	●
RF modulator	○	○	○	● (output only)
NTSC Output				
Maximum resolution (pixels)	640 × 480	768 × 480	640 × 480	640 × 480
Maximum number of colors	256	256	256	256
Supports separate sync	○	●	○	○
Allows screen blanking	●	●	●	●
Overscan/underscan controls	○/○	●/●	○/●	○/○
Vertical/horizontal controls	○/○	●/●	○/○	●/●
Video Effects and Editing				
Software-controlled keying	●	○	●	●
Grabs video in single frame	○	○	○	○
Freezes video in a frame	○	○	○	○
Converts video-in to gray 1–1 scale	○	○	○	○
Converts video-in to negative	○	○	○	○
Provides image fade-in or fade-out	○	●	●	○
Changes RGB values	○	○	○	○
Hue/Saturation	○/○	○/○	○/○	○/○
Brightness/Contrast	○/○	○/○	○/○	○/○
Anti-jitter/anti-flicker filter	○/○	●/●	○/○	○/○
VGA Characteristics				
VGA	Pass-through	Pass-through	On-board	On-board
VGA controller	N/A	N/A	Tseng ET4000	Tseng 3000AX
BIOS version	N/A	N/A	Tseng 8.00	Willow/Tseng 1.11
On-board display memory	N/A	N/A	1Mb	512K
Video standards:				
1,280 × 1,024	N/A	N/A	○	○
1,024 × 768 noninterlaced	N/A	N/A	○	○
1,024 × 768 interlaced	N/A	N/A	●	●
Super VGA (800 × 600)	N/A	N/A	●	●
VGA (640 × 480)	N/A	N/A	●	●
Maximum addressable resolution	N/A	N/A	1,024 × 768	640 × 480
Maximum displayable resolution	N/A	N/A	1,024 × 768	640 × 480
Maximum number of colors simultaneously displayable (resolution)	N/A	N/A	256 (1,024 × 768)	256 (640 × 480)
Drivers	N/A	N/A	AutoCad, Lotus 1-2-3, Microsoft Windows, Ventura Publisher, WordPerfect	AutoCad, Gem, Lotus 1-2-3, Microsoft Windows, Ventura Publisher, WordPerfect
Technical Support and Warranty				
Technical support hours (Eastern time)	12:00–7:00 M–F	11:00–8:00 M–F	8:00–6:00 M–F	10:00–6:00 M–F
Toll-free number	○	●	○	●
BBS	●	●	●	●
Warranty	2 years	1 year	1 year	3 years

●—Yes   ○—No   N/A—Not applicable   INA—Information not available

End ■

SOUND BOARDS

Sound Boards

(Products listed in alphabetical order by company name)	AdTech Sound 2000	Ad Lib Gold 1000	Advanced Gravis UltraSound	Alpha Systems Cyber Audio Card	ATI Stereo-F/X
List price	$	$	$	$	$
GENERAL FEATURES					
Add-in board or external box	Add-in board	Add-in board	Add-in board	Add-in board	Add-in board
ISA interface	16-bit	8-bit	16-bit	16-bit	8-bit
Dimensions of external box (HWD, in inches)	N/A	N/A	N/A	N/A	N/A
IRQ levels supported	2, 5, 7, 10–12	3–5, 7	2, 3, 5, 7, 11, 12, 15	2, 5, 10, 12	2, 3, 5, 7
Number of selectable addresses	8	8	6	4	7
Includes digital signal processor	●	●	○	●	○
Includes on-board VGA	○	○	○	○	○
Supports ADPCM data compression	●	●	○	●	●
WAVEFORM AUDIO					
Maximum sampling size (recording)	10-bit	12-bit	8-bit	12-bit	8-bit
Maximum sampling size (playback)	16-bit	12-bit	16-bit	16-bit	8-bit
Maximum sampling rate:					
Input (kHz)	44.1	44.1	44.1	44.1	44.1
Output (kHz)	44.1	44.1	44.1	44.1	44.1
Stereo output (kHz)	44.1	44.1	44.1	44.1	22.05
MIDI SYNTHESIZER					
MIDI Synthesizer chip	Sierra ST8002 Aria Synthesizer	Yamaha OPL3	ICS GF1 Custom ASIC	Sierra ST8002 Aria Synthesizer	Yamaha OPL3
Synthesizer type	Wavetable lookup	FM synthesis	Wavetable lookup	Wavetable lookup	FM synthesis
Number of operators	N/A	4	N/A	N/A	2
MIDI interface	Optional	Optional	Optional	Optional	Optional
Supports General MIDI standard	●	●	●	●	●
Maximum number of simultaneous multitimbred voices	32	20	32	32	11
Maximum number of simultaneous polyphonic notes	32	18	32	32	9
MIXING CAPABILITIES					
Number of channels (recording mixer)	1	3	3	3	2
Number of channels (playback mixer)	1	7	5	4	2
Number of volume settings per channel	N/A	100	256	256	8
Mixes audio sources from:					
CD audio	●	●	●	●	○
Microphone	●	●	●	●	●
PC internal speaker	○	○	○	○	○
Stereo DAC	●	●	●	●	●
Stereo line-in	●	●	●	●	●
Stereo synthesizer	●	●	●	●	●
COMPATIBILITY					
Ad Lib Music Synthesizer Card	●	●	●	●	●
Creative Labs Sound Blaster	●	○	●	●	●
Roland MPU-401	●	○	○	●	○
CUSTOMER SUPPORT					
BBS/Toll-free support number	○/○	●/●	●/○	●/○	●/○
Telephone technical support hours (Eastern time)	11:00–9:00 M–F	10:00–5:00 M–F	11:00–7:30 M–F	10:00–7:00 M–F	9:00–5:00 M–F
Warranty	1 year	1 year	1 year	2 years	2 years (5 years on parts)

●—Yes   ○—No   N/A—Not applicable   INA—Information not available

Table Continues →

ZIFF-DAVIS PRESS

Sound Boards

	ATI VGAStereo-F/X	AVM Alta Pro Synthesizer	Aztech Sound Galaxy NX Pro	Cardinal SoundVision	CompuAdd Spectrum 16 Multimedia Sound Card
List price	$	$	$	$	$
GENERAL FEATURES					
Add-in board or external box	Add-in board	Add-in board	Add-in board	Add-in board	Add-in board
ISA interface	16-bit	16-bit	16-bit	16-bit	16-bit
Dimensions of external box (HWD, in inches)	N/A	N/A	N/A	N/A	N/A
IRQ levels supported	2, 3, 5, 7	2, 5, 7, 9–12	2, 3, 5, 7, 10	3, 5	2, 3, 5, 7
Number of selectable addresses	7	10	2	3	3
Includes digital signal processor	○	●	○	○	○
Includes on-board VGA	●	○	○	●	○
Supports ADPCM data compression	●	●	●	●	●
WAVEFORM AUDIO					
Maximum sampling size (recording)	8-bit	12-bit	8-bit	12-bit	16-bit
Maximum sampling size (playback)	8-bit	16-bit	8-bit	12-bit	16-bit
Maximum sampling rate:					
Input (kHz)	44.1	44.1	44.1	44.1	44.1
Output (kHz)	44.1	44.1	44.1	44.1	44.1
Stereo output (kHz)	22.05	44.1	22.05	44.1	44.1
MIDI SYNTHESIZER					
MIDI Synthesizer chip	Yamaha OPL2	Sierra ST8004 Aria Synthesizer	Yamaha OPL3	Yamaha OPL3	Yamaha OPL3
Synthesizer type	FM synthesis	Wavetable lookup	FM synthesis	FM synthesis	FM synthesis
Number of operators	2	N/A	4	4	4
MIDI interface	●	●	Optional	●	Optional
Supports General MIDI standard	●	●	●	●	●
Maximum number of simultaneous multitimbred voices	11	32	20	20	20
Maximum number of simultaneous polyphonic notes	9	32	18	18	18
MIXING CAPABILITIES					
Number of channels (recording mixer)	2	3	6	6	7
Number of channels (playback mixer)	2	4	6	6	8
Number of volume settings per channel	8	256	16	100	256
Mixes audio sources from:					
CD audio	○	●	●	●	●
Microphone	●	●	●	●	●
PC internal speaker	○	○	●	○	●
Stereo DAC	●	●	●	●	●
Stereo line-in	●	●	●	●	●
Stereo synthesizer	●	●	●	●	●
COMPATIBILITY					
Ad Lib Music Synthesizer Card	●	●	●	●	●
Creative Labs Sound Blaster	●	●	●	○	●
Roland MPU-401	○	●	○	○	○
CUSTOMER SUPPORT					
BBS/Toll-free support number	●/○	○/●	●/●	●/○	●/●
Telephone technical support hours (Eastern time)	9:00–5:00 M–F	10:00–7:00 M–F	10:00–8:00 M–F	8:00–5:00 M–F	24 hours a day, 7 days a week
Warranty	2 years (5 years on parts)	2 years	1 year	1 year	3 years

●—Yes   ○—No   N/A—Not applicable   INA—Information not available

Sound Boards

	Computer Peripherals ViVa Maestro 16VR	Covox Sound Master II	Creative Labs Sound Blaster	Creative Labs Sound Blaster 16 ASP	Creative Labs Sound Blaster Pro
List price	$	$	$	$	$
GENERAL FEATURES					
Add-in board or external box	Add-in board	Add-in board	Add-in board	Add-in board	Add-in board
ISA interface	16-bit	8-bit	8-bit	16-bit	16-bit
Dimensions of external box (HWD, in inches)	N/A	N/A	N/A	N/A	N/A
IRQ levels supported	7, 9, 10, 12	2, 3, 5, 7	2, 5, 7, 10	2, 5, 7, 10	2, 5, 7, 10
Number of selectable addresses	4	4	2	4	2
Includes digital signal processor	●	○	○	●	○
Includes on-board VGA	○	○	○	○	○
Supports ADPCM data compression	○	●	●	○	●
WAVEFORM AUDIO					
Maximum sampling size (recording)	12-bit	8-bit	8-bit	16-bit	8-bit
Maximum sampling size (playback)	16-bit	8-bit	8-bit	16-bit	8-bit
Maximum sampling rate:					
Input (kHz)	44.1	25.1	15	44.1	44.1
Output (kHz)	44.1	44.1	44.1	44.1	44.1
Stereo output (kHz)	44.1	N/A	N/A	44.1	22.05
MIDI SYNTHESIZER					
MIDI Synthesizer chip	Sierra ST8003 Aria Synthesizer	Yamaha OPL2	Yamaha 1312	Yamaha OPL3	Yamaha OPL3
Synthesizer type	Wavetable lookup	FM synthesis	FM synthesis	FM synthesis	FM synthesis
Number of operators	N/A	2	2	4	4
MIDI interface	Optional	●	Optional	Optional	●
Supports General MIDI standard	●	●	○	○	○
Maximum number of simultaneous multitimbred voices	32	11	11	20	20
Maximum number of simultaneous polyphonic notes	32	9	9	18	18
MIXING CAPABILITIES					
Number of channels (recording mixer)	3	1	2	2	2
Number of channels (playback mixer)	4	1	2	2	2
Number of volume settings per channel	256	2	8	32	8
Mixes audio sources from:					
CD audio	●	○	●	●	●
Microphone	●	○	●	●	●
PC internal speaker	○	○	○	●	●
Stereo DAC	●	○	○	●	●
Stereo line-in	●	○	○	●	●
Stereo synthesizer	●	○	○	●	●
COMPATIBILITY					
Ad Lib Music Synthesizer Card	●	●	●	●	●
Creative Labs Sound Blaster	●	○	●	●	●
Roland MPU-401	●	○	○	●	○
CUSTOMER SUPPORT					
BBS/Toll-free support number	●/●	●/○	●/●	●/●	●/●
Telephone technical support hours (Eastern time)	10:00–7:00 M–F	11:00–8:00 M–F	10:00–9:00 M–F	10:00–9:00 M–F	10:00–9:00 M–F
Warranty	1 year	1 year	1 year	1 year	1 year

●—Yes ○—No N/A—Not applicable INA—Information not available

Table Continues →

Sound Boards

	Media Vision Audioport	Media Vision Pro Audio-Spectrum 16	Microsoft Windows Sound System	Midi Land Okey Dokey Sound Card	National Semiconductor Tyln 2000
List price	$	$	$	$	$
GENERAL FEATURES					
Add-in board or external box	External box	Add-in board	Add-in board	Add-in board	Add-in board
ISA interface	N/A	16-bit	16-bit	8-bit	16-bit
Dimensions of external box (HWD, in inches)	0.25 × 2.25 × 4.25	N/A	N/A	N/A	N/A
IRQ levels supported	N/A	2, 3, 5, 7	7, 9–11	2–5, 7	2–15
Number of selectable addresses	N/A	3	3	1	4
Includes digital signal processor	○	○	○	●	●
Includes on-board VGA	○	○	○	○	○
Supports ADPCM data compression	○	●	●	●	●
WAVEFORM AUDIO					
Maximum sampling size (recording)	8-bit	16-bit	16-bit	8-bit	8-bit
Maximum sampling size (playback)	8-bit	16-bit	16-bit	8-bit	8-bit
Maximum sampling rate:					
Input (kHz)	22.05	44.1	44.1	11.025	11.025
Output (kHz)	22.05	44.1	44.1	22.05	22.05
Stereo output (kHz)	N/A	44.1	44.1	N/A	N/A
MIDI SYNTHESIZER					
MIDI Synthesizer chip	Yamaha OPL2	Yamaha OPL3	Yamaha OPL3	Yamaha OPL2	None
Synthesizer type	FM synthesis	FM synthesis	FM synthesis	FM synthesis	N/A
Number of operators	2	4	4	2	N/A
MIDI interface	○	Optional	○	Optional	○
Supports General MIDI standard	●	●	●	●	N/A
Maximum number of simultaneous multitimbred voices	11	20	20	11	N/A
Maximum number of simultaneous polyphonic notes	9	18	18	9	N/A
MIXING CAPABILITIES					
Number of channels (recording mixer)	6	7	2	1	1
Number of channels (playback mixer)	6	8	3	1	1
Number of volume settings per channel	62	256	N/A	N/A	N/A
Mixes audio sources from:					
CD audio	○	●	○	○	○
Microphone	○	●	○	○	●
PC internal speaker	○	●	○	○	●
Stereo DAC	○	●	○	○	○
Stereo line-in	○	●	●	○	○
Stereo synthesizer	○	●	●	○	○
COMPATIBILITY					
Ad Lib Music Synthesizer Card	●	●	●	●	○
Creative Labs Sound Blaster	●	●	○	●	○
Roland MPU-401	○	○	○	●	○
CUSTOMER SUPPORT					
BBS/Toll-free support number	●/●	●/●	○/●	○/●	●/○
Telephone technical support hours (Eastern time)	11:00–8:00 M–F	11:00–8:00 M–F	9:00–9:00 M–F	12:00–8:00 M–F	8:00–8:00 M–F
Warranty	3 years	3 years	1 year	1 year	5 years

●—Yes ○—No N/A—Not applicable INA—Information not available

Sound Boards

	Omni Labs AudioMaster	Orchid Sound Producer Pro	Sigma WinStorm	Turtle Beach MultiSound	Video Associates MicroKey/AudioPort
List price	$	$	$	$	$
GENERAL FEATURES					
Add-in board or external box	Add-in board	Add-in board	Add-in board	Add-in board	External box
ISA interface	16-bit	16-bit	16-bit	16-bit	N/A
Dimensions of external box (HWD, in inches)	N/A	N/A	N/A	N/A	2 × 3.5 × 0.5
IRQ levels supported	2–5, 7, 9–12	2, 5, 7, 10	2–7, 10–12, 15	5, 7, 9–12, 15	N/A
Number of selectable addresses	3	2	7	8	N/A
Includes digital signal processor	○	○	○	●	●
Includes on-board VGA	○	○	●	○	○
Supports ADPCM data compression	○	●	○	○	●
WAVEFORM AUDIO					
Maximum sampling size (recording)	12-bit	8-bit	16-bit	16-bit	12-bit
Maximum sampling size (playback)	12-bit	8-bit	16-bit	16-bit	12-bit
Maximum sampling rate:					
Input (kHz)	44.1	44.1	44.1	44.1	44.1
Output (kHz)	44.1	44.1	44.1	44.1	44.1
Stereo output (kHz)	44.1 (no stereo input)	22.05	44.1	44.1	N/A
MIDI SYNTHESIZER					
MIDI Synthesizer chip	Motorola 68008	Yamaha OPL3	Yamaha OPL3	E-mu Proteus 1XR	None
Synthesizer type	Wavetable lookup	FM synthesis	FM synthesis	Wavetable lookup	N/A
Number of operators	N/A	4	4	N/A	N/A
MIDI interface	Optional	●	Optional	Optional	○
Supports General MIDI standard	●	○	●	●	N/A
Maximum number of simultaneous multitimbred voices	24	20	20	16	N/A
Maximum number of simultaneous polyphonic notes	24	18	18	32	N/A
MIXING CAPABILITIES					
Number of channels (recording mixer)	3	2	6	1	1
Number of channels (playback mixer)	3	2	6	4	1
Number of volume settings per channel	64	16	256	127	N/A
Mixes audio sources from:					
CD audio	●	●	●	●	○
Microphone	●	●	●	○	○
PC internal speaker	○	●	○	○	○
Stereo DAC	●	●	○	●	○
Stereo line-in	●	●	●	●	○
Stereo synthesizer	●	●	●	●	○
COMPATIBILITY					
Ad Lib Music Synthesizer Card	Optional	●	●	○	○
Creative Labs Sound Blaster	Optional	●	●	○	○
Roland MPU-401	○	○	●	○	○
CUSTOMER SUPPORT					
BBS/Toll-free support number	○/○	●/○	●/○	●/○	●/●
Telephone technical support hours (Eastern time)	12:00–8:00 M–F	10:00–8:00 M–F	10:00–8:00 M–F	9:00–5:30 M–F	9:30–6:30 M–F
Warranty	1 year	4 years	5 years	1 year	1 year

●—Yes ○—No N/A—Not applicable INA—Information not available

End ■

SURGE SUPPRESSORS

APPENDIX

L

Surge Suppressors

(Products listed in alphabetical order by company name)	AESI/ StediWatt Diagnostic Power Refinery, Model 718	American Power Conversion Surge Arrest Plus with telephone suppression	Brooks Surge Reactor BN6-6	Brooks Power Systems Surge Stopper BPS-BN6-6	Control Concepts Supertrac ST6D
List price	$	$	$	$	$
PHYSICAL CHARACTERISTICS					
Power cord length (inches)	75	72	72	72	60
Case material	Aluminum	Plastic	Metal	Aluminum	Plastic
Number of outlets	7	7	6	6	6
Socket arrangement	Single row	Single row	Single row	Single row	Two rows
TECHNOLOGY					
Capacitators	●	●	●	●	●
Inductors	●	●	●	●	●
Gas tubes	○	○	○	○	○
Numbers of MOVs (metal oxide varistors)	6	7	3	5	6
Size (mm)	22	20	20	20	20
Silicon avalanche diodes	○	○	●	●	○
UL ratings (pass-through voltage):					
Hot-to-neutral line	330V	330V	330V	330V	330V
Neutral-to-ground line	330V	330V	330V	330V	400V
Hot-to-ground line	330V	330V	330V	330V	400V
Phone jack	$20.00	●	○	○	●
GENERAL FEATURES					
Separate on/off switches for individual outlets	○	○	○	○	○
Suppression light	●	●	●	●	●
Circuit breaker	15 amps	15 amps	15 amps	15 amps	15 amps
Technical support hours (Eastern time)	8:00–6:00 M–F	8:00–8:00 M–F	8:00–5:00 M–F	9:00–7:00 M–F	8:00–5:00 M–F
Standard warranty	5 years	Lifetime	Lifetime	Lifetime	10 years
Warranty covers damage to equipment plugged in	●	●	○	●	○

●—Yes　○—No　N/A—Not applicable　INA—Information not available

Table Continues →

Surge Suppressors

	Current Technology Power Siftor Pro 15	Curtis Manufacturing Ruby Plus	Datashield S100	EFI PowerTrax 2000	Electripak Model 6SSU
List price	$	$	$	$	$
PHYSICAL CHARACTERISTICS					
Power cord length (inches)	72	72	72	72	48
Case material	Aluminum	Plastic	Plastic	Plastic	Metal
Number of outlets	6	6	6	6	6
Socket arrangement	Single row	Two rows	Two rows	Single row	Single row
TECHNOLOGY					
Capacitators	○	●	●	●	●
Inductors	○	●	●	●	○
Gas tubes	○	○	●	○	○
Numbers of MOVs (metal oxide varistors)	14	6	4	6	3
Size (mm)	20	14	22	18	20
Silicon avalanche diodes	○	○	○	●	○
UL ratings (pass-through voltage):					
Hot-to-neutral line	330V	400V	400V	330V	330V
Neutral-to-ground line	330V	400V	400V	330V	330V
Hot-to-ground line	330V	400V	400V	400V	330V
Phone jack	●	●	○	●	○
GENERAL FEATURES					
Separate on/off switches for individual outlets	○	○	○	○	● (4 switched, 2 unswitched)
Suppression light	○	●	○	●	●
Circuit breaker	15 amps	15 amps	10 amps	15 amps	15 amps
Technical support hours (Eastern time)	7:00–4:00 M–F	8:00–5:00 M–F	7:00–5:30 M–F	9:00–6:00 M–F	8:00–5:00 M–F
Standard warranty	Lifetime	Lifetime	Lifetime	Lifetime	5 years
Warranty covers damage to equipment plugged in	○	○	●	●	○

●—Yes   ○—No   N/A—Not applicable   INA—Information not available

Surge Suppressors

	GC-Thorsen Power Management System 64-631	Geist Ultimate SRF-6MO/S-DP	GE Wiring Devices SurgePro SP-6000NS	General Semiconductor Industries 1206K6	Hubbell Circuit Guard SS6
List price	$	$	$	$	$
PHYSICAL CHARACTERISTICS					
Power cord length (inches)	72	72	72	72	72
Case material	Steel	Plastic	Plastic	Metal	Steel
Number of outlets	6	6	6	6	6
Socket arrangement	Single row	Two rows	Two rows	Single row	Single row
TECHNOLOGY					
Capacitors	●	●	●	○	○
Inductors	○	●	●	○	○
Gas tubes	○	○	○	○	○
Numbers of MOVs (metal oxide varistors)	3	4	2	8	4
Size (mm)	14.5	20	14	20	20
Silicon avalanche diodes	○	●	○	●	○
UL ratings (pass-through voltage):					
Hot-to-neutral line	330V	330V	600V	330V	330V
Neutral-to-ground line	330V	330V	600V	330V	330V
Hot-to-ground line	330V	330V	600V	330V	330V
Phone jack	●	●	○	○	○
GENERAL FEATURES					
Separate on/off switches for individual outlets	○	○	○	○	○
Suppression light	●	●	●	●	●
Circuit breaker	15 amps	15 amps	15 amps	15 amps	15 amps
Technical support hours (Eastern time)	7:00–4:00 M–F	7:00–4:00 M–F	8:00–5:00 M–F	7:00–4:00 M–F	8:00–4:30 M–F
Standard warranty	5 years	Lifetime	None	5 years	1 year
Warranty covers damage to equipment plugged in	○	●	N/A	○	○

●—Yes   ○—No   N/A—Not applicable   INA—Information not available   **Table Continues** →

Surge Suppressors

	Inland 3 Mode Surge Protector	Innovative Technology SPIU-6	Jayco Electronics Supress-All AC-6	Joslyn Model 1203-03 Surge Suppressor	Kensington Microware Ltd. Power Tree 50
List price	$	$	$	$	$
PHYSICAL CHARACTERISTICS					
Power cord length (inches)	48	60	72	72	108
Case material	Plastic	Plastic	Plastic	Aluminum	Plastic and steel
Number of outlets	6	6	6	6	6
Socket arrangement	Single row	Two rows	Two rows	Two rows	Two rows
TECHNOLOGY					
Capacitators	●	●	●	●	●
Inductors	○	●	○	●	●
Gas tubes	○	INA	○	●	○
Numbers of MOVs (metal oxide varistors)	3	INA	6	10	3
Size (mm)	14	INA	20	20	23
Silicon avalanche diodes	○	INA	●	○	○
UL ratings (pass-through voltage):					
Hot-to-neutral line	400V	330V	330V	330V	330V
Neutral-to-ground line	400V	330V	330V	330V	500V
Hot-to-ground line	400V	330V	330V	330V	500V
Phone jack	○	$20.00	○	○	●
GENERAL FEATURES					
Separate on/off switches for individual outlets	○	○	○	○	○
Suppression light	●	●	●	●	●
Circuit breaker	15 amps	10 amps	10 amps	15 amps	15 amps
Technical support hours (Eastern time)	8:30–5:30 M–F	8:00–5:00 M–F	9:00–5:00 M–F	10:30–7:30 M–F	11:00–8:30 M–F
Standard warranty	Lifetime	5 years	10 years	5 years	5 years
Warranty covers damage to equipment plugged in	○	○	●	○	●

●—Yes   ○—No   N/A—Not applicable   INA—Information not available

Surge Suppressors

	L.E.A. Dynatech CS-615	L.E.A. Dynatech Transient Tamer TT 415	NCR Pyramid	NCR Series 4000 Model 4070	Pacific Electricord XP
List price	$	$	$	$	$
PHYSICAL CHARACTERISTICS					
Power cord length (inches)	72	72	72	72	72
Case material	Plastic	Plastic	Plastic	Plastic	Plastic
Number of outlets	6	4	6	7	6
Socket arrangement	Two rows	Two rows	Two rows	Horseshoe	Single row
TECHNOLOGY					
Capacitators	○	●	○	●	●
Inductors	○	●	●	●	○
Gas tubes	○	○	●	●	○
Numbers of MOVs (metal oxide varistors)	5	7	3	6	3
Size (mm)	20	20	20	20	15
Silicon avalanche diodes	●	○	●	○	○
UL ratings (pass-through voltage):					
Hot-to-neutral line	330V	330V	330V	330V	400V
Neutral-to-ground line	330V	330V	330V	330V	400V
Hot-to-ground line	330V	330V	330V	330V	400V
Phone jack	○	●	○	●	○
GENERAL FEATURES					
Separate on/off switches for individual outlets	○	○	○	○	○
Suppression light	●	●	●	○	●
Circuit breaker	15 amps	15 amps	15 amps	15 amps	15 amps
Technical support hours (Eastern time)	7:00–6:00 M–F	7:00–6:00 M–F	24 hours a day	8:00–5:00 M–F (local time)	10:00–8:00 M–F
Standard warranty	Lifetime	Lifetime	2 years	5 years	2 years
Warranty covers damage to equipment plugged in	●	●	○	●	●

●—Yes   ○—No   N/A—Not applicable   INA—Information not available

Table Continues →

Surge Suppressors

	Panamax Max 6	Pass & Seymour/Legrand SpecGuard C6L	Perma Power RS-610	Power Sentry Surge Protector 300 Plus Model 106	ProTek Devices Surgebuster Model 1206K6
List price	$	$	$	$	$
PHYSICAL CHARACTERISTICS					
Power cord length (inches)	72	72	72	48	72
Case material	Plastic	Plastic	Steel	Plastic	Metal
Number of outlets	6	6	6	6	6
Socket arrangement	Two rows	Two rows	Single row	Single row	Single row
TECHNOLOGY					
Capacitators	●	●	○	●	●
Inductors	●	●	●	●	●
Gas tubes	○	○	○	○	○
Numbers of MOVs (metal oxide varistors)	6	6	3	3	8
Size (mm)	20	20	22	17	20
Silicon avalanche diodes	○	○	●	○	●
UL ratings (pass-through voltage):					
Hot-to-neutral line	330V	400V	330V	400V	330V
Neutral-to-ground line	330V	400V	330V	400V	330V
Hot-to-ground line	330V	400V	330V	400V	330V
Phone jack	○	○	○	○	○
GENERAL FEATURES					
Separate on/off switches for individual outlets	○	○	○	○	○
Suppression light	●	●	●	●	○
Circuit breaker	15 amps	15 amps	15 amps	15 amps	15 amps
Technical support hours (Eastern time)	10:30–8:00 M–F	8:00–5:30 M–F	9:00–7:00 M–F	10:00–10:00 M–F	10:00–7:00 M–F
Standard warranty	Lifetime	Lifetime	Lifetime	2 years	2 years
Warranty covers damage to equipment plugged in	●	○	●	●	○

●—Yes ○—No N/A—Not applicable INA—Information not available

Surge Suppressors

	Proxima Network-Grade Surge Protector Model S500	Proxima ProLine 30	SL Waber Surge Sentry DL6D	SL Waber Wave Tracker WT6SS	SRW Computer Components SRW GS-2
List price	$	$	$	$	$
PHYSICAL CHARACTERISTICS					
Power cord length (inches)	72	72	72	72	72
Case material	Plastic	Plastic	Plastic	Aluminum	Plastic
Number of outlets	7	6	6	6	6
Socket arrangement	Single row	Single row	Single row	Two rows	Single row
TECHNOLOGY					
Capacitators	●	●	○	●	●
Inductors	●	○	○	●	○
Gas tubes	○	○	○	●	○
Numbers of MOVs (metal oxide varistors)	6	6	1	5	3
Size (mm)	18	18	20	20	25
Silicon avalanche diodes	○	○	○	●	○
UL ratings (pass-through voltage):					
Hot-to-neutral line	330V	330V	330V	330V	340V
Neutral-to-ground line	330V	330V	330V	330V	340V
Hot-to-ground line	330V	330V	330V	330V	340V
Phone jack	○	●	○	○	○
GENERAL FEATURES					
Separate on/off switches for individual outlets	○	○	○	○	○
Suppression light	●	●	●	●	●
Circuit breaker	15 amps	15 amps	15 amps	15 amps	15 amps'
Technical support hours (Eastern time)	11:00–9:00 M–F	11:00–9:00 M–F	8:00–5:00 M–F	8:00–5:00 M–F	11:00–7:30 M–F
Standard warranty	Lifetime	Lifetime	Lifetime	Lifetime	Lifetime
Warranty covers damage to equipment plugged in	●	●	●	●	○

●—Yes   ○—No   N/A—Not applicable   INA—Information not available

Table Continues →

Surge Suppressors

	Tandy 6-Outlet Power Center	Tripp Lite Isobar 6 Ultra	Tripp Lite Isobar 8	Woods 5623 Surge Suppressor	Zaptech Model MSS-206	Zero Surge ZS1800 Surge Eliminator
List price	$	$	$	$	$	$
PHYSICAL CHARACTERISTICS						
Power cord length (inches)	72	72	144	48	72	72
Case material	Plastic	Steel and aluminum	Metal	Plastic	Plastic	Steel
Number of outlets	6	6	8	6	6	6
Socket arrangement	Two rows	Two rows	Single row	Single row	Two rows	Two rows
TECHNOLOGY						
Capacitors	●	●	●	●	●	●
Inductors	INA	●	○	●	○	●
Gas tubes	○	○	○	○	●	○
Numbers of MOVs (metal oxide varistors)	3	8	8	7	3	None
Size (mm)	INA	20	22	14	15	N/A
Silicon avalanche diodes	○	○	○	○	○	○
UL ratings (pass-through voltage):						
Hot-to-neutral line	340V	330V	330V	330V	400V	330V
Neutral-to-ground line	340V	330V	330V	330V	400V	N/A
Hot-to-ground line	340V	330V	330V	330V	400V	N/A
Phone jack	○	●	○	●	○	○
GENERAL FEATURES						
Separate on/off switches for individual outlets	○	○	○	○	●	○
Suppression light	●	●	○	●	○	○
Circuit breaker	15 amps	12 amps	15 amps	15 amps	15 amps	15 amps
Technical support hours (Eastern time)	9:00–6:30 M–F	7:00–5:30 M–F	8:00–6:30 M–F	8:00–5:00 M–F	12:00–9:00 M–F	9:00–5:00 M–F
Standard warranty	1 year	Lifetime	Lifetime	Lifetime	2 years	10 years
Warranty covers damage to equipment plugged in	○	●	●	○	○	●

●—Yes ○—No N/A—Not applicable INA—Information not available

End ■

INDEX TO *PC MAGAZINE* PRINTER REVIEWS (1984–1992)

A P P E N D I X

M

OVER THE LAST NINE YEARS, PC Magazine Labs has tested more than 900 printers for reviews in nine annual issues. Of those reviewed units, over 200 are still available from the manufacturers and are included in this index.

We have listed engine types, current prices (as of 9/1/92), and, for most products, speed scores on PC Labs' text speed test. For the color PostScript printers, we list the graphics speed score. For your reference, we have also provided the

INDEX TO *PC MAGAZINE* PRINTER REVIEWS (1984–1992)

volume, issue, and page numbers of the original reviews. Products whose names are followed by * (asterisk) have been replaced by upgraded models, but these upgrades were not considered significant enough to warrant a new review in *PC Magazine,* or, in certain cases, the company chose not to submit an upgraded machine for review. The prices listed for those machines are those of the upgraded models; please refer to the vendor for more specific product information. For printers that have stayed the same while their names have changed, we use the new names.

Since most dot-matrix printers are now available with color options, we no longer differentiate between monochrome and color-capable dot-matrix printers. The price listed in each case is for the standard printer, without a color option. Because color PostScript printers belong in a category of their own, we have indicated which thermal wax transfer and solid-ink PostScript-compatible printers handle color.

PC Labs' text speed test has remained virtually unchanged since our first printer issue; the Graphics Speed test has changed more significantly. You should keep this in mind when comparing speeds across nine years of products. Page printer speeds are measured in pages per minute (ppm); dot-matrix and ink-jet speeds are measured in characters per second (cps); line printers in lines per minute (lpm); and this year's color PostScript printers in graphics pages per minute (gppm). For most dot-matrix and ink-jet printers, we indicate draft text speed, unless the product offers a quality mode only. While laser print speed is not directly comparable with dot-matrix or ink-jet speed, a score of 1 page per minute falls roughly within a range of 25 to 30 characters per second for double-spaced text, or 50 to 60 cps single-spaced.

Company name	Product	Type	Speed	Price	Vol.	No.	Pg.
Advanced Matrix Technology	Accel–212	DM	122 cps	$469	11	20	327
Advanced Matrix Technology	Accel–214	DM	122 cps	$529	11	20	327
Advanced Matrix Technology	Accel–242	DM	118 cps	$529	11	20	327
Advanced Matrix Technology	Accel–244	DM	117 cps	$595	11	20	327
Advanced Matrix Technology	Accel–292	DM	151 cps	$795	11	20	327
Advanced Matrix Technology	Accel–294	DM	119 cps	$895	11	20	327
Advanced Matrix Technology	TracJet Laser Printer	L	14.7 ppm	$4,995	11	20	224
Advanced Matrix Technology	Accel-500*	DM	161 cps	$1,485	8	19	345
AEG Olympia	**NP 136-24**	**DM**	**118 cps**	**$395**	**8**	**19**	**246**
AEG Olympia	NP 136SE	DM	145 cps	$314	9	19	334
AEG Olympia	NP 80-24	DM	115 cps	$369	8	19	246
AEG Olympia	NP 80-24E	DM	105 cps	$327	9	19	334
AEG Olympia	NP 80SE	DM	126 cps	$330	9	19	334
AEG Olympia	NPC 136-24	DM	96 cps	$495	8	19	345
AGFA	P3400 PS	L	10.5 ppm	$6,495	8	19	117
ALPS	Allegro 500	DM	113 cps	$499	9	19	345
ALPS	Allegro 500XT	DM	138 cps	$799	9	19	345
ALPS	ASP1600	DM	59 cps	$299	9	19	339

C—color, DM—dot matrix, DS—dye sublimation, DW—daisy wheel, IJ—ink jet, L—laser, SI—solid ink, TT—thermal transfer
Boldface—*PC Magazine* Editor's Choice

* This machine has been replaced by an upgraded model.

INDEX TO *PC MAGAZINE* PRINTER REVIEWS (1984-1992)

Company name	Product	Type	Speed	Price	Vol.	No.	Pg.
ALPS	DMX800	DM	265 cps	$2,195	11	20	352
ALPS	ALPS LSX1600	L	13.6 ppm	$3,295	11	20	230
Apple	LaserWriter IIf	L	7.1 ppm	$3,299	11	20	158
Apple	LaserWriter IIg	L	7.1 ppm	$4,299	11	20	158
Apple	LaserWriter IINT	L	6.4 ppm	$3,999	7	18	116
Apple	LaserWriter IINTX	L	6.8 ppm	$4,999	7	18	116
Apple	Personal LaserWriter NTR	L	3.9 ppm	$2,199	11	20	158
Apple	Personal LaserWriter NT	L	3.9 ppm	$2,599	9	19	152
AT&T	570*	DM	124 cps	$755	8	19	250
AT&T	583	DM	94 cps	$1,295	8	19	348
Axonix	LiteWrite	DM	50 cps	$529	8	19	326
Axonix	MilWrite	DM	95 cps	$1,395	11	20	361
Axonix	ThinWrite 100	DM	60 cps	$499	6	19	255
Bézier	BP4040	L	3.9 ppm	$1,895	10	20	150
Brother	HJ–100i	IJ	42 cps	$499	11	14	331
Brother	HL-4PS	L	3.9 ppm	$2,595	10	20	156
Brother	HL–4Ve	L	4 ppm	$1,595	11	20	159
Brother	**HL-8PS**	**L**	**7.4 ppm**	**$4,495**	**8**	**19**	**120**
Brother	HL-8V	L	7.6 ppm	$2,495	10	20	156
Brother	HL–10V	L	9 ppm	$1,995	11	20	159
Brother	HT-500PS	CTT	0.2 gppm	$4,995	11	20	259
Brother	M-1309	DM	105 cps	$299	10	20	414
Brother	M-1324	DM	106 cps	$399	10	20	414
Brother	M-1809	DM	83 cps	$549	8	19	350
Brother	M-1824L	DM	121 cps	$749	8	19	352
Brother	M-1909	DM	129 cps	$699	9	19	345
Brother	M-1924L	DM	122 cps	$949	9	19	346
Brother	M-2518	DM	123 cps	$1,295	7	18	240
Brother	M-4018	DM	258 cps	$1,795	6	19	260
Brother	M-4309A	DM	258 cps	$2,195	11	10	352
Bull	Compuprint 4/22	DM	117 cps	$375	9	19	348
Bull	Compuprint 4/23	DM	116 cps	$525	9	19	348
Bull	Compuprint 4/24	DM	113 cps	$640	9	19	351
Bull	Compuprint 4/40	DM	154 cps	$935	9	19	351
Bull	Compuprint 4/43	DM	142 cps	$1,995	9	19	352
Bull	Compuprint 4/66	DM	235 cps	$2,395	6	19	302
Bull	Compuprint 4/68	DM	192 cps	$1,895	9	19	358
Bull	Compuprint 970	DM	284 cps	$2,595	10	20	415
Calcomp	ColorMaster Plus 6603PS	CTT	0.9 gppm	$4,995	10	20	329
Calcomp	ColorMaster Plus 6613PS	CTT	0.3 ppm	$6,995	11	20	262
Canon	BJ-10ex Bubble Jet Printer	IJ	42 cps	$499	11	14	331
Canon	BJ-20 Bubble Jet Printer	IJ	45 cps	$599	11	20	292
Canon	BJ-10e	IJ	40 cps	$499	9	19	276
Canon	BJ-130	IJ	68 cps	$1,095	7	18	243
Canon	**BJ-300 Bubble Jet Printer**	**IJ**	**198 cps**	**$699**	**10**	**20**	**366**
Canon	**BJ-330 Bubble Jet Printer**	**IJ**	**198 cps**	**$849**	**10**	**20**	**366**
Canon	BJC-800 Bubble Jet Printer	IJ	74 cps	$2,795	11	20	292
Canon	LBP-4*	L	3.9 ppm	$1,545	9	19	156
Canon	LBP-8 Mark III*	L	7.3 ppm	$2,495	8	19	124
Canon	LBP-8 Mark IIIR	L	7.4 ppm	$3,795	9	19	165
Canon	LBP-8 Mark IIIT	L	7.5 ppm	$3,295	9	19	165
CIE	C-815	DM	195 cps	$2,295	6	19	268
CIE	CI-250 LXP	DM	349 lpm	$2,295	10	20	420

C—color, DM—dot matrix, DS—dye sublimation, DW—daisy wheel, IJ—ink jet, L—laser, SI—solid ink, TT—thermal transfer
Boldface—*PC Magazine* Editor's Choice

* This machine has been replaced by an upgraded model.

INDEX TO *PC MAGAZINE* PRINTER REVIEWS (1984–1992)

Company name	Product	Type	Speed	Price	Vol.	No.	Pg.
CIE	CI-500	DM	370 lpm	$5,795	10	20	420
CIE	CI-1000	DM	388 cps	$7,695	9	19	364
CIE	CI-5000	DM	250 cps	$1,995	9	19	358
Citizen	GSX-130	DM	127 cps	$399	10	20	421
Citizen	GSX-140	DM	94 cps	$499	9	19	361
Citizen	GSX-140 Plus	DM	112 cps	$499	10	20	421
Citizen	GSX-145	DM	100 cps	$599	10	20	421
Citizen	GSX-240	DM	130 cps	$499	11	20	362
Citizen	PN48 Notebook Printer	DM	24 cps	$469	11	14	338
Citizen	HSP-500	DM	151 cps	$499	8	19	357
Citizen	HSP-550	DM	156 cps	$699	8	19	357
Citizen	**PN48**	**TT**	**24 cps**	**$469**	**10**	**20**	**421**
Citizen	**200GX**	**DM**	**108 cps**	**$299**	**9**	**19**	**360**
Citizen	200GX Fifteen	DM	100 cps	$499	10	20	421
Compaq	**PageMarq 15**	**L**	**12.8 ppm**	**$3,999**	**11**	**20**	**233**
Compaq	**PageMarq 20**	**L**	**16.5 ppm**	**$5,499**	**11**	**20**	**233**
C-Tech	C.Itoh ProWriter CI-4	L	4 ppm	$1,245	10	20	164
C-Tech	ProWriter C-240	DM	113 cps	$449	9	19	365
C-Tech	ProWriter C-245	DM	110 cps	$559	9	19	365
C-Tech	ProWriter C-310 XP	DM	157 cps	$739	5	19	174
C-Tech	ProWriter C-315 XP	DM	150 cps	$919	5	19	174
C-Tech	ProWriter C-510	DM	111 cps	$639	9	19	368
C-Tech	ProWriter C-515	DM	110 cps	$749	9	19	368
C-Tech	ProWriter C-610+	DM	113 cps	$799	9	19	368
C-Tech	ProWriter C-610C+	DM	112 cps	$859	9	19	368
C-Tech	ProWriter C-610II	DM	120 cps	$799	11	20	361
C-Tech	**ProWriter C-615II**	**DM**	**124 cps**	**$1,175**	**11**	**20**	**361**
C-Tech	ProWriter C-645	DM	168 cps	$1,395	9	19	371
C-Tech	ProWriter C-715A	DM	145 cps	$1,499	6	19	267
C-Tech	ProWriter CI-4	L	4 ppm	$1,245	10	20	164
C-Tech	ProWriter CI-8	L	7.4 ppm	$2,395	11	20	162
C-Tech	ProWriter CI-8E	L	7.5 ppm	$1,695	11	20	162
Dataproducts	8070 Plus	DM	250 cps	$1,795	7	18	261
Dataproducts	9030	DM	136 cps	$669	9	19	372
Dataproducts	9044	DM	104 cps	$1,132	9	19	372
Dataproducts	LX 455	DM	443 lpm	$4,595	11	20	366
Dataproducts	LZR 960	L	8.1 ppm	$2,195	10	20	164
Dataproducts	LZR 1555	L	12.5 ppm	$5,995	11	20	236
Dataproducts	LZR 1560	L	12.3 ppm	$5,695	11	20	236
Datasouth	DS 180	DM	128 cps	**	3	23	223
Datasouth	DS 220	DM	150 cps	$1,695	3	23	226
Datasouth	Performax	DM	207 cps	$2,995	10	20	432
Datasouth	XL-300	DM	184 cps	$1,595	10	20	432
DCS/Fortis	**DM2215**	**DM**	**132 cps**	**$495**	**8**	**19**	**268**
DCS/Fortis	DM3215	DM	125 cps	$699	9	19	391
DCS/Fortis	DQ4110	DM	100 cps	$499	8	19	270
DCS/Fortis	DQ4210	DM	122 cps	$589	8	19	273
DCS/Fortis	DQ4215	DM	100 cps	$899	8	19	364
Digital Equipment Corp.	DECmultijet 1000	IJ	69 cps	$329	11	14	342
Digital Equipment Corp.	DEClaser 1150	L	3.9 ppm	$1,799	10	20	166
Digital Equipment Corp.	DEClaser 2100	L	7.5 ppm	$1,599	9	19	232
Digital Equipment Corp.	DEClaser 2150	L	7.4 ppm	$2,299	10	20	166
Digital Equipment Corp.	DEClaser 2200	L	7.6 ppm	$2,599	9	19	232

C—color, DM—dot matrix, DS—dye sublimation, DW—daisy wheel, IJ—ink jet, L—laser, SI—solid ink, TT—thermal transfer
Boldface—*PC Magazine* Editor's Choice

* This machine has been replaced by an upgraded model.

** Available by special order only

INDEX TO *PC MAGAZINE* PRINTER REVIEWS (1984-1992)

Company name	Product	Type	Speed	Price	Vol.	No.	Pg.
Digital Equipment Corp.	DEClaser 2250	L	7.4 ppm	$3,699	10	20	166
Digital Equipment Corp.	DEClaser 3250	L	14.1 ppm	$4,799	11	20	236
Digital Equipment Corp.	LA70 Personal Printer	DM	105 cps	$299	9	19	376
Digital Equipment Corp.	LA75 Plus Companion	DM	140 cps	$549	11	20	367
Digital Equipment Corp.	LA75 Companion Printer	DM	142 cps	$835	9	19	377
Digital Equipment Corp.	LA210	DM	138 cps	$1,549	3	23	213
Digital Equipment Corp.	LA324 Multiprinter	DM	162 cps	$1,995	9	19	377
Digital Equipment Corp.	LA424 Multiprinter	DM	178 cps	$1,349	11	20	367
Digital Equipment Corp.	DECmultiJET 2000	IJ	79 cps	$539	11	20	304
Digital Equipment Corp.	LJ252 Companion Color Printer	IJ	62 cps	$1,549	9	19	276
Digital Equipment Corp.	LN03R-AA	L	7.4 ppm	$3,000	5	19	276
Eastman Kodak	Diconix 150 Plus	IJ	70 cps	$519	8	19	327
Eastman Kodak	Diconix Color 4 Printer	IJ	64 cps	$895	10	20	374
Eastman Kodak	Diconix 180si Printer	IJ	68 cps	$399	11	14	357
Eastman Kodak	Diconix 701 Printer	IJ	60 cps	$549	11	14	357
Eastman Kodak	Ektaplus 7008	L	7.4 ppm	$1,395	10	20	177
Eastman Kodak	Ektaplus 7016 PS	L	14.7 ppm	$5,795	10	20	276
Eicon Technology	EiconLaser	L	7.3 ppm	$5,595	10	20	180
Epson	DFX-5000	DM	307 cps	$2,199	7	18	267
Epson	**DFX-8000**	**DM**	**264 cps**	**$3,699**	**9**	**19**	**380**
Epson	EPL-7000	L	5.7 ppm	$1,399	10	20	181
Epson	EPL-7500	L	5.9 ppm	$2,999	10	20	181
Epson	FX-850	DM	138 cps	$499	7	18	267
Epson	**FX-1050**	**DM**	**141 cps**	**$699**	**8**	**19**	**260**
Epson	LQ-200	DM	89 cps	$399	10	20	441
Epson	**LQ-570**	**DM**	**103 cps**	**$499**	**10**	**20**	**441**
Epson	LQ-860	DM	128 cps	$949	9	19	383
Epson	**LQ-870**	**DM**	**141 cps**	**$749**	**10**	**20**	**441**
Epson	**LQ-1170**	**DM**	**140 cps**	**$1,049**	**10**	**20**	**441**
Epson	LQ-2550	DM	105 cps	$1,499	8	19	362
Epson	**LX-810**	**DM**	**94 cps**	**$269**	**8**	**19**	**266**
Everex Systems	LaserScript LX	L	6 ppm	$1,995	10	20	187
Facit	B1200*	DM	74 cps	$307	9	19	384
Facit	B2400	DM	111 cps	$699	8	19	266
Facit	B3100*	DM	149 cps	$792	6	19	284
Facit	B3450	DM	134 cps	$1,349	9	19	386
Facit	B3550C*	DM	181 cps	$1,479	8	19	363
Facit	P6060	L	5.7 ppm	$1,599	9	19	180
Fujitsu	DL1200 PC PrintPartner	DM	101 cps	$649	11	20	374
Fujitsu	DL3400	DM	143 cps	$699	6	19	291
Fujitsu	DL3600	DM	154 cps	$799	10	20	444
Fujitsu	DL4600	DM	169 cps	$1,199	9	19	392
Fujitsu	DL5600	DM	230 cps	$2,195	7	18	276
Fujitsu	**DL5800**	**DM**	**213 cps**	**$1,995**	**11**	**20**	**374**
Fujitsu	**Print Partner 10**	**L**	**10.1 ppm**	**$1,995**	**11**	**20**	**164**
Fujitsu	RX7300E	L	14.8 ppm	$7,150	8	19	146
GCC Technologies	BLP II	L	4.2 ppm	$1,799	10	20	191
GCC Technologies	BLP IIS	L	7.9 ppm	$2,599	10	20	191
General Parametrics	Spectra*Star 430	CTT	0.8 ppm	$6,995	10	20	336
Genicom	1020	DM	111 cps	$1,218	5	19	194
Genicom	1040	DM	103 cps	$1,799	8	19	368
Genicom	3320 Quiet	DM	144 cps	$2,144	4	19	166
Genicom	3410XLQ	DM	150 cps	$2,375	8	19	273

C—color, DM—dot matrix, DS—dye sublimation, DW—daisy wheel, IJ—ink jet, L—laser, SI—solid ink, TT—thermal transfer
Boldface—*PC Magazine* Editor's Choice

* This machine has been replaced by an upgraded model.

INDEX TO *PC MAGAZINE* PRINTER REVIEWS (1984–1992)

Company name	Product	Type	Speed	Price	Vol.	No.	Pg.
Genicom	**3840E**	**DM**	**212 cps**	**$2,595**	**10**	**20**	**445**
Genicom	4440 XT	DM	326 lpm	$7,795	11	20	375
Genicom	Model 7170	L	14.7 ppm	$4,495	11	20	241
Hewlett-Packard	**DeskJet 500**	**IJ**	**62 cps**	**$599**	**9**	**19**	**290**
Hewlett-Packard	DeskJet 500C	IJ	81 cps	$779	11	20	309
Hewlett-Packard	DeskJet 550C	IJ	78 cps	$1,099	11	20	309
Hewlett-Packard	LaserJet IIP Plus	L	4 ppm	$1,249	11	20	170
Hewlett-Packard	**LaserJet IIP**	**L**	**3.9 ppm**	**$1,295**	**8**	**19**	**152**
Hewlett-Packard	**LaserJet III**	**L**	**7.5 ppm**	**$2,395**	**9**	**19**	**184**
Hewlett-Packard	**LaserJet IIID**	**L**	**7.6 ppm**	**$3,595**	**9**	**19**	**184**
Hewlett-Packard	**LaserJet IIIP**	**L**	**4 ppm**	**$1,595**	**10**	**20**	**192**
Hewlett-Packard	**LaserJet IIISi**	**L**	**14.6 ppm**	**$5,495**	**10**	**20**	**289**
Hewlett-Packard	**LaserJet 4**	**L**	**7.9 ppm**	**$2,199**	**11**	**20**	**170**
Hewlett-Packard	**LaserJet 4M**	**L**	**7.9 ppm**	**$2,999**	**11**	**20**	**170**
Hewlett-Packard	PaintJet	IJ	78 cps	$1,095	6	19	297
Hewlett-Packard	PaintJet XL	IJ	65 cps	$2,595	9	19	290
Hewlett-Packard	**PaintJet XL300**	**IJ**	**19 ppm**	**$3,495**	**11**	**20**	**309**
Hewlett-Packard	RuggedWriter	DM	173 cps	$1,895	7	18	280
Hewlett-Packard	ThinkJet	IJ	70 cps	$595	3	23	172
IBM/Lexmark. *See* LexMark							
Kentek Information Systems	K30D	L	27 ppm	$21,430	11	20	242
Kyocera	F-1000A	L	9.4 ppm	$2,895	7	18	152
Kyocera	**FS-1500A**	**L**	**9.3 ppm**	**$2,395**	**11**	**20**	**172**
Kyocera	F-1800A	L	15.2 ppm	$4,495	9	19	195
Kyocera	F-2010	L	6.8 ppm	$4,295	6	19	188
Kyocera	F-5000A	L	13.6 ppm	$7,995	10	20	297
Laser Computer	Laser 190E	DM	90 cps	$219	8	19	288
LaserMaster	LM 1000	L	INA	$5,995	9	19	211
LaserMaster	TrueTech 800/4	L	3.7 ppm	$3,695	10	20	203
LaserMaster	TrueTech 1000	L	7.2 ppm	$5,995	10	20	203
LaserMaster	TrueTech 1200	L	14.9 ppm	$16,995	10	20	307
LaserMaster	Unity 1000	L	7 ppm	$6,995	11	20	180
LaserMaster	Unity 1200xl	L	4.4 ppm	$9,995	11	20	180
LaserMaster	WinPrinter 400	L	4 ppm	$1,195	10	20	204
LaserMaster	WinPrinter 800	L	INA	$1,595	11	20	180
Lexmark	**ExecJet Printer**	**IJ**	**198 cps**	**$1,099**	**10**	**20**	**378**
Lexmark	LaserPrinter	L	8.9 ppm	$2,395	8	19	156
Lexmark	LaserPrinter 5e	L	4.5 ppm	$1,595	10	20	194
Lexmark	LaserPrinter 6	L	5.7 ppm	$1,895	10	20	194
Lexmark	LaserPrinter 6P	L	5.8 ppm	$2,295	11	20	182
Lexmark	**LaserPrinter 10**	**L**	**9.1 ppm**	**$2,395**	**10**	**20**	**194**
Lexmark	LaserPrinter 10L	L	8.9 ppm	$2,995	10	20	292
Lexmark	**LaserPrinter 10P**	**L**	**9.1 ppm**	**$3,795**	**11**	**20**	**182**
Lexmark	LaserPrinter 4019	L	8.9 ppm	$2,125	8	19	156
Lexmark	LaserPrinter 4019E	L	4.8 ppm	$999	9	19	190
Lexmark	**LaserPrinter E**	**L**	**4.8 ppm**	**$1,495**	**9**	**19**	**190**
Lexmark	Personal Printer Series II 2380	DM	153 cps	$499	10	20	448
Lexmark	Personal Printer Series II 2381	DM	162 cps	$699	10	20	448
Lexmark	Personal Printer Series II 2390	DM	112 cps	$499	10	20	448
Lexmark	Personal Printer Series II 2391	DM	120 cps	$699	10	20	448
Lexmark	Proprinter 24P	DM	102 cps	$499	10	20	448
Lexmark	Proprinter X24E	DM	100 cps	$859	8	19	286
Lexmark	**Proprinter XL24E**	**DM**	**159 cps**	**$1,099**	**8**	**19**	**286**

C—color, DM—dot matrix, DS—dye sublimation, DW—daisy wheel, IJ—ink jet, L—laser, SI—solid ink, TT—thermal transfer
Boldface—*PC Magazine* Editor's Choice

* This machine has been replaced by an upgraded model.

INDEX TO *PC MAGAZINE* PRINTER REVIEWS (1984-1992)

Company name	Product	Type	Speed	Price	Vol.	No.	Pg.
Lexmark	**4226 Printer**	**DM**	**229 cps**	**$2,295**	**10**	**20**	**448**
Mannesmann Tally	MT82	DM	73 cps	$499	10	20	455
Mannesmann Tally	MT 150/9	DM	150 cps	$699	11	20	386
Mannesmann Tally	MT 151/9	DM	151 cps	$749	11	20	386
Mannesmann Tally	MT 150/24	DM	156 cps	$899	11	20	386
Mannesmann Tally	MT 151/24	DM	159 cps	$999	11	20	386
Mannesmann Tally	**MT661**	**DM**	**674 lpm**	**$6,999**	**10**	**20**	**455**
Mannesmann Tally	MT735	TT	6.3 ppm	$999	10	20	206
Mannesmann Tally	MT908	L	7.6	$1,995	11	20	162
Mannesmann Tally	MT911 PS	L	9 ppm	$3,195	10	20	206
Mannesmann Tally	81	DM	73 cps	$259	8	19	298
Mannesmann Tally	87	DM	113 cps	$599	6	19	317
Mannesmann Tally	130/9	DM	131 cps	$699	9	19	401
Mannesmann Tally	130/24	DM	128 cps	$899	9	19	402
Mannesmann Tally	131/9	DM	120 cps	$799	9	19	401
Mannesmann Tally	131/24	DM	127 cps	$999	9	19	402
Mannesmann Tally	230/24	DM	108 cps	$1,799	7	18	291
Mannesmann Tally	290	DM	133 cps	$1,399	5	19	208
Mannesmann Tally	330	DM	190 cps	$2,349	6	19	320
Mannesmann Tally	340	DM	150 cps	$2,449	7	18	292
Mannesmann Tally	490	DM	247 cps	$3,779	5	19	250
Mannesmann Tally	645	DM	313 cps	$5,999	9	19	342
Mannesmann Tally	906 PS	L	5.8 ppm	$2,795	9	19	196
Microtek Lab	TrueLaser	L	6.1 ppm	$1,995	10	20	227
Mitek Systems	130TE	L	7.5 ppm	$6,850	9	19	199
Mitsubishi	DiamondColor Print 300PS	CDS	0.1 gppm	$17,995	11	20	274
Mitsubishi	CHC-S446i ColorStream/DS	CDS	0.2 gppm	$11,900	11	20	279
NCR	6417-0101	DM	162 cps	$600	9	19	406
NCR	6421-0201	DM	134 cps	$1,050	9	19	407
NCR	6436-0301*	L	12.4 ppm	$6,795	10	20	308
NEC	Colormate PS Model 40	CTT	1.8 ppm	$5,995	10	20	338
NEC	Pinwriter P3200	DM	104 cps	$342	10	20	456
NEC	Pinwriter P3300	DM	102 cps	$497	10	20	456
NEC	**Pinwriter P6200**	**DM**	**144 cps**	**$621**	**9**	**19**	**407**
NEC	**Pinwriter P6300**	**DM**	**146 cps**	**$945**	**9**	**19**	**407**
NEC	Pinwriter P9300	DM	162 cps	$1,326	10	20	456
NEC	Silentwriter LC 890XL	L	7.4 ppm	$5,995	8	19	164
NEC	**Silentwriter 95**	**L**	**6 ppm**	**$1,749**	**11**	**20**	**196**
NEC	**Silentwriter2 90**	**L**	**5.8 ppm**	**$2,373**	**9**	**19**	**205**
NEC	Silentwriter2 990	L	7.5 ppm	$3,734	10	20	229
NewGen Systems	TurboPS/300p	L	3.8 ppm	$1,995	11	20	205
NewGen Systems	TurboPS/360	L	2.1 ppm	$4,995	9	19	220
NewGen Systems	TurboPS/400p	L	3.9 ppm	$2,595	11	20	205
NewGen Systems	TurboPS/480	L	2.1 ppm	$7,495	9	19	220
NewGen Systems	TurboPS/630En	L	7.3 ppm	$3,995	11	20	205
NewGen Systems	TurboPS/660	L	7.1 ppm	$3,795	11	20	205
NewGen Systems	TurboPS/840	L	7.2 ppm	$5,495	11	20	205
NewGen Systems	TurboPS/880	L	7.2 ppm	$5,495	11	20	205
NewGen Systems	TurboPS/1200T	L	9 ppm	$14,994	11	20	244
Océ Graphics	G5241-PS	CTT	1.2 ppm	$7,990	10	20	343
OCTuS Inc.	LaserPro 810	L	7.5 ppm	$3,495	5	19	292
OCTuS Inc.	LaserPro 1510	L	13.5 ppm	$5,795	7	18	156
Okidata	Microline 172	DM	83 cps	$289	8	19	299

C—color, DM—dot matrix, DS—dye sublimation, DW—daisy wheel, IJ—ink jet, L—laser, SI—solid ink, TT—thermal transfer
Boldface—*PC Magazine* Editor's Choice

* This machine has been replaced by an upgraded model.

INDEX TO *PC MAGAZINE* PRINTER REVIEWS (1984–1992)

Company name	Product	Type	Speed	Price	Vol.	No.	Pg.
Okidata	Microline 182 Turbo	DM	95 cps	$339	8	19	300
Okidata	Microline 184 Turbo	DM	117 cps	$359	11	20	395
Okidata	**Microline 320**	**DM**	**164 cps**	**$499**	**7**	**18**	**300**
Okidata	**Microline 321**	**DM**	**157 cps**	**$699**	**7**	**18**	**300**
Okidata	Microline 380	DM	89 cps	$349	9	19	414
Okidata	Microline 390 Plus	DM	140 cps	$699	9	19	419
Okidata	Microline 391 Plus	DM	140 cps	$949	9	19	419
Okidata	Microline 393 Plus	DM	167 cps	$1,499	9	19	420
Okidata	Microline 393C	DM	163 cps	$1,599	7	18	302
Okidata	OL400	L	4.1 ppm	$1,099	9	19	224
Okidata	OL810	L	8 ppm	$1,699	11	20	207
Okidata	OL820	L	8.1 ppm	$1,999	9	19	226
Okidata	**OL830**	**L**	**8.1 ppm**	**$1,999**	**10**	**20**	**232**
Okidata	OL840	L	7.7 ppm	$2,599	9	19	227
Okidata	**PaceMark 2410**	**DM**	**216 cps**	**$2,599**	**4**	**19**	**168**
Okidata	PaceMark 3410	DM	226 cps	$1,999	11	20	395
Output Technology Corp.	560DL	DM	147 cps	$1,895	8	19	301
Output Technology Corp.	DuraLine	DM	217 cps	$2,595	10	20	465
Output Technology Corp.	Euroline 400	DM	365 lpm	$6,995	11	20	396
Output Technology Corp.	**Euroline 600**	**DM**	**477 lpm**	**$5,495**	**11**	**20**	**396**
Output Technology Corp.	LaserMatrix 1000 Model 5	L	14.1 ppm	$5,695	11	20	245
Output Technology Corp.	TriMatrix 850XL	DM	307 cps	$2,095	6	19	330
Panasonic	KX-P1123	DM	92 cps	$350	10	20	466
Panasonic	KX-P1124i	DM	107 cps	$500	10	20	466
Panasonic	**KX-P1180**	**DM**	**59 cps**	**$270**	**8**	**19**	**303**
Panasonic	KX-P1180i	DM	59 cps	$270	8	19	303
Panasonic	KX-P1624	DM	96 cps	$600	9	19	428
Panasonic	KX-P1695	DM	140 cps	$630	9	19	428
Panasonic	KX-P2180	DM	89 cps	$300	11	20	399
Panasonic	KX-P2123	DM	91 cps	$420	11	20	399
Panasonic	**KX-P2124**	**DM**	**116 cps**	**$550**	**11**	**20**	**399**
Panasonic	**KX-P2624**	**DM**	**111 cps**	**$650**	**10**	**20**	**466**
Panasonic	KX-P4410	L	4.5 ppm	$1,095	11	20	207
Panasonic	KX-P4420 Laser Partner	L	7.4 ppm	$1,395	9	19	235
Panasonic	KX-P4430	L	4.7 ppm	$1,495	11	20	207
Panasonic	KX-P4450i Laser Partner	L	10.2 ppm	$2,095	9	19	236
Panasonic	KX-P4455 Laser Partner	L	10.2 ppm	$2,995	10	20	236
Primages	Primage 90-GT	DW	56 cps	$1,500	6	19	386
Printek	FormsPro 2000	DM	111 cps	$2,095	5	19	247
Printronix	L1016	L	14.8 ppm	$6,995	11	20	247
Printronix	L2324 Page Printer	L	20.9 ppm	$14,495	8	19	167
Printronix	P3240	DM	290 lpm	$6,195	10	20	470
Printware	720 IQ Professional-II	L	7.5 ppm	$7,990	9	19	240
Printware	Printware Pro-III	L	8.5 ppm	$15,990	10	20	311
QMS	**ColorScript 100 Model 10**	**CTT**	**2.8 ppm**	**$6,995**	**8**	**19**	**217**
QMS	ColorScript 100 Model 10p	CTT	1.2 ppm	$5,995	10	20	347
QMS	ColorScript 100 Model 30si	CTT	0.5 gppm	$9,995	11	20	281
QMS	PS-410	L	3.6 ppm	$1,995	9	19	251
QMS	PS-810	L	6.7 ppm	$3,995	7	18	165
QMS	PS-810 Turbo	L	7.5 ppm	$5,495	9	19	252
QMS	PS-815	L	7.5 ppm	$3,295	10	20	240
QMS	PS-815 MR	L	7.3 ppm	$3,995	10	20	240
QMS	PS-820	L	6.9 ppm	$4,995	8	19	172

C—color, DM—dot matrix, DS—dye sublimation, DW—daisy wheel, IJ—ink jet, L—laser, SI—solid ink, TT—thermal transfer
Boldface—*PC Magazine* Editor's Choice

* This machine has been replaced by an upgraded model.

INDEX TO *PC MAGAZINE* PRINTER REVIEWS (1984-1992)

Company name	Product	Type	Speed	Price	Vol.	No.	Pg.
QMS	PS-820 Turbo	L	7.5 ppm	$6,495	9	19	252
QMS	PS-825	L	7.4 ppm	$3,995	10	20	240
QMS	PS-1500	L	8.8 ppm	$7,995	8	19	174
QMS	PS-1700	L	14.7 ppm	$6,995	11	20	248
QMS	**PS-2000**	**L**	**17.2 ppm**	**$12,995**	**10**	**20**	**314**
QMS	**PS-2210**	**L**	**17.3 ppm**	**$5,795**	**9**	**19**	**256**
Qume	CrystalPrint Express	L	2.6 ppm	$3,495	9	19	242
Qume	CrystalPrint Publisher	L	5.1 ppm	$3,499	8	19	176
Qume	CrystalPrint Publisher II	L	5.2 ppm	$2,995	9	19	245
Qume	CrystalPrint Series II	L	6.5 ppm	$1,499	9	19	245
Qume	CrystalPrint Super Series II	L	6 ppm	$1,999	9	19	246
Qume	Sprint 11/55 Plus	DW	54 cps	$2,498	3	23	340
Royal	CJP 450	IJ	62 cps	$500	11	20	314
Samsung Electronics America	Finalé 8000	L	7.5 ppm	$1,995	11	20	208
Seiko	ColorPoint PSX Model 4	CTT	0.9 ppm	$7,999	10	20	352
Seiko	ColorPoint PSX Model 14	CTT	0.6 ppm	$11,999	10	20	352
Seikosha	BP 5460	DM	238 cps	$1,999	8	19	307
Seikosha	BP 5780	DM	221 cps	$2,200	10	20	471
Seikosha	LT 20	DM	23 cps	$499	10	20	471
Seikosha	SBP-10AI	DM	314 cps	$4,495	7	18	309
Seikosha	SBP-10 Plus	DM	314 cps	$4,495	7	18	309
Seikosha	SK-3005AI	DM	170 cps	$849	6	19	349
Seikosha	SK-3005 Plus	DM	170 cps	$854	6	19	349
Seikosha	SL-90	DM	63 cps	$499	9	19	429
Seikosha	SL-90 Plus	DM	63 cps	$549	9	19	429
Seikosha	SL-230AI*	DM	77 cps	$998	8	19	307
Seikosha	SP-2000*	DM	86 cps	$329	9	19	429
Seikosha	SP-2400	DM	96 cps	$329	11	20	400
Seikosha	SP-2415	DM	94 cps	$549	11	20	400
Sharp	JX-9500H	L	8.5 ppm	$995	10	20	252
Sharp	JX-9500PS	L	6.5 ppm	$2,849	10	20	252
Sharp	JX-9700	L	14.4 ppm	$2,295	10	20	317
Siemens Nixdorf	Ink Jet PT 88S-32	IJ	97 cps	$718	8	19	312
Siemens Nixdorf	Ink Jet PT 90-12	IJ	136 cps	$1,500	8	19	309
Star Micronics	LaserPrinter 4	L	4 ppm	$1,395	10	20	254
Star Micronics	LaserPrinter 4 StarScript	L	4 ppm	$1,995	10	20	254
Star Micronics	NX-1001 Multi-Font	DM	97 cps	$229	10	20	472
Star Micronics	NX-1020 Rainbow	DM	96 cps	$299	10	20	472
Star Micronics	NX-1500 Multi-Font	DM	91 cps	$499	9	19	430
Star Micronics	NX-2410 Multi-Font	DM	91 cps	$399	9	19	436
Star Micronics	NX-2415 Multi-Font	DM	100 cps	$559	9	19	436
Star Micronics	NX-2420 Multi-Font	DM	94 cps	$449	10	20	472
Star Micronics	NX-2420 Rainbow	DM	90 cps	$499	10	20	472
Star Micronics	**NX-2430 Multi-Font**	**DM**	**90 cps**	**$399**	**11**	**20**	**400**
Star Micronics	**StarJet SJ-48**	**IJ**	**38 cps**	**$499**	**10**	**20**	**378**
Star Micronics	XB-2410 Multi-Font	DM	117 cps	$699	8	19	313
Star Micronics	**XB-2415 Multi-Font**	**DM**	**110 cps**	**$899**	**8**	**19**	**374**
Star Micronics	XB-2420 Multi-Font	DM	136 cps	$749	10	20	472
Star Micronics	XB-2425 Multi-Font	DM	135 cps	$949	10	20	472
Star Micronics	XR-1020 Multi-Font	DM	137 cps	$549	10	20	472
Star Micronics	XR-1500 Multi-Font	DM	127 cps	$749	8	19	313
Star Micronics	XR-1520 Multi-Font	DM	137 cps	$699	10	20	472
Talaris	1590-T Printstation	L	11 ppm	$8,990	8	19	187

C—color, DM—dot matrix, DS—dye sublimation, DW—daisy wheel, IJ—ink jet, L—laser, SI—solid ink, TT—thermal transfer
Boldface—*PC Magazine* Editor's Choice

* This machine has been replaced by an upgraded model.

INDEX TO *PC MAGAZINE* PRINTER REVIEWS (1984–1992)

Company name	Product	Type	Speed	Price	Vol.	No.	Pg.
Tandy	DMP 135	DM	99 cps	$320	10	20	478
Tandy	DMP 136	DM	108 cps	$250	10	20	478
Tandy	DMP 202	DM	71 cps	$400	10	20	478
Tandy	DMP 240	DM	98 cps	$400	9	19	441
Tandy	DMP 300	DM	132 cps	$599	8	19	316
Tandy	DMP 310 Slimline	DM	43 cps	$500	11	20	402
Tandy	DMP 2102	DM	136 cps	$899	8	19	318
Tandy	DMP 2130	DM	108 cps	$899	9	19	438
Tandy	LP 950	L	6.2 ppm	$1,599	10	20	256
Tektronix	Phaser II PXe	CTT	0.6 gppm	$4,995	11	20	282
Tektronix	Phaser II PXi	CTT	1.2 ppm	$7,995	10	20	357
Tektronix	Phaser IIsd	CDS	0.2 gppm	$9,995	11	20	282
Tektronix	**Phaser III PXi**	**CSI**	**0.5 ppm**	**$9,995**	**10**	**20**	**357**
Texas Instruments	880 AT	DM	172 cps	$2,195	5	19	252
Texas Instruments	885	DM	195 cps	$2,295	6	19	365
Texas Instruments	8930	DM	174 cps	$2,545	9	19	441
Texas Instruments	microLaser[*]	L	6.3 ppm	$999	9	19	258
Texas Instruments	microLaser Turbo	L	8.3 ppm	$1,749	11	20	208
Texas Instruments	microLaser XL Turbo	L	14.5 ppm	$3,649	11	20	249
Texas Instruments	microLaser XL PS35	L	14.7 ppm	$3,149	10	20	320
Texas Instruments	OmniLaser 2015	L	7.1 ppm	$5,995	5	19	296
Texas Instruments	OmniLaser 2115	L	9.5 ppm	$7,995	6	19	234
Toshiba America Information Systems	ExpressWriter 201	DM	18 cps	$499	11	14	367
Toshiba America Information Systems	PageLaser GX200	L	7.6 ppm	$1,799	11	20	211
Toshiba America Information Systems	PageLaser GX400	L	14.8 ppm	$4,499	11	20	241
Unisys	AP 1324	DM	117 cps	$1,695	8	19	319
Unisys	**AP 1371**	**DM**	**281 cps**	**$3,295**	**11**	**20**	**402**
Unisys	AP 9215-1	L	13.4 ppm	$5,995	8	19	190
Unisys	AP 9230	L	21.5 ppm	$16,750	8	19	195
U.S. Laser Corp.	EiconLaser[*]	L	7.3 ppm	$5,595	10	20	180
Varityper	**VT600P**[*]	**L**	**7.9 ppm**	**$11,995**	**8**	**19**	**197**
Xante Corp.	Accel-a-Writer 8000	L	7.7 ppm	$3,295	11	20	211
Xerox	4045 Laser CP Model 160	L	9.2 ppm	$5,000	5	19	294

C—color, DM—dot matrix, DS—dye sublimation, DW—daisy wheel, IJ—ink jet, L—laser, SI—solid ink, TT—thermal transfer
Boldface—*PC Magazine* Editor's Choice

[*] This machine has been replaced by an upgraded model.

DIRECTORY OF MANUFACTURERS

APPENDIX

N

THIS APPENDIX IS A COMPREHENSIVE LISTING of manufacturers of computers, mice and miscellaneous peripherals, modems and telecommunications equipment, monitors and video-related equipment, and printers, scanners, and related equipment.

DIRECTORY OF MANUFACTURERS

This table was produced using Computer Select™, a comprehensive computer products database for buyers of hardware, software, and communications products. Computer Select is a first-rate, easy-to-use reference for current computer product specifications and reviews. Each monthly CD-ROM contains over 70,000 articles from the most recent year's worth of issues of over 140 computer, business, and technical periodicals. Computer Select also includes specifications for over 70,000 hardware, software, and data communications products and profiles of the over 12,000 companies that make those products. The product specifications and reviews are taken from Data Sources™, the most comprehensive directory of the computer industry in print.

Computer Select and Data Sources are products of the Computer Library division of Ziff Communications Company. For more information or to subscribe to Computer Select or Data Sources, contact Computer Library at 212–503–4400.

DIRECTORY OF MANUFACTURERS

Computers

ABC Computer Corp.
2531 237th St., Ste. 122
Torrance, CA 90505
310-325-4005
fax: 310-325-6369

Abest Computer Co.
17800 S. Main St., Ste. 406
Carson, CA 90248
310-768-8004
fax: 310-768-8359

Able Technologies, Inc. (Abletec Division)
46791 Fremont Blvd.
Fremont, CA 94538
510-659-1544

ABTECH, INC.
1431 N. Potrero Ave., Unit B
South El Monte, CA 91733
800-992-1978; 818-575-0007
fax: 818-575-1500

ACC, Inc.
34360 Glendale
Livonia, MI 48150
313-422-4444
fax: 313-422-8891

ACCTON Technology Corp.
46750 Fremont Blvd., Ste. 104
Fremont, CA 94538
510-226-9800
fax: 510-226-9833

Acer America Corp.
401 Charcot Ave.
San Jose, CA 95131
800-538-1542; 408-922-0333
fax: 408-922-0176
Technical support: 800-637-7000

ACMA Computers, Inc.
117 Fourier Ave.
Fremont, CA 94539
510-623-1212
fax: 510-623-0818

A.C.T. International
10772 Noel St.
Los Alamitos, CA 90720
714-952-8999
fax: 714-952-3804

Adtech
2701 Lasiter Lane
Turlock, CA 95380
800-326-6548; 209-669-6111

Advance Data Systems, Inc.
9272 Jeronimo Rd., Ste. 114
Irvine, CA 92718
714-581-3850
fax: 714-583-9367

Advance Electronic Diagnostics, Inc.
10850 North 24th Ave., Ste. 101
Phoenix, AZ 85029
602-861-9359
fax: 602-678-4471

Advanced Computer Products, Inc.
1310C E. Edinger Ave.
Santa Ana, CA 92705
800-366-3227; 714-558-8813
fax: 714-558-1603

Advanced Group Innovations, Inc. (AGI)
48431 Milmont Dr.
Fremont, CA 94538 800-821-0806;
510-683-2800
fax: 510-683-2400

Advanced Logic Research, Inc.
9401 Jeronimo
Irvine, CA 92718
800-444-4257; 714-581-6770
fax: 714-581-9240
Technical support: 714-458-0863

Advantage Computer Corp., Inc.
117 Walnut Ave., NE
Canton, OH 44702
800-622-6691; 216-452-2842

AEG Olympia, Inc.
3140 Rt. 22, Box 22
Somerville, NJ 08876-0022
800-999-6872; 908-231-8300
fax: 908-526-6349
Technical support: Use main number

AGI Computer, Inc.
48431 Milmont Dr.
Fremont, CA 94538
510-683-2200

Agilis Corp.
1390 Shorebird Way
Mountain View, CA 94043-1349
415-962-9400
fax: 415-962-9202

AIRIS Computer Corp.
1824 N. Besly Court
Chicago, IL 60622
312-384-5608
fax: 312-384-5609

Allbest International Corp.
45-03 Junction Blvd.
Corona, NY 11368
800-262-9942; 718-760-2210
fax: 718-760-1937

Alloy Computer Products, Inc.
165 Forest St.
Marlborough, MA 01752
800-544-7551; 508-481-8500
fax: 508-481-7711

AlphaNumeric International, Inc.
13360 E. Firestone Blvd., Ste. F
Santa Fe Springs, CA 90670
310-921-8689
fax: 310-921-8661

ALR—Advanced Logic Research, Inc.
9401 Jeronimo
Irvine, CA 92718
800-444-4257; 714-581-6770

Altec Technology Corp.
18555 E. Gale Ave.
City of Industry, CA 91748
800-255-9971; 818-912-8688

Altima Systems, Inc.
1390 Willow Pass Rd., Ste. 1050
Concord, CA 94520
800-356-9990; 510-356-5600
fax: 510-356-2408

Altos Computer Systems
2641 Orchard Pkwy.
San Jose, CA 95134
800-258-6787; 408-432-6200
fax: 408-433-9335

Amax Applied Technology, Inc.
3001-A W. Mission Rd.
Alhambra, CA 91803
818-300-8828
fax: 818-282-9992

AMAX Engineering Corp.
47315 Mission Falls Court
Fremont, CA 94539
800-888-2629; 510-651-8886
fax: 510-651-3720

Amdek Corp.
3471 N. First St.
San Jose, CA 95134
408-922-5700

American Computer Products, Inc.
511 Valley Way
Milpitas, CA 95035
800-229-0123; 408-946-9746
fax: 408-434-0859

American Computer Security Industries, Inc.
2517 Lebanon Rd.
Nashville, TN 37214
615-883-6741
fax: 615-872-0676

American Digital Data Associates
434 Cloverleaf Dr., Unit A
Baldwin Park, CA 91706
818-369-2332
fax: 818-369-5109

American Mitac Corp.
410 E. Plumeria Dr.
San Jose, CA 95134
800-648-2287; 408-432-1160
fax: 408-432-8519
Technical support: Use toll-free number

American Research Corp.
1101 Monterey Pass Rd.
Monterey Park, CA 91754
800-346-3272; 213-265-0835
fax: 213-265-1973
Technical support: 213-265-0523

American Systec Corp.
2860 E. Imperial Hwy.
Brea, CA 92621
714-993-0882
fax: 714-996-3903

Ameritek International
1061 N. Shepard St., Bldg. C
Anaheim, CA 92806
714-666-0210
fax: 714-666-0340

AMI (American Micronics, Inc.)
3002 Dow Ave., Ste. 224
Tustin, CA 92680
714-573-9005
fax: 714-573-9008

Amkly Systems, Inc.
60 Technology Dr.
Irvine, CA 92718
800-367-2655; 714-727-0788

Amplicom
7985 Dunbrook Rd., Ste. H
San Diego, CA 92126
619-693-9127
fax: 619-693-3368

Computers

AMREL Technology, Inc.
9952 E. Baldwin Place
El Monte, CA 91731
800-88-AMREL; 818-575-5110
fax: 818-575-0801

AMT International
2393 Qume Dr.
San Jose, CA 95131
408-432-1790
fax: 408-944-9801

Andrex Corp.
365 S. Milpitas Blvd.
Milpitas, CA 95035
408-263-3993
fax: 408-263-3899

Angel Business Machines Co.
15439 Valley Blvd.
City of Industry, CA 91746
818-961-1919
fax: 818-369-5488

APEX Computer, Inc.
1279 S. Willow St.
Manchester, NH 03103
603-641-5335
fax: 603-641-5338

A-Plus Computer, Inc.
10016 Pioneer Blvd., Ste. 102
Santa Fe Springs, CA 90670
800-443-5373; 310-949-9345
fax: 310-949-4125

Apple Computer, Inc.
20525 Mariani Ave.
Cupertino, CA 95014
408-996-1010
Technical support: 800-776-2333

**Applied Digital Data Systems, Inc.
(ADDS)**
100 Marcus Blvd., P.O. Box 18001
Hauppauge, NY 11788
800-231-5445; 516-231-5400
fax: 516-231-7378

Apricot in Canada
111 Granton Dr. #401
Richmond Hill, Ontario
Canada L4B 1L5
416-492-2777; 416–492–2513

Aquiline, Inc.
449 Main St.
Bennington, VT 05201
800-221-1119; 802-442-1526
fax: 802-442-8661

Arche Technologies, Inc.
48881 Kato Rd.
Fremont, CA 94539
800-422-4674; 510-623-8100
fax: 510-683-6754
Technical support: 800-322-2724

Ares Microdevelopment, Inc.
23660 Research Dr., Unit A
Farmington Hills, MI 48335
800-322-3200; 313-473-0808

Ariel Design, Inc.
45 Pond St.
Norwell, MA 02061
800-55ariel; 617-982-8800
fax: 617-982-9095

Arima Computer Corp.
15775 N. Hillcrest, Ste. 508
Dallas, TX 75248
800-332-7462; 214-404-9119

Ark Research Corp.
3012 Scott Blvd.
Santa Clara, CA 95054
408-988-6192
fax: 408-988-0435

Arlington Electronics
P.O. Box 5699
Woodland Park, CO 80866
800-833-3590; 719-687-0969

Arm Systems
1455 E. Francisco Blvd., Ste. K
San Rafael, CA 94901
415-454-7601
fax: 415-454-1736

Associates Mega Sub-System, Inc.
4801 Little John St., Unit A
Baldwin Park, CA 91706
800-955-1089; 818-814-8851
fax: 818-814-0782

AST Research Inc.
P.O. Box 19658, 15215 Alton Pkwy.
Irvine, CA 92713-9658
800-727-1278; 714-727-4141
fax: 714-727-9355
Technical support: Use toll-free number

Astarte Computer Systems, Inc.
1035 Pearl St., 5th Fl.
Boulder, CO 80302
303-449-9970
fax: 303-449-2773

Atari
1196 Borregas
Sunnyvale, CA 94088
408-745-2000
fax: 408-745-4306
Technical support: 408-745-2004

Atlas Industries, Inc.
11601 Wilshire Blvd., Ste. 1820
Los Angeles, CA 90025
800-ATLAS-11; 310-478-6920
fax: 310-479-2334

ATR Systems, Inc.
1725 McCandless Dr.
Milpitas, CA 95035
408-945-4302
fax: 408-945-0105

A-Tronic Computer & Office Machines
15703 E. Valley Blvd.
City of Industry, CA 91744
800-888-6118; 818-333-0193
fax: 818-961-4337

ATronics International Inc.
1830 McCandless Dr.
Milpitas, CA 95035
408-942-3344
fax: 408-942-1674

AT&T Computer Systems
1776 On The Green
Morristown, NJ 07960
800-247-1212; 201-898-8000
fax: 201-644-9768
Technical support: Use main number

Austin Computer Systems
10300 Metric Blvd.
Austin, TX 78759
800-752-1577; 512-339-3500
fax: 512-454-1357
Technical support: 512-339-7932

Automated Computer Technology Corp.
10849 Kinghurst
Houston, TX 77099
800-521-9237; 713-568-1778
fax: 713-568-1779

AUVA Computer
960 Industrial Dr.
Elmhurst, IL 60126
800-879-2882
fax: 708-832-2858

Avant Industries, Inc.
12020 Mora Dr., Unit 1
Santa Fe Springs, CA 90670
310-946-7706
fax: 310-946-9476

Avantech Solutions, Inc.
3 W. Columbia Ave.
Palisades Park, NJ 07650
201-941-1961
fax: 201-941-4345

AVI Systems, Inc.
1830 Embarcadero
Oakland, CA 94606-5226
510-535-0905
fax: 510-535-0905

Axik Computer Inc.
1031 F E. Duane Ave.
Sunnyvale, CA 94086
800-234-2945; 408-735-1234
fax: 408-735-1437

Basic Time
3280 Victor St.
Santa Clara, CA 95054
408-727-0877
fax: 408-727-7983

BCC
1610 Crane Court
San Jose, CA 95112
800-827-4222; 408-944-9000
fax: 408-944-0657
Technical Support: 800-827-4333

Benchmarq Corp.
2611 Westgrove, Ste. 101
Carrollton, TX 75006
800-966-0011; 214-407-0011
fax: 214-407-9845

Best Computer, Inc.
5017 Telegraph Rd.
Los Angeles, CA 90022
800-634-7920; 213-265-0900
fax: 213-265-4234

Bethel Computer, Inc.
1723 21st St.
Santa Monica, CA 90404
310-828-1415
fax: 310-828-0460

Bi-Link Computer, Inc.
11606 E. Washington Blvd., Ste. A
Whittier, CA 90606
800-888-5369; 310-692-5345
fax: 310-695-9623

DIRECTORY OF MANUFACTURERS

Binary Technology, Inc.
17120 Dallas Pkwy., Ste. 212
Dallas, TX 75248
800-776-7990; 214-931-3777
fax: 214-248-1571

Bioanalytical Systems, Inc. (BAS)
2701 Kent Ave.
West Lafayette, IN 47906
317-463-4527
fax: 317-497-1102

BIOS Trading Co., Ltd.
7313 Grove Rd.
Frederick, MD 21701
800-777-6050; 800-492-5316 (in Maryland);
301-695-5300
fax: 301-695-0478

Bi-Tech Enterprises, Inc.
10 Carlough Rd.
Bohemia, NY 11716
516-567-8155
fax: 516-567-8266

Bitwise Designs, Inc.
701 River St.
Troy, NY 12180
800-367-5906; 518-274-0755
fax: 518-274-0764
Technical support: Use main number

Blackship Computer Systems, Inc.
2031 O'Toole Ave.
San Jose, CA 95131
800-531-7447; 408-432-7500
fax: 408-432-1443
Technical support: Use toll-free number

Blue Dolphin Computers
1010 Morse St., Ste. 9
Sunnyvale, CA 94089
408-720-0298

Blue Star Computer, Inc.
2312 Central Ave., NE
Minneapolis, MN 55418
800-950-8884; 612-788-1404
fax: 612-788-3442
Technical support: 800-950-8894

Bona International
P.O. Box 337
Piscataway, NJ 08855
800-999-BONA

Bondwell Industrial Co., Inc.
47485 Seabridge Dr.
Fremont, CA 94538
510-490-4300
fax: 510-490-5897
Technical support: 800-288-4388

Boss Technology Corp.
6050 McDonough Dr.
Norcross, GA 30093
800-628-1787; 404-368-2077

Broadax Systems, Inc. (BSI)
9440 Telstar Ave., Ste. 4
El Monte, CA 91731
800-872-4547; 818-442-0020
fax: 818-442-4527

BRYSIS Data, Inc.
17431 E. Gale Ave.
City of Industry, CA 91748
818-810-0355
fax: 818-810-4555

BSM Corp.
1355 Glenville Dr.
Richardson, TX 75081
800-888-3475; 214-699-8300
fax: 214-699-8404

Bull Dog Computer
3241 E. Washington Rd.
Martinez, GA 30907
404-860-7364

Burham Computer Center
908 E. Main St.
Alhambra, CA 91801
818-570-0396
fax: 818-570-0936

Burr-Brown Corp.
P.O. Box 11400
Tucson, AZ 85734
800-548-6132; 602-746-1111
fax: 602-741-3895

Bus Computer Systems
135 West 26th St.
New York, NY 10010
800-451-5289; 212-627-4485

BusinessNet, Inc.
2950 Airway Ave.
Costa Mesa, CA 92626
714-662-7969

Cache Computers, Inc.
46714 Fremont Blvd.
Fremont, CA 94538
510-226-9922
fax: 510-226-9911

Caching Technology Corp.
1250 N. Lakeview Ave.
Anaheim, CA 92807
714-777-2818
fax: 714-777-3608

CAF Technology, Inc.
600 S. Date Ave.
Alhambra, CA 91803
800-289-8299; 818-289-8299
fax: 818-289-8752

Caliber Computer Corp.
1500 McCandless Dr.
Milpitas, CA 95035
408-942-1220
fax: 408-942-1345

Canon U.S.A., Inc.
One Canon Plaza
Lake Success, NY 11042
516-488-6700
fax: 516-354-5805
Technical support: 800-423-2366

Cardinal Technologies, Inc.
1827 Freedom Rd.
Lancaster, PA 17601
800-722-0094; 717-293-3000
fax: 717-293-3055
Technical support: 717-293-3124

CBM Associates, Inc.
1500 Jerusalem Ave.
North Merrick, NY 11566
516-483-5300
fax: 516-483-3924

CCS Custom Computer Systems, Inc.
191 Woodport Rd.
Sparta, NJ 07871
201-729-6762

fax: 201-729-0966

CD Technology, Inc.
780 Montague Expwy., Ste. 407
San Jose, CA 95131
408-432-8698
fax: 408-432-0250
Technical support: Use main number

CDS Systems, Inc.
14050 21st Ave., N
Minneapolis, MN 55447-4686
612-559-7459

Centrix Computer
15316 E. Valley Blvd.
Industry, CA 91746
818-855-2800
fax: 818-330-9618

Chaintech Computer U.S., Inc.
10450 Pioneer Blvd., Unit 8
Santa Fe Springs, CA 90670
310-944-2291
fax: 310-946-6633

Chaplet Systems, Inc.
252 N. Wolf Rd.
Sunnyvale, CA 94086
408-732-7950
fax: 408-732-6050

Chaumont & Associates
805 Bayou Pines, Ste. A
Lake Charles, LA 70601
800-673-2271; 318-436-2294

Cheetah Computer Systems, Inc.
7075 Flying Cloud Dr.
Eden Prairie, MN 55344
800-243-3824; 612-943-8690
fax: 612-943-8790

Chicony America, Inc.
3002 Dow Ave., Ste. 122
Tustin, CA 92680 714-573-0456
fax: 714-573-0673
Technical support: 714-380-0928

Clone Computers
2544 W. Commerce St.
Dallas, TX 75212
800-527-0347; 214-637-5400
fax: 214-634-8303

Clone Technologies, Inc.
1213 Bittersweet Rd.
Lake Ozark, MO 65049
314-365-2050
fax: 314-365-2080

Clover Computer Systems, Inc.
1430 Koll Circle #102
San Jose, CA 95112
800-925-6837; 408-436-0444
fax: 408-436-0494

Club American Technologies, Inc.
3401 W. Warren Ave.
Fremont, CA 94539
510-683-6600
fax: 510-490-2687
Technical support: Use main number

CMS Enhancements, Inc.
2722 Michelson Dr.
Irvine, CA 92715
714-222-6000
fax: 714-549-4004
Technical support: 714-222-6058

Computers

CNet Technology, Inc.
62 Bonaventura Dr.
San Jose, CA 95134
408-954-8000
fax: 408-954-8866

Colby Systems Corp.
2991 Alexis Dr.
Palo Alto, CA 94304
415-941-9090
fax: 415-949-1019

Comex Computer Corp.
3450 S. Broadmont, Ste. 110
Tucson, AZ 85713
800-826-9577; 602-792-3609

Commax Technologies, Inc.
2031 Concourse Dr.
San Jose, CA 95131
800-526-6629; 408-435-5000
fax: 408-435-5005

Commodore Business Machines, Inc.
(Computer Systems Division)
1200 Wilson Dr.,
Brandywine Industrial Park
West Chester, PA 19380
215-431-9100
fax: 215-431-9156

Compaq Computer Corp.
P.O. Box 692000
Houston, TX 77269-2000
800-231-0900; 713-370-0670
fax: 713-374-1402
Technical support: 800-345-1518

Compeq USA/Focus Technology
18226 W. McDurmott
Irvine, CA 92714
800-852-0105; 714-553-8626
fax: 714-553-8548
Technical support: 213-404-1686

CompuAdd Corp.
12303 Technology Blvd.
Austin, TX 78727
800-531-5475; 512-250-1489
fax: 512-250-5760
Technical support: 800-999-9901

Compudyne, Inc.
15167 Business Ave.
Dallas, TX 75244
800-932-2667; 214-888-5700
fax: 214-888-5742
Technical Support: 800-447-3895

Compulan Technology, Inc.
1842 Daltrey Way
San Jose, CA 95132
408-922-6888
fax: 408-954-8299

CompUSER, Inc.
15151A Surveyor
Addison, TX 75244
800-932-COMP; 214-484-8500
fax: 214-702-0300

Computer Creations, Inc.
88 Westpark Rd.
Dayton, OH 45459
513-438-2777

Computer Expo Superstore, Inc.
11312 Westheimer Rd.
Houston, TX 77077
800-229-3976; 713-531-0990
fax: 713-496-4600

Computer Extension Systems, Inc.
16850 Titan Dr.
Houston, TX 77058
800-562-1699; 713-488-8830
fax: 713-488-7631

Computer Information Specialists
910 Page Ave.
Fremont, CA 94538
800-552-4953; 510-623-1300
fax: 510-623-9466

Computer Market Place, Inc.
450 Park Way
Broomall, PA 19008
800-545-7397; 215-359-0750

Computer Peripherals, Inc.
667 Rancho Conejo Blvd.
Newbury Park, CA 91320
800-854-7600; 805-499-5751
fax: 805-498-8848
Technical support: 800-235-7618

Computer Products Corp.
4657 MacArthur Lane
Boulder, CO 80301
800-338-4273; 303-442-4747
fax: 303-442-7985
Technical support: Use main number

Computer Sales Professional
764 Easton Ave.
Somerset, NJ 08873
800-950-6660; 201-563-9628

Computer Systems Corp.
205 W. Grand Ave., Ste. 112
Bensenville, IL 60106
800-284-7746; 708-860-5807

Computer Systems Research
370 North St.
Teterboro, NJ 07608
201-288-6655
fax: 201-288-2739

Computer Terminal International, Inc.
4246 Ridge Lea Rd.
Amherst, NY 14226
800-223-4492; 716-833-6723
fax: 716-833-7101

ComputersFirst, Inc.
27 West 20th St.
New York, NY 10011
800-875-7580; 212-366-6673
fax: 212-366-6686

Computop, Inc.
14634 Firestone Blvd.
La Mirada, CA 90638
714-994-0605
fax: 714-994-0658

CompuTrend
1306 John Reed Court
City of Industry, CA 91745
818-333-5121
fax: 818-369-6803

Comtek Solutions, Inc.
1739 Northwest 16th St.
Oklahoma City, OK 73106
800-767-0668; 405-524-0668
fax: 405-525-9154

Comterm, Inc.
110 Hymus Blvd.
Pointe-Claire, Quebec
Canada H9R 1E8
514-694-4332
fax: 514-694-4123

Comtrade
1016-B Lawson St.
City of Industry, CA 91748
800-969-2123; 818-964-6688

Continental Resources, Inc.
175 Middlesex Tpke., P.O. Box 9137
Bedford, MA 01730
800-937-4688; 617-275-0850
fax: 617-275-6563

Continental Technology, Inc.
300 McGaw Dr.
Edison, NJ 08837
908-255-1166
fax: 908-225-8999

Copam Electronics Corp.
45875 Northport Loop East
Fremont, CA 94538
800-326-4567; 510-623-8911
fax: 510-623-8551

Cordata Technologies, Inc.
1055 W. Victoria St.
Compton, CA 90220
800-233-3602; 800-524-2671 (in California);
310-603-2901
fax: 310-763-0447

Core International
7171 N. Federal Hwy.
Boca Raton, FL 33487
407-997-6005
fax: 407-997-6009

Corman Technologies, Inc.
75 Bathurst Dr.
Waterloo, Ontario
Canada N2V 1N2
519-884-4430
fax: 519-884-0204

Cornerstone Computers
55851 East Ave.
Mishawaka, IN 46545
800-999-3957; 219-259-9004

Coté Computers of Arizona, Inc.
1817 S. Home, Ste. 6
Mesa, AZ 85204
800-562-4084; 602-892-8737

CPT Corp.
8100 Mitchell Rd.
Eden Prairie, MN 55344-9833
800-447-1189; 612-937-8000
fax: 612-937-1858

CPU, Inc.
385 N. Anaheim Blvd.
Orange, CA 92668
800-999-9033; 714-939-9133
fax: 714-939-9144

CSS Laboratories, Inc.
1641 McGaw Ave.
Irvine, CA 92714
714-852-8161
fax: 714-852-9464

DIRECTORY OF MANUFACTURERS

CTI, U.S.A.
1249 Commerce Dr.
Richardson, TX 75081
214-680-8737
fax: 214-680-8744

C2 Micro Systems, Inc.
47448 Fremont Blvd.
Fremont, CA 94538
510-683-8888
fax: 510-683-8893

CTXT Systems, Inc.
9205 Alabama Ave., Ste. E
Chatsworth, CA 91311
800-872-2898; 800-438-2898 (in California);
818-341-4227

CUBE Computer Corp.
150 Clearbrook Rd.
Elmsford, NY 10523
800-522-2823; 914-592-8282
fax: 914-592-3482

CUI
1680 Civic Center Dr. #101
Santa Clara, CA 95050
800-458-6686; 408-241-9170
fax: 408-241-2487

Cumulus Corp.
23500 Mercantile Rd.
Cleveland, OH 44122
216-464-2211
fax: 216-464-2483

Cyber Research, Inc.
25 Business Park Dr.
Banford, CT 06405
800-341-2525; 203-483-8815
fax: 203-483-9024

Daedalus Group
4750 Wiley Post Way
Salt Lake City, UT 84116
800-456-2587; 801-575-6600
fax: 801-575-6621

Daetech Computer Technologies Corp.
5512 E. Hastings St., Ste. 103
Burnaby, BC
Canada V5B 1R3
604-294-6135
fax: 604-294-0349

Dale Computer Corp.
2367 Science Pkwy.
Okemos, MI 48864
800-336-7483; 517-349-0200
fax: 517-349-7812

D.A.P. Technologies
5401 W. Kennedy Blvd., Ste. 480
Tampa, FL 33609
800-363-1993; 813-289-2822
fax: 813-286-1270

Dariana Technology Group, Inc.
6945 Hermosa Circle
Buena Park, CA 90620
714-994-7400
fax: 714-587-2221

Darius Technology, Ltd.
2808 Ingleton Ave.
Burnaby, BC
Canada V5C 6G7
604-436-1027
fax: 604-436-0882

Data Bank Computer, Inc.
48363 Warm Springs Blvd.
Fremont, CA 94539
800-777-3842; 510-490-5002
fax: 510-490-3519

Data General Corp.
4400 Computer Dr.
Westboro, MA 01580
800-328-2436; 508-366-8911
fax: 508-366-1299
Technical support: 800-537-6084

Data Technology Products
P.O. Box 3497
Costa Mesa, CA 92628
800-336-7060; 714-650-7060
fax: 714-650-0346

Data/Voice Solutions Corp. (DVSC)
16842 Von Karman, Ste. 200
Irvine, CA 92714
714-474-0330
fax: 714-474-8794

Datalux Corp.
2836 Cessna Dr.
Winchester, VA 22601
800-328-2589; 703-662-1500
fax: 703-662-1682

DataMemory Systems Corp.
6130 Variel Ave.
Woodland Hills, CA 91367-3799
818-704-9500
fax: 818-704-6637

Datavue
One Meca Way
Norcross, GA 30093-2919
404-564-5555
fax: 404-564-5528

Dataworld
3733 San Gabriel River Pkwy.
Pico Rivera, CA 90660-1495
800-736-8080; 310-695-3777
fax: 310-695-7016
Technical support: 800-776-8088

DATOM Technologies, Inc.
511 Baddour Pkwy., P.O. Box 1363
Lebanon, TN 37087
800-874-1795; 615-449-2449
fax: 615-449-7850

Dauphin Technology, Inc.
1125 E. St. Charles Rd.
Lombard, IL 60148
800-782-7922; 708-627-4004
fax: 708-627-7618
Technical support: Use main number

DCS/Fortis
1820 West 220th St., Ste 220
Torrance, CA 90501
800-736-4847; 310-782-6090
fax: 310-782-6134

Decision Data
One Progress Ave.
Horsham, PA 19044
800-523-5357; 215-674-3300
fax: 215-675-1931

Dee Van Enterprise USA, Inc.
3817 Spinnaker Court
Fremont, CA 94538
800-878-0691; 510-623-0628
fax: 510-623-0529

DEICO Electronics, Inc.
2800 Bayview Dr.
Fremont, CA 94537
800-321-8990; 510-651-7800
fax: 510-651-6109

Dell Computer Corp.
9505 Arboretum Blvd.
Austin, TX 78759-7299
800-426-5150; 512-338-4400
fax: 512-338-8421
Technical support: 800-624-9896

Delta Phase International
22262 Chestnut Lane
El Toro, CA 92630
714-768-6842
fax: 714-768-1417

DerbyTech Computers, Inc.
718 15th Ave.
East Moline, IL 61244
800-24-DERBY; 309-755-2662

Destiny Computers
754 Whitney St.
San Leandro, CA 94577
800-366-4272; 510-430-8810
fax: 510-430-1858

DFI, Inc.
2544 Port St.
West Sacramento, CA 95691
916-373-1234
fax: 916-373-0221
Technical support: Use main number

DFM Systems, Inc.
1601 48th St.
West Des Moines, IA 50265
800-DFM-LITE; 515-225-6744
fax: 515-225-7183

Diamond Micro Solutions
1615 Alvarado St.
San Leandro, CA 94577
800-366-4367; 510-351-4700
fax: 510-352-1089

Diamond Technologies
17155 Von Karman Ave., Ste. 103
Irvine, CA 92714
714-252-1008
fax: 714-252-1508

Digipro, Inc.
102 Lowry St.
Huntsville, AL 35805
205-536-2047

Digital Equipment Corp.
146 Main St.
Maynard, MA 01754-2571
508-493-5111
fax: 508-493-8780
Technical support: 800-332-8000

Digital Technology Exchange
700 S. John Rodes Blvd.
Melbourne, FL 32904
407-728-0172
fax: 407-722-2216

Digitech Research, Inc.
800 Monterey Pass Rd.
Monterey Park, CA 91754
800-999-7957; 213-267-1638
fax: 213-267-1583

Computers

Discovery Electronics
1351 Dividend Dr., SE, Ste. N
Marietta, GA 30067
800-346-8243; 404-980-9664
fax: 404-980-9754

DMS Computers, Inc.
222 Cedar Lane, Ste. 200
Teaneck, NJ 07666-3309
201-907-0462
fax: 201-907-0463

Dolch Computer Systems
372 Turquoise St.
Milpitas, CA 95035
800-538-7506; 408-957-6575
fax: 408-263-6305
Technical support: Use main number

DTK Computer, Inc.
17700 Castleton St., Ste. 300
City of Industry, CA 91748
818-810-8880
fax: 818-810-5233
Technical support: 818-810-0098

Dyna Computers, Inc.
3081 N. First St.
San Jose, CA 95134
408-943-0100

Dyna Micro, Inc.
30 W. Montague Expy.
San Jose, CA 95134
800-336-DYNA; 408-943-0100
fax: 408-943-0714

Dynabook Technologies
6150 Stoneridge Mall Rd., Ste. 225
Pleasanton, CA 94566
510-847-0660
fax: 510-847-0664

Dynamac Computer Products, Inc.
555 17th St., Anaconda Tower, Ste. 1850
Denver, CO 80202
800-234-2349; 303-296-0606
fax: 303-296-9540

Dynamic Decisions, Inc.
134 West 26th St.
New York, NY 10001
800-869-9888; 212-242-0108

Edge Technologies, Inc.
3531 Ryder St.
Santa Clara, CA 95051
800-886-3688; 408-736-8688
fax: 408-736-8689

ELCO Computers
215 S. Raymond Ave.
Alhambra, CA 91803
818-284-3281
fax: 818-281-3449

Eltech Research, Inc.
47266 Benicia St.
Fremont, CA 94538
510-438-0990
fax: 510-438-0663

Emerald Computers
7324 S.W. Durham Rd.
Portland, OR 97224
503-620-6094

Emerson Computer Corp.
5500 E. Slauson Ave.
Commerce, CA 90040
310-722-9800
fax: 310-722-3216

EMPAC International Corp.
47448 Fremont Blvd.
Fremont, CA 94538
510-683-8800
fax: 510-683-8662

Engineering Systems, Inc.
601 E. William St., Ste. 3
Ann Arbor, MI 48104
313-668-8154

EPS Technologies, Inc.
P.O. Box 278
Jefferson, SD 57038
800-447-0921; 605-966-5586
fax: 605-966-5482

Epson America, Inc.
20770 Madrona Ave.
Torrance, CA 90509-2842
800-289-3776; 310-782-0770
Technical support: 310-782-2600

Ergo Computing, Inc.
One International Way
Peabody, MA 01960
800-633-1925

ESC Computers, Inc.
7042 Owensmouth Ave.
Canoga Park, CA 91303
800-747-4372; 818-888-0188
fax: 818-888-7090

Event Solutions
N. 15217 Ferrall
Mead, WA 99021
509-467-7351

Everest Computer Corp.
1153 Tasman Dr.
Sunnyvale, CA 94089
408-734-2604
fax: 408-734-8469

Everex Systems, Inc.
48431 Milmont Dr.
Fremont, CA 94538
800-821-0806; 510-498-1111
fax: 510-651-0728
Technical support: 510-498-4411

Evergreen Systems, Inc.
1510 Grant Ave., Ste. 102
Novato, CA 95945
415-897-8888
fax: 415-897-6158

Everlasting Technology International Corp.
10450 Pioneer Blvd., Unit 8
Santa Fe Springs, CA 90670
310-946-5241
fax: 310-946-6633

Expo Tech Computers
800 N. Church St.
Lake Zurich, IL 60047
800-284-3976
fax: 800-947-3976

Express Micro Mart, Inc.
5520 Drake Rd.
West Bloomfield, MI 48322
800-533-0177; 313-788-0133

FastMicro
3721 E. Grove St.
Phoenix, AZ 85040
800-441-3278; 602-437-8975

Federal Data Corp.
4800 Hampden Lane, Ste. 1100
Bethesda, MD 20814
301-986-0800
fax: 301-961-3892

Fifth Force
2550 W. Main St., Ste. 202
Alhambra, CA 91803
818-281-6956
fax: 818-281-3449

Finetek, Inc.
135-18 Northern Blvd.
Flushing, NY 11354
516-864-3310
fax: 516-864-2842

First Class Systems, Inc.
2875 Northwestern Pkwy.
Santa Clara, CA 95051
408-980-0200
fax: 408-748-9044

First Computer Systems, Inc.
3951 Pleasantdale Rd., Ste. 224
Atlanta, GA 30340
800-325-1911; 404-441-1911
fax: 404-441-1856
Technical support: 404-447-8324

First International Computer
of America, Inc.
30077 Ahern St.
Union City, CA 94587
510-475-7885

FiveStar Computers
2100 N. Greenville Ave.
Richardson, TX 75081
800-752-5555; 214-470-9000
fax: 214-470-0191

Flash Technology, Inc.
55 W. Hoover Ave., Ste. 9
Mesa, AZ 85210
800-448-2031; 602-464-9272
fax: 602-464-9856

Floppy's Computer House
317 Forestview Dr.
Wintersville, OH 43952
614-264-0859
fax: 614-264-1930

Flytech Technology (U.S.A.), Inc.
3008 Scott Blvd.
Santa Clara, CA 95054
408-727-7373
fax: 408-727-7375

Fora, Inc.
3081 N. First St.
San Jose, CA 95134
800-FOR-FORA; 408-944-0393
fax: 408-944-0392

Forefront Technology Corp. (MA)
50 Mall Rd., Executive Place III, Ste. G12
Burlington, MA 01803
617-270-9733
fax: 617-270-9313

Fornet Corp.
46718 Fremont Blvd.
Fremont, CA 94538
800-232-4NET; 510-623-7800
fax: 510-623-0771

DIRECTORY OF MANUFACTURERS

Fortron Corp.
6818-G Patterson Pass Rd.
Livermore, CA 94550
800-821-9771; 510-373-1008
fax: 510-373-1168

Fountain Technologies, Inc.
12K Worlds Fair Dr.
Somerset, NJ 08873
908-563-4800
fax: 908-563-4999

Franklin Datacom
733 Lakefield Rd.
Westlake Village, CA 91361
805-373-8688
fax: 805-373-7373

Futura Systems
40 Bayfield Dr.
North Andover, MA 01845
800-448-1461; 508-685-1925
fax: 508-685-5017

FutureTech Systems, Inc.
Six Bride St., Bridge Plaza
Hackensack, NJ 07601
800-275-4414; 201-488-4414
fax: 201-488-4405

Gallant International Corp.
2705 N. Durfee Ave.
El Monte, CA 91732
800-848-0088; 818-575-0866
fax: 818-575-3780

Gateway 2000
610 Gateway Dr.
North Sioux City, SD 57049
800-523-2000; 605-232-2000
fax: 605-232-2023
Technical support: 800-248-2031

G&C Computer Products, Inc.
1977 O'Tool Ave., Ste. B105
San Jose, CA 95131
408-954-0982
fax: 408-954-0666

GCH Systems, Inc.
201 Ravendale Dr.
Mountain View, CA 94043
800-366-4560; 415-968-3400
fax: 415-964-9747

GEM Computer Products
3624 Pierce Rd.
Bakersfield, CA 93308
805-323-0707
fax: 805-323-9747

Gemini Computers
31-00 47th Ave.
Long Island City, NY 11101
718-472-0220
fax: 718-472-0231

Gems Computers, Inc.
2115 Old Oakland Rd.
San Jose, CA 95131
408-432-7380
fax: 408-432-8622

GenTech
P.O. Box 20555
Cranston, RI 02920
800-444-3683; 401-732-5556
fax: 401-732-5518

GoldStar Technology, Inc.
3003 N. First St.
San Jose, CA 95134-2004
408-432-1331
fax: 408-432-6053
Technical support: 800-777-1192

GRiD Systems Corp.
P.O. Box 5003, 47211 Lakeview Blvd.
Fremont, CA 94537-5003
800-222-4743; 510-656-4700
fax: 510-683-0902
Technical support: 800-654-4743

GST, Inc.
6900 Hermosa Circle
Buena Park, CA 90620
800-821-2792; 714-739-0106
fax: 714-670-6404

GVC Technologies, Inc.
99 Demarest Rd.
Sparta, NJ 07871
800-289-4821; 201-579-3630
fax: 201-579-2702
Technical support: Use main number

Halskar, Inc.
45260 Industrial Dr.
Fremont, CA 94538
800-728-4348; 510-490-4009
fax: 510-490-4069

Handok Information Systems Corp.
250 Santa Ana Court
Sunnyvale, CA 94086
408-736-3191
fax: 408-749-0477

HAST, Ltd.
2781 Brower Ave.
Oceanside, NY 11572
800-253-7922; 516-678-9165
fax: 516-678-9430

HCI (Hyosung Computer & Information Systems)
671 E. Argues Ave.
Sunnyvale, CA 94086
408-733-0810
fax: 408-733-2638

Heath Co.
P.O. Box 1288
Benton Harbor, MI 49022
800-253-0570; 616-982-3200
fax: 616-982-5577

HEREX Computer Technology, Inc.
2237 E. Division
Arlington, TX 76011
817-652-1144
fax: 817-652-1656

Hertz Computer Corp.
325 Fifth Ave.
New York, NY 10016
800-232-8737; 212-684-4141
fax: 212-684-3685

Hewlett-Packard Co.
3000 Hanover St.
Palo Alto, CA 94304
800-752-0900; 415-857-1501
Technical support: Use toll-free number

HIMS, Inc.
368 Montaque Expwy.
Milpitas, CA 95035
800-367-2924; 408-946-9711
fax: 408-946-9744

HiQuality Systems, Inc.
740 N. Mary Ave.
Sunnyvale, CA 94086
800-827-5836; 408-245-5836

HiTech International, Inc.
712 Charcot Ave.
San Jose, CA 95131
408-435-8827
fax: 408-435-3023

Husky Computers, Inc.
13921 ICOT Blvd.
Clearwater, FL 34620
800-486-7774; 813-530-4141
fax: 813-536-9906

Hyundai Electronics America
166 Baypointe Pkwy.
San Jose, CA 95134
800-544-7808; 408-473-9200
fax: 408-943-9567
Technical support: 800-234-3553

i Corp Computers, Inc.
398 Columbus Ave., Ste. 395
Boston, MA 02116-6008
617-424-7080
fax:617-354-9632

IBM (International Business Machines)
Old Orchard Rd.
Armonk, NY 10504
800-426-2468; 914-765-1900
Technical support: Use toll-free number

IBS Computer Corp.
5915 Graham Court
Livermore, CA 94550
510-443-3131
fax: 510-449-1179

ICL Business Systems
9801 Muirlands Blvd.
Irvine, CA 92718
714-458-7282
fax: 714-458-6257

Identity Systems Technology, Inc.
1347 Exchange Dr.
Richardson, TX 75081
800-723-8258; 214-235-3330
fax: 214-907-9227

IMC Computer, Inc.
11100 S. Wilcrest St., Ste. H
Houston, TX 77099
713-561-8857

Impulse Systems, Inc.
85 Bornett Ave.
San Francisco, CA 94131
415-641-9197
fax: 415-641-9226

IndTech Systems, Inc.
1349B Moffett Park Dr.
Sunnyvale, CA 94089
408-743-4300

Infomatic Power Systems Corp.
9832 Alburtis Ave.
Santa Fe Springs, CA 90670
310-948-2217
fax: 310-948-5264

Informtech International, Inc.
3349 S. La Cienega
Los Angeles, CA 90091
213-836-8993
fax: 213-836-8992

Computers

Innovation Computer Corp.
1325 Juniper St.
Cleveland, WI 53015
414-693-3416
fax: 414-693-3165

Insight Computers
1912 West 4th St.
Tempe, AZ 85281
800-776-7600; 602-350-1176
fax: 602-829-9193
Technical support: 800-488-0007

Intelec
6075 Northwest 82nd Ave.
Miami, FL 33166
800-683-0969; 305-594-0001
fax: 305-477-9074

Intelligence Technology Corp.
P.O. Box 671125
Dallas, TX 75367
214-250-4277

Intelligent Data Systems, Inc.
6319 E. Alondra Blvd.
Paramount, CA 90723
310-633-5504
fax: 310-408-1550

Intelligent MicroSystems
1633 Babcock, Ste. 424
San Antonio, TX 78229
800-777-7757

International Communications
Equipment Corp.
17945G Skypark Circle
Irvine, CA 92714
800-486-7800; 714-660-0191
fax: 714-660-0927

International Instrumentation, Inc.
2282 Townsgate Rd.
Westlake Village, CA 91361
800-543-DISK; 800-346-DISK (in
California); 818-991-9614
fax: 805-379-0701

**International Systems Marketing, Inc.
(ISM)**
943 A Russell Avenue
Gaithersburg, MD 20879
301-670-1813

Intra Electronics USA, Inc.
1133 N. Fair Oaks Ave.
Sunnyvale, CA 94086
408-744-1706
fax: 408-744-1871

I.S.C. Power Systems
2629 Manhattan Ave., Ste. 235
Hermosa Beach, CA 90254
800-933-5161; 310-379-9209
fax: 310-318-0555

Isotropic Computer, Inc.
East 5920 Seltice Way
Post Falls, ID 83854
208-667-1447
fax: 208-765-8130

Iverson Computer Corp.
1356 Beverly Rd., P.O. Box 6250
McLean, VA 22106-6250
703-749-1200
fax: 703-893-2396
Technical support: 800-677-7881

Jade Computer Products, Inc.
4901 W. Rosecrans Ave., Box 5046
Hawthorne, CA 90251-5046
800-421-5500; 800-262-1710 (in California);
310-973-7707
fax: 310-675-2522

Jameco Electronics
1355 Shoreway Rd.
Belmont, CA 94002
415-592-8097
fax: 415-592-2503

Jawin Computer Products
565 W. Lambert, Ste. C
Brea, CA 92621
800-543-5107; 714-990-2097

JC Information Systems
44036 S. Grimmer
Fremont, CA 94538
510-659-8440
fax: 510-659-8449

JCC Products, Inc.
10675 E. Rush St.
South El Monte, CA 91733
800-421-1771; 818-575-7951
fax: 818-575-8198

Jetta International, Inc.
51 Stouts Lane, Ste. 3
Monmouth Junction, NJ 08852
800-445-3882; 908-329-9651
fax: 908-329-0105

Jinco Computers, Inc.
5122 Walnut Grove Ave.
San Gabriel, CA 91776
818-309-1108
fax: 818-309-1107

JKL Computers
717 Ellsworth Dr.
Silver Spring, MD 20910
800-553-0386; 301-587-3232
fax: 800-828-0486

Join Data Systems, Inc.
14838 Valley Blvd., Ste. C
City of Industry, CA 91746
818-330-6553
fax: 818-330-6865

Joy Systems
2380 Bering Dr.
San Jose, CA 95131
408-435-0980

J-Tech Corp.
15358 Valley Blvd.
City of Industry, CA 91746
800-543-2525; 818-369-1332
fax: 818-333-5000

Kanix, Inc.
13111 Brooks Dr., Ste. F
Baldwin Park, CA 91706
818-814-3997
fax: 818-814-0248

Kaypro Corp.
4174 Sorrento Valley Blvd.
San Diego, CA 92121
800-452-9776; 619-535-2155
fax: 619-535-2170

Kelleco Technologies
7101 S. Adams St.
Willowbrook, IL 60521
800-323-3244; 708-887-0330
fax: 708-887-0448

Keydata International, Inc.
111 Corporate Blvd.
South Plainfield, NJ 07080
800-486-4800; 908-755-0350
fax: 908-756-7359
Technical Support: 800-756-7410

KFC Computek Components Corp.
31 E. Mall
Plainview, NY 11803
516-454-0262
fax: 516-454-0265

Kingtech
13918 Equitable Rd.
Cerritos, CA 90701
310-404-5611
fax: 310-404-4982

KISS Computer Corp.
2604 Washington Rd.
Kenosha, WI 53140-2375
800-GET-KISS; 414-652-5477

KLH Computers
10310 Harwin St.
Houston, TX 77036
800-347-1777; 713-995-4433

Kontron Elektronik
66 Cherry Hill Dr.
Beverly, MA 01918
508-927-6575
fax: 508-927-6511

KRIS Technologies
260 E. Grand Ave.
South San Francisco, CA 94080
800-282-5747; 415-875-6729
fax: 415-877-8048
Technical support: Use main number

Laguna Systems, Inc.
731 E. Ball Rd., Ste. 101
Anaheim, CA 92805
714-758-9943

Lan Technologies, Inc.
520 Fellowship Rd., Ste. B-208
Mt. Laurel, NJ 08054
800-899-LAN1; 609-234-8777
fax: 609-234-4454

Lancer Research, Inc.
557 W. Covina Blvd.
San Dimas, CA 91773
800-966-8866; 714-592-6003
fax: 714-592-5871

Laser Computer, Inc.
800 N. Church St.
Lake Zurich, IL 60047
708-540-8086
fax: 708-540-8335
Technical support: 708-540-5022

Laser Digital, Inc.
1257B Tasman Ave.
Sunnyvale, CA 94086
800-826-4225; 408-747-1966
fax: 408-747-1971

DIRECTORY OF MANUFACTURERS

Leading Edge Products, Inc.
117 Flanders Rd.
Westboro, MA 01581-5020
800-874-3340; 508-836-4800
fax: 508-836-4501
Technical support: 900-370-4800

Leading Technology, Inc.
10430 Southwest 5th St.
Beaverton, OR 97005-3447
800-999-5323; 503-646-3424
fax: 503-626-7845
Technical support: 800-999-4888

Liberty Electronics USA, Inc.
270 E. Grand
South San Francisco, CA 94080
415-742-7000
fax: 415-952-9588

Librex Computer Systems, Inc.
1731 Technology, Ste. 700
San Jose, CA 95110
800-441-9520; 408-441-8500
fax: 408-441-7842

Lightning Computers, Inc.
340 Brannan St., Ste. 200
San Francisco, CA 94107
800-347-4486; 415-543-3111
fax: 415-543-3532

Link Computer, Inc.
560 S. Melrose St.
Placentia, CA 92670
714-993-0800
fax: 714-993-0705

Linus Technologies, Inc.
11130 Sunrise Valley Dr.
Reston, VA 22091
703-476-1500
fax: 703-264-0389

LONGSHINE Technology, Inc.
2013 N. Capitol Ave.
San Jose, CA 95132
408-942-1746
fax: 408-942-1745

LSE Electronics, Inc.
77 W. Nicholai St.
Hicksville, NY 11801
516-931-1670
fax: 516-931-2565

Lucky Computers
1701 N. Greenville, Ste. 602
Richardson, TX 75081
214-690-6110
Technical support: 800-966-5825

L&W MicroComputing Corp.
278 D W Hwy.
Nashua, NH 03060
800-882-7830; 603-888-8288
fax: 603-888-8289

Mag Computronic (USA) Inc.
17845-E Skypark Circle
Irvine, CA 92714
714-927-3998
fax: 714-827-5522

Magic Computer Corp.
13177 Romona Blvd., Ste. B
Irwindale, CA 91706
818-813-1210

Magitronic Technology, Inc.
10 Hub Dr.
Melville, NY 11747
516-454-8255
fax: 516-454-8268

Mandax Computer, Inc.
14935 Northeast 95th St.
Redmond, WA 98052
206-867-1973

Marathon Computers
4915 Prospect, NE
Albuquerque, NM 87110
800-525-8363; 505-881-0077
fax: 505-889-9575

Martec Associates, Inc.
1510 Jarvis Ave.
Elk Grove Village, IL 60007
708-956-8090

Mascot Computer Corp.
42-20 College Point Blvd.
Flushing, NY 11355
718-321-1944
fax: 718-321-0136

Master Computer, Inc.
10742 5th Ave., NE
Seattle, WA 98125
206-365-1156

Matrix Digital Products, Inc.
1811 N. Keystone St.
Burbank, CA 91504
800-227-5723; 818-566-8567
fax: 818-566-1476

Maxtron
1825A Durfee Ave.
South El Monte, CA 91733
800-266-5706; 818-350-5706
fax: 818-350-4965

ME—Micro Express
1801 E. Carnegie Ave.
Santa Ana, CA 92705
800-989-9900; 714-852-1400
fax: 714-852-1225
Technical support: 800-762-3378

Mead Computer Corp.
1000 Nevada Hwy., Ste. 101
Boulder City, NV 89005
800-654-7762; 702-294-0204
fax: 702-294-1168

Mectel International, Inc.
3385 Viso Court
Santa Clara, CA 95054
800-248-0255; 408-980-4709
fax: 408-980-4713

Mega Computer Systems
16980 Via Tazon
San Diego, CA 92127
619-487-8888
fax: 619-485-1518

Megadata Corp.
35 Orville Dr.
Bohemia, NY 11716-2598
800-634-2827; 516-589-6800
fax: 516-589-6858

Memorex Telex Corp.
6422 East 41st St.
Tulsa, OK 74135
800-950-3465; 918-627-1111
fax: 918-624-4581
Technical support: Use main number

Metra Information Systems, Inc.
657 Pastoria Ave.
Sunnyvale, CA 94086
800-733-9188; 408-730-9188
fax: 408-730-5933

Micro Base Technologies
3000 Scott Blvd., Ste. 203
Santa Clara, CA 95054
800-345-4479; 408-727-6276
fax: 408-727-7307

Micro Experts
2055 Beaver Ruin Rd.
Norcross, GA 30071
404-368-9176

Micro Express
1801 E. Carnegie Ave.
Santa Ana, CA 92705
800-642-7621; 714-852-1400
fax: 714-852-1225
Technical support: 800-762-3378

Micro Generation
300 McGaw Dr.
Edison, NJ 08837
800-872-2841; 908-225-8899
fax: 908-225-8999

Micro Image International, Inc.
1010 W. Fulleton, Unit G
Addison, IL 60101
708-628-0344
fax: 708-543-1859

Micro-Net International
60 S. Park Victoria
Milpitas, CA 95035
408-262-9444
fax: 408-262-0708

Micro 1 Inc.
557 Howard St.
San Francisco, CA 94105
800-338-4061; 415-974-5439

Micro Palm Computers
13773-500 ICOT Blvd.
Clearwater, FL 34620
813-530-0128
fax: 813-530-0738

Micro Smart, Inc.
200 Homer Ave.
Ashland, MA 01721
800-333-8841; 508-872-9090
fax: 508-881-1520

Micro-Technology Concepts, Inc.
258 Johnson Ave.
Brooklyn, NY 11206
800-366-4860; 718-456-9100
fax: 718-456-1200

Micro Telesis, Inc.
1260 A Logan Ave., Ste. A2
Costa Mesa, CA 92626
714-557-2003
fax: 714-557-9729

Computers

Microage-Bay Area Computers
130 Sansome St.
San Francisco, CA 94104
800-233-2778; 415-393-9600
fax: 415-393-9640

Microchip Technology
2900 Northwest 72nd Ave.
Miami, FL 33122
305-592-5739
fax: 305-592-5738

Microcom Computers
48890 Milmont Dr.
Fremont, CA 94537
800-248-3398; 510-623-3628
fax: 510-623-3620

Microlab
23976 Freeway Park Dr.
Farmington Hills, MI 48335
800-677-7900; 313-474-7711
fax: 313-474-0843

Micronics Computers, Inc.
232 E. Warren Ave.
Fremont, CA 94539
800-234-4386; 510-651-2300
fax: 510-651-5612
Technical support: Use main number

MicroServe Corp.
2504 BuildAmerica Dr.
Hampton, VA 23666
804-838-0806
fax: 804-827-7464

MicroSlate, Inc.
9625 Ignace St., Ste. D
Brossard, Quebec
Canada J4Y 2P3
514-444-3680
fax: 514-444-3683

MicroStar Computer Technology, Inc.
3211 Olympic Blvd.
Santa Monica, CA 90404
800-633-8088; 310-453-7500
fax: 310-453-8888

Microsystems Group
2500 W. Higgins Rd., Ste. 450
Hoffman Estates, IL 60195
708-882-5666

Microwriter, Inc.
1101 N. Elm St., Ste. 1002
Greensboro, NC 27401
919-274-6040
fax: 919-274-6022

Midern Computer, Inc.
18005 Cortney Court
City of Industry, CA 91748
800-669-1624; 818-964-8682
fax: 818-964-2381

Mini-Micro Supply Co., Inc.
2050 Corporate Court
San Jose, CA 95131
800-628-3656; 408-456-9500
fax: 408-434-9242

Minta Technologies Co.
11 Deerpark Dr., Ste. 116, Princeton Corp.
Plaza IV
Monmouth Junction, NJ 08852
800-82-MINTA; 908-329-2020
fax: 908-329-2219

Mitsuba Corp.
1925 Wright Ave.
La Verne, CA 91750
800-648-7822; 714-392-2000
fax: 714-392-2021
Technical support: 714-392-2019 (Laptop);
714-392-2018 (Desktop)

Mitsubishi Electronics America, Inc.
991 Knox St.
Torrance, CA 90502
800-556-1234, ext. 54M; 800-441-2345, ext.
54M (in California); 310-515-3993
fax: 310-527-7693
Technical support: Use main number

Model American Computer Corp.
233 Needham St.
Newton, MA 02164
800-843-3838; 617-969-0093
fax: 617-969-2596

Modgraph, Inc.
83 Second Ave.
Burlington, MA 01803
800-327-9962; 617-229-4800
fax: 617-272-3062

Monolith Corp.
335 S. White St.
Wake Forest, NC 27587
800-255-7425; 919-556-6664
fax: 919-556-1920

Morse Technology, Inc.
17531 Railroad St., Unit I
City of Industry, CA 91748
818-854-8681
fax: 818-854-8682

MSO Computers, Inc.
463 Montague Expwy.
Milpitas, CA 95035
800-YES-4-MSO; 408-945-4270
fax: 408-945-1742

M2 Lab
315 Cloverleaf Dr., Ste. 1D
Baldwin Park, CA 91706
818-968-0643
fax: 818-968-8848

Multi Connection Technology
3518 Arden Rd.
Hayward, CA 94545
510-670-0633
fax: 510-670-0790

Multi-Industry Technology, Inc.
777 New Durham Rd.
Edison, NJ 08817
800-999-6481; 201-906-9206
fax: 201-906-9209

Multi-Pal International, Inc.
17231 E. Railroad St., Ste. 500
City of Industry, CA 91748
818-913-4188
fax: 818-912-9149

Myoda, Inc.
1053 Shore Rd.
Naperville, IL 60563
800-562-1071; 708-369-5199
fax: 708-369-6068

National Computer
9823 Mira Mesa Blvd.
San Diego, CA 92131
619-530-2446

National Micro Systems (NMS)
2833 Peterson Place
Norcross, GA 30071
404-446-0520

NCR Corp.
1700 S. Patterson Blvd.
Dayton, OH 45479
513-445-5000
fax: 513-445-2008
Technical support: 800-CALL-NCR

NEC Technologies, Inc.
1414 Massachusetts Ave.
Boxborough, MA 01719
800-826-2255; 508-264-8000
fax: 508-264-8673
Technical support: 508-264-4300

Neotech Systems
8125 Catalpa, Ste. A
El Paso, TX 79925
915-779-1722

Netcom Research, Inc.
36 Mauchly, Ste. C
Irvine, CA 92718
714-727-0724
fax: 714-727-0732

Netis Technology Inc.
1544 Century Pointe Dr.
Milpitas, CA 95035
408-263-0368

Network Centre, Inc.
1915 Peters Rd., Ste. 306
Irving, TX 75061
817-498-2262
fax: 817-438-7247

**Network & Communication
Technology, Inc.**
24 Wampum Rd.
Park Ridge, NJ 07656
201-307-9000
fax: 201-307-9404

The Network Connection, Inc.
1324 Union Hill Rd.
Alpharetta, GA 30201
800-327-4853; 404-751-0889
fax: 404-751-1884

Network Interface Corp.
15019 West 95th St.
Lenexa, KS 66215
800-343-2853; 913-894-2277
fax: 913-894-0226

New MMI Corp.
2400 Reach Rd.
Williamsport, PA 17701
800-221-4283; 717-327-9575
fax: 717-327-1217

Norand Corp.
550 Second St., SE
Cedar Rapids, IA 52401
800-553-5971; 319-369-3100

Northgate Computer Systems, Inc.
P.O. Box 59080
Minneapolis, MN 55459-0080
800-548-1993; 612-943-8181
fax: 612-943-8336
Technical support: 800-446-5037

DIRECTORY OF MANUFACTURERS

Notebook Computer Co.
1000 Louisiana, Ste. 1080
Houston, TX 77002
713-651-0800
fax: 713-651-0513

NoteStar
5A Joanna Court
East Brunswick, NJ 08816
908-254-0555
fax: 908-254-5218

Novacor, Inc.
1841 Zanker Rd.
San Jose, CA 95112
800-486-6682; 408-441-6500
fax: 408-441-6811

Nycom Technologies Distribution, Inc.
3 Riverview Dr.
Somerset, NJ 08873
908-469-7800
fax: 908-757-6334
Technical support: 800-477-8776

Oak Microsystems, Ltd.
13 Technology Dr.
Setauket, NY 11733
516-689-6171
fax: 516-689-6081

Ocean Interface Co.
515 Spanish Lane
Walnut, CA 91789-3042
714-595-1212
fax: 714-595-9683

Octave Systems, Inc.
1715 Dell Ave.
Campbell, CA 95008
408-866-8424
fax: 408-866-4252

Ogivar Technologies
7200 Trans-Canada Hwy.
Ville Saint-Laurent, Quebec
Canada H4T 1A3
800-361-3694; 800-363-2252 (in Canada);
514-737-3340
fax: 514-737-4729

Olivetti USA
P.O. Box 6945, 765 U.S. Hwy. 202, S
Bridgewater, NJ 08807-0945
800-527-2960; 908-526-8200
fax: 908-526-8405
Technical support: 908-704-6501

Omnidata International, Inc.
750 West 200 North, P.O. Box 3489
Logan, UT 84321
801-753-7760
fax: 801-753-6756

ONYX Computer, Inc.
30799 Pinetree Rd., Ste. 303
Cleveland, OH 44124
800-486-5005; 216-591-0489

Opus Systems
329 N. Bernardo Ave.
Mountain View, CA 94043
800-873-6787; 415-960-4040
fax: 415-960-4001

Osicom Technologies, Inc.
198 Green Pond Rd.
Rockaway, NJ 07866
800-922-0881; 201-586-2550
fax: 201-586-9740

Outbound Systems, Inc.
4840 Pearl East Circle
Boulder, CO 80301
800-444-4607; 303-786-9200
fax: 303-786-8611

Owl Computer Services
5950 Keystone Dr.
Bath, PA 18014
800-245-6228; 215-837-1917

Pacific Computer
9945 Lower Azusa
Temple City, CA 91780
800-346-7207; 800-421-1102 (California);
818-442-9112

Packard Bell
9425 Canoga Ave.
Chatsworth, CA 91311
818-773-4400
fax: 818-773-9521
Technical support: 800-733-4411

PACKinTELL Electronics USA
11369 Sunrise Gold Circle
Rancho Cordova, CA 95742
800-447-2515; 916-635-2784
fax: 916-635-4836

**Panasonic Communications & Systems Co.
(Office Automation Group)**
2 Panasonic Way
Secaucus, NJ 07094
201-348-7000
Technical support: 800-222-0584

Panther Systems Ltd.
111 Great Neck Rd., Ste. 305
Great Neck, NY 11021
800-272-6843; 516-466-6108

Pan-United Corp.
2 Ethel Rd., Ste. 203B,
Durham Business Center
Edison, NJ 08817
908-248-0848
fax: 908-248-0498

Paravant Computer Systems
305 East Dr.
Melbourne, FL 32904
800-848-8529; 407-727-3672
fax: 407-725-0496

PC Brand, Inc.
954 W. Washington St.
Chicago, IL 60607
800-722-7263; 312-226-5200
fax: 312-226-6841
Technical support: Use toll-free number

PC & C Research Corp.
1100 Avenida Acaso
Camarillo, CA 93012
800-843-1239; 805-484-1685
fax: 805-987-8088

PC Craft, Inc.
640 Puente St.
Brea, CA 92621
800-733-6666; 714-256-5000
fax: 714-256-5025

PC Designs, Inc.
2504 N. Hemlock Circle
Broken Arrow, OK 74012
800-322-4872; 918-251-5550
fax: 918-251-7057

PC-Ease, Inc.
67 Melrose Rd.
Amherst, NY 14221
716-626-0315

PC House
841 E. Artesia Blvd.
Carson, CA 90746
310-324-8621
fax: 310-324-8654

PC Link Corp.
29 West 38th St.
New York, NY 10018
800-221-0343; 212-730-8030
fax: 212-221-7132

PC MAX
8025 Deering Ave.
Canoga Park, CA 91304
818-888-8880
fax: 818-888-5309

PC-Plus Technologies
Loft Plaza, 65 Southbridge St.
Auburn, MA 01501
800-422-4947; 508-831-9826
fax: 508-799-9941

PC Pros/Touche Micro Technologies
8205 S. Cass Ave.
Darien, IL 60559
800-999-9490; 708-810-1010

PC Time Data
43038 Christy St.
Fremont, CA 94538
800-878-3868; 510-623-8862
fax: 510-623-8865

PCA Personal Computer Associates, Inc.
85 Chambers Dr., Ste. 7
Ajax, ON, CD L1Z 1E2
800-263-7535; 416-427-6612
fax: 416-427-0934

PCI Systems, Inc.
5690 Sonoma Dr. Ste. D
Pleasanton, CA 94566
510-484-2818
fax: 510-484-3088

PCQT, Inc.
12930 Saratoga Ave., Ste. B7
Saratoga, CA 95070
408-255-1131
fax: 408-255-7610

PCW Sales
P.O. Box 4, 115 Essex St.
New York, NY 10002
718-271-0238
fax: 718-760-1744

Peregrine Computers
110 E. Canal St.
Troy, OH 45373
800-326-7015; 515-399-3151
fax: 513-339-6272

Personal Computer & Communication, Inc.
3 Musick
Irvine, CA 92718
714-587-1369
fax: 714-587-1136

Computers

Philips Consumer Electronics Co.
One Philips Dr., P.O. Box 14810
Knoxville, TN 37914-1810
615-521-4316
fax: 615-521-4406
Technical support: 800-722-6224

Philips Information Systems Co.
1435 Bradley Lane, Ste. 100
Carrollton, TX 75007
800-527-0204; 214-323-8238
fax: 214-991-6572

Phoenix Computer Corp.
3815 North U.S. 1, Ste. 118
Cocoa, FL 32926
800-525-7283; 407-631-0473
fax: 407-631-0476

PH6 Technologies Corp.
5819 Uplander Way
Culver City, CA 90230
800-522-6838; 310-216-0055
fax: 310-216-4931

Plamar Computer Systems
7101 Adams St.
Willowbrook, IL 60521
800-535-7885
fax: 708-323-3442

Polywell Computers, Inc.
61-C Airport Blvd.
South San Francisco, CA 94080
800-999-1278; 415-583-7222
fax: 415-583-1974

Poqet Computer Corp.
5200 Patrick Henry Dr.
Santa Clara, CA 95054
800-624-8999; 408-982-9500
Technical support: 408-764-9400

Positive Corp.
P.O. Box 2101
Chatsworth, CA 91313-2101
800-452-6345; 800-252-6345 (in California);
818-341-5400

Precision Systems Group
3728-48 Phillips Hwy.
Jacksonville, FL 32207
800-326-4774

Premier Computer Innovations
10310 Harwin Dr.
Houston, TX 77036
800-347-1777; 713-995-4433
fax: 713-995-4751

President Micro Systems Corp.
1300 Pioneer, Ste. C
Brea, CA 92621
213-691-1553
fax: 213-691-2151

Primax Data Products
52 Bramwin Court
Brampton, Ontario
Canada L6T 5G2
416-792-7330
fax: 416-792-6537

Private Label PCs, Inc.
1356 Beverly Rd.
McLean, VA 22101
800-666-PVLB; 703-790-4690
fax: 703-893-2396

Proteus Technology Corp.
377 Rt. 17, S, Airport Center
Hasbrouck Hgts., NJ 07604
800-878-6427; 201-288-2041
fax: 201-288-2045

Proton Corp.
5630 Cerritos Ave.
Cypress, CA 90630
714-952-6900

PSION, Inc.
118 Echo Lake Rd.
Watertown, CT 06795
800-548-4535; 203-274-7521
fax: 203-274-7976

QANTEL Business Systems, Inc.
4142 Point Eden Way
Hayward, CA 94545-3781
800-227-1894; 510-887-7777
fax: 510-782-6195

QIC Research, Inc.
3401 W. Warren Ave.
Fremont, CA 94539
510-623-2050

QSI Corp.
95 Rockwell Place
Brooklyn, NY 11217
718-834-4545
fax: 718-834-5318

Quadrant Components
4378 Enterprise St.
Fremont, CA 94538
510-656-9988
fax: 510-656-2208

Quick Technology Corp.
1642 McGaw Ave.
Irvine, CA 92714
714-660-4948
fax: 714-660-8809

Quill Corp.
P.O. Box 4700
Lincolnshire, IL 60197-4700
708-634-4800
fax: 708-634-5708
Technical support: 708-634-6650

Qume Corp.
500 Yosemite Dr.
Milpitas, CA 95035
408-942-4000
fax: 408-942-4052
Technical support: 408-942-4138 (Monitors,
Terminals); 408-942-4100 (Printers)

Racore Computer Products, Inc.
170 Knowles Dr., Ste. 204
Los Gatos, CA 95030
800-635-1274; 408-374-8290
fax: 408-374-6653

Radix II, Inc.
(Sophos Integrated Systems Division)
6230 Oxon Hill Rd.
Oxon Hill, MD 20745
800-334-SISI; 301-567-5200
fax: 301-839-0836

RALPH Associates
305 Wilson Rd.
Cherry Hill, NJ 08002

Reason Technology
290 Coon Rapids Blvd.
Minneapolis, MN 55433
800-800-4860; 612-780-4792; 612-780-4797

Recortec, Inc.
1290 Lawrence Station Rd.
Sunnyvale, CA 94089
800-729-7654; 408-734-1290
fax: 408-734-2140

Reply Corp.
4435 Fortran Dr.
San Jose, CA 95134
800-955-5BY5; 408-942-4804
fax: 408-942-4897
Technical support: Use toll-free number

Republic Technology Corp.
1161 Headway Circle, Bldg. 3
Austin, TX 78754
800-622-2177; 512-834-2222
fax: 512-834-1111

**Research, Development & Innovations,
Inc.**
6696 Mesa Ridge Rd., Bldg. A
San Diego, CA 92121
619-944-6381
fax: 619-558-4720

Rio Computers
8900 San Pedro, Ste. 127
San Antonio, TX 78216
512-878-7774
fax: 512-828-1155

Rose Hill Systems
4865 Scotts Valley Dr.
Scotts Valley, CA 95066
800-248-ROSE; 408-438-3871
fax: 408-438-3642

SAI Systems Laboratories, Inc.
911 Bridgeport Ave.
Shelton, CT 06484
800-331-0488; 203-929-0790
fax: 203-929-6948

St. Croix Computer Corp.
6640 Shady Oak Rd., 3rd Fl.
Eden Prairie, MN 55344
800-950-0174; 612-943-8618
fax: 612-943-3854

Sampo Corp. of America
(Industrial Products Division)
5550 Peachtree Industrial Blvd.
Norcross, GA 30071
404-449-6220
fax: 404-447-1109

**Samsung Information Systems
America, Inc.**
3655 N. First St.
San Jose, CA 95134-1708
800-446-0262; 408-434-5400
fax: 408-434-5653
Technical support: Use main number

Sanyo Business Systems Corp.
(Computer Division)
51 Joseph St.
Moonachie, NJ 07074
800-524-0047; 201-440-9300, ext. 318
fax: 201-440-1775
Technical support: Use main number

DIRECTORY OF MANUFACTURERS

Scantech Computer Systems, Inc.
12981 Ramona Blvd., Units H&I
Irwindale, CA 91706
818-960-2999
fax: 818-962-4819

Scenario, Inc.
260 Franklin St., Ste. 520
Boston, MA 02110
617-439-6611
fax: 617-439-6644

SCI/Fortune
2000 Ringwood Ave.
San Jose, CA 95131
800-443-7072; 408-943-6200
fax: 408-943-6249

Semi-Tech Microcomputers, Ltd.
131 McNabb St.
Markham, Ontario
Canada L3R 5V7
416-475-2670
fax: 416-475-1552

SF Micro, Inc.
1143 Post St.
San Francisco, CA 94109
800-237-5631; 415-929-1505
fax: 415-922-1187

Sharp Electronics Corp.
(Professional Products Division)
Sharp Plaza, P.O. Box 650
Mahwah, NJ 07430
201-529-8200
fax: 201-529-9636
Technical support: 800-732-8221

Sherwood/Kimtron
4181 Business Center Dr.
Fremont, CA 94538-6355
800-777-8755; 510-623-8900
fax: 510-623-8945

Siemens Nixdorf Information Systems, Inc.
200 Wheeler Rd.
Burlington, MA 01803
800-225-1484; 617-273-0480
fax: 617-221-0231
Technical support: Use main number

SIIG, Inc.
5369 Randall Place
Fremont, CA 94538
510-657-0567
fax: 510-657-5962

Silicon Electronics
3350 Scott Blvd., Ste. 1201
Santa Clara, CA 95054
408-988-4408
fax: 408-988-4431

Sirex U.S.A., Inc.
132-14 11th Ave.
College Point, NY 11356
800-722-0404; 718-746-7500
fax: 718-746-0882

Softworks Development Corp.
5985 N. Lilly Rd.
Menomonee Falls, WI 53051
800-332-3475; 414-252-2020

Soletek Computer Supply, Inc.
47400 Seabridge Dr.
Fremont, CA 94538
510-438-0160
fax: 510-438-0243

Solidtech, Inc.
2014 Rt. 22, E
Scotch Plains, NJ 07076
800-321-8922

Sony Microsystems Co.
645 River Oaks Pkwy.
San Jose, CA 95134
408-434-6644
fax: 408-954-1057

Soyo USA, Inc.
148 Eighth Ave., Ste. H
City of Industry, CA 91746
818-330-1712
fax: 818-968-4161

Spear Technology, Inc.
710A Landwehr Rd.
Northbrook, IL 60062
708-480-7300
fax: 708-480-9538

SST—Sirus Systems Technology, Inc.
4344 Young St.
Pasadena, TX 77504
800-424-0724; 713-946-0724
fax: 713-946-5451

Standard Computer Corp.
12803 Schabarum Ave.
Irwindale, CA 91706
818-338-4668
Technical support: 800-662-6111

Star Industries, Inc.
7655 E. Redfield Rd., Ste. 10
Scottsdale, AZ 85260
800-782-7286; 602-483-2854
fax: 602-483-7138

Storage System Engineering Service
3350 Scott Blvd., Ste. 1902
Santa Clara, CA 95054
408-727-6040
fax: 408-727-6042

Sun Moon Star
(North America Personal Computer Division)
1941 Ringwood Ave.
San Jose, CA 95131
800-545-4SUN; 408-452-7811
fax: 408-452-1411

SunnyTech, Inc.
17 Smith St., Ste. 7
Englewood, NJ 07631
800-367-1132; 201-569-7773
fax: 201-569-6279

Sunnyvale Memories
1400 Dell Ave., Ste. F
Campbell, CA 95008
800-262-3475; 408-378-8378

Suntronics, Inc.
12603 Crenshaw Blvd.
Hawthorne, CA 90250
800-545-9777; 310-644-1140

Super Computer, Inc.
17910 S. Adria Maru Lane
Carson, CA 90746
310-532-2133
fax: 310-532-6342

Supercom
410 S. Abbott Ave.
Milpitas, CA 95035
408-456-8888
fax: 408-770-0513

Supernet Computer, Inc.
1001 Baltimore Pike
Springfield, PA 19069
215-544-7722

Swan Technologies
3075 Research Dr.
State College, PA 16801
800-468-9044; 814-238-1820
fax: 814-237-4450
Technical support: 800-468-7926

Symbionics, Inc.
P.O. Box 687, Redwood Center
Dripping Springs, TX 78620
800-873-4619; 512-288-2113
Technical support: 512-288-4408

Syncomp International Corp.
1400 W. Lambert Rd., Ste. D
Brea, CA 92621
213-690-1011
fax: 213-690-6380

Syntax Manufacturing Co.
5680 Bandini Blvd.
Bell, CA 90201
800-552-8900; 310-262-1300
fax: 310-261-1300

Syntrex, Inc. (Network Systems Division)
246 Industrial Way, W
Eatontown, NJ 07724
800-526-2829; 908-542-1500
fax: 908-542-3957

Sys Technology, Inc.
10655 Humbolt St.
Los Alamitos, CA 90720
310-493-6888
fax: 310-493-2816

SYSTEK
5310 West 161st St., Ste. E
Brookpark, OH 44142
800-777-7077; 216-676-6511
fax: 216-676-6521

System Ave., Inc.
14946 Shoemaker Ave., Ste. N
Santa Fe Springs, CA 90670
310-926-9849
fax: 310-926-4472

Systems Integration Associates
222 E. Pearson, Ste. 502
Chicago, IL 60611
312-440-1275

Tadpole Technology, Inc.
8310 Capital of Texas Hwy., N, Ste. 375
Austin, TX 78731
512-338-4221

TALBOTT Corp.
6295 Harrison Dr.
Las Vegas, NV 89120
702-795-8815
fax: 702-795-0129

Computers

Tandem Computers, Inc.
19333 Vallco Pkwy., Location 4-40
Cupertino, CA 95014-2599
800-538-3107; 408-725-6000
fax: 408-285-0505
Technical support: Use main number

Tandon Corp.
301 Science Dr.
Moorpark, CA 93021
805-523-0340
fax: 805-529-4450
Technical support: 800-487-8324

Tandy Corp.
1800 One Tandy Center
Ft. Worth, TX 76102
817-390-3011
fax: 817-390-2774
Technical support: 817-390-3861

Tangent Computer, Inc.
197 Airport Blvd.
Burlingame, CA 94010
800-223-6677; 415-342-9388
fax: 415-342-9380
Technical support: Use toll-free number

Tartan Computers
44 W. Ferris St.
E. Brunswick, NJ 08816
908-390-1900
fax: 908-390-9380

Tatung Co. of America, Inc.
2850 El Presidio St.
Long Beach, CA 90810
800-827-2850; 310-979-7055
fax: 310-637-8484
Technical support: Use main number

Tech Data Corp.
5350 Tech Data Dr.
Clearwater, FL 34620
800-237-8931; 813-539-7429
fax: 813-530-0108

TECO Information Systems, Inc.
24 E. Harbor Dr.
Lake Zurich, IL 60047
708-438-3998
fax: 708-438-8061

Teconomics, Inc.
755 5th Ave., SW
Calgary, Alberta
Canada T2P 0N2
403-265-0707
fax: 403-265-1067

Telemart
8804 North 23rd Ave.
Phoenix, AZ 85021
800-426-6659; 602-944-0402
Technical support: Use toll-free number

TeleVideo Systems, Inc.
550 E. Brokaw Rd., P.O. Box 49048
San Jose, CA 95161-9048
800-835-3228; 408-954-8333
fax: 408-954-0623

Tenex Computer Express
56800 Magnetic Dr.
Mishawaka, IN 46545
800-776-6781; 219-259-7051
fax: 219-255-1778

Texas Instruments, Inc.
P.O. Box 655012, M/S 57
Dallas, TX 75265
800-527-3500; 214-995-2011
fax: 214-995-4360
Technical support: 512-250-7407

Texas Microsystems, Inc.
10618 Rockley Rd.
Houston, TX 77099
800-627-8700; 713-933-8050
fax: 713-933-1029
Technical support: Use main number

Thoroughbred Microsystems, Inc.
616 Bark Cove Dr.
Owensboro, KY 42303
502-926-3968
fax: 502-683-0101

3Com Corp.
P.O. Box 51845, 5400 Bayfront Plaza
Santa Clara, CA 95052-8145
800-638-3266; 408-764-5000
fax: 408-764-5032
Technical support: 800-876-3266

Top-Link Computer, Inc.
48810 Kato Rd.
Fremont, CA 94538
510-226-8600
fax: 510-623-7132

Topline Technologies, Inc.
330 E. Orangethorpe Ave.
Placentia, CA 92670
714-524-6900
fax: 714-572-3784

TOPPCs International, Inc.
648 N. Eckhoff
Orange, CA 92668
714-939-1416
fax: 714-939-0103

**Toshiba America Information Systems,
Inc. (Computer Systems Division)**
9740 Irvine Blvd.
Irvine, CA 92718
800-334-3445; 714-583-3000
Technical support: 800-999-4273

Touche MicroTechnologies
8205 S. Cass Ave.
Darien, IL 60559
708-810-1010
fax: 708-810-9490

Trans PC System, Inc.
11849 E. Firestone Blvd.
Norwalk, CA 90650
310-868-6930
fax: 310-864-2249

Transource Services Corp.
2033 W. North Lane #18
Phoenix, AZ 85021
800-235-8191; 602-997-8101

Treasure Chest
4668 Portrait Lane
Plano, TX 75024
800-245-3040; 214-233-2880

Triad Computing, Inc.
1711 Belmont Ave.
Youngstown, OH 44504
800-933-9223; 216-743-2922
fax: 216-743-2934

TriGem Corp.
2388 Walsh Ave., Bldg. B
Santa Clara, CA 95051
408-970-0844
fax: 408-970-0870

Tri-Star Computers
1520 W. Mineral Rd.
Tempe, AZ 85283
602-838-1222

Triton Technology Laboratory, Corp.
1804 Plaza Ave., Ste. 4
New Hyde Park, NY 11040
516-488-8852
fax: 516-488-8856

Tussey Computer Products, Inc.
P.O. Box 1006
State College, PA 16804
800-468-9044

TW Casper Corp.
47430 Seabridge Dr.
Fremont, CA 94538
510-770-8500
fax: 510-770-8509

Twinhead Corp.
1537 Centre Pointe Dr.
Milpitas, CA 95035
408-945-0808
fax: 408-945-1080

Ultra-Comp
11988 Dorsett Rd.
Maryland Heights, MO 63043
800-435-2266; 314-298-1998
fax: 314-991-0437
Technical support: Use main number

UNIQ Technology, Inc.
49090 Milmont Dr.
Fremont, CA 94538
800-878-3656; 510-226-9988
fax: 510-266-1188

Unisys Corp.
P.O. Box 500
Blue Bell, PA 19424-0001
215-542-4011
Technical support: 800-448-1424

United Electronics Systems, Inc.
601 N. Vermont Ave., Ste. 100
Los Angeles, CA 90004
213-669-1234
fax: 213-668-1234

Unitek Systems Corp.
7540 Quincy St., Ste. D
Willowbrook, IL 60521
708-323-3395
fax: 708-887-0448

Unitron, Inc.
736 Stimson Ave.
City of Industry, CA 91749
818-333-0280
fax: 818-968-1388

US Integrated Technologies (USIT)
3023 Research Dr.
Richmond, CA 94806
510-223-1001
fax: 510-223-2766

DIRECTORY OF MANUFACTURERS

U.S. Micro Engineering, Ltd.
P.O. Box 17728
Boulder, CO 80308
303-939-8700
fax: 303-939-8791

USA Flex
471 Brighton Dr.
Bloomingdale, IL 60108
800-876-5607; 708-351-7334
fax: 708-351-7204
Technical Support: 800-441-5416

UTI Computers
3640 Westchase Dr.
Houston, TX 77042
800-237-4961

U-tron, Inc.
47381 Bayside Pkwy.
Fremont, CA 94535
800-933-7775; 510-656-3600
fax: 510-656-7688

Vector Computer Research, Inc.
803 S. Adams
Fredericksburg, TX 78624
512-997-6001
Vector Computers Corp.
3901 E. Blanche St.
Pasadena, CA 91107
818-946-0879

Vektron International
1841 Wilderness Trail
Grand Prairie, TX 75052
214-606-0280
fax: 214-606-1278

Veridata Research, Inc.
11901 Goldring Rd., Ste. A&B
Arcadia, CA 91006
818-303-0613
fax: 818-303-0626

Vertex Advanced Research, Inc.
1111 Town and Country Rd., Ste. 50
Orange, CA 92668
800-521-4892; 714-835-1919
fax: 714-835-3238

VIP Computer, Inc.
2 Gourmet Lane
Edison, NJ 08837
908-494-2400
fax: 908-494-2411

VIPC Computers
384 Jackson, Ste. 1
Hayward, CA 94544
800-222-5657; 510-881-1772

VNS America Corp.
910 Boston Post Rd., Ste. 270
Marlboro, MA 01752
800-252-4212; 508-481-7192
fax: 508-481-2218

Wang Laboratories, Inc.
One Industrial Way, M/S 014-A1B
Lowell, MA 01851
800-835-9264; 508-459-5000
Technical support: 800-247-9264

Wedge Technology, Inc.
1587 McCandless Dr.
Milpitas, CA 95035
408-263-9888
fax: 408-263-9886

Wells American Corp.
3243 Sunset Blvd.
West Columbia, SC 29169
803-796-7800

West Coast Peripherals
48521 Warm Springs Blvd., Ste. 306
Fremont, CA 94539
510-226-1844
fax: 510-226-1848

Win Laboratories, Ltd.
11090 Industrial Rd.
Manassas, VA 22110
703-330-1426

WLT Systems, Inc.
800 Chelmsford St.
Lowell, MA 01851
800-272-9771; 508-656-8590
fax: 508-656-8540

WYSE Technology
3471 N. First St.
San Jose, CA 95134
800-438-9973; 408-473-1200
fax: 408-473-1222
Technical support: 408-922-5700

Xerox Corp. (U.S. Marketing Group)
P.O. Box 24
Rochester, NY 14692
800-832-6979

Xinetron, Inc.
2330B Walsh Ave.
Santa Clara, CA 95051
408-727-5509
fax: 408-727-6499

Xtek Electronics, Inc.
92 Argonaut, Ste. 160
Aliso Viejo, CA 92656
714-455-4660
fax: 714-455-4666

Xtron Computer Equipment Corp.
716 Jersey Ave.
Jersey City, NJ 07302
800-854-4450; 201-798-5000
fax: 201-798-4322

YKE International, Inc.
76-16 Jamaica Ave.
Woodhaven, NY 11421
718-296-0101
fax: 718-296-0070

Zenith Data Systems (ZDS)
2150 E. Lake Cook Rd.
Buffalo Grove, IL 60088
800-533-0331; 708-808-5000
Technical support: Use main number

Zeno Computer Products, Inc.
P.O. Box 3518
Ontario, CA 91761
714-923-4841
fax: 714-923-6519

Zeny Computer Systems
4033 Clipper Court
Fremont, CA 94538
510-659-0386
fax: 510-659-0468

Zeos International, Ltd.
530 5th Ave., NW
St. Paul, MN 55112
800-423-5891; 612-633-4591
fax: 612-633-1325
Technical support: Use toll-free number

Input Devices

Abaton
48431 Milmont Dr.
Fremont, CA 94538
800-444-5321; 510-683-2226
fax: 510-683-2870
Technical support: 510-498-4433

Acco International, Inc.
770 S. Acco Plaza
Wheeling, IL 60090-6070
800-222-6462; 708-541-9500
fax: 708-541-9638

Adaptec, Inc.
691 S. Milpitas Blvd.
Milpitas, CA 95035
408-945-8600
fax: 408-262-1845
Technical support: 408-945-2550

ADI Systems, Inc.
2121 Ringwood Ave.
San Jose, CA 95131
800-228-0530; 800-232-8282 (in California);
408-944-0100
fax: 408-944-0300

Adobe Systems, Inc.
1585 Charleston Rd., P.O. Box 7900
Mountain View, CA 94039-7900
800-922-3623; 415-961-4400
fax: 415-961-3769
Technical support: 415-961-4992

Advanced Digital Corp.
5432 Production Dr.
Huntington Beach, CA 92649
714-891-4004
fax: 714-893-1546

**Advanced Gravis Computer
Technology, Ltd.**
7033 Antrim Ave.
Burnaby, BC
Canada V5J 4M5
800-663-8558; 604-434-7274
fax: 604-434-7809

Aedex Corp.
1070 Ortega Way
Placentia, CA 92670
714-632-7000
fax: 714-632-1334

Alarmcard Co.
14700 N.E. Eight St., Ste. 205
Bellevue, WA 98007
800-635-9083; 206-747-0824
fax: 206-644-2190

Alloy Computer Products, Inc.
165 Forest St.
Marlborough, MA 01752
800-544-7551; 508-481-8500
fax: 508-481-7711

Input Devices

ALPS America
3553 N. First St.
San Jose, CA 95134
800-828-2577; 408-432-6000
fax: 408-432-6035
Technical support: 800-950-2577

AlteCon Data Communications, Inc.
1333 Strad Ave.
North Tonawanda, NY 14120
800-888-8511; 716-693-2121
fax: 716-693-9799

Altra
1200 Skyline Dr.
Laramie, WY 82070
800-726-6153; 307-745-7538
fax: 307-745-3627

AMAC South, Inc.
2055 S. Congress Ave.
Delray Beach, FL 33445
407-243-2405
fax: 407-243-2408

American Advantech Corp.
1310 Tully Rd., Ste. 115
San Jose, CA 95122
408-293-6786
fax: 408-293-4697

AMKLY Systems, Inc.
60 Technology Dr.
Irvine, CA 92718
800-367-2655; 714-727-0788

AMX Remote Control Systems
12056 Forestgate Dr.
Dallas, TX 75243
800-222-0193; 214-644-3048
fax: 214-907-2053

Anacom General Corp.
1335 S. Claudina St.
Anaheim, CA 92805-6235
714-774-8080
fax: 714-774-7388

Anakin Research, Inc.
100 Westmore Dr.
Rexdale, Ontario
Canada M9V 5C3
416-744-4246
fax: 416-744-4248

Analog Devices, Inc.
P.O. Box 9106, One Technology Way
Norwood, MA 02062-9106
617-329-4700
fax: 617-326-8703

Analog Technology Corp.
1859 Business Center Dr.
Duarte, CA 91010
818-357-0098
fax: 818-303-4993

Anchor Pad International, Inc.
4483 McGrath St., Ste. 3
Ventura, CA 93003
800-426-2467; 800-626-2467 (in California);
805-658-2661
fax: 805-658-6432

Antec Inc.
4555 Cushing Pkwy.
Fremont, CA 94538
510-770-1200

Apollo Audio Visual
60 Trade Zone Court
Ronkonkoma, NY 11779
800-777-3750; 516-467-8033
fax: 516-467-8996

Apple Computer, Inc.
20525 Mariani Ave.
Cupertino, CA 95014
408-996-1010
Technical support: 800-776-2333

Applied Computer Sciences, Inc.
11711 Northcreek Pkwy., S, Ste. 107
Bothell, WA 98011
800-525-5512; 206-486-2722
fax: 206-485-4766

Appoint
1332 Vendels Circle
Paso Robles, CA 93446
800-448-1184; 805-239-8976
fax: 805-239-8978
Technical support: Use main number

Arche Technologies, Inc.
48502 Kato Rd.
Fremont, CA 94538
800-437-1688; 510-623-8100
fax: 510-683-6754
Technical Support: 510-623-8162

Ark International, Inc.
1950 Ohio St.
Lisle, IL 60532
800-232-6221; 708-960-7463
fax: 708-960-7472

Arrick Computer Products/MicroSync, Inc.
1655 Hickory Dr., Ste. B
Haltom, TX 76017
800-543-0161; 817-831-7816
fax: 817-354-1034

ASP Computer Products, Inc.
1026 W. Maude Ave., Ste. 305
Sunnyvale, CA 94086
800-445-6190; 408-746-2965
fax: 408-746-2803
Technical support: Use main number

Asuka Technologies, Inc.
17145 Von Karman Ave., Ste. 110
Irvine, CA 92714
714-757-1212
fax: 714-757-1288

Aten Research, Inc.
340 Thor Place
Brea, CA 92621
714-255-0566
fax: 714-255-0275

Aura Systems
P.O. Box 4576
Carlsbad, CA 92008
800-365-AURA; 619-440-2304
fax: 619-447-8982

Avalon Design and Manufacturing, Inc.
130 McCormick Ave., Ste. 113
Costa Mesa, CA 92626
800-247-6166; 714-432-7227
fax: 714-432-7482

Aydin Controls
414 Commerce Dr.
Ft. Washington, PA 19034
800-347-4001; 215-542-7800
fax: 215-628-4372

Az-Tech Software, Inc.
305 E. Franklin
Richmond, MO 64085
800-227-0644; 816-776-2700
fax: 816-776-8398

Bay Technical Associates, Inc.
200 N. Second St., P.O. Box 387
Bay St. Louis, MS 39520
800-523-2702; 601-467-8231
fax: 601-467-4551

Behavior Tech Computer (USA) Corp.
46177 Warm Spring Blvd.
Fremont, CA 94539
510-657-3956
fax: 510-657-3965

Belkin Components
14550 S. Main St.
Gardena, CA 90248
800-223-5546; 310-515-7585
fax: 310-329-3236

Biopac Systems
275 S. Orange Ave., Ste. E
Goleta, CA 93117
805-967-6615
fax: 805-967-6043

Bitstream, Inc.
215 First St.
Cambridge, MA 02142
800-522-FONT; 617-497-6222
fax: 617-868-4732
Technical support: 617-497-7514

Black Box Corp.
P.O. Box 12800
Pittsburgh, PA 15241
412-746-5500
fax: 412-746-0746

Bondwell Industrial Co., Inc.
47485 Seabridge Dr.
Fremont, CA 94538
510-490-4300
fax: 510-490-5897
Technical support: 800-288-4388

Boxlight Corp.
19689 7th Ave., NE, Ste. 143
Poulsbo, WA 98370
800-762-5757; 206-697-4008
fax: 206-779-3299

Brady Office Machine Security, Inc.
11056 S. Bell Ave.
Chicago, IL 60643
312-779-8349

Brookrock Corp.
20 Shea Way, Ste. 201
Newark, DE 19713
800-345-0315; 302-292-6060
fax: 302-292-6072

Brown & Co., Inc.
P.O. Box 2443
South Hamilton, MA 01982
508-486-7464

Bubbl-tec
6800 Sierra Court
Dublin, CA 94568
510-829-8700
fax: 510-829-9796

DIRECTORY OF MANUFACTURERS

Buffalo Products, Inc.
2805 19th Ave., SE
Salem, OR 97302-1520
800-345-2356; 503-585-3414
fax: 503-585-4505

Burham Computer Center
908 E. Main St.
Alhambra, CA 91801
818-570-0396
fax: 818-570-0936

Burr-Brown Corp.
P.O. Box 11400
Tucson, AZ 85734
800-548-6132; 602-746-1111
fax: 602-741-3895

Bus Computer Systems
135 West 26th St.
New York, NY 10010
800-451-5289; 212-627-4485

ByteBrothers
3602 Lake Washington Blvd., N
Renton, WA 98056
206-271-9567

CalComp Plotter Products Group
P.O. Box 3250, 2411 W. La Palma Ave.
Anaheim, CA 92803
800-932-1212; 714-821-2000
fax: 714-821-2832
Technical support: Use main number

Camintonn Corp.
22 Morgan St.
Irvine, CA 92718-2022
800-843-8336; 714-454-6500
fax: 714-454-6599
Technical support: Use main number

Canon U.S.A., Inc.
One Canon Plaza
Lake Success, NY 11042
516-488-6700
fax: 516-354-5805
Technical support: 800-423-2366

Cardinal Technologies, Inc.
1827 Freedom Rd.
Lancaster, PA 17601
800-722-0094; 717-293-3000
fax: 717-293-3055
Technical support: 717-293-3124

Carroll Touch
P.O. Box 1309
Round Rock, TX 78680
512-244-3500
fax: 512-244-7040

CDCE, Inc.
2992 E. LaPalma, Ste. D
Anaheim, CA 92806
800-373-5353; 714-630-4633
fax: 714-630-5022

CH Products
970 Park Center Dr.
Vista, CA 92083
619-598-2518
fax: 619-598-2524

Chaplet Systems, Inc.
252 N. Wolf Rd.
Sunnyvale, CA 94086
408-732-7950
fax: 408-732-6050

The Cherry Corp.
3600 Sunset Ave.
Waukegan, IL 60087
708-662-9200
fax: 708-360-3566

Chicony America, Inc.
3002 Dow Ave., Ste. 122
Tustin, CA 92680
714-573-0456
fax: 714-573-0673
Technical support: 714-380-0928

Chisholm
910 Campisi Way
Cambell, CA 95008
800-888-4210; 408-559-1111
fax: 408-559-0444

CMS Enhancements, Inc.
2722 Michelson Dr.
Irvine, CA 92715
714-222-6000
fax: 714-549-4004
Technical support: 714-222-6058

Cole-Parmer Instrument Co.
7425 N. Oak Park Ave.
Chicago, IL 60648
800-323-4340; 708-647-7600
fax: 708-647-9660

Commax, Inc.
15 Shire Way
Middletown, NJ 07748
908-671-0775
fax: 908-671-0804

Communications Specialties, Inc.
89A Cabot Court
Hauppauge, NY 11788
516-273-0404
fax: 516-273-1638

CompuAdd Corp.
12303 Technology Blvd.
Austin, TX 78727
800-531-5475; 512-250-1489
fax: 512-250-5760
Technical support: 800-999-9901

ComputAbility Corp.
40000 Grand River, Ste. 109
Novi, MI 48375
800-433-8872; 313-477-6720

Computer Elektronik Infosys
of America, Inc.
512-A Herndon Pkwy.
Herndon, VA 22070
800-322-3464; 703-435-3800
fax: 703-435-5129

Computer Friends, Inc.
14250 N.W. Science Park Dr.
Portland, OR 97229
800-547-3303; 503-626-2291
fax: 503-643-5379
Technical support: Use main number

Computer Peripherals, Inc.
667 Rancho Conejo Blvd.
Newbury Park, CA 91320
800-854-7600; 805-499-5751
fax: 805-498-8848
Technical support: 800-235-7618

Computer Support Corp.
15926 Midway Rd.
Dallas, TX 75244
214-661-8960
fax: 214-661-5429

Computer System Associates, Inc.
7564 Trade St.
San Diego, CA 92121
619-566-3911
fax: 619-566-0581

ComputerVideo
215 Salem St., Ste. 5
Woburn, MA 01801
617-937-0888

Comspec Communications, Inc.
74 Wingold Ave.
Toronto, ON, CD M6B 1P5
416-785-3553
fax: 416-785-3668

Connect Computer Co., Inc.
9855 West 78th St., Ste. 270
Eden Prairie, MN 55344
612-944-0181
fax: 612-944-9298

Connecticut Microcomputer, Inc.
P.O. Box 186
Brookfield, CT 06804
800-426-2872; 203-354-9395
fax: 203-355-8258

CONNEXPERTS
8333 Douglas Ave., Ste. 700
Dallas, TX 75225
800-433-5373; 214-739-4200
fax: 214-696-3925

Consolink
600 S. Sunset
Longmont, CO 80501
303-651-2642
fax: 303-678-8360

Contek International Corp.
66 Field Crest Rd.
New Canaan, CT 06840
203-972-3406
fax: 203-972-0156

Covid, Inc.
2400 West 10th Place, Ste. 4
Tempe, AZ 85281
800-638-6104; 602-966-2221
fax: 602-966-6728

CPT Corp.
8100 Mitchell Rd.
Eden Prairie, MN 55344-9833
800-447-1189; 612-937-8000
fax: 612-937-1858

Creative Computer Products, Inc.
6369 Nancy Ridge Dr.
San Diego, CA 92121
800-231-5413; 800-523-5441 (in California);
619-458-1965
fax: 619-458-9024

CTI Electronics Corp.
200 Benton St.
Stratford, CT 06497
203-386-9779
fax: 203-378-4986

Input Devices

Cubix Corp.
2800 Lockheed Way
Carson City, NV 89706
800-829-0550; 702-883-7611
fax: 702-882-2407

Cumulus Corp.
23500 Mercantile Rd.
Cleveland, OH 44122
216-464-2211
fax: 216-464-2483

Curtis Manufacturing Co., Inc.
30 Fitzgerald Dr.
Jaffrey, NH 03452-1931
800-548-4900; 603-532-4123
fax: 603-532-4116

Cyber Research, Inc.
25 Business Park Dr.
Banford, CT 06405
800-341-2525; 203-483-8815
fax: 203-483-9024

Cybex Corp.
2800-H Bob Wallace Ave.
Huntsville, AL 35805
205-534-0011
fax: 205-534-0010

Daisy Data, Inc.
333 S. Enola Dr.
Enola, PA 17025-2897
717-732-8800
fax: 717-732-8806

Data General Corp.
4400 Computer Dr.
Westboro, MA 01580
800-328-2436; 508-366-8911
fax: 508-366-1299
Technical support: 800-537-6084

DataDesk International
9330 Eton Ave.
Chatsworth, CA 91311
800-328-2337; 818-998-4200
fax: 818-998-0330
Technical support: Use main number

Data-Doc Electronics, Inc.
4903 Commercial Park Dr.
Austin, TX 78724-2638
800-328-2362; 512-928-8926
fax: 512-928-8210

Dataflow Technologies, Inc.
1300 York Rd., Ste. 30
Lutherville, MD 21093
301-296-2630
fax: 301-321-6524

Datalux Corp.
2836 Cessna Dr.
Winchester, VA 22601
800-328-2589; 703-662-1500
fax: 703-662-1682

Dataworld
3733 San Gabriel River Pkwy.
Pico Rivera, CA 90660-1495
800-736-8080; 310-695-3777
fax: 310-695-7016
Technical support: 800-776-8088

Davis USA
540 N. La Salle St.
Chicago, IL 60610
312-751-7500
fax: 312-751-7448

Dell Computer Corp.
9505 Arboretum Blvd.
Austin, TX 78759-7299
800-426-5150; 512-338-4400
fax: 512-338-8421
Technical support: 800-624-9896

Delta Phase International
22262 Chestnut Lane
El Toro, CA 92630
714-768-6842
fax: 714-768-1417

Design Technology
1050-R Pioneer Way
El Cajon, CA 92020
619-440-7666
fax: 619-440-8048

Designs By Royo
320 H St.
Marysville, CA 95901
916-741-3937
fax: 916-743-0427

DFI, Inc.
2544 Port St.
West Sacramento, CA 95691
916-373-1234
fax: 916-373-0221

Dianachart, Inc.
101 Round Hill Dr.
Rockaway, NJ 07866
201-625-2299
fax: 201-625-2449

Dickerson Enterprises, Inc.
8101 N. Milwaukee Ave.
Niles, IL 60648
800-247-5419; 708-966-4884
fax: 708-966-0294

Digital Communications Associates, Inc. (DCA)
1000 Alderman Dr.
Alpharetta, GA 30201-4199
800-348-3221; 404-442-4000
fax: 404-442-4361
Technical support: 404-740-0300 (Micro Products)

Digital Equipment Corp.
146 Main St.
Maynard, MA 01754-2571
508-493-5111
fax: 508-493-8780
Technical support: 800-332-8000

Digital Products, Inc.
108 Water St.
Watertown, MA 02172
800-243-2333; 617-924-1680
fax: 617-924-7814

DP-Tek, Inc.
3031 W. Pawnee St.
Wichita, KS 67213
800-727-3130; 316-945-8600
fax: 316-945-8629

Dragoon Corp.
1270 Avenida Acaso, Unit F
Camarillo, CA 93010
805-987-4911
fax: 805-987-4358

Dresselhaus Computer Products
8560 Vineyard Ave., Ste. 405
Rancho Cucamonga, CA 91730
800-368-7737; 714-945-5600
fax: 714-989-2436

Dual Group, Inc.
P.O. Box 13944
Torrance, CA 90503
310-542-0788
fax: 310-214-0697

Dukane Corp.
2900 Dukane Dr.
St. Charles, IL 60174
708-584-2300
fax: 708-584-2370

Dunamis, Inc.
3620 Hwy. 317
Suwanee, GA 30174
800-828-2443; 404-932-0485
fax: 404-932-0486

Edimax Computer Co.
3350 Scott Blvd., Bldg. 9A
Santa Clara, CA 95054
408-496-1105
fax: 408-980-1530

Edmark Corp.
14350 Northeast 21st St.
Bellevue, WA 98007
800-426-0856; 206-746-3900
fax: 206-746-3962

Educational Systems, Inc.
3175 Commercial Ave.
Northbrook, IL 60062
800-333-0551; 708-498-3780
fax: 708-498-0185

Eiki International, Inc.
27882 Camino Capistrano
Laguna Niguel, CA 92677-8000
714-582-2511

Elesys, Inc.
528 Weddell Dr.
Sunnyvale, CA 94089
800-637-0500; 408-747-0233
fax: 408-747-0131

Eliashim Microcomputers, Inc.
520 W. Hwy. 436, Ste. 1180-30
Altamonte Springs, FL 32714
800-771-SAFE; 407-682-1587
fax: 407-869-1409
Technical support: Use main number

Elite Business Applications, Inc.
36-J Rt. 3, N, P.O. Box 593
Millersville, MD 21108
800-942-0018; 301-987-9050
fax: 301-987-9098
Technical support: Use main number

Elographics, Inc.
105 Randolph Rd.
Oak Ridge, TN 37830
615-482-4100
fax: 615-482-4943

EMAC
48431 Milmont Dr.
Fremont, CA 94538
800-821-0806; 510-683-2585
fax: 510-651-0728
Technical support: 510-498-4440

DIRECTORY OF MANUFACTURERS

Enigma Research, Inc.
15760 Ventura Blvd., Ste. 910
Encino, CA 91436
818-501-6698

EuroComm, Inc.
629 S. Rancho Santa Fe Rd., Ste. 394
San Marcos, CA 92069
619-471-9362, ext. 5
fax: 619-471-5054

Everex Systems, Inc.
48431 Milmont Dr.
Fremont, CA 94538
800-821-0806; 510-498-1111
fax: 510-651-0728
Technical support: 510-498-4411

Evergreen Systems
31336 Via Colinas, Dept. 3/336
Westlake Village, CA 91362
818-991-7835
fax: 818-991-4036

Excellink, Inc.
1430 Tully Rd., Ste. 415
San Jose, CA 95122
408-295-9000
fax: 408-295-9011

ExecRak, Inc.
115 Gun Ave.
Pointe Claire, Quebec
Canada H9R 3X2
514-697-8855
fax: 514-697-8763

EXP Computer, Inc.
568 45th St.
Bay Ridge, NY 11220
718-972-2799
fax: 718-854-4826

Extended Systems
P.O. Box 4937, 6123 N. Meeker Ave.
Boise, ID 83704
800-235-7576; 208-322-7575
fax: 208-377-1906

Extron Electronics
13554 Larwin Circle
Sante Fe Springs, CA 90670
800-633-9876; 310-802-8804
fax: 310-802-2741

EZ-Tek Industries
500 Hidden Valley Rd.
Grants Pass, OR 97527
503-474-2192
fax: 503-474-0787

Fifth Generation Systems, Inc.
10049 N. Reiger Rd.
Baton Rouge, LA 70809
800-873-4384; 504-291-7221
fax: 504-295-3268
Technical support: 504-291-7283

Fischer International Systems Corp.
P.O. Box 9107, 4073 Mercantile Ave.
Naples, FL 33942
800-237-4510; 800-331-2866 (in Florida);
813-643-1500
fax: 813-643-3772

Flytech Technology (U.S.A.), Inc.
3008 Scott Blvd.
Santa Clara, CA 95054
408-727-7373
fax: 408-727-7375

FMJ, Inc.
1954 Gladwick St.
Compton, CA 90220
800-322-3365; 310-632-9751
fax: 310-635-6407

Focus Electronic Corp.
9080 Telstar Ave., Ste. 304
El Monte, CA 91731
818-280-0416
fax: 818-280-4729

Forte Communications, Inc.
1050 E. Duane Ave., Ste. J
Sunnyvale, CA 94086
800-331-3903; 408-733-5100
fax: 408-733-5600

4G Data Systems, Inc.
96 Fulton St.
New York, NY 10038
212-233-4300
fax: 212-233-2627

Johnathon Freeman Technologies
P.O. Box 880114
San Francisco, CA 94118
800-288-4357; 415-822-8451
fax: 415-822-8611

FTG Data Systems
P.O. Box 615, 10801 Dale St., Ste. J-2
Stanton, CA 90680
800-962-3900; 714-995-3900
fax: 714-995-3989

Fujikama O.A. Distribution
150 Ormont Dr.
Weston, Ontario
Canada M9L 1N7
800-265-7761; 416-748-1668
fax: 416-748-0447

Fulcrum Computer Products
25084 Asti Rd.
Cloverdale, CA 95425
707-433-0202

FuncKey Enterprises
Rt. 1, Box 639G
Sanger, TX 76266
800-777-WORX; 817-482-6613

Galil Motion Control, Inc.
575 Maude Court
Sunnyvale, CA 94086
408-746-2300
fax: 408-746-2315

GEC-Marconi Software Systems
12110 Sunset Hills Rd., Ste. 450
Reston, VA 22090
703-648-1551
fax: 703-476-8035

Generation Systems
1185-C Bordeaux Dr.
Sunnyvale, CA 94089
800-325-5811; 408-734-2100
fax: 408-734-4626
Technical support: 800-323-9825

Genovation, Inc.
17741 Mitchell, N
Irvine, CA 92714
714-833-3355
fax: 714-833-0322

Gentek International, Inc.
305 Trapper Circle
Windsor, CT 06095
203-683-1160
fax: 203-683-2146

Glenco Engineering, Inc.
270 Lexington Dr.
Buffalo Grove, IL 60089
800-562-2543; 708-808-0300
fax: 708-808-0313

GRiD Systems Corp.
47211 Lakeview Blvd.
Fremont, CA 94537
800-222-4743

Grimes
115 S. Arovista Circle
Brea, CA 92621
714-671-3931
fax: 714-671-1426

Groundhog Graphics, Inc.
P.O. Box 325, 101 E. Mahoning St.
Punxsutawney, PA 15767
800-GRAPH-99; 814-938-8943
fax: 814-938-7035

GW Instruments
35 Medford St.
Somerville, MA 02143
617-625-4096
fax: 617-625-1322

HEI, Inc.
P.O. Box 5000, 1495 Steiger Lake Lane
Victoria, MN 55386
800-776-6688; 612-443-2500
fax: 612-443-2668

Hertz Computer Corp.
325 Fifth Ave.
New York, NY 10016
800-232-8737; 212-684-4141
fax: 212-684-3685

Hewlett-Packard Co.
3000 Hanover St.
Palo Alto, CA 94304
800-752-0900; 415-857-1501
Technical support: Use toll-free number

HMW Enterprises, Inc.
604 Salem Rd.
Etters, PA 17319
717-938-4691
fax: 717-938-4095

Honeywell, Inc. (Keyboard Division)
4171 N. Mesa, Bldg. D
El Paso, TX 79902
800-445-6939; 915-543-5503
fax: 915-543-5126

Hooleon Corp.
Page Springs Rd., P.O. Box 230
Cornville, AZ 86325
800-937-1337; 602-634-7515
fax: 602-634-4620

Hornet Technology U.S.A. Corp.
330 E. Orangethorpe Ave., Ste. D-E
Placentia, CA 92670
714-572-3781
fax: 714-572-3784

Input Devices

Houston Computer Services, Inc.
11331 Richmond Ave., Ste. 101
Houston, TX 77082
713-493-9900

IBM (International Business Machines)
Old Orchard Rd.
Armonk, NY 10504
800-426-2468; 914-765-1900
Technical support: Use toll-free number

ICD, Inc.
1220 Rock St.
Rockford, IL 61101-1437
815-968-2228
fax: 815-968-6888

Idea Courier/Servcom, Inc.
P.O. Box 29039
Phoenix, AZ 85038
800-528-1400; 602-894-7000

Identity Systems Technology, Inc.
1347 Exchange Dr.
Richardson, TX 75081
214-235-3330

Identix, Inc.
510 N. Pastoria Ave.
Sunnyvale, CA 94086
408-739-2000
fax: 408-739-3308

IMSI
1938 Fourth St.
San Rafael, CA 94901
800-833-4674; 415-454-7101
fax: 415-454-8901

In Focus Systems, Inc.
7770 S.W. Mohawk St.
Tualatin, OR 97062
800-327-7231; 503-692-4968
fax: 503-692-4476

In Touch Systems
11 Westview Rd.
Spring Valley, NY 10977
914-354-7431

Infogrip, Inc.
812 North Blvd.
Baton Rouge, LA 70802
504-336-0033
fax: 504-336-0063

Information Strategies, Inc.
888 S. Greenville Ave., Ste. 121
Richardson, TX 75081
214-234-0176

Inmac Corp.
P.O. Box 58031, 2465 Augustine Dr.
Santa Clara, CA 95054
800-547-5444; 408-727-1970
Technical support: 800-446-6224

Intel Corp. (Personal Computer Enhancement Operation)
5200 N.E. Elam Young Pkwy., M/S CO3-07
Hillsboro, OR 97124
503-696-8080
Technical support: 503-629-7000

Intellicom
20415 Nordhoff St.
Chatsworth, CA 91311
800-992-2882; 818-407-3900
fax: 818-882-2404
Technical support: Use main number

Interaction Systems, Inc.
86 Coolidge Ave.
Watertown, MA 02172
617-923-6001
fax: 617-923-2112

Intercon Associates, Inc.
1850 Winton Rd., S, 1 Cambridge Place
Rochester, NY 14618
800-422-3880; 716-244-1250
fax: 716-473-4387

International Data Acquisition & Control, Inc.
The Meeting Place, P.O. Box 397
Amherst, NH 03031
603-673-0765
fax: 603-673-0767

International Machine Control Systems (IMCS)
1332 Vendels Circle
Paso Robles, CA 93446
800-448-1184; 805-239-8976 (in California)

Intertech Marketing, Inc.
8820 Six Forks Rd., NCNB Bank Bldg.,
Ste. 100
Raleigh, NC 27615
800-762-7874; 919-870-8404
fax: 919-870-8343

Iocomm International Technology Corp.
12700 Yukon Ave.
Hawthorne, CA 90250
310-644-6100
fax: 310-644-6068

IOLINE Corp.
12020-113th Ave., NE
Kirkland, WA 98034
206-821-2140
fax: 206-823-8898

IOtech, Inc.
25971 Cannon Rd.
Cleveland, OH 44146
216-439-4091
fax: 216-439-4093

IQ Engineering
685 N. Pastoria
Sunnyvale, CA 94086
800-765-3668; 408-733-1161
fax: 408-733-2585
Technical support: Use toll-free number

ITAC Systems, Inc.
3121 Benton St.
Garland, TX 75042
800-533-4822; 214-494-3073
fax: 214-494-4159

Jasco Products Co., Inc.
P.O. Box 466
Oklahoma City, OK 73101
800-654-8483; 405-752-0710
fax: 405-752-1537

JLCooper Electronics
13478 Beach Ave.
Marina del Rey, CA 90292
213-306-4131
fax: 213-822-2252

Don Johnston Developmental Equipment, Inc.
P.O. Box 639, 1000 N. Rand Rd., Bldg. 115
Wauconda, IL 60084-0639
800-999-4660; 708-526-2682
fax: 708-526-4177

JOYCE Associates
215 Franklin St.
Clayton, NJ 08312

K & C Technologies, Inc.
5075 Moorpark Ave.
San Jose, CA 95129
408-257-1445
fax: 408-259-2490

K. S. Brotherbox (U.S.A.) Co.
14140 Live Oak Ave., Unit D
Baldwin Park, CA 91706
818-814-0516
fax: 818-814-0323

Kansai International, Inc.
2005 Hamilton Ave., Ste. 220
San Jose, CA 95125
800-733-3374; 408-377-7062
fax: 408-782-8559

KDS Corp.
934 Cornell St.
Wilmette, IL 60091
708-251-2621
fax: 708-251-6489

KEA Systems, Ltd.
3738 N. Fraser Way, Unit 101
Burnaby, BC
Canada V5J 5G1
800-663-8702; 604-431-0727
fax: 604-431-0818

Keithley Instruments, Inc.
(Instruments Division)
28775 Aurora Rd.
Cleveland, OH 44139
800-552-1115; 216-248-0400
fax: 216-248-6168

Kennect Technology
120-A Albright Way
Los Gatos, CA 95030
800-552-1232; 408-370-2866
fax: 408-370-0484

Kensington Microware, Ltd.
2855 Campus Dr.
San Mateo, CA 94403
800-535-4242; 415-572-2700
fax: 415-572-9675
Technical support: Use main number

Key Concepts, Inc.
316 S. Eddy St.
South Bend, IN 46617
800-526-6753; 219-234-4207
fax: 219-234-6414

Key-Tech
7315 Lahser
Birmingham, MI 48010
800-383-1210; 313-644-4993
fax: 313-644-5901

Key Tronic Corp.
P.O. Box 14687
Spokane, WA 99214
800-262-6006; 509-928-8000
fax: 509-927-5216
Technical support: Use toll-free number

Keytime
3147 Fairview, E, Ste. 200
Seattle, WA 98102
206-324-7219
fax: 206-323-6494

DIRECTORY OF MANUFACTURERS

Kingston Technology Corp.
17600 Newhope St.
Fountain Valley, CA 92708
800-835-2545; 714-435-2600
fax: 714-435-2699
Technical support: Use main number

Koala Acquisitions, Inc.
70 North 2nd St.
San Jose, CA 95113
408-287-6278
fax: 408-971-2494

Kofax Image Products, Inc.
3 Jenner St.
Irvine, CA 92718
714-727-1733
fax: 714-727-3144

Kraft Systems, Inc.
450 W. California Ave.
Vista, CA 92083
619-724-7146
fax: 619-941-1770
Technical support: Use main number

Kurta Corp.
3007 E. Chambers St.
Phoenix, AZ 85040
800-445-8782; 602-276-5533
fax: 602-276-7823

KYE International, Inc.
2605 E. Cedar St.
Ontario, CA 91761
800-456-7593; 714-923-3510
fax: 714-923-1469

Lama Systems, Inc.
2100 Kramer Lane
Austin, TX 78758
512-835-0888

Laser Storage & Graphics Co.
644 Forest Ridge Dr.
Marietta, GA 30067
404-973-3860

LaserGo, Inc.
9369 Carroll Park Dr., Ste. A
San Diego, CA 92121
619-450-4600
fax: 619-450-9334

Lasergraphics
20 Ada
Irvine, CA 92718
714-727-2651
fax: 714-727-2653

LaserPlex Corp.
304 S. Abbott Ave.
Milpitas, CA 95035
408-946-2298
fax: 408-946-0232

LaserTools Corp.
1250 45th St., Ste. 100
Emeryville, CA 94608-2907
800-767-8004; 510-420-8777
fax: 510-420-1150
Technical support: 800-767-8005

Lightek
11000 Three Chopt Rd., Ste. B
Richmond, VA 23233
804-270-4291

Lite-On, Inc.
720 S. Hillview Dr.
Milpitas, CA 95035
408-946-4873
fax: 408-942-1527

Liuski International
10 Hub Dr.
Melville, NY 11747
516-454-8220

The Lock Box
22546 Summit Rd.
Los Gatos, CA 95030
408-685-1000
fax: 408-353-1007

Logitech, Inc.
6505 Kaiser Dr.
Fremont, CA 94555
800-999-9846; 510-795-8500
fax: 510-792-8901
Technical support: 510-795-8100

Lucas Deeco Corp.
31047 Genstar Rd.
Hayward, CA 94544
510-471-4700
fax: 510-489-3500

Lynx Computer Products
120 Linden Ave.
Long Beach, CA 90802
800-321-LYNX; 310-590-9990
fax: 310-495-1258

The Lyra Group
P.O. Box 4297
Brick, NJ 08723
908-920-9667

MacSema
29383 Lamb Dr.
Albany, OR 97321
800-344-7228; 503-757-1520
fax: 503-754-7189

Mandrill Corp.
P.O. Box 33848
San Antonio, TX 78265
800-531-5314; 512-341-6155

Marconi Circuit Technology Corp.
160 Smith St.
Farmingdale, NY 11735
516-293-8636
fax: 516-293-0061

Mark of the Unicorn, Inc.
222 Third St.
Cambridge, MA 02142
617-576-2760

Market Central, Inc.
600 N. Main St.
Houston, PA 15342-1615
412-746-6000

Marstek
17795-F Skypark Circle
Irvine, CA 92714
800-366-4620; 714-833-7740
fax: 714-833-7813
Technical support: Use main number

Maxi Switch Inc.
2901 E. Elvira Rd.
Tucson, AZ 85706
602-294-5450
fax: 602-294-6890

Merak Industries
8704 Edna St.
Warren, MI 48093
800-231-4310 ext. 768; 313-562-9768

Meridian Data, Inc.
5615 Scotts Valley Dr.
Scotts Valley, CA 95066
408-438-3100
fax: 408-438-6816
Technical support: 800-755-TECH

Merlan Scientific, Ltd.
247 Armstrong Ave.
Georgetown, ON, CD L7G 4X6
800-387-2474; 416-877-0171
fax: 416-877-0929

Mextel, Inc.
159 Beeline Dr.
Bensenville, IL 60106
800-888-4146; 708-595-4146
fax: 708-595-4149

Micro Security Systems, Inc.
4750 Wiley Post Way, Ste. 180
Salt Lake City, UT 84116
800-456-2587; 801-575-6600
fax: 801-575-6621

MicroComputer Accessories, Inc.
5405 Jandy Place, P.O. Box 66911
Los Angeles, CA 90066-0911
800-521-8270; 213-301-9400
fax: 213-306-8379

Micron Technology, Inc.
2805 E. Columbia Rd.
Boise, ID 83706-9698
800-642-7661; 208-368-4000
fax: 208-368-4558
Technical support: 208-368-3900

Microsafe Products Co.
P.O. Box 2393
Kirkland, WA 98083-2393
206-881-6390

Microsoft Corp.
One Microsoft Way
Redmond, WA 98052-6399
800-426-9400; 206-882-8080
fax: 206-883-8101
Technical support: 206-454-2030

MicroSpeed
44000 Old Warm Springs Blvd.
Fremont, CA 94538
800-232-7888; 510-490-1403
fax: 510-490-1665
Technical support: Use main number

MicroTouch Systems, Inc.
55 Jonspin Rd.
Wilmington, MA 01887
508-694-9900
fax: 508-694-9980

Minatronics Corp.
3046 Penn Ave.
Pittsburgh, PA 15201
412-281-5050

Mitchell Pacific
10303 Jasper Ave., Ste. 1050
Edmonton, Alberta
Canada T5J 3N6
403-425-0100
fax: 403-420-0900

Input Devices

Mitsumi Electronics Corp., Inc.
35 Pinelawn Rd.
Melville, NY 11747
516-752-7730
fax: 516-752-7490

Mobius Technologies, Inc.
5835 Doyle St.
Emeryville, CA 94608
800-669-0556; 510-654-0556
fax: 510-654-2834

Modular Instruments, Inc.
81 Great Valley Pkwy.,
Great Valley Corp. Center
Malvern, PA 19355
215-640-9292
fax: 215-644-0190

Monterey Electronics, Inc.
2355 Paragon Dr., Ste. B
San Jose, CA 95131
408-437-5496

Mouse Systems Corp.
47505 Seabridge Dr.
Fremont, CA 94538
510-656-1117
fax: 510-770-1924

Msound International, LP
550 Kirkland Way, Ste. 100
Kirkland, WA 98033
800-366-1794; 206-828-8182
fax: 206-828-2149

Multi-Pal International, Inc.
17231 E. Railroad St., Ste. 500
City of Industry, CA 91748
818-913-4188
fax: 818-912-9149

National Semiconductor Corp.
(Quadram Products Group)
219 Perimeter Center Pkwy.
Atlanta, GA 30346
404-551-1000

NEFF Instrument Corp.
700 S. Myrtle Ave.
Monrovia, CA 91016
800-423-7151; 818-357-2281
fax: 818-303-2286

Neotec International
20468 Carrey Rd.
Walnut, CA 91789
909-595-0509
fax: 909-594-1968

Netcor/Giltronix, Inc.
850 Auburn Court
Fremont, CA 94538
800-531-1300; 510-623-3700
fax: 510-623-3717

Network Technologies, Inc.
7322 Pettibone Rd.
Chagrin Falls, OH 44022
800-742-8324; 216-543-1646
fax: 216-543-5423

NewCo Technology, Inc.
3243 Sunset Blvd.
West Columbia, SC 29169
800-662-9005; 803-794-4300
fax: 803-794-0810

NMB Technologies, Inc.
9730 Independence Ave.
Chatsworth, CA 91311
800-321-3536; 818-341-3355
fax: 818-341-8207

Northgate Computer Systems, Inc.
P.O. Box 59080
Minneapolis, MN 55459-0080
800-548-1993; 612-943-8181
fax: 612-943-8336
Technical support: 800-446-5037

Numonics Corp.
101 Commerce Dr.
Montgomeryville, PA 18936
800-247-4517; 215-362-2766; 215-361-0167

Nutmeg Systems, Inc.
25 South Ave.
New Canaan, CT 06840
800-777-8439; 203-966-7972

NVIEW Corp.
11835 Canon Blvd.
Newport News, VA 23606
800-736-8439; 804-873-1354
fax: 804-873-2153

Office Automation Systems, Inc.
9940 Barnes Canyon Rd.
San Diego, CA 92121
619-452-9400
fax: 619-452-2427

OIS Optical Imaging Systems, Inc.
1896 Barrett St.
Troy, MI 48084
313-362-2738
fax: 313-362-4866

OMNIfax
8700 Bellanca Ave.
Los Angeles, CA 90045
800-221-8330; 213-641-3690
fax: 213-670-8578

OpCode Systems
3641 Haven Dr., Ste. A
Menlo Park, CA 94025-1010
415-369-8131
fax: 415-369-1747
Technical support: 415-369-1676

Orange Micro, Inc.
1400 N. Lakeview Ave.
Anaheim, CA 92807
800-223-8029; 714-779-2772
fax: 714-779-9332

Our Business Machines, Inc.
12901 Ramona Blvd., Unit J
Irwindale, CA 91706
800-443-1435; 818-337-9614
fax: 818-960-1766

Pacific Data Products, Inc.
9125 Rehco Rd.
San Diego, CA 92121
619-552-0880
fax: 619-552-0889
Technical support: 619-587-4690

Pacific Rim Data Sciences
47307 Rancho Higuera Dr.
Fremont, CA 94539
510-651-7935
fax: 510-226-9691

PACKinTELL Electronics USA
11369 Sunrise Gold Circle
Rancho Cordova, CA 95742
800-447-2515; 916-635-2784
fax: 916-635-4836

PAMCO Electronics
377 Carowinds Blvd., Ste. 121
Fort Mill, SC 29715
800-255-6265; 803-548-6740
fax: 803-548-3419

PC Craft, Inc.
640 Puente St.
Brea, CA 92621
800-733-6666; 714-256-5000
fax: 714-256-5025

PC Guardian
118 Alto St.
San Rafael, CA 94901
800-288-8126; 415-459-0190
fax: 415-459-1162

PC Horizons, Inc.
1710-M Newport Circle
Santa Ana, CA 92705
714-953-5396

PC House
841 E. Artesia Blvd.
Carson, CA 90746
310-324-8621
fax: 310-324-8654

PC Power & Cooling, Inc.
31510 Mountain Way
Bonsall, CA 92003
800-722-6555; 619-723-9513
fax: 619-723-0075
Technical support: Use main number

The Pendulum Group, Inc.
333 W. Hampden Ave., Ste. 1015
Englewood, CO 80110
800-772-6483; 303-781-0575
fax: 303-761-2440

Penny & Giles Controls, Inc.
163 Pleasant St., Ste. 4
Attleboro, MA 02703
508-226-3008
fax: 508-226-5208

Personal Computer Card Corp.
5015 S. Florida Ave.
Lakeland, FL 33813
800-336-6644; 813-644-5026
fax: 813-644-1933
Technical support: Use main number

Personal Computer Products, Inc. (PCPI)
10865 Rancho Bernardo Rd.
San Diego, CA 92127
800-225-4098; 800-262-0522 (in California);
619-485-8411
fax: 619-487-5809

Personal Writer, Inc.
1900 Avenue of the Stars, Ste. 2870
Los Angeles, CA 90067
800-322-4744; 213-556-1001
fax: 213-556-1164

Pointer Systems, Inc.
1 Mill St.
Burlington, VT 05401
800-537-1562; 802-658-3260
fax: 802-658-3714

DIRECTORY OF MANUFACTURERS

Polytel Computer Products Corp.
1287 Hammerwood Ave.
Sunnyvale, CA 94089
800-245-6655; 408-745-1540
fax: 408-745-6340

Power Source Computer Systems, Inc.
10020 San Pablo Ave.
El Cerrito, CA 94530
510-527-6908
fax: 510-527-3823

Practical Peripherals, Inc.
31245 La Baya Dr.
Westlake Village, CA 91362
800-442-4774; 818-706-0333
fax: 818-706-2474
Technical support: Use main number

Practical Solutions
1135 Jones Blvd.
Tucson, AZ 85716
602-322-6100
fax: 602-322-9271

Preh Electronics Industries, Inc.
470 E. Main St.
Lake Zurich, IL 60047-2578
708-438-4000
fax: 708-438-5522

Premier Computer Innovations
10310 Harwin Dr.
Houston, TX 77036
800-347-1777; 713-995-4433
fax: 713-995-4751

Presentation Electronics, Inc.
4320 Anthony Court, Ste. 8
Rocklin, CA 95677
800-888-9281; 916-652-9281
fax: 916-652-9286

Primax Electronics (USA), Inc.
2531 West 237th St., Ste. 102
Torrance, CA 90505
310-326-8018
fax: 310-326-7504
Technical support: 800-338-3693;
408-379-6482

The Printer Works
3481 Arden Rd.
Hayward, CA 94545
800-235-6116; 510-887-6116
fax: 510-786-0589

ProCorp
10 Hub Dr.
Melville, NY 11747
516-454-8220
fax: 516-454-8266

ProHance Technologies, Inc.
1558 Siesta Dr.
Los Altos, CA 94022
415-967-5679

ProTech Marketing, Inc.
9600 J Southern Pines Blvd.
Charlotte, NC 28217
800-843-0413; 704-523-9500
fax: 704-523-7651

Proxima Corp.
6610 Nancy Ridge Dr.
San Diego, CA 92121-9639
800-582-2580; 800-582-0852 (in California);
619-457-5500
fax: 619-457-9647
Technical support: Use main number

QMS, Inc.
P.O. Box 81250
Mobile, AL 36689
800-631-2692; 205-633-4300
fax: 205-633-0013
Technical support: 205-633-4500

Qualitas Trading Co.
6907 Norfolk Rd.
Berkeley, CA 94705
510-848-8080
fax: 510-848-8009

Quality Computer Products, Inc.
2288 Tripaldi Way
Hayward, CA 94545
510-785-4225
fax: 510-786-2356

Qualtec Data Products, Inc.
47767 Warm Springs Blvd.
Fremont, CA 94539
800-628-4413; 510-490-8911
fax: 510-490-8471

QuaTech, Inc.
662 Wolf Ledges Pkwy.
Akron, OH 44311
800-553-1170; 216-434-3154
fax: 216-434-1409

Questar Technologies, Inc.
500 Alden Rd., Ste. 212A
Markham, Ontario
Canada L3R 5H5
416-477-1918
fax: 416-477-1143

Qumax Corp.
2380 Qume, Ste. D
San Jose, CA 95131
408-954-8040
fax: 408-954-8043

Radius, Inc.
1710 Fortune Dr.
San Jose, CA 95131
800-227-2795; 408-434-1010
fax: 408-434-0770
Technical support: 408-434-1012

Radix II, Inc.
(Sophos Integrated Systems Division)
6230 Oxon Hill Rd.
Oxon Hill, MD 20745
800-334-SISI; 301-567-5200
fax: 301-839-0836

Rainbow Technologies, Inc.
9292 Jeronimo Rd.
Irvine, CA 92718
800-852-8569; 714-454-2100
fax: 714-454-8557

Rapid Systems
433 North 34th St.
Seattle, WA 98103
206-547-8311
fax: 206-548-0322

Reactive Systems, Inc.
222 Cedar Lane
Teaneck, NJ 07666
201-907-0100
fax: 201-907-0270

Recortec, Inc.
1290 Lawrence Station Rd.
Sunnyvale, CA 94089
800-729-7654; 408-734-1290
fax: 408-734-2140

Reflection Technology
240 Bear Hill Rd.
Waltham, MA 02154
617-890-5905
fax: 617-890-5918

Reliable Communications, Inc.
20111 Stevens Creek Blvd.
Cupertino, CA 95014
800-222-0042; 408-996-0230
fax: 408-996-3367

Remote Measurement Systems, Inc.
2633 Eastlake Ave., E, Ste. 200
Seattle, WA 98102
206-328-2255
fax: 206-328-1787

Renton Products
P.O. Box 16271
Seattle, WA 98116
206-682-7341
fax: 206-624-5610

George Risk Industries, Inc.
802 S. Elm St., GRI Plaza
Kimball, NE 69145
800-445-5218; 308-235-4645

Roland Digital Group
1961 McGaw Ave.
Irvine, CA 92714
714-975-0560
fax: 714-975-0569

Rose Electronics
P.O. Box 742571
Houston, TX 77274
800-333-9343; 713-933-7673
fax: 713-933-0044
Technical support: Use main number

SAI Systems Laboratories, Inc.
911 Bridgeport Ave.
Shelton, CT 06484
800-331-0488; 203-929-0790
fax: 203-929-6948

Sam Systems, Inc.
P.O. Box 2339
Hammond, IN 46323
219-844-2327

Sarasota Technologies, Inc.
2215 Stickney Point Rd.
Sarasota, FL 34231
813-923-9504

Sayett Technology, Inc.
100 Kings Hwy., Ste. 1800
Rochester, NY 14617
800-836-7730; 716-342-0700
fax: 716-342-1621

Seasoned Systems, Inc.
P.O. Box 3720
Chapel Hill, NC 27515-3720
800-334-5531; 919-732-9391
fax: 919-732-9392

Second Wave, Inc.
9430 Research Blvd., Echelon II, Ste. 260
Austin, TX 78759
512-343-9661
fax: 512-343-9663

Input Devices

Sector Technology, Inc.
5109 Leesburg Pike, 6 Skyline Place,
Ste. 900
Falls Church, VA 22041-3201
703-379-1800
fax: 703-845-0323

Secure-It, Inc.
18 Maple Court
East Longmeadow, MA 01028
800-451-7592; 413-525-7039

Security Microsystems, Inc.
215 Cromwell Ave.
Staten Island, NY 10305
800-345-7390; 718-667-1019
fax: 718-667-0131

Se-Kure Controls, Inc.
5685 N. Lincoln Ave.
Chicago, IL 60659
800-322-2435; 312-728-2435
fax: 312-728-6464

Selectech, Ltd.
30 Mountain View
Colchester, VT 05446
802-655-9600
fax: 802-655-5149

Sentient Systems Technology
5001 Baum Blvd.
Pittsburgh, PA 15213
412-682-0144

Server Technology, Inc.
2332 A Walsh Ave.
Santa Clara, CA 95051
800-835-1515; 408-738-8377
fax: 408-738-0247

Sharp Electronics Corp.
(Professional Products Division)
Sharp Plaza, P.O. Box 650
Mahwah, NJ 07430
201-529-8200
fax: 201-529-9636
Technical support: 800-732-8221

Simgraphics Engineering Corp.
1137 Huntington Dr.
South Pasadena, CA 91037
213-255-0900
fax: 213-255-0987

Singular Solutions
959 E. Colorado Blvd.
Pasadena, CA 91106
818-792-9567
fax: 818-792-0903

SmarTEAM, Inc.
19205 Parthenia St., #J
Northridge, CA 91324
800-233-7327; 818-886-9726

Software Security, Inc.
1011 High Ridge Rd.
Stamford, CT 06905
800-333-0407; 203-329-8870
fax: 203-329-7428

Softworks Development Corp.
5985 N. Lilly Rd.
Menomonee Falls, WI 53051
800-332-3475; 414-252-2020

Sophisticated Circuits, Inc.
19017 120th Ave., NE, Ste. 106
Bothell, WA 98011
206-485-7979

Spark International, Inc.
1939 Waukegan Rd., Ste. 107
Glenview, IL 60025
708-998-6640
fax: 708-998-8840

Spatial Systems, Inc.
900 Middlesex Tpke., Bldg. 8
Billerica, MA 01821
508-670-2720

Spies Laboratories
4040 Spencer St., Bldg. Q
Torrance, CA 90503
800-255-9433; 800-992-9433 (in California);
310-214-2345
fax: 310-214-0751

Staff Computer Technology Corp.
440 San Lucas Dr.
Solana Beach, CA 92075
619-259-1313

Starion Corp.
3002 Dow Ave., Ste. 226
Tustin, CA 92680
800-828-9098; 714-573-0626
fax: 714-573-0695

Suncom Technologies
6400 Gross Point Rd.
Niles, IL 60648
708-647-4040
fax: 708-459-8095

Sunland Micro Systems
11 Musick, Fairbanks Business Park
Irvine, CA 92718
714-380-1958
fax: 714-380-0918

Support Systems International Corp.
150 S. Second St.
Richmond, CA 94804
800-777-6269; 510-234-9090
fax: 510-233-8888

Swan Technologies
3075 Research Dr.
State College, PA 16801
800-468-9044; 814-238-1820
fax: 814-237-4450
Technical support: 800-468-7926

Syncomp International Corp.
1400 W. Lambert Rd., Ste. D
Brea, CA 92621
213-690-1011
fax: 213-690-6380

System General Corp.
244 S. Hillview Dr.
Milpitas, CA 95035
408-263-6667
fax: 408-262-9220

Tall Tree Systems
P.O. Box 50690, 2585 E. Bayshore Rd.
Palo Alto, CA 94303
415-493-1980
fax: 415-493-7639

Talton/Louley Engineering
9550 Ridge Haven Court
San Diego, CA 92123
619-565-6656

Tandy Corp.
1800 One Tandy Center
Ft. Worth, TX 76102
817-390-3011
fax: 817-390-2774
Technical support: 817-390-3861

Tash, Inc.
70 Gibson Dr., Unit 12
Markham, Ontario
Canada L3R 4C2
416-475-2212
fax: 416-475-2422

TeleSensory Systems, Inc.
P.O. Box 7455, 455 N. Bernardo Ave.
Mountain View, CA 94039-7455
800-227-8418; 415-960-0920
fax: 415-969-9064

Telex Communications, Inc.
9600 Aldrich Ave., S
Minneapolis, MN 55420
800-828-6107; 612-884-4051
fax: 612-884-0043

Texas Instruments, Inc.
P.O. Box 655012, M/S 57
Dallas, TX 75265
800-527-3500; 214-995-2011
fax: 214-995-4360
Technical support: 512-250-7407

ThumbScan, Inc.
1919 S. Highland Ave., Ste. 118C
Lombard, IL 60148
708-932-8844
fax: 708-495-0279

Thunderware, Inc.
21 Orinda Way
Orinda, CA 94563
510-254-6581
fax: 510-254-3047

Toshiba America Information Systems, Inc.
9740 Irvine Blvd.
Irvine, CA 92718
800-334-3445; 714-583-3000
Technical support: 800-999-4273

Total Technologies, Ltd.
2110 S. Anne St.
Santa Ana, CA 92704
800-669-4885; 714-241-0406
fax: 714-557-5838

Touchstone Technology, Inc.
955 Buffalo Rd.
Rochester, NY 14624
800-828-6968; 716-235-8358
fax: 716-235-8345

Transcend Information, Inc.
9159 La Rosa Dr.
Temple City, CA 91780
818-287-7892
fax: 818-287-5782

Transfinite Systems Co., Inc.
P.O. Box N, MIT Branch P.O.
Cambridge, MA 02139
617-969-9570

Trantor Systems, Ltd.
5415 Randall Place
Fremont, CA 94538
510-770-1400
fax: 510-770-9910

DIRECTORY OF MANUFACTURERS

Trend Micro Devices, Inc.
2421 West 205th St., Ste. D-100
Torrance, CA 90501
800-228-5651; 310-782-8190
fax: 310-328-5892
Technical support: Use main number

Trimarchi, Inc.
P.O. Box 560
State College, PA 16804
800-356-6638; 814-353-9120
fax: 814-353-9132
Technical support: Use main number

T. S. MicroTech, Inc.
12565 Crenshaw Blvd.
Hawthorne, CA 90250
800-356-5906; 310-644-0859
fax: 310-644-0567

T&t Research
44 George St.
Etobicoke, Ontario
Canada M8V 2S2
416-252-4789

UCI Corp.
948 Cherry St.
Kent, OH 44240
216-673-5155
fax: 216-673-1811

UDP Data Products, Inc.
2908 Oregon Court, Unit I2
Torrance, CA 90503
800-888-4413; 310-782-9800
fax: 310-782-1577

Ultima Electronics Corp.
1156 Aster Ave., Ste. A
Sunnyvale, CA 94086
408-246-9208
fax: 408-246-9207

Unisys Corp.
P.O. Box 500
Blue Bell, PA 19424-0001
215-542-4011
Technical support: 800-448-1424

Unit Technology America
15237 Texaco Ave.
Paramount, CA 90723
310-602-2392
fax: 310-602-2497

Universal Vectors Corp.
580 Herndon Pkwy., Ste. 400
Herndon, VA 22070
703-435-2500
fax: 703-435-9638

Vatell Corp.
P.O. Box 66
Christiansburg, VA 24073
703-961-2001

Vernier Software
2920 Southwest 89th St.
Portland, OR 97225
503-297-5317
fax: 503-297-1760

Versa Computing, Inc.
7260 West 90th St.
Westchester, CA 90045
213-338-0065

Vertex Industries, Inc.
23 Carol St., P.O. Box 996
Clifton, NJ 07014-0996
201-777-3500
fax: 201-472-0814

Visualon, Inc.
9000 Sweet Valley Dr.
Cleveland, OH 44125
216-328-9000
fax: 216-328-9099

Wang Laboratories, Inc.
One Industrial Way, M/S 014-A1B
Lowell, MA 01851
800-835-9264; 508-459-5000
Technical support: 800-247-9264

Warp Speed Light Pens, Inc.
1086 Mechem Dr.
Ruidoso, NM 88345
800-874-4315; 505-258-5713
fax: 505-258-5744

Wen Technology Corp.
11 Clearbrook Rd.
Elmsford, NY 10523
800-377-4WEN; 914-347-4100
fax: 914-347-4128

Wespercorp
17032 Murphy
Irvine, CA 92714
800-854-8737; 714-261-0606
fax: 714-261-0894

Western Telematic, Inc.
5 Sterling
Irvine, CA 92718
800-854-7226; 714-586-9950
fax: 714-583-9514

Wink Data
720 132nd St., SW, Ste. 202
Everett, WA 98204
800-624-2101; 206-742-4145
fax: 206-742-3666

Winner Products (U.S.A.), Inc.
821 S. Lemon Ave., Ste. A-9
Walnut, CA 91789
714-595-2490
fax: 714-595-1483

World Precision Instruments, Inc.
375 Quinnipiac Ave.
New Haven, CT 06513-4445
203-469-8281
fax: 203-468-6207

Xante Corp.
23800 Hwy. 98, P.O. Box 518
Montrose, AL 36559
800-926-8839; 205-990-8189
fax: 205-990-8489

XCP, Inc.
40 Elm St.
Dryden, NY 13053
800-647-7020; 607-844-9143
fax: 607-844-8031

Z-Nix Co., Inc.
211 Erie St.
Pomona, CA 91768
714-629-8050
fax: 714-629-4792
Technical support: 714-629-3018

Zenion Industries, Inc.
5430 Commerce Blvd.
Rohnert Park, CA 94928
800-477-5297; 707-584-3663
fax: 707-584-4664

Zeny Computer Systems
4033 Clipper Court
Fremont, CA 94538
510-659-0386
fax: 510-659-0468

ZEOS International, Ltd.
530 5th Ave., NW
St. Paul, MN 55112
800-423-5891; 612-633-4591
fax: 612-633-1325
Technical support: Use toll-free number

Zoltrix, Inc.
41394 Christy St.
Fremont, CA 94538
510-657-1188
fax: 510-657-1280

Modems and Telecommunications Equipment

ACCTON Technology Corp.
46750 Fremont Blvd., Ste. 104
Fremont, CA 94538
510-226-9800
fax: 510-226-9833

Adtech Micro Systems, Inc.
43120 Christy St.
Fremont, CA 94538
510-659-0756
fax: 510-659-9364

Advanced Microcomputer Systems, Inc.
1321 Northwest 65 Place
Ft. Lauderdale, FL 33309
800-972-3733; 305-975-9515
fax: 305-975-9698
Technical support: Use main number

American Mitac Corp.
410 E. Plumeria Dr.
San Jose, CA 95134
800-648-2287; 408-432-1160
fax: 408-432-8519
Technical support: Use toll-free number

AMT International Industries, Inc.
3857 Birch St., Ste. 258
Newport Beach, CA 92660
714-955-2440

Anchor Automation, Inc.
20675 Bahama St.
Chatsworth, CA 91311
818-998-6100
fax: 818-407-5330

Apple Computer, Inc.
20525 Mariani Ave.
Cupertino, CA 95014
408-996-1010
Technical support: 800-776-2333

Modems and Telecommunications Equipment

Applied Engineering
P.O. Box 5100
Carrollton, TX 75011
214-241-6060
fax: 214-484-6587

Aprotek
9323 W. Evans Creek Rd.
Rogue River, OR 97537
503-582-2120
fax: 503-582-2149

ATI Technologies, Inc.
3761 Victoria Park Ave.
Scarborough, Ontario
Canada M1W 3S2
416-756-0718
fax: 416-756-0720
Technical support: 416-756-0711

AT&T Computer Systems
1776 On The Green
Morristown, NJ 07960
800-247-1212; 201-898-8000
fax: 201-644-9768
Technical support: Use main number

AT&T Paradyne
8545 126th Ave., N, P.O. Box 2826
Largo, FL 34649-2826
800-482-3333, ext. 448; 813-530-2000
fax: 813-530-2109

Barr Systems, Inc.
4131 Northwest 28 Lane
Gainesville, FL 32606
800-227-7797; 904-371-3050
fax: 904-371-3018
Technical support: Use toll-free number

Bay Technical Associates, Inc.
200 N. Second St., P.O. Box 387
Bay St. Louis, MS 39520
800-523-2702; 601-467-8231
fax: 601-467-4551

BCH Equipment Corp.
2601 Ulmerton Rd., E, Ste. 101
Largo, FL 34641
800-237-8121; 813-530-9177

Best Data Products, Inc.
9304 Deering Ave.
Chatsworth, CA 91311
800-632-BEST; 818-773-9600
fax: 818-773-9619
Technical support: Use main number

Black Box Corp.
P.O. Box 12800
Pittsburgh, PA 15241
412-746-5500
fax: 412-746-0746

BT North America, Inc.
2560 North 1st St., P.O. Box 49019
San Jose, CA 95161-9019
800-872-7654; 408-922-0250
fax: 408-922-7030

Calculus, Inc.
522 Mercury Dr.
Sunnyvale, CA 94086-4018
408-733-7800

Cardinal Technologies, Inc.
1827 Freedom Rd.
Lancaster, PA 17601
800-722-0094; 717-293-3000
fax: 717-293-3055
Technical support: 717-293-3124

Cardkey Systems, Inc.
101 W. Cochran St.
Simi Valley, CA 93065
805-522-5555
fax: 805-526-0064

Cermetek Microelectronics, Inc.
1308 Borregas Ave.
Sunnyvale, CA 94088
800-882-6271; 408-752-5000
fax: 408-752-5004

CLEO Communications
3796 Plaza Dr.
Ann Arbor, MI 48108
800-233-2536; 313-662-2002
fax: 313-662-1965
Technical support: Use main number

CMS Enhancements, Inc.
2722 Michelson Dr.
Irvine, CA 92715
714-222-6000
fax: 714-549-4004
Technical support: 714-222-6058

CNet Technology, Inc.
62 Bonaventura Dr.
San Jose, CA 95134
408-954-8000
fax: 408-954-8866

Com 1 Data Communication Corp.
5120 Avenida Encinas, Ste. C
Carlsbad, CA 92008
800-289-COM1; 619-431-5606
fax: 619-431-5744

ComData Corp.
7900 N. Nagle Ave.
Morton Grove, IL 60053
800-255-2570; 708-470-9600

Commtech, Inc.
8622 Mt. Vernon Court
Wichita, KS 67207
316-651-0077
fax: 316-651-0758

CompuCom Corp.
1275 Palamus Ave.
Sunnyvale, CA 94089
800-228-6648; 408-732-4500
fax: 408-732-4570

Compulan Technology, Inc.
1842 Daltrey Way
San Jose, CA 95132
408-922-6888
fax: 408-954-8299

Compuquest, Inc.
801 Morse Ave.
Schaumburg, IL 60193
708-529-2552
fax: 708-894-6048

Computer Friends, Inc.
14250 N.W. Science Park Dr.
Portland, OR 97229
800-547-3303; 503-626-2291
fax: 503-643-5399
Technical support: Use main number

Computer Peripherals, Inc.
667 Rancho Conejo Blvd.
Newbury Park, CA 91320
800-854-7600; 805-499-5751
fax: 805-498-8848
Technical support: 800-235-7618

Computer Products, Inc.
(Measurement & Control Division)
2900 Gateway Dr.
Pompano Beach, FL 33069
305-974-5500
fax: 305-979-7371

Computer Systems & Technology, Inc.
226 Sherwood Ave.
East Farmingdale, NY 11735
516-420-1470
fax: 516-420-1503

COMSPEC Digital Products, Inc.
2313 W. Sam Houston Pkwy., N, Ste. 145
Houston, TX 77043
713-461-4487
fax: 713-461-8846

Comstat DataComm Corp.
1720 Spectrum Dr., NW
Lawrenceville, GA 30243
800-248-9496; 404-822-1962
fax: 404-822-4886

Connect, Inc.
10101 Bubb Rd.
Cupertino, CA 95014
800-262-2638; 408-973-0110
fax: 408-973-0497

Continental Resources, Inc.
175 Middlesex Tpke., P.O. Box 9137
Bedford, MA 01730
800-937-4688; 617-275-0850
fax: 617-275-6563

Cumulus Corp.
23500 Mercantile Rd.
Cleveland, OH 44122
216-464-2211
fax: 216-464-2483

CXR Telcom Corp.
521 Charcot Ave.
San Jose, CA 95131
800-537-5762; 408-435-8520
fax: 408-435-1276

Daetech Computer Technologies Corp.
5512 E. Hastings St., Ste. 103
Burnaby, BC, CD V5B 1R3
604-294-6135
fax: 604-294-0349

Dallas Fax, Inc.
13771 North Central Expwy., #1001
Dallas, TX 75243
800-876-8581; 214-699-8999
fax: 214-699-9079

Data Race, Inc.
11550 IH 10, W, Ste. 395
San Antonio, TX 78249
512-558-1900
fax: 512-558-1929

DataTrek
4505 Wyland Dr.
Elkhart, IN 46516
219-522-8000
fax: 219-522-0822

DCB of Champaign, Inc.
807 Pioneer
Champaign, IL 61820
800-637-1127; 217-352-3207
fax: 217-352-0350

DIRECTORY OF MANUFACTURERS

DigiBoard
6751 Oxford St.
Minneapolis, MN 55426
800-344-4273; 612-943-9020
fax: 612-922-4287
Technical support: Use main number

Digicom Systems, Inc.
188 Topaz St.
Milpitas, CA 95035
800-833-8900; 408-262-1277
fax: 408-262-1390

Digital Equipment Corp.
146 Main St.
Maynard, MA 01754-2571
508-493-5111
fax: 508-493-8780
Technical support: 800-332-8000

Dowty Communications, Inc.
55 Carnegie Plaza, Cherry Hill Industrial
Center
Cherry Hill, NJ 08003
800-424-4451; 609-424-4451
fax: 609-424-8065
Technical support: 800-284-2273

Dowty Direct
55 Carnegie Plaza
Cherry Hill, NJ 08003
800-553-6989; 609-751-2456
fax: 609-751-0136

E-Tech Research, Inc.
3525 Ryder St.
Santa Clara, CA 95051
408-730-1388
fax: 408-730-2488

Edimax Computer Co.
3350 Scott Blvd., Bldg. 9A
Santa Clara, CA 95054
408-496-1105
fax: 408-980-1530

Edsun Laboratories, Inc.
564 Main St.
Waltham, MA 02154
617-647-9300
fax: 617-894-6927

Eicon Technology Corp.
2196 32nd Ave.
Montreal, Quebec
Canada H8T 3H7
514-631-2592
fax: 514-631-3092

Elec & Eltek (USA) Corp.
545 Weddell Dr.
Sunnyvale, CA 94089
800-428-2839; 408-734-4223
fax: 408-734-8352

Electronic Innovations Corp. (EIC)
3107 W. Hampden Ave.
Englewood, CO 80110
303-789-0424
fax: 303-789-0809

EMAC
48431 Milmont Dr.
Fremont, CA 94538
800-821-0806; 510-683-2585
fax: 510-651-0728
Technical support: 510-498-4440

Emerson Computer Corp.
5500 E. Slauson Ave.
Commerce, CA 90040
213-722-9800
fax: 213-722-3216

Everex Systems, Inc.
48431 Milmont Dr.
Fremont, CA 94538
800-821-0806; 510-498-1111
fax: 510-651-0728
Technical support: 510-498-4411

Farallon Computing, Inc.
2000 Powell St.
Emeryville, CA 94608
510-596-9000
fax: 510-596-9020

FastComm Communications Corp.
45472 Holiday Dr.
Sterling, VA 22170
800-521-2496; 703-318-7750
fax: 703-878-4625
Technical support: Use toll-free number

Forval America, Inc.
6985 Union Park Center, Ste. 425
Midvale, UT 84047
800-367-8251; 801-561-8080
fax: 801-561-8777

Franklin Datacom
733 Lakefield Rd.
Westlake Village, CA 91361
805-373-8688
fax: 805-373-7373

Galacticomm, Inc.
4101 Southwest 47th Ave., Ste. 101
Ft. Lauderdale, FL 33314
305-583-5990
fax: 305-583-7846

Galaxy Networks, Inc.
8937 DeSoto Ave., Ste. 4
Canoga Park, CA 91304
818-998-7851
fax: 818-998-1758

Gandalf Data, Inc.
1020 Noel Ave.
Wheeling, IL 60090
800-426-3253; 708-541-6060
fax: 708-541-6803
Technical support: Use main number

GCH Systems, Inc.
201 Ravendale Dr.
Mountain View, CA 94043
800-366-4560; 415-968-3400
fax: 415-964-9747

Gecco Computers
1325 W. 21st St.
Tempe, AZ 85282
800-486-1000; 602-967-7500
fax: 602-967-3610

General DataComm, Inc.
1579 Straits Tpke.
Middlebury, CT 06762-1299
800-777-4005; 203-574-1118
fax: 203-758-8507
Technical support: 203-598-7526

Global Village Communication, Inc.
1204 O'Brien Dr.
Menlo Park, CA 94025
415-329-0700
fax: 415-327-3808

GoldStar Technology, Inc.
3003 N. First St.
San Jose, CA 95134-2004
408-432-1331
fax: 408-432-6053
Technical support: 800-777-1192

GVC Technologies, Inc.
99 Demarest Rd.
Sparta, NJ 07871
800-289-4821; 201-579-3630
fax: 201-579-2702
Technical support: Use main number

Hayes Microcomputer Products, Inc.
P.O. Box 105203
Atlanta, GA 30348
404-449-8791
Technical support: 404-441-1617

Holmes Microsystems, Inc.
2620 South 900 West
Salt Lake City, UT 84119
800-658-8418; 801-975-9929
fax: 801-975-9726
Technical support: Use main number

HT Communications, Inc.
16776 Bernardo Center Dr., Ste. 110B
San Diego, CA 92128
619-489-0206
fax: 619-743-3826

Hyundai Electronics America
166 Baypointe Pkwy.
San Jose, CA 95134
800-544-7808; 408-473-9200
fax: 408-943-9567
Technical support: 800-234-3553

IBM (International Business Machines)
Old Orchard Rd.
Armonk, NY 10504
800-426-2468; 914-765-1900
Technical support: Use toll-free number

Identity Systems Technology, Inc.
1347 Exchange Dr.
Richardson, TX 75081
214-235-3330

Image Communications
6 Caesar Place
Moonachie, NJ 07074
201-935-8880

Imavox Corp.
550 Lakeside Dr., Ste.2
Sunnyvale, CA 94086
408-736-3500

INCOMM Data Systems, Inc.
652 S. Wheeling Rd.
Wheeling, IL 60090
800-346-2660; 708-459-8881
fax: 708-459-0189
Technical support: Use main number

Modems and Telecommunications Equipment

Inmac Corp.
P.O. Box 58031, 2465 Augustine Dr.
Santa Clara, CA 95054
800-547-5444; 408-727-1970
Technical support: 800-446-6224

Intel Corp. (Personal Computer Enhancement Operation)
5200 N.E. Elam Young Pkwy., M/S CO3-07
Hillsboro, OR 97124
503-696-8080
Technical support: 503-629-7000

Intelligence Technology Corp.
P.O. Box 671125
Dallas, TX 75367
214-250-4277

ITS, Inc. (MI)
205 Hillbrady Rd.
Battle Creek, MI 49015
800-999-9ITS; 616-969-0500

Join Data Systems, Inc.
14838 Valley Blvd., Ste. C
City of Industry, CA 91746
818-330-6553
fax: 818-330-6865

LaCie, Ltd.
19552 Southwest 90th Court
Tualatin, OR 97062
503-691-0771
fax: 503-692-8289
Technical support: 800-288-9919

LAN Systems, Inc.
784 Ulloa St.
San Francisco, CA 94127
415-566-4798
fax: 415-566-4804

Lava Computers
28A Dansk Court
Rexdale, Ontario
Canada M9W 5V8
416-674-5942

Leading Edge Products, Inc.
117 Flanders Rd.
Westboro, MA 01581-5020
800-874-3340; 508-836-4800
fax: 508-836-4501
Technical support: 900-370-4800

Leading Technology, Inc.
10430 Southwest 5th St.
Beaverton, OR 97005-3447
800-999-5323; 503-646-3424
fax: 503-626-7845
Technical support: 800-999-4888

Logicode Technology, Inc.
5320-R Derry Ave.
Agoura Hills, CA 91301
818-879-0533
fax: 818-879-1034

LONGSHINE Technology, Inc.
2013 N. Capitol Ave.
San Jose, CA 95132
408-942-1746
fax: 408-942-1745

MacProducts USA, Inc.
8303 Mopac Expwy., Ste. 218
Austin, TX 78759
512-343-9441

Mastercom Communication Products
13701 Gramercy Place
Gardena, CA 90249
800-759-0148; 310-538-5000
fax: 310-324-9000

MaxLogic, Inc.
48350 Milmont Dr.
Fremont, CA 94538
510-490-4199
fax: 510-683-4782

Maya Computer Co.
P.O. Box 680, Bridge St. Market Place
Waitsfield, VT 05673
800-541-2318; 802-496-6982
fax: 802-496-8110

Megahertz Corp.
4505 S. Wasatch Blvd.
Salt Lake City, UT 84124
800-527-8677; 801-272-6000
fax: 801-272-6077
Technical support: Use toll-free number

Memotec Data, Inc.
600 McCaffrey St.
Montreal, Quebec
Canada H4T 1N1
800-361-1962; 514-738-4781
fax: 514-738-4436

MFI International, Inc.
18662 MacArthur Blvd., Ste. 103
Irvine, CA 92715
800-243-6654; 714-660-1110
fax: 714-660-1640

MICOM Communications Corp.
P.O. Box 8100, 4100 Los Angeles Ave.
Simi Valley, CA 93062-8100
800-642-6687; 805-583-8600
fax: 805-583-1997

Micro Electronic Technologies
35 South St.
Hopkinton, MA 01748
800-766-SIMM; 508-435-9057
fax: 508-435-6481

Micro Integrated Communications Corp. (MiCC)
3255 Scott Blvd., Bldg. 3, Ste. 102
Santa Clara, CA 95054
800-289-6422; 408-980-8061
fax: 408-980-9568
Technical support: Use toll-free number

Micro-Technology Concepts, Inc.
258 Johnson Ave.
Brooklyn, NY 11206
800-366-4860; 718-456-9100
fax: 718-456-1200

Microcom, Inc.
500 River Ridge Dr.
Norwood, MA 02062-5028
800-822-8224; 617-551-1000
fax: 617-551-1968
Technical support: Use main number

MicroGate Corp.
P.O. Box 27350
Austin, TX 78755
800-444-1982; 512-345-7791
fax: 512-343-9046

Micronet Computer Systems, Inc.
6970 Aragon Circle, Bldg. 3
Buena Park, CA 90620
800-468-6273; 714-739-2244
fax: 714-739-4220

Mirror Technologies, Inc.
2644 Patton Rd.
Roseville, MN 55113
800-654-5294; 612-633-4450
fax: 612-633-3136
Technical support: 612-633-2105

Misco
One Misco Plaza
Holmdel, NJ 07733
800-876-4726; 908-264-1000
fax: 908-264-5955

Mitsuba Corp.
1925 Wright Ave.
La Verne, CA 91750
800-648-7822; 714-392-2000
fax: 714-392-2021
Technical support: 714-392-2019 (Laptop);
714-392-2018 (Desktop)

Morton Management, Inc.
12079 Tech Rd.
Silver Spring, MD 20904
800-548-5744; 301-622-5600
fax: 301-622-5438

Motorola Codex
20 Cabot Blvd.
Mansfield, MA 02048
800-446-6336; 508-261-4000
fax: 508-261-1203
Technical support: 800-544-0062

Multi-Tech Systems, Inc.
2205 Woodale Dr.
Mounds View, MN 55112
800-328-9717; 612-785-3500
fax: 612-785-9874
Technical support: Use main number

NEC America, Inc. (Data and Video Communication Systems Division)
110 Rio Robles
San Jose, CA 95134
800-222-4NEC, ext. 1276; 408-433-1250
fax: 408-433-1239

NetQuest Corp.
129 H Gaither Dr.
Mt. Laurel, NJ 08054
609-866-0505
fax: 609-866-2852

Network Equipment Technologies, Inc. (N.E.T.) (Access Products Division)
26 Castilian Dr.
Santa Barbara, CA 93117
800-235-6935; 805-685-1411
fax: 805-562-3300

Network Software Associates, Inc.
39 Argonaut
Laguna Hills, CA 92656
714-768-4013
fax: 714-768-5049

Nokia Data Communications Corp.
2300 Tall Pines Dr., Ste. 100
Largo, FL 34641
813-535-6999
fax: 813-536-4773

DIRECTORY OF MANUFACTURERS

Octocom Systems, Inc.
255 Ballardvale St.
Wilmington, MA 01887
508-658-6050
fax: 508-658-0376

Okidata Corp.
532 Fellowship Rd.
Mt. Laurel, NJ 08054
800-654-3282; 609-235-2600
fax: 609-778-4184
Technical support: 609-273-0300

OmniTel, Inc.
3500 W. Warren Ave.
Fremont, CA 94538
800-OMNITEL; 510-490-2202
fax: 510-657-4079
Technical support: Use toll-free number

Osicom Technologies, Inc.
198 Green Pond Rd.
Rockaway, NJ 07866
800-922-0881; 201-586-2550
fax: 201-586-9740

Outbound Systems, Inc.
4840 Pearl East Circle
Boulder, CO 80301
800-444-4607; 303-786-9200
fax: 303-786-8611

Packard Bell
9425 Canoga Ave.
Chatsworth, CA 91311
818-773-4400
fax: 818-773-9521
Technical support: 800-733-4411

Patton Electronics Co.
7958 Cessna Ave.
Gaithersburg, MD 20879
301-975-1000
fax: 301-869-9293

PCA Personal Computer Associates, Inc.
85 Chambers Dr., Ste. 7
Ajax, Ontario
Canada L1Z 1E2
800-263-7535; 416-427-6612
fax: 416-427-0934

PCS Performance Computer Systems, Inc.
35520 Mound Rd.
Sterling Heights, MI 48310
800-473-7369; 313-795-9209
fax: 313-268-3313

Penril DataComm Networks
1300 Quince Orchard Blvd.
Gaithersburg, MD 20878
800-4-PENRIL; 301-921-8600
fax: 301-921-8376
Technical support: Use main number

Practical Peripherals, Inc.
31245 La Baya Dr.
Westlake Village, CA 91362
800-442-4774; 818-706-0333
fax: 818-706-2474
Technical support: Use main number

Premier Computer Innovations
10310 Harwin Dr.
Houston, TX 77036
800-347-1777; 713-995-4433
fax: 713-995-4751

Premier Telecom Products, Inc.
600 Industrial Pkwy.
Industrial Airport, KS 66031
800-321-0057; 913-791-7000
fax: 913-791-7022

Processing Innovations, Inc.
10471 S. Brookhurst
Anaheim, CA 92804
714-535-8161

Prodatel Communications, Inc.
720 Montgolfier, Ste. 201
Ville de Laval, Quebec
Canada H7W 4Z2
514-686-0232
fax: 514-686-0239

Product R & D Corp.
1194 Pacific St., Ste. 201
San Luis Obispo, CA 93401
800-321-9713; 805-546-9713
fax: 805-546-9716

Prometheus Products, Inc.
7225 S.W. Bonita Rd.
Tigard, OR 97223
800-477-3473; 503-624-0571
fax: 503-624-0843
Technical support: 503-624-0953

PTXI
P.O. Box 167688, 2000 Westridge Dr.
Irving, TX 75016-7688
800-527-0177; 214-518-1200
fax: 214-580-7503

Racal-Milgo
1601 N. Harrison Pkwy.
Sunrise, FL 33323-2899
800-722-2555; 305-846-1601
fax: 305-846-4942
Technical support: 305-846-4600

Racal-Vadic
1708 McCarthy Blvd.
Milpitas, CA 95035
800-482-3427; 408-432-8008
fax: 408-434-0188
Technical support: 408-922-3350

Reliable Communications, Inc.
20111 Stevens Creek Blvd.
Cupertino, CA 95014
800-222-0042; 408-996-0230
fax: 408-996-3367

RJD Associates, Inc.
10885 G Kalama River
Fountain Valley, CA 92708
800-543-8234; 714-841-8791
fax: 714-855-6265

SAI Systems Laboratories, Inc.
911 Bridgeport Ave.
Shelton, CT 06484
800-331-0488; 203-929-0790
fax: 203-929-6948

Sharp Digital Information Products, Inc.
16841 Armstrong Ave.
Irvine, CA 92714-4979
800-562-7427; 714-261-6224
fax: 714-261-9321

Sharp Electronics Corp.
(Professional Products Division)
Sharp Plaza, P.O. Box 650
Mahwah, NJ 07430
201-529-8200
fax: 201-529-9636
Technical support: 800-732-8221

Shiva Corp.
One Cambridge Center
Cambridge, MA 02142
800-458-3550; 617-252-6300
fax: 617-252-6852
Technical support: 617-252-6400

Star Logic, Inc.
238 E. Caribbean Dr.
Sunnyvale, CA 94089
408-747-0903
fax: 408-747-0954

Sunhill, Inc.
500 Andover Park, E
Seattle, WA 98188
800-544-1361; 206-575-4131
fax: 206-575-3617

Supra Corp.
1133 Commercial Way
Albany, OR 97321
800-727-8772; 503-967-9075
fax: 503-926-9370
Technical support: 503-967-9081

Swan Technologies
3075 Research Dr.
State College, PA 16801
800-468-9044; 814-238-1820
fax: 814-237-4450
Technical support: 800-468-7926

Tandy Corp.
1800 One Tandy Center
Ft. Worth, TX 76102
817-390-3011
fax: 817-390-2774
Technical support: 817-390-3861

Tek-Com Corp.
2343 Bering Dr.
San Jose, CA 95131
800-346-6597; 408-435-9515
fax: 408-435-9514

Telcor Systems Corp.
4 Strathmore Rd.
Natick, MA 01760
800-826-2938; 508-653-3995
fax: 508-651-0065

Telebit Corp.
1315 Chesapeake Terr.
Sunnyvale, CA 94089
800-835-3248; 408-734-4333
fax: 408-734-3333
Technical support: 408-734-5200

Telenetics Corp.
5109 E. La Palma Ave.
Anaheim, CA 92807
800-826-6336; 714-779-2766
fax: 714-779-1255

Terminal Data Corp.
15733 Crabbs Branch Way
Rockville, MD 20855
301-921-8282
fax: 301-921-8353

Monitors and Video-Related Equipment

TIL Systems, Inc.
225 Stedman St., Ste. 27
Lowell, MA 01851
508-970-1189
fax: 508-970-1295

Toshiba America Information Systems, Inc. (Computer Systems Division)
9740 Irvine Blvd.
Irvine, CA 92718
800-334-3445; 714-583-3000
Technical support: 800-999-4273
(Computers)

Tri-Data Systems, Inc.
3270 Scott Blvd.
Santa Clara, CA 95054-3011
800-874-3282; 408-727-3270
fax: 408-980-6565

TriGem Corp.
2388 Walsh Ave., Bldg. B
Santa Clara, CA 95051
408-970-0844
fax: 408-970-0870

UDS Motorola
5000 Bradford Dr.
Huntsville, AL 35805-1993
800-451-2369; 205-430-8000
fax: 205-830-5657
Technical support: 205-430-8047

Universal Data Systems, Inc.
5000 Bradford Dr.
Huntsville, AL 35805-1993
800-631-4869; 205-430-8000

US Robotics, Inc.
8100 McCormick Blvd.
Skokie, IL 60076
800-342-5877; 708-982-5001
fax: 708-982-5235
Technical support: 800-982-5151

Ven-Tel, Inc.
2121 Zanker Rd.
San Jose, CA 95131
800-538-5121; 408-436-7400
fax: 408-436-7451
Technical support: Use main number

Visionary Electronics, Inc.
141 Parker Ave.
San Francisco, CA 94118
415-751-8811

Vocal Technologies, Ltd.
3032 Scott Blvd.
Santa Clara, CA 95054
408-980-5181
fax: 408-980-8709

Wang Laboratories, Inc.
One Industrial Way, M/S 014-A1B
Lowell, MA 01851
800-835-9264; 508-459-5000
Technical support: 800-247-9264

Western DataCom Co., Inc.
P.O. Box 45113
Westlake, OH 44145-0113
800-262-3311; 216-835-1510
fax: 216-835-9146

X-Alt, Inc.
42 Digital Dr.
Novato, CA 94949
800-899-9258; 415-883-9611
fax: 415-883-9628

Xecom, Inc.
374 Turquoise St.
Milpitas, CA 95035
408-945-6640
fax: 408-942-1346

Yang Automatic Machines
4920 E. La Palma Ave.
Anaheim, CA 92807
800-233-4208; 714-693-0333
fax: 714-693-0705

Zenith Data Systems
2150 E. Lake Cook Rd.
Buffalo Grove, IL 60089
708-808-5000

Zoltrix, Inc.
41394 Christy St.
Fremont, CA 94538
510-657-1188
fax: 510-657-1280

Zoom Telephonics, Inc.
207 South St.
Boston, MA 02111
800-631-3116; 617-423-1072
Technical support: 617-423-1076

Monitors and Video-Related Equipment

Aamazing Technologies, Inc.
5980 Lakeshore Dr.
Cypress, CA 90630
714-826-9680
fax: 714-826-9681

Aapps Corp.
756 N. Pastoria Ave.
Sunnyvale, CA 94086
408-735-8550
fax: 408-735-8670

AccuSys, Inc.
3695 Kings Row
Reno, NV 89503
800-247-6413; 702-746-1111
fax: 702-746-2306

Acer America Corp.
401 Charcot Ave.
San Jose, CA 95131
800-538-1542; 408-922-0333
fax: 408-922-0176
Technical support: 800-637-7000

ACS International, Inc.
1325 Capital Pkwy., Ste. 109
Carrollton, TX 75006
214-242-0884
fax: 214-245-1559

Actix Systems, Inc.
4701 Patrick Henry Dr., Ste. 1701
Santa Clara, CA 95054
408-986-1625
fax: 408-986-1646

Ad Lib, Inc.
220 Grande Allée, E, Ste. 960
Quebec City, Quebec
Canada G1R 2J1
800-463-2686; 418-529-9676
fax: 418-529-1159

Adara Technology, Inc.
680 Knox St.
Torrance, CA 90502
310-327-1059
fax: 310-538-1090

ADEX Corp.
1750 Junction Ave.
San Jose, CA 95112
408-436-9700
fax: 408-436-9706

ADI Systems, Inc.
2121 Ringwood Ave.
San Jose, CA 95131
800-228-0530; 800-232-8282 (in California);
408-944-0100
fax: 408-944-0300

Advanced Digital Corp.
5432 Production Dr.
Huntington Beach, CA 92649
714-891-4004
fax: 714-893-1546

Advanced Digital Imaging
22 Rocky Knoll
Irvine, CA 92714
714-725-0154

Advanced Logic Research, Inc.
9401 Jeronimo
Irvine, CA 92718
800-444-4257; 714-581-6770
fax: 714-581-9240
Technical support: 714-458-0863

Advent Computer Products, Inc.
449 Santa Fe Dr., Ste. 213
Encinitas, CA 92024
619-942-8456
fax: 619-942-0648

Aedex Corp.
1070 Ortega Way
Placentia, CA 92670
714-632-7000
fax: 714-632-1334

Ahead Systems, Inc.
44244 Fremont Blvd.
Fremont, CA 94538
510-623-0900
fax: 510-623-0960

Aitech International
830 Hillview Court, Ste. 145
Milpitas, CA 95035
408-946-3291
fax: 408-946-3597

Alacrity Systems, Inc.
43 Newburg Rd.
Hackettstown, NJ 07840
908-813-2400
fax: 908-813-2490

Alacron, Inc.
71 Spitbrook Rd., Ste. 204
Nashua, NH 03060
603-891-2750
fax: 603-891-2745

Allen Communication, Inc.
5225 Wiley Post Way, Ste. 140
Salt Lake City, UT 84116
800-325-7850; 801-537-7800
fax: 801-537-7805

DIRECTORY OF MANUFACTURERS

Alloy Computer Products, Inc.
165 Forest St.
Marlborough, MA 01752
800-544-7551; 508-481-8500
fax: 508-481-7711

Allstar Microsystems Corp.
13885 Alton Pkwy.
Irvine, CA 92718
714-951-1884

Alpha Microsystems
3501 Sunflower
Santa Ana, CA 92704
714-957-8500
fax: 714-957-8705

Amdek Corp.
3471 N. First St.
San Jose, CA 95134
800-PC-AMDEK; 408-473-1200

American Advantech Corp.
1310 Tully Rd., Ste. 115
San Jose, CA 95122
408-293-6786
fax: 408-293-4697

American Mitac Corp.
410 E. Plumeria Dr.
San Jose, CA 95134
800-648-2287; 408-432-1160
fax: 408-432-8519
Technical support: Use toll-free number

Answer Software Corp.
20045 Stevens Creek Blvd., Ste. 1E
Cupertino, CA 95014
408-253-7515

Antex Electronics Corp.
16100 S. Figueroa St.
Gardena, CA 90248
800-338-4231; 310-532-3092
fax: 310-532-8509

AOC International (U.S.A.), Ltd.
10991 N.W. Airworld Dr.
Kansas City, MO 64153
800-443-7516; 816-891-8066
fax: 816-891-7882

Appian Technology, Inc.
477 N. Matilda Ave.
Sunnyvale, CA 94088
408-730-8800

Apple Computer, Inc.
20525 Mariani Ave.
Cupertino, CA 95014
408-996-1010
Technical support: 800-776-2333

Applied Data Sciences, Inc.
P.O. Box 814209
Dallas, TX 75381
214-243-0113
fax: 214-243-0217

Applied Data Systems, Inc.
409A E. Preston St.
Baltimore, MD 21202
800-541-2003; 301-576-0335

Ara-Tech, Inc.
18040 Sherman Way, Ste. 105
Reseda, CA 91335
818-996-8801
fax: 818-996-1946

Ariel Corp.
433 River Rd.
Highland Park, NJ 08904
908-249-2900
fax: 908-249-2123

Artic Technologies
55 Park St., Ste. 2
Troy, MI 48083
313-588-7370
fax: 313-588-2650

Artist Graphics
2675 Patton Rd.
St. Paul, MN 55113
800-999-9678; 612-631-7800
fax: 612-631-8424
Technical support: Use main number

AST Research Inc.
P.O. Box 19658, 15215 Alton Pkwy.
Irvine, CA 92713-9658
800-727-1278; 714-727-4141
fax: 714-727-9355
Technical support: Use toll-free number

ATI Technologies, Inc.
3761 Victoria Park Ave.
Scarborough, Ontario
Canada M1W 3S2
416-756-0718
fax: 416-756-0720
Technical support: 416-756-0711

Atlaz International, Ltd.
616 Burnside Ave., P.O. Box 110
Inwood, NY 11696
516-239-1854
fax: 516-239-1939

ATronics International, Inc.
1830 McCandless Dr.
Milpitas, CA 95035
408-942-3344
fax: 408-942-1674

AT&T Computer Systems
1776 On The Green
Morristown, NJ 07960
800-247-1212; 201-898-8000
fax: 201-644-9768
Technical support: Use main number

Autofax Corp.
9666 Hwy. 9
Ben Lomond, CA 95005
408-336-5171

Autograf, Inc.
2730 S. Harbor Blvd.
Santa Ana, CA 92704
714-641-0700
fax: 714-641-0171

Autrec, Inc.
4305-40 Enterprise Dr., Ste. A
Winston-Salem, NC 27106
919-759-9493

Avalon Design and Manufacturing, Inc.
130 McCormick Ave., Ste. 113
Costa Mesa, CA 92626
800-247-6166; 714-432-7227
fax: 714-432-7482

AView Technology, Inc.
2 St. Clair Ave., Ste. 1600
Toronto, Ontario
Canada M4V 1L5
800-263-7288; 416-922-6555
fax: 416-967-6036

Barco, Inc.
1000 Cobb Place Blvd.
Kennesaw, GA 30144
404-590-7900

Beaver Computer Corp.
174 Component Dr.
San Jose, CA 95131-1119
408-944-9000
fax: 408-944-9001

Behavior Tech Computer (USA) Corp.
46177 Warm Spring Blvd.
Fremont, CA 94539
510-657-3956
fax: 510-657-3965

Bell & Howell Quintar Co.
370 Amapola Ave., Ste. 106
Torrance, CA 90501
800-223-5231; 310-320-5700
fax: 310-618-1282

Bit 3 Computer Corp.
8120 Penn Ave., S
Minneapolis, MN 55431-1393
612-881-6955
fax: 612-881-9674

BleuMont Inc.
4900 Jean-Talon West #220
Montreal, Quebec
Canada H4P 1W9
514-340-9992

Boca Research, Inc.
6413 Congress Ave.
Boca Raton, FL 33487-2839
407-997-6227
fax: 407-997-0918

Bus Computer Systems
135 West 26th St.
New York, NY 10010
800-451-5289; 212-627-4485

Business Technology Manufacturing, Inc. (BTM)
42-20 235th St.
Douglaston, NY 11363
718-229-8080

CalComp Plotter Products Group
P.O. Box 3250, 2411 W. La Palma Ave.
Anaheim, CA 92803
800-932-1212; 714-821-2000
fax: 714-821-2832
Technical support: Use main number

Cardinal Technologies, Inc.
1827 Freedom Rd.
Lancaster, PA 17601
800-722-0094; 717-293-3000
fax: 717-293-3055
Technical support: 717-293-3124

Carroll Touch
P.O. Box 1309
Round Rock, TX 78680
512-244-3500
fax: 512-244-7040

CCSI/The Voice Connection
8258 Kingslee Rd.
Bloomington, MN 55438
612-944-1334

Monitors and Video-Related Equipment

Centcircuit International, Inc.
3400 Corporate Way, Ste. F
Duluth, GA 30136
404-623-3937
fax: 404-623-3941

Chaplet Systems, Inc.
252 N. Wolf Rd.
Sunnyvale, CA 94086
408-732-7950
fax: 408-732-6050

Cheetah Computer Systems, Inc.
7075 Flying Cloud Dr.
Eden Prairie, MN 55344
800-243-3824; 612-943-8690
fax: 612-943-8790

Chicony America, Inc.
3002 Dow Ave., Ste. 122
Tustin, CA 92680
714-573-0456
fax: 714-573-0673
Technical support: 714-380-0928

Chugai Boyeki (America) Corp.
55 Mall Dr.
Commack, NY 11725
800-422-6707; 516-864-9700
fax: 516-543-5426

Clary Corp.
(Precision Instruments Division)
320 W. Clary Ave.
San Gabriel, CA 91776
818-287-6111
fax: 818-286-7216

CMS Enhancements, Inc.
2722 Michelson Dr.
Irvine, CA 92715
714-222-6000
fax: 714-549-4004
Technical support: 714-222-6058

Colorburst
P.O. Box 3091
Nashua, NH 03061
603-891-1588
fax: 603-881-7600

Colorgraphic Communications Corp.
5388 New Peachtree Rd.
Atlanta, GA 30341
404-455-3921
fax: 404-458-0616

Command Corp., Inc.
3675 Crestwood Pkwy.
Duluth, GA 30136
404-925-7950

Commax Technologies, Inc.
2031 Concourse Dr.
San Jose, CA 95131
800-526-6629; 408-435-5000
fax: 408-435-5005

**Communication Automation &
Control, Inc.**
1642 Union Blvd., Ste. 200
Allentown, PA 18103-1510
800-367-6735; 215-776-6669
fax: 215-770-1232

Communication Inter-Globe
633 McCaffrey
St. Lawrence, Quebec
Canada H4T 1N3
514-738-6580

Compaq Computer Corp.
P.O. Box 692000
Houston, TX 77269-2000
800-231-0900; 713-370-0670
fax: 713-374-1402

Compeq USA/Focus Technology
18226 W. McDurmott
Irvine, CA 92714
800-852-0105; 714-553-8626
fax: 714-553-8548
Technical support: 213-404-1686

Comprehensive Video Supply
148 Veterans Dr.
Northvale, NJ 07647
800-526-0242; 201-767-7990
fax: 201-767-7377

CompuAdd Corp.
12303 Technology Blvd.
Austin, TX 78727
800-531-5475; 512-250-1489
fax: 512-250-5760
Technical support: 800-999-9901

Computer Friends, Inc.
14250 N.W. Science Park Dr.
Portland, OR 97229
800-547-3303; 503-626-2291
fax: 503-643-5379
Technical support: Use main number

Computer Voice Systems
6290 Montrose Rd.
Rockville, MD 20852
301-984-1400

Comy Technology
62 Bonaventura Dr.
San Jose, CA 95134
408-456-0333
fax: 408-456-0366

Conographic Corp.
16802 Aston St.
Irvine, CA 92714
714-474-1188

Conrac Display Products, Inc.
1724 S. Mountain Ave.
Duarte, CA 91010
818-303-0095
fax: 818-303-5484

Control Vision
P.O. Box 596
Pittsburg, KS 66762
800-292-1160; 316-231-6647

Copam Electronics Corp.
45875 Northport Loop East
Fremont, CA 94538
800-326-4567; 510-623-8911
fax: 510-623-8551

Cordata Technologies, Inc.
1055 W. Victoria St.
Compton, CA 90220
800-233-3602; 800-524-2671 (in California);
310-603-2901
fax: 310-763-0447

CORECO, Inc.
(The COmputer REsearch CO.)
6969 Trans-Canada Hwy., Ste. 113
St. Laurent, Quebec
Canada H4T 1V8
800-361-4914; 514-331-1301
fax: 514-333-1388

Cornerstone Technology
1990 Concourse Dr.
San Jose, CA 95131
800-562-2552; 408-435-8900
fax: 408-435-8998

Creative Labs, Inc.
2050 Duane Ave.
Santa Clara, CA 95054
408-986-1461
fax: 408-986-1777
Technical support: 408-982-9226

CSP, Inc.
40 Linnell Circle
Billerica, MA 01821
800-325-3110; 617-272-6020
fax: 508-663-0150

CSS Laboratories, Inc.
1641 McGaw Ave.
Irvine, CA 92714
714-852-8161
fax: 714-852-9464

CTX International, Inc.
20530 Earlgate St.
Walnut, CA 91789
714-595-6146
fax: 714-595-6293

Cubix Corp.
2800 Lockheed Way
Carson City, NV 89706
800-829-0550; 702-883-7611
fax: 702-882-2407

Dakota Microsystems, Inc.
301 E. Evelyn Ave., Bldg. A
Mountain View, CA 94041
800-999-6288; 415-967-2302

Darius Technology, Ltd.
2808 Ingleton Ave.
Burnaby, BC, CD V5C 6G7
604-436-1027
fax: 604-436-0882

Data Business Systems
11640 Coley River Circle
Fountain Valley, CA 92708
800-543-2983; 714-662-3282
fax: 714-662-1906

Data Translation, Inc.
100 Locke Dr.
Marlboro, MA 01752
508-481-3700
fax: 508-481-8620

Data/Voice Solutions Corp. (DVSC)
16842 Von Karman, Ste. 200
Irvine, CA 92714
714-474-0330
fax: 714-474-8794

Datacube
4 Dearborn Rd.
Peabody, MA 01960
508-535-6644
fax: 508-535-5643

Datafox Computer Products
2215 E. University
Phoenix, AZ 85034
800-821-6387; 215-879-7080

DIRECTORY OF MANUFACTURERS

Definicon International Corp.
17282 Eastman St.
Irvine, CA 92714
800-253-7223; 714-261-8313
fax: 714-851-1286

DEICO Electronics, Inc.
2800 Bayview Dr.
Fremont, CA 94537
800-321-8990; 510-651-7800
fax: 510-651-6109

Dell Computer Corp.
9505 Arboretum Blvd.
Austin, TX 78759-7299
800-426-5150; 512-338-4400
fax: 512-338-8421
Technical support: 800-624-9896

Desktop Computing, Inc.
4600 Bohannon Dr., Ste. 220
Menlo Park, CA 94022
415-323-5535

DFI, Inc.
2544 Port St.
West Sacramento, CA 95691
916-373-1234
fax: 916-373-0221
Technical support: Use main number

Diamond Computer Systems, Inc.
532 Mercury Dr.
Sunnyvale, CA 94086
408-736-2000
fax: 408-730-5750

Diaquest, Inc.
1440 San Pablo Ave.
Berkeley, CA 94702
510-526-7167
fax: 510-526-7073

Digidesign, Inc.
1360 Willow Rd., Ste. 101
Menlo Park, CA 94025
800-333-2137; 415-327-8811
fax: 415-327-0777
Technical support: Use main number

Digital F/X, Inc.
755 Ravendale Dr.
Mountain View, CA 94043
415-961-2800

Digital Technology International (DTI)
500 West 1200 South
Orem, UT 84058
801-226-2984
fax: 801-226-8438

Digital Vision, Inc.
270 Bridge St.
Dedham, MA 02026
800-346-0090; 617-329-5400
fax: 617-329-6286

Distributed Image Systems Corp.
(DISCORP)
290 Easy St., Ste. 5
Simi Valley, CA 93065
805-584-0688
fax: 805-584-0795

Dome Imaging Systems, Inc.
20 Powdermill Rd.
Maynard, MA 01754
508-897-3144
fax: 508-897-3927

Dragon Systems, Inc.
90 Bridge St., Chapel Bridge Park
Newton, MA 02158
617-965-5200
fax: 617-527-0372

DSM ComputerSystems Corp.
388 S. Abbott Ave.
Milpitas, CA 95035
408-946-0655
fax: 408-946-0908

DSP Technology, Inc.
48500 Kato Rd.
Fremont, CA 94538-7385
510-657-7555
fax: 510-657-7576

DTK Computer, Inc.
17700 Castleton St., Ste. 300
City of Industry, CA 91748
818-810-8880
fax: 818-810-5233
Technical support: 818-810-0098

Du Pont Electronics Imaging Division
(Computing Products Group)
P.O. Box 6099
Newark, DE 19714-6099
302-733-9692
Technical support: 800-225-8414

EECS
1753 Mass Ave.
Cambridge, MA 02140
617-498-9838
fax: 617-491-6808

Ehman, Inc.
97 S. Redwillow Rd.
Evanston, WY 82930
800-257-1666; 307-789-3830
fax: 307-789-4656
Technical support: Use main number

Electrograph Systems, Inc.
175 Commerce Dr.
Hauppauge, NY 11788
800-776-5768; 516-436-5050
fax: 516-436-5227

Electrohome, Ltd.
809 Wellington St., N.
Kitchener, Ontario
Canada N2G 4J6
519-744-7111; 519-749-3131

Eletech Electronics, Inc.
1262 E. Katella Ave.
Anaheim, CA 92805
714-385-1707
fax: 714-385-1708

Elite Business Applications, Inc.
36-J Rt. 3, N, P.O. Box 593
Millersville, MD 21108
800-942-0018; 301-987-9050
fax: 301-987-9098
Technical support: Use main number

Elitegroup Computer Systems, Inc.
365 Ravendale Dr.
Mountain View, CA 94043
415-969-1000
fax: 415-969-0343

ELSA America, Inc.
400 Oyster Point Blvd., Ste. 109
South San Francisco, CA 94080
800-272-3572; 415-588-6285
fax: 415-588-0113

Emerson Computer Power
15041 Bake Pkwy., Ste. L
Irvine, CA 92718
800-BACK-UPS; 714-380-1005
fax: 714-380-0456

E-Machines, Inc.
9305 S.W. Gemini Dr.
Beaverton, OR 97005
503-646-6699
fax: 503-641-0946
Technical support: 503-626-5163

Enertronics Research, Inc.
1801 Beltway Dr.
St. Louis, MO 63114
800-325-0174; 314-427-7578
fax: 314-427-7522

EPIX, Inc.
310 Anthony Trail
Northbrook, IL 60062
708-498-4002
fax: 708-498-4321

Epson America, Inc.
20770 Madrona Ave.
Torrance, CA 90509-2842
800-289-3776; 310-782-0770
Technical support: 310-782-2600

Ericsson Information Systems
715 N. Glenville Dr.
Richardson, TX 75081
214-997-0492
fax: 214-669-1374

EuroComm, Inc.
629 S. Rancho Santa Fe Rd., Ste. 394
San Marcos, CA 92069
619-471-9362, ext. 5
fax: 619-471-5054

Everex Systems, Inc.
48431 Milmont Dr.
Fremont, CA 94538
800-821-0806; 510-498-1111
fax: 510-651-0728
Technical support: 510-498-4411

Everlasting Technology International Corp.
10450 Pioneer Blvd., Unit 8
Santa Fe Springs, CA 90670
310-946-5241
fax: 310-946-6633

Extended Systems
P.O. Box 4937, 6123 N. Meeker Ave.
Boise, ID 83704
800-235-7576; 208-322-7575
fax: 208-377-1906

Face Technologies, Inc.
3711 Plaza Dr., Ste. 1
Ann Arbor, MI 48108
313-662-8008
fax: 313-662-5904

Falco Data Products, Inc.
440 Potrero Ave.
Sunnyvale, CA 94086-4117
800-835-8765; 408-745-7123
fax: 408-745-7860
Technical support: Use main number

Focus Information Systems, Inc.
42840 Christy St.
Fremont, CA 94538
510-657-2845
fax: 510-657-4158

Monitors and Video-Related Equipment

Fora, Inc.
3081 N. First St.
San Jose, CA 95134
800-FOR-FORA; 408-944-0393
fax: 408-944-0392

Forefront Technology Corp.
50 Mall Rd., Executive Place III, Ste. G12
Burlington, MA 01803
617-270-9733
fax: 617-270-9313

FTG Data Systems
P.O. Box 615, 10801 Dale St., Ste. J-2
Stanton, CA 90680
800-962-3900; 714-995-3900
fax: 714-995-3989

Fujikama O.A. Distribution
150 Ormont Dr.
Weston, Ontario
Canada M9L 1N7
800-265-7761; 416-748-1668
fax: 416-748-0447

General Business Machines Corp.
6053 Bristol Pkwy.
Culver City, CA 90230
800-228-3349; 310-649-9199
fax: 310-649-9177

Generation Systems
1185-C Bordeaux Dr.
Sunnyvale, CA 94089
800-325-5811; 408-734-2100
fax: 408-734-4626
Technical support: 800-323-9825

Genesis Development Corp.
15850 W. Bluemound Rd., Ste. 307
Brookfield, WI 53005
414-796-1005
fax: 414-797-0727

Genius Technologies, Inc.
755 East 31st St., P.O. Box 455
Hastings, MN 55033
800-328-9524; 612-437-2233
fax: 612-437-7325

Genoa Systems Corp.
75 E. Trimble Rd.
San Jose, CA 95131
800-423-6211; 408-432-9090
fax: 408-434-0997

Golden Dragon
110 Dynamic Dr., Unit 41
Scarborough, Ontario
Canada M1V 5C7
416-297-1202
fax: 416-754-2240

GoldStar Technology, Inc.
3003 N. First St.
San Jose, CA 95134-2004
408-432-1331
fax: 408-432-6053
Technical support: 800-777-1192

Graphic Software Systems, Inc.
9590 S.W. Gemini Dr.
Beaverton, OR 97005
503-641-2200
fax: 503-643-8642

**GreatWest Technology, Ltd.
(SYSDYNE Products Division)**
31129 Wiegman Rd., P.O. Box 30728
Hayward, CA 94544-7820
510-429-2000
fax: 510-487-2250

Greenleaf International, Inc.
136 Wolfe Rd.
Sunnyvale, CA 94086
408-735-7056
fax: 408-735-7057

Groundhog Graphics, Inc.
P.O. Box 325, 101 E. Mahoning St.
Punxsutawney, PA 15767
800-GRAPH-99; 814-938-8943
fax: 814-938-7035

GTK Technology, Inc.
708 N. Valley St., Ste. H
Anaheim, CA 92801
714-772-7393
fax: 714-772-7508

**HCI (Hyosung Computer & Information
Systems)**
671 E. Argues Ave.
Sunnyvale, CA 94086
408-733-0810
fax: 408-733-2638

Headland Technology, Inc.
46221 Landing Pkwy.
Fremont, CA 94538
800-238-0101; 800-962-5700 (in California);
510-623-7857
fax: 510-656-0397
Technical support: 800-248-1850

Hearsay, Inc.
307 76th St.
Brooklyn, NY 11209
718-836-0990
fax: 718-836-1159

Hercules Computer Technology, Inc.
921 Parker St.
Berkeley, CA 94710
800-532-0600; 510-540-6000
fax: 510-540-6621
Technical support: 510-540-0749

Hewlett-Packard Co.
3000 Hanover St.
Palo Alto, CA 94304
800-752-0900; 415-857-1501
Technical support: Use toll-free number

High Res Technologies
P.O. Box 76
Lewiston, NY 14092
416-497-6493
fax: 416-497-1988

Hitachi America, Ltd. (OAS Division)
110 Summit Ave.
Montvale, NJ 07645
800-448-2244; 201-573-0774
fax: 201-573-7660

HNC, Inc.
5501 Oberlin Dr.
San Diego, CA 92121
619-546-8877
fax: 619-452-6524

Hydra Systems, Inc.
1340 S. Saratoga-Sunnyvale Rd., Ste. 106
San Jose, CA 95129
408-253-5800
fax: 408-253-1113

HYPERSPEED Technologies, Inc.
10696 Marbury Ave.
San Diego, CA 92126-2838
619-578-4893
fax: 619-271-6717

Hyundai Electronics America
166 Baypointe Pkwy.
San Jose, CA 95134
800-544-7808; 408-473-9200
fax: 408-943-9567
Technical support: 800-234-3553

IBM (International Business Machines)
Old Orchard Rd.
Armonk, NY 10504
800-426-2468; 914-765-1900
Technical support: Use toll-free number

Ideatech, Inc.
1806 T St., NW
Washington, DC 20009
800-247-4332; 202-667-4559
fax: 202-667-9498

IDEC, Inc.
1195 Doylestown Pike
Quakertown, PA 18951
215-538-2600
fax: 215-538-2665

Idek North America
650 Louis Dr. #120
Warminster, PA 18974
215-957-6543

Identity Systems Technology, Inc.
1347 Exchange Dr.
Richardson, TX 75081
214-235-3330

IEV Corp.
3030 S. Main St., Ste. 300
Salt Lake City, UT 84115
800-438-6161; 801-466-9093

Iiyama North America, Inc.
650 Louis Dr., Ste. 120
Warminster, PA 18974
215-957-6543
fax: 215-957-6551

Ikegami Electronics (U.S.A.), Inc.
37 Brook Ave.
Maywood, NJ 07607
201-368-9171
fax: 201-569-1626

Image Processing Systems, Inc.
3075 14th Ave.
Markham, Ontario
Canada L3R 0G9
416-940-0300
fax: 416-940-0301

Image Systems Corp.
11543 K-Tel Dr.
Hopkins, MN 55343
800-462-4376; 612-935-1171
fax: 612-935-1386

DIRECTORY OF MANUFACTURERS

Imaging Technology, Inc.
600 W. Cummings Park
Woburn, MA 01801-6343
800-532-3500; 617-938-8444
fax: 617-938-1757

Imagraph Corp.
11 Elizabeth Dr.
Chelmsford, MA 01824
508-256-4624
fax: 508-250-9155

Imtec, Inc.
P.O. Box 809 Imtec Lane
Bellows Falls, VT 05101
802-463-9502
fax: 802-463-4334

InfoChip Systems, Inc.
2840 San Tomas Expwy., Ste. 200
Santa Clara, CA 95051
800-447-0200; 408-727-0514
fax: 408-727-4190
Technical support: Use main number

Infotronic America, Inc.
8834 N. Capital of Texas Hwy., Ste. 200
Austin, TX 78759
512-345-9646
fax: 512-345-9895

Intecolor Corp.
2150 Boggs Rd., Bldg. 200
Duluth, GA 30126
404-623-9145
fax: 404-623-9163

Integrated Workstations, Inc.
1648 Mabury Rd.
San Jose, CA 95133
800-832-6526; 408-923-0301
fax: 408-923-0427

Intel Corp.
3065 Bowers Ave.
Santa Clara, CA 95051
408-765-8080
fax: 408-765-1821

Intelec
6075 Northwest 82nd Ave.
Miami, FL 33166
800-683-0969; 305-594-0001
fax: 305-477-9074

Intelligent Resources Integrated Systems, Inc.
1626 Colonial Pkwy.
Inverness, IL 60067-4732
708-705-9388
fax: 708-705-9410

Interceptor Security Systems, Inc.
10900 Northeast 4th, Ste. 604
Bellevue, WA 98004
206-637-2819
fax: 206-451-8546

International Meta Systems, Inc.
23842 Hawthorne Blvd.
Torrance, CA 90505
310-375-4700
fax: 310-378-7643

Intertec International
762 Big Tree Dr.
Longwood, FL 32750
800-749-1877; 407-834-7777
fax: 407-767-8720

Intra Electronics USA, Inc.
1133 N. Fair Oaks Ave.
Sunnyvale, CA 94086
408-744-1706
fax: 408-744-1871

Iocomm International Technology Corp.
12700 Yukon Ave.
Hawthorne, CA 90250
800-998-8919
fax: 310-644-6068

ITT PowerSystems Corp.
3400 Britannia Dr.
Tucson, AZ 85706
602-889-7600
fax: 602-294-1808

Jodan Technology, Inc.
177 Bedford St., P.O. Box 362
Lexington, MA 02173-0362
617-863-8898
fax: 617-863-0462

Jovian Logic Corp.
47265 Fremont Blvd.
Fremont, CA 94538
510-651-4823
fax: 510-651-1343

JOYCE Associates
215 Franklin St.
Clayton, NJ 08312

JVC Information Products Co. of America
2903 Bunker Hill Lane
Santa Clara, CA 95054
408-988-7506
fax: 408-727-7533

Keithley MetraByte
440 Myles Standish Blvd.
Taunton, MA 02780
508-880-3000
fax: 508-880-0179

KFC Computek Components Corp.
31 E. Mall
Plainview, NY 11803
516-454-0262
fax: 516-454-0265

KLH Computers
10310 Harwin St.
Houston, TX 77036
800-347-1777; 713-995-4433

Korea Data Systems Co., Ltd.
6 Blackstone Valley Pl.
Lincoln, RI 02865
401-334-0100

Lapis Technologies, Inc.
1210 Marina Village Pkwy., Ste. 100
Alameda, CA 94501
510-748-1600
fax: 510-748-1645

Laser Computer, Inc. (a Video Technology Co.)
800 N. Church St.
Lake Zurich, IL 60047
708-540-8086
fax: 708-540-8335
Technical support: 708-540-5022

LaserMaster Technologies Corp.
7156 Shady Oak Rd.
Eden Prairie, MN 55344
612-944-9330
fax: 612-944-0522
Technical support: 612-944-9331

Lava Computers
28A Dansk Court
Rexdale, Ontario
Canada M9W 5V8
416-674-5942

Lazerus
2821 Ninth St.
Berkeley, CA 94710
510-339-6263
fax: 510-845-1237

Leading Technology, Inc.
10430 Southwest 5th St.
Beaverton, OR 97005-3447
800-999-5323; 503-646-3424
fax: 503-626-7845
Technical support: 800-999-4888

Levco Sales
6181 Corner Stone Court, E, Ste. 101
San Diego, CA 92121
619-457-2011

Link Computer, Inc.
560 S. Melrose St.
Placentia, CA 92670
714-993-0800
fax: 714-993-0705

Lite-On, Inc.
720 S. Hillview Dr.
Milpitas, CA 95035
408-946-4873
fax: 408-942-1527

Logitech, Inc.
6505 Kaiser Dr.
Fremont, CA 94555
800-999-8846; 510-795-8500
fax: 510-792-8901

Logix Microcomputer, Inc.
375 Morgan Lane
West Haven, CT 06516
800-248-2140; 203-937-7725
fax: 203-932-3154

Logos Systems International
100 Royal Oak
Scotts Valley, CA 95066
408-438-5012
fax: 408-439-9440

Logos Technology Corp.
809 S. Lemon Ave.
Walnut, CA 91789
714-869-7789
fax: 714-869-7980

LSI Logic Corp.
1551 McCarthy Blvd.
Milpitas, CA 95035
800-433-8778; 408-433-8000
fax: 408-434-6457

MacSema
29383 Lamb Dr.
Albany, OR 97321
800-344-7228; 503-757-1520
fax: 503-754-7189

Monitors and Video-Related Equipment

MacTel Technology Corp.
3007 N. Lamar
Austin, TX 78705
800-950-8411; 512-451-2600
Technical support: 512-458-2222

Mag Computronic (USA) Inc.
17845-E Skypark Circle
Irvine, CA 92714
714-927-3998
fax: 714-827-5522

Magni Systems, Inc.
9500 S.W. Gemini Dr.
Beaverton, OR 97005
800-624-6465; 503-626-8400
fax: 503-626-6225

MAI Systems Corp.
14101 Myford Rd.
Tustin, CA 92680
714-731-5100
fax: 714-730-3312

Mass Microsystems, Inc.
810 W. Maude Ave.
Sunnyvale, CA 94086-3528
800-522-7979; 408-522-1200
fax: 408-733-5499
Technical support: 800-442-7979

Matrox Electronic Systems, Ltd.
1055 St. Regis Blvd.
Dorval, Quebec
Canada H9P 2T4
800-361-4903; 514-685-2630
fax: 514-685-2853

Maxa Corp.
22120 Clarendon Ave., Ste. 230
Woodland Hills, CA 91367
800-289-6292; 818-593-2100
fax: 818-999-6737

MaxLogic, Inc.
48350 Milmont Dr.
Fremont, CA 94538
510-490-4199
fax: 510-683-4782

Media Vision, Inc.
47221 Fremont Blvd.
Fremont, CA 94538
800-348-7116; 510-770-8600
fax: 510-770-8648

MegaGraphics, Inc.
439 Calle San Pablo
Camarillo, CA 93012
800-487-6342; 805-484-3799
fax: 805-484-5870

Metheus Corp.
1600 N.W. Compton Dr.
Beaverton, OR 97006-6905
800-547-5315; 503-690-1550
fax: 503-690-1525

Method Systems, Inc.
3511 Lost Nation Rd., Ste. 202
Willoughby, OH 44094
800-533-6116; 216-942-2100
fax: 216-942-1674

Micro-Base Corp.
562 E. Congress Park Dr.
Centerville, OH 45459
800-922-1360; 513-434-7072
fax: 513-434-7513

Micro Display Systems, Inc.
1310 Vermillion St.
Hastings, MN 55033
612-437-2233

Micro Express
1801 E. Carnegie Ave.
Santa Ana, CA 92705
800-642-7621; 714-852-1400
fax: 714-852-1225
Technical support: 800-762-3378

Micro-Labs, Inc.
7309 Campbell Rd.
Dallas, TX 75248
214-702-8654
fax: 214-702-0655

Micro Solutions Computer Products
132 W. Lincoln Hwy.
DeKalb, IL 60115
815-756-3411
fax: 815-756-2928

The Micro Works, Inc.
1942 S. El Camino Real
Encinitas, CA 92024
619-942-2400

Microdyne Corp.
491 Oak Rd.
Ocala, FL 32672
904-687-4633
fax: 904-687-3392

Microfield Graphics, Inc.
9825 S.W. Sunshine Court
Beaverton, OR 97005
800-334-4922; 503-626-9393
fax: 503-641-9333

Micron Technology, Inc.
2805 E. Columbia Rd.
Boise, ID 83706-9698
800-642-7661; 208-368-4000
fax: 208-368-4558
Technical support: 208-368-3900

Microtek Lab, Inc.
680 Knox St.
Torrance, CA 90502
800-654-4160; 310-321-2121
fax: 310-538-1193
Technical support: Use main number

Microvitec, Inc.
1943 Providence Court, Airport Perimeter
Business Center
College Park, GA 30337
404-991-2246
fax: 404-996-2387

MicroWay, Inc.
P.O. Box 79, Research Park
Kingston, MA 02364
508-746-7341
fax: 508-746-4678

Mirror Technologies, Inc.
2644 Patton Rd.
Roseville, MN 55113
800-654-5294; 612-633-4450
fax: 612-633-3136
Technical support: 612-633-2105

Mitsuba Corp.
1925 Wright Ave.
La Verne, CA 91750
800-648-7822; 714-392-2000
fax: 714-392-2021
Technical support: 714-392-2019 (Laptop);
714-392-2018 (Desktop)

Mitsubishi Electronics America, Inc.
991 Knox St.
Torrance, CA 90502
800-556-1234, ext. 54M; 800-441-2345, ext.
54M (in California); 310-515-3993
fax: 310-527-7693
Technical support: Use main number

**Mitsubishi Electronics America, Inc.
(Professional Electronics Division)**
800 Cottontail Lane
Somerset, NJ 08873
800-445-0755; 908-563-9889
fax: 908-563-9196
Technical support: Use main number

Mobius Technologies, Inc.
5835 Doyle St.
Emeryville, CA 94608
800-669-0556; 510-654-0556
fax: 510-654-2834

Modgraph, Inc.
83 Second Ave.
Burlington, MA 01803
800-327-9962; 617-229-4800
fax: 617-272-3062

Moniterm Corp.
5740 Green Circle Dr.
Minnetonka, MN 55343-9074
800-343-4969; 612-935-4151
fax: 612-933-5701
Technical support: Use main number

Monitronix, Inc.
929 Eastwind Dr., Ste. 220
Westerville, OH 43081
800-365-5646; 614-891-3232
fax: 614-891-2192

Monolithic Systems Corp.
7050 S. Tucson Way
Englewood, CO 80112
800-525-7661; 303-790-7400
fax: 303-790-7118
Technical support: Use main number

Morse Technology, Inc.
17531 Railroad St., Unit I
City of Industry, CA 91748
818-854-8681
fax: 818-854-8682

MTI, Inc.
14711 Northeast 29th Place, Ste. 245
Bellevue, WA 98007
206-881-1789
fax: 206-883-7136

Multi-Pal International, Inc.
17231 E. Railroad St., Ste. 500
City of Industry, CA 91748
818-913-4188
fax: 818-912-9149

Music Quest, Inc.
P.O. Box 260963
Plano, TX 75026
800-876-1376; 214-881-7408

DIRECTORY OF MANUFACTURERS

Mylex Corp.
34551 Ardenwood Blvd.
Fremont, CA 94555-3607
800-77-MYLEX; 510-796-6100
fax: 510-745-7564
Technical support: Use main number

Myoda, Inc.
1053 Shore Rd.
Napierville, IL 60563
800-562-1071; 708-369-5199
fax: 708-369-6068

Nanao USA Corp.
23535 Telo Ave.
Torrance, CA 90505
800-800-5202; 310-325-5202
fax: 310-530-1679
Technical support: Use main number

National Design, Inc.
9171 Capital Texas Hwy., N, Houston
Bldg., Ste. 230
Austin, TX 78759
512-343-5055
fax: 512-343-5053
Technical support: 512-343-5054

National Instruments Corp.
6504 Bridge Point Pkwy.
Austin, TX 78730-5039
800-433-3488; 512-794-0100
fax: 512-794-8411
Technical support: Use toll-free number

National Semiconductor Corp.
(Quadram Products Group)
219 Perimeter Center Pkwy.
Atlanta, GA 30346
404-551-1000
Technical support: Use main number

NEC Technologies, Inc.
1414 Massachusetts Ave.
Boxborough, MA 01719
800-826-2255; 508-264-8000
fax: 508-264-8673
Technical support: 508-264-4300

Nemonix, Inc.
25 South St.
Hopkinton, MA 01748
800-435-8650; 508-435-9087
fax: 508-435-6127

New Media Graphics Corp.
780 Boston Rd.
Billerica, MA 01821
508-663-0666
fax: 508-663-6678

Newbridge Microsystems
603 March Rd.
Kanata, Ontario
Canada K2K 2M5
800-267-7231; 613-592-0714
fax: 613-592-1320

NewVoice
8500 Leesburg Pike, Ste. 409
Vienna, VA 22182-2409
703-448-0570
fax: 703-448-1078

Nissei Sangyo America, Ltd. (NSA)
800 South St.
Waltham, MA 02154
617-893-5700

Norpak Corp.
10 Hearst Way
Kanata, Ontario
Canada K2L 2P4
613-592-4164
fax: 613-592-6560

Novacor, Inc.
1841 Zanker Rd.
San Jose, CA 95112
800-486-6682; 408-441-6500
fax: 408-441-6811

Nth Graphics
1908 Kramer Lane, Ste. A
Austin, TX 78758
800-624-7552; 512-832-1944
fax: 512-832-5954
Technical support: Use main number

Number Nine Computer Corp.
18 Hartwell Ave.
Lexington, MA 02173
800-438-6463; 617-492-0999
fax: 617-864-9329

Nutmeg Systems, Inc.
25 South Ave.
New Canaan, CT 06840
800-777-8439; 203-966-7972

Nuvo Star, Inc.
30941 W. Agoura Rd., Unit 306
Westlake Village, CA 91361
800-527-NUVO; 818-597-8691
fax: 818-597-0503

Omnicomp Graphics Corp.
1734 W. Sam Houston Pkwy., N
Houston, TX 77043
713-464-2990
fax: 713-827-7540

Omnitronix, Inc.
760 Harrison St.
Seattle, WA 98109
800-765-5576; 206-624-4985
fax: 206-624-5610

Online Products Corp.
20251 Century Blvd.
Germantown, MD 20874
800-922-9204; 301-428-3700
fax: 301-428-2903

Opta Corp.
2525 E. Bayshore Rd., Ste. 2
Palo Alto, CA 94303
415-354-1120

Optiquest
12070 Telegraph Rd., Ste. 101
Santa Fe Springs, CA 90670
800-THE-OPTI; 310-903-1030
fax: 310-903-1036

Opus Systems
329 N. Bernardo Ave.
Mountain View, CA 94043
800-873-6787; 415-960-4040
fax: 415-960-4001

Orange Micro, Inc.
1400 N. Lakeview Ave.
Anaheim, CA 92807
800-223-8029; 714-779-2772
fax: 714-779-9332

Orchid Technology, Inc.
45365 Northport Loop West
Fremont, CA 94538
800-767-2443; 510-683-0300
fax: 510-490-9312
Technical support: Use main number

Our Business Machines, Inc.
12901 Ramona Blvd., Unit J
Irwindale, CA 91706
800-443-1435; 818-337-9614
fax: 818-960-1766

Packard Bell
9425 Canoga Ave.
Chatsworth, CA 91311
818-773-4400
fax: 818-773-9521
Technical support: 800-733-4411

PACKinTELL Electronics USA
11369 Sunrise Gold Circle
Rancho Cordova, CA 95742
800-447-2515; 916-635-2784
fax: 916-635-4836

Panasonic Communications & Systems Co.
(Office Automation Group)
2 Panasonic Way
Secaucus, NJ 07094
201-348-7000
Technical support: 800-222-0584

Paradise Systems, Inc.
99 S. Hill Dr.
Brisbane, CA 94005
415-468-7300

Parallax Graphics, Inc.
2500 Condensa St.
Santa Clara, CA 95051
408-727-2220
fax: 408-980-5139

Parsytec, Inc.
245 W. Roosevelt Rd., Bldg. 9, Unit 60&61
West Chicago, IL 60185
708-293-9500
fax: 708-293-9525

PC Brand, Inc.
954 W. Washington St.
Chicago, IL 60607
800-722-7263; 312-226-5200
fax: 312-226-6841
Technical support: Use toll-free number

PC Craft, Inc.
640 Puente St.
Brea, CA 92621
800-733-6666; 714-256-5000
fax: 714-256-5025

PC Tech, Inc.
907 North 6th St.
Lake City, MN 55041
612-345-4555
fax: 612-345-5514

Performance Xpress
14807 North 73rd St., Ste. 103
Scottsdale, AZ 85260
800-654-4331; 602-998-3122
fax: 602-998-3092

Performix Technology Corp.
47000 Warm Springs Blvd., Ste. 455
Fremont, CA 94539
510-659-0100

Monitors and Video-Related Equipment

The Periscope Co., Inc.
1197 Peachtree St., Plaza Level
Atlanta, GA 30361
800-722-7006; 404-875-8080
fax: 404-872-1973

Personal Computer & Communication, Inc.
3 Musick
Irvine, CA 92718
714-587-1369
fax: 714-587-1136

Personal Computer Graphics Corp.
3914 Del Amo Blvd.
Torrance, CA 90503
310-214-0550

Personal Computer Peripherals Corp.
4710 Eisenhower Blvd., Bldg. A
Tampa, FL 33634
800-622-2888; 813-884-3092
fax: 813-886-0520

Philips Consumer Electronics Co.
One Philips Dr., P.O. Box 14810
Knoxville, TN 37914-1810
615-521-4316
fax: 615-521-4406
Technical support: 800-722-6224

Pinnacle Micro, Inc.
15265 Alton Pkwy.
Irvine, CA 92718
800-553-7070; 714-727-3300
fax: 714-727-1913

Pixel Engineering, Inc.
40491 Encyclopedia Circle
Fremont, CA 94539
510-656-1338

Pixelworks, Inc.
7 Park Ave.
Hudson, NH 03051
800-247-2476; 603-880-1322
fax: 603-880-6558

Pixielink Corp.
8 Kane Industrial Dr.
Hudson, MA 01749
508-562-4803

Portacom Technologies, Inc.
3235 Kifer Rd. #310
Santa Clara, CA 95051
408-736-9135

Powercard Supply
12231 Southwest 129 Court
Miami, FL 33186
800-63-PCPWR; 305-251-5855
fax: 305-251-2334

Poynting Products, Inc.
P.O. Box 1227
Oak Park, IL 60304
312-489-6638

Premier Computer Innovations
10310 Harwin Dr.
Houston, TX 77036
800-347-1777; 713-995-4433
fax: 713-995-4751

Princeton Graphic Systems
P.O. Box 100040, 1100 Northmeadow
Pkwy., Ste. 150
Roswell, GA 30076
800-221-1490; 404-664-1010
fax: 404-664-1510
Technical support: Use main number

Princeton Publishing Labs
101 Business Park Dr., Ste. 100
Skillman, NJ 08558
609-924-1153
fax: 609-924-6465

Prism Imaging Systems
5309 Randall Place
Fremont, CA 94538
510-490-9360
fax: 510-490-9342

Processor Sciences, Inc.
180 Bear Hill Rd.
Waltham, MA 02154
617-890-0292
fax: 617-890-3345

Programming Sciences
7194 Clairmont Mesa Blvd.
San Diego, CA 92111
619-569-0774
fax: 619-569-5073

Progressive Image Technology
120 Blue Ravine Rd., Ste. 2
Folsom, CA 95630
916-985-7501
fax: 916-985-7507

Prometa USA, Inc.
5929 Southwest 36th Way
Gainesville, FL 32608
800-283-6382; 904-335-6382

Proton Corp.
5630 Cerritos Ave.
Cypress, CA 90630
714-952-6900

PSI Integration, Inc.
851 E. Hamilton Ave., Ste. 200
Campbell, CA 95008
800-622-1722; 408-559-8544
fax: 408-559-8548

Purart, Inc.
P.O. Box 189
Hampton Falls, NH 03844
603-772-9907

QANTEL Business Systems, Inc.
4142 Point Eden Way
Hayward, CA 94545-3781
800-227-1894; 510-887-7777
fax: 510-782-6195

Q/Cor
One Quad Way
Norcross, GA 30093-2919
800-548-3420; 404-923-6666
fax: 404-564-5528
Technical support: Use main number

QDI Computer, Inc.
11552 E. Washington Blvd., Unit D
Whittier, CA 90606
213-908-1029
fax: 213-908-1033

Quadtel
3190-J Airport Loop Dr.
Costa Mesa, CA 92626
714-754-4422
fax: 714-754-4426

Questel, Inc.
10175 Joerschke Dr., P.O. Box 752
Grass Valley, CA 95945
916-477-5000

Qume Corp.
500 Yosemite Dr.
Milpitas, CA 95035
408-942-4000
fax: 408-942-4052
Technical support: 408-942-4138 (Monitors,
Terminals); 408-942-4100 (Printers)

Radius, Inc.
1710 Fortune Dr.
San Jose, CA 95131
800-227-2795; 408-434-1010
fax: 408-434-0770
Technical support: 408-434-1012

Rapid Systems
433 North 34th St.
Seattle, WA 98103
206-547-8311
fax: 206-548-0322

Rasterex USA
1908 Cliff Valley Way, Ste. 2010
Atlanta, GA 30329
800-648-7249; 404-320-0800
fax: 404-315-7645

RasterOps Corp.
2500 Walsh Ave.
Santa Clara, CA 95051
408-562-4200
fax: 408-562-4065
Technical support: 800-729-2656

Redlake Corp.
15005 Concord Circle
Morgan Hill, CA 95037
800-543-6563; 408-779-6464
fax: 408-778-6256

REDMS Group, Inc.
20160 Paseo Del Prado, Ste. D
Walnut, CA 91789
714-598-8209
fax: 714-598-7321

Relax Technology
3101 Whipple Rd., Ste. 22
Union City, CA 94587
510-471-6112
fax: 510-471-6267
Technical support: Use main number

Reliable Communications, Inc.
20111 Stevens Creek Blvd.
Cupertino, CA 95014
800-222-0042; 408-996-0230
fax: 408-996-3367

Relisys
320 S. Milpitas Blvd.
Milpitas, CA 95035
408-945-9000
fax: 408-945-0587

Renaissance GRX, Inc.
2265 116th Ave. Northeast
Bellevue, WA 98004
206-454-8086

**Sampo Corp. of America
(Industrial Products Division)**
5550 Peachtree Industrial Blvd.
Norcross, GA 30071
404-449-6220
fax: 404-447-1109

DIRECTORY OF MANUFACTURERS

Samsung Information Systems America, Inc.
3655 N. First St.
San Jose, CA 95134-1708
800-446-0262; 408-434-5400
fax: 408-434-5653
Technical support: Use main number

Samtron
14251 E. Firestone Blvd., Ste. 101
La Mirada, CA 90638
213-802-8425
fax: 213-802-8820

SANYO/ICON International, Inc.
764 E. Timpanogos Pkwy.
Orem, UT 84057
800-US-SANYO; 801-225-6888
fax: 801-226-0651

SCION Corp.
152 W. Patrick St.
Frederick, MD 21701
301-695-7870
fax: 301-695-0035

Seawell Microsystems, Inc.
3808 39th Ave., SW
Seattle, WA 98116
206-938-5420

Sefco East
41-37 24th St.
Long Island City, NY 11101
718-786-2001

Seiko Instruments U.S.A., Inc.
(PC Products Division)
1130 Ringwood Court
San Jose, CA 95131
800-873-4561; 408-922-5900
fax: 408-922-5835
Technical support: 800-553-5312

Sherwood/Kimtron
4181 Business Center Dr.
Fremont, CA 94538-6355
800-777-8755; 510-623-8900
fax: 510-623-8945

Sigma Designs, Inc.
46501 Landing Pkwy.
Fremont, CA 94538
510-770-0100
fax: 510-770-2640

Signal Analytics Corp.
374 Maple Ave., E, Ste. 204
Vienna, VA 22180
703-281-3277
fax: 703-281-2509

SIIG, Inc.
5369 Randall Place
Fremont, CA 94538
510-657-0567
fax: 510-657-5962

Silicon Composers, Inc.
208 California Ave.
Palo Alto, CA 94306
415-322-8763

Silicon Graphics, Inc.
2011 N. Shoreline Blvd.
Mountain View, CA 94039-7311
415-960-1980
Technical support: 800-800-4744

Silicon Shack
512 Campbell Ave., Ste. 112
San Jose, CA 95130
408-446-4521
fax: 408-374-4412

Sirex U.S.A., Inc.
132-14 11th Ave.
College Point, NY 11356
800-722-0404; 718-746-7500
fax: 718-746-0882

SONY Corporation of America
(Component Peripheral Products Co.)
655 River Oaks Pkwy.
San Jose, CA 95134
408-432-0190
fax: 408-943-0740

SONY Corporation of America
(Information Products Division)
Sony Dr.
Park Ridge, NJ 07656
800-222-7669; 201-930-1000
fax: 201-573-8608
Technical support: Use main number

SONY Corporation of America
(Microcomputer Products Division)
Sony Dr.
Park Ridge, NJ 07656
201-930-1000
fax: 201-573-8608

Sota Technology, Inc.
559 Weddell Dr.
Sunnyvale, CA 94089
800-237-1713; 408-745-1111
fax: 408-745-1640

Spark International, Inc.
1939 Waukegan Rd., Ste. 107
Glenview, IL 60025
708-998-6640
fax: 708-998-8840

Spectragraphics Corp.
9707 Waples St.
San Diego, CA 92121
800-821-4822; 619-450-0611
fax: 619-450-0218
Technical support: 619-587-6853

Spectral Innovations, Inc.
4633 Old Ironsides Dr., Ste. 450
Santa Clara, CA 95054
408-727-1314
fax: 408-727-1423

Spectre Corp.
600 W. Cummings Park, Ste. 6500
Woburn, MA 01801
617-932-8640

Spectrum Signal Processing, Inc.
3700 Gilmore Way, Ste. 301, Discovery Park
Burnaby, BC
Canada V5G 4M1
800-323-1842; 604-438-7266
fax: 604-438-3046

Stac Electronics
5993 Avenida Encinas
Carlsbad, CA 92008
800-522-7822; 619-431-7474
Technical support: 800-522-5335

STB Systems, Inc.
1651 N. Glenville, Ste. 210
Richardson, TX 75081
214-234-8750
fax: 214-234-1306

Street Electronics Corp.
6420 Via Real
Carpinteria, CA 93013
805-684-4593
fax: 805-684-6628

Strobe Data, Inc.
13240 Northup Way, Ste. 19A
Bellevue, WA 98005-2077
206-641-4940
fax: 206-641-1303

SunRiver Corp.
11500-01 Metric Blvd., Ste. 150
Austin, TX 78758
512-835-8001
fax: 512-835-8026

Sunshine Technologies, Inc.
725 Brea Canyon Rd., Ste. 1
Walnut, CA 91789
714-598-9686
fax: 714-598-6323

SuperMac Technology
485 Potrero Ave.
Sunnyvale, CA 94086
800-624-8999; 408-245-2202
fax: 408-735-7250
Technical support: 408-245-0646

Swan Technologies
3075 Research Dr.
State College, PA 16801
800-468-9044; 814-238-1820
fax: 814-237-4450
Technical support: 800-468-7926

Symbolics, Inc.
8 New England Exec. Park
Burlington, MA 01803
617-221-1000
fax: 617-221-1099

Symmetric Research
15 Central Way, Ste. 9
Kirkland, WA 98033
206-828-6560

Syncomp International Corp.
1400 W. Lambert Rd., Ste. D
Brea, CA 92621
213-690-1011
fax: 213-690-6380

Syscom, Inc. (CA)
2362-D Qume Dr.
San Jose, CA 95131
800-624-8007; 408-432-8153

Systems Consulting, Inc.
P.O. Box 111209
Pittsburgh, PA 15238-0609
412-781-5280
fax: 412-963-1624

Systems Peripherals, Inc.
134 Newbury St.
Peabody, MA 01960
508-535-6196
fax: 508-535-6191

Monitors and Video-Related Equipment

Systran Corp.
4126 Linden Ave.
Dayton, OH 45432-3068
513-252-5601
fax: 513-258-2729

Talon Technology Corp.
1819 Firman Dr., Ste. 137
Richardson, TX 75081
214-680-9913
fax: 214-690-1001

Tandy Corp.
1800 One Tandy Center
Ft. Worth, TX 76102
817-390-3011
fax: 817-390-2774
Technical support: 817-390-3861

Tatung Co. of America, Inc.
2850 El Presidio St.
Long Beach, CA 90810
800-827-2850; 310-979-7055
fax: 310-637-8484
Technical support: Use main number

Taxan America, Inc.
161 Nortech Pkwy.
San Jose, CA 95134
800-829-2641; 408-946-3400
fax: 408-262-9059
Technical support: Use main number

Technical Solutions, Inc.
P.O. Box 1148
Mesilla Park, NM 88047
505-524-2154
fax: 505-525-5801

Tecmar
6225 Cochran Rd.
Solon, OH 44139
800-624-8560; 216-349-0600
fax: 216-349-0851
Technical support: 800-344-4463

TECO Information Systems, Inc.
24 E. Harbor Dr.
Lake Zurich, IL 60047
708-438-3998
fax: 708-438-8061

Tektronix, Inc.
Howard Vollum Park, P.O. Box 500
Beaverton, OR 97077-0001
800-835-9433; 503-627-7111
fax: 503-627-5502
Technical support: 800-835-6100

Ten X Technology, Inc.
4807 Spicewood Springs Rd.
Bldg. 3, Ste. 3200
Austin, TX 78759
800-922-9050; 512-346-8360
fax: 512-346-9580

Texas Instruments, Inc.
P.O. Box 655012, M/S 57
Dallas, TX 75265
800-527-3500; 214-995-2011
fax: 214-995-4360
Technical support: 512-250-7407

Texas Microsystems, Inc.
10618 Rockley Rd.
Houston, TX 77099
800-627-8700; 713-933-8050
fax: 713-933-1029
Technical support: Use main number

Thomson Information Systems Corp.
5731 W. Slauson Ave.
Culver City, CA 90230
800-325-0464

3Lynx Technologies Corp.
1450 Seareel Lane
San Jose, CA 95131
800-243-5969; 408-432-8833
fax: 408-434-0466

TIMESLIPS Corp.
239 Western Ave.
Essex, MA 01929
800-338-5314; 508-768-6100
fax: 508-768-7660
Technical support: 508-768-7490

Toshiba America Electronic Components, Inc.
One Parkway, N, Ste. 500
Deerfield, IL 60015-2547
800-843-2108; 708-945-1500
fax: 708-945-1044

Trident Microsystems, Inc.
321 Soquel Way
Sunnyvale, CA 94086
800-348-8808; 408-738-3194
fax: 408-738-0905

Truetech, Inc.
181 B W. Orangethorpe
Placentia, CA 92670
714-961-0438
fax: 714-961-0952

TrueVision, Inc.
7340 Shadeland Station
Indianapolis, IN 46256-3921
800-858-8783; 317-841-0332
fax: 317-576-7700
Technical support: Use main number

Tseng Laboratories, Inc.
10 Pheasant Run, Newtown Commons
Newtown, PA 18940
215-968-0502
fax: 215-860-7713

TTX Computer Products, Inc.
1255 Laquinta Dr., Ste. 118
Orlando, FL 32809
407-826-0186
fax: 407-826-0267

Turtle Beach Systems
P.O. Box 5074
York, PA 17405
717-843-6916
fax: 717-854-8319

TVM Professional Monitor Corp.
1109 West 9th St.
Upland, CA 91786
800-822-8168; 714-985-4788
fax: 714-978-8377

TW Casper Corp.
47430 Seabridge Dr.
Fremont, CA 94538
510-770-8500
fax: 510-770-8509

Unisys Corp.
P.O. Box 500
Blue Bell, PA 19424-0001
215-542-4011
Technical support: 800-448-1424

Univation, Inc.
513 Valley Way
Milpitas, CA 95035
800-221-5842; 408-263-1200
fax: 408-263-1474

Univision Technologies, Inc.
Three Burlington Woods
Burlington, MA 01803
617-221-6700
fax: 617-221-6777

US Integrated Technologies (USIT)
3023 Research Dr.
Richmond, CA 94806
510-223-1001
fax: 510-223-2766

US Power
743 N. Main St.
Orange, CA 92668
714-997-0388
fax: 714-538-3323

U.S. Trade Research
1134/C Buckingham Dr.
Costa Mesa, CA 92626
714-557-6709
fax: 714-662-2783

US VIDEO
62 Southfield Ave., One Stamford Landing
Stamford, CT 06902-9950
203-964-9000
fax: 203-964-1824

UVC Corp.
16800 Aston St.
Irvine, CA 92714
714-261-5336

Vectrix Corp.
204 S. Olive St.
Rolla, MO 65401
314-364-7500
fax: 314-364-9533

VENT (Video Enhanced New Technologies)
110 Pioneer Way
Mountain View, CA 94041
415-961-3671
fax: 415-964-7715

Ventek Corp.
31336 Via Colinas, Ste. 102
Westlake Village, CA 91362
818-991-3868
fax: 818-991-4097

Vermont Microsystems, Inc.
11 Tigan St., P.O. Box 236
Winooski, VT 05404-0236
800-354-0055; 802-655-2860
fax: 802-655-9058

Video Associates Labs
4926 Spicewood Springs Rd.
Austin, TX 78759
800-331-0547; 512-346-5781
fax: 512-346-9407

Video Dynamics
155 Bryant St., Ste 612
San Francisco, CA 94103
415-863-3023

DIRECTORY OF MANUFACTURERS

Video Seven, Inc.
46221 Landing Pkwy.
Fremont, CA 94538
800-238-0101; 800-248-1850

VideoLogic, Inc.
245 First St.
Cambridge, MA 02142
617-494-0530
fax: 617-494-0534

Videomail, Inc.
568-4 Weddell Dr.
Sunnyvale, CA 94089
408-733-5166
fax: 408-733-2075

ViewSonic
12130 Mora Dr.
Santa Fe Springs, CA 90670
310-946-0711

VIP Computer, Inc.
2 Gourmet Lane
Edison, NJ 08837
908-494-2400
fax: 908-494-2411

Vision Technologies
48431 Milmont Dr.
Fremont, CA 94538
510-683-2900
fax: 510-657-0601

Visionetics International
21311 Hawthorne Blvd., Ste. 235
Torrance, CA 90503
310-316-7940
fax: 310-543-2117

Voice Technologies
120 Village Sq., Ste. 143
Orinda, CA 94563
510-283-7586
fax: 510-283-3661

Vortex Systems, Inc.
800 Vinial St.
Pittsburgh, PA 15212
412-322-7820
fax: 412-322-8888

Wang Laboratories, Inc.
One Industrial Way, M/S 014-A1B
Lowell, MA 01851
800-835-9264; 508-459-5000
Technical support: 800-247-9264

Ward Systems Group, Inc.
245 W. Patrick St.
Frederick, MD 21701
301-662-7950
fax: 301-662-5666

Warp Speed Light Pens, Inc.
1086 Mechem Dr.
Ruidoso, NM 88345
800-874-4315; 505-258-5713
fax: 505-258-5744

Western Digital Imaging
800 E. Middlefield Rd.
Mountain View, CA 94043
800-331-8127; 415-960-3353
fax: 415-960-1584
Technical support: 800-832-4778

Willow Peripherals, Inc.
190 Willow Ave.
Bronx, NY 10454
800-444-1585; 212-402-9500
fax: 212-402-9603

Workstation Technologies, Inc.
18004 Sky Park Circle
Irvine, CA 92714
714-250-8983

Wyse Technology
3471 N. First St.
San Jose, CA 95134
800-438-9973; 408-473-1200
fax: 408-473-1222
Technical support: 408-922-5700

Xerox Corp.
1960 East Grand Ave.
El Segundo, CA 90245
310-333-8718

Xtron Computer Equipment Corp.
716 Jersey Ave.
Jersey City, NJ 07302
800-854-4450; 201-798-5000
fax: 201-798-4322

Xycom, Inc.
750 N. Maple Rd.
Saline, MI 48176
800-AT-XYCOM; 313-429-4971
fax: 313-429-1010

YARC Systems Corp.
27489 W. Agoura Rd.
Agoura Hills, CA 91301
818-889-4388
fax: 818-889-2658

Zenith Data Systems
2150 E. Lake Cook Rd.
Buffalo Grove, IL 60089
708-808-5000

Printers and Related Equipment

Abaton
48431 Milmont Dr.
Fremont, CA 94538
800-444-5321; 510-683-2226
fax: 510-683-2870
Technical support: 510-498-4433

Acer America Corp.
401 Charcot Ave.
San Jose, CA 95131
800-538-1542; 408-922-0333
fax: 408-922-0176
Technical support: 800-637-7000

AcuPrint, Inc.
5235 Avenida Encinas, Ste. A
Carlsbad, CA 92008
619-931-9316
fax: 619-431-1188

Advanced Communications, Inc.
1031 E. Duane, Ste. D
Sunnyvale, CA 94086
408-749-9845
fax: 408-749-0409

Advanced Matrix Technology, Inc.
765 Flynn Rd.
Camarillo, CA 93010
800-992-2264; 805-388-5799
fax: 805-499-4147
Technical support: Use main number

Advanced Technologies International
355 Sinclare-Frontage Rd.
Milpitas, CA 95035
408-942-1780
fax: 408-942-1260

AEG Olympia, Inc.
3140 Rt. 22, Box 22
Somerville, NJ 08876-0022
800-999-6872; 908-231-8300
fax: 908-526-6349
Technical support: Use main number

AgFa Compugraphic
200 Ballardbale St.
Wilmington, MA 01887
800-822-5524; 508-658-5600
fax: 508-658-6285

ALPS America
3553 N. First St.
San Jose, CA 95134
800-828-2577; 408-432-6000
fax: 408-432-6035
Technical support: 800-950-2577

American Computer Hardware Corp.
2205 S. Wright St.
Santa Ana, CA 92705
800-447-1237; 714-549-2688
fax: 714-662-0491

Amstrad, Inc.
1915 Westridge Dr.
Irving, TX 75038
214-518-0668
fax: 214-578-0922

Anritsu America, Inc.
15 Thornton Rd.
Oakland, NJ 07436
800-255-7234; 201-337-1111
fax: 201-337-1033

Apollo Computer, Inc.
300 Apollo Dr.
Chelmsford, MA 01824
508-256-6600
fax: 508-256-9374
Technical support: 800-227-6556

Apple Computer, Inc.
20525 Mariani Ave.
Cupertino, CA 95014
408-996-1010
Technical support: 800-776-2333

AT&T Computer Systems
1776 On The Green
Morristown, NJ 07960
800-247-1212; 201-898-8000
fax: 201-644-9768
Technical support: Use main number

Autographix, Inc.
63 Third Ave.
Burlington, MA 01803
800-548-8558; 617-272-9000

Autologic, Inc.
1050 Rancho Conejo Blvd.
Newbury Park, CA 91320
805-498-9611
fax: 805-499-1167

Printers and Related Equipment

Axis Communications, Inc.
130 Centre St.
Danvers, MA 01923
508-777-7957
fax: 508-777-9905

Axonix Corp.
1214 Wilmington Ave.
Salt Lake City, UT 84106
800-866-9797; 801-466-9797
fax: 801-485-6204

BDT Products, Inc.
17152 Armstrong Ave.
Irvine, CA 92714
800-346-3238; 714-660-1386
fax: 714-474-0480

Bézier Systems, Inc.
1190 Saratoga Ave.
San Jose, CA 95129
408-345-0345
fax: 408-345-0350

BGL Technology Corp.
438 Constitution Ave.
Camarillo, CA 93012
805-987-7305
fax: 805-987-7346

Blue Chip International
P.O. Box 4090
Mesa, AZ 85274
602-731-6980

Bren Instruments, Inc.
(Printing Systems Division)
308 Century Court
Franklin, TN 37064
800-826-3991; 615-794-7478

Brother International Corp.
(Office Systems Division)
200 Cottontail Lane
Somerset, NJ 08875-6714
908-356-8880
fax: 908-469-5167

Bull HN Information Systems, Inc.
2 Wall St., Technology Park, M/S 111N
Billerica, MA 01821-4199
508-294-6000
fax: 508-294-4508

C-Tech Electronics, Inc.
2515 McCabe Way, P.O. Box 19673
Irvine, CA 92713-9673
800-347-4017; 714-833-1165
fax: 714-757-4533

CalComp Plotter Products Group
P.O. Box 3250
2411 W. LaPalma Ave.
Anaheim, CA 92803
800-932-1212; 714-821-2000
fax: 714-821-2832

Canon U.S.A., Inc.
One Canon Plaza
Lake Success, NY 11042
516-488-6700
fax: 516-354-5805
Technical support: 800-423-2366

Chinon America, Inc.
(Information Equipment Division)
660 Maple Ave.
Torrance, CA 90503
800-441-0222; 310-533-0274
fax: 310-533-1727
Technical support: Use main number

CIE America, Inc.
2515 McCabe Way, P.O. Box 19663
Irvine, CA 92713-9663
800-877-1421; 714-660-1421
fax: 714-757-4488

Citizen America Corp.
2450 Broadway Ave., Ste. 600
Santa Monica, CA 90404-3060
310-453-0614
fax: 310-453-2814

C. Itoh Electronics Co.
2505 McCabe Way
Irvine, CA 92714-6297
800-347-2484; 714-660-1421

Colorocs Corp.
P.O. Box 1828, 2830 Peterson Place
Norcross, GA 30071
800-966-2579; 404-840-6500
fax: 404-446-1771

Computer Communications, Inc.
2610 Columbia St.
Torrance, CA 90503
800-421-1178; 310-320-9101
fax: 310-533-8502

Computer Language Research, Inc.
2395 Midway Rd.
Carrollton, TX 75006
800-FORM-FREE; 214-250-7000
fax: 214-250-1014

Computer Products Plus, Inc.
16351 Gothard St.
Huntington Beach, CA 92647
800-274-4277; 714-847-1799
fax: 714-848-6850

Comterm, Inc.
110 Hymus Blvd.
Pointe-Claire, Quebec
Canada H9R 1E8
514-694-4332
fax: 514-694-4123

CPT Corp.
8100 Mitchell Rd.
Eden Prairie, MN 55344-9833
800-447-1189; 612-937-8000
fax: 612-937-1858

CSS Laboratories, Inc.
1641 McGaw Ave.
Irvine, CA 92714
714-852-8161
fax: 714-852-9464

Data General Corp.
4400 Computer Dr.
Westboro, MA 01580
800-328-2436; 508-366-8911
fax: 508-366-1299
Technical support: 800-537-6084

Data Systems Hardware
22560 Glenn Dr., Ste. 112
Sterling, VA 22170
703-450-1700
fax: 703-450-5726

Dataproducts Corp.
6219 De Soro Ave., P.O. Box 746
Woodland Hills, CA 91365-0746
800-624-8999, ext. 588; 818-887-8000
fax: 818-887-4789
Technical support: 818-888-4242

Datasouth Computer Corp.
4216 Stuart Andrew Blvd.
Charlotte, NC 28217
800-476-2120; 704-523-8500
fax: 704-523-9298

DCS/Fortis
1820 West 220th St., Ste 220
Torrance, CA 90501
800-736-4847; 310-782-6090
fax: 310-782-6134

Decision Data
One Progress Ave.
Horsham, PA 19044
800-523-5357; 215-674-3300
fax: 215-675-1931

DeRex, Inc.
3650 Coral Ridge Dr.
Coral Springs, FL 33065
800-245-7282; 305-753-0840
fax: 305-753-0944

Desktop Systems, Inc.
48431 Milmont Dr.
Femont, CA 94538
800-444-5321; 510-683-2727
fax: 510-683-2151

Dianachart, Inc.
101 Round Hill Dr.
Rockaway, NJ 07866
201-625-2299
fax: 201-625-2449

Digital Design, Inc.
8400 Baymeadows Way
Jacksonville, FL 32256
800-733-0908; 904-737-0908
fax: 904-737-1162

Digital Equipment Corp.
146 Main St.
Maynard, MA 01754-2571
508-493-5111
fax: 508-493-8780
Technical support: 800-332-8000

Digitec
959 Cheney Ave.
Marion, OH 43302
614-387-3444
fax: 614-383-6254

DSI, Inc.
1440 S. Lipan
Denver, CO 80223
800-641-5215; 303-777-8211
fax: 303-778-0689

Eastman Kodak Co.
(Copy Products Division)
343 State St.
Rochester, NY 14650
800-242-2424; 716-724-4000
fax: 716-724-0663
Technical support: Use main number

Epson America, Inc.
20770 Madrona Ave.
Torrance, CA 90509-2842
800-289-3776; 310-782-0770
Technical support: 310-782-2600

Everex Systems, Inc.
48431 Milmont Dr.
Fremont, CA 94538
800-821-0806; 510-498-1111
fax: 510-651-0728
Technical support: 510-498-4411

DIRECTORY OF MANUFACTURERS

Facit, Inc.
400 Commercial St., P.O. Box 9540
Manchester, NH 03108-9540
800-733-2248; 603-647-2700
fax: 603-647-2724
Technical support: Use main number

Florida Digital, Inc.
295-F North Dr.
Melbourne, FL 32934
407-242-2842
fax: 407-242-3059

Fortis Information Systems, Inc.
Rickenbacker Rd.
Commerce, CA 90040
213-727-1227

Fujitsu America, Inc.
(Computer Products Group)
3055 Orchard Dr.
San Jose, CA 95134-2022
800-626-4686; 408-432-1300
fax: 408-434-0475
Technical support: 800-826-6112

GCC Technologies, Inc.
580 Winter St.
Waltham, MA 02154
800-422-7777; 617-890-0880
fax: 617-890-0822
Technical support: Use toll-free number

General Business Technology, Inc.
1891 McGaw Ave.
Irvine, CA 92714
800-521-1891; 714-261-1891
fax: 714-261-8285

General Parametrics Corp.
1250 Ninth St.
Berkeley, CA 94710
800-223-0999; 510-524-3950
fax: 510-524-9954

Genicom Corp.
Genicom Dr.
Waynesboro, VA 22980
800-443-6426; 703-949-1000
fax: 703-949-1392
Technical support: 703-949-1031

Gulton Graphic Instruments
Gulton Industrial Park
East Greenwich, RI 02818
800-343-7929; 401-884-6800
fax: 401-884-4872

Harris Adacom Corp.
P.O. Box 809022, 16001 Dallas Pkwy.
Dallas, TX 75380-9022
214-386-2000
fax: 214-386-2159

Hewlett-Packard Co.
3000 Hanover St.
Palo Alto, CA 94304
800-752-0900; 415-857-1501
Technical support: Use toll-free number

Howtek, Inc.
21 Park Ave.
Hudson, NH 03051
800-44-HOWTEK; 603-882-5200
fax: 603-880-3843
Technical support: Use main number

Hyundai Electronics America
166 Baypointe Pkwy.
San Jose, CA 95134
800-544-7808; 408-473-9200
fax: 408-943-9567
Technical support: 800-234-3553

IBM (International Business Machines)
Old Orchard Rd.
Armonk, NY 10504
800-426-2468; 914-765-1900
Technical support: Use toll-free number

Idea Courier/Servcom, Inc.
P.O. Box 29039
Phoenix, AZ 85038
800-528-1400; 602-894-7000

IDEAssociates, Inc.
29 Dunham Rd.
Billerica, MA 01821
800-257-5027; 508-663-6878
fax: 508-663-8851

The Identification Business
18079 Edison Ave.
Chesterfield, MO 63005
314-537-8400
fax: 314-537-8535

Image Systems, Inc.
2515 McCabe Way, P.O. Box 19743
Irvine, CA 92713-9743
800-347-4027; 714-833-0155
fax: 714-757-4418

Infoscribe/CTSI International, Inc.
75 Mall Dr.
Commack, NY 11725-5703
800-233-4442; 516-864-5200
fax: 516-864-5878

Interface Systems, Inc.
5855 Interface Dr.
Ann Arbor, MI 48103
800-544-4072; 313-769-5900
fax: 313-769-1047

JOYCE Associates
215 Franklin St.
Clayton, NJ 08312

KCR Technology
One Riverview Sq., Ste. 1
East Hartford, CT 06108
800-527-7055; 203-291-0842
fax: 203-528-1880

Kentek Information Systems, Inc.
2945 Wilderness Place
Boulder, CO 80301
303-440-5500

Konica Business Machines USA, Inc.
500 Day Hill Rd.
Windsor, CT 06095
800-456-6422; 203-683-2222
fax: 203-688-0700

Kyocera Unison, Inc.
1321 Harbor Bay Pkwy.
Alameda, CA 94501
800-367-7437; 510-748-6680
fax: 510-748-6963

Laser Computer, Inc.
(a Video Technology Co.)
800 N. Church St.
Lake Zurich, IL 60047
708-540-8086
fax: 708-540-8335
Technical support: 708-540-5022

LaserMaster (Macintosh Products Division)
6900 Shady Oak Rd.
Eden Prairie, MN 55344
612-944-9696
fax: 612-943-3469
Technical support: 612-944-8008

LaserMaster Technologies Corp.
7156 Shady Oak Rd.
Eden Prairie, MN 55344
612-944-9330
fax: 612-944-0522
Technical support: 612-944-9331

LaserSmith, Inc.
430 Martin Ave.
Santa Clara, CA 95050
408-727-7700
fax: 408-727-7888

Lee Data
10230 West 70th St.
Eden Prairie, MN 55344
800-533-3282; 612-828-0400
fax: 612-828-5799

Lexi Computer Systems Corp.
231 Sutton St.
North Andover, MA 01845
800-222-5394; 508-681-1118
fax: 508-681-0851

Linotype-Hell
425 Oser Ave.
Hauppauge, NY 11788-9890
800-633-1900; 516-434-2000

Magnetec Corp.
61 W. Dudleytown Rd.
Bloomfield, CT 06092
203-243-8941
fax: 203-243-5152

Mannesmann Tally Corp.
8301 South 180th St.
Kent, WA 98032-0413
800-843-1347; 206-251-5500
fax: 206-251-5520
Technical support: 206-251-5593

Memorex Telex Corp.
6422 East 41st St.
Tulsa, OK 74135
800-950-3465; 918-627-1111
fax: 918-624-4581
Technical support: Use main number

Microtek Lab, Inc.
680 Knox St.
Torrance, CA 90502
800-654-4160; 310-321-2121
fax: 310-538-1193
Technical support: Use main number

Miltope Business Products Corp.
1770 Walt Whitman Rd.
Melville, NY 11747
516-420-0200
fax: 516-756-7606

Minolta Corp.
(Document Imaging Systems Division)
101 Williams Dr.
Ramsey, NJ 07446
201-825-4000
fax: 201-444-8736

Printers and Related Equipment

Mirror Technologies, Inc.
2644 Patton Rd.
Roseville, MN 55113
800-654-5294; 612-633-4450
fax: 612-633-3136
Technical support: 612-633-2105

Mitsubishi Electronics America, Inc.
(Information Systems Division)
991 Knox St.
Torrance, CA 90502
800-556-1234, ext. 54M; 800-441-2345, ext.
54M (in California); 310-515-3993
fax: 310-527-7693
Technical support: Use main number

Mosier, Scott and Associates, Inc.
(Protocol Division)
9839 Whithorn Dr.
Houston, TX 77095
713-550-4550
fax: 713-550-5037

Motorola Commercial Systems
10700 N. De Anza Blvd.
Cupertino, CA 95014
800-556-1234, ext. 165; 800-441-2345, ext.
165 (in California); 408-366-4000
fax: 408-366-4402
Technical support: 800-624-8999, ext. 165

NBS Southern, Inc.
11451 S. Belcher Rd.
Largo, FL 34643
800-327-5602; 813-541-2200
fax: 813-546-8042

NCR Corp.
1700 S. Patterson Blvd.
Dayton, OH 45479
800-544-3333; 513-445-5000
fax: 513-445-2008
Technical support: 800-CALL-NCR

NEC Information Systems, Inc.
1414 Massachusetts Ave.
Boxborough, MA 01719
800-826-2255; 508-264-8000
fax: 508-264-8673
Technical support: 508-264-4300

NewGen Systems Corp.
17580 Newhope St.
Fountain Valley, CA 92708
714-641-8600
fax: 714-641-2800

NeXT, Inc.
900 Chesapeake Dr.
Redwood City, CA 94063
800-848-NEXT; 415-366-0900
fax: 415-780-3714
Technical support: Use toll-free number

Nissei Sangyo America, Ltd. (NSA)
800 South St.
Waltham, MA 02154
617-893-5700

Nissho Electronics (U.S.A.) Corp.
17320 Red Hill Ave., Ste. 200, Inwood Park
Irvine, CA 92714
800-233-1837; 714-261-8811
fax: 714-261-8819

Novatek Corp.
3700 Northwest 124th Ave., Ste. 137
Coral Springs, FL 33065
305-341-7700
fax: 305-345-9334

Océ Graphics USA, Inc.
385 Ravendale Dr., P.O. Box 7169
Mountain View, CA 94039-7169
800-545-5445; 415-964-7900
fax: 415-961-6152

Office Automation Systems, Inc.
9940 Barnes Canyon Rd.
San Diego, CA 92121
619-452-9400
fax: 619-452-2427

Okidata Corp.
532 Fellowship Rd.
Mt. Laurel, NJ 08054
800-654-3282; 609-235-2600
fax: 609-778-4184
Technical support: 609-273-0300

Olivetti Office USA
P.O. Box 6945, 765 U.S. Hwy. 202, S
Bridgewater, NJ 08807-0945
800-527-2960; 908-526-8200
fax: 908-526-8405
Technical support: 908-704-6501

Output Technology Corp.
East 9922 Montgomery, Ste. 6
Spokane, WA 99206-4199
800-468-8788; 509-926-3855
fax: 509-922-4742

OWEN Associates, Inc.
22 Princeton Dr.
Delran, NJ 08075

Packard Bell
9425 Canoga Ave.
Chatsworth, CA 91311
818-773-4400
fax: 818-773-9521
Technical support: 800-733-4411

PACKinTELL Electronics USA
11369 Sunrise Gold Circle
Rancho Cordova, CA 95742
800-447-2515; 916-635-2784
fax: 916-635-4836

Panasonic Communications & Systems Co.
(Office Automation Group)
2 Panasonic Way
Secaucus, NJ 07094
201-348-7000
Technical support: 800-222-0584

Pentax Technologies Corp.
100 Technology Dr.
Broomfield, CO 80021
800-543-6144; 303-460-1600
fax: 303-460-1628

Personal Computer Products, Inc. (PCPI)
10865 Rancho Bernardo Rd.
San Diego, CA 92127
800-225-4098; 800-262-0522 (in California);
619-485-8411
fax: 619-487-5809

Philips Information Systems Co.
1435 Bradley Lane, Ste. 100
Carrollton, TX 75007
800-527-0204; 214-323-8238
fax: 214-991-6572

Primages, Inc.
151 Trade Zone Dr., Trade Plaza 5
Ronkonkoma, NY 11779
800-821-0066; 516-585-8200
fax: 516-585-2134

Printek, Inc.
1517 Townline Rd.
Benton Harbor, MI 49022
800-368-4636; 616-925-3200
fax: 616-925-8539

Printer Systems Corp. (PSC)
207 Perry Pkwy.
Gaithersburg, MD 20877
800-638-4041; 301-258-5060
fax: 301-926-7333

Printronix, Inc.
P.O. Box 19559, 17500 Cartwright Rd.
Irvine, CA 92713-9559
800-826-3874; 714-863-1900
fax: 714-660-8682

Printware, Inc
1385 Mendota Heights Rd.
St. Paul, MN 55120
800-456-1616; 612-456-1400

Q/Cor
One Quad Way
Norcross, GA 30093-2919
800-548-3420; 404-923-6666
fax: 404-564-5528
Technical support: Use main number

QANTEL Business Systems, Inc.
4142 Point Eden Way
Hayward, CA 94545-3781
800-227-1894; 510-887-7777
fax: 510-782-6195

QMS, Inc.
P.O. Box 81250
Mobile, AL 36689
800-631-2692; 205-633-4300
fax: 205-633-0013
Technical support: 205-633-4500

Qume Corp.
500 Yosemite Dr.
Milpitas, CA 95035
408-942-4000
fax: 408-942-4052
Technical support: 408-942-4138 (Monitors,
Terminals); 408-942-4100 (Printers)

Remanco Systems, Inc.
300 Rosewood Dr.
Danvers, MA 01923
508-777-4100
fax: 508-774-2010

Ricoh Corp.
5 Dedrick Place
West Caldwell, NJ 07006
800-327-8349; 201-882-2000
fax: 201-882-2506

Rosetta Technologies Corp.
9417 Princess Palm Ave.
Tampa, FL 33619
800-937-4224; 813-623-6205
fax: 813-620-1107

The ScanSoft Group, Inc.
1531 Sam Rittenberg Blvd.
Charleston, SC 29407
803-571-2430
fax: 803-571-6230

Seiko Instruments U.S.A., Inc.
(PC Products Division)
1130 Ringwood Court
San Jose, CA 95131
800-873-4561; 408-922-5900
fax: 408-922-5835
Technical support: 800-553-5312

DIRECTORY OF MANUFACTURERS

Seikosha America, Inc.
10 Industrial Ave.
Mahwah, NJ 07430
800-338-2609; 800-477-7468 (NJ);
201-327-7227
fax: 201-818-9075
Technical support: 800-477-7468

Sharp Electronics Corp.
(Professional Products Division)
Sharp Plaza, P.O. Box 650
Mahwah, NJ 07430
201-529-8200
fax: 201-529-9636
Technical support: 800-732-8221

Shinwa of America, Inc.
5915 Lincoln Ave.
Morton Grove, IL 60053
708-470-1600
fax: 708-470-0858

Siemens Nixdorf Printing Systems
5500 Broken Sound Blvd.
Boca Raton, FL 33487
407-997-3100

Singer Data Products
790 Maple Lane
Bensenville, IL 60106
708-860-6500
fax: 708-860-3672

Spear Technology, Inc.
710A Landwehr Rd.
Northbrook, IL 60062
708-480-7300
fax: 708-480-9538

Stafford Computer Corp.
RR 1, Box 90-C
Bringhurst, IN 46913
317-566-3724
fax: 317-852-9852

Star Micronics America, Inc.
420 Lexington Ave., Ste. 2702
New York, NY 10170
800-447-4700; 212-986-6770
fax: 212-286-9063
Technical support: 714-768-3192

Storage Technology Corp.
2270 South 88th St.
Louisville, CO 80028-4310
303-673-5151, ext. 5020
fax: 303-673-5019

Stratus Computer, Inc.
55 Fairbanks Blvd.
Marlboro, MA 01752
508-460-2000
fax: 508-481-8945

Sun Microsystems, Inc.
2550 Garcia Ave.
Mountain View, CA 94043
800-821-4643; 800-821-4642 (in California);
415-960-1300
fax: 415-969-9131
Technical support: 800-USA-4SUN

Synergystex International, Inc.
2967 Nationwide Pkwy., Ste. 5
Brunswick, OH 44212
216-225-3112
fax: 216-225-0099

Syntest Corp.
40 Locke Dr.
Marlboro, MA 01752
508-481-7827
fax: 508-481-5769

Talaris Systems, Inc.
P.O. Box 261580,
6059 Cornerstone Court, W
San Diego, CA 92196
619-587-0787
fax: 619-587-6788

Tandem Computers, Inc.
19333 Vallco Pkwy., Location 4-40
Cupertino, CA 95014-2599
800-538-3107; 408-725-6000
fax: 408-285-0505
Technical support: Use main number

Tandon Corp.
301 Science Dr.
Moorpark, CA 93021
805-523-0340
fax: 805-529-4450
Technical support: 800-487-8324

Tandy Corp.
1800 One Tandy Center
Ft. Worth, TX 76102
817-390-3011
fax: 817-390-2774
Technical support: 817-390-3861

Taneum Computer Products, Inc.
201 Southwest 41st St.
Renton, WA 98055
800-829-7768; 206-251-0711
fax: 206-251-6332

TEC America Electronics, Inc.
2710 Lakeview Court
Fremont, CA 94538
510-651-5333
fax: 510-651-6914

Tektronix, Inc.
Howard Vollum Park, P.O. Box 500
Beaverton, OR 97077-0001
800-835-9433; 503-627-7111
fax: 503-627-5502
Technical support: 800-835-6100

Terminal Data Corp.
5898 Condor Dr.
Moorpark, CA 93021
805-529-1500
fax: 805-529-6538

Texas Instruments, Inc.
P.O. Box 655012, M/S 57
Dallas, TX 75265
800-527-3500; 214-995-2011
fax: 214-995-4360
Technical support: 512-250-7407

Top-Link Computer, Inc.
48810 Kato Rd.
Fremont, CA 94538
510-226-8600
fax: 510-623-7132

Toshiba America Information Systems,
Inc. (Computer Systems Division)
9740 Irvine Blvd.
Irvine, CA 92718
800-334-3445; 714-583-3000
Technical support: 800-999-4273

TrendCOM
46309 Warm Springs Blvd.
Fremont, CA 94539
510-490-1291

Troy
2331 S. Pullman St.
Santa Ana, CA 92705
800-332-MICR; 714-250-3280
fax: 714-250-8972

Unisys Corp.
P.O. Box 500
Blue Bell, PA 19424-0001
215-542-4011
Technical support: 800-448-1424

Varityper
11 Mt. Pleasant Ave.
East Hanover, NJ 07936
800-631-8134; 201-887-8000, ext. 999

Vistron, Inc.
20380 Town Center Lane, Ste. 140
Cupertino, CA 95014
408-996-1824
fax: 408-996-1829

Wang Laboratories, Inc.
One Industrial Way, M/S 014-A1B
Lowell, MA 01851
800-835-9264; 508-459-5000
Technical support: 800-247-9264

Xerox Corp. (U.S. Marketing Group)
P.O. Box 24
Rochester, NY 14692
800-832-6979

Xpoint Corp.
5600 Oakbrook Pkwy., Ste. 240
Norcross, GA 30093
404-446-2764
fax: 404-446-6129

Xtron Computer Equipment Corp.
716 Jersey Ave.
Jersey City, NJ 07302
800-854-4450; 201-798-5000
fax: 201-798-4322

Backup and Storage

Alloy Computer Products, Inc.
165 Forest St.
Marlborough, MA 01752
800-544-7551; 508-481-8500
fax: 508-481-7711

CD Technology, Inc.
780 Montague Expwy., Ste. 407
San Jose, CA 95131
408-432-8698
fax: 408-432-0250
Technical support: Use main number

Chinon America, Inc.
660 Maple Ave.
Torrance, CA 90503
800-441-0222; 310-533-0274
fax: 310-533-1727
Technical support: Use main number

Accessories

Colorado Memory Systems, Inc.
800 S. Taft Ave.
Loveland, CO 80537
800-346-9881

COREtape
CORE International, Inc.
7171 N. Federal Hwy.
Boca Raton, FL 33487
800-688-9910; 407-997-6055

Everex Systems
48431 Milmont Dr.
Fremont, CA 94538
800-821-0806; 510-498-1111
fax: 510-651-0728
Technical support: 510-498-4411

Genesis Development Corp.
15850 W. Bluemound Rd., Ste. 307
Brookfield, WI 53005
414-796-1005
fax: 414-797-0727

Hitachi America, Ltd. (OAS Division)
110 Summit Ave.
Montvale, NJ 07645
800-448-2244; 201-573-0774
fax: 201-573-7660

IBM (International Business Machines)
Old Orchard Rd.
Armonk, NY 10504
800-426-2468; 914-765-1900
Technical support: Use toll-free number

**Irwin Magnetic Systems, Inc.
(Distribution Division of Maynard
Electronics)**
2101 Commonwealth Blvd.
Ann Arbor, MI 48105
800-421-1874

LMSI—Laser Magnetic Storage Int'l. Co.
4425 Arrows W. Dr.
Colorado Springs, CO 80907
800-777-5674

Maynard Electronics, Inc.
36 Skyline Dr.
Lake Mary, FL 32746
800-821-8782

Micro Solutions Computer Products
132 W. Lincoln Hwy.
DeKalb, IL 60115
815-756-3411
fax: 815-756-2928

Mountain Network Solutions, Inc.
240 Hacienda Ave.
Campbell, CA 95008
800-458-0300

NEC Technologies, Inc.
1414 Massachusetts Ave.
Boxborough, MA 01719
800-826-2255; 508-264-8000
fax: 508-264-8673
Technical support: 508-264-4300

PLI—Peripheral Land, Inc.
47421 Bayside Pkwy.
Fremont, CA 94538
800-288-8754

Procom Technology, Inc.
200 McCormick
Costa Mesa, CA 92626
800-800-8600; 714-549-9449

**SONY Corporation of America
(Microcomputer Products Division)**
Sony Dr.
Park Ridge, NJ 07656
201-930-1000
fax: 201-573-8608

Summit Memory Systems, Inc.
100 Technology Circle
Scotts Valley, CA 95066-3520
800-523-4767

Tallgrass Technologies Corp.
11100 W. 82nd St.
Lenexa, KS 66214
800-825-4727

Tandy Corp.
1800 One Tandy Center
Ft. Worth, TX 76102
817-390-3011
fax: 817-390-2774
Technical support: 817-390-3861

Tecmar
6225 Cochran Rd.
Solon, OH 44139
800-624-8560; 216-349-0600
fax: 216-249-0851
Technical support: 800-344-4463

Texel America, Inc.
1080 E. Duane Ave.
Sunnyvale, CA 94086
800-886-3935; 408-736-1374

Todd Enterprises, Inc.
224-49 67th Ave.
Bayside, NY 11364
800-445-8633; 718-343-1040

**Toshiba America Information Systems,
Inc. (Computer Systems Division)**
9740 Irvine Blvd.
Irvine, CA 92718
800-334-3445; 714-583-3000
Technical support: 800-999-4273

Wangtek, Inc.
41 Moreland Rd.
Simi Valley, CA 93065
800-992-9916

Accessories

**Advanced Gravis Computer
Technology, Ltd.**
3750 N. Fraser Way, Ste. 101
Burnaby, BC
Canada V5J 5E9
800-663-8558; 604-431-5020
fax: 604-431-5155
Technical support: 604-431-1807

AESI (Advanced Electronics Systems, Inc.)
2005 Lincoln Way, E
Chambersburg, PA 17201
800-345-1280; 717-263-5681
fax: 717-263-1040
Technical Support: 800-733-3155

American Power Conversion Corp.
132 Fairgrounds Rd.
P.O. Box 278
West Kingston, RI 02892
800-788-2208; 401-789-5735
fax: 401-789-3710
Technical Support: 800-800-4272

AVM Technology, Inc.
655 East 9800 South
Sandy, UT 84070
800-880-0041; 801-571-0967
fax: 801-566-2952

Brooks Electronics, Inc.
4001 N. American St.
Philadelphia, PA 19140
800-523-0130; 215-228-4433
fax: 215-227-7687

CD Technology, Inc.
780 Montague Expwy., Ste. 407
San Jose, CA 95131
408-432-8698
fax: 408-432-0250

Chinon America, Inc.
660 Maple Ave.
Torrance, CA 90503
800-441-0222; 310-533-0274
fax: 310-533-1727

Control Concepts
328 Water St.
P.O. Box 1380
Binghamton, NY 13902-1380
800-288-6169; 607-724-2484
fax: 607-722-8713

Covox, Inc.
675 Conger St.
Eugene, OR 97402
800-432-8970; 503-342-1271
fax: 503-342-1283

Current Technology, Inc.
101 W. Buckingham Rd.
Richardson, TX 75081
800-238-5300
fax: 214-238-0911

Curtis Manufacturing Co., Inc.
30 Fitzgerald Dr.
Jaffrey, NH 03452-1931
800-955-5544; 603-532-4123
fax: 603-532-4116

DataShield
500 N. Orleans St.
Chicago, IL 60610
312-239-1601
fax: 312-644-6505

EFI Electronics Corp.
2415 South 2300 West
Salt Lake City, UT 84119
800-877-1174; 801-977-9009
fax: 801-977-0200

Electripak
1555 Lynnfield Rd., Ste. 250
Memphis, TN 38119
800-888-0211; 901-682-7766

GC Electronics Co.
1801 Morgan St.
Rockford, IL 61102
800-435-2931; 815-968-9661
fax: 815-968-9731

Geist, Inc.
P.O. Box 83088
Lincoln, NE 68501
800-432-3219; 402-474-3400
fax: 402-474-4369

DIRECTORY OF MANUFACTURERS

General Semiconductor Industries, Inc.
2001 W. Tenth Pl.
Tempe, AZ 85281
800-927-8743; 602-968-3101

Genesis Development Corp.
15850 W. Bluemound Rd., Ste. 307
Brookfield, WI 53005
414-796-1005
fax: 414-797-0727

GE Wiring Devices
225 Service Ave.
Warwick, RI 02886
401-886-6200
fax: 401-886-6250

Hitachi America, Ltd. (OAS Division)
110 Summit Ave.
Montvale, NJ 07645
800-448-2244; 201-573-0774
fax: 201-573-7660

**Hubbell, Inc.
(Wiring Device Division)**
1613 State St.
Bridgeport, CT 06605-0933
203-337-3100
fax: 203-579-2892

IBM (International Business Machines)
Old Orchard Rd.
Armonk, NY 10504
800-426-2468; 914-765-1900

Inland Datapak
65909 Sims
Sterling Heights, MI 48313
800-969-3705; 313-795-9135
Technical Support: 313-795-3640

Innovative Technology, Inc.
15470 Flight Path Dr.
Brooksville, FL 34609
904-799-0713

Jayco Electronics, Inc.
10 Sunray St., Unit 1
Whitby, Ontario
Canada L1N 9B5
800-668-6587; 416-430-7100

Joslyn Electronic Systems Corp.
P.O. Box 817
Goleta, CA 93116
800-752-8068; 805-968-3551
fax: 805-968-0922

Kensington Microware, Ltd.
2855 Campus Dr.
San Mateo, CA 94403
800-535-4242; 415-572-2700
fax: 415-572-9675

L.E.A. Dynatech, Inc.
6520 Harney Rd.
Tampa, FL 33610
800-654-8087; 813-621-1324
fax: 813-621-8980

Liberty Systems, Inc.
160 Saratoga Ave., Ste. 38
Santa Clara, CA 95051
408-983-1127
fax: 408-243-2885

LMSI—Laser Magnetic Storage Int'l. Co.
4425 Arrows W. Dr.
Colorado Springs. CO 80907
800-777-5674

MacProducts USA, Inc.
608 West 22nd Street
Austin, TX 78705-5116
800-622-3475;512-472-8881
Direct sales: 800-MAC-USA1
fax: 512-499-0888

MIDI Land, Inc.
398 Lemon Creek Dr., Ste. L
Walnut, CA 91789
714-595-0708
fax: 714-595-4106

NEC Technologies, Inc.
1414 Massachusetts Ave.
Boxborough, MA 01719
800-826-2255; 508-264-8000
fax: 508-264-8673
Technical support: 508-264-4300

Pacific Electricord Co.
747 W. Redondo Beach Blvd.
P.O. Box 10
Gardena, CA 90247
800-326-8887; 310-532-6600
fax: 310-532-5044

Panamax
150 Mitchell Blvd.
San Rafael, CA 94903-2057
800-472-5555; 415-499-3900
fax: 415-472-5540

Pass & Seymour/Legrand
P.O. Box 4822
Syracuse, NY 13221
800-776-4035; 315-468-6211
fax: 315-468-6296

Perma Power Electronics, Inc.
5601 W. Howard Ave.
Niles, IL 60714
800-323-4255; 708-647-9414
fax: 312-763-8330
Technical Support: 800-437-3762

Philips Consumer Electronics Co.
One Philips Dr.
P.O. Box 14810
Knoxville, TN 37914-1810
800-835-3506; 615-521-4316
Direct sales: 615-475-8869
fax: 615-521-4406
Technical support: 900-555-5500

PLI—Peripheral Land, Inc.
47421 Bayside Pkwy.
Fremont, CA 94538
800-288-8754

Power Sentry, Inc.
6543 City West Pkwy.
Minneapolis, MN 55344
800-852-4312; 612-942-6655

Procom Technology, Inc.
200 McCormick
Costa Mesa, CA 92626
800-800-8600; 714-549-9449

Proxima Corp.
6610 Nancy Ridge Dr.
San Diego, CA 92121-9639
800-447-7694; 619-457-5500
fax: 619-558-1408

SL Waber, Inc.
520 Fellowship Rd., Ste. 306
Mt. Laurel, NJ 08054
800-634-1485; 609-866-8888
fax: 609-866-9845

**SONY Corporation of America
(Microcomputer Products Division)**
Sony Dr.
Park Ridge, NJ 07656
201-930-1000
fax: 201-573-8608

SRW Computer Components Co., Inc.
1402 Morgan Circle
Tustin, CA 92680
800-331-7248; 800-547-7766 (CA);
714-259-7500
fax: 714-968-1543

Storage Devices, Inc.
6800 Orangethorpe Ave.
Buena Park, CA 90620
800-USA-SDI1; 714-562-5500
fax: 714-562-5505

Tandy Corp.
1800 One Tandy Center
Ft. Worth, TX 76102
817-390-3011
fax: 817-390-2774
Technical support: 817-390-3861

Texel America, Inc.
1080 E. Duane Ave.
Sunnyvale, CA 94086
800-886-3935;408-736-1374

Todd Enterprises, Inc.
224-49 67th Ave.
Bayside, NY 113643
800-445-8633; 718-343-1040

**Toshiba America Information Systems,
Inc. (Computer Systems Division)**
9740 Irvine Blvd.
Irvine, CA 92718
800-334-3445; 714-583-3000
Technical support: 800-999-4273

Tripp Lite
500 N. Orleans
Chicago, IL 60610-4188
312-329-1777
fax: 312-644-6505
Technical Support: 312-329-1601

Woods Wire Products, Inc.
510 Third Ave.
Carmel, IN 46032
800-428-6168; 317-844-7261
fax: 317-843-1675

Zaptech International Corp.
1902 Orange Tree Ln. #100
Redlands, CA 92374
909-792-2229
fax: 909-792-5269

Zero Surge
103 Clairmont Rd.
Bernardsville, NJ 07924
908-766-4220

GLOSSARY

adapter   Also known as an add-on card, controller, or I/O card. Adapters are installed in expansion slots to enhance the processing power of the computer or to communicate with other devices. Examples of adapters include asynchronous communication, floppy disk-controller, and expanded memory.

address   A unique memory location permitting reading or writing of data to/from that location. Network interface cards and CPUs often use shared addresses in RAM to move data between programs.

alpha channel   The upper 8 bits of a 32-bit data path in some graphics adapters. The alpha channel is used by some software for controlling the color information contained in the lower 24 bits.

Alt key   The alternate key on the keyboard is similar to the control key. It is like a Shift key in that when used simultaneously with another key it creates a command or, in certain applications, a graphics character. The Alt key is more common in telecommunications programs and TSR (terminate and stay resident) programs than in regular programs. It is often used in multitasking enviroments (OS/2, Windows, DESQview X).

analog-to-digital converter (ADC)   A device that converts analog input signals to digital output signals used to represent the amplitude of the original signal.

ANSI (American National Standards Institute)   An organization that develops and publishes standards for codes, alphabets, and signaling schemes.

API (application program interface)   A set of standard software interrupts, calls, and data formats that application programs use to initiate contact with network services, mainframe communications programs, or other program-to-program communications.

application software   A computer program designed to help people perform a certain type of work. An application can manipulate text, numbers, graphics, or a combination of elements. Some application packages focus on a single task and offer greater computer power while others, called integrated software, offer less power but include several applications, such as word processing, spreadsheet, and database programs. An application may also be referred to as *software, program, instructions,* or *task*.

GLOSSARY

areal density   The amount of data that can be stored in one area of a disk—hard or floppy.

ASCII (American Standard Code for Information Interchange)   The data alphabet used in the IBM PC to determine the composition of the 7-bit string of 0s and 1s that represents each character (alphabetic, numeric, or special). It is a standard way to transmit characters.

aspect ratio   A video term that refers to the proportion of a pixel's width to its height. In VGA and Super VGA mode, this ratio is 1:1, which means the pixels are as tall as they are wide.

asynchronous communication   A type of serial communication by which data is passed between devices. "Asynchronous" means that the timing of each character transmitted is independent of other characters. Also known as ASYNC.

AT command set   Commands used by Hayes and Hayes-compatible modems. Every command starts with the letters *AT,* for ATtention. The most common commands include ATDT (dial a number), ATA (manually answer the phone), ATZ (reset modem), ATS0=0 (disable auto-answer), and ATH (hang up the phone). You can use several commands on one line; you only need "AT" before the first one. Some modems require commands typed in capital letters. The AT command set is an industry standard set of commands.

autosizing   True autosizing occurs when a monitor maintains a constant image size when moving across low and high resolutions.

average access time   The time (in milliseconds) that a disk drive takes to find the right track in response to a request (the seek time), plus the time it takes to get to the right place on the track (the latency).

back up   To make a copy of a file, group of files, or the entire contents of a hard disk.

barrel distortion   Barrel distortion occurs in monitors at the edges of the screen. The sides of the affected image seem to bow out—like a fun-house mirror—and resemble a barrel. It is the inverse of *pincushioning*.

baud rate   A measure of the actual rate of symbols transmitted per second, which may represent more than one bit. A given baud rate may have

GLOSSARY

more than one bps (bits per second) rate. Baud rate is often used interchangeably with bps, although this is technically incorrect.

binary   A numbering system with two digits, 0 and 1, used by computers to store and process information.

BIOS (basic input/output system)   A collection of primitive computer routines (stored in ROM in a PC) that control peripherals such as the video display, disk drives, and keyboard.

bisynchronous   Computer communications in which both sides simultaneously transmit and receive data. Also called BISYNC.

bit   A binary digit: the smallest piece of information that can be recognized and processed by a computer. A bit is either 0 or 1. Bits can form larger units of information called nibbles (4 bits), bytes (8 bits), and words (usually 16 bits).

bit-BLT (bit-block transfer)   A video term to identify the operation in which a block of pixel data in one area of the frame buffer is copied to another area of the frame buffer through the computer's video memory. By performing bit-block transfers, graphics coprocessors can dramatically improve video display speeds, since a displayed object is treated as one unit rather than as many individual pixels.

bits per second (bps)   The number of data bits sent per second between two modems. Used as a measure of the rate at which digital information is handled, manipulated, or transmitted. Similar, but not identical, to baud rate.

buffer   An area of RAM (usually 512 bytes plus another 16 for overhead) in which DOS stores data temporarily.

bulletin board system (BBS)   A computer (generally a microcomputer) set up to receive calls and act as a host system. BBSs allow users to communicate through message bases and to exchange files.

bus   A group of wires used to carry a set of related signals or information within a computer from one device to another.

business software   Any computer application designed for use in business (as opposed to scientific use or entertainment). These applications include word processing, spreadsheets, databases, and communications as

GLOSSARY

well as accounting, payroll, financial planning, project management, support systems, PIMs, and office management.

byte   A sequence of adjacent binary digits that the computer considers a unit. A byte consists of 8 bits.

C   A programming language used predominantly by professional programmers to write applications software.

cache   An amount of RAM set aside to hold data that is expected to be accessed again. The second access, which finds the data in RAM, is very fast. (Pronounced like "cash.")

CAD/CAM (computer-aided design/computer-aided manufacturing)
A term describing the use of computers in both the design and manufacturing of a product, such as a machine part, in which the product is designed with a CAD program and the finished design is translated into a set of instructions to be used by machines in the fabrication, assembly, and process control stages.

CGA   IBM's first color graphics standard, capable of 320 by 320 resolution at four colors (or gray shades on laptops), or 640 by 200 at two colors (black and white). CGA-only laptops are behind the times.

chip   An integral part of the PC. These are very tiny, square or rectangular slivers of material (usually silicon) with electrical components built in. Some of the chips in a computer aid in memory, but the most important chip is the microprocessor. This is the "8088", "286", "386", or "486" that every salesperson will speak of when talking about a specific machine's features.

clone   An IBM PC/XT- or AT-compatible computer made by another manufacturer.

cluster   A hard-disk term that refers to a group of sectors, the smallest storage unit recognized by DOS. On most modern hard disks, four 512-byte sectors make up a cluster, and one or more clusters make up a track.

CMOS (complementary metal oxide semiconductor)   An integrated circuit requiring low power. Most laptop CPUs use CMOS.

GLOSSARY

coding   The act of programming a computer; specifically, generating source code in the language of the program's choice. The most popular languages used by programmers are Pascal, C, and C++.

COM   Communications port or serial port used by modems, mice, and some printers. DOS assigns these ports as COM1, COM2, and sometimes COM3 and COM4. DOS also lets you refer to the first communications port as AUX. Note: Some programs count communications ports starting with 0, so "Port 0" or "Communications Port 0" would be COM1, and "Port 1" would be COM2.

communications parameters   Settings that define how your communications software will handle incoming data and transmit outgoing data. Parameters include bits per second, parity, data bits, and stop bits.

control key (Cntrl or Ctrl)   This is like a Shift key or Alt key in that when used simultaneously with another key it makes a new graphic character or command.

convergence   A video term that describes the way in which the three beams that generate the three color dots (red, green, blue) should meet. When all three dots are excited at the same time and their relative distance is perfect, the result is pure white. Deviation from this harmony (due to an incorrect relationship of the beams to each other) results in poor convergence. This causes white pixels to show bits of color and can decrease image sharpness and resolution.

CPU (central processing unit)   The functional "brain" of a computer; the element that does the actual adding and subtracting of 0s and 1s and the manipulation and moving of data that is essential to computing.

database   A file consisting of a number of records or tables, each of which is constructed of fields (in column format) of a particular type, together with a collection of operations that facilitate searching, sorting, recombination, and similar acts.

data bits   The bits sent by a modem. These bits make up characters and don't include the bits that make up the communications parameters.

DB-9   A 9-pin connector, usually for serial ports. The connector attached to your laptop is typically a male DB-9. The device at the other end (an external modem, most likely) almost always has a 25-pin (DB-25) connector and is always female. This means the cable you want to buy is 9-pin

GLOSSARY

female (computer end) to 25-pin male (modem end). Some older laptops with EGA video connectors will have a 9-pin female connector on the laptop.

DB-15   A 15-pin connector stuffed in the space of a DB-9 connector, used to connect VGA monitors to the laptop.

DB-25   A 25-pin connector for parallel ports and some serial ports (mostly on desktop PCs). At the computer end, the parallel port is female and the serial port is male. At the other end, the connector is a 36-pin Centronics male (parallel) or 25-pin female (serial). For printers, specify a DB-25 male to a Centronics cable. For serial devices, specify a DB-25 female to a DB-25 male cable.

Del (Delete key)   In most word-processing programs, this key will delete the characters to the right of the cursor.

device   Any piece of computer hardware.

device-level interface   An interface that uses an external controller to connect the disk drives to the PC. Among its other functions, the controller converts the serial stream of data read from the drive into parallel data for the host computer's bus. ST506 and ESDI are device-level interfaces.

dial-up line   A communications circuit established with a modem by dialing a destination over a commercial telephone system.

digital-to-analog converter (DAC)   A circuit that accepts digital input signals and converts them to analog output signals. Sometimes called DAC chips, they are used in VGA video cards, for example.

DIN connector   Plug and socket conforming to the DIN (Deutsche Industrie Norm) standard. Many keyboard connectors are DIN.

directory   A list of file names and locations of files on a disk.

disk   A circular metal platter or mylar diskette with magnetic material on both sides that stores programs and data. Disks are rotated continuously so that read/write heads mounted on movable or fixed arms can read or write programs or data to and from the disk.

GLOSSARY

disk cache   A portion of a computer's RAM set aside for temporarily holding information read from a disk. The disk cache does not hold entire files as does a RAM disk, but information that has either been recently requested from a disk or has previously been written to a disk.

disk defragmenter   Defragmentation is the rewriting of all the parts of a file on contiguous sectors. When files on a hard disk drive are being updated, the information tends to be written all over the disk, causing delays in file retrieval. Defragmentation reverses this process, and is often achieved with special defragmentation programs that provide up to 75 percent improvement in the speed of disk access and retrieval.

disk drive   The motor that actually rotates the disk, plus the read/write heads and associated mechanisms, usually in a mountable housing. Sometimes used synonymously to mean the entire disk subsystem.

disk format   Refers to the method in which data is organized and stored on a floppy or hard disk.

DOS (disk operating system)   A set of programs that control the communications between components of the computer. Examples of DOS functions are: displaying characters on the screen, reading and writing to a disk, printing, and accepting commands from the keyboard. DOS is a widely used operating system on IBM-compatible personal computers (PCs).

dot matrix   A type of printer technology using a print head with pins to poke out arrays of dots that form text and graphics.

dot pitch   A monitor characteristic; specifically, the distance between the holes in the *shadow mask.* It indirectly describes how far apart the individual dots are on screen. The smaller the dot pitch, the finer the image's "grain." Some color monitors, such as the Sony Trinitron, use a slot mask (also known as an aperture grille) that is perforated by strips, not holes, in the shadow mask. In this case, the dots are arranged in a linear fashion, and their density is called striped dot pitch. (Monochrome monitors do not use a shadow mask and therefore do not have a dot pitch.)

download   To receive information from another modem and computer over the telephone lines. It is the opposite of upload.

GLOSSARY

DRAM (dynamic random-access memory)   The most commonly used type of memory, found on video boards as well as on PC system boards. DRAM is usually slower than VRAM (video random-access memory), since it has only a single access pathway.

drift   Together with jitter and swim, describes unwanted motion in a line of text displayed on a monitor. The three terms refer to different periods of time between on-screen wavers.

drive array   A storage system composed of several hard disks. Data is divided among the different drives for greater speed and higher reliability.

DSDD (double-sided, double-density)   On PCs and laptops, DSDD means 720K 3^1/$_2$-inch diskettes or 360K 5^1/$_4$-inch diskettes.

DSHD (double-sided, high-density)   On PCs and laptops, DSHD means 1.44Mb 3^1/$_2$-inch diskettes or 1.2Mb 5^1/$_4$-inch diskettes.

EGA   IBM's second graphics standard (1984), capable of 640 by 300 resolution at 16 colors.

EIA (Electronic Industries Association)   Standards-setting body of manufacturers. Sets the RS-232C standard, now technically the EIA 232D standard.

EISA (Extended Industry Standard Architecture)   Primarily a desktop specification for high-performance computers. Competes with IBM's Micro Channel architecture (MCA). EISA computers can use existing PC, XT, and AT add-in cards; MCA computers can't.

E-mail (electronic mail)   The exchange of messages via a bulletin board or on-line service. One user leaves the message on the service "addressed" to another user. The other user later connects to the same service and can read the message and reply to it.

EMM (expanded memory manager)   The software driver used to implement the Expanded Memory Specification. Drivers written for the 80386 and 80486 microprocessors usually allow you to use extended memory to simulate expanded memory.

EMS (expanded memory specification)   A description of a technique for expanding memory in an IBM-compatible microcomputer. Also called LIM EMS because it was developed by Lotus, Intel, and Microsoft.

GLOSSARY

ESDI (enhanced small device interface)   A device-level interface designed for a disk drive as a successor to ST-506 but with a higher transfer rate (1.25Mb to 2.5Mb per second).

Enter   When pressed, this key lets the computer know a command has been issued; in a word processing document, this key is used like a typewriter's Return key to add a line feed. Also called the Return key.

Esc (Escape key)   A key that will usually back you out of a program, a menu, a dialog box, or a command.

expanded memory   Memory that can be used by some DOS software to access more than the normal 640K (technically, more than 1Mb). 80386, 80386SX, and 80486 computers can create expanded memory readily by using an EMS (expanded memory specification) driver provided with DOS, through Microsoft Windows, or through a memory manager such as Quarterdeck QEMM or Qualitas 386 To The Max. To use expanded memory, a program must be EMS-aware or run under an environment such as Microsoft Windows. 8088- and 80286-based computers often need special hardware to run expanded memory.

extended memory   Memory above 1Mb in 80286 and higher computers. Can be used for RAM disks, disk caches, or Microsoft Windows, but requires the processor to operate in a special mode (protected mode or virtual real mode). With a special driver, you can use extended memory to create expanded memory.

file   A collection of related records treated as a unit. In a computer system, a file can exist on magnetic tape, disk, or as an accumulation of information in system memory. A file can contain data, programs, or both.

fixed disk   Also called an internal disk, a hard disk, or a Winchester. An early IBM disk drive was called the 30–30 (like the rifle), hence the nickname "Winchester." A bulk storage system with nonremovable, rotating, rigid, magnetic storage disks. There are some types of hard disk with removable rigid media in the form of disk packs.

flicker   A monitor term that describes two different effects. True flicker, where the screen seems to blink rapidly on and off, is caused by a slow refresh rate or low vertical frequency. This means the screen isn't rewritten quickly enough to fool the eye into seeing a steady image. The second kind of flicker looks more like a jiggling of horizontal lines, caused by interlacing. To avoid both kinds of flicker you need a high

GLOSSARY

vertical frequency (at least 60 Hz, but often more) and a noninterlaced video scheme—currently an expensive combination.

floppy disk   A removable, rotating, flexible magnetic storage disk. Floppy disks come in a variety of sizes, but 3½-inch and 5¼-inch are the most popular. Storage capacity is usually between 360K and 1.44Mb. Also called flexible disk or diskette.

floppy drive   A disk drive designed to read and write data to a floppy disk for transfer to and from a computer.

form factor   Fancy way of saying size (width, depth, height).

format   A DOS command that records the physical organization of tracks and sectors on a disk.

frame buffer   A large section of memory used to store an image to be displayed on-screen as well as parts of the image that lie outside the limits of the display.

function   An operation, a set of tasks for a computer to do.

function keys (F-keys)   Keys numbered from F1 to F12 that are used to perform special functions. They are used to standardize software interfaces. For example, F1 in most software will activate the help screen. Function keys also make word processing packages easier to use by serving as shortcuts for often-used commands.

gateway   An ad hoc connection between two on-line services. A gateway exists when you are provided with a means of accessing one on-line service through another. For instance, users of CompuServe can access MCI Mail through a gateway.

GCR (group coded recording)   A hard-disk term for a storage process where bits are packaged as groups, with each group assigned to and stored under a particular code. Used by RLL drives.

graphics coprocessor   Similar to a math coprocessor in concept, a programmable chip that can speed video performance by carrying out graphics processing independently of the microprocessor. Graphics coprocessors can speed up performance in two ways: by taking over tasks the main processor would lose time performing and by optimizing for graphics. Video adapter cards with graphics coprocessors are expensive

GLOSSARY

compared to those without them, but they speed up graphics operations considerably. Among the coprocessor's common abilities are drawing graphics primitives and converting vectors to bitmaps.

handshaking   A modem term that describes the initial exchange between modems. It's like "are you there?" with the response "I am here."

hard disk   A mass storage device that transfers data between the computer's memory and the disk storage media.

hardware   The physical components of a computer.

head actuator   In a disk drive, the mechanism that moves the read/write head radially across the surface of the platter of the disk drive.

high-speed modem   A modem operating at speeds from 9,600 to 19,200 bits per second.

Home   This key is supposed to move the cursor to the upper-left corner of the screen. In reality, it does a number of different things, depending on how the software program has been written to use it. Sometimes it will work as it's supposed to, other times it will move the cursor to the top of the current page, but often it does nothing.

horizontal scan frequency   The frequency per second at which a monitor repaints the horizontal lines that make up an image. This frequency is measured in kHz (kilohertz). A standard VGA signal requires a 31.5-kHz horizontal scan frequency.

host system   In telecommunications, the system that you have called up and to which you are connected, such as a BBS (bulletin board system) or an on-line service such as CompuServe.

Hz (Hertz)   A unit of measurement. This used to be called cycles per second.

IDE (integrated drive electronics)   A disk drive with its own controller electronics built in to save space and money. Many laptops use IDE drives.

IEEE (Institute of Electrical and Electronic Engineers)   A standards-setting group.

GLOSSARY

Ins (Insert key)   A key that in many instances is a "toggle." (This means that if you press the key it will turn a function on or off.) The Insert key will turn the insert mode on or off. If you turn off the insert mode, move your cursor to within a line of text, and begin to type, you will write over existing text instead of adding text. With the insert mode on you would place new text between existing text.

Intel   A major manufacturer of integrated circuits used in computers. Intel makes the 8086 family of microprocessors and its derivatives: the 8088, 80286, 80386SX and DX, and 80486SX and DX. These are the chips used in the IBM PC family of computers and all the computers discussed in this book.

integrated circuit (IC)   A tiny complex of electronic components and their connections that is produced in or on a slice of material (such as silicon). A single IC can hold many electronic elements. Also called a chip.

interlaced and noninterlaced scanning   Two monitor schemes with which to paint an image on the screen. Interlaced scanning takes two passes, painting every other line on the first pass and filling in the rest of the lines on the second pass. Noninterlaced scanning paints all the lines in one pass and then paints an entirely new frame. Noninterlaced scanning is preferable because it reduces screen flicker, but it's more expensive.

interleaving   A hard-disk term that describes a method of arranging disk sectors to compensate for relatively slow computers. Spreads sectors apart instead of arranging them consecutively. For example, 3:1 interleaving means your system reads one out of every three tracks on one rotation. The time required for the extra spin lets the read/write head catch up with the disk drive, which might otherwise outrun the head's ability to read the data. Thanks to track buffering and the speed of today's PCs, interleaving is obsolete. Look for a "1:1 interleaving," which indicates a noninterleaved drive.

I/O (input/output)   Input is the data flowing into your computer. Output is the data flowing out. I/O can refer to the parallel and serial ports, keyboard, video display, and hard and floppy disks.

IRQ (interrupt request)   A request for attention and service made to the CPU. The keyboard and the serial and parallel ports all have interrupts. Setting two peripherals to the same IRQ is a cause of hair pulling among desktop PC users; laptops don't suffer the problem as badly because they have few, if any, add-on products that need interrupts set.

GLOSSARY

ISA (Industry Standard Architecture)   Computers using the same bus structure and add-in cards as the IBM PC, XT, and AT. Also called classic bus. It comes in an 8-bit and 16-bit version. Most references to ISA mean the 16-bit version. Many machines claiming ISA compatibility will have both 8- and 16-bit connectors on the motherboard.

JPEG (Joint Photographic Experts Group)   The image compression standard developed by an international committee of the same name. JPEG was developed to compress large still images, such as photographs, single video frames, or scanned pictures, to reduce the amount of memory required to store them.

kilo   One thousand, but in computers, it's typically 1,024 (2 to the tenth power).

kilobyte   1,024 bytes. Sometimes abbreviated as k (lowercase), K-byte, K, or KB for kilobyte and Kb for kilobit (1,024 bits). When in doubt about whether an abbreviation refers to kilobytes or kilobits, it's probably kilobytes, with these exceptions: the speed of a modem (as in 2.4 kilobits per second) and the transfer rate of a floppy disk (as in 500 kilobits per second).

local area network (LAN)   A small- to moderate-size network in which communications are usually confined to a relatively small area, such as a single building or campus.

logical drive   A drive that has been created by the disk operating system (DOS). This is done either at the preference of the user or because the DOS version does not allow a formatted capacity in excess of 32Mb. A user with a 100Mb hard disk will want to use more than 32Mb, so a program will tell DOS there are a bunch of "logical" drives that add up to 100Mb. DOS 5.0 eliminates this need.

log on or log off   The process of connecting or disconnecting your computer to another system by modem.

LPT Printer port (short for line printer)   LPT1 is the first printer port. DOS also allows you to use PRN to describe the printer port.

mega   One million, but with computers it typically means 1,048,576 (1,024 times 1,024).

GLOSSARY

megabyte (Mb)   1,048,576 bytes (1,024 times 1,024). Used to describe the total capacity of a hard or floppy disk or the total amount of RAM. Sometimes abbreviated as Mb, M, MB, or meg for megabyte; and Mb, M-bit, or Mbit for megabit. When in doubt, it's probably megabyte, not megabit, with these exceptions: the capacity of a single memory chip (a 1-megabit chip; you need eight chips plus an optional ninth parity-checking chip to get 1 megabyte of memory), the throughput of a network (4 megabits per second), and the transfer speed of a hard disk (5 megabits per second).

memory   A device that stores data in a computer. Internal memories are very fast and are either read/write random-access memory (RAM) or read-only memory (ROM). Bulk storage devices are either fixed disk, floppy disk, tape, or optical memories; these hold large amounts of data, but are slower to access than internal memories.

MFM (modified frequency modulation)   A hard-disk method of magnetically encoding information that creates a one-to-one correspondence between data bits and flux transitions (magnetic changes) on a disk. It uses smaller storage densities and lower transfer speeds than RLL.

MHz (megahertz)   One million cycles per second, typically used in reference to a computer's clock rate. Both the clock rate and the processor type (80286, 80386, etc.) determine the power and speed of a computer.

Micro Channel architecture (MCA)   The basis for the IBM Micro Channel bus, used in high-end models of IBM's PS/2 series of personal computers.

microprocessor   An integrated circuit (IC) that communicates, controls, and executes machine language instructions.

microsecond   1/1,000,000 (one-millionth) of a second.

millisecond (ms)   1/1,000 (one-thousandth) of a second. Hard disks are rated in milliseconds. Modern laptop hard disks have drives of 20 to 40 milliseconds, meaning they can find the average piece of data in $1/25$ to $1/50$ of a second. Older hard disks were about 100 milliseconds. Higher numbers mean slower performance.

MNP (Microcom Network Protocol)   MNP classes (or levels) 1–4 cover error correction. MNP 5 covers data compression and can compress data up to 2:1, providing twice the effective speed (4,800 bps on a 2,400-bps

GLOSSARY

modem). MNP levels 6–10 are less widely accepted, although MNP 10 may gain ground as an error-correcting protocol for cellular communications. MNP is likely to be superseded by V.42 error correction and V.42bis data correction. V.42 incorporates MNP 1–4; V.42bis does not incorporate MNP 5, but many V.42bis modems include it anyway.

modem   A combination of the words *modulate* and *demodulate.* A device that allows a computer to communicate with another computer over telephone lines.

MTBF (mean time between failures)   How long your computer or other equipment runs before it breaks, based on component testing.

multimedia   The presentation of information on a computer using sound, graphics, animation, video, and text.

nanosecond   1/1,000,000,000 (one-billionth) of a second. Memory chips are rated in nanoseconds, typically 80 to 150 nanoseconds. Higher numbers indicate slower chips.

NetWare   A popular series of network operating systems and related products made by Novell.

network   A continuing connection between two or more computers that facilitates sharing files and resources.

OEM (original equipment manufacturer)   This is a company that puts parts from other companies together and sells the resultant product under its own brand name.

online/offline   When connected to another computer via modem and telephone lines, a modem is said to be online. When disconnected, it is offline.

operating system (OS)   A set of programs residing in ROM and/or on disk that controls communications between components of the computer and the programs run by the computer. MS-DOS is an operating system.

OS/2 (Operating System/2)   An operating system developed by IBM and Microsoft for use with Intel's microprocessors. Unlike its predecessor, DOS, OS/2 is a multitasking operating system. This means many programs can run at the same time.

GLOSSARY

OS/2 Extended Edition IBM's proprietary version of OS/2; it includes built-in communications and database-management facilities.

parallel port A port that transmits or receives 8 bits (1 byte) of data at a time between the computer and external devices. Mainly used by printers. LPT1 is a parallel port, for example.

PCL (printer command language) Usually refers to Hewlett Packard laser printers. Most HP compatibles support PCL 4. HP's newest printers (the III series) use PCL 5, which includes scalable fonts and monochrome support for HPGL.

PEL Picture element or pixel. It represents one dot on your computer screen.

peripheral A device that performs a function and is external to the system board. Peripherals include displays, disk drives, and printers.

PgUp and PgDn keys Move the cursor up or down 25 lines—usually a full page. In telecommunications programs these keys are used to begin to send or to get ready to receive files.

PIM (personal information manager) A program that manages a person's collection of personal information, keeping track of notes, memos, time planning, telephone numbers, and addresses.

pincushioning A monitor term that describes an unwanted curve of an image that usually occurs at the edges of the screen. The sides of an image appear to curve inward.

Piracy The act of making or distributing an unauthorized copy of a copyrighted software product for financial gain. In most countries such an act is prohibited by law.

pixel (See *PEL*.) A pixel is the smallest information building block of an on-screen image. On a color monitor screen, each pixel is made of one or more triads (red, green, and blue). Resolution is usually expressed in terms of the number of pixels that fit within the width and height of a complete on-screen image. In VGA, the resolution is 640 by 480 pixels; in SuperVGA, it is 800 by 600 pixels.

platter The actual disk inside a hard-disk drive; it carries the magnetic recording material. All but the thinnest disk drives have multiple platters,

GLOSSARY

most of which have two sides that can be used for data storage. (On multiple-platter drives, one side of each platter is usually reserved for storing control information.)

port   The channel or interface between the microprocessor and peripheral devices.

print server   A computer on the network that makes one or more attached printers available to other users. The server usually requires a hard disk, to spool the print jobs while they wait in a queue for the printer.

print spooler   The software that holds print jobs sent to a shared printer over a network when the printer is busy. Each file is saved in temporary storage and then printed when the shared printer is available.

programming language   Any artificial language that can be used to define a sequence of instructions that can ultimately be processed and executed by the computer.

PROM (programmable read-only memory)   A (usually) permanent memory chip programmed after manufacture (unlike a ROM chip). EPROMs (erasable PROMs) and EEPROMs (electrically erasable PROMs) can be erased and reprogrammed several times.

protocol   Rules governing communications, including flow control (start-stop), error detection or correction, and parameters (data bits, stop bits, parity). If they use the same protocols, products from different vendors can communicate.

QWERTY   The keyboard arrangement on computers and typewriters, after the Q-W-E-R-T-Y layout of the top row of the alphabet keys.

RAM (random-access memory)   Also known as read-write memory; the memory used to execute application programs.

RAM disk   VDISK (virtual disk) that can be used in place of a hard or floppy disk for frequently accessed files. A RAM disk is dangerous for storing data because the contents are lost if the computer crashes or if power is turned off. Most users with extra RAM use it for a disk cache rather than as a RAM disk.

GLOSSARY

read/write head   The part of the hard disk that writes data to or reads data from a platter. It functions like a coiled wire that reacts to a changing magnetic field by producing a minute current that can be detected and amplified by the electronics of the disk drive.

restore   To replace files on a disk from a backup copy.

RF (radio frequency)   A generic term referring to the technology used in cable television and broadband networks. It uses electromagnetic waveforms, usually in the megahertz (MHz) range, for transmission. It can also refer to the emissions coming from a computer that cause interference with TV reception.

RGB (red, green, blue)   The triad, the three colors that make up one pixel of a color monitor.

RJ-11/RJ-45   Designations for commonly used modular telephone connectors. RJ-11 is the 8-pin connector used in most voice connections. RJ-45 is the 8-pin connector used for data transmission over twisted-pair telephone wire.

RLL (run length limited)   A hard-disk method of encoding information magnetically that uses a scheme (GCR) to store blocks of data instead of single bits of data. It allows greater storage densities and higher transfer speeds than the other method in use (MFM).

ROM (read-only memory)   The memory chip(s) that permanently store computer information and instructions. Your computer's BIOS (basic input/output system) information is stored in a ROM chip. Some laptops even have the operating system (DOS) in ROM.

roping   A video term to describe image distortion that gives solid, straight lines a helical or twisted appearance. The problem is caused by poor convergence.

RS-232C   An electrical standard for the interconnection of equipment established by the Electrical Industries Association; the same as the CCITT code V.24. RS-232C is used for serial ports.

SCSI (small computer system interface)   A system-level interface designed for general purpose applications that allows up to seven devices to be connected to a single host adapter. It uses an 8-bit parallel connection

GLOSSARY

that produces a maximum transfer rate of 5Mb per second. The term is pronounced "scuzzy."

sector   The basic storage unit on a hard disk. On most modern hard disks, sectors are 512 bytes each, four sectors make up a cluster, and there are 17 to 34 sectors in a track—although newer drives may have a different number of sectors.

serial port   The "male" connector (usually DB-9 or DB-25) on the back of your computer. It sends out data one bit at a time. It is used by modems and, in years past, for daisy-wheel and other printers. The other port on your computer is the parallel port, which is a "female" connector. It is used for printers, backup systems, and mini-networking (LANs). See also *COM* port.

shadow mask   Inside the color monitor just behind the screen, it is drilled with small holes, each of which corresponds to a triad. The shadow mask helps guide the electron beams so that each beam hits only one phosphor dot in the triad.

shareware   Copyrighted software that is distributed free of charge but is usually accompanied by a request for a small payment from satisfied users to cover costs and registration for documentation and program updates. These programs range from fully functional programs to ones having only limited features.

shell   A piece of software providing direct communication between the user and the operating system. The main inner part of the system, called the kernel, is enclosed by the shell program, as in a nut.

slot mask   Also known as an aperture grille, serves the same function as the shadow mask on a monitor.

spindle   One part of a hard disk, around which the platters rotate.

software   Programming tools such as languages, assemblers, and compilers; control programs such as operating systems; or application programs such as electronic spreadsheets and word processors. Software instructs the computer to perform tasks.

spreadsheet   An application commonly used for budgets, forecasting and other finance-related tasks. Data and formulas to calculate those data

GLOSSARY

are entered into ledger-like forms (spreadsheets or worksheets) for analysis, tracking, planning, and evaluation of impacts on economic strategy.

ST-506 A hard-disk device-level interface (a connection between the hard disk and the computer system); the first interface used with PCs. It provides a maximum data-transfer rate of less than 1Mb per second (625k per second with MFM encoding, or 984k per second with RLL encoding.)

start bit A data bit used in asynchronous transmission to signal the start of a character and indicate that the channel is active. It signifies that what follows is the data.

stop bit A data bit used in asynchronous transmission to signal the end of a character and indicate that the channel is idle. It is a mark signal lasting at least for the duration of 1 bit.

street price The real or typical selling price of computers, hardware, and software. Most laptop and desktop computers sell for about 25 percent below list price. Software may be discounted even more.

synchronous communication Fixed-rate serial communication, eliminating the need for transmitting inefficient start-stop information. PC-to-mainframe communication may be synchronous; most PC-to-PC communication is asynchronous. Most laptop modems are asynchronous only. If you're not sure whether you need a synchronous-asynchronous modem, you probably don't.

system-level interface A connection between the hard disk and its host system that puts control and data-separation functions on the drive itself (and not on the external controller). SCSI and IDE are system-level interfaces.

SysReq (System request key) The seldom-used key used to get attention from another computer.

telecommunication Using your computer to communicate with another computer via telephone lines and your modem.

TMS 34010 A popular graphics coprocessor chip from Texas Instruments that is one of the leading choices for coprocessed video adapter boards.

GLOSSARY

track   The circular path traced across the spinning surface of a disk platter by the read/write head inside the hard-disk drive. The track consists of one or more clusters.

track buffer   Memory sometimes built into disk-drive electronics, sufficient to store the contents of one full track. This allows the drive to read the entire track quickly, in one rotation, then slowly send the information to your CPU. It eliminates the need for interleaving and can speed up drive operation.

transfer rate   The speed at which a disk drive can transfer information between its platters and your CPU. The transfer rate is typically measured in megabytes per second, megabits per second, or megahertz.

triad   Three phosphor-filled dots (one red, one green, one blue) arranged in a triangular fashion within a monitor. Each of the three electron guns is dedicated to one of these colors. As the guns scan the screen, each active triad produces a single color, which is determined by the combination of excited color dots and by how active each dot is.

TTL (transistor-transistor logic)   Another way of saying digital, as in TTL monitor. CGA and EGA monitors are TTL. VGA monitors are analog.

TTY (teletype terminal or dumb terminal)   In communications or printing, the simplest form of terminal or printer. If you choose a TTY printer, you don't get any boldfacing, underlining, or other print enhancements. TTY is also the name of a DOS device referring to the keyboard and display.

UART (universal asynchronous receiver transmitter)   The circuit that controls the serial port, converting bytes to bits and bits to bytes, and adding and stripping start and stop bits. Buying tip: Look for a computer with a 16550A or 16550AF UART instead of the older, slower 16450 or 8250 UARTs if you're planning to do high-speed data communications (19,200 bps between your computer and modem).

UNIX   An operating system used mostly by minicomputers.

utility program   A program designed to perform maintenance work on a system or on system components, e.g. a storage backup program, a disk and file recovery program, or a resource editor.

GLOSSARY

V.   The CCITT international communications standards, pronounced "vee-dot." Various V. standards cover speed (modulation), error correction, data compression, and signaling characteristics. The ones listed in this glossary are the most important.

V.22   1,200-bps modem speed, about 120 characters per second. Most 1,200-bps communication in the United States uses the Bell 212A standard instead. Above 1,200 bps, all standards are the same around the world.

V.22bis   2,400-bps modem speed.

V.29   9,600-bps data communications (also 4,800 and 7,200) used by Group III fax machines and PC fax modems. Fax modems, at least of the same brand, can exchange nonfax data at 9,600 bps, usually in half-duplex mode (one way at a time).

V.32   9,600-bps data communications (also 4,800). Most but not all 9,600-bps modems support V.32 or V.32bis.

V.32bis   A follow-on to V.32 that allows 14,400-bps (also 4,800, 7,200, 9,600, and 12,000) data communications. V.29 is 9,600 bps, but it can't talk to V.32.

V.42   Emerging error-control standard. Uses a protocol called LAPM or LAP-M (link access protocol-modem). Incorporates MNP error-control levels 1–4 for compatibility with existing modems. If you have a V.42 modem, it has MNP 1–4 error correction whether the specifications say it or not.

V.42bis   Emerging data-compression standard, better than MNP 5 data compression because it compresses data up to 4:1 (versus 2:1). Includes the V.42 error-control standard, so even if a modem is listed as having V.42bis but not V.42, it has both. Buying caution: A "V.42bis-compatible" modem may only have MNP 5, not LAPM; a "V.42bis-compliant" modem should have both. Ask before you buy.

VAR (value-added retailer)   Similar to a dealer, but VARs take a computer, add special software to run on it, and price it higher than a dealer would since it has "value added."

vertical frequency   This is also called the vertical refresh rate, or the vertical scan frequency. It is a monitor term that describes how long it

GLOSSARY

takes to draw an entire screenful of lines, from top to bottom. Monitors are designed for specific vertical and horizontal frequencies. Vertical frequency is a key factor in image flicker. Given a low enough vertical frequency (53 Hz, for example) nearly everyone will see a flicker because the screen isn't rewritten quickly enough. A high vertical frequency (70 Hz on a 14-inch monitor) will eliminate the flicker for most people.

VESA (Video Electronics Standards Assoication)   A consortium of manufacturers formed to establish and maintain industry-wide standards for video cards and monitors. VESA is responsible for establishing the Super VGA recommendations that many manufacturers follow today.

video bandwidth   The highest input frequency a monitor can handle. It determines the monitor's resolution capabilities. Video bandwidth is measured in MHz (megahertz).

VGA   IBM's third (1987) and current mainstream graphics standard, capable of 640-by-480-pixel resolution at 16 colors or gray shades. SuperVGA (800 by 600) resolution is important on desktop PCs. A handful of laptops support SuperVGA when connected to an external monitor; they use regular VGA when driving the built-in display. Caution: Some laptop vendors use "text mode" VGA, which means the monitor displays only 400 pixels, not 480, vertically, and uses either EGA (640 by 350) or double-scan CGA (640 by 400) for graphics.

VLSI (very large scale integration)   A group of a bunch of different chips and their functions jammed onto a single silicon chip. Over 100,000 transistors can be integrated into one, and the amazing thing is that as one chip they consume little power and can perform extremely complex functions.

VRAM (video random-access memory)   Special-purpose RAM with two data paths for access, rather than the one path in conventional RAM. The two paths let a VRAM board handle two functions at once: display refresh and processor access. VRAM doesn't force the system to wait for one function to finish before starting the other, so it permits faster operation for the video subsystem.

wide area network (WAN)   Usually a moderate to large network in which communications are conducted over the telephone lines using modems.

GLOSSARY

window   An area of a screen that displays information. Some programs support several windows that can be viewed simultaneously or sequentially.

write protection   Keeping a file or disk from being written over or deleted. $3^1/_2$-inch floppy disks use a sliding write-protect tab in the lower-left corner (diagonally across from the beveled corner of the disk) to keep the computer from writing to the disk. When the opening is hidden by the tab (no light passes), you can write to the disk; tab open, you can't write. This can be confusing because it's the exact opposite of how a $5^1/_4$-inch disk works. Most file management utilities allow you to write-protect individual files.

XMA (extended memory specification)   Interface that lets DOS programs cooperatively use extended memory in 80286 and higher computers. One such driver is Microsoft's HIMEM.SYS, which manages extended memory and HMA (high memory area), a 64K block just above 1Mb.

X Window   A network-based windowing system that provides a programmatic interface for graphic window displays. X Window permits graphics produced on one networked workstation to be displayed on another.

INDEX

INDEX

INDEX

INDEX

INDEX

INDEX

INDEX

INDEX

INDEX

INDEX